MUSIC
BUSINESS
HANDBOOK
AND CAREER GUIDE

MUSIC BUSINESS HANDBOOK

AND CAREER GUIDE
SEVENTH EDITION

DAVID BASKERVILLE, Ph.D

Published in association with
Sherwood Publishing Partners

Sage Publications, Inc.
International Educational and Professional Publisher
Thousand Oaks ▪ London ▪ New Delhi

For information

Sage Publications, Inc.
2455 Teller Road
Thousand Oaks, California 91320
E-mail: order@sagepub.com

Sage Publications Ltd.
6 Bonhill Street
London EC2A 4PU
United Kingdom

Sage Publications India Pvt. Ltd.
M-32 Market
Greater Kailash I
New Delhi 110 048 India

Printed in the United States of America

Library of Congress Cataloging-in-Publication Data

Baskerville, David.
    Music business handbook & career guide / David Baskerville — 7th ed.
        p.   cm.
    Includes bibliographical references and index.
    ISBN 0-7619-1667-9
    1. Music—Vocational guidance—United States—Handbooks, manuals, etc.
2. Music trade—Vocational guidance—United States—Handbooks, manuals, etc.
I. Title.
    ML3795.B33   2000
    780'.23'73—dc21   00-008014

This book is printed on acid-free paper.

01   02   03   04   05   9   8   7   6   5   4   3   2   1

Acquiring Editor:	Marquita Flemming
Editorial Assistant:	Mary Ann Vail
Production Editor:	Astrid Virding
Editorial Assistants:	Cindy Bear/Karen Wiley
Designer/Typesetter:	Janelle LeMaster
Indexer:	Cristina Haley
Cover Designer:	Ravi Balasuriya

To my family, and
to those in the business
who care about the music, too

Staff for the Seventh Edition
  Editor—Tim Baskerville
  Managing Editor—Lynnette Pennings
  Senior Editor—Janet Nepkie, Ph.D.
  Developmental Editors—Marilyn Power Scott, Susan Hellman
  Research Editor—Elizabeth Lubaczewski
  Editorial Consultant—Roberta Baskerville

CONTENTS

Part II SONGWRITING, PUBLISHING, COPYRIGHT

Part III BUSINESS AFFAIRS

Part V   MUSIC IN BROADCASTING AND FILM

Part VI   CAREER PLANNING AND DEVELOPMENT

Part VII   CANADIAN MUSIC INDUSTRY AND INTERNATIONAL COPYRIGHT

Part VIII   APPENDIX

FOREWORD

Stan Cornyn
Recording Industry Pioneer

I t's never easy. The road to success in the music business is as rife with ruts and detours as that of any other field. No pat personality profile, no set philosophy guarantees entry to the big time. The men and women who've carved out positions of respect and influence in the industry are an amalgam of many different styles, psyches, temperaments. Some have come a long way; others took shortcuts. Some are incredulous that they are where they are; for others, the goal was inevitable.

One certainty unites them all: Nothing in this business is certain. The achievers have all exhibited, in one form or another, an ability to adapt, to alter longstanding opinions, to substitute professional intuition for conventional logic. They take chances. There are two kinds of people in the world, talkers and doers, men and women of action, of inaction. I don't want to downgrade a very critical element of this business—one very near and dear to me—that of articulating your point, but for some people that's as far as it goes. Anyone can think of a great idea and pin your ear to the wall detailing it, and most people at some time do. But only doers can take a plan out of the gray matter and put it into action. The individuals who attain some level of leadership in the recording community are as good as their word—and deed.

Recording companies do not, however, turn people loose in their corridors just because they have a few plans to carry out. Those who have ideas had better also have quite a few facts at their disposal. And it takes years to develop a full understanding of all the elements needed to make a hit, from recording it, to packaging it, to publicizing it, to airing it, to selling it. We're concerned, then, with the nuts-and-bolts side of the business as well as with the more nebulous concept of "art" in the industry, an equally ongoing dilemma in the realms of literature and film.

Selling music is not exactly selling blenders. I won't deny an album's objective presence. That recording's every move is followed until it shows up, it is hoped, on computer runs in the "sold" column. That's what the business is about.

But not completely. We're dealing with artists, personalities—not objects— and that makes this business quite unlike any other.

We're selling taste and emotion, not cellular phones or rear-window defoggers. This casts much of what we do in a very subjective light, raising age-old questions about the relationship between art and commerce. If it's not commercial, how do we sell it? Don't certain "uncommercial" works of music deserve to exist on artistic merit alone? If so, which ones? And how do you persuade the public, even your own staff, of the value and viability of unfamiliar, challenging musical concepts?

In contrast to other businesses, some of which have been in operation for hundreds of years, the recording industry as recently as 30 years ago was by and large a backroom affair. Street-corner groups were sent into dingy 1- and 2-track studios with a $400 budget to turn out hits that made millions for the label, but not a cent for them. Serious recordings were never expected to be profitable.

Today, the recording business is coming of age, and we have college texts on the subject to prove it. Those entering the business have the challenge of giving it new form and focus.

In the more than 30 years I've spent in the business, the business has not gotten any less open to executives who will *do* something new. This business is still open to those who will *do* that new thing, who will create with that new talent, and who will please us old-timers with a fresh way of doing *anything* in this business. Many times over the years, young people wanting a job in the business have come to me for advice. Invariably, they speak of their passion for music, their obsession with the recording business.

I disillusion them. To love the music makes you a good consumer. To become a good employee, bring to this industry a fresh skill, and find your own way to put it into operation. In 30 years that has not changed. Nor will it in the next 30.

Stan Cornyn's background includes positions as Executive Vice President of Warner Bros. Records Inc. and President of Warner New Media.

ACKNOWLEDGMENTS

The editors wish to thank those people who were helpful in generously sharing their knowledge of many facets of the music and entertainment business during the preparation of the seventh edition of this book.

Special thanks go to Janet Nepkie of State University of New York, College at Oneonta for her expert work on copyright and legal issues, specifically Chapters 4 through 8 and 16. Much gratitude also goes to Alan Bergman, Bergman & Associates, Inc., who gave us the benefit of his experience as a successful music business attorney, with particular emphasis on the recording and publishing part of the industry and the new business traditions being established in the digital world. Thanks also extend to Robert Clarida of Cowan, Liebowitz & Latman, whose thoughtful and precise explanation of copyright law was extremely helpful.

We acknowledge the unique contribution of Richard Flohil, Toronto-based music industry veteran and author of the chapter on the Canadian music industry in Part VII of this book. We are also grateful to Phil Hardy and Dave Laing, editors of *Financial Times Music & Copyright,* London, authors of the chapter on international copyright in Part VII.

The performance rights organizations were generous with their help, particularly Gary Roth and David Sanjek of BMI, Jim Steinblatt and Charles Reimer of ASCAP, and Crystal Caviness of SESAC.

The National Music Publishers Association/Harry Fox Agency, Inc., were well represented in our book by attorney Charles Sanders. For help with information on their respective organizations, thanks go to Chester Lane of the ASOL, Elizabeth Cecchetti and Jamie Driver of Opera America, John Munger of Dance/USA, Virginia Cohen of the NEA, and Gina Giuffreda of the U.S. Copyright Office.

The music business associations, unions, and guilds also offered helpful reviews and clarifications. Our appreciation goes to Ann Chaitovitz and Ralph Braun of AFTRA, Dennis Drieth and Jeff Tomberg of AFM, Louis Ross of the NACA, Harriet Slaughter of the League of American Theatres and Producers, Christopher Wilson of the Dramatists Guild, Greg Krizman from SAG, George Wurzbach of SGA, and Gerald W. Purcell and Stan Evans of NCPM. Al Baumanis gave valuable help with information about the American Music Therapy Association. Special thanks go to Pat Page of NAMM for going the extra mile for us.

Other professionals, educators, and experts were very generous with their time. Heartfelt thanks go to all of them:

Dick Moore of Dick Moore and Associates, Inc., gave a very useful description of AFTRA and other artist guilds and unions.

Louis Aborn from Tams-Witmark provided an accurate picture of the modern music print business.

Victoria Shaw of Nashville graciously contributed the reflections of a successful songwriter.

Gene Perla of Sound Design Studios and Andrew Kautz of Emerald Studios were especially helpful with studio information.

Stephen Marcone of William Paterson College, Larry Fitzgerald and Gina Miller of Fitzgerald/Hartley Management, and Gary Borman of Gary Borman Management all gave wise counsel on artist management.

Kenton Frorip, recently retired from St. Cloud State University, provided excellent help in arts administration.

Richard Bellis and Richard McIlvery, both of University of Southern California, were immensely helpful with the content and restructuring, respectively, of Chapter 24, "Dramatic Scoring for Motion Pictures and TV," and for information updating Chapter 22, "Music in Television."

Wade Jessen and Geoff Mayfield, both of *Billboard,* provided prompt and valuable help on record market information.

Ron Rodriguez and Adam Jacobson of *Radio and Records* contributed in-depth work to the revision of Chapter 21, "Music in Radio." Lynne Kite of WUSN Chicago and Steven Graybow also gave helpful definitions.

Bob Scott of KDB Radio and Nick Rail of Nick Rail Music, both of Santa Barbara, California, gave insight and valuable information regarding their fields.

Bobby Roberts of the Bobby Roberts Company helped us update material on concert promotion.

Drew Murphy of Pace Theatrical gave perspective on music and theater.

Ron Romero of Sony Trans Com contributed greatly to our understanding of in-flight music.

James F. Slutz, Indiana State University, lent his expert and extensive contribution to the revision of Chapter 12, "Music Product Merchandising."

Arthur Bernstein of the Liverpool Institute of Performing Arts offered a helpful perspective on international matters.

Matthew O'Brien, of Middle Tennessee State University, did expert revision work on Chapter 14, "Scope of the Recording Industry," and offered additional legal assistance.

Greg Seese of Capitol Records, David Lang of CD World, and David Hazan of Putumayo World Music gave helpful commentary on record promotion, distributing, and retailing.

Jay Boberg and Alicia Graham of MCA Records, Inc., updated record production information.

Jonathan Yarbrough of Rubin Postaer and Associates, John Osborn, and Jeffrey Mordos of BBDO contributed expertise in advertising.

Barry Freeman, Producer/Talent Acquisition, ABC Radio Network/Nashville, was generous with his help, as was Lark Baskerville, Vice President, Director, Human Resources, of Rubin Postaer and Associates.

Special thanks go to the many educators who gave us advice and information used throughout the book. We are especially grateful to Scott Fredrickson of University of Massachusetts at Lowell; Tim Hays of Elmhurst College, Illinois; Marcia Lewis of Valparaiso University, Indiana; Richard Weissman of University of Colorado, Denver; and Steve Widenhofer of Millikin University, Illinois, for their general commentary that helped guide this revision.

Many people have contributed to the development of this book in earlier editions, including Dr. Alfred Reed, who, along with Dr. William Lee, established the first university degree program in music merchandising at the University of Miami.

Always helpful was attorney Jay L. Cooper, in addition to David Ludwick, Mike Milom, Craig Hayes, and Jeffrey Cunard.

Educators who offered useful suggestions include Geoffrey P. Hull, Richard Barnet, Dr. Newton J. Collins, and David P. Leonard.

Others who shared their knowledge with us were Alberta Arthurs, Ellen S. Buchwalter, David Bartlett, Brian Chin, Jan Holmquist, John Parikhal, Steven Ship, Mike Shalett, Paul Sweeting, Angela Corio, and Ira Mayer.

Insights of Patrick Williams, Tom Scott, Brian Ingoldsby, Dave Grusin, Bones Howe, and the late Nelson Riddle are reflected here, as are those of critic Henry Pleasants, Robert Young, Adam Somers, Mickey Granberg, John Devarion, Ralph Peer II, and Jay Morgenstern.

Among others who have been helpful over the years are Dave Dannheiser, John Fagot, Janet Bozeman, John Dobel, Walt Love, B. Aaron Meza, and David Bosca, as well as Bruce Stevens, Harley Drew, Monica Logan, Norm Visger, Al Tavera, Jim Taber, Chris Kershaw, Alan Ett, and Gail Kantor.

To all of those mentioned here and to many other friends who have shared their knowledge of the music business with us—thank you.

—The Editors

Part I

MUSIC IN THE MARKETPLACE

OVERVIEW

I never cared much for poverty.

—*Igor Stravinsky*

Did someone say "the music *business*?" What happened to the *art* of music? The shortest possible answer to that question is, "Billions!"—the windstorm of money swirling worldwide around the art and business of music today. But the question of what is happening to musical art in the modern marketplace calls for a serious answer, and that is what this book is all about. Not only do we examine the radical changes in music and its audiences, we also set forth in detail just who produces the music who "consumes" it, and how the artists and merchants share those billions.

Art and commerce make very strange bedfellows. This ever-present linkage is inherently contradictory, for musicians and merchants are, in many respects, natural enemies. They seem to hold generally conflicting views on what music should be and do. But when communications technology developed into mass media in the 1940s, artists and the business world learned how to work together to get their music into the marketplace.

Most musicians trying to function as full-time professionals find it desirable, even imperative, to cooperate with a number of helpers to assist them in their careers and their search for steady income. These musicians' helpers now outnumber the composers and performers and are indispensable in today's world of music making. The successful musician can hardly function without the ongoing professional assistance of a whole array of associates—agents, managers, promoters, producers, sound engineers, broadcasters, merchants, attorneys, business advisers, and accountants.

← A computer musician at Stanford University conducts a computer-generated orchestra by waving wands.

The *music business* (the term is used here to include the art, the profession, and the business of music) has grown so rapidly in recent decades it could be said that the decision makers are still trying to figure out how to run the store. Music is produced and consumed today at a rate that could not have been imagined even a few decades ago.

Perceptions of the profession and business of music are usually at wide variance from reality. This is partly because the field is so diverse and changes so rapidly. But it can be understood. It is argued that the music business, particularly the recording industry, is fundamentally irrational. But most of what really goes on in the business and the profession does submit to rational analysis.

We can begin to understand the music business, or any large and diverse activity, once we examine each of its components. That is our method here. But before we do this, let's consider the overall magnitude of the music business today. These facts can provide a perspective:

▶ Americans spend more money buying prerecorded music and videos than they do going to the movies or attending sporting events.

▶ One out of five Americans plays a musical instrument. These musicians spend more than $5 billion a year on instruments, accessories, and sheet music.

▶ The annual sales of cassettes, discs, and videos, combined with their prime delivery medium, broadcasting, exceeds the gross national product of more than 80 countries in the United Nations.

▶ We own more radios, CD players, and VCRs than bathtubs.

This pervasive interest in music and entertainment begins with a young audience: By the time teenagers have left high school, they have spent more time watching television and listening to music than they have in school!

MORE THAN POP

A glance at the world of music making today might suggest that the new mass audience is found only in the field of popular music. This is not true. The American Symphony Orchestra League reports that there are more than 27,000 symphony concerts given every year. This particular audience now numbers around 32 million patrons each season. Opera continues to attract its loyal audience, now being served by more than 300 professional and semiprofessional companies in this country. As for dance (ballet, modern), this ancient art has increased its audience many times over in recent decades; about 9 million people attend at least one ballet performance in the United States each year.

The tremendous growth in music production and consumption is not unique to the United States. The rate of growth is even faster in some foreign countries, for instance, those in Latin America.

One of the mysteries of the music scene is that many of those involved in it—composers, performers, businesspeople, educators—do not understand how it really works. Many artists and music merchants lack even basic information. Worse yet, much of what they believe they "know" is either out of date or incorrect. The profession and the business change so radically, few people, including the educators, are able to keep up with it.

The result of this pervasive ignorance about the business and the profession has been tragic. Only about 15% of the musicians' union (American Federation of Musicians, or AFM) members work steadily in music. Top graduates of our conservatories fail to get their careers even started. The turnover among personnel already working in the business end of music is alarming. Many of these folks resign or get fired because they do not know enough about their jobs to hold them. Employers keep searching for people who know how to function effectively in the field.

So what does the artist or the business executive do about this predicament? How can one get the information needed to function effectively in this field? Four sources are suggested. Start by reading the "trades," the music business magazines and papers. Rarely does a music business office not have these publications in evidence. Who reads the trades? Everybody, from **gofers** to presidents. Because the business changes so rapidly, the trades are an indispensable source of current information.

Another source is the various professional meetings. These national (and international) affairs are sponsored by industry associations and trade magazines and sometimes by artists' unions. Many of these industry associations will send valuable booklets and pamphlets upon request. Certain information can be found in books on such subjects as copyright and pop songwriting.

The most reliable sources of information for the serious student can be found in a select group of colleges and universities. Following the leadership of the University of Miami in the mid-1960s, increasing numbers of accredited institutions are offering courses and degrees in the music business field.

Qualified professionals in the business can now be found throughout North America. Many are located in one of the three major recording centers—New York, Nashville, or Los Angeles. This is because most of the music business is based on the star system—specifically, the recording star system. Because it costs so much money to launch a performer's career and finance concert tours, investors are reluctant to put their money behind any individual who lacks star potential. But predicting stardom is usually impossible, so performers and investors continue to gamble in the music game.

Only a limited number of performers can attain star status, so it is fortunate that the music business system offers many opportunities for individuals needed to help make the system function. No performer today can ascend to stardom or hang there in orbit without an array of qualified supporting satellites. As this book unfolds, we shall examine how stars and their satellites make the music business work.

ART VERSUS COMMERCE

Many who do not share in the prosperity of the music industry view it with resentment, even hostility. They suggest it be spelled "the mu$ic bu$ine$$."

Criticisms of the cheap and tawdry in the music business are richly deserved. Too much of the material is derivative and uninspired trash. *Rolling Stone* magazine, relentless advocate of rock and roll, has said that too much of today's music suffers from a "glittering vacuity." Apt phrase. Too many untalented and overhyped composers and performers enjoy undeserved "success," at least for a while. Far too many genuinely talented people have not found their places in the profession because talent is only one among many requirements for success in a business more concerned with mass sales than with art. As long as the music industry remains personality oriented, there will always be "undeserved" successes from a purely musical perspective.

These are some of the negative aspects of the music business. But there are positive things to observe, too. From the management side, it is clear the industry is now run more rationally. Corporate stockholders in the entertainment industry today demand cost-effective management.

Another positive aspect of the music business is that musicians are no longer restricted in their expression by the laws of acoustics. New electronic ways to make music are invented every year, offering a composer or video producer more controls than 10 fingers can handle. The people with access to newer technology are limited in their expressive capacities only by their imaginations.

In our search for positive things to observe about the music business today, can we come up with something complimentary for our pop songwriters? Perhaps the reason many new songs sound bad is that they are. The truth is that the insatiable demands of the marketplace exceed the creativity of the suppliers. At no period in music history have composers been expected to create several hundred new songs every week. Any scan of the radio tuner proves that such an achievement is impossible.

Defenders of contemporary music argue that some of the songwriters since the early 1960s rank with the Gershwins and Kerns of earlier decades. What about the film composers? The best film composers today are producing music of a quality superior to the work of many so-called serious composers—and a number of them operate in both those worlds.

As for the dominant popular musical styles of our time, they are the most ridiculed, the most loved, and the most profitable of any genre in the history of music.

HISTORICAL DEVELOPMENT: FINDING A PAYING AUDIENCE

History books provide only spotty information on how the musician fared in earlier times as a professional. Music historians, most of them tenured behind the protective walls of universities, have rarely shown concern for the bread-and-butter needs of the working musician. This traditional lack of concern for the professional status and financial condition of musicians dates from earliest times. We can assume that in the beginning, music making was undertaken by individuals and groups simply for their own pleasure. The performer was also the composer. If there was an audience, it was a social or religious gathering; it did not occur to the early musicians that they might develop an audience that would pay to hear them sing their songs.

Among the first important professional musicians in Western civilization were the mimes of the Greek and Roman theater. They were singing-dancing actors. Roman law held them to be disreputable types, calling them *infami* (outlaws). In the Middle Ages, the minstrels of Germany and the jongleurs of France were the first professionals. Accounts of their activities read like a review from *Variety*.

These musicians were actually vaudevillians, and their acts might include not only singing and dancing but also juggling, card tricks, even knife throwing and trained animals. Show business had begun—in the Middle Ages.

A handful of musicians involved in secular music managed to earn at least part of their livelihood during the Middle Ages and Renaissance. But in the religious sector, almost no musicians enjoyed real professional status. The choirboys and men of the Western church performed in the cathedral choirs as just another part of their Christian service. Professional composers in the religious field seem to have first appeared in Paris around 1100 A.D. at Notre Dame cathedral. But musicologists cannot provide a satisfactory account of how the profession of composing music took shape in the following centuries. To this day, church musicians in most communities are either unpaid or paid below professional rates.

Conditions for the working musician were somewhat better in Germany in the 15th and 16th centuries. The tradition of guilds included the music trade. Musicians' guilds influenced not only working conditions but also creative and artistic standards. These early guilds were active in organizing composition and singing contests and formulated elaborate rules for them (an accurate account of these proceedings may be found in Richard Wagner's opera, *Die Meistersinger Von Nürnberg*).

In the following period in Europe, increasing numbers of artists were employed by the nobility as house musicians. Composers and performers were put on the royal payroll to make music in the salons, ballrooms, and chapels for their wealthy patrons. But nobility looked on these artists as servants, and they were expected to use the rear entrances to royal buildings. In addition, musicians' royal patrons would frequently pay them later than promised or not at all. Despite some advances in status, modern-day musicians sometimes complain that they still do not receive appropriate respect for their talents and professional stature.

In our own time and place, the champion for elevating the status of the music profession has been the AFM of the United States and Canada. The AFM **locals**[1] receive requests regularly from sponsors of civic events, political rallies, and community benefits. These requests are usually sung in the same key: "Please, would you just send over some musicians for our event? They'll really enjoy it and, of course, we'll have some nice refreshments for them." Most musicians have been willing to play benefits, but they have also been exploited by those who would have them "share their art" just for the inherent pleasure of it. AFM locals have developed an effective response for unreasonable requests of this kind: They offer to supply union musicians without fee, provided the other trades and professions—stagehands, waiters, teamsters, bartenders—also work without pay. It is a fair offer; there are few takers.

Gradually, musicians acquired recognition as professionals with the development of a new phenomenon, the paying audience. This first occurred in the musical theater and opera, particularly in Italy and England. When the public began to pay its way into a room to hear music, the *music business* had begun. By the 1800s, the public had accepted the idea that you had to buy a ticket to hear a professional. Increasing numbers of paid concerts developed, not only in European cities such as Vienna, London, and Paris but also in New York, Philadelphia, and Boston.

We lack reliable accounts of who organized and promoted the earliest paid employment for professional musicians. Perhaps the earliest notable artist's manager or agent was Mozart's father, Leopold Mozart. Young Mozart's talent was discovered by his father before the youngster had barely graduated from diapers. When Wolfgang was 6 years old, father Leopold started presenting his son to all of Europe. But Mozart's father did not teach his son much about career management. Mozart junior earned considerable sums in his short lifetime but seems to have died a pauper. Mismanagement of money and careers is not unique to the current century.

A more recent ancestor of today's music entrepreneur was the circus genius, P. T. Barnum. In 1850, when Jenny Lind, "The Swedish Nightingale," came to America, Barnum presented her around the country as if she were a star acrobat. Barnum's bookings earned the artist $130,000 in her American tour, big money indeed in those days.

Barnum understood that the public likes a good show, and the music business grew, even in the classical field, in a razzle-dazzle, show-biz atmosphere. At the same time Barnum was touring opera star Jenny Lind, other entrepreneurs were developing enthusiastic audiences for that unique American contribution to theater—the minstrel show. This is not the place to treat the racist aspects of that phenomenon; our interest in minstrelsy here must be limited to how it fostered the development of the popular music business. As early as the Middle Ages, musicians from Africa were in Europe entertaining whites. But it was not until the mid-19th century, with the development of the minstrel show, that blacks began to find a place in the white musical world as full professionals. Though most of the performers were white, increasing numbers of blacks began to take part.

This development turned out to be of historical significance, for it would be impossible even to conceive of music in the 20th century without the pervasive influence of black musicians.

The increasing popularity of minstrelsy in the 1850-1900 period enlarged public awareness and appreciation of popular music and the entertainment business. Near the end of the Reconstruction period, the size and affluence of the middle class grew. By the 1890s, the piano was a standard adornment in the parlors of upper-middle-class families. On thousands of piano racks across the land, one would probably find, in addition to some Stephen Foster songs and a hymnal, a copy of *After the Ball.* The year was 1892, and this song was the first million-seller (in a 12-month period). It eventually sold 10 million copies of sheet music.

By this time, a number of large publishing houses had developed, such as E. B. Marks, Witmark Bros., T. B. Harms, Leo B. Feist, Mills Music, and Shapiro, Bernstein & Co. Some of these firms remain active and prosperous today. These popular music publishers took pride in being able to spot potential hits. When they couldn't find them, the publishers wrote the songs themselves or put composers on weekly salaries to work **in-house.**

These late-19th-century publishers developed the merchandising methods that prevailed until radio came on strong in the 1920s. Songs were introduced in a number of ways. In the final days of minstrelsy (which died around 1900), song pluggers would attempt to persuade the performers to use material coming off the presses. When vaudeville and burlesque began to displace the minstrel shows, pluggers contacted the headliners and even the lesser acts to try to get them to use the songs their firms were pushing at the time. A publisher who could come up with a piece of material that some vaudeville headliner like Al Jolson or Eddie Cantor would sing was almost assured of a hit, for these were the superstars of their day.

In the 1920s, the music industry felt the huge impact of new media of mass communication. The sale of records was excellent; the first million-seller came along. Industry leaders misjudged radio broadcasting; they held a view exactly opposite the conventional wisdom of today. When radio started in the 1920s, the publishers fought it, believing that "giving music away" through this medium would hurt sheet music sales. Overexposure via radio broadcasting, they argued, was killing songs in 6 weeks; potential customers could not get down to the store to make a purchase before the song's popularity had waned. It should be pointed out that publishers' income from broadcast performances at that time was zero.

Another significant development in the entertainment field occurred in 1927 when the "talkies" began. Movie producers discovered, with the very first sound film (a musical titled *The Jazz Singer*, starring Al Jolson), that audiences would buy a lot of theater tickets to hear songs sung on "the silver screen." The major studios began scrambling for **synchronization rights** to enable them to add music to films and turn out musical films in rapid succession.

During the Great Depression of the 1930s, million-selling records disappeared, and sales of sheet music collapsed. Attendance at vaudeville theaters dropped, too, with the growing popularity of the movie musical. Concurrent with these depressions in the music market, radio broadcasting grew rapidly. Music publishers now shifted their attention from plugging vaudeville performers to the new stars of radio. The network broadcasts at that time emanated mostly from New York, Chicago, and Los Angeles. Publishers closed their regional offices across the land and focused their plugging efforts on these new broadcasting centers. It worked. The publishers quickly discovered that they should point their promotional efforts toward the big bands and their singers who had weekly, sometimes nightly, radio broadcasts (which, at that time, were referred to as "remotes"). Song-plugging had grown from a local to a national enterprise with the development of network radio.

Publishers were not the only ones to benefit from the coming of network broadcasting. Big bands became name bands because of network radio. Then the name bands became the record stars. Management noticed that the best-selling big band records featured the band's singer. Alert talent handlers pulled the singers off the bandstand (Frank Sinatra, Doris Day, Ella Fitzgerald, etc.) and started them working alone—for much more money. This was the beginning of the present era of the dominance of the popular singer; they became the new stars and superstars, with the help of recordings and films.

During World War II, the whole world seemed to discover the appeal of America's popular music. Much of this worldwide popularity was fostered by the Armed Forces Radio network. With over 90 stations broadcasting American-made records around the world, millions of listeners, not just the G.I.s for whom the broadcasts were intended, heard the great entertainment available from this kind of music. By the late 1940s, the American style had become a world style. And so it is today.

When the G.I.s returned home, they bought large quantities of records. Music instrument factories, which had been shut down earlier to produce weapons, were now spewing out guitars, organs, pianos, and wind and percussion instruments in quantity. The music industry was reaching a mass market.

Record companies were moving millions of singles in the 1940s. When Columbia came out with the long-playing record, the music business again experienced a development of overwhelming significance. Now, instead of 2 songs per record, songwriters and publishers could place 12 songs on each release. Income could thus be increased by 600%. On the new LP, record buyers could hear an entire Broadway show; opera buffs could carry home an entire opera in a box; complete symphonies could easily fit on one LP. The dollar volume of classical records grew to 10% of the market.

Concurrent with the growing popularity of LPs was the increasing availability of low-cost tape recorders. Add to this the boom in high-fidelity sound. For a relatively low cost, consumers could hear recorded or broadcast music with a quality of sound that was better, audiophiles believed, than that offered at their local concert halls.

The music business began to attract not only new capital but also a new breed of merchants, some of whom were quite savvy. New distribution and merchandising methods developed. The most significant marketing development at the time was the discovery that people would buy records wherever they shopped. Enter the **rack jobber.** This new kind of music merchant set up record racks in supermarkets, variety stores, department stores—anywhere shoppers passed by.

Large corporations began to notice that people in the music publishing and record business were making lots of money. They decided to buy in. By the 1970s, even conservative bankers got the message: Music enterprise was now an acceptable risk. They began making loans to music publishers, record producers, and artists' managers, types of people they used to classify with street vendors. The main attraction to these new investors was record production. In what other kind of business enterprise could an individual or a bank invest, say, $20,000 in a master tape, then receive from it royalties one hundred times that amount, if the record hit? To the inexperienced investor, the music business began to look like a money tree.

Investors of all types tried to buy into the music industry, whether or not they knew anything about its hazards. By the 1970s, the buying and selling of music companies resulted in the majority of firms becoming controlled by a handful of giant corporations. This trend continues, as major labels buy up smaller, independent record companies, and giant multinational firms swallow many major labels.

INFLUENCE OF MASS MEDIA

The unique phenomenon in music in the 20th century was the discovery of new audiences. The world has always been full of music lovers, but it was not until the development of mass communication technology that so many "new" audiences were discovered. Until the 1920s, most professional music making was addressed to a small, elite audience that was accustomed to buying tickets to attend the opera, the symphony, perhaps a Broadway musical. When radio, records, and television came along, that elite audience not only continued, it grew. But now it was joined and immeasurably augmented by whole new audiences for folk music, country and western songs, blues, and jazz. Mass media forever changed the size and composition of the music audience, and merchants were quick to respond to the new millions of paying customers.

Diverse as these audiences are, the largest segment of consumers is still found "in the middle." For now, we shall refer to this group as the popular audience. Music addressed to this audience experienced its greatest change in the 1950s when performers such as Elvis Presley began to merge the styles of country, gospel, and rhythm and blues. Then the Beatles came along, and the new style rocked and rolled around the world like a sonic boom. An entire generation of music lovers was electrified. The Beatles soon won over just about everybody. This can be attributed to their natural vocal, instrumental, and songwriting talent; brilliant record production; and personalities that viewed the whole phenomenon with a disarming sense of humor.

The Beatles had a great sense of theater, as did Elvis. They established what might be called rock theater, where the performer engages the eye as much as the ear. Mick Jagger adopted James Brown's moves into his own style and created modern rock's definition of the frontman. David Bowie later redefined rock performance as theater, with the electrifying singer assuming his song characters on stage.

The drama of rock theater lent itself naturally to the new genre of music videos, which in turn made a path for ever more adventurous aural/visual combinations fed by evolving technology in ventures that transcend the music business.

THE ARTS AND ENTERTAINMENT INDUSTRY

In this always-fascinating journey, we see the interrelation of the European classical tradition, African American influence, recording technology, **telecommunications,** and computer science. Artist, merchant, and scientist are working side by side, building on the past, creating the future.

As we shall see, the music business is but one component of the arts, entertainment, and communications industry, the whole often locked together with a few microchips and a Web browser. This amalgam is complex and ever-changing. But it can be understood when examined as a *system,* composed of a number of subsystems. That is our approach in the chapters that follow.

NOTE

1. Words in boldface type indicate inclusion in the glossary section.

THE MUSIC
BUSINESS SYSTEM

We have no art. We do everything as well as possible.

—*Balinese musician*

The music industry can be described as having two essential elements: the musician and the audience. Drawing them together is the *business* of music. Despite evidence of a prevailing anarchy, the music industry operates much like other large commercial activities. The main difference between the music business and other industries is, of course, the "product" itself and the constant demand for new product. In examining the business aspects of music, it is the rapid change of product that makes this business almost unique.

GETTING THROUGH THE MAZE

The music industry today is a group of interrelated subsystems, each of which can be analyzed and understood. This chapter examines how each subsystem relates to the other components that make up the music business.

Before analyzing these relationships in detail, let's consider two different ways of viewing the industry as a whole. First, study the flowchart shown in Figure 2.1. It graphically illustrates the music business system and its principal subsystems. This flowchart can serve as a framework on which to hang additional subsystems.

A second way of grasping the big picture is to examine the sequence of events that often occurs as a new song finds its way to market. As you will observe, the following list sets forth much of the same information appearing on the flowchart in Figure 2.1.

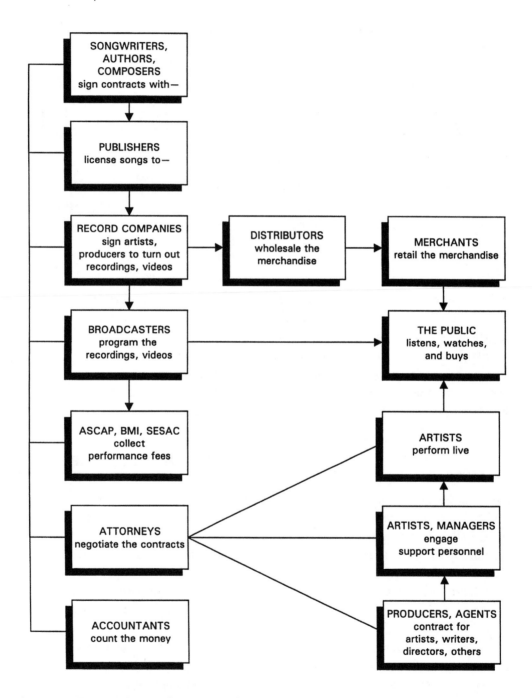

Figure 2.1   The Music Business System and Its Principal Subsystems

1. The composer writes a song and signs with a publisher.
2. The publisher persuades an artist (or that artist's producer) to record the song.
3. The recording company produces a recording and, probably, a video version of the song.
4. Promoters persuade programmers to broadcast the recording and the video.
5. The recording company ships the merchandise to distributors, who sell it to retailers.
6. A talent agency contacts promoters and books a concert tour. (Meanwhile, the attorneys are negotiating the contracts.)
7. Concert promoters enlist cosponsors and sell the tickets.
8. The road manager moves the people and the equipment.
9. The concert production manager dresses the stage, lights it, reinforces the sound.
10. The artists perform; the performing rights organizations collect performance royalties.
11. The accountants count the money; the participants pay their bills.
12. The government collects the taxes.

Since the end of World War II, the music business has grown so rapidly that companies could not find enough qualified people to handle their affairs. And until recently, our schools and colleges have not been much help in preparing people for these new kinds of careers.

The rapid growth of the industry meant that most people had to learn on the job. It was a slow and expensive process. It was also inefficient. Most people learned only one job at one company. When they were let go, as often happened, they had to start all over again and try to learn how their new employers operated. Even today, this hit-and-miss, on-the-job training causes considerable "floating" of music business personnel, because many employees in this field lack the solid educational backgrounds demanded today by business enterprises.

The good news is that help did finally arrive, from a predictable source.

Instructor and students in Trebas Institute's digital sound design lab.
Photo courtesy of Trebas Institute. Photo by Malcolm P. Gibson.

MUSIC BUSINESS STUDIES IN HIGHER EDUCATION

As the music business became larger and much more complex, it required a new kind of leadership: individuals possessing competence in such diverse fields as music, business administration, accounting, and law. The only places such a broad education can be acquired are colleges, universities, and certain specialized institutes.

Pressure for new curricula in the music business came from several sources. The students observed the burgeoning business of music and started asking their instructors how they might prepare themselves for jobs in such fields as recording, broadcasting, or music **publishing.** Most college faculty lacked experience in the "commercial" side of the profession. But a handful of their colleagues did have backgrounds in such areas as music merchandising, recording, and performance. Some were jazz educators who knew the "gigging" side of the music profession. This group of college teachers heard the students' concerns, perceived the need, and began to develop music business courses, then complete degree programs. These on-campus instructors were often assisted by local music merchants, broadcasters, and sometimes, entertainment lawyers.

Thus, music business studies in higher education were born. After a slow start, we now have somewhere around 200 universities, institutes, and colleges offering educational programs designed to prepare the new professionals for positions of leadership in the music and entertainment industry.

These educational offerings are diverse, but most of them include studies in the fields the new leadership must understand—music, certainly, but also business administration, accounting, marketing, business law, and copyright. In addition, many colleges and technical schools now offer studies and even degrees in recording technology and audio/video production.

Graduates of these programs cannot know it all, of course. But they are far better prepared than anyone else to meet the wide-ranging demands of today's music industry.

These young people can be called "the new professionals," the new leaders in the art and business of music. Their most striking attribute is their versatility. The breadth of their music business studies helps them perform effectively, not just in one area but in all the major facets of the field, ranging from merchandising to recording, from artist management to broadcasting.

HELP WANTED!

College study of the music business is supplying increasing numbers of industry leaders. But the field attracts more aspiring professionals than it can accommodate.

The reason some aspirants fail to achieve their goal is not so much a shortage of opportunity as a lack of sufficient talent and an understanding of how the music business system works. But many (though not all) ambitious newcomers do make it. Why: Luck? Timing? Education? These factors have helped launch many successful careers in both the music and business ends of the field. There are four

Music Business/Management class at Berklee College of Music, Boston.
Don Gorder, Chairman, standing center rear, and faculty member Sky Traughber
standing right. Photo courtesy of Berklee; photo copyright © by Kimberly Grant.

other factors contributing to the success of those who "win" in the music business:

1. They are strongly motivated; they really want to win.
2. They are talented—and they surround themselves with talented associates.
3. They persevere; they hang in there until they win.
4. They get the important information.

The first three items depend totally on you. This book deals only with Item 4. The music business offers excellent career opportunities for the really talented individual, provided that individual gets the important information—and acts on it. The essential core of that information is offered here.

Part II

SONGWRITING, PUBLISHING, COPYRIGHT

3 PROFESSIONAL SONGWRITING

There should be a single Art Exchange in the world, to which the artist would simply send his works and be given in return as much as he needs. As it is, one has to be half a merchant on top of everything else, and how badly one goes about it!

—*Ludwig van Beethoven*[1]

THE MARKET

Everything begins with the songwriter. One creative individual must first produce before anyone else in the music business can make a sound. Or a dollar. The music industry continues to thrive on the great standards, but even these wonderful evergreens are not immortal. The demand for new songs has increased exponentially, because mass media have expanded the audience. The music business gobbles up hundreds of new songs every week.

If the demand for new songs is insatiable, why do so many amateur songwriters fail to find acceptance for their material?

Publishers and performers are inundated with submissions. Eager young songwriters descend on the recording centers like locusts. Probably 10% of the people flowing through the Greyhound stations in Nashville and Hollywood are carrying a suitcase full of **demo** tapes.

Major publishers and recording companies receive in excess of 200 unsolicited songs each week. The problem is not that the industry lacks enough songs. The omnipresent concern is that it *cannot discover enough good ones*. We have abundant proof of this: A large number of weak songs get recorded. This is not so

← Radio City Music Hall. © Digital Vision/PNI.

much because the producers lack taste (although they are not immune to this). Rather, it is that they publish and record the best they can find. When a poor song gains initial acceptance, everyone gets hurt. The powerful promotion machinery of a rich label can often crank up initial enthusiasm for a new recording. But note how quickly a weak song disappears from the **charts.** Most poor songs have a life expectancy of about 1 month, if they are lucky. That means that every individual and every company that has anything to do with that weak song loses money. So the search begins anew for material good enough to survive long enough in public favor to generate enough income to at least break even.

PREDICTORS OF SUCCESS

Is it possible to define a "good" song? Yes, if you know what to look for. Can anyone predict professional acceptance? Quite often, if you know how. Does anyone know which songs will become lasting hits? No one on this earth. Can a creatively talented songwriter break in? Very likely—if determined to learn the craft as well as the business.

What makes a Franz Schubert, a Richard Rodgers, a Duke Ellington, or a John Lennon? Can we identify the elements in their songs that make us love them? We would be on safe ground when we identify the songs that are well crafted musically and lyrically. As for commercial success, it is immediately apparent from sales figures. But how far can we go in predicting how a song will fare in the marketplace? Until the Beatles came along and turned the world on its ear, musicians and merchants had a working understanding of what a "popular song" was. They knew what a C&W (country and western) song was. R&B (rhythm and blues) was identifiable. Today, these tidy classifications don't serve nearly as well. From 11th-century chansons to this week's charts, the all-time favorite is the love song. But then, there are an infinite number of ways to express love. We once had a hit on the charts that concerned a hot love affair between two muskrats. So even within the love song genre, it is difficult to classify songs or to predict what might be commercially successful. Hits come from everywhere. And it is this unpredictability that encourages the amateur to try to get lucky.

Although it is difficult to identify specific ingredients that might bring a song artistic or commercial success, we can critically examine the great songs of the past and see what they have in common. A really great song tends to exhibit these six characteristics:

1. The song is memorable; it sticks in the mind. This is accomplished particularly by use of a **hook**—a catchy phrase or refrain that repeats several times during the song.
2. The song has immediate appeal.
3. The text uses some kind of special imagery. Not "Your beauty makes me love you,"but perhaps, "Your touching makes me tremble."
4. The song is well crafted: It has a beginning, a middle, and an end.
5. Everything lyrical and musical holds to the central theme of the song. No digressions.
6. A great love song has an element of mystery, an indefinable enchantment. It transports the spirit and we don't know why.

If a song has potential for making it in the marketplace, the following events can be critical:

1. The song gets an appealing initial performance (by a well-known performer, it is hoped) that is captured on tape.
2. The recording company promotes strong **airplay** for the recording.
3. The song and the recording suit the taste of the current market.
4. The recording is distributed effectively and made readily available nationally.

THE CRAFT

Not all songwriters are endowed with creative gifts. We lack evidence that *creativity* can be taught. But the *craft* of songwriting can be learned through formal study or private instruction.

All colleges accredited by the National Association of Schools of Music (NASM) offer at least 2 academic years of theory study—harmony, ear training, music reading, orchestration, and counterpoint. This may be the most certain way for a musician to acquire a solid theoretical background. And some colleges offer composition classes that include popular songwriting as well as the traditional classical fare.

What about the various "how-to" books addressed to songwriters? Many contain useful information. Some of them are lightweight, get-rich-quick publications. And what about private instruction? Excellent, if you can find good teachers and can afford it.

Probably nothing could be more useful to a songwriter, amateur or pro, than to select 100 of the leading standards, then study them, phrase by phrase, line by line, chord by chord. To guide you in this kind of analysis, you might well study Alec Wilder's excellent book, *American Popular Song: The Great Innovators, 1900-1950*. Wilder, himself a first-rate songwriter, theorist, and contemporary music historian, studied, not 100 songs, but several thousand. Borrow Wilder's technique: If you can examine the internal workings of 100 great melodies, 100 great lyrics, you will have at least begun a serious study of the songwriting craft.

Collaboration

Some of the most creative artists in the popular song field have managed to write both words and music. If you can do this as well as Irving Berlin, Cole Porter, and Paul Simon, the world awaits. But if your strong point is music, find yourself a lyricist. If you are good at lyrics and lack musical talent, don't try to fake it as a composer. If you write only words or only music, don't feel that you are second class. Consider Rodgers and Hammerstein, George and Ira Gershwin, and others.

There are no formulas for locating a collaborator. Try hanging out with other writers and performers. Get the word out around town that you are looking. Contact regional performing rights organizations (ASCAP, BMI, etc.) or call their headquarters for suggestions on regional workshops and other sources. Check local clubs for songwriting nights. Songwriters of every description will surface. Some good writing teams got started through placement of classified ads in trade papers. One suggestion: If the collaborator you hook up with is not studying the craft as seriously as you are, drop that person for someone who knows there is still a lot to learn. Learn, grow together.

Whatever you do, don't hire a collaborator. Don't respond to ads soliciting song poems. Don't pay any so-called publisher to "publish" your songs or add music or add words. *Legitimate publishers never charge writers a dime.* They pay *you.*

When two coauthors are ready to approach publishers, they should have worked out a clear understanding, preferably in writing, covering the essential issues of their relationship. The agreement should provide answers to these questions:

1. Is all income generated by the collaboration to be shared equally?
2. May one writer make changes in the material unilaterally?
3. Under what conditions may one writer withdraw the words or music from the collaborative work if the work remains unpublished or otherwise unsuccessful?
4. Under what circumstances will the collaborative relationship terminate?
5. May the writers concurrently write alone or with a different collaborator?

Mention should be made that a special kind of working relationship exists between the composer who doesn't read music and a chosen arranger. Some naturally gifted songwriters never bother to learn how to read and write music. They get by with their intuitive talent for inventing appealing melodies that turn out to be commercially acceptable. They usually sing their simple tunes into a tape recorder, then hire an arranger to clean up the rhythm, fix the phrasing, add the harmony, and transcribe the results onto **leadsheets.** Such a composer should, however, gain command of the songwriting craft, thus legitimizing the claim to be a professional composer.

Work Habits

Most successful songwriters write all the time. They write, not dozens, but hundreds of songs. Many professionals like to work out a schedule, perhaps setting aside every morning for creative work. They isolate themselves for several hours, not permitting anything or anybody to interfere with their work time. Other writers are more productive working in spurts. They might stay away from their studio for days or weeks. Then they get some ideas or have to meet a deadline.

The truly professional songwriter works at the profession full-time. This means that when not writing, that creator is promoting what has been written. Publishers are quick to spot a writer who understands that professional success comes only from continual hustling. Some professionals think of their work week as about one half writing and one half selling. Professional songwriters not only help their publishers and recording companies push their material, they are on the street and in the studios and around the watering holes where the pros gather. They spread the good word. If they don't, who will know what they have written lately? How will the writer learn what people are looking for in songs? Writing and promoting, promoting and writing. This is the professional song-writer's life.

Having described the full-time professional writer, we must recognize those professionals who divide their time between composing and performing (or be-tween writing music and some other kind of activity relating to the business). Many writers begin as performers, particularly in the fields of rock, folk, and country music. In the rock field especially, practically every successful group in-cludes instrumentalists and singers who also write for the act.

INCOME SOURCES

When a writer manages to get published and experiences some success, income from a variety of sources will be realized. Table 3.1 gives a convenient summary, and Figure 3.1 shows how writers' and publishers' incomes are related.

Income From a Hit Recording

One of the principal sources of income for a writer is **mechanicals**—mechani-cal royalties. This term and other terms relating to a writer's licensing royalties are defined in the chapters that follow. But here is a preview of what a songwriter will earn from just mechanicals. Assume the following: (a) The recorded song goes "gold," sells 500,000 copies; (b) the writer in question is the composer of two songs on the album; and (c) the current mechanical royalty rate (it changes year to year) is 8 cents per song per album.

500,000 albums sold × 8 cents per song × two songs = $80,000.
50-50 split between publisher and writer = $40,000 each.

If this same writer wrote all 10 songs on an album that went gold (500,000 copies sold), it is obvious that $400,000 would be earned from that hit album. After de-ductions and chargebacks have been made, most recorded songs do not produce

TABLE 3.1   Writers' Potential Income Sources

Type of Music Use	Who Pays the Writer
Broadcast performances (TV—commercial and noncommercial)	Writer's performing rights organization
Nonbroadcast performance (clubs, hotels, stadiums, business music, in-flight music, aerobic and dance studios, etc.)	Writer's performing rights organization
Mechanical royalties (tape and CD sales)	Recording company pays writer's publisher, who shares 50-50 with writer
Sheet music sales	Publisher pays percentage on "paper" sales
Synchronization of music to film or tape (movies, videos)	Publisher shares 50% of fees received with writer
Special permissions, licenses (merchandising deals)	Users pay publisher, who shares with writer
Jukeboxes	Performing rights organization pays publisher, who shares 50-50 with writer
Dramatic (or grand) rights	Publisher shares with writer (unless writer or agent retains dramatic rights)

NOTE: All these uses are for *nondramatic* music, except the last item, dramatic (or grand) rights.

anything close to these figures. To generate a steady living wage, the writer must write and write all the time—and must somehow get the material published and recorded on as regular a basis as possible.

Additional Income Sources

Mechanical royalties provide just one potential source of income for songwriters. Performance royalties (payable when a song has been broadcast or otherwise performed) will equal, and often surpass, mechanical income. Additional potential income sources are listed in Table 3.1.

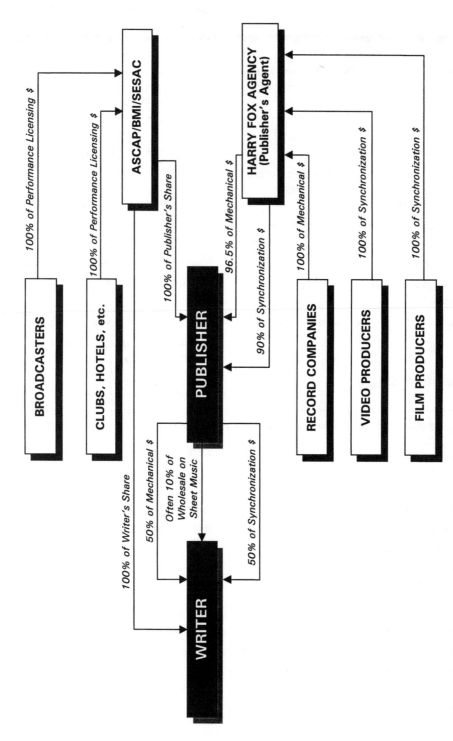

Figure 3.1   Songwriters' and Publishers' Income Sources

PUBLISHING OPTIONS

If the writer manages to compose works that appear to possess commercial potential, a number of **publishing** options may surface. These are among the most common arrangements:

1. The writer can simply search out an established publisher and sign that firm's contract. Here, the writer would participate only in writer's income.
2. The writer can negotiate a contract with a publisher in which the writer gets a piece of the publisher's share of the income. This kind of deal is often called "splitting the publishing"—the two parties usually share equally in the publisher's income.
3. The writer can set up a publishing company.
4. If the writer is also a recording artist, the personal manager under contract (or an attorney) might set up a publishing company owned by the writer and administered by the manager for a commission.
5. The writer might enter into a partnership or set up a corporation with others to operate a publishing company. If the writer in a corporate structure were a full-time professional writer, the corporation might pay the writer as a regular employee. Whether the writer also received a salary "override" on writer's royalties would be determined by the provisions of the employment contract.
6. The writer might be offered a staff job by a publisher.

Staff Writers

Publishers who can afford it will sometimes place promising writers on staff and demand their exclusive services on a full-time basis. Most staff writers receive a weekly salary; it may be just a token payment or a living wage. Whatever the size of the salary, it is treated as an advance on the writer's future royalty earnings. Remember, the bigger the advance, the more may have to be paid back or done without when the royalties start coming in—it's not free money.

Another kind of staff writer is also on salary, often full-time, for exclusive services. But the big difference here is that the writer is engaged to perform "work made for hire" for the publisher—meaning that the songs remain the exclusive property of the employer, and the writer can never claim copyright. If the publisher fails to **exploit** the songs (very common), the writer cannot recapture them

ASCAP Nashville Songwriter's Workshop participants
Max T. Barnes, Harlan Howard, Max D. Barnes (seated), unidentified,
ASCAP's Chris Dubois, and Laura Putty (standing). Photo courtesy of ASCAP.

after 35 years, as is provided under the 1976 Copyright Act. If any of the songs gain the status of a standard, this forfeiture of the right to recapture could represent a substantial financial loss for the writer and the writer's heirs. This kind of staff writer owns nothing.

Early in a career, a writer might be so hungry that accepting a work-made-for-hire job is the only option. But it would be well to seek a more attractive long-term alternative as soon as possible.

Label-Affiliated Deals

Songwriters who learn to take care of business discover that their best opportunity to make a financial killing in the music industry is to present themselves as not just writers but performing artists. The hottest property in the business is the singer-songwriter, who can earn both writer's royalties and artist's royalties. Because of this potential for big earnings, everybody in the business wants a piece of that pie. A small label will pressure, sometimes coerce, a prospective writer-performer to assign some or all of the publishing rights to the label. If the writer declines to share at least administration rights, the firm may **pass** on that writer—decline to sign a recording contract. Similar pressure on the singer-songwriter comes from many independent production companies. Typical dialogue: "Hey kid, we're gonna make you a big star, but it'll be expensive. We must have your publishing rights to help us recoup our recording costs and promotion expenses." The aspiring singer-songwriter has been cautioned to "hang on to your publishing" but may have to choose between signing it away to a production company or not getting signed as a recording artist.

Throughout the industry, recording companies now generally include a *controlled composition clause* in their artists' agreements. This states that the recording company will pay only a percentage (typically, 75%) of the current mechanical royalty rate to the composer and publisher for any song written or coauthored by that artist/composer.

And in recent years, some publishers in Nashville have been successful in contractually drawing from a songwriter's performance income, as well as mechanical royalties, to recoup advance money. This point can be negotiable, if the writer is willing to take less in the way of an advance.

EVALUATING PUBLISHERS

If the writer does not sign with the publishing wing of the recording label or a production company or if the writer is not a recording artist, an outside solution must be found—if not by setting up a publishing company, then by locating a publisher independent of affiliation with a recording company or production company.

How does a thoughtful writer evaluate a prospective publisher? Very carefully. Sharks and wolves abound where big dollars are available. Let us assume the writer is unknown. If there has been a struggle to gain the interest of a publisher, the writer may be ready to sign with just about any firm that shows interest. An unpublished writer should withstand the temptation to sign the first contract that is offered.

The following questions can help inexperienced composers judge a prospective publisher:

1. What is the publisher's reputation for integrity? Is your information objective, trustworthy, and current?
2. How good is the firm's leadership? How competent? How stable?
3. What is the firm's long-term track record? Is it coasting on its catalog of golden oldies or is it currently active with contemporary material?
4. Is the company making money? Says who?
5. Who in the company cares about you and your material? Do you know the professional manager or are you dealing with a subordinate person in the firm? Is there at least one individual in the firm who likes your songs enough personally to exert real effort on your behalf? This kind of personal enthusiasm is sometimes the key to successful promotion.
6. What are the firm's resources? Do the professional manager and field promoters have valuable contacts with record producers and other important people in the business? Does the company agree to produce high-quality demos of your songs? Does the company have enough working capital to carry it over lean periods?
7. If your songs hit, does the company understand the print business and the income available from licensing for sale a variety of different editions?
8. If your songs hit, does the company know how to set up licensing arrangements abroad to produce foreign income?

An unknown writer on the verge of signing a first contract with a publisher may be afraid to pose such pointed questions for fear of blowing the deal. But the answers are needed.

Whatever publishing arrangement the writer ultimately pulls together, the decision should be based on which person or firm can most successfully exploit the music over the long term. Is the publisher a genuine publisher with the know-how and contacts to truly exploit those copyrights internationally? Or only someone posing as a publisher, functioning merely as a collection agency for the writer's royalties? A shockingly high percentage of so-called publishers are only collecting agents and are not qualified to offer complete and genuine publishing services.

THE SONGWRITERS GUILD OF AMERICA

One of the important organizations representing the creative community in music is the Songwriters Guild of America (SGA). The organization bearing this name was originally formed in 1931 as the Songwriters Protective Association. For many years, it was called the American Guild of Authors and Composers (AGAC); it changed to its current name in the 1980s.

The organization provides a variety of useful services to its members: (a) offers a standard writers' publishing contract; (b) collects royalties, charging 5.75% to a ceiling of $1,750, with no charge thereafter; (c) reviews members' publishing contracts, free of charge; (d) audits publishers; (e) maintains a copyright renewal service; (f) administers writer-publishers' catalogs (CAP, the Catalog Administration Plan); (g) provides a collaboration service; (h) maintains the Songwriters Guild Foundation; (i) operates an estates administration service; (j) provides financial evaluation of songs and catalogs to members and nonmembers; (k) offers workshops for writers; and (l) lobbies actively in Washington, D.C., on behalf of songwriters.

The Songwriters Guild of America Contract

The guild urges its members to attempt to negotiate acceptance of its Popular Songwriters Contract. As one would assume, it is heavily weighted in favor of the writer. Many publishers refuse to sign it. But writers can use it at least as a negotiating document. These provisions should be studied in tandem with the draft contract provisions in Chapter 4.

The agreement's main features are the following:

1. The writer warrants that the composition is the writer's "sole, exclusive and original work" and that the writer has the right and power to make the contract and that "there exists no adverse claim to or in the composition."

2. The publisher pays at least some advance, deductible from the writer's royalties.

3. Royalties on printed editions are based on the wholesale selling price and are 10% on the first 200,000 copies sold in the United States and Canada, 12% on sales in excess of 200,000, and 15% when sales reach 500,000.

Guest speaker Marshall Crenshaw with ASCAP's Marcy Drexler at ASCAP's Advanced Songwriter Workshop held in New York. Photo courtesy of ASCAP.

4. The publisher pays the writer 50% of the publisher's receipts from all sources outside the United States and Canada.

5. The writer shares 50-50 with the publisher on income derived from all other sources, for example, mechanical royalties, synchronization rights, transcriptions, and block licenses. The publisher may discount any payments made to a collecting agent, such as the Harry Fox Agency, Inc.

6. The publisher must obtain the writer's consent before granting use of the composition in a movie, broadcast commercial, or dramatico-musical presentation.

7. The writer's royalties must be held in trust by the publisher and not used for any other purpose.

8. If the publisher fails to get a commercial recording of the composition within 1 year, the contract terminates. But the writer may grant an extension of 6 months, providing the publisher pays the writer $250.

9. The publisher must print and offer for sale regular piano copies or provide such copies or leadsheets to the writer.

10. The publisher must pay the writer 50% of foreign advances received by the publisher on a single song or a group of songs by the same writer.

11. The term (length) of the contract may be for any number of years but not more than 40 years "or 35 years from the date of first release of a commercial sound recording of the composition, whichever term ends earlier, unless this contract is sooner terminated in accordance with the provisions hereof."

12. When the contract terminates, the publisher revests in the writer all rights in the composition.

13. The publisher supplies a royalty statement at least every 6 months. The writer may demand an audit of the publisher's books upon supplying appropriate notice.

14. All disputes between the parties are to be submitted to the American Arbitration Association, and the parties agree "to be bound by and perform any award rendered in such arbitration."

15. The publisher may not assign (turn over to another publisher) the contract without the writer's consent (except on a sale of a full catalog).

16. The writer and publisher must agree on future use—the exploitation of a composition in a manner not yet contemplated and therefore not specifically covered by the contract.

CONTRACT REASSIGNMENT OR DEFAULT

The writer and publisher may negotiate at length to shape a contract that is equitable. The relationship may turn out to be mutually profitable, even congenial. But it is the nature of the business that writers and publishers frequently want to terminate contracts. This does not mean the songs under contract must then die for lack of promotion. Rather, the copyrights may be reassigned.

Reassignments are common and can be to the advantage of the writer. From the writer's point of view, a reassignment is perhaps even advantageous if the songs are included in a bona fide sale of the first publisher's catalog, or in the event of a merger, or if the assignment is to a subsidiary or affiliated company. In each of these circumstances, the writer should demand from the first publisher a written instrument that states that the assignee-publisher assumes all obligations of the original (first) publisher.

The songwriter must continually police the contract to make sure that its terms are being carried out. Default is a common occurrence. It may not involve unfairness or dishonesty or fraud at all. More likely, a publisher defaults if unable to get the song recorded, or royalty statements are incorrect or incomplete, or the publisher just can't come up with royalty payments when they are due, or becomes too burdened working on other properties. If the writer believes the publisher is guilty of default, and if the publisher has been given the chance to **cure** the **default** if such cure was stipulated in the contract, whatever the reasons, there are some options. The first is to break the contract unilaterally. Courts take a dim view of unilateral action of this kind, for it is the court that must determine if a contract **breach** is "material" and whether the publisher has flagrantly disregarded appeals from the writer for **remedy**. Second, a lawsuit can be filed asking to be released from the contract. Third, a letter of termination can be sent to the publisher, stating that the publisher is in default and that henceforth the rights to any songs that have not yet been delivered to the publisher (known as *future rights*) will go to another publisher.

BREAKING IN

Breaking into the field of professional songwriting is not as mysterious as generally believed. Many unknown writers are discovered every year, but few make it on luck alone. When we check out the so-called overnight success stories, we learn that most of these individuals used certain promotion techniques. We cannot articulate a breaking-in "formula." But we can describe what works for most new writers (see Table 3.2).

To increase your chances of success, you should undertake three levels of self-promotion: (a) Establish a local reputation and local contacts, (b) contact publishers by mail, and (c) meet with publishers directly.

TABLE 3.2   Seven Steps to Success

1. The first step is the most critical. Before spending time and money seeking a professional career, it is of overriding importance that a songwriter first find out whether or not the talent is there. Your songs may go over just great with your family and friends. These reactions can be heartwarming—and they can be seriously misleading. What you as an amateur need at this point is an objective appraisal of your creative talents.

2. Make certain you know your craft. A writer may not be a creative genius but can learn to be a craftsman.

3. Arm yourself with professional leadsheets, lyric sheets, and demonstration recordings.

4. Focus your promotion efforts on the specific market your songs fit.

5. Thoroughly promote your songs in your own locale before risking a trip to "the big city."

6. Employ the promotion techniques outlined in these pages; learn the business.

7. Persist. Most of your competitors will become discouraged and give up. The persistent writer can beat the competition by hanging in there.

Local Promotion

Prove yourself locally. The amateur needs a place to make mistakes, to experiment with different kinds of promotional efforts. The home town provides a space more private for this breaking-in period than the big recording-center cities.

Look within your own circle of family and friends for a connection to the music business, no matter how small. If you don't have one, start with professional performers in your area. Observe them in performance; visit their rehearsals. Hang out, get acquainted. If your songs suit their style, you may persuade them to try your material and give you their reactions. At this stage, it does not matter whether these professionals are well known. One day, they may be, and making their acquaintance may initiate a contact that will bear fruit later.

Contact your local radio stations and try to persuade program directors, disc jockeys, and music librarians to listen to your demos. They will be unable to use your songs, but their opinions of your work could be valuable to you, for they are full-time professional appraisers of recordings and have ears tuned to popular tastes.

See if it's possible to collaborate with people writing and producing college shows in your area. Colleges also are among the most important bookers of visiting artists. Traveling performers often pick up useful material on the road. With some performers, it is more effective to get your songs to people *around* the artist, such as the performer's musical director, arranger, or manager—some managers are influential song pickers.

Some smaller cities are headquarters for publishing companies. Do not rule out small publishers. If you evaluate them according to the guidelines listed in this chapter and if they measure up, go with them if you do not have a more attractive option at the time. Contact local advertising agencies and commercial production companies. Communities with populations of 100,000 and up will have such firms. They are in constant need of melodies and musical ideas for broadcast commercials.

If you begin to receive favorable local reaction to your writing, you just might be ready for the next step in promoting your songs.

Promotion by Mail

Amateur songwriters have frequently been successful in landing their first publishers through the mail. This is a special technique, however, and efforts of this kind often fail because they are not handled effectively. But the writer who follows the procedures outlined has a reasonably good chance of getting songs heard.

1. Study the record charts and find out the names of publishers who are currently active in handling the type of music you write. Select a dozen or so, perhaps two dozen, names.
2. Locate the addresses and telephone numbers of these publishers. Your local telephone company and public library have directories for large cities, and you can try the Web. Another source is *Billboard's International Buyers Guide*, published annually.
3. Even if these sources list the name of the firm's professional manager, you should write a short letter of inquiry or place a telephone call to make sure the position is still held by that individual.

4. After getting the name of the professional manager, write that person a letter requesting permission to mail in some of your songs. The letter should be short, well written, and to the point. Briefly state what reception your songs have already experienced with professional performers. The publisher will be uninterested in your success at that Rotary Club luncheon. Drop a name or two, if you can, of established artists who have reacted favorably to your songs. If permission is received, mail in not more than three or four songs. Don't expect any publisher to examine more than that; send only your best work. Your package should contain, at a minimum, a demo recording of each song (put all three of them on the same cassette) *and* separate lyric sheets for each song, neatly typed or printed, with your name, address, and telephone number on each sheet. Inclusion of professionally prepared leadsheets is optional with some publishers, but play it safe and include them. Your package should contain a brief cover letter. Because many publishers won't bother to answer your letter, a better response can probably be obtained if you mail the publisher a self-addressed, stamped postcard.

All mail addressed to publishers should be sent first class. Do not send certified or registered mail; many publishers seem to feel that such mail could mean trouble, and they often refuse to accept it unless they recognize the sender's name.

Wait 3 weeks. If you receive no reply, call the publisher to be sure that your material has arrived. If your songs have been received but have not gained acceptance, continue the process with other publishers until you receive a favorable reaction.

Very few publishers today will open unsolicited mail. They are concerned not only about being accused of stealing material; a greater concern is that 99% of unsolicited songs and demos are just awful. Publishers cannot take time to dig through the hundreds of songs received every week just in the hope that 1% might be worth serious consideration. But when a writer has been professional enough to obtain permission from the publisher to submit material, whatever is mailed in is viewed entirely differently. Publishers at least know that a well-written letter of request has been authored by an individual who understands something about how a publishing company functions. An unknown writer, so appraised, may have a better chance to be heard than the run-of-the-mill amateurs who clog the mails with unacceptable material. Take a look at the sample first-contact letter that follows

---

Mr. John Doe, Professional Manager
XYZ Music Publishing Company
Address

Dear Mr. Doe: Date:

Please indicate your response to the following question and then mail this card back to me (it is already addressed and stamped).

Will you examine my songs for publication?

Yes _____   **No** _____

Your response will be sincerely appreciated.

Thank you.
(Signed here)
Austin Hopeful
Address/Telephone

Direct Contact With Publishers

Even though many amateur songwriters manage to create publisher interest through mail contacts, most songs get published following a direct, personal contact with the publisher.

Because popular music publishers have offices in the leading recording centers, the amateur writer who would be professional must eventually invade the forbidding precincts of New York, Nashville, or Los Angeles. Publishers in these cities vary in the manner in which they will see uninvited guests who visit their offices. Many publishers will see unknown songwriters, but it is unwise for the newcomer to walk directly from the bus station to the publisher's office. Often, publishers recommend that the songwriter who is unknown first write a letter to the publisher. Here again, the U.S. mail can open the door for you.

Your letter can be about the same as the sample given earlier, but its purpose is to ask permission to present your material to the publisher in person rather than by mail. If you are only visiting the city, ask for an appointment as soon as possible, but don't pressure the publisher. Leave your local telephone number. It may be more convenient for the publisher's office to telephone you than write you a letter. Publishers will often see people who write them a sensible letter of this kind. Does this tactic result in publishers signing new songwriters? Rarely. Why? For the reasons already stated: Very few really good songs are presented to them.

Yet another approach to getting to a direct contact with a publisher is to telephone and ask for an appointment. Here again, the receptionist must be the gatekeeper. Chances of soliciting an appointment through a letter or a telephone call are about equal.

Once you have met with a publisher, be sure to write a thank-you note for the time and the opportunity to discuss your work. Keep up that valuable contact even if you may not have new material. Then, when you are ready to submit more songs—whether in person or by mail—you will be on the inside track.

The foregoing promotional methods are the most effective ones a person can use, at least until that time when the writer can contact a publisher cold and say, "Your friend and mine, Jane Doe, suggested I get in touch with you about my songs . . ." If this Jane Doe is truly a mutual friend, the publisher's attitude toward seeing the unknown writer is immediately transformed, for someone whose judgment is respected has already functioned for the publisher as a preliminary gatekeeper. The publisher's door is now open, at least temporarily. If a writer can develop these kinds of inside contacts, a good start has been made. But once "inside," the material had better be good, or the inside contact will prove valueless.

Demonstration Recordings

Demonstration recordings (**demos**) are used in a variety of ways:

- ▶ A songwriter records a demo to introduce the songs to a publisher.
- ▶ A publisher produces demos to persuade an artist or record producer to record the publisher's new songs.
- ▶ A performer records a demo to showcase the performer's talents to a prospective employer, such as a recording company, an agent, or a **contractor.**
- ▶ A composer prepares a demo to induce an advertising agency to use the material for broadcast commercials.

▶ An ad agency produces a demo to show a client, or prospective client, how a broadcast commercial might sound.

Effective demos can be performed by a singer or small group. The minimum accompaniment is piano or guitar. The maximum appropriate accompaniment would include a **rhythm section** and one or two front-line players. Under special circumstances, elaborate demos with full instrumentation and written charts are produced. As for the style of performance, the singing should be straightforward, with a minimum amount of styling. With a songwriter's demo, the listener wants to judge the song. Of course, if the demo is not of a song but of an auditioning performer, the artist will do whatever possible to simulate a live performance.

Demos made for publishers or by publishers are most commonly recorded on high-quality audiocassettes. Each cassette should be clearly labeled, on the box as well as the cassette itself, with an accompanying log of songs: their sequence numbers, song titles, and full names of composers. Tape one copy of the log outside the case and fold another copy inside. Be sure your own name, address, and phone number are on every piece of material you submit.

Songwriters who sing passably well can produce their own demos—on home recording equipment, if it is of reasonably good quality, and there is more and more available with the current advances in technology. Professional demo producers are readily available in larger cities. They provide a professional singer accompanied by piano or guitar. Rates rise, of course, for more backup musicians, but producers offer special rates for more than one song. Elaborately produced demos with written-out arrangements, full orchestra, perhaps a group of singers, recorded **multitrack** can be very expensive. Such demos, properly mixed down and equalized, can attain the quality of a master. Some do, and are subsequently released commercially. Such releases are illegal unless they are properly licensed by the copyright owners of the material and the appropriate payments are made to the American Federation of Musicians (AFM) and American Federation of Television and Radio Artists (AFTRA) artists involved.

All demos should include two notices of copyright: the letter P in a circle (℗), to protect the phonorecord, and the letter C in a circle (©), to protect the music contained in the recording. Such notices offer some protection from unauthorized use of the tapes. Demos are frequently lost because of inadequate identification and careless handling. Mailed demo packages should also bear a complete return address and return postage. Mail them first class. Send copies, of course, not the masters.

Performing artists' unions have regulations concerning demo production, but circumvention in most cities is widespread. Check local practices before recording.

Who Pays?

Simple demos can be produced for just the cost of the tape and the electricity needed to power the home recorder. The cost of the songwriter's demos may rise a bit if someone else is hired to sing or play. But many publishers find homemade demos unacceptable and prefer to go into a demo studio with professional performers. Costs can run to several hundred dollars and, under special circumstances, perhaps several thousand dollars, if the publisher believes a master tape could be produced.

So who should pay for demo production costs? Views differ in the industry. Some publishers attempt to charge all demo costs against a contract writer's potential royalties—in other words, making these costs recoverable. Other publishers try to get the writer to split demo costs 50-50, again charging the writer's share against recoupable royalties. Most writers believe that all promotional costs, including demo expenses, should be considered the publisher's responsibility.

NOTE

1. Letter to Franz Anton-Hoffmeister dated January 15, 1801.

MUSIC PUBLISHING

Years ago, music publishers printed copies of music and placed them in stores for sale to the public. Today, the process is much more complex. In the popular music field, the great majority of new songs are not printed at all. They exist, at first, only in the form of tapes or professional copies (**leadsheets**) that are distributed in manuscript form without cost to artists and record producers. Music publishers, then, are not printers. When they believe that printing their copyrighted works might prove profitable, most publishers license others to provide these services (see Chapter 5 for more information on copyrights).

The heart of the music **publishing** business today lies not in the print business, as it is called, but in the rights to the original music. A publisher's principal sources of income derive from record royalties and from **performance** royalties received from the American Society of Composers, Authors and Publishers (ASCAP), Broadcast Music Incorporated (BMI), or SESAC for performances of music copyrighted by the publisher. Most performance royalties are generated from performances of recordings on radio and of songs on television or other media. Those with long experience in the music business know publishing to be a lucrative and steady source of income. That is why just about everyone in the performing and recording fields is involved in some way in music publishing.

To gain a perspective on how this field has become the rich giant that it is, Table 4.1 shows how the industry developed historically.

← Paul McCartney celebrates more than 6 million broadcasts of "Yesterday" as the most performed song in BMI's catalog as of 1993. McCartney is shown here with BMI Vice President, European Writer/Publisher Relations Phil Graham. Photo courtesy BMI.

TABLE 4.1   Development of Music Publishing

1640:	The first book published in America—and it happens to be a music book—is *The Bay Psalm Book*, which first used musical notation in the edition of 1698.
1770:	The first native-born American composer, William Billings, gets his music published.
1790:	First U.S. Congress passes first copyright law.
1850-1900:	Minstrel shows are widely popular and increase public interest in popular music. Publishers begin to prosper.
1890s:	The player piano becomes popular, creating a demand for player piano rolls. Large music publishing firms are established in the last two decades of the 1800s. Merchandising methods develop, and publishers begin to discover that if enough people hear a good song, it will probably be a hit. The most effective song promoters now are the performers in various theaters and vaudeville houses that develop around the turn of the century.
1900:	Popular music publishing becomes big business. In this first decade, an estimated 100 songs each sell a million copies or more within a 1-year period. This occurs at a time when the population of the United States is about 90 million. The U.S. Congress passes the historic 1909 Copyright Law that provides publishers, for the first time, with *mechanical rights* in recorded music. Initially, this revenue derives largely from player piano rolls.
1920s:	ASCAP, established in 1914, becomes a major force as a performing rights organization. For the first time in this country, publishers and writers begin to receive income from performances of their music. Radio broadcasting begins and is initially fought by publishers. They believe radio hurts sheet music sales. Sound movies ("talkies") begin. Film producers negotiate fees for music synchronization rights. The Harry Fox Agency is established. Sheet music sales drop with the rise of radio. Publishers now close most of their branch offices to concentrate promotion efforts on the radio network broadcasting centers that, at this time, are New York City, Chicago, and Los Angeles.
1930s:	The Great Depression severely hurts the music publishing business but increasing income from movie producers helps. The "big bands" develop and become the most important source for plugs for new songs, particularly if the band has a remote wire for radio broadcasting. National Music Publishers' Association expands the Harry Fox Agency to include mechanical licensing of copyrights. SESAC is formed, with headquarters in New York City, in response to European publisher concerns about performance royalty income from the United States.
1940s:	During and after World War II, people spend larger shares of their incomes on music, instruments, records, movies. The LP record appears in 1948, now producing publishers' royalties on 10 to 12 songs per record, not just 2. National Association of Broadcasters (NAB) forms BMI in reaction to increasing demands from ASCAP. The big band singers (Perry Como, Frank Sinatra, Doris Day, others) go solo and become the dominant source for introducing new songs. American gospel music becomes a mainstay of SESAC's representation.

1950s:	Rapid growth of television kills live music on the radio. Disc jockeys become the new hit-makers. Rock and roll comes to dominate popular music, exploding the record market. BMI now succeeds in capturing the majority of copyrights in the rock and country fields. SESAC repertory expands to include country music.
1960s:	Increasing dependence of publishers on radio to break new songs. The print business improves, particularly editions for the amateur and the educational field. Harry Fox Agency becomes a wholly owned subsidiary of National Music Publishers Association (NMPA).
1970s:	Radio broadcasters shorten their playlists below the Top 40, forcing companies to promote airplay in secondary and tertiary markets, located in smaller cities. The print business in the pop song folio and educational field continues to grow, but inflating costs cause many publishers to quit all print activity and assign such rights to subpublishers and licensees here and abroad. Publishers' incomes from ASCAP and BMI continue to rise. New musical genres continue to develop.
1980s:	Old copyrights enjoy financial boom due to widespread popularity of CDs. Huge mergers and acquisitions dominate the publishing business and all the music industry. Music becomes an even more significant part of films, television programs, and commercials. MTV begins broadcasting music videos 24 hours a day. Increased music use via new media, particularly home videocassettes, computer games, and video jukeboxes, increases publisher revenues.
1990s:	Publishers, recording companies, and other music users contemplate new ways to exploit their product with the advent of the Internet. The European Economic Community moves to ease restrictions among its member countries, and the United States seeks to make trade agreements that will help it remain competitive and to update and harmonize its legislation. New musical genres, including rap and alternative, challenge rock and roll for dominance of the market. Success in foreign markets remains critical to the overall success of an artist as a performer or composer. Communication and entertainment companies with related interests, such as cable, Internet-based music sites, telephone, motion picture, record, television and radio stations, software and hardware companies, theme parks, and retail stores, continue to merge or to make cooperative agreements.
2000:	The industry enters the new millennium grappling with technological issues such as digital media delivery and transmission standards.

TYPES OF PUBLISHERS

The music publishing business is a maze of full-line publishers, **subpublishers,** publishing groups, administered and administering companies, print licensees, manager-publishers, lawyer-publishers, independent publishers, and multinational conglomerates.

When a small publisher starts to become successful, large firms take notice and may offer to enter into a **copublishing** relationship or even to buy part or all of the smaller firm.

Big firms seek to acquire smaller ones in the music field for many of the same reasons such transactions occur all the time in other industries—among them the notion that bigger is better and more efficient. Although some small publishers can deal successfully in foreign markets, joining a publisher's group or otherwise connecting with a larger firm can increase opportunities abroad. All large music publishers have affiliates or licensees abroad, and these relationships afford opportunities for reciprocal sharing of royalties in foreign territories. Music publishers have learned a valuable lesson from the movie producers, who discovered decades ago that foreign income may be as large as, or larger than, money derived from domestic markets.

Several years ago, there were more than 30 major music publishers. Today, there are fewer than 10, and their international control of the industry is enormous. Through an unprecedented surge of mergers and large acquisitions, some companies currently boast catalogs of more than 500,000 copyrights. These megapublishers may seem more focused on administration and collection than on development and exploitation of songs and songwriters. But new companies are rising to fill the void, and the giants say they are returning to the fine old art of "song-plugging," not only to earn the kind of publisher's shares that would justify their purchases but also because the future of the industry depends on finding and publishing new material as well as making money from the sale of rights to songs in existing catalogs.

Full-Line Companies

Prior to the great expansion of the recording industry, many of the older music publishers included practically all types of music in their catalogs—classical, educational, movie and show music, and pop. New firms with this broad a repertoire are scarce today. But firms such as Warner/Chappell, BMG Music, MCA Music, Universal Music Group, and Sony Music, for example, attempt to be active in all musical styles. These giants are all affiliated with record and, in some cases, film companies. Representative Warner/Chappell owns, administers, or subpublishes more than a million copyrights here and abroad. Full-line publishers trace their origins to the music of Hollywood, Broadway, or the great pop writers of **Tin Pan Alley**. Each full-line firm has developed its own administrative structure, but Figure 4.1 shows a typical organization of this scope. Department names vary from company to company.

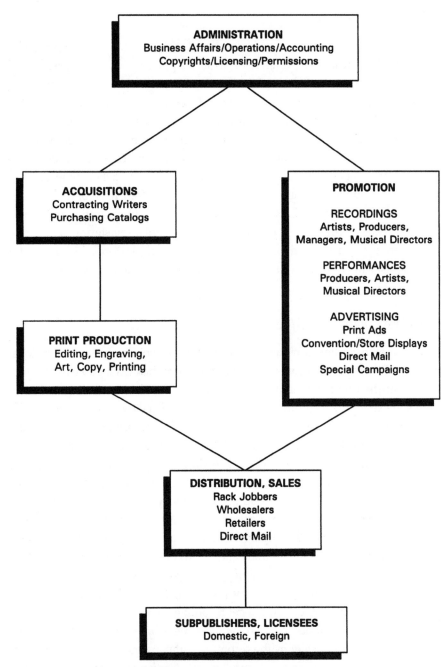

Figure 4.1   Full-Line Music Publisher

Independent Publishers

Some firms are not affiliated with a multinational publishing organization or a recording label; the industry often refers to such a publisher as an *independent*. Independents range in size from the one-person operation to firms controlling multimillion-dollar catalogs. Many of the independents are members of the Association of Independent Music Publishers. Some publishing firms are proud of their independence and do not actively seek to be acquired by a larger organization; others try to build up their catalogs to become attractive to a prospective buyer. Some independent publishers are administrative publishers who perform basic administrative duties in return for a percentage (often 10%) of the publishing income they administer. Responsibilities of such administrative publishers include collecting royalties, licensing use of copyrights, registering new copyrights, and royalty accounting. They do little or no **exploitation,** which is fine for their clients, who are usually artists or writers who promote themselves.

Recording Company Affiliates

Almost all recording companies own or control publishing companies. Most of these affiliates are expected to show a profit from their own publishing activities, rather than be dependent on their alliance with their recording company. Others are set up by recording companies as merely a depository for copyrights of songs written by their contract recording artists. Recording companies find that they need to affiliate with an ASCAP, BMI, or SESAC publishing operation to negotiate contracts with their artists involving both publishing and recording rights. Recording company publishing affiliates, many of whom are among the largest publishers in the world, also acquire catalogs from other publishers or writers. When such catalogs are acquired, advances are generally paid. Critics argue that these interlocking companies create conflicts of interest. Others argue that such arrangements restrain trade and are in conflict with antitrust laws. Historically, newer writers and artists were sometimes coerced into placing their copyrights with a recording company publisher. Those who refused to do so sometimes found it more difficult to get recording contracts.

Many recording contracts contain *controlled composition* language that calls for a reduced *mechanical royalty* by the recording company on any song recorded by the artist that was also written or controlled by the artist. The term *controlled composition* refers to control of the copyright of a composition. Whoever controls the copyright has the right to agree to a reduced mechanical payment from the recording company. Most of these clauses reduce the label's payment to the artist/writer and the song publisher to 75% of the statutory rate, but it may be even less because of the imposition of a maximum rate usually 10 times the three-fourths statutory rate for all the songs on an album. The recording company may impose a controlled composition clause on songs performed by the artist on an album even if the artist was not the composer of all the songs on the album. In this case, the artist is often required to make up the difference between the three-fourths rate and the full statutory rate to the composer and publisher of the songs that were recorded. Some recording companies will not insist on controlled composition clauses with writers who agree to place their works in the recording company's affiliated publishing company.

Nonetheless, for most performer-songwriters, a recording contract is the best way to promote their songs. Despite the associated reduced mechanical payments, publishing/recording deals, when fairly handled, are still the most important income source other than personal appearance, which usually becomes significant later in an artist's career.

Artist-Owned Companies

Many recording artists who write their own material form their own publishing companies. The reason is simple: They see no need to give up the extra income to anyone else. Royalties to the publisher of the copyrights accrue from all record sales. As a result, artists, usually with assistance from their managers (and attorneys), set up publishing companies in order to keep control over their music. Because most artists are largely concerned with recording and performing, their publishing activities are almost always limited to their own compositions. They do not generally get involved in the print business or conventional domestic distribution, although they may have subpublishing deals abroad usually negotiated by their attorneys or administrative publisher.

Writer-Owned Companies

Hundreds of very small publishing operations are owned by individual writers. Most often, these small firms have been set up by writers who have been unable to get their music accepted by other publishers. Some writer-owned firms

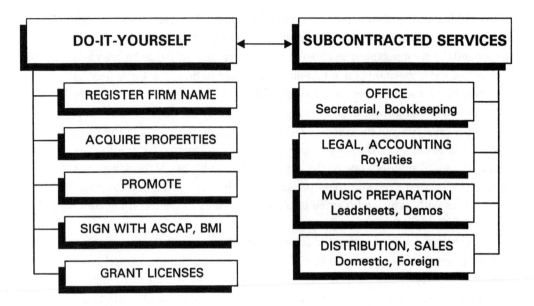

Figure 4.2   Writer-Owned Publishing Company

have been set up by composers who were previously under contract but who came to believe their material was not receiving sufficient promotion—so they go it alone.

One reason for the prevalence of so many writer-owned firms is that an individual can set up shop for an absurdly low amount of capital—perhaps less than $500. At the end of this book are recommendations on how to set up your own company. Also, see Figure 4.2, which shows how very small music publishing firms can be structured.

Educational Field

Some publishers in the United States limit their catalogs primarily to music intended for use by students and schools from elementary grade levels through college. The biggest sellers are for piano, organ, and guitar, followed by strings and percussion. Part of these sales are known as *bench packs*—educational materials given by the equipment manufacturer to the customer upon sale of a new piano or organ. The instrument manufacturer pays the copyright owners for these materials. The biggest-selling editions scored for schools are for pop, jazz, choir, marching band, and concert band compositions.

Specialty Publishers

Many publishers limit their catalogs to just one kind of music. Publishers active only in the country field, for example, are among the nation's largest. Most specialty houses are, however, relatively small, preferring to restrict their activities to a field they understand best, such as choral music, gospel, children's music, and so-called stage band (big bands in schools and colleges playing pop and jazz music). One of the larger kinds of specialty houses publishes what is called "Christian music." These firms, many of them located in Nashville, prosper not only through large sales of their music on records but also from a good-sized print business.

Included on the list of specialty publishers should be those who limit their catalogs to contemporary serious (classical) and avant-garde music. Most of these kinds of publishers are subsidized by a foundation or university; they usually have sizable catalogs of foreign copyrights. Some of them publish only privately distributed editions. Recordings of their music are also largely subsidized.

Concert Music

Concert (or classical) music is that repertoire generally associated with opera, symphony, ballet, recital, choral, and church music. Only a handful of publishers limit their catalogs to these fields. Representative concert music publishers include G. Schirmer, Peters, and Theodore Presser.

Classical music publishers make up for their marginal properties with an array of special editions of the classics for school orchestras and choirs, as well as studies for keyboard, strings, solo instruments, and voice. Much of the income of classical publishers derives from the rental and licensing of scores and instrumental and vocal parts.

Besides maintaining catalogs of older music, nearly all of it from Europe, these houses provide a special service. They publish the works of 20th-century serious composers despite the lack of financial gain from this area of music. Some of these losses are offset by offering dramatic works and extended pieces through the rental of the parts rather than the sale of printed editions.

Subpublishers, Licensees

Most publishers, including many of the largest ones, find it necessary to farm out some of their services. Firms providing these services are called subpublishers, licensees, or **selling agents** (application of these terms is not always precise; many professionals use them interchangeably).

The service most commonly assigned to an outside firm is the print business or the production and sale of printed editions. Because few popular music publishers print and market printed editions of their copyrights, they license another company to do this for them. Among the largest of these licensee publishers are Hal Leonard, Inc. and Warner/Chappell. A publisher not wanting to get into the print business will normally strike a deal that provides for the licensee (the print firm) to bear the full costs of preparing, printing, and distributing the printed edition; then the licensee pays the licensor a royalty on sales, often in the range of 20% of the wholesale price. In deals of this kind, the licensee is sometimes called a selling agent. A less common arrangement involves the copyright owner (prime publisher) bearing all preparation and printing costs, then paying the subpublisher or selling agent a distribution fee of 20% on sales. These kinds of licensing deals are most common for major catalogs where the licensor is in a position to bear the production costs in return for a larger slice of the proceeds.

Publisher-subpublisher arrangements are also common in print editions for the educational market. One of the largest licensee/selling agents in this field is Hal Leonard, Inc.

Foreign Territories

The publishing business is worldwide, and many American publishers receive a large percentage of their income from foreign territories. Some large companies have branch offices in foreign countries that function much like the American parent firm. First, they try to exploit the American catalog by promoting the original recording, getting **cover records,** selling printed editions, and collecting mechanical and performance royalties. This may involve the branch office arranging for translations of English lyrics into the indigenous language. Second, branch offices usually involve themselves not only in pushing the catalog of the home office, but also in exploiting new copyrights on their own.

An American publisher lacking branch offices abroad calls on firms that do possess them. Many publishers, large and small, retain the subpublishing services of the giants. Although royalty splits vary from country to country, the most common sharing between the prime publisher and licensee is 75% to 80% for the prime publisher and 20% to 25% for the licensee. Percentages usually correlate to how the parties share the production and promotion expenses.

If an American publisher lacks foreign offices of its own and chooses not to license its copyrights through a large U.S. firm that has foreign offices, it may seek out one or more foreign-based independent publishers as a subpublisher or licensee. Most of these deals are for at least 3 years. The American company will expect the subpublisher to exploit the American copyrights through release and promotion of the original recording, arranging cover records, providing printed editions, and collecting performance royalties. The performing rights organization functioning in a given territory will be forwarding the writer's share to ASCAP, BMI, or SESAC, but the American firm's subpublisher is usually expected to receive the publisher's share and make sure that performances are being fully licensed and money is paid for them.

With regard to foreign collections, some distinction should be made between a collection deal and a subpublishing deal. In a collection deal, the subpublisher is merely expected to collect the income, taking 10% or 15% as an administrative fee and remitting the rest. In a subpublishing deal, the percentages are more favorable to the local publisher and usually involve advances to the original publisher supplying the catalog. Although performance rights societies may collect performance royalties for writers and publishers, many subpublishing deals often allow the local publisher to collect 100% of the full publisher's share.

At-Source Deals and Receipts-Basis Deals

Payment of royalties earned at the source is a concept most favorable to the writer: The writer's share is calculated on income earned in the foreign territory. In contrast, in a receipts-basis agreement, the share is only on income received by the publisher in the United States (after payments or deductions to a subpublisher have been made). At-source deals are usually available only from publishers who have wholly owned affiliates in foreign territories, such as multinational companies like BMG and Warner/Chappell. The writer gets paid as if the writer were in the country where the money is made so the writer is entitled to the writer's share (50% or more) as well as a copublishing share if there is a copublishing deal. An at-source deal means that the writer would get 50% of income earned at the source, in the foreign territory, before deductions for subpublishers are made, no matter what money is eventually remitted to the United States. In an at-source deal, if $100 is earned in Australia, the writer's share would be $50. In a receipts deal, the writer would get royalties based on monies received by the publisher. If $100 is earned in Australia and the publisher had a 75/25 deal with the Australian subpublisher, the American publisher would receive $75 and the writer's share would be $37.50 (half of that 75%).

American firms may contract for subpublishers to cover more than one country. For example, it is common for a subpublisher based in Germany to cover Germany, Austria, and German-speaking Switzerland, the territory of GEMA, the German performance rights society. French-based subpublishers would probably service the French-speaking territories in Africa, the SACEM territory. A Scandinavian subpublisher would probably have jurisdiction over Norway, Sweden, Denmark, Iceland, and Finland.

The Music Publishers' Forum, representing a number of independent publishers centered in Nashville, recommends that subpublishers be limited to licenses covering performance, mechanical, and print royalties. The group believes that American publishers should wholly retain lyric and video rights, **jingle** licenses, and **grand rights,** or at least be able to approve and control these kinds of uses.

The ideal subpublishing situation would include a person on the spot who understands the language and knows the music business, especially with regard to registering copyrights with local societies and collecting performance royalties. For instance, Germany's performance rights society, GEMA, not only collects performance royalties but collects mechanical royalties as well. Independent publishers lacking the resources to set up subpublishing deals can retain the Harry Fox Agency to meet many of their basic needs for services in foreign territories through the agency's reciprocal agreements with foreign societies (see Table 3, Foreign Affiliates, in the "International Copyright" chapter).

ADMINISTRATION

Administration of publishing companies varies greatly according to the size of the firm. Independent companies may have a small staff, with each individual performing a variety of tasks to keep the company functioning properly. For example, a small, independent publisher might be run entirely by the owner-songwriter and a part-time secretary. Contrast this type of operation with the management structure of a full-line publisher (see Figures 4.1 and 4.2).

Large publishers will have a central administration consisting of a president (or vice president in charge of administration), department heads, and support personnel. Firms vary in the labels they apply to departments. What follows is a description of the administrative structure of a typical major publisher.

Royalty Department

The royalty department is managed by an individual, usually an accountant or financial person, who supervises assistants handling receipts and disbursements, accounting, data processing, payroll, insurance, and purchasing.

Copyright Department

Most publishers have at least one employee who heads a department that handles copyrights. Larger firms would have several persons in this department. A qualified department head of copyrights must know the U.S. Copyright Laws of 1909, the 1976 revisions, and basic international laws and agreements ("conventions") covering foreign copyrights.

The firm's copyright department performs a number of essential tasks. Among the most important are the following:

1. Conducting a title search. The copyright department must first determine who really owns the work. The Library of Congress will assist in this research. Copyright ownership can get complicated. If the work has coauthors, what are their claims of ownership and are the claims valid? What if the work was published before? What if the music or the lyrics

have been revised? How does a publisher determine if some of the rights have been assigned to another firm or individual or estate? After the copyright department has performed this research, questions remaining unclear are referred to a copyright attorney, who might or might not be on the publisher's staff.

2. Registering claims of copyright.

3. Recording transfers of copyright ownership.

4. Forming a liaison with the Harry Fox Agency, particularly with respect to **mechanical licenses** and synchronization fees. Publishing firms may also choose to issue their own mechanical licenses and synchronization licenses.

5. Keeping records of **subsisting** copyrights and their pending expiration dates. Recommending renewal, extension, sale, or abandonment of subsisting copyrights. In matters of this importance, top management would, of course, be directly involved.

Legal or Business Affairs

Music publishers must have lawyers expert in copyright law and music publishing. They also need expert tax lawyers experienced in artist management and the recording industry. Nearly all publishing transactions are based on contracts, and the ongoing services of qualified attorneys are essential in negotiating them. Small firms employ these specialists by the hour or day. Larger firms not only retain counsel part-time, as needed, but employ one or more lawyers on their staffs full-time. Attorneys from outside firms may also be employed for specific projects, such as to facilitate a major acquisition.

Print Publishing Operations

After a copyright title has been cleared and the author is signed to a contract, and after the arrangers and editors have performed their tasks (assuming the work is printed), the music must go through a number of additional operations before it can be distributed and sold. Many firms group these activities, such as printing, warehousing, inventory control, and shipping, under an operations department.

Distribution

Publishers vary in how they handle the distribution and sale of printed editions. Some of the typical patterns include the following:

- From publisher to print publisher to jobber to retailer to customer
- From print publisher to **rack jobber** to retailer to customer
- From print publisher via direct mail or electronic distributions to customer

Some print publishers are licensed to handle everything for the prime publisher—arranging, editing, printing, advertising, distribution. Such printers/distributors may also work with rack jobbers, who service a variety of retail outlets.

The Professional Manager

Years ago, all publishers in the popular music field employed what were known at that time as song pluggers. Their place in the world of show business has been portrayed colorfully in the movies and other media, occasionally with accuracy. In the late 1940s, it became unfashionable to call these operatives song pluggers. Gradually, they came to be known as professional managers. Since World War II, the professional manager has had to assume a role much broader in scope than song-plugging. Here are the principal responsibilities of the professional manager:

1. Discover and sign new writers.
2. Maintain good working relationships with writers under contract.
3. Persuade artists and producers to record the writer's music.
4. Negotiate favorable rates when licensing uses of the writer's copyrights.
5. Search out ancillary uses of those copyrights such as jingles and merchandising tie-ins.

Except for smaller, newer firms, most professional managers working for established publishers are individuals with long experience and lots of street knowledge, who form that indispensable link between the composer, the artist, and particularly, the record producer. Inexperienced musicians should plan on several years of pavement pounding, listening, and learning before attempting to fill the shoes of a professional manager. Still, small firms offer a good training ground, and some versatile individuals managing small publishing firms rise fast.

ACQUIRING NEW MATERIAL

The single most important enterprise of a music publisher is to locate new music and sign writers. This unending search for new talent and new material is of primary importance to the success of a publishing company, for the music publishing business cannot manufacture its own raw material. Rather, publishers must discover talented writers among the hundreds of thousands of composers who think their music is just what the publisher wants.

In searching for new material, a publisher will first turn to writers of recent success. Such composers are as sought after as recording stars. Songwriters with songs on the current **charts** can pick and choose their own publishers. To persuade writers to place their next new material with them, publishers offer a variety of inducements. In fact, many successful writers change publishers frequently, ever seeking a better contract, stronger promotion, perhaps more congenial associates.

A second source of good writers for publishers comes through the recommendation of insiders, those in the music business whose musical judgment appears trustworthy or whose track record in the field has been impressive.

A third source of usable new material is writers already under contract. Professional managers often find it necessary to prod their own staff writers, urging them to keep turning out material for the insatiable market.

Quite often the recording company and publisher are seeking the same talent. Most new writers signed by publishers are potential recording artists who have not yet come to the attention of the label A&R (artist and repertoire) staff. At this stage, the publisher can sign the artist or group to a publishing deal with the intent of then placing them with a label. This has two important advantages: (a) The publisher getting involved at this early stage usually pays less in advances, and (b) the artist/writer is getting some much needed money at a crucial time while establishing a relationship with an influential ally who can provide creative as well as business assistance. On the other hand, lawyers and managers usually prefer to sign an artist to a label first and then either make a bigger publishing deal for the now more valuable artist or have the artist retain the publishing, at least in the United States.

Acceptance Criteria

Successful popular music publishers have developed criteria that often serve well to distinguish acceptable material. Most publishers, knowingly or intuitively, seem to judge material based on these criteria:

1. Does the **demo** hit you? If the music in the recording doesn't appeal to you in the first eight bars, that demo probably will never be heard to its end.

2. Has the composer been successful lately? Popular preferences shift so rapidly, a publisher is safer going with a currently charted writer than with someone with an impressive history but no recent success.

3. What artists might record the song? What recording producers can the publisher contact who might be persuaded to consider the song?

4. Does the material fill a current need in the catalog? Most publishers seek, over a period of time, some kind of balance among the types of songs they accept. They have learned it is unprofitable to try to push, say, in one season, all country songs or all rock songs. Prudent publishers seek not only diversity but balance. Someone might submit a very attractive piece of material, but if that particular publisher is currently loaded with that kind of song, a good piece of material will probably be rejected.

5. Does the material appear to show inherent quality? Most of the decision makers in the business love music. Although they can go broke if they pander too often to their own personal tastes, many music publishers know that the best way to build a catalog of lasting value is to continue searching not just for the surface appeal of a new song but also for music that seems to have inherent quality, music that might also appeal to listeners of the next generation.

Catalog Acquisitions

The purchase and sale of entire catalogs have always been common in the industry, for reasons described earlier. If the firm on the block is small and headed by a successful writer-manager, the buyer will probably seek to contract for the ongoing services of the management team that developed the firm's early success. The price of the acquisition is usually based on a multiple of the average annual net earnings over a 3- to 5-year period. This multiple is generally between 5 and 10, but it can be much lower, depending on the demand, the steadiness of earnings, and the remaining copyright life of the compositions being purchased.

When whole catalogs are bought, the seller normally assigns all rights of copyright and ownership, including subsisting contracts with writers. This means that if the first publisher has contracted with a composer to publish that composer's music for the next several years, the new publisher must honor that contract. The new publisher also, of course, assumes all obligations for payment of royalties.

Editing for Print Publications

Nearly all music submitted for print publication needs to be edited. Very few composers, even those classically trained, are familiar with the proper way to prepare a manuscript for the printer. Even a simple leadsheet should be prepared by an arranger qualified in this specialized field. At this stage, the arranger-editor must correct errors in notation, perhaps even rewrite portions that do not make good musical sense. Some editors may be called on to polish lyrics, although this, too, is a field that should be left to professional lyricists or "lyric doctors." Print publication has changed dramatically in recent years due to the introduction of computerized ordering, editing, and printing and the use of computerized graphics.

The Print Production Line

If a publisher determines that a newly acquired piece of music should be offered for sale in printed form, that music goes down a production line somewhat like other products, progressing from raw material to vendable commodity. Here is a typical line of production for a piece of printed music headed for the marketplace:

1. The publisher's acquisitions committee (or an authorized individual) determines that the piece of music should be accepted for publication and, in this instance, that it should be made available in at least one printed edition.

2. The publisher's copyright department determines that the title (ownership) of the music is clear (unencumbered), and a contract is negotiated with the author.

3. The publisher registers a claim to copyright with the Copyright Office and places copies on file with the Library of Congress.

4. The publisher's arranger (or a freelance arranger) scores a piano-voice version of the music. The editor makes sure it is in acceptable form, then directs the preparation of digital files or camera-ready art. At some point, it is usually submitted to the writer for approval.

5. After proofreading, if the editor approves the completed work, the printer (**in-house** or external) prints the music. First printings in the educational field are normally 1,000 copies. In the case of popular song folios, a first printing may run 25,000 copies or more.

6. The printer (in-house or external) then ships and **drop ships** (ships directly to the customer but bills through the retailer) copies of the music according to instructions from the publisher. No set distribution patterns prevail, but two are fairly common: A publisher may ship directly to its jobbers and larger retail outlets or may assign to a subpublisher a license to promote, distribute, and sell the entire edition.

7. Meanwhile, the publisher's or licensee's promotion/advertising people have been trying to generate sales both here and abroad. If they have been successful, purchasers put down their money and everyone is happy.

8. The publisher pays the author royalties based on sales volume of the printed editions.

TALENT DEVELOPMENT

Some music publishers pride themselves on discovering raw talent and developing it, perhaps employing what might be called song doctors to work with young contract writers whose material may lack professional polish. The music business continues to change rapidly, however, and many publishers spend a great deal of time in finding new artist/songwriters, making demos, and then "shopping" those demos by trying to find a record deal for the artist/songwriter.

CONTRACTS WITH WRITERS

In the preceding chapter, we discussed the Songwriters Guild of America (SGA) contract, which is heavily weighted in favor of the writer. In the past, at least, some publishers would not only refuse to sign it, but they would also require their writers to sign a contract heavily favoring the publisher. Although the SGA contract is a single-song agreement, it would be useful to bear in mind the issues presented in the SGA agreement when considering an exclusive-term contract between a writer and publisher.

In an ideal world, writer and publisher would work out a contract that balances the interests of both parties. The draft that follows might serve as a model for two parties coming to the table with about equal bargaining power. They give and take and just might end up with something comparable to the following agreement:

ASSUMPTIONS

Any consideration of contract negotiations requires knowledge of the background of the parties and their relative bargaining strengths. In this draft contract, we make the following assumptions:

About the Writer: This is a creative person who writes both songs and instrumental pieces in the popular music genre. Prior to entering into these negotiations with our imaginary publisher, the writer enjoyed some publishing success through modest sales of recordings of music and has some music "in the trunk," compositions not yet copyrighted or published, that could be assigned to the publisher for the right kind of deal. Wanting to advance in this career, not only as a writer but also as a recording artist, the writer can be persuaded to assign copyrights in works covered by the contract to the publisher exclusively if the offer is good enough.

About the Publisher: The firm is well established and moderately successful, an ancillary operation of a parent recording company with multinational distribution. The label's publishing wing has not yet fully established its operations in foreign territories. The publisher farms out all its printed music activity. The publisher has strong faith in the potential earning power of the prospective writer and seeks the writer's exclusive services.

DRAFT CONTRACT

AGREEMENT made (date) _____ by and between _____,
the Writer, and _____, the Publisher

1.0. **Appointment.** The Publisher engages the Writer as a composer, lyricist, arranger, orchestrator, and/or music editor, and the Writer's services as a writer shall be rendered exclusively for the Publisher. Services performed under this agreement shall not be deemed to be work made for hire as defined under U.S. copyright law.

2.0. **Term.** This agreement starts on (date) _____ and ends on (date) _____.[1] The Publisher is granted options to extend this agreement, by 1-year increments of extension for additional years, but not to exceed an aggregate total of _____ years,[2] on the identical terms and conditions of the initial term. The foregoing notwithstanding, the Writer retains the option to deny these extension options unless the Publisher has obtained, directly or indirectly, _____[3] commercially released recordings of the Controlled Compositions during the time period of _____. This shall be referred to hereafter as The Recording Goal.[4]

> *The writer would not have the option to deny extensions of the initial term if advances had been paid and unrecouped. The same agreement, in rare circumstances, could be negotiated to provide a reversion of copyright after a period of years but only if all advances have been recouped.*

2.1. If the Publisher's affiliated recording company terminates the Writer's contract as a royalty artist, this Writer's contract shall be coterminous with that recording contract.[5]

> *In situations where there is an affiliated recording company, the publishing deal will often be a copublishing deal, rather than the 50/50 writer-publisher split described below.*

3.0. **Assignment.** The Writer assigns to the Publisher all rights throughout the world in the compositions listed on Schedule A attached hereto (prior compositions).[6] Throughout this contract the word *composition* shall include music, words, and title. During the term of this agreement, the Writer agrees to deliver _____ newly recorded compositions.

3.1. The Writer also assigns to the Publisher all rights in the compositions created by the Writer during the term and under the conditions of this agreement. The foregoing notwithstanding, these works are offered to the Publisher on a first-refusal basis only. If the Publisher does not agree to accept them for publication and exploitation within 60 days of their being offered, the Writer reserves the right to assign them to any other publisher.

> *A first-refusal deal would only be made if no advances were paid. If the writer has been paid an advance by the publisher, the publisher will not allow the writer to sign with another publisher.*

All works listed on Schedule A, together with all works described under 3.1 that the Publisher accepts, are referred to hereinafter as the Controlled Compositions.

4.0. **Warranty.** The Writer warrants that the Writer has the right to enter into this agreement and that the Controlled Compositions are original, and as the sole author and composer, the Writer has not paraphrased or otherwise used any other copyrighted material for them.

4.1. The Writer indemnifies the Publisher against loss or damage and attorney fees arising out of a breach of warranty including a situation where any copyright infringement action is settled with the Writer's consent.

5.0. **Advances and Royalties.** In consideration of this agreement the Publisher agrees:

> 5.0-A. To pay the Writer $ _____ in twelve (12) equal monthly installments, and the receipt of the first installment is hereby acknowledged, as a nonreturnable advance against royalties, and these payments shall be deductible only from payments becoming due the Writer under this contract. Payment of such advances is dependent upon the Writer's prior delivery of the agreed upon number of compositions, and in the event of nondelivery, Publisher shall have the right to suspend payment of advance installments hereunder.

> 5.0-B. Subject to Paragraph 5.1 below, to pay the Writer one half of the Publisher's net receipts in the United States from all other licenses of Controlled Compositions under licenses relating to uses now known or hereafter developed.

5.1. The Writer shall not be entitled to receive any income from any performing rights organizations anywhere in the world designated as a Publisher's share nor shall the Publisher be entitled to receive any income from any performing rights organization anywhere in the world designated as a Writer's share.

5.2. The Publisher shall not grant any mechanical license at a rate lower than the prevailing statutory maximum to any individual or company with whom the Publisher has any affiliation or financial interest.[7]

> *If the artist has signed a recording contract that has record-contract controlled composition language, the lower mechanical rate might apply despite this prohibition in the publishing contract. The writer's attorney must reconcile this provision with that contract.*

5.3. To pay the Writer 10% of the wholesale price on the sale of all printed editions in the United States and Canada (except for piano/vocal copies where the royalty is usually stated in cents per copy).[8]

5.4. No cross-collateralization is permitted the Publisher in respect to any royalties or other payments made to the Writer by the Publisher's affiliated recording company.

> *If limitations are not put on so-called cross-collateralization language, the recording company and the publishing company affiliate may treat advances under the publishing agreement as being recoupable from royalties payable from the publishing agreement and/or the recording agreement. It could even be extended to allow recoupment of recording costs and advances under the record agreement from royalties payable under the publishing agreement. This cross-collateralization is obviously extremely favorable to the publisher/record company and would be agreed to only by an artist/writer who had very little bargaining power and over the vehement protests of the artist's entertainment attorney.*

5.5. Where a Controlled Composition has more than one author the shares of royalties among them shall be apportioned in relation to the creative contributions of each Writer as these apportionments have been negotiated by the parties. The Writer will have final approval over which additional co-writers or arrangers are used.

5.6. If the Publisher engages the Writer as an arranger, orchestrator, editor, or copyist, the Writer, if a union member, will be paid the appropriate AFM union scale for such services, and such payments shall be over and above all other advances and royalties provided for in this contract and shall not be recoupable from royalties hereunder.[9]

6.0. **Foreign Rights.** Publisher shall have the right to designate subpublishers, foreign licensees, or affiliates outside the territory of the United States on such terms as the Publisher in its reasonable business judgment shall determine pursuant to arm's length negotiations provided that in no event shall the percentage paid to the Publisher of income earned at the source be less than 75%.[10]

An arm's length agreement is negotiated between two unaffiliated parties acting in good faith to reach an understanding that benefits both parties. Such a stipulation would avoid the possibility of one party having an undue advantage over the other. An agreement between a parent company and its affiliate or a subsidiary company that favors the parent company at the expense of the subsidiary company is not an agreement negotiated at arm's length.

7.0. **Promotion Expense.** The Publisher shall be solely responsible for all promotion expense, including the production of audio and video demonstration tapes or discs.

The extent to which promotion expenses are recoupable is subject to negotiation. The demo costs are normally 50% recoupable.

7.1. If the ownership and copyright of any Controlled Composition should revert from the Publisher to the Writer, all demos on that composition shall also become the property of the Writer.

8.0. **Right to Audit.** The Publisher grants to the Writer the right to engage a qualified accountant to examine the Publisher's books and related financial documents, following receipt of reasonable notice. The cost of any such audit is to be borne entirely by the Writer except that if the Writer is found to be owed a sum equal to or greater than _____ %[11] of the sum shown on that royalty statement as being due the Writer, then the Publisher shall pay the entire cost of the audit, but not to exceed _____ %[12] of the amount shown to be due the Writer.

9.0. **Creative Rights.** The Publisher acknowledges that the Writer's reputation and potential income relate importantly to the originality and quality of the Controlled Compositions as well as to their use. The Writer acknowledges, however, that the Publisher has the right to make minimal changes in the compositions and has the day-to-day responsibility of determining the best way to exploit the compositions. To balance these interests of the parties in this respect, it is agreed that the Publisher has the right to do any or all of the following in this context only with the consent of the Writer:

9.0-A. Engage a lyricist to alter the Writer's lyrics materially or to write new lyrics.

9.0-B. Make substantive changes in the Writer's music.

9.0-C. Grant a synchronization license for a Controlled Composition, particularly for works such as X-rated movies that might harm the value of the composition or the image of the writer.

9.0-D. Use the Writer's likeness, photograph, or name to exploit a product or service without the Writer's consent in respect to appropriateness and good taste and without paying the Writer a royalty commensurate with the exploitation value.

9.0-E. License a Controlled Composition for use in connection with a broadcast commercial, print advertisement, or merchandising of a product or service.

9.0-F. Grant a Grand or Dramatic Right in connection with part of the production and performance of a Controlled Composition as a dramatic musical work.

Grand rights are often excluded in publishing contracts.

10.0. **Right of Assignment.** The Publisher reserves the right to assign this contract to another fully qualified publisher. The Writer consents to this right of assignment only if such assignment is part of a sale of a substantial portion of publisher assets, and provided the assignee assumes all the responsibilities and obligations of the first publisher hereafter.

11.0. **Reversion.** If the Recording Goal is not reached, the Writer will grant the Publisher an extension period of six (6) months beyond the initial term set forth under Item 2.0 of this contract. If, by the end of the extension period, the Recording Goal has still not been reached, and if no advances have been paid by the Publisher to the Writer, or if paid, recouped or re-paid to the Publisher, all rights in any Controlled Composition not released or recorded revert totally to the Writer.

12.0. **Default, Cure.** If either the Publisher or the Writer asserts that the other party is in default or breach of this contract, the aggrieved party shall provide written notice setting forth the nature of the default or breach. The accused party is then allowed 30 days to cure the alleged default, during which period no default or other grievances shall be deemed incurable.

13.0. **Arbitration.** The parties agree to submit all disputes to the American Arbitration Association and be bound by and perform any award rendered in such arbitration.

_____   _____
Publisher   Writer

_____   _____
Date   Date

County of _____   State of _____

SPLIT COPYRIGHTS, COPUBLISHING

Nowadays it is not unusual to find many of the songs on the pop charts copublished by two or more publishers. In reality, nearly all these **split publishing** deals are simply a number of persons or firms agreeing to share the publishing income, not the publishing responsibilities.

In a traditional arrangement, publishing money is divided equally between the artist/songwriter and the publisher; that is, the artist/songwriter gets 50% of the publishing income and the publisher gets the other 50% of the publishing income. In this case, the publisher usually owns all of the copyright.

If the artist who already has a record deal signs a publishing agreement, the publisher is often willing to give half of its publishing income and half of the copyright ownership to the artist/songwriter. In one kind of common copublishing deal, the parties are co-owners of the copyright, and the artist/songwriter receives 75% of the income (the writer's 50% plus 50% of the publisher's share). The administration of the copyright remains with the publisher.

When ownership of a copyright is split, administration of the property can be difficult. Where coauthors are involved, ASCAP, BMI, and SESAC will honor directions from the co-owners to divide performance royalties among the writers and publishers involved. With respect to mechanical royalties and synchronization fees, the Harry Fox Agency is accustomed to splitting monies in accordance with instructions it receives from **copyright proprietors.**

Joint administration of copyright requires specific contractual arrangements for sharing of synchronization fees. **Synchronization rights** apply worldwide, but differences of opinion prevail on how income from this source should be shared. In the past, most publishers have believed it equitable to attribute 50% of synchronization fee income to the United States and the balance to foreign sources. Administration of copyrights outside this country should be assigned entirely to one co-owner or the other, because sharing of the responsibility leads to confusion and lack of control. This is particularly important because in some foreign countries a unilateral commitment by one co-owner may be binding on the other.

Where a work has two authors, and two publishers split the copyright, one writer's share comes from one publisher, the other writer's share from the other publisher. Unless otherwise provided in a joint administration agreement, mechanical royalties will be equally divided by the two publishers, and each publisher will then be able to pay its writer.

Sometimes the copyright proprietor does not split ownership. Instead, the copyright owner may offer someone an income participation or **cut-in** from the copyright. If a new artist lacks the funds to rent a preferred studio or to hire a preferred producer, the artist/writer may offer a cut-in to the studio or producer in place of, or in addition to, payment up front. Under controlled circumstances, the cut-in can be fair and work even better than joint administration; a single administration is generally preferable to one that is shared. But a cut-in agreement should specify certain limitations: It should be limited to payments on mechanicals derived from a particular record by a specified artist for a finite period. If a work is recorded but never commercially released, the cut-in deal should be automatically voided or the proprietorship and copyright income should return to the original owner.

In yet another kind of cut-in, some songwriters or publishers have agreed to add the name of a prominent recording artist to a song in exchange for the artist recording the song.

COPYRIGHT PROTECTION: SAMPLING

As new technology develops, new concerns about copyright protection arise. For example, anyone who has access to the appropriate technical equipment can copy an entire recording or simply sample part of a song.

The word *sampling* is used in two different but related ways:

1. **Sampling** is actually the process by which the amplitude and frequency of some sound waves are measured and reproduced. The higher the sampling rate (the greater the number of samples taken), the truer the reproduction. Live sounds, such as bird calls or train whistles, can be sampled and used to create entirely new sounds. Previously recorded sounds can also be sampled and manipulated or used in new contexts.

2. In the music business, the meaning of the term **sampling** has been broadened to include the copying or taking of previously recorded sounds and music. These copied or sampled sounds are then used on new recordings. The **new use** may be instantly recognizable to the listener or it may be changed or altered to such an extent that it is very unlike the original. No matter how previously recorded sounds are used, permission to sample should be sought from the publisher and the recording company of the original recording. If permission is granted, a licensing fee will be paid by the user of the sampled music. Instead of a licensing fee, the original publisher may agree to split the copyright or income with the new user.

If music is sampled without the permission of the publisher and recording company, the sampler is infringing the copyrights in the original work and in the sound recording. The sampler is then subject to various penalties, including payment of actual or statutory damages, impoundment of recordings, and an injunction against further release of the infringing recording. Often, settlements or other agreements are made outside of court in such instances.

PROMOTION, ADVERTISING

Popular Music

The main concern of a publisher of popular songs is getting music recorded and broadcast. Although the promotion methods discussed here are ultimately meant to encourage the public to consume more music, much of the promotion process is initially aimed at professionals who are already in the music business. Publishers persuade artists and record producers to record their music generally through direct, personal contacts. Even though the publishing and recording industries are huge, much of the power and control are in the hands of a relatively small number of insiders: the recording artists, record producers, established composers, and important managers. Publishers place on their payrolls the kind of promotion personnel who know the insiders, the power brokers, understand their needs, keep track of market trends and changing tastes, then deliver the right material.

Song Casting. One of the most critical functions of a publisher is to attempt to match songs with performers. A professional manager and staff analyze each song and search out those particular recording artists they believe have a performing style that is right for the material. This is often called song casting; it is as critical a task as casting a TV show or Broadway play. This matching of artist to repertoire used to be the principal concern of staff record producers, hence their appellation, **A&R producers.** Those persons who know how to do this well are scarce, in high demand, and well paid.

One of the largest popular music publishers has said that the song casting process often works in reverse for prestigious publishers: Recording producers will contact the publisher, listing their current needs, and ask the publisher to supply material the publisher believes right for a particular recording project. A publisher enjoying this kind of prestige has a good share of work done by producers and artists who believe the firm has good casting judgment and strong material.

Experienced publishers understand that, at the outset, only a select number of recording artists will even consider their material because so many acts in popular music are *self-contained*—the individual performer or group uses only its own material. Rarely do self-contained acts accept outside songs.

Cover Records. The publisher who has a self-contained act under contract understands, or should understand, that once the material is initially recorded by that act, the publisher's job has only begun. Now the principal concern is getting cover records—inducing other artists to record the song. Whatever the size of a publisher's catalog, the long-range income of the firm largely depends on the number of covers generated over the years.

Getting cover records will be very difficult unless the publisher has shown good judgment in choosing the material placed in the catalog. The unending search is for potential hit material. Knowledgeable song promoters generally limit the material they submit to songs they believe might make it as singles, passing on material that appears to be just album cuts. Most recording artists already have available, from their own hands or from insiders and friends, all the album-cut material they believe they can use. Of course, no one can always predict hit material, but successful publishers, especially in the country area, often guess correctly.

Another aspect of publisher promotion is offering services directly to recording companies. The two kinds of companies, their economic interests almost identical, work out cooperative promotion campaigns for new material, frequently in connection with personal appearances of recording artists.

Additionally, electronic exploitation is an important new income source. Record companies are able to promote, license, and sell CDs or download music directly over the Web; independent labels and individual artists are able to bypass the major distribution companies to promote and distribute their own product. The National Music Publishers Association (NMPA), Recording Industry Association of America (RIAA), and other trade associations have worked to establish standards for "watermarking" and other means of electronic "tagging" of music so that people who upload and download music can be identified, and when appropriate, charged a license fee or sales charge.

The Internet provides a new and immediate global market for publishers' catalogs, greatly increasing access to worldwide music and new genres that might remain unheard if dependent on the more traditional promotion via a record label. Many industry professionals say that the Internet has made a more level playing field for artists who are trying to break into the music business.

Educational Field

Promotion of printed music intended for student and school use is accomplished in two ways. First, publishers active in the educational field spend most of their advertising budgets on direct mail campaigns. Music educators receive dozens of these promotional mailings every month. Along with recordings of arrangements, printed samples of new releases are included in these mailings in the form of *thematics*—short samples of themes from complete works. The educator, when "sold" by such mailings, places an order through a store or by telephone, fax, mail, or the Internet.

A second promotional scheme involves publishers placing display ads in music education journals. Media of this type with the largest circulation include *Music Educators Journal, Jazz Educators Journal*, the *Instrumentalist*, and *Down Beat*.

A unique promotional device used in the educational and church fields is the reading clinic. Large retailers or an educational group will cohost daylong readings of new publications. Educators attend these readings (school ensembles are commonly used) and subsequently place orders with their dealers to cover their needs for the school or church year.

Classical Field

Publishers of chamber music, art songs, operas, and ballets have their own ways of acquainting potential buyers with their music. Unlike the pop and educational fields that focus on new music, classical music publishers are usually engaged in reminding customers of, rather than promoting, the great music of the past. They periodically enliven their catalogs with new compositions and arrangements, but the bulk of their sales comes from reprints and new editions of the classics.

New serious works of any length are rarely printed, because anticipated sales would not usually produce enough money to cover costs of production. In lieu of direct sales, such works as new operas, ballets, and symphonic works are made available through rental of the scores and parts for performance and recording. In regard to dramatic musical works, publishers often get additional income by charging performance fees. Dramatic works by major contemporary composers produce fairly good income for both publishers and writers.

Classical music is also promoted through display ads placed in music journals. A large part of the classical and semiclassical repertoire spills over into the educational field, and most publishers sell to schools and colleges either the original scores or else parts or arrangements scored specifically for school use.

Income for publishers of classical music from recordings is negligible, because most of the repertoire is in the **public domain.**

INCOME SOURCES

One of the reasons publishing income can become large is that it is generated from so many diverse sources. The most important ones are shown in Table 4.2. Over the long term, the all-time money earner is probably the Broadway musical. If we were to aggregate the income of a dramatico-musical work such as *South Pacific* or *A Chorus Line*—including grand rights, performance income of

TABLE 4.2   Publisher's Potential Income Sources

Type of Music Use	Who Pays the Publisher
Broadcast performances (TV, radio, cable, Internet)	Publisher's performing rights organization
Nonbroadcast performances (clubs, hotels, stadiums, environmental music, in-flight music, aerobic and dance studios, etc.)	Publisher's performing rights organization
Mechanical royalties (disc, tape, and CD sales)	Recording company
Sheet music sales	Publisher's licensee
Synchronization of music to film or tape (movies, videos, Internet, DVD)	Movie and video producers
Special permissions, licenses (merchandising deals such as musical greeting cards, toys and dolls, lyrics used in books and magazines, etc.)	Music users
Jukeboxes	Publisher's performing rights organization
Dramatic (or grand) rights	Producer of the dramatic performance
Foreign rights	Subpublishers, licensees abroad; reciprocating performing rights organizations (through ASCAP, BMI, and SESAC)

hits from the show, print rights, movie rights, mechanical royalties—these receipts would probably exceed all the money generated by the stage production at the box office. Not all publishers own these kinds of multimillion-dollar properties, but standards of lesser value and current hits are in demand for merchandising tie-ins for such diverse uses as computer software, greeting cards, apparel, posters, and stationery. Licensing fees, individually considered, for uses of this kind will rarely be high, but when aggregated, money from these ancillary sources can generate a respectable share of a publisher's annual income.

Except where a compulsory license is involved (see Chapter 5), a publisher has the option of granting permissions-to-use either on a royalty basis (a percentage of sales) or for a one-time flat fee. The latter option will be preferred where only small sums are involved, in that a one-time license fee is simpler to collect and does not require extended bookkeeping or royalty fees accounting.

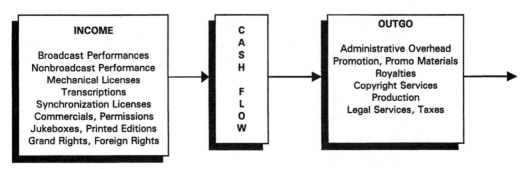

Figure 4.3   Publisher's Cash Flow

TRADE ASSOCIATIONS

The trade association most representative of publishers in the popular music field is NMPA. NMPA performs important services for thousands of American publishers through its licensing subsidiary, the Harry Fox Agency, which provides licensing services for its music publishing principals.

NMPA is deeply immersed in the process of providing leadership for the music publishing/songwriting community and in helping to formulate policy regarding copyright infringement, the protection of copyrights in an age of advancing technology, and the payment of royalties for electronic delivery of music throughout the world.

Today, NMPA/Harry Fox Agency licenses a large percentage of the uses of music in the United States on records, tapes, CDs, imported **phonorecords,** and new technology uses. It also licenses music on a worldwide basis on behalf of its publisher principals for use in films, commercials, television programs, and all other types of audiovisual media.

Harry Fox Agency, Inc.

NMPA established the Harry Fox Agency, Inc., in 1927 to provide an information source, clearinghouse, and monitoring service for licensing musical copyrights. The Harry Fox Agency provides the following services in the United States on behalf of its publisher principals:

1. Licensing copyrighted musical compositions for use on commercial records, tapes, CDs, and computer chips to be distributed to the public for private use (mechanical licensing).

2. Worldwide licensing of copyrighted musical compositions for use in audiovisual works including motion pictures, broadcast and cable television programs, CD videos, and home **videograms** (synchronization licensing).

3. Licensing copyrighted musical compositions for use in TV and radio commercial advertising.

4. Licensing musical compositions in recordings for other than private use, such as background music, in-flight music, computer chips, syndicated radio services, sounds and effects for **MIDI** (musical instrument digital interface) use, karaoke, and multimedia.

5. Licensing musical compositions in recordings made outside of the United States and imported into this country for sale, pursuant to Section 602 of the U.S. Copyright Act, which bars importation into the United States of recordings containing U.S. copyrighted musical compositions without the authorization of the U.S. copyright owner (import licensing).

6. Licensing theatrical motion picture performing rights in the United States only.

7. Collecting and distributing royalties derived from the uses of copyrighted musical compositions pursuant to the licenses issued.

8. Auditing books and records of licensees using copyrighted musical compositions pursuant to the licenses issued.

The Harry Fox Agency does not act in the area of licensing public performance (except as indicated above), grand and dramatic rights, print rights, and derivative uses (music arrangements). Further information on how the agency functions is found in Chapter 6.

NOTES

1. This kind of exclusive-term contract in earlier times was often limited to 1 year. Even enterprising publishers are often unable to develop acceptance of a composition in the first year of a contract.

2. In California, a contract for personal services cannot normally be enforced for a period longer than 7 years. In New York state, there are precedents for contracts of this kind

being enforceable for up to 10 years. Five-year-term contracts are probably the most common today, whatever statutory limitations might prevail.

3. The SGA contract allows the publisher 1 year to obtain a commercially released recording of the particular song under contract, unless the publisher pays the writer a sum of money to "buy" 6 additional months' time to attain that goal. Failing this, all rights to the song revert to the writer.

4. A reasonable "recording goal" might be getting recording deals for one half of the Controlled Compositions. See 11.0 for the consequences if the recording goal is not reached.

5. Although coterminous contracts are often inadvisable for the writer, in this instance the writer would want to be released from the publishing contract to be free to negotiate a new publishing deal with another recording company.

6. This list would probably include all of the works the writer had in the trunk prior to signing this contract that had not been previously published or otherwise encumbered by prior commitment. Some lawyers recommend their clients grant only *administrative* rights to a writer's available works composed prior to a term contract.

7. This clause prevents the publisher from offering anyone a "sweetheart" deal and helps guard against the three-fourths statutory rate commonly found in controlled compositions clauses in artist contracts.

8. Instead of this, the parties might negotiate a graduated royalty rate. See the SGA formula.

9. If the income of the writer under this contract fails to aggregate a reasonable amount, the contract may not be enforceable in some states in that the publisher has the writer completely tied up as exclusive writing "property," thus denying the writer the opportunity of finding additional outside writing income. California law makes personal service agreements unenforceable if the artist or writer has failed to achieve a certain minimum level of income from entertainment contracts.

10. The parent contract is left open-ended here to provide the parties an opportunity to remain flexible in response to rapidly changing foreign markets. Although the parties might agree on a worldwide 50-50 split of income, equity might be better served by negotiating deals territory by territory.

11. The SGA contract calls for 5% here. Between 10% and 15% might be reasonable, at least from the publisher's point of view.

12. The SGA contract calls for 50% here.

 # MUSIC COPYRIGHT

Every serious student of copyright should acquire a complete copy of the Copyright Act, together with other special publications and bulletins relating to copyright. In addition to the act (Circular 92), Circular R1 (Copyright Basics) and Circular R50 (Copyright Registration for Musical Compositions) are especially useful. These documents are available, without charge, from the Register of Copyrights, Copyright Office, Library of Congress, Washington, D.C. 20559, or by calling the Forms Hotline (24 hours a day) at (202) 707-9100. They are also available on the Copyright Office Web site at http://lcweb.loc.gov/copyright. The Copyright Office Public Information Office number is (202) 707-3000. If legal advice or other expert assistance is required, the services of a competent professional should be sought.

BACKGROUND

Congress enacted the first U.S. copyright law in 1790, under the authority of Article I, Section 8 of the Constitution, which states, "The Congress shall have power . . . to promote the Progress of Science and useful Arts, by securing for Limited Times to Authors and Inventors the Exclusive Right to their respective Writings and Discoveries." Comprehensive revisions were enacted in 1831, 1870, and 1909. The current copyright act was enacted by Congress in 1976 (U.S. Code, Title 17, Copyrights) and became generally effective on January 1, 1978.

The United States became a party to the Universal Copyright Convention in 1955, and in 1989 it became a party to the Berne Convention. Accession to these treaties helped the United States to enhance the protection of its copyrights internationally as well (see the International Copyright chapter).

From the outset, the goal of Congress was to seek a balance of interests between copyright owners and users.[1] This search for balance and fairness took place under the watchful eye and with the vigorous participation of a number of special interest groups representing the motion picture, music, radio, and TV industries as well as educators, librarians, the cable industry, and other public interest groups. And when ultimately enacting the 1976 Copyright Act, Congress stated its intent was that implementation of the law "would minimize any disruptive impact on the structure of the industries involved and on generally prevailing industry practices."[2]

The 1976 act has been interpreted in widely varying ways by the different courts, and it is useful to remember that copyright law involves not only examining the "letter of the law" but developing persuasive *interpretations* of the statute. In addition, copyright law can develop through new laws written by Congress and through interpretations by the courts in current cases and based on legal precedent (the decisions in previous court cases). The ultimate authority for the law is, however, the U.S. Constitution.

Before viewing the entire landscape of copyright law, it is necessary to become familiar with the law's basic terms and provisions.

ESSENTIAL PROVISIONS

Following are seven essential provisions of the 1976 act and subsequent amendments:

1. The statute preempts nearly all other copyright laws—federal, state, and **common law.**

2. Duration of copyright was lengthened and now conforms more closely to practices prevailing throughout most of the rest of the world: life of the author plus 70 years.

3. Performance royalties are not paid to copyright owners of sound recordings except for certain performances by digital transmission over the Internet.

4. Public broadcasters, cable systems, and jukebox operators were compelled to start paying for the use of copyrighted music, as were schools and col-

leges. A by-product of accession to the Berne Convention was amendment of the copyright act to provide for **negotiated licenses** between jukebox operators and music copyright owners (through performing rights organizations) rather than the statutorily mandated compulsory licenses.

5. Congress codified the principles previously enunciated in case law as to what constitutes the "fair use defense" to otherwise infringing activity. Four discrete factors are to be considered by the courts in determining the applicability of the fair use defense, and courts may also look to other factors as appropriate to a particular case.

6. Policies and rates of music use licenses were to be periodically reexamined.

7. Some formal procedures were treated more permissively, and others were eliminated entirely.

KEY TERMS

An understanding of copyright is dependent on awareness of how the current law defines its terms. Most of the definitions that follow are quoted directly from section 101 of the Copyright Act. (Language not relating to music has been deleted.)

"Audiovisual works" are works that consist of a series of related images that are intrinsically intended to be shown by the use of machines or devices such as projectors, viewers, or electronic equipment, together with accompanying sounds, if any, regardless of the nature of the material objects, such as films or tapes, in which the works are embodied.

The **"best edition"** of a work is the edition, published in the United States at any time before the date of deposit, that the Library of Congress determines to be the most suitable for its purposes.

A **"collective work"** is a work, such as a periodical issue, anthology, or encyclopedia, in which a number of contributions, constituting separate and independent works in themselves, are assembled into a collective whole.

A **"compilation"** is a work formed by the collection and assembling of preexisting materials or of data that are selected, coordinated, or arranged in such a way that the resulting work as a whole constitutes an original work of authorship. The term *compilation* includes collective works.

"Copies" are material objects, other than **phonorecords,** in which a work is fixed by any method now known or later developed, and from which the work can be perceived, reproduced, or otherwise communicated, either directly or with the aid of a machine or device. The term *copies* includes the material object, other than a phonorecord, in which the work is first fixed.

"Copyright owner," with respect to any one of the exclusive rights comprised in a copyright, refers to the owner of that particular right.

A work is **"created"** when it is fixed in a copy or phonorecord for the first time; where a work is prepared over a period of time, the portion that has been fixed at any particular time constitutes the work as of that time, and where the work has been prepared in different versions, each version constitutes a separate work.

A **"derivative work"** is a work based on one or more preexisting works, such as a translation, musical arrangement, dramatization, fictionalization, motion picture version, sound recording, art reproduction, abridgment, condensation, or any other form in which a work may be recast, transformed, or adapted. A work consisting of editorial revisions, annotations, elaborations, or other modifications that, as a whole, represent an original work of authorship is a derivative work.

A **"device," "machine,"** or **"process"** is one now known or later developed.

To **display** a work means to show a copy of it, either directly or by means of a film, slide, television image, or any other device or process or, in the case of a motion picture or other audiovisual work, to show individual images nonsequentially.

An **"establishment"** is a store, shop, or any similar place of business open to the general public for the primary purpose of selling goods or services in which the majority of the gross square feet of space that is nonresidential is used for that purpose, and in which nondramatic musical works are performed publicly.

A work is **"fixed"** in a tangible medium of expression when its embodiment in a copy or phonorecord, by or under the authority of the author, is sufficiently permanent or stable to permit it to be perceived, reproduced, or otherwise communicated for a period of more than transitory duration. A work consisting of sounds, images, or both that are being transmitted is "fixed" for purposes of this title if a fixation of the work is being made simultaneously with its transmission.

A **"food service or drinking establishment"** is a restaurant, inn, bar, tavern, or any other similar place of business in which the public or patrons assemble for the primary purpose of being served food or drink in which the majority of the gross square feet of space that is nonresidential is used for that purpose and in which nondramatic musical works are performed publicly.

To **"perform"** a work means to recite, render, play, dance, or act it, either directly or by means of any device or process, or in the case of a motion picture or other audiovisual work, to show its images in any sequence or to make the sounds accompanying it audible.

"Phonorecords" are material objects in which sounds, other than those accompanying a motion picture or other audiovisual work, are fixed by any method now known or later developed, and from which the sounds can be perceived, reproduced, or otherwise communicated, either directly or with the aid of a machine or device. The term *phonorecord* includes the material object in which the sounds are first fixed.

A **"pseudonymous work"** is a work on the copies or phonorecords of which the author is identified under a fictitious name.

"Publication" is the distribution of copies or phonorecords of a work to the public by sale or other transfer of ownership, or by rental, lease, or lending. The *offering* to distribute copies or phonorecords to a group of persons for purposes of further distribution, public performance, or public display constitutes publication. A public performance or display of a work does not of itself constitute publication.

To perform or display a work **"publicly"** means

1. To perform or display it at a place open to the public or at any place where a substantial number of persons outside of a normal circle of a family and its social acquaintances are gathered; or
2. To transmit or otherwise communicate a performance or display of the work to a place specified by clause (1) or to the public, by means of any device or process, whether the members of the public capable of receiving the performance or display receive it in the same place or in separate places and at the same time or at different times.

"Registration" means a registration of a claim in the original or the renewed and extended term of copyright.

"Sound recordings" are works that result from the fixation of a series of musical, spoken, or other sounds, but not including the sounds accompanying a motion picture or other audiovisual work, regardless of the nature of the material objects, such as discs, tapes, or other phonorecords, in which they are embodied.

A **"transfer of copyright ownership"** is an assignment, mortgage, exclusive license, or any other conveyance, alienation, or hypothecation of a copyright or of any of the exclusive rights comprised in a copyright, whether or not it is limited in time or place of effect, but not including a nonexclusive license.

A **"transmission program"** is a body of material that, as an aggregate, has been produced for the sole purpose of transmission to the public in sequence and as a unit.

To **"transmit"** a performance or display is to communicate it by any device or process whereby images or sounds are received beyond the place from which they are sent.

A **"useful article"** is an article having an intrinsic utilitarian function that is not merely to portray the appearance of the article or to convey information. An article that is normally a part of a useful article is considered a useful article.

A **"work made for hire"** is (a) a work prepared by an employee within the scope of his or her employment; or (b) a work specially ordered or commissioned for use as a contribution to a collective work, as a part of a motion picture or other audiovisual work, as a translation, as a supplementary work, as a compilation, as an instructional text, as a test, as answer material for a test, or as an atlas, if the parties expressly agree in a written instrument signed by them that the work shall be considered a work made for hire. For the purpose of the foregoing sentence, a "supplementary work" is a work prepared for publication as a secondary adjunct to a work by another author for the purpose of introducing, concluding, illustrating, explaining, revising, commenting upon, or assisting in the use of the other work, such as a musical arrangement.

COVERAGE

Copyright protection does not extend to ideas themselves, but only to the expression of those ideas. This important distinction prevents someone from legally protecting the idea of "reggae music," for example. A particular expression (e.g., a reggae song by Ziggy Marley) may be protected, but the idea itself (the beat, the general concepts defining the genre, etc.) cannot. This allows the normal development of musical forms, which typically involves heavy borrowing from other sources, but prohibits exploitation of a particular artist's expression of an idea.

Copyright protection is granted to original works of authorship. Such works must be "fixed in any tangible medium of expression, from which they can be perceived, reproduced, or otherwise communicated, either directly or with the aid of a machine or device." Works of authorship include[3]:

- ▶ Literary works
- ▶ Musical works, including any accompanying words
- ▶ Dramatic works, including any accompanying music
- ▶ Pantomimes and choreographic works
- ▶ Pictorial, graphic, and sculptural works
- ▶ Motion pictures and other audiovisual works
- ▶ Sound recordings
- ▶ Architectural works

The works listed above are subject to protection under the law even if unpublished, without regard to the nationality or domicile of the author. With respect to published works, protection is accorded if any of the following is true:

1. On the date of first publication, one or more of the authors is a national or domiciliary of the United States, or is a national, domiciliary, or sovereign authority of a foreign nation that is a party to a copyright treaty to which the United States is also a party, or is a stateless person, wherever that person may be domiciled; or

2. The work is first published in the United States or in a foreign nation that, on the date of first publication, is a party to the Universal Copyright Convention[4]; or

3. The work is a sound recording that was first fixed in a nation that is a treaty party; or

4. The work is a pictorial, graphic, or sculptural work that is incorporated in a building or other structure, or an architectural work that is embodied in a building or structure located in the United States or a treaty party; or

5. The work is first published by the United Nations; or

6. The work comes within the scope of a Presidential proclamation.

Copyright protection can cover compilations and derivative works as well. But this protection does not extend to any part of a compilation or derivative work in which such material has been used unlawfully. Also, copyright in compilations and derivative works extends only to the material contributed by the author of such work (as distinguished from the preexisting material employed in the work) and does not imply any exclusive right in the preexisting material. The copyright in compilations and derivative works is independent of and does not affect or enlarge the scope, duration, ownership, or subsistence of any copyright protection in the preexisting material.

Copyright does not extend to publications of the U.S. government. An individual may quote from such publications without concern for copyright infringement.

EXCLUSIVE RIGHTS

Section 106 of the Copyright Act specifies six distinct exclusive rights vested in the author of a protected work. Subject to certain limitations, the act states that the owner of copyright has the exclusive right to do and to authorize any of the following:

Section 106. Exclusive Rights in Copyrighted Works

Subject to sections 107 through 121, the owner of copyright under this title has the exclusive rights to do and to authorize any of the following:

(1) to reproduce the copyrighted work in copies or phonorecords;

(2) to prepare derivative works based upon the copyrighted work;

(3) to distribute copies or phonorecords of the copyrighted work to the public by sale or other transfer of ownership, or by rental, lease, or lending;

(4) in the case of literary, musical, dramatic, and choreographic works, pantomimes, and motion pictures and other audiovisual works, to perform the copyrighted work publicly;

(5) in the case of literary, musical, dramatic, and choreographic works, pantomimes, and pictorial, graphic, or sculptural works, including the individual images of a motion picture or other audiovisual work, to display the copyrighted work publicly; and

(6) in the case of sound recordings, to perform the copyrighted work publicly by means of a digital audio transmission.

These are referred to as the **bundle of rights.**

FAIR USE OF COPYRIGHTED MATERIAL

In passing the legislation, Congress attempted to reconcile the rightful interests of the copyright owners with the legitimate, nonprofit interests of individuals, schools, libraries, churches, and noncommercial broadcasters in using copyrighted material. Much of the act, particularly sections 107 through 112, concerns the limitations of these rights.

Since the 19th century, the courts have held that certain kinds of uses of copyrighted material are "fair," within reason, and not an infringement or materially damaging to a copyright owner. This tradition was validated and codified, to a large extent, in the 1976 law. This law offers examples of what constitutes fair use.[5]

The fair use of a copyrighted work, including such use by reproduction in copies or phonorecords, or by any other means specified by section 106 of the law, for purposes such as criticism, comment, news reporting, teaching (including multiple copies for classroom use), scholarship, or research, "is not an infringement of copyright." In determining whether the use made of a work in any particular case is a fair use, four criteria have been established by prior court actions and are incorporated in the new law:

1. The purpose or character of the use, including whether such use is of a commercial nature or is for nonprofit educational purposes
2. The nature of the copyrighted work
3. The amount and substantiality of the portion used in relation to the copyrighted work as a whole
4. The effect of the use on the potential market for or value of the copyrighted work

The **fair use doctrine,** a legal defense to a copyright infringement claim, essentially allows minimal takings of copyrighted material for the furtherance of purposes such as scholarship, research, and news reporting. Even within these favored areas, however, any substantial taking is likely to be looked upon by the court as an infringement.

Some analysts point out a potential conflict between First Amendment free speech rights and the fair use doctrine of copyright law. Although copyright law provides an incentive for authorship, some critics say it gives creators monopoly rights that may conflict with public interest in the dissemination of information. A counterargument runs that copyright protection extending only to the expression of ideas (as opposed to the ideas themselves) allows free speech to flourish.

The law identifies certain kinds of performances that are considered to be exceptions to the copyright owner's exclusive rights; these performances are not infringements:[6]

1. The performance or display of a work by instructors or pupils in the course of face-to-face teaching activities of a nonprofit educational institution
2. Performance of a nondramatic literary or musical work, display of a work, by or in the course of a transmission, if

    a. the performance or display is a regular part of the systematic instructional activities of a governmental body or a nonprofit educational institution

    b. the performance or display is directly related and of material assistance to the teaching content of the transmission

    c. the transmission is made primarily for reception in classrooms or similar places devoted to instruction

3. Performance of a nondramatic literary or musical work or of a dramatico-musical work of a religious nature in the course of religious services

4. Performance of a nondramatic literary or musical work (otherwise than in a transmission to the public) without any direct or indirect purpose of commercial advantage and without payment of any fee or other compensation for the performance to any of its performers, promoters, or organizers, if

    a. there is no direct or indirect admission charge; or

    b. the proceeds, after deducting reasonable costs of production, are used exclusively for educational, religious, or charitable purposes and not for private financial gain

5. Communication by an establishment of a transmission or retransmission embodying a performance or display of a nondramatic musical work intended to be received by the general public, originated by a radio or television broadcast station, or, if an audiovisual transmission, by a cable system or satellite carrier, if that establishment contains less than 3,750 gross square feet, or, for those establishments containing more than 3,750 gross square feet, if (1) their audio use is via 6 or fewer speakers with not more than 4 in any one room, or (2) their audio/visual use is via not more than 4 TVs, of which no more than 1 TV is in any room unless a direct charge is made to see or hear the transmission, or the transmission thus received is further transmitted to the public. Those non-food service and beverage establishments that contain more than 2,000 gross square feet must meet the requirements of (1) and (2) above in order to be exempt.

6. Performance of a nondramatic musical work by a vending establishment where the sole purpose of the performance is to promote the retail sale of copies or phonorecords of the work or of the devices used in performing the work

COPYRIGHT OWNERSHIP

Copyright ownership vests initially and exclusively in the author of the work.[7] This ownership includes the six exclusive rights under copyright (the bundle of rights).

Where there are multiple authors, these authors share ownership of the copyright. In the popular song field, it is customary for the composer(s) of the music to share ownership equally with the lyricist(s). Multiple authors may, however, set up, through a written agreement, disproportionate shares of ownership in a work in which they collaborated. Examples:

	Composers' Share (50%)	Lyricists' Share (50%)
Ex. 1	One composer: owns 50%	One lyricist: owns 50%
Ex. 2	First composer: owns 25% Second composer: owns 25%	First lyricist: owns 25% Second lyricist: owns 15% Third lyricist: owns 10%

Ownership Limitation

Ownership of copyright, or any of the exclusive rights under a copyright, is distinct from ownership of any material object in which the work may be embodied, such as sheet music, discs, or tapes. Transfer of ownership of any such material objects in which the work is first fixed does not of itself convey any rights in the copyrighted work embodied in these objects (see First Sale Doctrine section below). Thus, the ownership of the physical master tapes on which a song is recorded does not carry with it any ownership of copyright in the underlying song.

Collective Works

Copyright in each separate contribution to a collective work is distinct from copyright in the collective work as a whole and vests initially in the author of the contribution. In the absence of an express transfer of the copyright, the owner of the copyright in the collective work is presumed to have acquired only the privilege of reproducing and distributing the contribution as part of that particular collective work, any revision of that collective work, and any later collective work in the same series.

Film Music

Copyright in music, and accompanying words, written for theatrical films and TV movies is often covered by the overriding copyright in the movie itself as an audiovisual work; however, additional copyrights may preexist for music a film producer licenses for inclusion in this production. In this kind of situation, the two copyrights coexist. The film producer would be required to obtain a synchronization license for use of the preexisting copyrighted music. But even in this situation, the complete audiovisual work—the movie itself—could still be protected by a blanket copyright covering its particular combination of component parts.

TRANSFER OR ASSIGNMENT

Although all six exclusive rights of authorship vest initially in the author(s) of a work, the law states that any or all of these rights may be transferred or assigned to other persons. As a matter of fact, most original copyright owners find it necessary to transfer or assign some or all of their rights in order to generate income from their properties. Some writers own their own publishing companies and recording labels, but the great majority assign publishing and recording rights to others, usually through the granting of licenses (see Chapter 6).

The law even permits subdivisions of individual rights. As explained elsewhere, this often occurs with publishing rights, where authors "split the publishing."

Recordation of Transfer

When copyright owners assign or grant an exclusive license for any of their copyrights, the action does not become valid until the parties (or their agents) execute a written agreement confirming the transfer. This written instrument may then be filed with the Copyright Office in accordance with procedures set by that office, although such filing is not necessary for the transfer to be effective. Filers must also pay the specified fee. Following these actions, the Copyright Office issues a Certificate of Recordation.

This recordation serves to provide all persons with what lawyers call "constructive notice" of the facts stated in the Certificate of Recordation.

Occasionally, a situation arises where two transfers are in conflict. In such instances, the one executed first prevails if it has been properly recorded and otherwise conforms to the regulations of the Copyright Office.

Termination or Recapture

In the case of any work other than a work made for hire, the exclusive or non-exclusive "grant of a transfer" or license of copyright or any right under a copyright, executed by the author on or after January 1, 1978, is subject to termination under conditions cited in section 203. The essential conditions cited there are the following:

1. Termination of the grant may be effected at any time during a period of 5 years beginning at the end of 35 years from the date of execution of the grant; or

2. If the grant covers the right of publication of the work, the period begins at the end of 35 years from the date of publication of the work under the grant or at the end of 40 years from the date of execution of the grant, whichever term ends earlier.

3. Advance notice of intent to terminate must be in writing, signed by the number and proportion of owners of termination interests required under section 203, or by their duly authorized agents, served upon the grantee or the grantee's successor in title. The notice shall state the effective date of the termination, which shall fall within the 5-year period specified in section 203, and the notice shall be served not less than 2 or more than 10 years before that date. To be in effect, this notice must be recorded in the Copyright Office before the effective date of termination. An individual intending to file a notice of termination must comply with the form, content, and manner of service prescribed by the Register of Copyrights.

4. Termination of a grant may be effected notwithstanding any agreement to the contrary, including an agreement to make a will or to make any further grant.

5. Upon the effective date of termination, all rights under this title that were covered by the terminated grant revert to the author(s).

6. Unless and until termination is effected under section 203, the grant, if it does not provide otherwise, continues in effect for the term of copyright provided by law.

Section 203 thus establishes the outer limits of copyright assignability by providing statutory termination guidelines. In practice, however, writers and publishers may negotiate a shorter term (typically, 1 to 5 years) to balance the writer's interest in recapturing copyrights that have not been effectively "worked" by the publisher against the publisher's interest in controlling the property long enough to promote it.

In the case of any copyright **subsisting** in either its first or renewal term on January 1, 1978, other than a copyright in a work made for hire, the exclusive or nonexclusive grant of a transfer or license of the renewal copyright or any right under it, executed before January 1, 1978, by an author or any statutory successors, is also subject to termination.

The termination of the grant may be effected at any time during a period of 5 years beginning at the end of 75 years from the date copyright was originally secured. Termination of the grant may be effected notwithstanding any agreement to the contrary, including an agreement to make a will or to make any future grant.

WORK MADE FOR HIRE

The term *work made for hire*[8] has special meaning under copyright law and is of overriding significance to composers, publishers, and movie producers. Whenever a composer is engaged on a work-made-for-hire basis, the employer is considered under the law as the author of any resulting creative work. And the "author," under copyright law, is thus the owner of the works.

This arrangement was first developed in the 1920s and 1930s in the **Tin Pan Alley** days, when large publishing companies employed salaried songwriters to work in-house on a full-time basis. Songwriters today typically operate as independent contractors with much less supervision.

Occasionally, however, a music publisher will attempt to claim authorship rights in a work produced by a writer who is effectively working as an independent contractor. If asked to sign a work-made-for-hire agreement, check with an attorney before signing.

Section 101 describes (but does not clearly define) conditions in which certain "creations" are to be considered works made for hire:

1. Work prepared by an employee within the scope of employment; or

2. Work specifically ordered or commissioned for use in one of several categories, the most relevant for composers being "as part of a motion picture or other audiovisual work."Even if the work falls into one of the nine categories, the parties must sign an agreement saying the work is made for hire.

Some disputes center on the language of the first condition. To resolve these disputes, bills are periodically introduced in Congress that attempt to clarify the meaning of "employee" by, for example, attaching social security benefits and withholding of taxes to the definition. The Supreme Court spoke to the question of when a creative artist may be considered an employee, listing no less than 13 factors to be considered.[9] The case dealt with whether ownership of a sculpture rested with the sculptor or the group that commissioned its creation. Although the original court decision found for the organization, that decision was reversed on appeal and the U.S. Supreme Court affirmed the reversal finding the sculptor to be the owner of copyright in the commissioned work.

MUSICAL ARRANGEMENTS

Copyright law provides that the original holder of the copyright has the exclusive right "to prepare derivative works based upon the copyrighted work."Because musical arrangements are usually considered derivative (or supplementary) works, it is clear that arrangers must first obtain permission of the copyright owner before scoring their own version of the material. In actual practice, this permission is sought and granted only under particular circumstances, especially when the proposed arrangement might substantially alter or distort the original. In the recording industry, publishers are usually delighted that anyone is interested in recording the song in the first place and welcome the potential exposure and income that result from a **cover record.** Most publishers issue a negotiated **mechanical license** (see Chapter 6) to record one of their properties. Implicit in this license is the understanding that the record producer may create a new arrangement consisting of small changes that will suit the style of the recording artist. Copyright law provides that when a compulsory (mechanical) license is issued, that license "includes the privilege of making a musical arrangement of the work to the extent necessary to conform it to the style or manner of interpretation of the performance involved" for the recording. This industry practice is not so much a specific permission to create such an arrangement. Rather, it is a tacit agreement by the publisher not to raise any objection to it.

With respect to arrangements made primarily for educational use, many publishers give their approval by accepting the standard form, Request for Permission to Arrange. The fine print on this form states that the publisher owns the arrangement made and limits its use.

Arrangers' Rights

Most people in the music business understand that the role of the music arranger is often at least as creative as that of the original composer of the song. Arrangers usually create work for hire—receiving a flat, one-time fee based on the American Federation of Musicians (AFM) scale for "orchestration," or whatever the traffic will bear. Except for work on music in the **public domain,** arrangers who work under such agreements generally enjoy no rights of copyright ownership and receive no royalties from record sales, nor do they share in income generated for composers and publishers from licensing of performances of their arrangements.

Public Domain

A different condition prevails when an arranger creates an original chart of a work in the public domain. The arranger's publisher of such material may demand and receive mechanical royalties from producers of recordings, then usually splits one half of such receipts with the arranger. In respect to performance income, ASCAP, BMI, and SESAC are accustomed to paying (often reduced) royalties to authors and publishers of arrangements based on works in the public domain. Arrangers of works in the public domain may also receive royalties from their publisher's sale of printed editions.

Arrangers are accorded more privileges in certain European countries, for example, France and England. There, arrangers are not always required to secure publishers' approval to render new arrangements of copyrighted material. Furthermore, arrangers in some European countries are often accorded parallel rights, which provide a share of royalties derived from mechanical licensing and performances of their charts.

SOUND RECORDINGS

One potentially confusing aspect of the 1976 Copyright Act and subsequent amendments is that a musical work (the underlying song with lyrics) is categorically differentiated from a sound recording (see definitions at the beginning of this chapter). The recording company typically holds the copyright in the sound recording, while the publisher holds the copyright in the musical work. These two factions may be divisions of the same company.

Section 114 states that the copyright owner of a sound recording has these exclusive rights:

1. To reproduce the copyrighted work to duplicate the sound recording in the form of phonorecords (or copies of motion pictures and other audiovisual works). Note that this right is limited to duplicating the actual sounds fixed in the recording.

2. To prepare derivative works based on the copyrighted material—to make and distribute phonorecords that are new arrangements or versions of the copyrighted work (sound recording).

3. To distribute phonorecords to the public by sale or other transfer of ownership, or by rental, lease, or lending.

4. To perform by digital audio transmission.

Performance Right Exclusion

The 1976 law and subsequent amendments specifically excluded **performance rights** in sound recordings, and generally speaking, sound recordings still do not enjoy a full performance right. Thus, except for the new performance right relative to digital transmission of sound recordings discussed below, owners of sound recordings do not receive performance royalties when music from sound recordings is broadcast or otherwise performed. This exclusion is one of the most significant and controversial sections of the law. The United States is out of step with other countries in this respect: More than 50 Western countries have laws providing for collection of such royalties, or the broadcasters voluntarily pay them.

The issue was debated at length by Congress, but the strong lobby representing broadcasters persuaded Congress to exclude payment of performing fees for sound recordings. The Register of Copyrights was instructed to study the issue, hold hearings of interested parties, then report back to Congress as to whether the exclusion should be amended or eliminated. In 1978, the Register of Copyrights reported to Congress, expressing the opinion that the exclusion of a performing right in sound recordings was not at all justified and that the 1976 Copyright Act should be amended accordingly.

Repeatedly, Congress debated bills that would provide for a performing right in records. Hopeful of eventual victory, performing artists and recording companies continued their lobbying efforts until they *finally* succeeded in passing a limited performance right for sound recordings in 1995. This right requires certain digital music transmission services, or *webcasters*, to pay royalties when they transmit sound recordings over the Internet.

Imitation Exclusion

The exclusive rights of the owner of copyright in a sound recording with respect to the preparation and reproduction of derivative works do not extend to the making or duplicating of another sound recording that consists entirely of an independent fixation of other sounds, even though such sounds imitate or simulate those in the copyrighted sound recording. In other words, imitations that mimic the original recording are legally permissible, but the imitative recording cannot simply be a recorded copy of the original. Furthermore, it is not legal to market the mimicked recordings as if they feature the original artists or in any way that might confuse the public.

COMPULSORY MECHANICAL LICENSE

One of the most important copyright provisions concerns the conditions under which a person is permitted to produce and distribute phonorecords of nondramatic musical works. The law provides that copyright owners of nondramatic music have complete control over recording rights of their properties until they license the material for the first recording. But after this first recording is distributed to the public, they are compelled by law to license any other person to produce and distribute recordings of the copyrighted music in exchange for a fixed statutory royalty, which is adjusted periodically. This provision stems in part from an important goal in copyright law: the increased dissemination of works to the public.

According to section 115, copyright owners become "subject to compulsory licensing." This kind of licensing requires special conditions, the most important of which are

1. "A person may obtain a compulsory license only if the primary purpose in making phonorecords is to distribute them to the public for private use, including by means of a digital phonorecord delivery." This sentence is very significant and clearly excludes from compulsory licensing all recordings that are generally classified under the term **transcriptions.** In the music field, that term is applied, not to phonorecords intended for purchase and use by the public, but to discs or tapes leased or sold for special uses, such as theme music for broadcast programs or wired music services such as Muzak.

2. "A person may not obtain a compulsory license for use of the work in the making of phonorecords duplicating a sound recording fixed by another, unless (i) such sound recording was fixed lawfully; and (ii) the making of the phonorecords was authorized by the owner of copyright in the sound recording or, if the sound recording was fixed before February 15, 1972 [the date when sound recordings first became subjects of statutory copyright protection in this country], by any person who fixed the sound recording pursuant to an express license . . . for use of such work in a sound recording." [The purpose of this provision was to prevent pirates and counterfeiters from availing themselves of the compulsory license.]

3. "A compulsory license includes the privilege of making a musical arrangement of the work to the extent necessary to conform it to the style or manner of interpretation of the performance involved." But the law also states that the arranger shall not change the basic melody or fundamental character of the work. Furthermore, the new arrangement shall not be subject to protection as a derivative work, except with the express consent of the copyright owner.

4. The person planning to obtain a compulsory license must notify the copyright proprietor of this intention before or within 30 days after making, and before distributing, any phonorecords of the work. If the person cannot locate the owner of the work, "it shall be sufficient to file notice of intention in the Copyright Office." Failure to serve or file notice forecloses the possibility of a compulsory license and, in the absence of a negotiated

license, renders the making and distribution of phonorecords actionable as acts of infringement.

Compulsory License Bypass

Compulsory mechanical license provisions in the copyright statute are so stringent, particularly in respect to notice and accounting requirements, that the industry typically uses an alternative, the negotiated mechanical license. This alternative kind of license is permitted by law and is explained in Chapter 6.[10]

ROYALTY PAYMENTS (SECTION 115[c])

After permitting the initial recording of a song, publishers are limited as a practical matter by the statute as to what royalty rate they may charge record makers. The statutory rate provided in the 1976 act was "2.75 cents, or one-half of one cent per minute of playing time or fraction thereof, whichever amount is larger" for each work embodied in a phonorecord. By 1998, this "statutory rate" increased to 7.1 cents or 1.35 cents per minute, whichever amount is larger, and continues to rise periodically. The Copyright Office has announced the mechanical compulsory license rates for phonorecords as follows:

2000/2001: 7.55 cents or 1.45 cents per minute

2002/2003: 8 cents or 1.55 cents per minute

2004/2005: 8.5 cents or 1.65 cents per minute

2006 and later: 9.1 cents or 1.75 cents per minute

To be entitled to receive royalty payments under a compulsory license, the copyright owner must be identified in the registration or other public records of the Copyright Office. The owner is entitled to royalties for phonorecords made and distributed after being so identified, but is not entitled to recover for any phonorecords previously made and distributed.

Except as provided above, the royalty under a compulsory license shall be payable for every phonorecord made and distributed in accordance with the license. "For this purpose, a phonorecord is considered 'distributed' if the person exercising the compulsory license has voluntarily and permanently parted with its possession."This language helps reduce the ambiguity prevalent until 1978 relative to liability for royalty payments. It appears that the manufacturer is not liable for royalty payments on records returned to it that have not been sold, for such records did not leave the manufacturer's possession permanently, as the law provides. "Giveaways"such as free goods and promotional copies do, however, trigger royalty payments, as the definition doesn't require a sale.

DURATION OF COPYRIGHT

Copyright protection obtained prior to enactment of the 1976 act could last no more than a total of 56 years: a 28-year initial term, followed by an optional 28-year renewal term. Under section 302 of the Copyright Act, copyright in a work created on or after January 1, 1978, lasts for 70 years from the author's death.

Subsisting Copyrights in Their First Term on January 1, 1978 (Section 304)

Copyrights still in their first terms continue, under the 1976 law, for their original 28 years. At the expiration of the original term of copyright, the copyright shall endure for a renewed and extended further term of 67 years, which

1. If the application to register a claim to such further term has been made to the Copyright Office within 1 year before the expiration of the original term of copyright, and the claim is registered, shall vest in the proprietor of the copyright who is entitled to claim the renewal of copyright at the time the application is made; or
2. If no such application is made or the claim is not registered, shall vest, upon the beginning of such further term, in the person or entity that was the proprietor of the copyright as of the last day of the original term of copyright.

Renewal Registration

As the result of a 1992 renewal amendment to the Copyright Act, there is no longer a requirement to register a renewal of a pre-1978 copyright during the 28th year to keep the work from falling into the public domain. It is, however, advisable to make such renewal registration to ensure validity of the copyright during its renewed and extended term. Renewal registration will also determine who has the right to use derivative works prepared under a grant of a transfer or license made before the expiration of the original term.

Subsisting Copyrights in Their Renewal Term

As Congress stated, the 1976 law creates an entirely new property right in the renewal term. The 1909 law provided a maximum of only 56 years of protection for pre-1978 works, which was later extended to 75 years by the original 1976 act. The current law provides, for these works, a total of 95 years of protection. The monetary value of many old, standard popular songs is high and, for this reason, authors and publishers have an interest in establishing claims on the additional 20 years of protection that Congress has granted for these works.

After 75 Years

Properties whose 75-year protection would otherwise expire under the original 1976 act are, under the new amendments, automatically granted copyright protection for a total of 95 years. If a writer wants to recapture a composition from a publisher to whom the renewal term has been assigned, the writer may, within a 5-year period following the original 75-year protection, terminate the grant of renewal term to the publisher by serving a notice of termination. This notice of termination must be given to the publisher not less than 2 years or more than 10 years ahead of the termination date decided on by the author. Once an author has thus reclaimed the publisher-owned renewal copyright, ownership by the author is free and clear. Failure to exercise the option to terminate within the 5-year period will permit a copyright to endure to the end of the renewal period.

After January 1, 1978

Copyright protection in works created on or after January 1, 1978, extends to a work from its creation and, except as provided under certain conditions, endures for a term consisting of the life of the author and 70 years after the author's death.

Joint Works. Where two or more authors prepared a joint work (and did not do the work for hire), they enjoy copyright for a term consisting of the life of the last surviving author and 70 years after such surviving author's death.

Work Made for Hire. In a work made for hire, copyright exists for 95 years from the date of its first publication, or a term of 120 years from the year of its creation, whichever expires first. Works made for hire are not included in the provisions concerning termination of grants for the 20-year extension period.

Works in the Trunk (Section 303)

Copyright in a work created before January 1, 1978, but not theretofore in the public domain or copyrighted, subsists from January 1, 1978, and endures for the life of the author and 70 years after the author's (or coauthor's) death. In no case, however, "shall the term of copyright in such a work expire before December, 2002; and, if the work is published on or before December 31, 2002, the term of copyright shall not expire before December 31, 2047."

FORMALITIES

The term *formalities* is used around the world in reference to the specific actions a claimant must take to validate claim to copyright.[11] These formalities include notice of copyright, deposit of copies, and registration of claim to copyright. The 1976 law is permissive in respect to some kinds of mistakes in following through on formalities. After March 1, 1989 (the effective date the United States joined the Berne Convention), these formalities for U.S. works became almost entirely optional. But to be on the safe side, claimants should put a proper notice on copyrighted material (see below).

Notice on Printed Music

The term *notice of copyright* refers to the public display of information concerning the date the work was published and who registered the claim. On printed editions, the law stipulates

1. Notice may be placed on all publicly distributed copies. The notice imprinted should be the symbol © or the word *Copyright* or the abbreviation *Copr.* and the year of first publication of the work. The type of notice most often seen is

© 2000 John Doe

2. In the case of compilations or derivative works incorporating previously published material, the year of the first publication of the compilation or derivative work is sufficient.

3. The notice must also include the name of the copyright owner. A recognizable abbreviation of the owner's name may be used.

4. The position of the notice shall be affixed to the copies so as to give reasonable notice of the claim to copyright.

Notice on Phonorecords (Section 402)

Whenever a sound recording protected under the 1976 law is published in the United States or elsewhere by authority of the copyright owner, a notice may be placed on all publicly distributed phonorecords of the sound recording. It is still prudent to do this. The form of the notice consists of three elements:

1. The symbol ℗,
2. The year of the first publication of the sound recording, and
3. The name of the owner of the copyright in the sound recording. A recognizable abbreviation may be used. If the producer of the sound recording is named on the phonorecord labels or containers, and if no other name appears in conjunction with the notice, the producer's name shall be considered a part of the notice.

Position of Notice. The notice shall be placed on the surface of the phonorecord, or on the phonorecord label or container, in such a manner and location as to give reasonable notice of the claim to copyright. A typical notice for a phonorecord is

℗ 2000 Smith Records

Audiovisual works do not require the symbol ℗ but rather the symbol ©, because they are not phonorecords.

Notice Errors or Omissions

For works first published between January 1, 1978, and March 1, 1989, as detailed in sections 401, 402, and 403, omission of notice from copies or phonorecords does not invalidate the copyright in a work (section 405) under any of the following conditions:

1. The notice has been omitted from no more than a relatively small number of copies or phonorecords distributed to the public.
2. Registration for the work has been made before or is made within 5 years after the publication without notice, and a reasonable effort is made to add notice to all copies or phonorecords that are distributed to the public in the United States after omission has been discovered.
3. The notice has been omitted in violation of an express requirement in writing that, as a condition of the copyright owner's authorization of the public distribution of copies or phonorecords, they bear the prescribed notice.

Also for pre-Berne Convention works (prior to March 1, 1989), an error in the date appearing in the copyright notice does not invalidate the copyright, for example,

1. When the year in the notice is earlier than the year in which the publication first occurred, any period computed from the year of first publication under section 302 is to be computed from the year of the notice.
2. When the year is more than 1 year later than the year in which the publication first occurred, the work is considered to have been published without any notice and is governed by the provisions of section 405.

Deposit (Section 407)

Deposit of works in the Library of Congress and registration of works are separate formalities. The performance of neither action is a condition of copyright, yet both are important. With respect to published copies, section 407 states that the copyright owner (or the publisher) must deposit, within 3 months after the date of publication, two complete copies of "the best edition" of the work. The deposit for sound recordings shall include two complete phonorecords of the best edition, together with any printed material or other visually perceptible material published with such phonorecords. Under the Berne Convention, notice of copyright is no longer required in deposit copies.

Under certain conditions, deposits made prior to any attempt to register the work may be used to satisfy the deposit requirements called for when the author (or the publisher) undertakes to register the work. If the author desires to have the initial deposit satisfy the deposit requirements specified on the registration forms, a letter must be enclosed with the initial deposit specifically directing the Library of Congress to hold those deposits for later connection with the author's registration application. If such a letter is not enclosed, the Copyright Office will require separate, additional deposits of a work, as specified on the registration form.

Congress has authorized modifications of deposit requirements from time to time, at the discretion of the Copyright Office. Although failure to deposit copies or phonorecords according to current regulations does not actually endanger the copyright, the Register of Copyrights does have the authority to demand copies and fine the laggard up to $250 per work and levy additional fines up to $2,500 for willful and repeated refusal to comply.

Registration (Section 408)

The law states that deposits and registration are "separate formalities," but this language can be confusing. The fact is that deposit can be made independent of registration, but registration of a claim to copyright must be accompanied by the deposit specified on the application form. Also, the law states that registration "is not a condition of copyright." But that language, too, can be misleading. Registration is strongly advised because, under certain conditions, an author's work left unregistered lacks certain advantages the work would otherwise enjoy. Most important, a work must be registered before the copyright owner can sue anyone for infringement.

A work may be registered at any time during the term of the copyright, whether it is published or unpublished. The registration may be made by the author or the publisher.

The acceptance of sound recordings, not just sheet music, in claims to copyright the underlying music was a significant advance over the 1909 law. In the popular music field, thousands of songwriters lack the ability to render their material in music notation. Now all they have to do is make a simple tape recording and submit it in lieu of sheet music. The acceptance of sound recordings also provides important advantages to persons desiring to copyright jazz improvisations, many of which are not easily transcribed into conventional music notation.

If the Register of Copyrights determines that all legal and formal requirements have been met, the Register will send the applicant a certificate of registration. If the claim is found invalid, the Register will refuse registration and notify the applicant in writing of the reasons for such refusal. (The Copyright Office has formulated an appeal procedure for applicants whose claims have been found invalid.) The effective date of copyright registration is the day on which an application, deposit, and fee have all been received in the Copyright Office.

If the author or the author's publisher made a mistake in an original registration of claim, or if either party wants to modify it, the Register of Copyright has established procedures and set fees to accommodate these matters.

Fees (Section 708)

The Copyright Office charges fees for certain services, such as registration of claims and recordation of transfers. For current rates, contact the Copyright Office, Library of Congress, Washington, D.C. 20559, or consult the Copyright Office Web site.

Copyright Royalty Tribunal and Copyright Arbitration Royalty Panel

The 1976 Copyright Act provided for the establishment of an instrumentality of the Congress to serve that legislative body in matters concerning copyright. That instrumentality was the Copyright Royalty Tribunal (CRT). The CRT set and periodically adjusted royalty rates and held hearings to determine whether rates and royalty distribution were fair and equitable.

The CRT was abolished in 1993 and replaced with ad hoc Copyright Arbitration Royalty Panels (CARPs) administered by the Librarian of Congress and the Copyright Office. If parties cannot come to agreement, a CARP may be impaneled to make determinations concerning the adjustment of royalty rates and/or the distribution of royalties including:

► Cable and satellite royalties
► Ephemeral sound recording rates

- ▶ Digital performance and phonorecord delivery royalties
- ▶ Mechanical royalties
- ▶ Jukebox royalties
- ▶ Educational broadcasting royalties

INFRINGEMENT, REMEDY

Copyright infringement is widespread, most of it going unnoticed and unpunished. Where infringement is "innocent" and of little or no financial consequence, courts may limit assessment of statutory damages (see below) to as little as $200. Where a library or school is involved with an infringement arising out of a lack of full understanding of the law, sometimes no damages at all are awarded.

Remedies. When infringements are not innocent offenses, the following remedies are available following a successful court action:

1. Injunction: A temporary or final injunction can be sought from any court having jurisdiction to prevent or restrain infringement of copyright.
2. Impoundment: The court may order impoundment of articles alleged to be involved with infringement. The impoundment can hold pending court determination of the merits of the claim of infringement. Impoundment could include printed copies, phonorecords, masters, even duplicating, manufacturing, and packaging equipment.
3. Destruction: The court could order, as part of a final judgment, destruction of inventories, such as printed copies and phonorecords.
4. Damages:
   a. The infringer is liable, except as the law otherwise provides, for (1) actual damages suffered by the copyright owner as a result of the infringement; and (2) any additional profits gained by the infringer as a result of acts of infringement.
   b. The copyright owner may elect, before final judgment is rendered, to seek statutory damages instead of actual damages and profits for all infringements in a sum not less than $500 or more than $20,000, "as the court considers just."

    c.   In a case where the copyright owner sustains the burden of proving, and the court finds "that infringement was committed willfully, the court at its discretion may increase the award of statutory damages to a sum of not more than $100,000." Lesser awards are made where the court finds the infringer was not aware and had no reason to believe the actions constituted infringement.

    d.   Costs and attorneys' fees may be recovered by the prevailing party, at the court's discretion. At today's legal rates, this amount is usually substantial.

    e.   Copyright owners may choose to sue for actual damages or statutory damages and may change to the latter course at any time before final judgment of the court. In the dynamic music market, successful artists with significant stakes at risk will often seek actual damages. Multi-million-dollar cases are not uncommon.

Neither statutory damages nor attorneys' fees can be awarded, however, if the copyright was not registered before the infringement began. This is the most important reason to register copyright in a work before making it available to potential infringers, whether within the music industry or the public at large.

RECORD COUNTERFEITING, PENALTIES

The 1976 law imposed strong penalties for counterfeit use of the copyright symbol ℗ on phonorecords. Owners of copyrights in sound recordings complained that the threat of fines and imprisonment were not adequate deterrents. The criminals appeared to view threatened sanctions simply as "the cost of doing business." Subsequently, Congress strengthened the penalties by passing the Piracy and Counterfeit Act of 1982. This law made both piracy and counterfeiting a felony. Among its other provisions, the 1982 law provided a maximum penalty of a $250,000 fine and jail terms. A person would receive this maximum penalty if found guilty of illegally manufacturing or distributing within a 180-day period at least 10 copies or phonorecords or one or more copyrighted works with a retail value of more than $2,500.

The trend in the United States and abroad is toward increasing penalties for copyright infringers.

CHANGING LAWS

Laws governing copyright have never been able to keep abreast of changes in the way music is produced, communicated, bought, and sold. This time lag is most hurtful to copyright owners in the matters of counterfeiting, home taping, **telecommunications,** direct satellite transmissions, or other alternative distribution via the Internet, cable, or cellular technology. Michael Greene, president/CEO of the National Academy of Recording Arts & Sciences, addressed the problems of information transfer by saying, "The rights of the creators must be protected from 'i-way' robbers."

As technological change thrusts new issues into the spotlight, two economic coalitions traditionally line up against each other, trying to persuade Congress and the courts to rule in their favor. On one side is the creative community: authors, composers, filmmakers, and those who hold copyrights on their creations—publishers, recording companies, movie producers, and so on. Lined up against the creative community are the users of copyrighted properties: broadcasters, hardware manufacturers, software merchants, and the consumer, who is understandably reluctant to pay for music uses and the royalties that may be demanded.

First Sale Doctrine

The principle of "first sale" was carried over from the 1909 statute to the 1976 copyright law (section 109[A]). Simply stated, the first sale principle provides that the copyright owner is entitled to compensation for the first sale of the copy or phonorecord embodying the copyrighted work. Thereafter, the owner of the physical copy may dispose of it or transfer it as the owner sees fit, with only a few exceptions. This provision, developed to facilitate dissemination of creative works, prevents copyright holders from exercising control (other than control over duplicating) over the product once it has left the distributors.

This became the legal basis for the video software rental business. Rentals reduce software sales, and the Motion Picture Association of America (MPAA), the group representing copyright owners of the most important movies rented on video software, initially launched a vigorous campaign with Congress and the public for modification of the first sale doctrine. MPAA and others have suggested that, to compensate copyright owners for financial losses, a royalty should be paid on home video rentals. This plea is similar to the one made with respect to home taping (audio or video): Copyright owners claim they are entitled to compensation for their losses through assessment of a royalty on blank tape and recording devices. The loudest voice raised against any royalties of this kind or any modification of the first sale doctrine has been a coalition of consumer electronics manufacturers and video retailers.

The Audio Home Recording Act of 1992

In 1992, Congress enacted the Audio Home Recording Act, which amended the 1976 Copyright Act by allowing home audio taping and by implementing a royalty payment system and a serial copy management system for digital audio recordings. As a direct result of the passage of this act, home taping is no longer an infringement of copyright, and certain additional copyright infringement actions were prohibited.

Definitions:

1. A **"digital audio copied recording"** is a reproduction in a digital recording format of a digital musical recording, whether that reproduction is made directly from another digital musical recording or indirectly from a transmission.
2. A **"digital audio interface device"** is any machine or device that is designed specifically to communicate digital audio information and related **interface** data to a digital audio recording device through a nonprofessional interface.
3. **"Serial copying"** means the duplication in a digital format of a copyrighted musical work or sound recording from a digital reproduction of a digital musical recording.

To prevent unauthorized digital copying, all digital audio recording devices or interface devices must conform to the serial copy management system or other approved system that prohibits unauthorized serial copying. It is illegal to circumvent such devices.

The importation, manufacture, and distribution of digital audio recording devices or interfaces that do not have a serial copy management system is prohibited. Persons who import, manufacture, and distribute such devices must pay specified royalties and must file statements with the Register of Copyrights.

Royalty Payments. Royalty payments made under this provision shall be distributed to any interested copyright party whose musical work or sound recording has been embodied in a digital or analog musical recording and distributed in the form of digital or analog recordings during the appropriate period and who has filed a claim for such payments.

Royalty payments shall be divided into two funds and paid to interested parties whose works have been embodied and distributed in digital or analog format during the appropriate period:

1. The Sound Recording Fund: 66.67% of royalties collected will be placed in this fund and will be divided as follows:

    2.625% for nonfeatured musicians on the recording

    1.375% for nonfeatured vocalists on the recording

    40% of the remaining royalty to featured recording artists

    60% of the remaining royalty to owners of sound recordings

2. The Musical Works Fund: 33.33% of royalties collected will be placed in this fund and will be divided as follows:

    50% to publishers

    50% to writers

RIGHTS IN NAMES AND TRADEMARKS

Rights in trade names and trademarks are not covered under copyright law in this country, but such rights are related. Company names and professional names of performers cannot be protected under copyright law, but are covered under a broader branch of law concerning unfair competition. In some states, it is a criminal offense to infringe on someone else's name or mark. (For more information, see the Federal Lanham Act, U.S. Code, Title 15.)

Individuals seeking federal registration of a name or mark must apply to the U.S. Patent and Trademark Office. Before proceeding, write to the Government Printing Office, Washington, D.C. 20402 (http://www.gpo.gov) for the pamphlet *General Information Concerning Trademarks.*

Selection of a Name

A new performing group should select its professional name with care to avoid duplication and possible confusion with another group using the same, or similar, name. Because most performing groups will have to register their professional names as "fictitious," they may discover at their own county and state government levels if any other group of performers in that geographic area has already registered the same name or a similar one (for details, see the Starting Your Own Business section in Chapter 25). To confirm the uniqueness of the group's name on a national level, the group should inquire of such organizations as artists' unions, ASCAP, BMI, and SESAC. Libraries often have publications such as *Index to the Trademark Register* that can be consulted. In addition, the group's attorney can provide the names of firms specializing in searches of this kind and can offer guidance on time restrictions for any filing that might be required under the Trademark Act.

Rights in a Name

Performing groups should, at the very outset, draw up a written agreement that explicitly states who owns the professional name, how the ownership is shared, and under what circumstances shares of ownership end or are modified when individual performers join or leave the group. Signing a basic agreement of this kind should help the artists avoid the kinds of costly lawsuits that have hurt less organized performing groups.

A FINAL NOTE ON LAW

Just as knowing how the law protects you is vital to success in the music business, so is an understanding of when the law will not protect you. Copyright protection extends to "expressions" but not "ideas." Anyone who is considering entering the recording and publishing part of the music and entertainment industry should be familiar with the Copyright Act; the Lanham Act; and issues of unfair competition, rights of privacy, and First Amendment issues relating to free speech. Contract law provides for additional remedies in many circumstances. No matter how well you may understand the law, however, court delays and attorneys' fees may effectively prevent access to a judicial decision on your issue.

NOTES

1. 1976 Copyright Act, Chapter 8. Section references throughout this chapter are from the 1976 act, unless otherwise noted.

2. 1976 Copyright Act, Chapter 8.

3. Section 102.

4. Section 104.

5. Section 107.

6. Section 110.

7. Section 201.

8. Section 201(b).

9. *Community for Creative Non-violence v. Reid,* 490 U.S. 730, 109 S.Ct. 2166, 104 L.Ed.2d 811 (1989).

10. See Chapter 6 of this volume concerning distinctions between a compulsory and a negotiated mechanical license.

11. Chapter 4 of the 1976 Copyright Act.

Part III

BUSINESS AFFAIRS

6 MUSIC LICENSING

MUSIC RIGHTS: AN OVERVIEW

Under U.S. copyright law, protected material generally can be used only after permission is obtained from the copyright owner. This consent is customarily given by the granting of a license. Because there are many different kinds of music uses and applications, copyright law and industry practice have developed an array of licenses and use permits.

The largest source of income for many composers and publishers is from licensed performances of their music. A performance occurs any time music is played, whether at a live concert or broadcast over radio, TV, the Internet, or other means of transmission. Because the music business is so large and diverse, writers and publishers affiliate themselves with performing rights organizations in order to collect performance royalties. In the United States, the performance rights of virtually every copyright are handled by one of three performing rights organization: ASCAP, BMI, and SESAC.

In addition to their principal functions of licensing public performances of music and distributing performance royalties to their affiliated writers and publishers, these organizations also distribute awards, lobby Congress, sue infringers, and promote music scholarship. They do not publish music[1] nor do they promote individual copyrights.

The uses of the licenses shown in Table 6.1 should be distinguished from the forms these licenses take. For instance, BMI, ASCAP, and SESAC typically issue *blanket* performance licenses, which allow their entire repertoire to be used by broadcasters and others for a single, annual fee. Some entertainment companies

← Ray Charles performs at the New Orleans Jazz Festival, 1980. © C. Fishman/Woodfin Camp/PNI.

TABLE 6.1   Music Licenses

Type of Music Use	Type of License Required
Commercial broadcast of nondramatic music	Performance license
Nonbroadcast performance of nondramatic music	Performance license
Phonorecord, audiocassette, compact disc, videocassette, videodisc sold for private use	Compulsory or "negotiated" mechanical license
Music video production used for broadcast or cable TV	Synchronization license and performance license
Movie, music video, other video software sold or rented to individuals for home use	Synchronization license that includes license to mechanically reproduce copies for sale
Motion picture for theatrical exhibition	Synchronization license that includes a right to exhibit (performance right)[a]
Broadcast commercial	Negotiated fees
Merchandising tie-ins, computer software applications, etc.	Negotiated fees
Business music (e.g., Muzak)	Transcription license that includes the right of performance
Dramatico-musical production (performed live)	Grand right or dramatic right
Public broadcasting station	Negotiated license
Jukebox	Negotiated license
Cable TV	Compulsory license for some, negotiated for others

a. Performing licenses for theaters outside the United States are often obtained by foreign performing rights organizations directly from movie theater operations. Costs of these kinds of licenses are scaled to a share of the box office receipts. ASCAP and BMI members sometimes share in this income through foreign performing rights organizations having reciprocal arrangements with ASCAP and/or BMI.

who feel it is unfair to have to pay for the complete catalog when they use only a small portion are demanding to be licensed at the *source* (through the program provider) or *direct* (from the copyright owner). These licenses allow broadcasters to negotiate a single fee for both performance and **synchronization rights.** The source and direct licenses bypass BMI, ASCAP, and SESAC by entailing direct negotiations between users such as broadcasters and publishers; therefore, performing rights organizations would have less bargaining power.

Although the Supreme Court's position on blanket licensing has traditionally been that the performing rights organizations offer the only feasible, efficient way of handling the large flow of information, there is evidence that the courts and Congress may be becoming increasingly sympathetic to broadcasters' arguments against the practice and its inherent monopoly over song rights. In 1987, for instance, a lower federal court ruled that ASCAP must offer per program licenses with surcharges for processing that are equivalent to blanket licenses in cost. ASCAP, BMI and SESAC also offer licenses permitting others to distribute music performances in a protected manner via the Internet. The blanket licensing issue may produce widespread industry changes, as judges and lawmakers balance the concerned parties' interests.

How much money do the performing rights organizations collect and distribute? A lot—fueled in part by the healthy growth in broadcasting. Other factors also contribute: (a) increasing acceptance by music users that they must obey the copyright laws and pay up; (b) increasing efficiency of the collecting agencies; (c) rising licensing rates; and (d) more efficient, comprehensive collections from reciprocating foreign collecting organizations.

The three American performing rights organizations currently collect nearly three quarters of a billion dollars a year from all sources, both foreign and domestic. ASCAP and BMI, which operate on a nonprofit basis, both retain 17% to 19% of their gross earnings for overhead, then distribute the rest to their members and affiliates. SESAC, a for-profit business, is not required to publish its operating expenses or the amount of collections that it retains for its profit, but maintains that its royalties are competitive with ASCAP and BMI.

PERFORMANCE LICENSING

The performance rights organizations license practically all radio **stations** and most TV stations, as well as broadcasting **networks.** They also have licensing contracts with MTV and cable and pay-TV program suppliers such as HBO. With respect to cable TV networks such as HBO, MTV, and USA, the main sources of performance information are program guides furnished by cable services and cue sheets. In addition to agreements with various kinds of broadcasters, rights organizations license clubs, hotels, arenas, colleges, restaurants, taverns, concert promoters, symphony orchestras, colleges, airlines, skating rinks, circuses, theme and amusement parks, background music services, and more.

A prospective licensee is initially contacted either by a field representative or by mail, in an attempt to educate the music user about the responsibilities that exist under U.S. copyright law. The prospective licensee generally enters into a licensing agreement at that time. If the party persists in using music without permission, a lawsuit is brought in the names of specific members for specific infringements under copyright law. Licensing organizations almost always win these legal battles, whether through persuasion or through the courts, for a simple reason: The law is on their side.

Clubs, bars, and other such facilities that present live music performances are normally asked to sign a 1-year blanket license. Hotel and motel licenses cover a 5-year period. The setting of the license rate takes into account (a) the seating capacity of the **venue,** (b) whether it charges admission, (c) its live music weekly budget, and (d) the number of hours of musical entertainment provided. It may also take into account the estimated gross income of the facility.

Neither BMI nor ASCAP surveys performances in such venues as clubs, hotels, skating rinks, or dance schools, because the cost of gathering such data would exceed the amounts that could be collected. Rather, the money generated by licensing such venues is distributed to members based on radio and television performances. Distributions are also made based on performances (broadcast or nonbroadcast) or commercial music services as well as live concerts.

Where a venue, such as a stadium or arena, offers musical entertainment only occasionally, performing rights organizations attempt to collect performance fees from the promoter or producer renting the facility. Where a facility offers entertainment on a regular basis, ASCAP, BMI, and SESAC will, however, normally look to the owner of the location to pay for the performance license.

With respect to concert music, a census technique is used, drawing evidence of live performances of composers' works by scrutinizing printed programs of concerts.

It should be emphasized that performing artists and their agents and managers normally are not expected to pay performance royalties to anyone. Rather, this responsibility and expense falls on either the venue management or the entertainment promoter or producer.

INCOME, ROYALTY DISTRIBUTION

If a writer can get a satisfactory answer about an accounting of performances, the next question is, "What is my fair share of the total royalties collected?"

TV and radio performances generate the majority of performance rights organizations' total revenue from performances. Nearly 15% of income from performances is generated by nonbroadcast sources, for example, clubs, hotels, arenas, and airlines.

A member's or affiliate's share of the total royalties collected is determined by the number and kind of performances. Royalties are paid quarterly.

Some songs have more than one writer, even more than one publisher. If they do not all belong to the same performing rights organization, the parties will earn differing amounts. This is because ASCAP, BMI, and SESAC use their own particular methods in determining royalty payments.

Performance rights earnings vary tremendously for individual members and affiliates. But the composers, authors, and publishers of widely performed copyrights earn royalties year after year going into six figures.

FOREIGN COLLECTIONS

The United States' adherence to the Berne Convention, an international treaty, is a significant development affecting foreign copyright royalty collections. Member countries treat foreigners as nationals for protection purposes, observing minimum standards that raise the integrity of cooperative worldwide copyright enforcement (in Part VII, see "International Copyright: The World Market Outside the United States").

The foreign **subpublisher** remains a dominant source of foreign collections. For those publishers who cannot depend on subpublishers outside this country to supervise collection of performance fees, ASCAP, BMI, and SESAC perform a valuable service by helping maintain reciprocal agreements with all of the important music licensing organizations abroad. They receive performance royalties from these foreign organizations, then pay members their share, withholding 3% to 10% for servicing foreign accounts.

ASCAP, BMI, and SESAC generally need to deal with only one licensing agency in each country; unlike the United States, most other countries have only one licensing organization each. Difficulties with collections abroad often arise with the problem of identifying songs when they are broadcast in the native language or when they are performed under a different title. In any event, foreign performance royalties for American writers and publishers are increasing rapidly as surveys and accounting procedures improve. Among the most lucrative foreign sources of income at this time are Canada, Japan, Germany, the United Kingdom, Holland, Denmark, France, Spain, Switzerland, and Italy.

How does one choose among ASCAP, BMI, and SESAC? Compare the organizations' current rates, policies on the issues of particular concern, and service to members and affiliates, then decide which better seems to meet one's needs. In general, once a member/affiliate strikes a relationship with one licensing organization, staying with that organization may be wise, for a disruption in the flow of income from performances can be costly. Most performance rights organization gains in membership occur through proselytizing of new writers and publishers, not from raiding each other's rosters.

AMERICAN SOCIETY OF COMPOSERS, AUTHORS AND PUBLISHERS

America's first performing rights organization, ASCAP (American Society of Composers, Authors and Publishers), was established, in great part, because of the passage of the U.S. Copyright Act of 1909. The act clearly provided that the right to perform a copyrighted work belongs to the owner(s) of the work; others wishing to perform the work must obtain permission from the owner(s) or a designated representative. In 1914, a small number of the leading American music creators and publishers of the day convened to form ASCAP to license and collect fees for the public performances of their works and to distribute the fees as royalties to the writer and publisher members.

The organization had a difficult time in its early days. Music users were reluctant to start paying for music performances they had traditionally enjoyed for free. Today, after decades of educating music users and after numerous court decisions in favor of copyright holders, the concept of payment of performance fees through music licensing organizations is now broadly accepted, although frequently with reluctance.

Income, Royalty Distribution

Some 20% to 25% of ASCAP's income derives from reciprocating foreign licensing organizations. Close to one half of ASCAP's income from licensed per-

ASCAP office building in Nashville. Photo courtesy of ASCAP.

formances comes from TV stations and networks. Radio generates about 25% of the total. Annual fees for most broadcasters are calculated on the basis of a small percentage of the broadcaster's adjusted gross income.

Membership

Until the mid-1940s, ASCAP's membership comprised mostly composers and lyricists of Broadway shows, movie musicals, and pop songs. Among the organization's charter members were Victor Herbert, John Philip Sousa, Jerome Kern, George M. Cohan, and Irving Berlin. Today, new members are admitted to ASCAP if they have at least one song published and distributed, or one song commercially recorded, available on rental, or performed in media licensed by the society.

ASCAP's board is made up of 12 writers and 12 publishers elected by its membership. Many of the greatest names in American music have served on ASCAP's board, including Harold Arlen, Sammy Cahn, and Virgil Thomson.

Music users have, from time to time, looked on the practices of music licensing organizations as monopolistic and unfair. Whatever the validity of that view, the U.S. Department of Justice, in actions in 1941, 1950, and 1960, agreed to a court-administered control of ASCAP with ASCAP's consent. The arrangement is known legally as a consent decree and was undertaken in respect to the antitrust laws of this country.[2] To this day, a court-appointed judge supervises ASCAP's affairs, particularly with respect to licensing music users and payments to ASCAP's members.

ASCAP conducts a public relations campaign to create goodwill among its members and the community. It offers prizes each year to composers and symphony orchestras. In addition to distribution of earned income, ASCAP has an extensive system of annual awards to its members.

ASCAP periodically hosts a variety of songwriter workshops and showcases across the country to help aspiring composers improve their writing, as well as their awareness of how the music business functions, and to bring these talents to the attention of the music industry. Since 1968, ASCAP has given its Deems Taylor Award to authors and publishers of outstanding books and articles on music. The second edition of this *Handbook* was honored with the award in 1980.

Sampling, Accounting

ASCAP obtains critical information on its member writers and publishers from their membership applications. This includes a listing of the titles in the applicants' catalogs. In addition, during the course of their membership writers and publishers supply the society with updated information on their new work.

Cue sheets for both television films and programs and theatrical films are used to assist in crediting television performances.

The society credits its members on the basis of census and sample surveys of performances. These surveys consist of a random sample of local commercial radio **airplay,** of local commercial television airplay, a census (i.e., complete count) of all performances on the major television networks, a sample of performances on wired music services (e.g., Muzak) and airlines, and certain circuses and ice skating shows. In addition, a census of all performances in symphony and concert halls and a random sample of performances in educational institutions are also taken. Besides this **sampling** of performances in commercial media, ASCAP also conducts a smaller sample of performances on PBS (the Public Broadcasting

System) and **NPR** (National Public Radio) and a smaller sample of college radio airplay.

ASCAP includes cable television in its survey, taking a census or sample of performances on the major cable channels.

In conducting its survey of network television performances, ASCAP uses program logs submitted by the networks as well as cue sheets obtained from program producers. In addition, ASCAP makes audiotapes and videotapes of network broadcasts to check on the accuracy of the performance information supplied.

The society's non-network television survey includes a combination of cue sheets, *TV Guide,* and information obtained from TV Data and Tribune Media Services. The latter two companies compile listings of every program shown on every local U.S. station. In cities where ASCAP maintains field offices, it will also tape broadcasts from television stations whose signals can be received by the field office.

ASCAP conducts its local radio survey through tape recordings made throughout the United States of actual on-the-air broadcasts by radio stations and logs submitted by stations. The tapes and logs are then sent to ASCAP's New York headquarters where a staff of experts analyzes the tapes and logs to identify individual performances.

With respect to cable TV networks such as HBO, MTV, and USA, the main sources of performance information are program guides furnished by cable services and cue sheets.

Weighting Performances

Licensing organizations use various formulas to calculate the relative value, or weight, of sampled performances. As part of its calculation, ASCAP takes into account the following:

1. The medium in which the performance takes place (e.g., local radio, local television, network television)
2. The weight of the station on which the performance is carried (each local radio and TV station has a weight that reflects its relative size in terms of the license fee it pays to ASCAP)

3. The weight of a TV network (the number of stations carrying a performance and the time of day a performance occurs)

4. The type of performance (whether it is a feature, theme, or background)

Background music underscoring a film is credited on a durational basis.

BROADCAST MUSIC INC.

Broadcast Music Inc. (BMI) is owned by stockholders, originally some 475 broadcasters in this country. The BMI board of directors is made up of its stockholders, who monitor overall performance of the company's management. BMI is managed by its president and executive cadre, who make all day-to-day decisions and design the company's strategy. BMI believes that this traditional business mode of operation is the most efficient and responsive way to serve its songwriters and publishers and its licensees.

When formation of BMI was first proposed in the late 1930s, the prospectus distributed to investors stated that stockholders could anticipate no dividends. None have ever been paid. BMI's first affiliates included songwriters from many genres of music that had not been previously represented by performance rights organizations. These genres included jazz, rhythm and blues (R&B), country, gospel, folk, and other indigenous American music. BMI was the representative of more than 90% of the composers in those genres whose work served as the foundation for the growth of the "Golden Age of Rock" that occurred in the 1960s.

Membership

BMI has no "members"; instead it has writer and publisher affiliates. BMI accepts a writer affiliate if that applicant has written a musical composition, alone or in collaboration with other writers, and the work is either commercially published or recorded or otherwise likely to be performed. As for admission of new publishers, BMI literature states, in part, that affiliation with BMI will be of practical benefit only to publishers who have the ability and financial resources to undertake broad-based exploitation of their works. BMI also requires that its publisher affiliates satisfy reasonable standards of literacy and integrity. BMI does not

BMI Nashville office. Photo courtesy of BMI. Photo Alan Mayor.

charge its affiliated writers any application fee or dues. BMI publisher affiliates pay an application fee.

BMI describes its attitude toward proselytizing new members as "the open door." It uses a number of publications and public relations projects to increase awareness of the advantages of BMI affiliation. BMI offers awards to school composers, unknown writers, and arts organizations such as symphony orchestras.

Important among these goodwill projects are the Songwriters' Workshops conducted to instruct inexperienced composers in how to create, then place, their unpublished material.

BMI is the sole sponsor of the Lehman Engel Musical Theater Workshop and the Jazz Composers' Workshop in New York City. In Los Angeles, BMI sponsors the Film and Television Composers Workshop; BMI also sponsors music business workshops in cooperation with universities.

Sampling, Accounting

To avoid separate dealings with the many thousands of music users, BMI conducts basic negotiations with established trade organizations. For example, it periodically negotiates industrywide rates with the American Hotel and Motel Association. In the classical field, BMI negotiates with the American Symphony Orchestra League. With respect to hotels, restaurants, and clubs, BMI works out license fees based in part on the establishment's weekly budget for music: for example, the size of the orchestra if any, the number of hours the business caters to the public, its seating capacity, and so forth. Licenses for such venues as theaters, concert halls, and stadiums are based largely on the frequency of their use and seating capacity.

College students have assisted BMI in auditing unlicensed facilities and live-logged all music heard in a club in a given evening of spot checking. These reports are turned over to BMI field representatives who then call upon and seek to sign up the establishment owner.

BMI believes it achieves a fair and accurate accounting by using a combination of sampling and census techniques. In the radio and television field, it is not economically feasible, due to the large number of individual stations, to attempt to account for all BMI performances every day of the year by each broadcaster. BMI therefore uses a sampling procedure. Every individual station is sampled once a year for a logging period of about 3 days. BMI reports that this technique generates about 440,000 sample hours from commercial stations and 50,000 sample hours from college stations each year. Selection of particular stations to be logged is made by an independent accounting firm, and the stations themselves do not know when they are being scrutinized. BMI believes this system maximizes objectivity of its sampling process.

With respect to broadcasting networks, a census technique is used. Broadcast network producers furnish BMI with daily logs or cue sheets of all music broadcast by them, including theme music, cue music, and songs. Logging of broadcasts (by individual stations and networks) of movies and syndicated shows is cross-checked with the same computer-stored information used by the nation's newspapers in preparing local listings of programming on broadcast TV stations.

Following accumulation of data via these logging, or census, procedures, the numbers are combined with information generated from the sampling process. These accumulated numbers are then used by BMI in an elaborate formula to determine royalty payments to its affiliated writers and publishers.

Income, Royalty Distribution

BMI's standard contract with writers and publishers (see the Appendix) does not cite payment rates, but BMI distributes its *Royalty Information Booklet* to anyone who cares to inquire. Payments are higher for songs that originate in a Broadway show or feature film. As a song's aggregate number of performances reaches certain plateaus, the copyright owners receive bonus payments from BMI, ranging from 1½ to 4 times the minimum rate.

Royalty rates are structured not only to attract new writers but also to discourage defection of present membership.

Foreign collections are an important factor in BMI's total income. BMI's foreign collections for U.S. writers and publishers have substantially increased in recent years because of the explosion of private radio and TV in Europe. BMI has reciprocal arrangements with all of the important music licensing organizations abroad. BMI receives performance royalties from these foreign organizations, then pays BMI members their share, withholding 3.6% for servicing foreign accounts.

SESAC

SESAC, Inc., a third performing rights organization, was founded in 1930 by Paul Heinecke, making it the second oldest performance licensing organization in the nation. While the acronym originally stood for Society of European Stage Authors and Composers, the company has been known only as SESAC since the 1960s. SESAC is a for-profit corporation. It was purchased in 1992 by Freddie Gershon, Ira Smith, and Stephen Swid and the merchant banking house of Allen & Company.

SESAC is the smallest U.S. performing rights society, by design. The company claims its smaller size enables it to position itself to respond to the needs and concerns of its affiliate songwriters and publishers and licensees.

Sampling, Accounting, Income, Royalty Distribution

In recent years, SESAC has established itself as the technological leader among U.S. performing rights organizations by being the first to embrace a vari-

SESAC office building in Nashville. Photo courtesy of SSAC.

ety of state-of-the-art tracking systems. In 1993, SESAC formed a division called SESAC Latina, which was dedicated to representing Spanish-language music. SESAC Latina formed an alliance with Broadcast Data Systems (BDS) to employ its monitoring system to track performances and distribute royalties based on the BDS data. (See Chapter 15 for more information.) Two years later, because of the success with SESAC Latina, SESAC expanded its BDS usage to track affiliates' music on adult contemporary, R&B, country, rock, and other major radio formats. With BDS, SESAC tracks 8.3 million broadcast hours.

For musical genres that are not monitored by BDS, such as jazz and Contemporary Christian, SESAC uses its chart payment system, which makes royalty payments based on chart positions in major trade publications, such as *Billboard, Gavin, Radio and Records,* and *College Music Journal.*

Although SESAC does not use a weighting system as such, when using the publications' charts, it uses the highest of the positions represented by those publications to determine the song's success.

SESAC also uses TV Data and other sources, such as cue sheets, to track television performances for its affiliates.

In 1998, SESAC became the first performing rights organization to sign an agreement with Aris Technologies, Inc., to use its MusiCode digital watermarking system for broadcast monitoring and royalty distribution. With MusiCode, segments of music as short as 3 seconds, which have historically been difficult to track, can be identified, enabling many composers, such as **jingle** and television writers, to receive the most accurate compensation for their works.

In the past, SESAC's catalog contained a large majority of gospel music and Contemporary Christian works. In recent years, the repertory has expanded to include virtually every genre of music, including country, New Age, R&B, dance, pop, A/C, rock, Latin, jingles, and television and film music.

SESAC licenses all types of establishments and broadcast facilities that use music in their business operations. Most SESAC licenses are entered into directly with an establishment.

SESAC conducts periodic song seminars for writers and writers' showcases for its affiliates, offers legal consultation for contracts in person or by mail, and helps pair up potential collaborators. It has agreements for foreign representation with approximately 60 foreign performing rights organizations. SESAC bases performance licenses on fixed fees instead of music users' income.

ASCAP and BMI operate under court consent decrees; SESAC does not.

Barry Mann and Cynthia Weil received the 1997 award for the
most-played song in BMI's repertoire, "You've Lost That Lovin' Feelin', "
which logged over 7 million performances. BMI President and
CEO Frances W. Preston stands between the two winners.
Photo courtesy of BMI.

MECHANICAL LICENSES

As explained in Chapter 5, "Music Copyright," recording manufacturers are required to obtain a **mechanical license** in order to produce and distribute records and tapes to the public. This type of license is limited to those who intend to make these recordings available only for private use—the kinds of recordings people buy and take home.

The copyright law sets forth procedures and fees for record producers to obtain a compulsory mechanical license. But in actual practice, most licenses of recordings for home use are negotiated mechanical licenses. Publishers and recording companies bypass the compulsory licensing route and work out their own license.

A negotiated mechanical license may differ from a statutory compulsory license in three ways:

1. The royalty rate may be lower.
2. Royalty accountings are usually quarterly rather than monthly as required under a statutory license.
3. The statutory requirement of "notice of intent" to record the copyrighted material is waived.

Most publishers use the Harry Fox Agency, Inc., the mechanical collection arm of the National Music Publishers Association (NMPA), to issue mechanical licenses. After publishers instruct Fox on the royalty to charge, the agency negotiates the license, collects the royalties, takes out a service fee of about 4%, and forwards the balance to the publisher.

Many publishers are not large enough to support strong branch offices in foreign territories to license their works and collect their international royalties. The Harry Fox Agency has reciprocal arrangements with most foreign collecting agencies, who normally charge Fox about 15% for their collecting service. Fox takes off its own service fee, then forwards the balance to the publisher client.

Royalty Rates

The first change in the statutory rate for a compulsory mechanical license since 1909 occurred in 1978 when Congress voted an increase to 2.75 cents for each work embodied in a **phonorecord** or one-half cent per minute of playing time or fraction thereof, whichever amount is larger. This rate is periodically adjusted. (See Chapter 5 for details.)

Collection Services

Publishers choosing not to retain the Harry Fox Agency to collect royalties have alternatives. For example, a firm offering licensing and collecting services for mechanical and synchronization rights is the American Mechanical Rights Association (AMRA). This association represents a number of foreign mechanical rights organizations, the largest of which is probably GEMA of Germany. AMRA finances its operation with a 5% service charge on gross collections.

Another service available to publishers is Copyright Management International (CMI). CMI provides licensing and collection services for mechanical and synchronization rights, but also offers full copyright administration services on a worldwide basis, including copyright registration, clearance of performing rights, and the preparation and maintenance of all legal documents such as assignments and **copublishing** agreements. CMI, which reports that it currently represents approximately 15% of domestic publishing revenues, takes a 10% service fee for its full administration service, and a 5% fee for those publishers using only its licensing services in the United States and Canada.

See Part VII for a discussion of the efforts of international associations to set worldwide copyright standards and enforce the collection of royalties.

SYNCHRONIZATION LICENSES

A producer of theatrical motion pictures must acquire two kinds of licenses in the United States. The first one is called a **synchronization license.** The term refers to the right to use music that is timed to synchronize with, or relate to, the action on the screen. Film producers ordinarily also seek a performance license for exhibitions in the United States.[3]

The producer who wants new music composed expressly for a film will engage a film music composer to write the original score, often buying these creative services on a work-made-for-hire basis. In this circumstance the producer, or employer, not only owns all the rights to the original music but is considered, under copyright law, the author of the work. Thus, the producer does not require a license of any kind from the composer of the music, because it is the producer's property.

If the film producer does not obtain the musical score on a work-made-for-hire basis, there are other ways to proceed. The producer may engage a film composer as an independent contractor, pay a fee, then negotiate publishing rights to the music. If the composer retains all publishing rights, the film producer must then obtain from the composer a synchronization license to use the music in a film.

Another source for film music is music already under copyright and published. A film producer who, for example, wants to use an established pop song must negotiate a synchronization license with the publisher. Most American publishers handle these arrangements through the Harry Fox Agency. After the publisher instructs Fox—the agency does not make basic decisions in this regard—on what to accept and what to charge, Fox negotiates with the film producer for the music use and the cost of the synchronization license.

Costs of synchronization licenses will be largely determined by the market value of the music, whether the music is to be performed on camera or just underscored, whether it is to be sung, and the duration of the performance in the film. When a producer does not know who owns a particular work, the Harry Fox Agency computer not only can reveal who publishes the music but can also call up on the same screen the licensing rates. If Fox doesn't have a record of the copyright, careful producers will normally engage a copyright researcher or law firm to assist.

It is very important for the film producer to obtain the broadest possible synchronization license, because a movie originally planned for theatrical exhibition in this country will probably be used later in foreign theaters, television broadcasts here and abroad, cable TV, and home video. The publisher may try to grant the film producer a limited license in order to maximize profits later when the film is used in different media.

With respect to performance licenses for film music, conditions in the United States differ from those in Europe. It is customary for film producers to acquire from publishers a performance license for theatrical exhibition of a film in this country. But in Europe and most other countries outside the United States, each country's own performance licensing organization grants to theaters in that country a blanket license for the performance of music accompanying films. These licensing organizations generally derive their income from film music by charging a small percentage of the net box office receipts. Nearly all performing rights organizations outside this country grant licenses for music controlled by ASCAP, BMI, and SESAC through reciprocal agreements with these performing rights organizations. American composers sometimes receive substantial performance royalties from music they have scored for films that become popular in theaters abroad.

TV Movie Rights

A different set of licensing problems arises when a film is originally produced for television broadcast. The producer will certainly go for the broadest possible synchronization license, in anticipation that the production will eventually be aired in other media and possibly foreign territories. The producer will normally not need a performance license for television broadcasts; the TV stations and networks already have a blanket performance license with ASCAP, BMI, and SESAC for all the music they broadcast. Broadcasters may, however, increasingly seek to use direct or source licensing to avoid paying for both performance and synchronization licenses.

New Use Rights

A film producer or TV movie producer frequently wants to use music already existing in a commercially released recording. One of the reasons this may appear attractive to the producer is that it is known beforehand how the music will sound and that it has been well received by the public. But obtaining permission to borrow a recording for a film score can become a complicated, expensive process. Negotiations of this kind will involve not only the recording company but also the performing artists, the artists' unions, and music publishers. The recording company contract with the artist may prohibit use of that artist's recordings in another medium. If so, special waivers and artist's compensation must be negotiated. Both artists' unions—American Federation of Musicians (AFM) and American Federation of Television and Radio Artists (AFTRA)—will require **new use** payments. The music publisher will demand from the film producer a synchronization license and a performing license.

CABLE TELEVISION LICENSES

Cable television systems (which pick up TV stations' signals, boost them, and wire the pictures into homes) are described in the 1976 Copyright Act as being in the business of offering **secondary transmissions** of primary material. As such, cable operators are required to operate under a compulsory license. These licenses are issued and administered by the Copyright Office. Rates are determined by an elaborate set of guidelines, including reports from the cable TV companies on the number of channels transmitted, number of subscribers, and adjusted gross receipts. After deducting administrative expenses, the Copyright Office then distributes this money to copyright owners. Rates set by the 1976 Copyright Act are periodically reevaluated with the assistance of a Copyright

Arbitration Royalty Panel (CARP), which is empowered by the Register of Copyrights to adjust them.

Individual members of the groups representing copyright owners, such as the three American performing rights organizations, for example, are encouraged to negotiate among themselves for fair apportionments. When disputes arise (and they often do), a CARP is empowered to determine fair shares.

Other Cable TV Licenses

Almost all cable operators offer not only relays of conventional TV programs but also additional channels as part of their standard service or for extra cost to their subscribers. Performing rights organizations negotiate separate licensing arrangements with these program suppliers, for example, MTV, HBO, and Showtime. These agreements are distinct from the compulsory licenses the law requires for cable TV operators.

With respect to music bounced off satellites and picked up by earth stations, copyright laws were clarified in the Satellite Home Viewer Act of 1988. Section 119 of the Copyright Act provides in general that secondary transmissions of a primary transmission made by a superstation, or of programming contained in a primary transmission made by a network station, and embodying a performance or display of a work, shall be subject to compulsory licensing if the secondary transmission is made by a satellite carrier to the public for private home viewing, and the carrier makes a direct or indirect charge for such retransmission service to each subscriber receiving the secondary transmission.

VIDEO LICENSES

The music video market grew rapidly in the early 1980s, and no industry standards were in place for licensing it. The matter was complicated by the failure of the 1976 Copyright Act to address the question.

Despite the initial skimpy guidance from copyright law, experienced entertainment lawyers and industry leaders gradually formed a consensus. Here is a summary of their views:

1. All videos, whether clips or albums, must be defined under copyright law as audiovisual works. As such, they are like little movies, and producers

must acquire synchronization licenses from music publishers or their agents.

2. Performance rights in the musical portion of videos must be acquired from the publisher by the party who shows the videos to the public. These rights are most conveniently negotiated with the publisher's performing rights organization. Where the video is shown through conventional TV, the broadcasters' blanket performance rights agreement is sufficient. Where the video is shown on cable TV, the exhibitor (e.g., MTV, HBO) must negotiate performance rights with ASCAP, BMI, or SESAC. If the video is shown in a club or similar venue, the venue's blanket performance license with ASCAP, BMI, or SESAC will suffice.

3. Video software manufacturers must pay publishers (or their agents, such as the Harry Fox Agency) for the right to reproduce the videos mechanically as cassettes or discs for home use. Courts have held that this right is not automatically considered part of a synchronization license, but must be addressed specifically. The parties, or their agents, can determine through negotiation whether the mechanical right is to be paid as a one-time flat fee or as a royalty based on software sales.

TRANSCRIPTION LICENSES

The term *transcription license* is applied imprecisely to cover music used by syndicated programs, Muzak, in-flight entertainment, and music **library services.** These kinds of music users require a mechanical license and a performance license. The two may be combined in one agreement or contracted separately.

A user seeking such licenses may negotiate directly with publishers or with the Harry Fox Agency or SESAC. With respect to the collection of performance fees, users negotiate agreements with ASCAP, BMI, or SESAC.

Firms such as Muzak usually obtain a master license from the performing rights organizations with fixed annual fees based on their current number of franchised dealers. Other transcription licenses may call, for example, for a payment of 5 cents per selection for each copy of the tape that is sold to users. This nickel would include 2 cents for the mechanical license and 3 cents for the performance right.

A somewhat different kind of transcription license is obtained by program syndicators and broadcasters' library services such as those described in the chapter on radio broadcasting (see Chapter 21). These transcription licenses for these packages must be negotiated with the Harry Fox Agency or directly with the music publishers.

With respect to in-flight entertainment, the supplier of the tapes and films must obtain rights of synchronization and mechanical reproduction from copyright owners. Negotiations may be directly with publishers or with the Harry Fox Agency. Concerning performance licenses, in-flight program suppliers normally negotiate directly with the performing rights organizations.

Special Use Permits

As explained in Chapter 4, "Music Publishing," music is often licensed for applications relating to various merchandising tie-ins, such as posters, apparel, greeting cards, even computer software. Licenses of this kind are simply referred to as *permissions* or *special use permits*. The music publisher may settle for a one-time fee or may prefer a royalty agreement tied to sales.

Broadcast Commercials

For many publishers, the highest earnings from special use permits are generated from broadcast commercials. An advertising agency or sponsor who wants to use all or part of a pop standard is often willing to pay several thousand dollars for the privilege. These kinds of music licenses often include the right to alter the words and music to suit the needs of the advertiser.

For music composed originally for broadcast commercials, the composer usually has the option of granting the advertiser a **buyout** deal or, more likely, permitting unlimited performances of the music if the usage is confined to advertising.

JUKEBOX LICENSES

Since 1978, jukebox owners have been required to obtain a public performance license for nondramatic music played on their machines. These licenses are negotiated between the jukebox operator and the copyright owner, often with the involvement of a performing rights organization.

ASCAP, BMI, SESAC, and the Amusement and Music Operators Association (AMOA) created the Jukebox License Office (JLO), which contacts jukebox operators and offers them one blanket license to cover the use of music from all three performance rights organizations. This **joint venture** handles the rebates and new jukebox registrations. Because licensing fees are negotiated based on standard rates recommended by the performing rights organizations, those interested should contact BMI, ASCAP, and/or SESAC directly.

DRAMATIC MUSIC RIGHTS

Study of U.S. copyright law reveals sharp distinctions between **dramatic music** and nondramatic music. Accordingly, the licensing of rights differs markedly.

The term *dramatic music* includes, for example, operas, musical plays, musical shows, and revues, in whole or in part. The term may also include music that did not originate in some kind of theatrical production but was written as part of a TV or radio show where the music was integral to the plot and where it contributed to carrying the drama forward. It is customary to refer to performing rights in dramatic music as **grand rights,** and grand rights must be negotiated with copyright owners separately from nondramatic rights, which are sometimes termed **small rights.**

With respect to Broadway musicals and similar productions, rights of authors, composers, and lyricists are set forth in contracts recommended by the Dramatists Guild, Inc. Under the guild's Approved Production Contract (APC), the separate rights in music and lyrics that comprise the dramatico-musical work are retained by the composers and lyricists and their publishers, sometimes with certain restrictions, as in the sale of movie rights. Also, there may be restrictions with respect to when the music and lyrics can be recorded (e.g., there may be a prohibition against releasing recordings of a show's songs on a single prior to the release of the original cast album).

A show's composers receive royalties from ASCAP, BMI, or SESAC for performances of individual songs on radio, TV, clubs and restaurants, and so forth. But when a dramatic musical work is performed as a whole or a substantial portion of it is performed—a scene including music and dialogue, for example—grand rights must be licensed. ASCAP does not involve itself in licensing grand rights of any of its repertoire. Its members usually assign that responsibility to one of the firms involved in grand rights licensing and rental of scores and parts. BMI licenses with broadcasters also grant only nondramatic rights but do grant the right to perform up to 30 minutes of a full-length dramatic or dramatico-musical work or an insubstantial portion of a shorter dramatic or dramatico-musical work. SESAC's standard contract with broadcasters excludes dramatic music. SESAC licenses such rights separately.

When a Broadway musical becomes a hit, its writers enjoy income from its performances long after its Broadway run. In this country, there are hundreds of regional theaters offering performances of these beloved shows. The author holds the so-called subsidiary rights to these shows, including motion pictures, band arrangements, live performance rights, TV usage, commercial jingle usage, and stage performance rights. Some companies act as agents who specialize in the licensing of subsidiary rights such as *stock and amateur* productions of musicals. Stock and amateur rights of a play are those rights reserved by the authors of a play and licensed to organizations such as Samuel French, Inc., Music Theatre International, Rogers and Hammerstein Music Library, and Tams-Witmark. These companies, mostly based in New York City, represent authors for specific works, rather than representing authors for every musical they write. The companies receive an agent's commission and handle the licensing of those shows to stock and amateur theaters around the country.

Each dramatic performance of this kind requires a license and royalty payment. Royalty rates are calculated on a percentage based on the seating capacity of the house, the number of performances, and the ticket prices. In addition to the license fee, the show's **book,** score, and parts must be rented from the licensing agency. Professional performances of Broadway shows (following a Broadway run) require a license involving a weekly minimum guarantee against 6% to 14% of the box office receipts. Professional productions also must rent the show's book, score, and parts. The producers are generally charged higher rates than those for amateur groups.

Performance licenses for touring companies vary. Some touring companies are under the aegis of the original Broadway producer; others are mounted independently. The producer usually has many options and a period of time after the opening (or close) of the producer's production of the play in which to exercise them, such as the right to send out a touring company. If the producer doesn't send out a touring company, the rights to license a touring company revert to the authors (this is one of the subsidiary rights that include motion picture rights, touring rights, and foreign rights). If the original show has run long enough that the producer is entitled to a share of subsidiary rights, the authors would then pay the producer a portion of their receipts just as they do with stock and amateur rights.

NOTES

1. BMI did publish music for a while in its early history (1940s) but no longer does so. Neither ASCAP nor SESAC has ever published music.

2. BMI is also under a consent decree, but it sets forth a different set of constraints.

3. For this license, the film producer will normally go to the publisher (or the publisher's agent) because a court decree has denied, to ASCAP at least, the right to require a performance license directly from movie theaters in the United States.

UNIONS AND GUILDS

7

W orkers involved in the music and entertainment fields have developed a large number of organizations to represent their interests. The number and kinds of representative organizations appear almost endless.[1] Here we have room to discuss only the larger organizations. They are structured in a variety of ways. Some, such as the American Federation of Musicians (AFM), are trade unions, connected with the AFL-CIO. Others are more accurately described as **guilds.** Still others are simply associations of independent contractors. If this were not complicated enough, we have entertainment industry guilds (e.g., the Dramatists Guild), whose members may own the company with whom they are supposed to negotiate for their services.

Discussed below are the AFM, the American Federation of Television and Radio Artists (AFTRA), the American Guild of Musical Artists (AGMA), the Screen Actors Guild (SAG), and the American Guild of Variety Artists (AGVA). Smaller unions and guilds are described at the end of this chapter.

When young artists start their careers, they are often reluctant to join their respective unions, seeing such an action as expensive and restrictive. But if a demand develops for the artist's services, opportunities will arise where union affiliation is not only advantageous but imperative. Most employment available to artists above the small-time level is union, meaning that if an individual wants to be a professional performer (or arranger, **copyist,** director, conductor, actor, dancer, etc.), those services will be under the jurisdiction and control of a union contract.

The arts organizations and industries employing artists have recognized, often reluctantly, the bargaining rights of AFM, AFTRA, and the other unions. But art-

← © David Austen/Stock, Boston/PNI.

ists' labor organizations have experienced, in recent years, the same problems affecting the labor movement as a whole: decreased bargaining power and loss of jobs through foreign competition and developing technologies.

AMERICAN FEDERATION OF MUSICIANS

The full name of the AFM is American Federation of Musicians of the United States and Canada. It is the oldest union in the United States representing individuals professionally active in the fields of entertainment and the arts, its history dating from the 19th century. AFM has always been the largest artists' labor organization. Through the decades, however, the AFM has been losing members and some of its power. Why? A number of reasons have been advanced: (a) difficulty in attracting many of the new, young professionals; (b) state and national laws restricting certain kinds of **collective bargaining;** (c) continuing displacement of live performances with recorded music; (d) increasing displacement of live musicians by electronic instruments; (e) continuing importation of music recorded abroad; and (f) increasing prevalence of nonunion performances, live and recorded. In recent years, in at least some local branches, the trend toward lower AFM membership has started to reverse itself, and membership numbers have begun to rise.

AFM membership includes professional instrumentalists, conductors, arrangers, **orchestrators,** copyists, music librarians, orchestra contractors, and proofreaders, as well as some related fields such as cartage people (or roadies) and, when there are no jurisdictional disputes, engineers. The union maintains no jurisdiction over the professional services of composers (although practically all composers professionally active in film, television, radio, commercials, and **syndication** are AFM members by virtue of their services as either conductors, instrumentalists, arrangers, or copyists).

If a musician sings professionally, it is not necessary to be an AFM member unless the musician also works professionally in one of the capacities listed for regular AFM membership.

Unlike a number of guilds and professional associations in the arts, the AFM is a bona fide labor union: Its members are employees and the AFM represents the interests of its members to employers.

The AFM functions on two levels, local and federation (United States and Canada). The local offices of the union have jurisdiction over all union work for musicians that is not covered by federation-wide contracts. AFM federation contracts embrace all services of musicians in the fields of recording, network broadcasting, theatrical film, television film and tape, **live-on-tape** network television, home video, syndicated programs and services, pay-TV, commercial announcements, and contracts covering the taped music for certain traveling productions such as circuses and ice shows.

Federation contracts are administered by the union's Electronic Media Services Division (EMSD), which is under the direct supervision of the AFM president. EMSD has resident representatives in New York City and Los Angeles.

AFM contracts, whether local or federation, generally include agreements on such issues as wages, hours, overtime, working conditions, instrument **doubling,** heavy-instrument cartage, class of **venue,** rehearsal fees, pay for leader and contractor, **tracking scale, reuse,** and **new use** of recorded material.

The AFM manages to negotiate reasonably satisfactory contracts, at least from the union's point of view, at the national level. But at the local level, union control over wages and benefits is weak. This is largely because certain states invoke their **right-to-work laws** and, more significantly, because of the constraints on union jurisdictions imposed by the Taft-Hartley Act (1947). Under a National Labor Relations Board interpretation of this law, absent a collective bargaining agreement (CBA), musicians are considered independent contractors. As such, they are prohibited from compelling purchasers of musicians' services to recognize the AFM as the musicians' collective bargaining agent. As a consequence, these purchasers of musicians' services (such as club owners, hotels) are not required to contribute to such employee benefits as unemployment insurance, FICA, and pension funds. Under these circumstances, however, a band leader may be considered the employer and therefore compelled to make benefit payments. Over a period of many years, the AFM has unsuccessfully urged Congress to modify the Taft-Hartley's limitations on musicians.

Union Finance

The union finances its activities with new members' initiation fees, annual dues, and work dues. The amount assessed as work dues varies from local to local and ranges from 1% to about 5% of union scale wages earned by members.[2]

A share of these monies collected by the locals is forwarded to AFM's international headquarters in New York City to finance the union's activities throughout the United States and Canada.

Other Services

The AFM attempts to license and control talent agents through franchising them. This process is described in Chapter 8. The union also seeks to protect its members from employers who don't pay union musicians what they are due.[3] Slow-paying or nonpaying employers are sometimes sued by the union. More often, they are simply blacklisted, in part through publication of the names of offenders in the musicians' monthly magazine, *International Musician.*

AFM contracts covering the record industry are described in Chapter 16. With respect to AFM employment in film scoring, see Chapter 24.

AMERICAN FEDERATION OF TELEVISION AND RADIO ARTISTS

The American Federation of Television and Radio Artists (AFTRA) represents professional singers and other vocalists, actors, news broadcasters, dancers, talk show hosts, disc jockeys, announcers and other television and radio personalities.[4] Among its membership are anonymous background singers and multimillionaire superstars.

Its jurisdiction includes live and taped television, radio, sound recordings, interactive media, and nonbroadcast material. The union has more than 30 regional offices, or locals. Like the AFM, AFTRA is affiliated with the AFL-CIO.

Like AFM, AFTRA is a real labor union: Its members are employees, and AFTRA's main business is working out labor agreements with employers. As with most national labor unions, AFTRA's leadership negotiates its national and local contracts with industry associations representative of the major sectors of the entertainment industry—record companies, TV and radio networks and stations, TV producers, and producers of commercial **spots** intended for broadcast.

When a singer gets an opportunity to perform for the first time in a field where AFTRA has jurisdiction, the **gig** may be accepted without joining the union, because the Taft-Hartley Act initially excuses the performer from this obligation. But the artist must join the union within 30 days thereafter to continue accepting jobs under AFTRA jurisdiction. The fee varies and is comparable to other performer unions. Members' dues vary widely and are determined by the individual's annual gross earnings on AFTRA jobs.

With respect to AFTRA's jurisdiction over professional singers, the union's contracts classify such artists as soloists, duos, or group singers. Scales are highest for soloists and duos; second-highest wages are earned by soloists who step out of an ensemble momentarily for a featured segment. Background singers are paid somewhat more when performing with duos and trios than they are in larger choral ensembles.

Of all the artists' performing unions, AFTRA has the most complicated schedule of wages. Particularly in the commercial spot field, **union stewards** must be able to tell a producer what costs will be for singers relative to the intended market for the spots whether they are for local, regional, or national broadcast. AFTRA wages rise according to the potential size of the market. In the commercial production industry, it is not unusual for large production companies and advertising agencies to have at least one full-time employee helping spot producers figure out the correct AFTRA scales. The only safe solution is for the producer to get current AFTRA scales directly from the union. Commercial contracts are identical for AFTRA and SAG, because they are jointly negotiated and administered.

One of the most important components of AFTRA contracts is the provision for new use or **extended use.** As with most other artists' union contracts, when an AFTRA member performs on a recording intended for one particular medium, additional money is earned if that recording is later used in a different medium, such as when a commercial recording might be licensed for use in a movie or a television show. AFTRA artists also earn additional wages when the use of a broadcast commercial extends beyond the initial term (often limited to 13 weeks). Because many spot campaigns are broadcast for long periods of time, even years after the initial use, earnings of AFTRA members from this source can become very large.

As with the AFM, AFTRA requires a union steward on the job if there are three or more background singers to make sure the producer meets all the obligations to the performers under contract. AFTRA is almost exclusively concerned with negotiating and implementing singers' activities covered by national contracts, particularly the recording and broadcasting industries. The performers' union has minimal control over singers performing on local shows and commercials outside of the recording centers of New York, Los Angeles, and Nashville.

AFTRA was the first talent union to provide its members with a pension and welfare plan. These benefits are funded by contributions made by employers.

For a discussion of AFTRA's involvement in the recording industry, see Chapter 16.

The 4As

AFTRA is a member of a loose alliance known in the industry as "the 4as." The term stands for Associated Actors and Artistes of America; all unions under this banner are affiliated with the AFL-CIO. This group includes the Actors' Equity Association, AGVA, AGMA, SAG, Guild of Italian-American Actors (GIAA), and Hebrew Actors Union (HAU). The 4As have helped reduce jurisdictional disputes among performers' unions, although each 4A member organization requires performers to belong to its particular union when jurisdictions appear to overlap. The AFM also zealously guards its own turf. For example, a singer who also plays an instrument on a network TV show must belong to both the AFM and AFTRA. A movie actor who appears on a TV show must hold a SAG card as a film actor and an AFTRA card as a television performer.

AFTRA and SAG have worked together in defining their jurisdictions in the field of music videos: Those shot on tape fall under AFTRA's jurisdiction, those shot on film under SAG's. In the early history of this field, practically all videos were knocked out on shoestring budgets too small to permit the payment of union wages, particularly for singers, dancers, and actors. Small, independent labels and the smaller production companies may continue to produce their videos with nonunion (or partly union) artists and crews. Music videos produced or financed by companies that have signed the AFTRA Sound Recording Code will be produced under AFTRA's jurisdiction. The larger firms increasingly use all union artists and production personnel.

AMERICAN GUILD OF MUSICAL ARTISTS

The American Guild of Musical Artists (AGMA) is one of the 4A unions (despite the word *Guild* in its title). AGMA was organized in the 1930s to serve the interests of singers and dancers working in the opera, dance, concert, oratorio, and recital fields.

AGMA employment agreements are often negotiated for a particular ensemble, such as the Met's chorus or the San Francisco Opera's corps de ballet. Such contracts cover the standard items in any labor agreement—wages, working conditions, and benefits. Most AGMA contract negotiations are with nonprofit arts organizations that own the performing groups, for example, the American Ballet Theatre Foundation, which owns and sponsors the American Ballet Theatre. The union negotiates several national Master Agreements for choristers, vocal soloists in opera and concert music, and dance corps members and dance soloists. Those agreements are used as a basis for individual agreements with companies such as the New York City Opera; the Dance Theatre of Harlem; the Alvin Ailey Dance Company, which operates under the umbrella organization of the Dance Theatre Foundation; and larger regional theaters such as the Portland Opera, the Michigan Opera Theatre, and the Cincinnati Ballet. Member companies agree to the conditions of the Master Agreement.

AMERICAN GUILD OF VARIETY ARTISTS

The American Guild of Variety Artists (AGVA) represents singers, dancers, comedians, ice skaters, jugglers, magicians, and others who perform live, primarily in such venues as clubs, casinos, resorts, and fairgrounds. AGVA includes in its membership not only the struggling regional performer but also world-famous artists drawing huge fees, performing live in Las Vegas and elsewhere. AGVA negotiates national agreements with venues in which its members perform. AGVA members include performers who work with variety acts and live theater.

ACTORS' EQUITY ASSOCIATION

Professional actors, directors, and stage managers on the legitimate stage in the United States are represented by the Actors' Equity Association, which theater people refer to simply as "Equity." **Equity** is the oldest of the major actors' unions, founded in 1913. Equity is a trade union and is affiliated with the AFL-CIO.

For many years, Equity membership was made up mostly of personnel working in New York City. Today, Equity has members all over the country. This has come about with the large growth of regional theaters, stock and dinner and small professional theaters, and acting companies in residence on college campuses.

There are 14 national contracts, 13 regional contracts, and 7 regional codes, which Equity either negotiates with collective bargaining partners or promulgates on its own. Actors and stage managers employed on Broadway work under the Production Contract that Equity negotiates with the League of American Theatres and Producers, Inc. Other negotiated contracts include the **Off-Broad-**

way Contract, and the LORT (League of Resident Theatres) contract, which governs employment in regional theaters.

Of all the artists' unions, Equity enjoys the best reputation with producers for its awareness of the economic variables within the theater industry: It knows that there are more members out of work than there are jobs for them to fill. While Equity will not permit the reduction of minimum salaries for Equity actors and stage managers, it may make other alterations (known as "concessions") in its agreement with a theater that can assist that theater in achieving financial stability.

One of Equity's primary responsibilities to its members is to require a bond, which protects the minimum guarantee of employment (usually 2 weeks), should a producer default on an obligation before or during rehearsal or during the performance period.

Equity also permits limited talent "showcases" in certain cities and regional areas to provide its members with the opportunity to gain experience, recognition, and, it is hoped, employment.

SCREEN ACTORS GUILD

The Screen Actors Guild (SAG) is probably the most widely known artists' union, in that so many of its members are world-famous performers. SAG has jurisdiction over all actors, singers, and on-screen instrumentalists who act in film; SAG shares jurisdiction with AFTRA over all actors, singers, and on-screen instrumentalists who act or appear on TV, in commercials, in music videos, and in industrial films. SAG is classified as a trade union, in that its members are employees whose services are rendered to employers through contracts negotiated by the union (guild). In Hollywood, the parent contract is negotiated with the Alliance of Motion Picture and Television Producers (AMPTP).

Like the AFM and AFTRA, the actors' union attempts to control behavior of actors' agents through a franchising system that specifies contract terms and percentages agents may charge. Again similar to AFM and AFTRA contracts, SAG contracts stipulate who is responsible for residual payments to actors when a production created for one medium is sold or licensed for exhibition through another medium.

INTERNATIONAL ALLIANCE OF THEATRICAL STAGE EMPLOYES[5]

The International Alliance of Theatrical Stage Employes, Moving Picture Technicians, Artists and Allied Crafts of the United States, Its Territories and Canada (IATSE) is the union having jurisdiction over stagehands in the legitimate theater and in the majority of motion picture and (filmed) television productions. Many motion picture camerapersons and movie projectionists also belong to IATSE, which represents members in all the crafts associated with video.

IATSE negotiates national contracts on behalf of its members, for example,

- ▶ Film exchange employee contracts
- ▶ National industrial and product demonstration contracts
- ▶ Traveling stage, wardrobe, and projectionist contracts (and others)

Organizations with whom IATSE has agreements include the following:

- ▶ All the major motion picture producers as well as scores of independents
- ▶ All the networks as well as local independent broadcasters in radio and television
- ▶ Most major opera, symphony, and ballet companies
- ▶ Most major arenas and civic centers
- ▶ Major producers of traveling theatrical productions

OTHER UNIONS AND GUILDS; RELATED ISSUES

National Association of Broadcast Employees and Technicians–Communications Workers of America

The National Association of Broadcast Employees and Technicians–Communications Workers of America (NABET-CWA) is another union that represents audio engineers and technicians and other workers in the field of broadcasting, including makeup artists and some on-air talent.

Dramatists Guild of America, Inc.

The Dramatists Guild is a trade association, not a labor union. It represents composers, lyricists, and **book** writers active in the musical theater. The guild also includes, as members, playwrights who write plays without music or plays that use music only incidentally.

The Dramatists Guild is a corporate member of the Authors League of America, which has two branches: the Dramatists Guild and the Authors Guild. The latter is a trade association of authors of books other than books for plays.

Royalty payments, maintenance of subsidiary rights, artistic control, and ownership of copyright have remained of paramount importance since the guild was established in 1919. The guild requires that the ownership and control of the music, lyrics, and book of a show remain in the hands of its authors and composers. The producer cannot claim publishing rights of this material. Guild members retain copyright in their material, including the licensing of performances of **dramatic music (grand rights)**. The guild also helps its members preserve the integrity of their works, in that producers and directors are not allowed to alter music, lyrics, or the book to a show without the composers' and authors' consent.

Related Unions and Guilds

Other unions and guilds related to the music and/or entertainment fields are the Writers Guild of America (west and east), the Directors Guild of America, the Producers Guild of America, the National Conference of Personal Managers, the Society of Stage Directors and Choreographers, and the United Scenic Artists.

Open Shop Agreements

Some situations have both union and nonunion employees. Often in such a case an *open shop* agreement is established. Open shop agreements generally stipulate that individuals employed in such a situation are subject to the collective bargaining agreement in effect between the pertinent union and the employer. In the event of a dispute, the terms of the collective bargaining agreement would govern the employment of the nonunion employee.

Audio Technicians

With respect to audio technicians working in recording studios and broadcasting, no one union has managed to gain complete jurisdiction. Many employers of these kinds of technicians have been able to avoid **union shop** status.

Other Issues

Additional concerns relating to unions and guilds have to do with the employment of minors, and the issues of immigration and work permits, where one country seeks to limit foreign artists from displacing its own citizens from job opportunities. Individuals needing definitive information on these kinds of problems are advised to search out current regulations and statutes through attorneys experienced in labor or immigration law.

NOTES

1. The following kinds of professionals are represented in some kind of organization: composers, arrangers, lyricists, instrumentalists, singers, playwrights, theatrical producers, directors, stage actors, screen actors, choreographers, dancers, scenic designers, scenery builders, stagehands, electricians, personal managers, record producers, audio technicians, and educators specializing in the fields of music management, merchandising, and recording technology.

2. In some cities, by mutual consent of the local and employer, the employer forwards a check directly to the union office to cover all union wages, benefits, and retirement funds. Then, upon the musicians' authorization, the union deducts musicians' work dues, deposits the benefits and all other special payments into their respective accounts, and writes a net paycheck for each musician employed on the date. Under different circumstances, the AFM will permit an employer to pay musicians through an artists' payroll service company, whose services are available in large cities. AFM contractors sometimes use this kind of company to handle wages, tax accounting, and benefit payments.

3. See Note 2.

4. In Canada, the comparable union is the Association of Canadian Television and Radio Artists (ACTRA).

5. This organization does indeed spell "Stage Employes" with only one "e."

AGENTS, MANAGERS, AND ATTORNEYS

The first thing we do, let's kill all the lawyers.
—Shakespeare, Henry VI, Part 2, Act IV, Scene II

Many professional artists find it desirable, even imperative, to call upon others to assist them in handling their business affairs and the development of their careers. Partly because of the glamour of the music and entertainment fields, performers of even modest success find themselves surrounded by individuals who claim they can help the artist find the path to fame and fortune. Although some performers of modest gifts have been brought from the unemployment line to at least temporary success through the efforts of clever management, many others, obviously very talented, continue to flounder in the small time for want of someone competent enough to guide their careers in the right direction.

Successful artists often find that their many business needs take time away from their creative work. To avoid this, they engage a team of assistants and professionals, probably including a personal manager, agent, business manager, road manager, attorney, publisher, and publicist. The services that support personnel perform often overlap and intertwine. In this chapter, the roles of agents, managers, and attorneys are defined and discussed as they relate to the arts and entertainment industry.

AGENTS

An agent represents clients by seeking employment for them, and, as an employment agent, must comply with state laws.

← Los Angeles skyline. Photo by Donna Carroll.

161

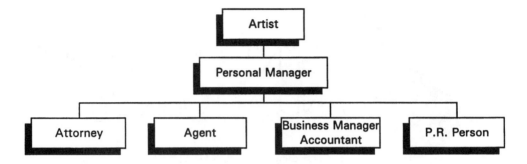

Figure 8.1a   The Team

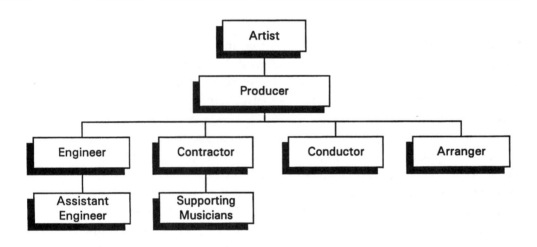

Figure 8.1b   The Team in Studio

Agents go by various names. Many people refer to them as *booking agents*, which most of them are. In California, they are known today as *talent agents*. Sometimes people in and out of the business use the term *manager* or *artist's manager* interchangeably with *agent*. A high percentage of agency work is conducted in California, so the word *agent* is used here the way California statutes define talent agent, that person who is in the full-time business of procuring employment primarily for performers, writers, producers, and directors.

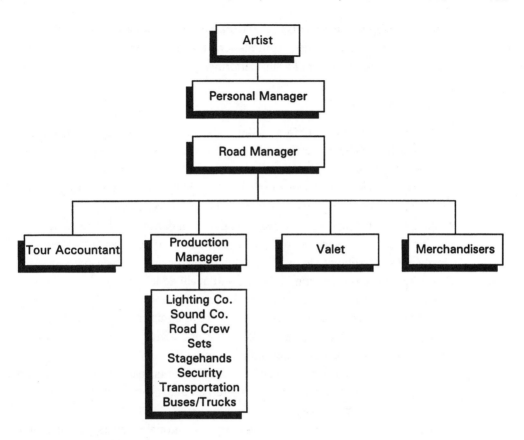

Figure 8.1c The Touring Team

The talent agent has two kinds of clients. The first is a roster of artists. The other kind of client is the buyer of such talent—primarily producers, promoters, and club owners. The talent agent's job is to deliver artists to talent buyers, to serve as the middleman, the negotiator who knows, or should know, what an artist is worth and what the buyer is willing and able to pay. If the agent prices the merchandise too high, the buyer won't deal. If the agent prices the merchandise too low, not only will there be a lower commission, but artist clients may be lost to other agents who are more aggressive.

The agents who are most successful over the long run have earned the respect and confidence of both buyers and sellers. It is the agent's task to obtain the highest possible fees for clients and to work closely with an artist's manager. If an agent can attract major artists, commissions may place the agent in an income bracket comparable to that of a star performer.

Regional Agencies

An agent often starts out in a medium-sized city working alone, quickly discovers it is hard to be very effective that way, and connects with one or two other local agents. Perhaps three of them can afford to rent a modest office and hire a secretary. Agencies of this size handle most local bookings. They try to persuade local club owners to try live music instead of a jukebox. One of their greatest challenges is locating acts attractive enough to pull dancers and drinkers into local clubs. Most of the acts sending them **demos** are, at best, semiprofessional— clearly not strong enough to justify the club owner paying them even union scale. So the agent keeps searching for buyers and qualified talents.

Until the agent can discover acts with some drawing power, there will rarely be a chance to build the booking business above a minimum survival level. But now and then, local acts create a following and start to command fees high enough to earn the agent a respectable income.

Agents with ambitions transcending the city limits search out contacts and joint bookings with national, and even international, agencies. Such deals ordinarily involve commission splits.

If a local agent learns the trade and develops national contacts, perhaps there will be a job with a large national booking agency. If the agent is aggressive, creative, and persevering, there might be a bright future ahead. National booking agencies employ hundreds of people and operate with offices in the major cities of the world. Agencies such as William Morris, International Creative Management (ICM), and Creative Artist's Agency (CAA) handle hundreds of artists and gross hundreds of millions of dollars a year. Such agencies generally take commissions of 10% to 15% of the artist's gross income from work generated by the agency or otherwise eligible for commission.

One of the principal reasons these large international outfits do well is their power to package or pull together, for a television network or movie company, not only the star performers but also supporting players, writers, directors, composers, even choreographers. It is big business in this league, and major talents generally seek exclusive representation by one of these international firms. In addition to their ability to package, the big companies represent artists in all fields of entertainment including concerts, television, recordings, films, commercials, and product endorsements. For rock tours, large agencies sometimes join forces with other agencies to package the tour.

Major agencies rarely sign unknown talents; they are preoccupied booking their stars. Unknown acts must struggle along with local agents, usually until they achieve some success as recording artists.

National Full-Service Agencies

Large talent-booking companies are sometimes described as full-service agencies. They generally demand that their artists grant them the right of exclusive representation in all fields. In the process of signing an artist, a large agency may submit a package of 10 or more contracts for the signature of the new client. Some of these agreements are form contracts used by that particular agency. Of the many contracts submitted to prospective new clients, only 4 are frequently used for contemporary recording artists or performing groups:

1. American Federation of Musicians (AFM) Exclusive Agent-Musician Agreement.
2. American Federation of Television and Radio Artists (AFTRA) Standard Exclusive Agency Contract.
3. American Guild of Variety Artists (AGVA) Exclusive Agency Contract.
4. The talent agency's own general services and materials agreement. This is a very comprehensive agreement that covers creative materials, services, TV and movie packages, and other kinds of entertainment packages.

Other agreements with agents cover areas not covered by the union employment contracts listed here. They generally provide that the agency serve as the artist's adviser and representative in respect to the artist's activity and participation in such fields as merchandising, testimonials, and commercial tie-ins. The general services contract that has been used by the California division of the William Morris Agency, one of the world's oldest and largest, incorporates language of the union contract that provides that the artist's approval is required prior to the agency committing the artist, that the agreement can be terminated if the agency can't find work for the artist for 4 consecutive months, that any disputes are to be referred to the Labor Commissioner of the State of California, that the agreement shall not negatively affect any union contracts involving the artist, and under what circumstances the agency has the right to assign the contract to a third party.

It is also possible for an artist to work with an agency on a nonexclusive basis, or even with no written agreement at all—a so-called handshake agreement. An agency might be hired to work with an artist in a limited or specific territory or kind of performance. An example of this kind of limited representation would be an artist who retains an agency to book live performance tours in a certain territory or for a specific tour but who does not use that agency for deals involving movie companies or recording contracts.

A full-service agency "general materials and packages" contract covers the artist's involvement in nonmusical creative properties (scripts, scenarios, and packaged shows, e.g., for television and film). But it is sometimes possible through negotiation to exclude professional activity as a composer. Accordingly, the artist's income from music publishing would be excluded. Agency representation for musical artists, particularly in rock, is usually restricted to matters relating to concerts and touring.

Changing Representation. Artists frequently change agencies in the hope that new representation will further their careers. Large agencies are often criticized for neglecting the individual artist unless that person is a star of some magnitude. Many lesser names feel they get lost in the shuffle of a big company attempting to find work for its huge stables. The major booking companies are aware of these negative views of their operations and attempt to offer each of their clients the personal attention of at least one particular agent on their staff who is assigned to keep the artist working and happy. The AFM agency agreement, for example, requires that the firm name the specific individual agents who are to handle the affairs of the musician under contract.

In addition, agents, like performers, are mobile. They frequently change companies or break off and set up their own firms. If the agent has performed well and leaves the agency, this causes consternation in the company, because the firm suffers disruption of continuity with the artist and probably a lot of goodwill among talent buyers. Often, personal relationships and confidences are built up between agent and artist. When the agent leaves, it is a common occurrence for those artists to seek relief from their contracts with the company, declaring their intention of following that agent. The agency is reluctant to terminate a contract with a valuable client and might refuse a release. A court battle may ensue. In general, in these kinds of altercations the courts have tended to find for the artist, recognizing that in the employment field, the element of personal relationships is entitled to special consideration. Many artists insist on inserting **key man clauses** into their agency agreements, making the agency agreement terminate if the "key man" is no longer present. This allows the artist to accompany a preferred agent should that agent depart the firm.

Regulation of Agents

Some of the colorful characterizations of booking agents on old movies might lead one to believe that the only qualifications needed by an agent are a tolerance for cigar smoke and a pair of alligator shoes. Although such images of unscrupulous agents may be interesting movie fiction, the modern talent agent is a professional whose success is measured, in large part, by the success of the talent or business entity represented.

Statutory Regulation. Agents and artist managers proliferated early in this century with the rapid growth of the movie industry. In the early days of agents' abuses of performers, wages would be skimmed or never paid; collusion between agents and employers would occur. Artists would be dispatched long distances to jobs that never existed. Because agents became particularly active in the early days of the film industry, California was one of the first states to attempt to regulate them. Following first attempts in 1913 to regulate employment agencies, California enacted its Labor Code in 1937. This code made a distinction between "motion picture employment agencies" and agents active primarily in booking vaudeville acts, circus performers, and actors for the legitimate stage.

In 1943, California added a new category, "artist's manager." In 1967, California repealed substantial portions of its Labor Code. "Theatrical employment agencies" and "motion picture employment agencies" were eliminated as separate categories. But the "artist's manager" category was retained and placed under the jurisdiction of the Labor Commissioner of the Department of Industrial Relations. "Employment agency" provisions were shifted to the jurisdiction of what is now the Department of Consumer Affairs.

In 1978, California altered its artist's manager statute, the principal change being one of nomenclature: Artist's managers were to be known as "talent agents."

Because of widespread abuse of artists by agents in the past, California laws today severely limit the activities of all persons involved in artist representation. Procurement of employment for artists and entertainers in California is strongly regulated by two state statutes: the Talent Agencies Act of 1978 and the Employment Agency Act.

Simply stated, all persons engaged in the procurement, or attempt of procurement, of employment for an artist must be licensed by the state to do so. Any contract can be canceled by either party or the state where an individual engaged in procuring employment lacks the required state license.

Union Regulation. In addition to state laws governing persons engaged in agency activity, talent agents representing union musicians are restricted severely on a national basis by the various performers' unions and **guilds.** The organizations most involved here are the AFM, AFTRA, AGVA, the American Guild of Musical Artists (AGMA), and the Screen Actors Guild (SAG).

Artists' guilds and unions vary in what they require when they franchise or license a talent agent, but the following requirements are typical of most agreements:

1. Maximum allowable commissions are stipulated. For example, AFTRA and SAG apply only a 10% ceiling on commissions applied to the artist's gross compensation. Artists are not permitted to pay both an agent and a manager more than an aggregate total of 10%. The AFM allows a 20% commission on one-night gigs, 15% if the job runs 2 days, and usually 10% on jobs running 3 days or longer. Under certain circumstances, the AFM will allow an additional 5% commission on engagements where the musician's wages equal or exceed twice the minimum union scale.

2. AFM, AFTRA, and SAG generally franchise only those agents who agree to limit their professional activity to procurement of employment for artists. This constraint is designed to protect the artist from paying superfluous or excessive commissions. The disadvantage of this restriction is that some professionals are barred from acting as agents because they also participate in other entertainment industry enterprises such as management, production, publishing, and recording.

3. Lengths of contracts are limited. AFTRA allows a maximum term of 3 years. Under certain conditions, SAG limits its members to contracts of 1 year's duration.

Getting Started. Individuals wanting to get a career started in the talent agency field often find it relatively easy. Sometimes, students can enter a talent agency as apprentices. Perhaps, after a short training period, they may be put on as assistant agents. Artists' unions license all owners of each franchised agency, then permit subagents to work under an individual owner's license.

MANAGERS

The arts and entertainment industry engages a number of different kinds of managers. The most influential among them is the artist's personal manager. Personal managers are expected to perform tasks ranging from negotiating multimillion-dollar contracts to checking on the star's wardrobe.

This chapter limits the discussion of personal managers to how they are regulated by state statutes and artists' unions. The manner in which management contracts are negotiated and how managers advance the careers of their clients is treated in some detail in the next chapter.

Regulation of Managers

California regulates artists' personal managers quite strictly. Because many management contracts are negotiated there, an understanding of California's regulations is most useful.

Statutory Regulation. As mentioned above, in California the only person allowed to procure employment for an artist is one who is licensed as a talent agent. Personal managers are supposed to be principally concerned with advising and counseling their clients about their careers, but they often become involved, directly or indirectly, in procuring jobs for their clients. Procurement of employment is supposed to be the responsibility of talent agents, but personal managers can rarely separate themselves totally from the talent agent's activities.

The California statute does not permit a personal manager to become involved even indirectly in procuring employment for an artist. Rulings of the California Labor Commission have held that any such activity of this kind by an unlicensed person is against the law.

If the personal manager in California wants to stay within the law and remain in the management profession, a talent agent's license would have to be obtained. But then the individual would have to function under the constraints imposed by artists' unions on talent agents. If the manager decides against becoming a licensed talent agent, there are other options:

1. The manager may voluntarily forgo commissions on all employment procured by a talent agent. California's Labor Commission has ruled, however, that this ploy is but a camouflage for what is really going on.

2. The manager may go into partnership with the artist. Both parties may find this unattractive, however, in that they are exposed to liability for their partner's actions.

3. The manager may employ the artist exclusively and supply the artist's services to third parties. This might serve the manager's interests, but will seriously disadvantage the artist by imposing restrictions on the artist's activities that could go well beyond the terms normally encountered in a regular management agreement.

4. The personal manager might set up a corporation that would deliver the artist's services to third parties. Some lawyers believe this may offer the best insulation available from the constraints of talent agent licensing requirements.

Next to California, the state that hosts the greatest number of personal management contract negotiations is New York. That state offers a more congenial environment for these proceedings than California. New York avoids the issue of licensing personal managers in that it defines theatrical agencies (booking agencies) as those that procure employment other than incidental to the manager-artist relationship. This would appear to exclude personal managers, in that most of their procurement activity is incidental.

Union Regulation. Personal managers of good reputation could obtain a franchise from an artists' union, but they would then fall under regulations far more constricting than they could tolerate. The unions would impose a ceiling on their commissions, the term of their contracts with clients would be shorter, and they would probably be required by the franchise to engage in employment procurement activity full-time and not engage in other business activities concurrently.

Few managers could function under these restrictions, in that it is the very nature of the business for them to be involved at any given time in a number of entertainment business activities, particularly publishing and recording. Generally, managers in New York are not union affiliated.

The personal manager in California has one other option: to take out a union franchise, then ignore the union's restraints. This is a temptation, in that unions have rarely enforced these rules. But ignoring union rules can be risky: No one can predict when the union might start enforcing its franchising agreements. Some California lawyers have publicly stated, however, that they believe this union-ignoring ploy may still be the personal manager's most attractive option to avoid the overriding power of the state's Labor Commission.

The end result of statutory and union constraints on personal managers is that, in California at least, many established and respectable personal managers opt against both state licensing and union franchising,[1] choosing instead to be guided by their own conception of ethical professional practices.

Assistants to Management

Most managers will try to be with their artists at all performances or events that are important for the artist's career. Few artists' managers attempt to travel regularly with their clients, however, and assign such duties to a road manager. Road managers handle the transportation of people and equipment, arrange for meals and lodging, ensure that adequate security is provided, hire tour accountants, supervise sound reinforcement and lighting personnel, check box office receipts, and collect performance income. Road managers who learn the business and know how to hustle often graduate to artist management jobs. Some have become producers.

Many young people break into show business by signing on as roadies, the label often used to describe persons hired to move and help set up the performance. Even though some roadies have previous training in such areas as lighting or sound, others seem to learn what is expected of them on the job.

The people hired on as road crew members for lesser known acts usually earn minimum salaries plus their travel expenses; such acts have little difficulty locating an adequate supply of individuals willing to work for low wages and high adventure. In contrast, today's top acts tour with highly disciplined, well-paid crews.

Whether the individual is a recording artist or some other kind of professional in the field, when income reaches a respectable level, other support personnel will be required to advance that performer's career. This is treated in Chapter 9, "Artist Management."

ATTORNEYS

Entertainment business attorneys hold positions of great power in the industry. Part of this power has come about by default. In the earlier years of the business, most executives, agents, and managers lacked the education and background to run big companies and handle the affairs of millionaire clients. Even today, executives lacking strong backgrounds in business management and business law keep their lawyers close at hand to protect them against unwise decisions and flawed contracts. With the continuing expansion of existing entertainment companies, not to mention the frequent acquisitions and consolidations, the role of the entertainment attorney is more crucial today than ever before.

Law practices are often roughly divided into litigation services and transactional services. The litigators present their matters before a judge, while transactional attorneys spend much of their time negotiating contracts. Although there are firms that specialize in entertainment litigation, most entertainment practice falls into the transactional category. The attorneys must be keenly aware of current industry conditions so that they can negotiate favorable contracts for their clients.

For the glamour fields of music, theater, and broadcasting, law schools are turning out at least twice as many interested graduates as seem to be needed. Despite the unemployment (or underemployment) among graduates generally now emerging from law schools, there is an actual shortage of lawyers fully qualified to practice in the entertainment field. Entertainment attorneys tend to specialize in chosen subareas of the business. Some work primarily with issues of copyright, trademark, and **intellectual property.** Some negotiate with recording and publishing companies; others work with clients who are involved with the theater or TV or movies. Some law firms employ a number of attorneys with different entertainment specialties.

The most experienced lawyers in copyright are found in Washington, D.C., New York City, the state of California, and Nashville. The best-qualified lawyers in general music business practice are found in the three recording centers in the

United States. In Canada, a handful of entertainment and sports industry lawyers practice in Toronto and Montreal. Nationally, we probably have some 200 to 300 attorneys who limit their practice exclusively to music business matters, trademarks, and copyright.

Retaining Legal Counsel

How can a person go about finding a qualified legal counselor? These questions might be asked:

1. What is the prospective attorney's reputation, and what is the source of your information? Is it objective? The fact that a lawyer has passed the state bar examination and offers all the appearances of respectability is insufficient reason for complete trust. The great majority are trustworthy, but check out your prospective legal counsel with as many persons as you can, both in terms of experience and ethical reputations. Read the trades, such as *Billboard*, to see who is active in the field. Find out which attorneys already represent successful artists, managers, and companies in the business.
2. Is the prospective lawyer sufficiently experienced in the music field to look out for the musician's interests in publishing, recording, performance rights, and foreign rights?
3. Is the prospective lawyer well informed in copyright?

Yet another way to check out lawyers is through the American Bar Association. But asking the local chapter of the American Bar Association for referrals will rarely be helpful outside those cities where the recording industry flourishes.

In addition to negotiating contracts, an attorney often can provide general legal services such as tax and estate counseling, investment counseling, negotiation of real and other property settlements, and dispute resolution. In the latter role, lawyers generally agree that the most skillful among them manage, whenever possible, to settle disputes without resorting to litigation.

As the role of the music attorney has significantly expanded in recent years, some clients retain attorneys primarily for their inside-industry connections. It is now common for lawyers to perform tasks that seem more appropriately handled by managers, such as circulating demo tapes to labels: Established lawyers are highly respected by A&R (artist and repertoire) executives. Some law firms even have separate artist management departments, and some of the most successful managers are or were lawyers. Before employing an attorney, be sure to know precisely what services may be provided.

Payment Options. One of the universal complaints against lawyers is their cost. Fees are generally so high that many individuals in need of counsel have to forgo the service. But when legal services are imperative, the client has a number of payment options.

The usual arrangement is paying an hourly fee. Before running up a bill, the prospective client should simply ask the lawyer, in an exploratory meeting, about the charges. If ongoing legal services are needed, the client may place the lawyer on a monthly retainer.

An alternative to these payment procedures is the contingent payment plan, which is common in the entertainment industry. The client pays a relatively low hourly rate, provided the gross compensation payable to the lawyer in any calendar month is not less than a specified percentage of the client's gross earnings. Some contingent fee arrangements call for no immediate monthly retainer fee, the lawyer's compensation being deferred until the client's income attains a prescribed level. In this kind of arrangement, the lawyer might, in addition, negotiate a percentage of the client's gross income, often set at 5% to 7.5%. Some lawyers charge as much as 15%.

Are contingent fee deals ethical? Yes, under certain conditions, according to the American Bar Association's Code of Professional Responsibility and opinions expressed by various state bar associations and state supreme courts. But they are considered ethical, as a rule, only where a contingent fee arrangement is to the advantage of the client and where the client may otherwise have no way to get legal services or is unable to pay a fixed fee. When the client is a production company or film producer, the lawyer might *participate,* a term used in the industry to describe sharing in an investment in a project or a company. A participating attorney might charge no legal fee, but "take points" instead—receive a percentage of the profits, if any. The lawyer may have a central role in finding a deal for the artist by shopping the artist's demo tape to record and publishing companies. If that is the case, the lawyer deserves compensation for contributing to the artist's success.

How much is a lawyer entitled to charge for services? State bar associations publish guidelines for their members.[2] Professional canons of ethics call for lawyers to follow them.

Form of Organization. When an attorney accepts a client, one of the first tasks in many entertainment industry situations is to determine the client's legal status. In business and legal relationships, will the client be best served by being self-employed, a partner, proprietor, or independent contractor—or would interests be better served by forming a corporation or taking part in **joint ventures**? The client (who may be a group of persons) will need the lawyer to explain the advantages and disadvantages of these options.

Contract Negotiations. As pointed out, nearly all significant events in the entertainment industry involve the negotiation of contracts. And that is the business of lawyers. The number and kinds of contracts commonly used in the industry are extensive. Typical agreements are

- ► Composer with a publisher, coauthor
- ► Performer with employer, agent, promoter, producer, contractor, performing group, lawyer, broadcaster, merchandiser, advertising agency, recording company, publisher
- ► Producer with a recording company, performer, recording studio, production company, publisher, distributor, merchandiser, lawyer
- ► Talent agent with a performer, promoter, club owner, producer, production company, recording company, film company, lawyer
- ► Artist's personal manager with an artist, recording company, broadcaster, accountant, auditor, road manager

The Adversarial Relationship. Individuals entering into contract negotiations are, by definition, adversaries. They may be the best of friends, but once they start negotiating a legal agreement, the parties should seek every legitimate advantage available. Contract negotiations need not be unfriendly encounters, but the parties are advised by their attorneys, as a rule, to go for whatever they can rightly get.

Each individual entering into contract negotiations should have separate legal counsel. When one lawyer attempts to represent both parties, there may be difficulty serving them impartially. The American Bar Association's Code of Professional Responsibility and most state bar associations' codes of ethics assert that in the absence of full disclosure and an agreement signed by all parties, lawyers should not represent adversaries and should urge prospective clients to retain their own attorneys.

Independent legal counsel is particularly important in situations where collateral contracts are entered into simultaneously, for example, an artist-manager contract and an artist-manager-publisher deal. If one of the parties to these collateral contracts happens to be a lawyer (very common in the industry), the potential exposure to conflicts of interest can be overwhelming. Disputes can arise out of collateral contracts. When they do, courts have sometimes found that a lawyer had taken advantage of the client's ignorance and subsequently determined that one or more of the contracts was unenforceable.

Extralegal Services. Clients frequently ask their attorneys to recommend agents and managers. If qualified people are unavailable, the client then often asks the lawyer to manage the career as well as the business. Lawyers frequently agree to do this, often protesting that the arrangement is to be only temporary. But then the lawyer-manager starts making more money in that capacity than in just practicing law. This outcome is frequent when a lawyer agrees to administer the client's publishing company. A lawyer attempting to provide a client with two different kinds of professional services is exposed to conflicts of interest. Among the sharpest critics of these practices have been lawyers themselves.

Bar associations state that lawyers shall not enter into a business transaction with a client or knowingly acquire a financial interest in an artist's enterprise potentially adverse to the client unless the transaction

> is fair and reasonable to the client and fully disclosed and transmitted in writing to the client in a manner and terms which should have reasonably been understood by the client . . . and the client is given reasonable opportunity to seek advice of independent counsel of the client's choice on the transaction . . . and the client consents in writing thereto.[3]

If a lawyer provides extralegal services and enters into business or investment deals with a client, legal ethics demand that all conduct be in accordance with the ethical and legal constraints imposed on a licensed **attorney-at-law.**

Termination. The law provides that a client can **discharge** a lawyer at any time.[4] But some courts have held that the discharge of a lawyer does not necessarily discharge a former client's liability. For example, dismissing an attorney where a contingent fee arrangement is in place can become sticky for the client. In this kind of situation, the former client will probably have to continue paying the attorney, after disengagement, on earnings flowing from contracts negotiated before the parties went separate ways.

Whether or not a contingent fee is involved, a client who discharges a lawyer should send written notice of termination. Where the artist is retaining a new attorney, the former attorney should be asked, in the notice of termination, to forward all material in the client's file to the new lawyer. Bar associations view this kind of procedure as a matter of professional courtesy.

BUSINESS MANAGEMENT TECHNIQUES

Authoritative studies have shown time and time again that some 90% of business failures result from poor management. Individuals planning careers in the music business as, for instance, agents, managers, attorneys, or entrepreneurs will probably increase their chances of success by studying business management.

Dozens of books and hundreds of college courses treat the subject. Although they differ in approach, it is interesting to observe that the most respected writers and teachers on the subject generally agree with this summary of what good management entails: planning, organizing, staffing, leading, and controlling.

NOTES

1. Nelville L. Johnson and Daniel Webb Lang, "The Personal Manager in the California Entertainment Industry," p. 175, in *Music Industry: Negotiations and the Law.* Toronto: Board of Governors, York University, 1980.

2. Language in the California Bar's *Rules of Professional Conduct* is typical: "A member of the State Bar shall not enter into an agreement for, charge or collect an illegal or unconscionable fee . . . when it is so exorbitant and wholly disproportionate to the service as to shock the conscience of lawyers of ordinary prudence practicing in the same community."

3. Quoted from p. 15 of "Ethical Constraints on Contingent Fee Arrangements" in *Rules of Professional Conduct.* Sacramento: California Bar Association.

4. Code of Civil Procedure, Section 284.

ARTIST
MANAGEMENT

Management, too, is an art.

—*Mozart's father (and manager)*

In the preceding chapter, personal management was discussed only from the standpoint of regulation by state statutes and artists' unions. This chapter examines financial relationships and the manager's functions in advancing the artist's career.[1]

How important is a good manager? Ask a recording company. Labels today prefer an artist who has good management. They believe it is not cost-effective to invest time and money in an artist whose career, even daily activities, are not thoughtfully planned. Good management is so important, in fact, that some labels will actually help certain artists find a good manager. However, undirected talent and unfocused careers remain commonplace in the music business. These performers may get lucky and land on the **charts** for a few weeks, but they quickly fade into oblivion, like thousands before them who lacked firm, knowledgeable management.

At what point do artists need a manager? About the time they discover they can earn more than union scale; suddenly they are in need of someone to handle their business affairs and develop their careers. This can be a difficult time, be-

← Violinist Isaac Stern performs with cellist Mstislave Rostropovich and the National Symphony Orchestra in Washington, D.C. © Richard Howard/Black Star/PNI.

cause they soon realize that many established managers are unwilling to take on a new, unproven act.

NATIONAL CONFERENCE OF PERSONAL MANAGERS

One way for an artist to find a manager is through an organization designed to facilitate a compatible match with a well-qualified and credible manager. The recognized professional association in the field is the National Conference of Personal Managers (NCPM). NCPM has about 150 members in its New York City-based eastern division, and about 100 in Los Angeles in its western division. Although NCPM does not represent the majority of professionals in the field, it includes many of the most powerful ones.

NCPM has attempted to establish ethical standards of conduct for the profession by first investigating a manager's references and business practices prior to acceptance for membership, then closely monitoring its managers for as long as they are associated with the organization.

DISCOVERING EACH OTHER

An artist searching for a personal manager should look for the person who

- ▶ Believes in the talent of the artist
- ▶ Is well organized, systematic
- ▶ Is straightforward and honest, and has a reputation to prove it
- ▶ Is an effective communicator, writes well, and is an articulate, persuasive oral communicator
- ▶ Won't try to fake expertise, if lacking competence in certain fields; will hire outside experts when needed
- ▶ Has good industry contacts; if not, is busy developing them
- ▶ Shares the artist's long-term vision and career goals

Some managers have a strong creative side as well as good business skills. A manager might help to put an act together by advising about choice of artistic personnel. The manager may also help to make decisions regarding production of an album and choice of material to be included on the album.

Some managers are closely involved with the negotiation of business contracts; others are not. Some handle an artist's books as well as helping to make creative decisions; others do not. Each artist-manager relationship should be structured to best serve the client.

Successful personal managers have one other kind of expertise: They know how to spot a potential star. They cannot afford to invest their time and money in anyone who lacks what the manager views as the potential talent to reach the top. And until a manager's clients develop strong earnings, there won't be many dollars available to produce commissionable income—the manager's livelihood.

Experienced managers and artists all agree on one issue: The relationship depends on strong personal ties of friendship and trust. When a manager and artist are considering joining forces, they might well enter into a short-term "trial" agreement, usually 1 year. If the manager achieves the objectives outlined in the trial agreement, the contract is generally extended to full **term**—3 or more years. A word of caution to the artist: Be sure that the management agreement is nontransferable, that is, the contract cannot be bought or sold.

THE FINANCIAL RELATIONSHIP

Established personal managers usually insist the artist agree in writing that the manager be authorized to handle all the artist's money—what comes in and what goes out. If an artist is fearful of granting the manager complete control over the money, the artist should not sign with that person.

As an alternative arrangement, the responsibility for receipts and disbursements could be handled by a business manager selected by both parties. Many artists of stature insist the money be entirely handled by such an independent third party—usually a business management firm. It is often a preferable arrangement where an act generates large sums of money.

Accounting

Whatever arrangements the parties agree on for business management, the personal manager's first responsibility in this regard is setting up the financial accounting. The astute personal manager will call in the accountants even in the formative stages of contract negotiations to make sure the parties agree on how they are going to control "the count" and report the taxes. The difficulty here is that, even in the entertainment capitals of the world, there are few accounting firms fully knowledgeable in these specialized areas of entertainment and communications industries. For example, a major recording star requires a financial adviser who understands international tax treaties and the exchange of foreign currencies and fluctuating money markets. Lacking specialized knowledge, an act of international stature can have little confidence that the accountants are sufficiently protective of the worldwide movement of royalties.

Although the personal manager should discover and recruit a qualified accountant, the selection of that individual or firm should be approved by the artist. A major act will also need auditors to examine the books periodically, not only those of the manager but of the publisher and recording company as well. Contracts with these parties must specify under what conditions audits will be acceptable and precisely who will be liable for the auditing expense.[2]

The artist's lawyer will recommend that audits requested by the artist must be undertaken by an individual or firm independent from the management firm.

Controlling Expense

It is not generally understood that a large percentage of working artists incur expenses larger than their incomes. This may be true even of some of the artists the public considers rich and famous. Because the "successful" artist will have to pay 10% to 25% of the gross to a manager, another 10% or so to a booking agency, perhaps additional fees to a business manager or accountant, the best hope of realizing a profit on what is left is to exert stringent control over all other expenses. Although a manager may make recommendations for expenditures, no expense over a certain dollar amount (agreed on by the artist and manager) is to be incurred without artist approval. The artist's attorney should include such spending constraints when the management contract is negotiated.[3]

However, many artists and managers have only a dim view of the realities of the rational business world. Many artists throw their money around, hoping that those royalties are going to keep rolling in forever. In such a case, a seasoned manager might persuade the artist to accept a weekly allowance. Show business stories abound of how former stars went through millions only to end up financially destitute. An artist submitting to a modest weekly expense account would increase the chances of surviving the late lean years when fame and income have faded.

Many personal managers also find it necessary to loan an act money to keep it alive, at least in its developing stage. The management contract should state, however, that the manager is under no obligation to loan money or advance money to the artist, no matter how serious the crisis may be.

MANAGER'S COMMISSION

It is standard practice in the industry for personal managers to earn compensation for their services through commissions on the artist's gross income. The equity of this practice is open to question, but managers who know how the business has operated in the past will rarely accept any other arrangement. Their argument is a simple one—and persuasive: The manager may be the person principally responsible for the rise and fall of the client's income. The manager invests time (and often personal funds) in getting a career off the ground and is entitled to participate in the artist's prosperity, should it ever come.

The informed artist's point of view on this issue is set forth in the draft contract appearing later in this chapter.

Going Rates

In recent years, certain "going rates" have become recognized in the industry for personal managers' commissions. They range from a low of 10% to a high of 25%. Here are some of the factors influencing these rates:

1. The stature and track record of the manager. A manager with powerful contacts in the industry may be worth 25% to an artist. A manager with little or no track record may earn a lower commission.

2. The income of the artist. If the artist has a high income, the manager will come out well even at a relatively low commission rate.

3. The extent of the manager's services. For example, if the manager farms out all business management, accounting services, and promotion services, top commission rates may not be appropriate.

An Argument for Reasonableness. A powerful manager can often get a very high commission even from an act that may be struggling to pay its rent. But if that artist later develops a high income, it may be tempting to renegotiate those commissions and reduce them to a reasonable level. More likely, the successful artist will be ready to dump the original manager and sign with a less expensive one. The manager who was greedy earlier in the relationship may well have lost an opportunity to come into really good earnings. Managers are well advised to keep their demands reasonable, because most artists are quick to discontinue association with support personnel, particularly personal managers, who fail to treat them fairly. Wise managers often volunteer to reduce or eliminate commissions on specific projects or concert dates. Such gestures go a long way in establishing long-term trust and goodwill between manager and artist.

Commission Base. Personal managers' commissions are usually based on the artist's gross income from all activity relating to the entertainment industry. In this context, "income"includes not only wages but also whatever is of value that comes to the artist from the entertainment industry, directly or indirectly, including such sources as royalties, an interest in, or ownership of, a production company, TV package, film, publishing or recording company, stock in a corporation, interest in a partnership, bonuses, merchandising, endorsements, tour sponsorship, commercials, video sales, even gifts.

The commission *base* can be more important than the commission *level*. If the artist has a competent, aggressive attorney, and if the personal manager lacks the clout of the artist, the commission base can sometimes be limited to what can be called the adjusted gross income. An artist negotiating from strength should be able to convince the manager to accept a commission based on the artist's actual income, not on all the money simply passing through the accounts to support other persons and other activities, such as record and video production and tour support from the artist's recording company. The artist will probably seek to exclude from commission such items as recording costs and **negative tour support** (money the label has advanced to make up for deficits the artist incurred while on tour). The pros and cons of this fundamental issue are set forth in the draft contract later in this chapter.

The Money Flow

The artist and manager may work together successfully for many years. But one day the relationship will end. As difficult as it may be, they should anticipate the problems of disengagement. Like marriage, an artist-manager relationship is easier to enter into than to leave. When the artist and manager get divorced, not only will they suffer the wrenching experience of ending a close personal relationship, they will also have to negotiate some kind of "property settlement." A divorcing couple can eventually agree on "who gets the house, who gets the car," and so forth, but the artist and manager have a much more complicated set of financial problems.

The essential difficulty here is that an established act has money flowing in from contracts the manager negotiated, and when the couple disengage (for whatever reason) that money continues to flow. Should the departing manager continue to receive commissions therefrom? Some lawyers make the argument that, unless negotiated otherwise, such commissions continue in perpetuity.

The richest source of these funds usually comes from publishing and recording contracts probably worked out during the period of service of the departing manager. Nearly all personal management contracts state the manager is entitled to full commissions on this money, without diminution, for the full term of those contracts. Part of the problem this creates for the artist is encountered during the search for new management. If the artist's major source of income is already tapped for years hence by the old manager, what has a new manager to gain by signing on with an act so encumbered with prior commitments?

A Possible Compromise

If it is assumed the parties possess about equal bargaining strength, one of the simplest compromises available is an across-the-board de-escalation of commissions over a year or two following termination of the contract. Figure 9.1 shows how this might work: The old manager continues to enjoy 100% of commissions for the first 6 months following disengagement from the artist. Then follows a 50% reduction for the next 6 months. At the start of the second year following disengagement, the artist pays the former manager only 25% of what would have otherwise been earned. After 12 months at this rate, all commissions to the former manager would end.

If the manager is negotiating from greater strength than the artist, the same de-escalation formula might still be used, but the percentages could be set higher and stretched out over a longer time. For instance, the old manager might earn a 100% commission indefinitely for deals he or she negotiated. The new manager might earn a 100% commission on all new deals set up for the artist. Commis-

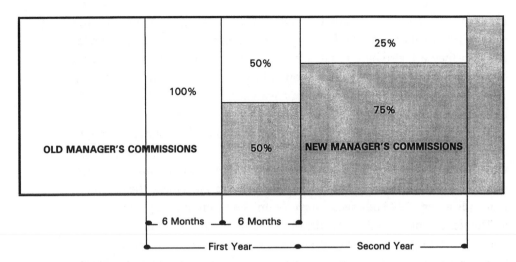

Figure 9.1   Artist's Money Flow to Managers

NOTE: The new manager receives *100%* commission from the *outset* on all business he or she generates.

sions on a holdover deal that changes will also be earned at 100% by the new manager.

One final advantage of a de-escalation formula: If the second manager accepts the plan suggested here, the parties should have little difficulty negotiating a similar de-escalation plan for the second manager as well when that relationship ends.

PRODUCING THE ACT

Once the artist and manager have negotiated their agreement, one of the first tasks they face is marketing the act—creating the presentation of the artist to the public. As we all know, the marketing of a commodity can be more valuable than the commodity itself. Many artists of modest gifts seem to get by well in the marketplace largely because they are presented so attractively.

If an artist is already established with a defined public image and personal style, the new manager may not want to alter a presentation materially that has been working well. But when a manager signs on a relatively new act, both parties have a lot of work to do. Unless the manager is fully qualified, the best help the artist can afford must be engaged. An objective appraisal must be made at the outset on these basic questions: (a) Just what kind of performer or act do we have? (b) To what audience does the artist appeal? (c) Can that audience be expanded? and (d) What must we do for the artist to fully **exploit** all the potential?

A useful tool for objective examination of an artist's performing strengths and weaknesses is videotape. The artist and coaches can use this medium to guide their work and measure progress toward the creation of truly polished performances.

In addition to engaging voice coaches, choreographers, wardrobe consultants, and more, the manager who takes the long view of the client's career will probably want to provide dramatic training, too. Nearly all musical performers who reach national prominence eventually receive opportunities to play dramatic roles.

Some managers provide important assistance when they have the ability to identify good musical material. Few artists—including those who write much of their own—ever seem to have a sufficient supply of high-quality songs. The manager may have to take time listening to demos and helping search out usable songs. The act may also need **special material,** songs and patter and routines created exclusively for that artist. Practically all stars booked into Las Vegas consider special material essential to a big-time presentation.

Coordinating the Elements

If the act has been fully prepared, the next move is to place it on stage, under flattering lighting, in an appropriate setting. Now, a theatrical producer is needed; if the manager can't handle this task, someone should be engaged who can. Major acts often tour with their own stage directors who supervise lighting, staging, and sound.

If cast in a touring Broadway show, the artist will be part of a company that travels, not only with its own sets, but its own lights, control board, audio system, even flooring.

Programming

Experienced managers representing powerful acts control the selection of opening and supporting acts, making sure that the headliner comes on at the best possible time and under the most advantageous circumstances. From the early days of vaudeville, headliners insisted on warm-up acts to preheat the audience. This sequencing of acts is called *programming,* and the manager must control it when possible. If the manager's client is to be introduced by an MC or some other person, the manager must make sure the introducer says the right things and says them briefly.

ADVANCING THE CAREER

The manager's main responsibility is advancing the career of the artist, whose reputation, and income, depend on how effectively this is done. A first-rate manager will design and execute a complete campaign for each artist, starting with people—with personalities, not organizations. Top managers develop extensive lists of key personnel in the industry. Most of these potential contacts will never be used. But when a manager must move quickly—which is most of the time—an up-to-date list of power brokers will prove essential.

Because the manager probably operates out of, or regularly travels to, one of the recording and publishing centers, it will become apparent who the decision makers are in the most active companies, as well as the important agents, promoters, and industry lawyers. The music industry is a giant, but only a few hundred individuals have positions of real power. Many of this group of decision makers know each other on a first-name basis. They rub shoulders together at industry conferences; they exchange information; they return each other's telephone calls; they trade favors. They even exchange jobs. When a manager is negotiating with one record company, the competing record companies for that contract have probably heard, privately, about what each side is offering. So the experienced manager discovers there are few secrets in the business at the top level. This inner circle of powerful people knows who the con artists are, who will keep an agreement, who can deliver.

How does a new manager crack this inner circle? By demonstrating credibility and competence.

The artist's manager must also develop good contacts wherever clients perform—the top music directors and programmers, retailers, distributors of recordings, media personnel, the important promoters, and agents. Given time, a network can be developed of key personnel in branch offices of recording labels with whom clients are under contract.

Care and Feeding of the Media

In executing a campaign to exploit an artist, the manager must develop contacts (and friends) with the purveyors of mass communications—particularly the press and broadcast media. This would include music video channels (e.g., MTV), networks, radio stations, wire service reporters, feature writers, syndicated columnists, and the *music press*—the writers and publications focusing on personalities in the music and entertainment fields. They are not difficult to contact: They look to artists, managers, and publicists to feed them information.

Materials. When contact is made, the manager must feed these sources with appropriate material. This is usually done with press kits or **promo packs.** They are expensive to assemble but essential to a publicity campaign. Depending on budget and circumstances, promo packs will often contain canned press releases, the artist's biography, news clips, previous media reviews, 8" × 10" photographs (glossies suitable for reproduction), perhaps 8" × 10" four-color photographs of the artist in performance; sample records and tapes, including videotapes; and perhaps additional gift items and novelties. If a recording company is involved, a major promotion will often include a material object (a novelty of some kind) that ties in with a new recording's release. The manager or the artist's publicist will help in getting these kits and trinkets to the press, disc jockeys, radio program directors, and perhaps to the employees of record distributors and retail outlets.

Interviews. Managers have learned one of the most economical techniques to generate strong publicity for a touring artist is to set up audio interviews in advance of the artist's arrival. Telephone or broadcast-quality audio interviews can be used in large cities when an artist lacks time to visit all the major broadcasting stations.

As the artist travels across the country, the label's publicity staff will set up news conferences. Most reporters and camera people are dispatched to these events by their assignment editors; they will appear where they are assigned to cover a story. But freelancers and stringers can often be persuaded to cover a press conference if free food and drink are available following the press conference. When the budget allows, some press conferences are planned as press parties. Enterprising publicists can often induce the press to show up for these happy hours even when the artist is relatively unknown.

In addition to news conferences, a manager or publicist can arrange for exclusive interviews. If a syndicated columnist or network TV host can be lined up, one interview or guest shot of this kind can yield more good PR than many open press conferences.

Artists' managers rarely attempt to handle all the PR for their clients and often retain a publicity firm to assist. Services of these companies can run from $100-a-week retainers to perhaps $6,000 a month, depending on the services required and the track record of the supplier. Competition among publicists is keen. In their effort to produce maximum attention, professional **flacks** will sometimes resort to outrageous publicity schemes. The media and the public may actually enjoy a crazy hype for a while. But it is the personal manager's responsibility to rein in PR types when they try too often to substitute promotion gimmicks for campaigns based on something approximating reality.

Billing. From the early days of the entertainment industry, it has been standard practice for managers and promoters to control what professionals call *billing*. Billing has to do with the size, emphasis, and position of artists' names in print ads and screen credits. If an artist ranks as a "star," the name might be set above the name of the production—in large, bold type.[4] If the artist is a "costar," the name will appear below the name of the production and in type smaller than that used for the star. If the artist is a "featured" player, the billing will be much less prominent and relegated to an inferior position in the layout.

As the manager's client gains prestige, attention must be given to the possibilities of negotiating for increasingly prominent billing. An astute manager will occasionally accept a lower fee for the client if the billing is strong.[5] In rock shows, the second act is often called "special guest star" and may receive 75% of the billing that the main act receives for the show, depending on the contract.

Controlling Performances

One of the personal manager's most useful services is controlling the client's performance opportunities. Once a career gains momentum, it is not unusual for the artist to receive more offers to perform than can be accepted. Both the agent and the manager are tempted to maximize income and accept every **gig** in sight. But it is the manager's responsibility to limit the frequency of performances to avoid exhausting the artist's energies and to avoid overexposure of the act. The manager will be particularly concerned with travel times between engagements.

As important as determining the frequency of performances is the selection of the kinds of engagement offers. The sharp manager understands the artist's unique identity and the nature of the artist's audience. Insensitive talent agents and promoters will offer the manager job opportunities from time to time that are totally unsuitable. The money might appear attractive, but placing an artist on a bill where the audience might have different tastes can do more harm than good for a career. In considering potential concert dates for a rock performer, the manager will consider the importance of the market, for instance, whether local radio stations are playing the client's music, record sales in that market, and the artist's product presence in local record retail outlets.

In addition to controlling the frequency and types of engagements, the manager must determine when the client is "ready." For example, if the performer is primarily a singer and the job offer also requires acting, the manager, in consultation with the client, should try to determine before they sign whether the artist can handle the role, whether the script is "right," and whether the production will be of respectable quality.

Landing a Recording Contract

Most young performers today find it impossible to graduate to the big time without a recording contract. This has not always been true. In earlier decades, a performer might acquire a national following through such media as network radio, television, the movies, Broadway, even vaudeville. Most of our older stars gained fame and wealth through this kind of exposure. Today, they sell few recordings, and might get $100,000 a week as a Las Vegas headliner, although this type of act is being rapidly replaced by the revue show.

The music business today revolves around recordings. A new act will find it difficult to get jobs, for example, in broadcasting or film before making it on records. Personal managers understand this and consider their most important responsibility is to somehow land recording contracts for their clients. Many performers engage a manager primarily for this purpose. Occasionally, the artist's attorney will recommend that a personal manager be engaged only if the manager can, indeed, secure a recording deal. No recording contract, no personal management agreement. To most aspiring young performers, a personal manager has little to offer without delivering at this level.

Even if we assume the artist in question has great talent, the manager will usually find it difficult to gain the serious attention of an established recording company. The manager must somehow persuade a recording company to invest very big money for production and promotion of a debut album of this unknown artist—just to get the recording career started.

Prospects for the manager's success in landing a record contract for a client will probably be determined by the answers to these kinds of questions:

▶ How strong are the manager's contacts in the industry?

▶ How strong is the manager's team (lawyer, accountant, support staff, etc.)?

▶ How strong, how unique is the artist's talent? Is there star potential there?

▶ Is the manager's approach timely? Is the label signing anyone at this time? Is the recording company undersupplied or oversupplied with artists who perform somewhat in the vein of the manager's client?

▶ Does the recording company believe in the manager? The label may love the artist but lack confidence in the manager's ability to deliver.

The Process. Let us assume that the manager is fully qualified and is respected in the industry, and represents an artist/writer who has star potential. Here is the sequence of events that might lead to the securing of a record contract:

1. The manager makes a frontal attack on the label itself, almost always starting with the A&R (artist and repertoire) department. If unable to gain the attention of the top decision makers, the manager works on the next level down. Recording companies are populated with employees trying to make points with the boss. If a label employee, in whatever position, can participate in the company's discovery of a new star, that employee believes it will be a personal career boost. Among the lower-level contacts the manager might pursue are promotion people and field personnel for the label. The alert ones are on the lookout for new talent.

2. The manager will try to work with the songwriter-client's publisher. If the client doesn't have a publishing deal, the manager will aggressively shop for one. Major publishing executives have excellent contacts with label executives and independent producers.

3. The manager fails to reach the attention of record companies and focuses on independent producers and production companies. The best of these have direct contact with record labels. The manager may determine an offer from a record production company looks more attractive than signing directly with a label; the production company may be able to present its services and the artist's services as a package to some label.

4. The manager arranges for third parties to catch the artist in showcase performance or watch a videotape demo. If some respected individual in the industry tells a friend (who tells a friend . . .) about a great new talent, the word may get back to a decision maker at some recording company. Word of mouth may turn out to be as effective as knocking on doors.

The Result. If the manager should fail to get the client a recording contract after 1 or 2 years' effort, the artist may need to search for a place in some other sector of the entertainment industry. But let's assume the manager succeeds in persuading a recording company to negotiate a contract. What is a "good" contract? How much dare be asked? Is the label excited and ready to get behind the new act with strong promotion and lots of money?

Let's assume the next step: The contract is signed; everyone is happy. At the moment, that is. Now the manager must badger the label to promote the recordings. If the effort is halfhearted, the artist's recordings may never gain **airplay** or reach the retailers. At this moment, the manager's greatest service will be prodding the label to perform on the contract, to deliver what was agreed. The manager must keep the artist a priority by talking to the label, to radio promo people, to the marketing department—even checking to make sure distribution is correct in filling orders. Efforts in this direction can never stop.

Let's make one more assumption in this scenario: The record label fulfills its promises of promotion and the recordings sell very well. Now the artist has so much money rolling in, it seems time to say to the manager, "My friends tell me your commission is out of line. I want to renegotiate our contract. Your new rate is now 10%, not 25%. If that is unacceptable, I will sign with this other management company that will probably do more for me—and for a lower commission than I've been paying you." This kind of scenario is not uncommon. Personal managers may struggle for years establishing an act. Their biggest problem may turn out to be success. When their clients start coming into really big money, they may defect to a manager who had nothing to do with building the act to high-income status. A lawsuit could result if a contract is in place and the artist tries to break it.

Why do bright people go into the personal management field? Probably because the really competent managers continue to be in high demand, and they often seem able to develop sufficient loyalty among their clients to be in on the receiving end when careers prosper. These kinds of managers can easily become millionaires.

Negotiating for Appearances

Once a manager has developed a successful artist, other talent buyers fall into line, seeking to cash in on the performer's growing stature, and it is not uncommon for an artist to have more than one agent. For instance, some artists may have a separate agent who deals only with commercials. Genuinely successful performing careers today often follow this sequence of events:

1. The artist gains initial recognition as a live performer in one geographic area, then signs with a personal manager.
2. Through competence, contacts, good luck, and timing, the manager lands the client a recording contract.
3. The artist's records gain airplay and the label helps underwrite a concert tour. Other live performances ensue.
4. The successful recording artist and concert performer attracts the attention of TV producers, who may engage the artist.
5. The artist, now successful on records and television, may attract the interest of film producers and Broadway producers. The manager has a major star and high income. The big task now is to try to figure out how to keep all these good things happening.

Developing Peripheral Income

Major stars receive additional opportunities to increase their incomes from such sources as product endorsements, broadcast commercials, and merchandising deals. It's up to the artist's manager to get those contracts and to know how to handle them to maximum advantage.

The field of product and service "merchandising" is bigger than most people realize. Major recording and touring stars may receive significant income from the sale of T-shirts, posters, and other concert souvenirs. Sponsorship fees from large companies may pay for the costs of an entire tour.

Each music souvenir merchandiser is licensed by the artist's manager to use the artist's name and image, then pays anywhere from 3% on up in royalties (at retail), depending on the clout of the individual artist, on each item sold. The manager may also receive invitations for clients to appear on broadcast commercials or endorse products and services. The manager, in consultation with the client, must determine whether these kinds of offers might help or hurt the artist's career.

In summary, it becomes evident that the personal manager is a key professional in the entertainment industry, often wielding more power and influence than any one person should be expected (or entitled) to handle. All that is asked of the manager is omniscience.

PERSONAL MANAGEMENT AGREEMENT

The artist and manager should both engage their own independent legal counselors and proceed to negotiate a contract. If their attorneys are well informed and aggressive, the artist and manager should negotiate for all they can get for themselves. Normal procedure is for one side to express demands—from a position, quite naturally, of maximum self-interest. The second party then counters with a position—similarly biased in that party's favor. At this juncture, the parties will need to negotiate compromises, with results being as satisfactory as possible to both parties.

The draft contract that follows assumes the parties start their negotiations in the sequence just described. Where issues are particularly controversial, we articulate the opening position of each party. Then follows an articulation of a compromise position—what might be a fair resolution and balance of interests if the parties had equal bargaining strength.

The compromise positions expressed here are a consensus of opinion prevailing among a number of distinguished entertainment industry attorneys.

Managers belonging to the NCPM are provided with contracts, and the organization provides board review and mediation as a part of its services when problems arise.

DRAFT AGREEMENT

AGREEMENT made (date) _____ by and between _____, the Artist, and _____, the Personal Manager (hereinafter called Manager).

WITNESSETH

Whereas the Artist wishes to obtain advice and direction in the advancement of his professional career, and

Whereas the Manager, by reason of his knowledge and experience, is qualified to render such advice and direction,

NOW THEREFORE, in consideration of the mutual promises set forth here, the Artist and Manager do agree:

DEFINITIONS

The "Artist"—the first party to this agreement—appoints the second party, the Personal Manager. The Artist may be one or more individuals comprising the professional performing group. If more than one individual signs this agreement as an Artist member of the performing group, then this Agreement shall be binding upon all such persons, individually and severally, and all of the representations, warranties, agreements, and obligations contained herein shall be deemed to be individual, joint, and several.[6]

This agreement covers all of the professional talents, activities, and services of the Artist in all sectors and media of the arts and entertainment industry, as an instrumentalist, singer, actor, entertainer, composer, writer, editor, arranger, orchestrator, publisher, executive, producer, manager, audio technician, promoter, and packager.

"Personal Manager" is used here to describe the individual who advises and counsels and directs the Artist's career and manages the Artist's business affairs.

"Third Party" is any individual, company, or corporation with whom the Artist and/or Manager do business relating to the agreement, such as talent agent, producer, publisher, record company, production company, promoter, business manager, accountant, auditor, union or guild, broadcaster, merchant, advertiser.

"Entertainment Industry" is used here, not only in its generally understood meaning, but also including all related aspects of literary activity, publishing, broadcasting, filming, telecommunications, promotion, merchandising, advertising, through all media of communication now known or later developed, of the arts and entertainment industry.

1.0. APPOINTMENT

Artist's Position: It is in the artist's interest to place strong language in the agreement setting forth precisely what the personal manager is obligated to do. To offer "advice and counsel" is ambiguous. The artist will seek a specific list of services to be rendered and require the manager to use the manager's "best efforts" to meet his responsibilities.

Manager's Position: The manager will seek only a general statement regarding his appointment. He may not accept the language committing him to his "best efforts," in that his commissions under such language might not be automatic.[7] The manager may prefer the expression "reasonable efforts."

Compromise Position:

The Artist appoints the Manager as his exclusive personal manager throughout the world in all fields related to the arts and entertainment industry. The Manager will offer the Artist advice and counsel and will use his best efforts to advance the Artist's career.

The Manager accepts the appointment as set forth here and agrees that, in fulfilling the appointment, he will (1) make himself available to the Artist at reasonable times and places; (2) devote his best efforts to the Artist's affairs; and (3) maintain an office and staff adequate to fulfill the appointment and his responsibilities thereunder.

1.1. Exclusivity. The Artist appoints the Manager as his exclusive personal manager and will engage no other personal manager during the term of this agreement. The Man-

ager's services to the Artist are nonexclusive; he may manage other artists concurrently and carry on other business activities, at his sole discretion.[8]

1.2. Business Management. The Manager shall be in charge of the Artist's business affairs personally or, with the consent of the Artist, engage a Third Party as business manager.

1.3. Representation. The Manager shall represent the Artist's best interests with Third Parties and supervise agreements with them.

2.0. EMPLOYMENT

Artist's Position: Despite the language in most contracts of this kind, the artist expects the manager to actively procure employment in the form of a recording agreement. This is the very reason most artists sign on with a particular manager.

Manager's Position: The manager will insist the agreement specifically excuse him from any obligation to procure employment for the artist. If the agreement is negotiated and "performed" in the state of California, the manager will require extra-strong language here disavowing any hint of even an attempt to procure employment or participation even indirectly in such activity.

Compromise Position:

The procurement of employment, or the attempt to procure employment, for the Artist is not an obligation of the Manager, and the Manager is not authorized, licensed, or expected to perform such services. But the Manager recognizes that the obtaining of employment is of the essence in advancing the Artist's career and that the Manager shall, after consultation with the Artist, engage, direct, and/or discharge such persons as talent agents, employment agents, as well as other persons and firms who may be retained for the purpose of securing engagement contracts for the Artist.

3.0. ASSIGNMENT

Artist's Position: The artist will attempt to deny the manager the right to transfer or assign the contract to another party. The artist enters into the agreement largely because of his feeling of confidence and trust in this particular manager. The artist could not be assured this same confidence and trust could be found in some other party who was allowed to take over the contract. To protect himself, the artist will seek a key man clause (below).

Manager's Position: The manager will seek to avoid inclusion of a key man clause, arguing that he may become disabled or otherwise unable to perform. He may develop different interests and want to be free to assign the contract. If the manager is employed by a management company, his company will probably insist it retain the right to assign the agreement.

Compromise Position:

The Manager is the key man in this agreement and is denied the option to assign this agreement without the prior written consent of the Artist. Any other party under consideration in this context shall agree to assume all the responsibilities assigned to the first Manager and be fully qualified, in the opinion of the Artist, to perform in a manner and at a level comparable to the first Manager.

4.0. TERM, TERMINATION

Artist's Position: Unless the artist is in an inferior negotiating position, he will seek an initial term of 1 to 2 years. He will try to avoid a longer first term on the possibility that the manager may do an inadequate job, and it may become necessary to free up the commission for a new manager; or alternatively, the artist may want to negotiate more favorable terms at the end of the first term—or seek to terminate his manager and engage a new one willing to serve for a lower commission.

Manager's Position: It is in the manager's best interests to negotiate a maximum term allowed by state statute for personal services contracts. He seeks maximum assurance that he has the artist tied up and can enjoy high income for years to come. He wants to recover his investment made during the lean years of the artist's career.

Compromise Position:

The initial term of the Agreement shall be for 2 years, provided the parties satisfactorily fulfill their mutual obligations. If either party has substantial cause to claim the other party has failed to perform under this Agreement, the claimant must send a written notice by registered mail, return receipt requested, citing specific reasons for the complaint, allowing the recipient of the written notice 30 days to cure and reasonably satisfy the complaint. If the aggrieved party does not receive a response that is reasonably satisfactory to the claimant, the claimant may then terminate this Agreement by sending written notice 10 days in advance to the other party.[9]

The Manager may then be given the right to exercise options to continue the Agreement beyond the initial term for additional 1-year periods, provided that certain performance criteria have been met, such as securing a recording agreement or generating a minimum amount of income as described below. The number of options should probably not exceed three.

4.1. Options. The Artist grants the Manager options to extend the initial term of this Agreement to a maximum aggregate total of _____ years,[10] provided the Artist has been offered opportunities for employment so that the Artist's gross income from the entertainment industry during the preceding year(s) aggregates these totals:

(A) First term:
     $ _____

(B) First Optional Extension Period of One Year
     (total of (A) and (B)):
     $ _____

(C) Second Optional Extension Period of One Year
     (total of (A) through (C)):
     $ _____

(D) Third Optional Extension Period of One Year
     (total of (A) through (D)):
     $ _____

The foregoing notwithstanding, the Artist grants these extension options only on the condition that the Manager fulfills, in the initial term and optional extensions thereof, all his responsibilities and obligations set forth herein.[11]

5.0. POWER OF ATTORNEY

Manager's Position: The manager will attempt to get general power of attorney, including, among other powers, the complete and unrestricted right to (1) collect and disburse all the artist's money; (2) negotiate and sign contracts on behalf of the artist; (3) engage and discharge personnel; (4) exploit the artist's personality, name, likeness, photographs, which would include commitment of the artist to product endorsements and commercial announcements; and (5) exert "creative control," including the selection or rejection of musical and literary materials, record producers, staging, and costuming.

Artist's Position: An artist will seek to limit a grant of power of attorney. Grant of general power of attorney is all-encompassing and affords exposure to conflicts of interest and abuse. The artist will probably be most resistant to extending power of attorney to creative control. Unless the manager is fully qualified to make artistic judgments, for example, the manager could impose poor decisions in such sensitive areas as selection of music to be recorded, the manner and style of presentation, and the selection of record producers. Whatever resolution the parties make in regard to creative control and constraints on decision making, the artist will probably demand that power of attorney be cancelable by the artist at any time.

Compromise Position:

The Artist agrees the Manager may need limited power of attorney from time to time for his convenience. Accordingly, the Artist grants limited power of attorney to the Manager to serve as the Artist's agent and attorney-in-fact in emergency situations only and denies the Manager this power without the prior written consent of the Artist (1) to accept any performing engagement on behalf of the Artist exceeding 1 week in duration; (2) to sign checks drawn upon the Artist-Manager's Trust Account with a face value greater than $1,000 and of an aggregate monthly amount in excess of $5,000 for all such draws; (3) to sign any agreement on behalf of the Artist that is of more than incidental importance or having a term longer than 1 month; (4) to engage or discharge support personnel; (5) to accept on the Artist's behalf any product or service endorsement; and (6) to limit the Artist's creative control over such matters as the selection of musical and literary material; determination of the manner and style of performance, including staging and costuming. The Artist may terminate this power of attorney at any time, without notice, in the event that the Manager misuses, in the sole opinion of the Artist, this power.

The manager usually insists on the right to collect the artist's income early on in the artist's career to ensure reimbursement, payment of expenses, and the receipt of his commission. The artist should, however, make provision for a third-party business manager to handle all of the money once income reaches a certain level, since abuses of artists' finances by personal managers are legendary in the music business.

6.0. ARTIST'S RESPONSIBILITIES, WARRANTIES

6.1. Encumbrance. The Artist warrants that he is under no restriction, disability, or prohibition in respect to the Artist's right to execute this Agreement and perform its terms and conditions. The Artist warrants that no act or omission by the Artist will violate, to the best of his knowledge, any right or interest of any person or firm or will subject the Manager to any liability or claim to any person.

6.2. Commitment. The Artist will devote his full time and attention to the advancement of his career.

6.3. Ownership. The Artist warrants that, to the best of his knowledge, he is the sole owner of his professional name,[12] _____, and that this warranty is restricted to adjudicated breaches.

6.4. Advice. The Artist will accept in good faith the advice and counsel of the Manager, in recognition of the Manager's special knowledge and experience in the entertainment industry.

6.5. Income. The Artist shall encourage all agents and employers to make payments of all monies due the Artist to the Manager, or to a Third Party approved by the Artist and Manager.

6.6. Employment. The Artist shall refer all offers of employment to the Manager, and the Artist shall not accept offers of employment without the consent of the Manager.

7.0. MANAGER'S COMPENSATION

Artist's Position: The artist will seek to sign the manager for a 10% to 15% commission. If this is unacceptable to the manager, the artist may offer to increase the rate as gross income rises.

Manager's Position: If the manager is new at the game and anxious to get into the field, he might accept a commission as low as 10%. An unknown manager will probably be able to attract only relatively unknown artists, so the parties must agree to struggle together in the early stages of their relationship. The astute manager who accepts a low starting income will seek commission increments when he can manage to increase his client's income substantially.

Compromise Position:

The Artist shall pay the Manager 15% of the Artist's gross income for the first year of this Agreement. "Gross income" shall include, without limitation, all fees, earnings, salaries, royalties, bonuses, shares of profit, stock, partnership interests, percentages, gifts of value, received directly or indirectly, by the Artist or his heirs, executors, administrators, or assigns, or by any other person, corporation, or firm on the Artist's behalf, from the arts and entertainment industry. The commission shall be 20% in the second year of this Agreement, provided the Artist's gross income for this second year increases _____ % over the first year. If this Agreement is extended to a third year, the commission shall rise to 25% provided the Artist's gross income increases _____ % over the prior year.

In other circumstances, the parties may choose to decrease the percentage as income rises, thereby acknowledging that the Manager may be contributing less significantly to the generation of income, but still resulting in more money for the Manager because the income is higher.

8.0. COMMISSION BASE

Artist's Position: An unknown artist may have to pay an established manager on the artist's unadjusted gross income. But an established artist with an aggressive lawyer may be able to obtain certain exclusions from that gross, such as those listed in the Compromise Position that follows.

Manager's Position: The manager will fight for the broadest possible commission base and seek to calculate his percentage on the artist's unadjusted gross income. But if the artist has any bargaining power, "gross income" will probably become an adjusted gross income.

Compromise Position:

The foregoing definition of the Artist's "gross income" notwithstanding, the following sums shall be deducted from the gross income for purposes of calculating the Manager's commission: (1) the first $25,000 aggregated income in any single year derived from the entertainment industry or $500 per calendar week, whichever is greater; (2) recording production expense where a Third Party provides same to the Artist; (3) record producers' fees, points, and percentages where a Third Party pays the Artist for same; (4) performance, production, and travel expense including salaries of support personnel connected thereto where a Third Party pays the Artist for same (often called "negative tour support"); (5) legal fees incurred by the Artist in dealings with the Manager and Third Parties in the negotiation and performance of agreements; and (6) passive income where the Artist receives money or other things of value from sources outside the entertainment industry or the Artist's income from investments inside or outside the entertainment industry.[13]

In any circumstances where the Manager has a financial interest with a Third Party or company with whom the Artist has any kind of business relationship, the Manager shall receive no commissions on any monies the Artist receives from such sources.[14]

When this Agreement and all extensions thereof terminate, the Artist shall pay the Manager 100% of his commissions for a period of 1 year from all income generated by contracts and agreements set up by the Manager during the term of the agreement. For the following 6 months, the Manager's commission is limited to 50% of the Artist's commissionable income. For the subsequent 6 months, the Manager's commission is limited to 25% of the Artist's commissionable income. Thereafter, all Manager's commissions on the Artist's commissionable income cease. Manager is not entitled to any commissions on albums released after his tenure has expired.[15]

9.0. FINANCIAL ACCOUNTING

Within thirty (30) days following the execution of this Agreement, the parties shall select, by mutual consent, a certified public accountant to provide accounting services for the Artist.

9.1. Records. The parties shall exchange informal financial records of all monies flowing through their hands that relate to this Agreement. The Manager's financial records shall account for all receipts, disbursements, commissions withheld, advances, loans, and investments, if any. Copies of the parties' financial reports shall be forwarded monthly to the accountant.

9.2. Audits. The Manager shall engage independent auditors, with the consent of the Artist, to conduct periodic audits of the Artist's publisher and record company to determine if these firms are fully paying royalties due the Artist and paying in a timely manner.

9.3. Limitations. The Manager may not incur any expense on behalf of the Artist in an amount larger than $ _____ for any one expense, without the consent of the Artist. The Manager may not incur monthly expenses on behalf of the Artist that exceed $ _____ without the consent of the Artist.

9.4. Loans. The Manager is not expected or required to make loans to the Artist or advance the Artist money. The Manager shall not make loans of the Artist's money to any other person or invest the Artist's money without the prior consent of the Artist.

If the Artist asks the Manager to loan him money, and if the Manager voluntarily agrees to do so, the Manager shall be entitled to recover when due such loaned money together with reasonable interest. If such repayments to the Manager are not made when due, the Manager may recover the amount outstanding from the Artist's current earnings from the entertainment industry.

9.5. Overhead. The Manager's office overhead is not recoupable from the Artist, nor the Manager's travel expense within a fifty (50) mile radius of his office. The Artist shall pay the Manager's travel expense outside this radius when the Manager is requested by the Artist to travel.

9.6. Liability. Neither party is liable to the other for debts and obligations they may incur that are not covered by the Agreement.

10.0. GENERAL ISSUES

The present Agreement constitutes the entire understanding between the parties, and no other agreement or commitment, oral or written, prevails between the parties. Neither party may change or modify any part of the present Agreement without the prior written consent of the other party.

If one or more parts of this Agreement is found to be illegal or unenforceable, for any reason or by any person, the same shall not affect the validity or enforceability of the remaining provisions of this Agreement.

10.1. Incorporation. If the Artist incorporates, he agrees to cause said corporation to sign an agreement with the Manager that provides no less favorable terms than the first agreement.

10.2. Default and Cure. If either party claims that the other is in default or breach of this agreement, the aggrieved party shall provide written notice setting forth the nature of the dispute. The accused party is then allowed thirty (30) days to cure the alleged default, during which period no default or other grievances shall be deemed incurable.

10.3. Arbitration. The parties agree to submit all disputes to the American Arbitration Association and be bound by and perform any award rendered in such arbitration.[16]

10.4. This Agreement is made under the laws of the state of _____

IN WITNESS WHEREOF, the parties hereto have executed this Agreement as of the day and year first indicated above.

_____

Artist

_____

Personal Manager

NOTES

1. In this chapter, the terms *artists* and *stars* refer not only to performers but also to other professionals who, from time to time, engage personal managers, such as writers, producers, directors, and choreographers.

2. When a major act audits a recording company, the expense can run from $30,000 to $100,000 or more.

3. Suppliers often try to overcharge entertainment business personalities, apparently assuming that such customers are not concerned enough to examine their bills critically.

4. Similar billings are used for producers, writers, directors, and others. In complex productions such as theatrical motion pictures, these participants may all joust for good billing, further complicated by the rules of competing unions. Some participants are so prestigious (or have invested so much money) that they receive star billing—their names positioned above the title of the production.

5. Contracts often specify billings in terms of relative percentages. For example, it might be required that an artist's name never be printed less than 50% as large as the production title—or that an artist's musical director's name appear 25% as large as the artist's name. These kinds of billings can be readily observed on Las Vegas hotel billboards.

6. The manager may require here that the members of the performing group are individually and severally liable for any claims against any other member of the group or the manager.

7. Joseph Taubman, *In Tune With the Music Business* (p. 80). New York: Law-Arts Publishers, 1980.

8. The artist may seek to limit the manager's freedom here by requiring a listing of current clients and agreement to limit future activity to those clients. This may help assure the artist that the manager will have sufficient time to serve the artist's best interests.

9. The parties may prefer that this option to terminate not be allowed and that all serious claims of failure to perform be referred to arbitration. But a powerful act may demand the right to terminate at any time, making the claim that the manager serves at the pleasure of the artist. But no prestigious manager would accept this, arguing possible vulnerability to a capriciously behaving artist.

10. States have statues of limitation on contracts involving "personal services."

11. Whatever the circumstances of termination or disengagement, the lawyers will need to exchange notices of release. These releases may include *executory provisions*—requirements for performance, payments, and so forth, following termination of the agreement.

12. Courts have held that the legal ownership of a trade name ultimately resides, not with the person first using it, but with the person or persons identified with the name when it acquires a "secondary meaning."

13. A manager with a strong track record and powerful contacts will probably not accept these commission exclusions—or not without a higher commission rate. The author's rationale for suggesting these exclusions is simple: Most of these exclusions are not the artist's income, they are his overhead. The manager is entitled to commissions on income, but not outflow.

14. The attorneys will need to negotiate how commissions, if any, are to be paid where the artist's services are provided by a corporation. The commission will be adjusted to reflect whether the artist, in this circumstance, has a financial interest in the corporation, is only an employee, or both.

15. This compromise of entirely eliminating the manager's commission after a relatively short period of time may be unacceptable to a manager. If the manager is responsible for securing a beneficial recording agreement for the artist, it may be that even a successful artist has little or no commissionable income during the first few years of the agreement. The manager may have invested a great deal of time, energy, and money over that period and would see essentially no return at all. For this reason, managers may justifiably seek to receive some reduced commission in perpetuity for every album produced under the contract they arranged, or at the very least, for every album produced during their tenure.

16. Many contracts include a compulsory arbitration clause calling for the parties to submit disputes to the American Arbitration Association. Although rulings can be prompt through arbitration proceedings, their implementation may still result in lawsuits; if, for instance, one party refuses to abide by the decision of the arbitration board, the other party would file for breach of contract.

Thousands delight in the Boston Pop's annual July 4th concert.
© Miro Vintoniv/Stock, Boston/PNI.

CONCERT PROMOTION

The promotion and production of live concerts employ large numbers of people and cause the flow of hundreds of millions of dollars. Those taking part hope that the money will flow in their direction. It looks so easy: You rent a facility, hire a star, and collect the money. This get-rich-quick illusion has caused many bankruptcies. Promoters and producers who know the concert field do well financially; those lacking competence do not survive in it.

GETTING STARTED

How does the aspiring concert promoter get started? Most professionals began simply by promoting and booking their own acts; others who go on to professional promotion work got their start working on a college campus entertainment committee. Many professional promoters paid their first dues putting on college concerts, shows, even lectures.

The new independent promoter must, first of all, get in touch with some money, perhaps by spending personal funds or persuading outside investors to gamble. In this start-up phase (true for starting any business), the promoter must usually register a firm name with the county clerk, license the business, and establish a business bank account. Assuming this preliminary homework has been done, an unknown concert promoter will have to provide cash deposits or surety bonds or a letter of credit to guarantee hall rentals and promotional expenses and may also have to come up with cash deposits required by most agents upon the signing of contracts for the performers. The freshman concert promoter may assume only part of the financial risk and consequently enjoy only a share in the profits, if there are any profits.

LOCATING COSPONSORS

Most promoters discover that the most efficient and profitable concert promotions are *cosponsored*, with two or more individuals or firms backing such a project.

Local Radio Stations

Concerts on and off campus are frequently sponsored or cosponsored by local radio stations. Stations and their employees find ways to ally themselves with live concerts, because they regard such events as excellent contacts with their broadcast audience. Concert promoters welcome cosponsorship of broadcasters, because the potential audience for the live event is largely made up of the same persons who listen to broadcast music.

Recording Companies

For many years, the most active cosponsor of concerts in the pop and rock fields has been the recording industry. Label executives know that the successful promotion of a new album may depend on coordination with a concert tour. Touring costs continue to rise—necessitating, in turn, ticket price increases that discourage some potential concertgoers from attending.

Despite the risks involved, recording companies will probably continue to be important sponsors or cosponsors of live concerts. When a label does help underwrite concerts, it cooperates with the artist's management in producing and supplying promotion materials. Most labels maintain "college departments" to coordinate record company support of college-sponsored performances. Some recording companies will buy blocks of tickets for concerts, then give them away to individuals and firms who have influence, or so they believe, over the record-buying public—disc jockeys, media personnel, and employees of record distributors and retail stores that sell recorded music. In addition to spreading goodwill among influential people, giving away tickets helps fill the house, thus giving the impression to the audience that the event is a huge success. This practice has been used for a long time on Broadway, too, and is known as **papering the house.**

A recording company strongly supporting a particular concert may send in one of its own publicists or product managers to assist. Yet another kind of promotional support involves participating in buying broadcast spots and print ads. In these efforts, the label and concert promoter may share such expenses with a local record retailer who wants to take part in the promotion.

An even more elaborate involvement by a recording company occurs when the label itself sets up a complete national tour. When this is undertaken for a new act, the artists may be so broke that their recording company must not only finance the purchase of equipment but also advance the group or artist funds for transportation, hotels, and meals. A label may invest heavily to finance a national tour of an act it believes may make it. Despite these descriptions of extensive tour support, artists' managers complain that their clients never get enough of this kind of backing.

ARENA SPONSORSHIP

Another trend in cosponsorship is the increasing involvement by the **venues** themselves. Although large arenas are still the leading choice for major artists, many small and midsize buildings have done well by promoting a variety of artists of lesser stature and occasionally accommodating the big act through a multinight schedule.

CORPORATE SPONSORSHIP

Evident to all is the corporate sponsorship of touring performers. A firm such as Pepsi-Cola is willing to spend $1 million or more for the right to associate its name and product with a star. These kinds of contracts may call for the corporation to underwrite entire tours.

Many of these endorsement contracts provide the sponsor the exclusive right to vend its products at the performances. For example, if Pepsi-Cola is the sponsor, Coca-Cola will not be sold at that concert. It can get complicated: Some facilities have endorsement contracts with competing sponsors, so conflicts are possible.

If the concert venue is owned by a municipality, the sponsor (or any vendor) is expected to pay the city a share of its gross. Ancillary revenue included in the gross can be substantial. In fact, many artists now earn as much or more from the sale of T-shirts, jackets, programs, and the like as they do from ticket sales. Buttressed by the high profits possible from arena refreshment sales, some concession companies have expanded into concert promotion.

NATIONAL PROMOTERS

After a local concert promoter has established a reputation in a particular area, national promoters (NPs) who need assistance in coordinating national tours will become aware of that success. Major acts and their agents usually prefer an NP to coordinate a whole tour because this arrangement affords greater continuity and smoother organization. All NPs need the local expertise of individual area promoters to recommend appropriate venues, **scale the house** (set seat prices), and arrange local promotional tie-ins with radio stations and record stores.

NPs are usually compensated on a share of net receipts—box office income less expenses. Local promoters' income usually comes out of the NP's share of income. Arguments often arise about "net profit." Contracts between NPs, local promoters, and artists must be precisely drawn to make sure the expenses charged against gross income are allowable and accurate.

COLLEGE SPONSORSHIP

A large percentage of the live concerts in the United States are sponsored or co-sponsored by colleges and universities that set up student-run committees to handle the school's annual budget for campus-sponsored entertainment. Sponsoring, promoting, and managing college concerts today is a big business. College students usually lack sufficient experience and knowledge in the field to handle these affairs by themselves. Increasing numbers of colleges find it necessary to bring in professional promoters and managers. Artists' agents find it helpful when a college involves a knowledgeable professional to work with them in handling the endless details and large sums of money involved. But due credit should be given to these students, some of whom begin to learn the promotion-management-production field while in school, then go on to find their places as professionals in the concert promotion or artist agent-management fields.

NATIONAL ASSOCIATION FOR CAMPUS ACTIVITIES

Major facets of the music business have their own trade associations. The one most representative of concert promotion focuses on the college field. It is NACA, the National Association for Campus Activities. It represents more than 1,200 colleges and offers associate memberships to agencies, managements, and individuals who supply related services or products. Every aspiring concert promoter should study NACA publications, particularly *Programming*, NACA's magazine.

NACA holds annual conventions that are attended not only by college representatives but also by talent agents and performing artists from both the pop and classical fields. NACA offers extensive educational and showcasing opportunities and allows students to meet a wide variety of talent agents and service companies related to live performance. Talent agencies and record companies sometimes send new acts to these conventions, and college promoters attend workshops to advance their knowledge of booking and promoting campus entertainments. Probably the most useful function of these conventions is providing a meeting ground where attendees can negotiate cooperative bookings of touring acts. NACA's national conventions include presentation of "Campus Entertainment" awards.

PREPARING BUDGETS

Early in the cycle of events leading to a live concert, the promoter will have formulated a budget. Inexperienced promoters are likely to underestimate certain costs and overlook certain kinds of overhead. Even if they follow the production management controls suggested here and budget expenses carefully, another danger area is *optimism*. Every year, hotshot new promoters jump into the field, full of confidence that they will show others in the field how it should be done.

They are optimistic beyond reason because they do not yet know enough about what they might encounter.

Before a promoter can start signing acts, an appropriate facility, referred to in the trade as a venue, must be located. Many communities' most attractive venues are tied up by other tenants or other promoters. Securing open dates can be difficult, and available dates are useless without the coincident availability of the acts the promoter wants. In selecting a concert venue, the promoter can usually rent the facility for a flat fee or a flat fee plus a percentage of the gross. The landlord normally furnishes the stage manager, box office manager, maintenance crew, security personnel, and ushers. The promoter's second rental option is called **four-walling:** The landlord furnishes the facility and the stage manager; the promoter brings in all other personnel—stagehands, ushers, security, and box office help—and foots the bill.

A critical issue is the number of seats. A 1,000-seat facility sold out at $20 a ticket grosses $20,000, obviously. The promoter with a budget of $17,500 (allowing $2,500 for profit) will probably lose money because few halls sell out. Even if every seat is sold, unanticipated expenses may gobble up the profit margin. Few concerts in the pop-rock fields can be put together and profit from a $20,000 gross. The promoter might be well advised to locate a 5,000- or 10,000-seat arena, book a headline act, and pull together enough money to finance a sizable promotional campaign. For a neophyte promoter, a budget of this kind may be less risky than the one described for the 1,000-seat facility.

Whatever the potential gross a particular venue might yield, the experienced promoter budgets the package to produce at least a break-even figure, not for an *SRO* (standing room only) audience, but for a *60% house*—meaning that the promoter estimates that 40% of the tickets just won't sell. Theater managers have used this 60% house figure since the 1800s in planning budgets.

Let us invent a concert budget for our freshman promoter-producer (see Table 10.1). This young promoter is very fortunate—and probably sets some kind of record for a first project: breaking even! Consider the things that were handled wisely.

The promoter:

▶ Hired a 10,000-seat arena, thus maximizing the potential gross

▶ Spent a bundle on a big-name act—to ensure strong ticket sales

▶ Was well covered against damaging lawsuits by taking out an expensive liability policy

TABLE 10.1   Sample Concert Budget

Potential income		
10,000 seats at $20 per seat		
Maximum gross	$200,000	
Less 40% for unsold tickets	−80,000	
Gross income		120,000
Estimated expense		
Hall rental (includes box office, ushers, stage crew)	10,000	
Star act	58,000	
Supporting act	6,500	
Liability insurance	2,000	
Surety bonds	500	
Advertising, promotion (15% of the gross)	18,000	
PA company	4,000	
Lighting/staging company	4,000	
Security company (rent-a-cop)	2,300	
ASCAP and BMI performance licenses	300	
Perquisites (special food, drink, etc.) for the star and entourage	400	
Cleanup	2,000	
Unforeseen expense		
(10% of estimated gross)	12,000	
		120,000
Profit/loss		0

▶ Budgeted 15% of anticipated gross revenue for advertising and promotion, an amount often recommended as a minimum by successful promoters

▶ Budgeted $2,000 for cleanup, just in case the audience left more mess than the arena rental contract would normally take care of as routine maintenance

▶ Budgeted 10% of the estimated gross revenue for unforeseen expense

If the first venture broke even, a promoter this smart can probably look forward to making a profit the next time around. The first venture produced another bonus: The people involved—agents, managers, artists, security people—all discovered this individual to be a level-headed businessperson who treats associates fairly. Next time around, there may be somewhat lower fees and more complete cooperation from these people.

The Colorado Symphony Orchestra performs in Denver, Colorado.
© Richard Pasley/Stock, Boston/PNI.

NEGOTIATING CONTRACTS

The concert promoter is obligated to enter into a number of written agreements before the entertainment can begin. For example, contracts must be signed with venue managements, talent agents, merchandisers, perhaps with NPs, with lighting and sound suppliers, insurance companies, transportation firms, even caterers, and there must be clear agreements with the city's police and fire departments.

With respect to security arrangements, the city or venue management will require the promoter to have a specified number of "rent-a-cops" on hand. Security requirements for classical performers, middle-of-the-road artists, and country acts will be minimal; for rock-and-roll and rap shows, where the potential for violence has historically been much higher, the promoter's costs for security are also likely to run higher.

City and county fire departments impose strict controls on the promoter in respect to hall capacity and standees. Fire departments have been known to close down performances where the promoter fails to control congestion of aisles or blocking of fire exits.

Signing Acts

Promoters normally contract for performers' services through talent agencies. Knowledgeable promoters try to work with agents of broad experience, who can be of invaluable service. Agents, in turn, usually prefer to work with seasoned promoters because they are more likely to share with them a successful experience. Agents will normally limit stars' bookings to promoters with good track records. Most stars are in a position to pick and choose where they will perform and need not take a chance on unknown concert promoters. But agents handling performers of lesser magnitude are frequently looking for concert dates, and the less-than-famous promoters can work out satisfactory contracts with them. Smart agents set artists' fees, whenever they can, to permit the promoter to make money, too. Contracts must be mutually profitable or the parties will shop elsewhere next time.

Promoters should make preliminary inquiry of agents concerning artists' usual fees and available dates. This information can set in motion preparatory steps, such as placing a hold on a concert facility. After the promoter has worked out a preliminary budget based on this information, it's time to contact the agent and nail down a firm agreement. If an acceptable fee can be negotiated for the acts, the promoter can then polish the budget, double-check the estimated income and expenses, then sign the contracts.

Some promoters permit themselves the luxury of booking the acts they personally prefer—if the price is within reach. Most experienced promoters favor their personal preferences, but are more likely to follow the weekly fluctuations of the trade charts, regional sales, and airplay—then do everything they can to book the acts that are the most recent successes in their concert territory. If the promoter's cosponsor aids in this research, they may develop a winning combination. Booking artists on the way down the charts has hurt many a promoter.

Once the promoter has signed the star act, there is pressure to accept a lead-off act or other secondary acts on the bill. Agents handling both the star and a favored lead-off act will do all they can to get the promoter to buy a package deal: "You can have my star if you'll give this new act a break and let them lead off." Or the promoter may hear this appeal from the recording company: "We just signed the Hitmakers group and if you buy them for your next bill, we'll fly in our promotion people to help you really push the date, for free. The act? Cheap!" Agents are on questionable legal ground when they attempt to coerce a talent buyer to buy an act on the condition that the buyer take another one in addition.

Technical Riders

Once the promoter and agent have come to terms on the acts and the prices, stars sometimes ask for additional agreements. Some concern the setup and expense for the sound system, lights, staging, and more. Details covering these items are attached as an addendum to the artist's contract in the form of a *technical rider.* Stars frequently specify the companies they want engaged to supply the sound reinforcement and staging. Others leave it to the promoter to engage the best local or regional suppliers and technicians. Audio and staging are usually determined by the star act. Lesser names on the bill are accustomed to accepting whatever the star has specified in technical services.

PROMOTION, ADVERTISING

Only a few superstars draw an SRO audience just by having their forthcoming appearance announced. These giant draws require the promoter to spend practically no money on advertising. That is fortunate, for a very high percentage of the gross has undoubtedly been signed away to the visiting superstar. More commonly, the promoter signs the acts, then has to shout and scream to inform the public that there are tickets, lots of tickets, for sale.

Some promoters prefer to handle publicity and advertising responsibilities personally. The promoter's advertising agency might have personnel to assist in the publicity campaign. More often, the promoter will hire a publicist or public relations (PR) firm to organize a campaign that will persuade the public to buy tickets. This process is aided by "promo kits" supplied by the managers of the artists (promotion materials are often supplied by the artist's recording company).

Another useful kind of press is the interview: "The Star" arrives; all newspapers and broadcast media in the concert territory are informed that at 2 p.m. in the Big Hotel, The Star will hold a press conference. Reporters present may turn in interview copy; their editors may or may not print it. More effective is the exclusive interview, where an individual reporter or newspaper columnist will be offered the exclusive right to interview The Star, provided reasonable assurance can be offered that the story will be written and printed.

If the bill features pop recording stars, the promoter knows the most effective advertising will be on the radio—not just spot announcements but the supporting chatter of jocks who are always searching for something musical to talk about.

Rock-pop audiences seem to be less attracted to print media. Older, non-rock music lovers, accustomed to following the entertainment pages of daily newspapers, may never be aware that a particular rock star has been in town, come and gone, sold out. In lieu of extensive newspaper ads, rock promoters focus their print ads on posters, locating them wherever young people gather—schools, college campuses, bookstores, for example. Recording labels can help promote a concert of one of their contract artists with special store displays, sometimes taking over whole windows to push the artist's latest release and local concert appearance. Some promoters learn that ad space bought in campus newspapers pays off, and the paper will usually run editorial copy, too. The Internet is another place for effective promotion: Many stars and groups have Web pages listing their appearance schedules, record companies and magazines on the Internet run ads, and cities often mention upcoming concerts in the current event listings on their Web pages.

PRODUCTION MANAGEMENT

The concert promoter is ultimately responsible not only for booking the talent and filling the hall but also for every detail relating to the presentation of that entertainment. Anyone attempting to enter the field should have the aptitude and desire to assume the management of a great variety of details. If your talents and inclinations lean mostly to actual promotion, an associate producer should assume the responsibility for managing details of the performance itself. This kind of associate producer might be called the production manager or stage director. Any individual presuming to function in this capacity must be experienced, as an amateur or professional, in theater and staging.

Although some promoters and stage managers do an adequate job with minimum controls, many of the best of them rely heavily on lists of things to do. It should help to work up *control sheets* as written guides for what to do and when to do it. The accompanying pages show the kind of production control sheets that can work efficiently in most situations. These forms will be particularly useful for college promoters.

The College Production Planning form (Table 10.2) identifies the myriad tasks that must be *back-timed* so that preparations for a performance can unfold in orderly fashion.

College students who acquire experience promoting campus concerts may find work with fully professional promotion companies, provided, of course, their track records as amateurs justify the confidence of potential employers.

Control Sheets

As preparations for a performance unfold, persons in charge start accumulating voluminous correspondence and telephone messages. Filing folders can become unmanageable. To maintain control, promoters, stage managers, and road managers might well pull all the data relating to the performance itself together on one sheet, called a control sheet, that is commonly used by experienced promoters. Try the one shown (Table 10.3) or prepare your own. Producers who favor assembling more detail than can be written on such a simple form will prefer to prepare their own summary sheets, perhaps on legal-sized paper or on computer spreadsheets, that can be duplicated to provide identical information for all key production personnel.

TABLE 10.2   College Production Planning

Lead Time	Control Number	Responsibility
6-12 months	1.	Research history of college promotions in your area. What has worked well in the past?
3-6 months	2.	Formulate budget for forthcoming school year; appeal for funding.
	3.	Place tentative holds on performance facilities.
	4.	Make preliminary contact with talent agents to learn of tentative costs, available artists, and dates.
3 months	5.	Get school's approval of your plans. Submit bid for artist, specifying date and price.
	6.	Get acceptance, rejection, or counteroffer from agents.
	7.	Negotiate contracts with agents. Pending formal execution of contracts, exchange written confirmation.
	8.	Confirm your hold on facility, then formulate a written agreement with the facility management.
2 months	9.	Execute contracts with agencies, including technical riders.
	10.	Contact artists' record companies for help with promotion. Ask for press kits, promotional materials, money for block-ticket purchases, cooperative ads, even promotion personnel.
	11.	Formulate promotion budget and campaign. Get print and broadcast ad costs.
	12.	Contract for outside suppliers, as needed, for sound reinforcement, lighting, security, caterers, etc.
6 weeks	13.	Place printing orders for tickets, posters, banners, etc.
	14.	Line up cooperative ads with record stores, radio stations, etc.
4 weeks	15.	Contract for ticket-selling outlets.
	16.	Seek store displays of posters, albums.
3 weeks	17.	Deliver printed tickets to outlets. Set strict controls for accounting.
	18.	Line up student volunteers for ushering, ticket takers, setting up/striking stage, publicity, gofers, box office, etc.
	19.	Clear plans with fire department: size of crowd, control of aisles, exits.
	20.	Clear security plans with police, sheriff, rent-a-cop firm, campus police. Discuss liabilities with school's legal counsel.
	21.	Distribute promotional materials to print and broadcast media. Schedule press conference, interviews. Mount banners, posters.
2 weeks	22.	Reconfirm arrangements with outside suppliers (sound, lighting, transport, caterers, etc.)
	23.	Check ticket sales. Adjust promotion budget accordingly.

(continued)

TABLE 10.2   Continued

Lead Time	Control Number	Responsibility
1 week	24.	Call a production planning meeting with facility manager, stage manager, production director, student volunteers. Issue written instructions to everybody concerning their responsibilities, schedule, contingency plans.
3 days	25.	*Reconfirm everything!* a. with artists' road managers regarding any changes in time of arrival of personnel, equipment b. with outside suppliers c. with facility stage manager d. with student crew chairpersons e. with ticket sellers (If sales are lagging, execute preconceived last-minute promotion campaign.)
Performance day	26.	Call production meeting 1 hour prior to scheduled arrival of equipment and roadies. Everyone charged with responsibilities relating to the production and performance attends this meeting and takes notes. Last-minute changes in plans discussed.
	27.	Set up. Confirm that all personnel and equipment are arriving per plan.
	28.	Pick up money and unsold tickets from outlets. Deposit money in bank, deliver unsold tickets to facility box office for sale there.
	29.	Welcome the performing artists and their entourage. Control issuing of backstage and auditorium passes. Save the best (free) seats for unexpected important guests.
Post-production	30.	If agreed contractually, join the road manager for a count of receipts and unsold tickets shortly after the box office closes. Make agreed payment, then arrange for secure place to store cash overnight.
	31.	Feed your people after the show, at least your volunteers. They've earned it!
	32.	Confirm facility cleanup is proceeding per plan. Did the place experience more-than-normal wear and tear? If so, discharge your contractual responsibilities.
	33.	Write a summary report, following a short meeting with your key personnel: What went wrong, what went well?
	34.	Thank the participants by telephone or letter for their cooperation, particularly those who worked as volunteers.
	35.	Pay your bills promptly to ensure goodwill for the school's next venture.

TABLE 10.3   Production Control

Performance facility (name/address/telephone/manager) _____

_____

_____

Performance date/time _____

_____

Producer/promoter/agent(s) _____

_____

_____

Featured artist(s) _____

_____

   Road manager _____

Stage (size/risers/pit/stairs/curtains/exits, etc.) _____

_____

_____

_____

_____

Lighting (spots/borders/foots/dimmer/voltage/supplier/operator) _____

_____

_____

Sound (supplier/technician/description) _____

_____

_____

Dressing rooms (number/size/furnishings/condition/location) _____

_____

_____

Loading dock (access/parking/security) _____

_____

_____

Performance licenses _____

_____

_____

Union jurisdictions _____

_____

_____

MUSIC AND THEATER

11

Music has played an integral part in the theater for centuries. Many of the master composers experienced their greatest success in the theater: Wagner, Stravinsky, Gershwin. In Western civilization, musical theater can be said to have started in the Jewish synagogue and the Roman Catholic church; most religious ceremony would be unthinkable without music. Much religious pageantry, of itself, is choreographed music.

Musical theater's earliest patronage, in addition to organized religion, came from the aristocracy who built and operated theaters right on their own premises. Later, men of wealth, for example, the merchants of Venice, the Medici family of Florence, became enthusiastic patrons of the arts. By the 17th century, public opera houses began operating, selling tickets (at the current equivalent of about 50 cents each) to cover production costs. In the 18th century, Handel, years before he scored his biggest hit, *Messiah*, was hustling around London, buying and managing theaters, booking talent, scoring, producing, conducting operas, even doubling as a **pit** musician (keyboards) in his own theater. Competing musical shows, particularly *The Beggar's Opera*, eventually drove impresario Handel out of the musical theater business, while other producers, whose ears were more in tune with current taste, established a musical theater tradition in London that flourishes to this day.

By the 19th century, musical theater in Europe and this country, including everything from grand opera to minstrel shows, was prospering, selling tickets, turning a profit. Early in the 20th century, opera and ballet production costs began to exceed box office income, and the musical *patron*, the big giver, reappeared to keep these art forms alive. Meanwhile, imported European operetta was being transformed in this country into such forms as the musical revue, musical comedy, light opera, and, since *Show Boat* (1927), the musical play. In our own time, it is musical theater that keeps Broadway and most regional theater going.

TYPES OF MUSICAL THEATER

Broadway Musicals

That piece of territory in New York known as Broadway has seen the production of contemporary musical theater's most treasured repertoire; it has been the working place for dozens of America's most gifted composers, lyricists, playwrights, producers, directors, and performers. Broadway would have collapsed had it not been for the musicals that kept it alive after 1945. Some Broadway musicals have produced more profit through record sales and publishing income than they ever generated through ticket sales. Royalties from successful Broadway musicals have earned enormous sums of money for the composers, lyricists, and *book authors* (the term *book* is used in the musical theater to describe the scenario and dialogue of the musical drama; it excludes music and lyrics). Stage musicals of genuine quality demonstrate a staying power unique in most popular music. The musical that lasts and experiences periodic revivals possesses two essential ingredients: a good book and memorable songs.

Broadway musicals have always been the most expensive kind of production to mount. In 1950, a sumptuous production cost $200,000. Today, a producer may have to raise $7 million or more to mount a first-class Broadway musical, and for most shows the investors could not expect to break even with a 52-week run: Many musical plays do not start turning a profit until they have run 2, even 3, years.

Costs are now out of hand because theater rentals are very expensive and stage production is a *handcraft enterprise* in a mechanized age. No matter how carefully a show is budgeted, a producer cannot increase the "efficiency" of live singers, dancers, and musicians. The live audience may total only 1,000 per performance, not the 20 million available on television. Investors have risked their money partly in anticipation that the Broadway run is but a preliminary phase of the potential profitable life of a musical through original cast recordings, perfor-

Tony Award ®. Photo courtesy of Tony Award Productions. Photo by Souders Studios.

mance licensing, national tours, perhaps even movie rights. Broadway producers with track records such as Harold Prince can raise money more easily than others. Some of them have a consortium of investors waiting to risk their money. The death of Broadway has been predicted since the 1930s, but this lively tradition refuses to attend its own funeral. Encouraged by the amount of money to be made by a hit, investors have been more willing to take risks.

Off-Broadway Theater

As rising costs began to reduce the number of shows mounted on Broadway, producers in the 1950s began to develop a theatrical movement that came to be known as **off-Broadway.** This movement away from New York's 10-block theater district centered on drama, particularly experimental theater. It had minimal impact on musical theater until 1967, when Joe Papp, noted producer of the New York Shakespeare Festival, purchased an about-to-be-demolished library and reopened it as the Public Theater. Dedicated to the production of new plays by American writers, the Public's first presentation was *Hair,* which became the first successful rock musical and moved to Broadway 6 months after its premiere. Going the same route some years later was *Two Gentlemen of Verona.* Unquestionably, the Public's most spectacular success came with *A Chorus Line,* which opened in 1975 and became one of Broadway's longest-running musicals ever. The income from *A Chorus Line* was undoubtedly the single most significant factor in keeping the New York Shakespeare Festival running. Because of the rising costs of musical theater production, even off-Broadway has become financially prohibitive for many small shows in New York City and elsewhere. For this reason, some shows are first presented in small theaters that are known as *off-off Broadway* productions.

School Productions

Concurrent with the off-Broadway movement, American universities began to increase their musical show production. Before a musical show can be performed at a school, the school must first get a license from the agent for the authors of that show. As described in Chapter 6, a specialized agent will license the right to present the show and will also rent the script and the musical parts. The agent traditionally gets 10% of the license fee. The other 90% of the license fee goes to the authors and their overall agent.

Regional Theater

Other regions of North America began developing indigenous theater at about the same time. At last, Broadway lost its monopoly on professional musical production. Regional theater includes amateur, semiprofessional, and fully professional productions. Actors, singers, and dancers now use university and regional theaters to learn their craft. These establishments help fill the void left by the death of vaudeville in the 1930s where, as the show business expression has it, a performer found "a place to be bad." Schools, colleges, and regional theaters now offer about the only training ground for aspiring professional singers, dancers, actors, and writers. They spawn many of the new television performers and some of the writers and producers.

Regional theaters find particularly strong public acceptance for plays, dances, and shows designed for children. Some children's theaters will break even at the box office. Regional theaters that focus on the classics or on experimental, noncommercial productions may receive financial support from the National Endowment for the Arts to help them stay alive and well. They also depend on grants and funding from private donors and foundations, as earned income through the sale of tickets is no longer sufficient for survival.

A particular kind of regional theater, dinner theaters, find that their biggest draws are productions of hit Broadway musicals. The public does not ever seem to tire of yet another production of *Camelot* or *Carousel.* Only very rarely do dinner theaters invest in the production of original musical plays. Many of these theaters cast leading roles with established performers, stars of lesser stature, or talented college students. But the kids get paid, and in this sense, dinner theaters can be considered part of the professional theater. These establishments rarely have a **proscenium** stage—they mount their productions in the round, use **blackouts** for curtains, employ a minimum number of dancers on their small stages, and make do with duo-piano accompaniment or a tiny pit band. Despite these limitations, some dinner theaters turn out attractive shows.

Summer Theater

Another component of musical theater is summer theater, so popular across the country. Cities with particularly successful summer theaters are Chicago, Kansas City, Houston, Sacramento, and Dallas. They mount proven Broadway musicals almost exclusively. Many of these productions are quite good. They usually hire name artists for the leads, support them with the best local talent (professional and semiprofessional singers-actors-dancers), and employ a full pit orchestra of AFM (American Federation of Musicians) musicians. Many summer theaters break even, perhaps even turn a profit, at the box office during their seasons, which may run from 2 to 6 weeks. Productions are mounted in old movie houses, community arts centers, parks, theaters, and even tents. These productions offer short-term professional employment, and some of their performing alumni go on to careers on Broadway, television, recording, and film.

National Tours

An important part of musical theater is touring shows. Most Broadway hit musicals develop at least one road company that begins touring just as soon as the investors believe the public has heard about its New York success. Major hits have more than one New York-mounted road company that not only prosper on tour but produce a lot of employment for singers, dancers, and musicians. Road companies generally tour with their own musical conductor, perhaps a percussionist, and one or two lead players, then fill in the pit orchestras with a dozen to three dozen local AFM members. The producer or musical director uses local AFM **contractors,** perhaps through the local promoter, to engage the pit musicians. These "casual" jobs provide considerable supplemental income for musicians across the country, many of whom are otherwise employed as music educators or as members of local symphony orchestras or **studio musicians.** There are "first-class tours" in so-called first-class cities, which are defined by tradition rather than other characteristics such as size of the city or **venue.** There are also so-called bus-and-truck tours that go into the smaller venues.

Classical and modern dance are a part of American musical theater. Resident and touring companies offer at least seasonal employment for dancers and the musicians who are engaged to accompany them. Many dance companies perform to recorded music, and the AFM has been unsuccessful in reducing this practice, which limits live employment of union musicians.

Las Vegas and Other Entertainment Centers

A significant part of musical theater in this country is found in Las Vegas and other entertainment centers such as Atlantic City and Branson, Missouri. The quality of the arrangers and players working in Las Vegas ranks with the best anywhere. A number of them were first drawn westward in search of work in Hollywood, then moved to Las Vegas and accepted steady employment there in preference to intermittent jobs in the Los Angeles area.

Revues have been gaining in popularity in Vegas, though headliners also continue to perform with their own music directors and nucleus of musicians, augmented by local instrumentalists.

Industrial Shows

Another component of American musical theater is the industrial show. When new products are introduced or national sales campaigns are being organized, companies such as Ford and IBM hire a producer or a production company to create commercial entertainment packages designed to motivate and instruct their sales staffs and to show appreciation to customers. These kinds of shows are not open to the public and are scheduled in major cities where the corporation might pull in its regional sales force. Industrial shows often have big budgets and offer seasonal employment for composers, arrangers, **copyists,** singers, dancers, and instrumentalists. Writers and producers of industrial shows are usually found among the group that also produces broadcast commercials. Several major cities have production companies set up to turn out the kind of shows major corporations want—Detroit, Chicago, Los Angeles, New York, and Philadelphia.

Amusement Parks and Cruise Ships

Many amusement parks around the country present musical stage revues, particularly during the peak summer and holiday seasons. These are usually original shows themed to each individual setting but can also feature Broadway or contemporary hit songs. Cruise ships also offer original musicals and abridged versions of Broadway shows.

THEATER ASSOCIATIONS

The League of Resident Theatres (LORT) is a multiemployer bargaining association representing individual, not-for-profit theaters. LORT represents member theaters in negotiation with three **collective bargaining** units: Actors' Equity Association, the Society of Stage Directors and Choreographers (SSDC), and the United Scenic Artists (USA). LORT members pay dues, which support the organization. Member benefits include centralized collective bargaining and legal advice.

Maury Yeston (right), Tony Award-winning composer/lyricist, directs Lehman Engel Musical Theatre Workshop. Photo courtesy of BMI Archives.

An organization that produces new works as well as the "standard" musicals both on and off Broadway is the Nederlander Producing Company of America, Inc. The Nederlander company, based in New York City, owns more than 35 theaters throughout the United States, as well as several theaters in London.

Also interested in the creation of new musicals is the National Alliance for Musical Theatre, an association of about 90 producing organizations that present theater on a cooperative basis. Any number of member companies pool their artistic and financial resources for one production of a show, rather than staging several separate productions of that same show.

PRODUCTION COMPONENTS

The Producer

For almost every theatrical production, everything begins and ends with one individual, the producer. Usually, all employment and all income is initially generated through the producer's imagination and money. In musical theater, the producer's work begins with acquisition of a *property*. Broadway's musicals are either original or based on an underlying property, such as a novel or dramatic play. The producer enters into an option agreement with the owner of the property (usually the playwright) providing that the producer will pay a nonreturnable advance against royalties to have the right for a period of time to develop and subsequently present the play. Sometimes, subsequent option periods are conditioned on certain additional requirements, such as the producer engaging a composer, a book writer, lyricist, or well-known director. If option conditions are met, the option period can be extended with the payment of additional money. The same concept is applied in the producer's contracts with the show's composer, lyricist, and book writer: The producer gets the exclusive right to create and present the show, which must happen during the option period(s) or the producer loses all such rights.

Producers are not always the only individuals seeking musical show properties. An influential director or aggressive agent can also put together a package, then seek out a producer to assume the overall responsibility of pulling the production together and mounting the show. Composers afflicted by the Broadway itch continually search various sources—novels, plays, even movies—for properties that they believe might form the basis for musical treatment. If they are successful in securing an option on a property, they then can take it to a producer. Sometimes the shows are put together by the authors without a producer. In that instance, a collaboration agreement is first entered into among the authors that spells out the parties' respective rights and obligations and contains options and elements similar to the ones in the agreement between the producer and the authors described earlier.

If the musical is heading for Broadway, the producer must negotiate contracts with the author of the book, the composer, and lyricist. The Dramatists Guild, Inc., has developed standards and procedures contained in the document known as the Approved Production Contract (APC). Its membership includes numerous playwrights and musical show book authors, composers, and lyricists active on Broadway.

Subsidiary Rights

The producer negotiates contracts with the show's book writer, composer, and lyricist that specify what these writers are to receive in advances, royalties, and credit and what the producer will receive from the author's exploitation of subsidiary rights. Once the show has completed its first run, the authors have the right to **exploit** the valuable subsidiary rights; the producer may receive a part of the income but has no control over the exploitation or disposition of these rights. Examples of subsidiary rights include movie rights, stock and amateur rights, touring rights to the extent that the producer doesn't exercise the producer's option with respect to them, and rights to do different productions and derivative works (e.g., the right to have a dramatic play turned into a musical). The book publishing rights of a play are usually retained by the book writer and not shared by the producer or the other authors. Separate rights to the music and lyrics are normally carved out by contract and retained only by the composer and lyricist and/or their music publisher.

Original Cast Album

The original cast album right is neither an author's subsidiary right nor exclusively a producer's right, but a hybrid right involving both. Generally, the producer negotiates for the right to make the cast album deal, providing certain conditions favorable to the author, such as a minimum royalty. Conditions might typically include an agreement about the division of recording company royalties that will be payable to the producer and to the author. An author might agree, for example, to allow the producer to make the cast album deal with a recording company if the recording company pays a royalty of 14% of the retail price of the album.

Option and Royalty Payments

The typical producer-writer contract provides for an option payment to be made during the period the show is being created, with an additional advance payment during rehearsals. With the APC, the author gets significant advances but the "royalty pool" concept also has been added, so after the advance payment, the author may not receive a significant amount of money beyond a guarantee in the early days of a show while the pool is in effect.

Approvals

These contracts also provide that when the show's director, cast, conductor, dance director, and designers for costumes, scenery, lighting, and sound are engaged, approval for these artists must first be obtained from the book writer, composer, and lyricist (such approval is either by unanimous or majority vote, depending on the arrangement made by the particular individuals involved). Furthermore, the producer cannot delete or add a song without the approval of the writers. The producer cannot make any changes at all to the authors' work without their approval, and the author involved owns all the changes. This is different from the movie industry, where the author has no ultimate control.

Costs

Concurrent with the effort to raise money for the show and sign the writers, the producer employs a general manager who prepares a preliminary budget and negotiates many of the creative contracts. One of the largest components of weekly running costs will be a combination of theater rental and labor-related expenses. Rent is generally a flat amount, but theater owners frequently negotiate a percentage of the adjusted gross box office receipts. There is no standard percentage amount on this profit sharing.

A producer schedules production time after estimating the date for opening on Broadway, then tries to locate a suitable theater that will be available. Most Broadway theaters are relatively small; the producer of a Broadway musical must locate a house that provides more than 1,000 seats in order to have sufficient capacity to generate adequate weekly box office income to be able to recoup the large costs of mounting and running a musical. Broadway theater owners know from long experience that the life expectancy of a new musical ranges from one performance to several years. They, too, must gamble with the show. A theater owner is reluctant to sign a rental agreement with any but a reliable producer and will be more willing to risk tying up the theater if the producer has a good track record, if the show's writers are well known, or if the cast includes a star. The rental agreement calls for the producer to reimburse the theater owner for all of the theater's operating expenses—fixed costs, such as utilities, heat, and air conditioning, and the salaries of ushers, box office staff, and other personnel—plus a rental fee that may be a percentage of the weekly gross box office receipts. All theater rental agreements have a "stop" clause that gives the theater owner and the producer the right to terminate, in the event that the show receipts fall below a certain negotiated amount. It is evident that a Broadway musical must do near-capacity business to stay alive.

The investor has a contract with the producer that says if there is any money left after the producer has paid the costs of mounting and running the show, the investors will next receive back all of the money that's left until they've recouped their investments. After recoupment has been achieved, the investors split the show's receipts, normally 50-50 with the producer, depending on the producer's share as outlined in the investment contract. The production company's receipts include the net receipts from the production company's presentation of the show and any portion of the subsidiary rights income to which the production company becomes entitled.

Typical weekly running costs of a full-line musical show will include most, possibly all, of the following:

1. Royalty payments of from 6% to 9% of the box office gross, divided among the author, composer, lyricist, director, choreographer, and designers, drawn from a *royalty pool.* The royalty pool is a complicated method of figuring that allocates a certain number of percentage points to each individual involved, with a minimum guarantee per point plus an allotment of the profits.

2. Salary (plus a possible weekly royalty) for the star.

3. Salaries for leading players (actors, singers, dancers).

4. Salaries for the stage manager and assistant stage manager.

5. Salaries (based on Actors' Equity scale) for supporting actors, dancers, singers.

6. AFM scale for the pit musicians and any musicians who might appear on stage.

7. Salaries for union stagehands, electricians (including audio technicians), carpenters, wardrobe personnel, hair and wig stylists, and other theater personnel, such as treasurers.

8. Office expense of the producer. The producer's "cash office charge" (usually between $750 and $1,500 per week) is provided in the agreement that defines the producer's rights in relation to the investors' rights. This agreement, although negotiable, often says that in addition to the cash office charge, the producer (who raised the money) will receive a producer's royalty each week equal to 1.5% to 2% of the gross weekly box office receipts before the investors get their money back and before the promoter-producer or the investors share net profits. The producer may also receive in-

come for providing electrical, sound, or other equipment for the production. There is usually a fee to the general manager of the show as well. This is normally a dollar amount, in the range of $750 to $1,500 a week, commencing a few weeks prior to rehearsals and ending a couple of weeks after the closing of the show. The general manager is the person who is knowledgeable about budgets and about how to negotiate an appropriate lease with the theater owner. A good general manager can be invaluable if the producer is good at raising money but doesn't know the nuts and bolts of producing.

9. Salaries for production assistants, retainers to public relations personnel, fees (or percentages) to theater party promoters who are part of the public relations efforts.

10. The rental payments under the theater lease.

Even if the show is a hit, the investors will not begin to get any of their investment returned until these weekly running costs are met, and the producer and investors will not receive any net profits until the investors' outlays have been returned. One of the reasons investors continue to put their money into this high-risk field is that income from subsidiary rights sometimes will not only help crack the production nut but will greatly exceed box office revenue.

Production of professional shows outside of New York is now extensive. Production overhead may include most of the salaries paid to persons connected with Broadway musicals, and in some cities, the rates are comparable to those in New York, particularly for stagehands and electricians. Some regional theaters and dinner theaters do not really "produce" musicals, they *reproduce* them, working only with proven material. Box office success is almost guaranteed when a theater announces a forthcoming production of, say, an *Oklahoma!* or a *Fiddler on the Roof.*

Regional theater producers often function in that gray area between the fully professional and the semiprofessional worlds. Actors' Equity regularly negotiates agreements with regional and community theaters that permit Equity members to perform in the same cast with non-Equity members. Regional producers often receive production money from city governments, light opera associations, and regional arts councils.

Producers of musical plays and operas are required to pay royalties to the copyright owners for performance of the show. When a producer licenses the rights to an existing show from the authors' agents, the producer has to negotiate for these **grand rights**. These kinds of performance licenses (see Chapter 6) are required for both amateur and professional productions.

If a song from a musical is performed separately (not as a part of the musical show), on radio, TV, or in live performance, the rights to nondramatic performance become part of the **small rights** that are licensed by the performing rights organizations, who collect a performance royalty from the music user and distribute that royalty to the composer, the lyricist, and the publisher of that song.

MUSIC PRODUCT MERCHANDISING

W ords such as *merchandising, marketing,* and *promotion* are not always used with precision in the music industry or, for that matter, in music business education. Some colleges call their music industry curricula "music merchandising" but offer a curriculum as broad as one named "music business studies," "music industry," or "music management." To add to the confusion, many people in the business limit their use of the term *music merchandising* to the licensing and vending of music souvenir items, such as posters and T-shirts.

Music product merchandising is a major part of the music business, bringing in over $5 billion annually in retail sales through music stores. In the United States, there are more than 60 million amateur instrumentalists, in addition to the professionals. These performers all need equipment and **accessories,** and it is the music products industry that sees to their needs.

For our purposes, the music products industry includes all musical hard goods and printed music. Musical hard goods include acoustic and electronic keyboard equipment, including home and church organs; wind, brass, percussion, and string instruments; and amplification and recording gear. The industry also includes the services needed for the customers to enjoy the products they purchase, such as repairs and lessons. This chapter takes a look at the retailing of these products (Chapter 18 covers merchandising of recorded music).

Effective merchandising takes close cooperation between the manufacturing, wholesaling, distributing, and retailing arms of the industry. These various branches provide jobs for many thousands of persons, many of them trained on the job. At the retail level, musicians often enter this field as a fall-back option to

← Photo courtesy of NAMM (International Music Products Association).

performing full-time but discover that music product merchandising becomes their number one choice for making their livings.

Tom Burzycki, President of the Selmer Music Company, has said, "To work in a music store, you have to feel that you're a part of it. You have to know the answers to any question which may arise about musical instruments and the music business."Retail music merchants are in an ever-changing field. They need to keep up with musical trends, new technology, and changing demographics of their potential customers, and they need to know how to work equally well with people who are 5 years old or 95 years old. They need to be able to speak knowledgeably about student- or professional-level instruments, provide information and service to schools, and understand the business trends of their communities. This business can be demanding—but rewarding.

SALES LEADERS

As shown in the following list, fretted products are the top leaders in sales (based on dollar volume), with the guitar proving once again to be the world's most popular instrument (source: *Music USA*, 1998).

1. Fretted products
2. Sound reinforcement products
3. Acoustic pianos
4. Wind instruments
5. Printed music
6. Single-unit amps
7. General accessories
8. Microphones
9. Percussion
10. **Multitrack** recording devices
11. Portable keyboards

Data on the music products industry do not include figures on the used-instrument market, which has been described as "extremely substantial but difficult to measure with even a semblance of accuracy."

Growth Areas. Sales of fretted products, particularly acoustic guitars, have been booming for years. Sales for sound reinforcement products, such as power amps, speaker enclosures, powered **mixers,** and mixing consoles, continue to improve, as does the electronic music market, aided by the development of the General MIDI standard—an industrywide standard of agreed-on features found on any instrument bearing the General MIDI logo.

Music Software and MIDI. MIDI stands for *musical instrument digital interface.* Developed in the early 1980s, MIDI is a protocol that allows different electronic musical instruments to communicate with each other. A simple patching job makes equipment **interface** easy and inexpensive. Several synthesizers can be played at once from a single keyboard, providing multitrack layers of sound. The principle behind the General MIDI is simply that any sequence produced should sound the same no matter what General MIDI instrument is used.

With prices continuing to drop for this equipment while quality goes up, bands and individuals are now able to produce their own good-quality demos. It's a boon for music retailers, not to mention the increased opportunities for creative musicians, amateur and pro, to let their imaginations roam. Electronic musical products are being used as part of multimedia productions in creative integration of musical instrument, pictures, and other sound.

DISTRIBUTION

Distribution begins after the product is manufactured. Most instruments are wholesaled directly to retailers; accessories typically go through independent jobbers, who then distribute to retailers.

Music Retailers

In big cities across the country, supermarkets for music are appearing, the "big box operations" of Mars, Sam Ash, and Guitar Center—the music equivalent of Wal-Mart and Borders. But most retailers still strive to offer knowledgeable, personal service to their customers. Music stores come in many varieties, from full-line stores handling all of the products to specialized stores handling only one area, as well as stores offering combinations that best reflect the needs of their

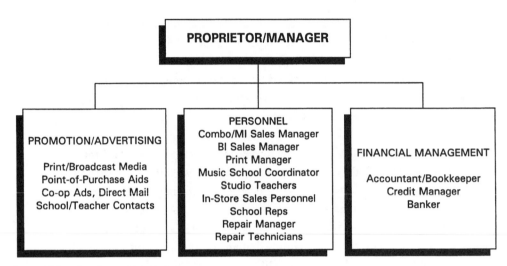

Figure 12.1   The General Music Store

communities or the knowledge and preferences of the store owners. Whatever the size and focus of the store, it's critical for merchants to provide good service and customer support. Generally, service is the key, not price. (For an understanding of the value of good service in any retail business, check out Spector and McCarthy's *The Nordstrom Way,* John Wiley, 1995.) Take a look at Figure 12.1 for an overview of the personnel involved in a general music store.

INSTRUMENTS AND EQUIPMENT

Combo (Guitar, Drum) Stores

In a full-line store, the *musical instruments* (MI) division deals with drums, guitars, amplifiers, speaker systems, audio mixing panels, public address systems, and lighting equipment—and the **accessory** items that go with them all, such as microphones and stands, cabling, drumsticks, snares, and the like. Recording equipment can also be found in this group, and it has become very saleable, with the vast improvement in technology, the significant drop in price, and the advent of the home recording studio.

Stand-alone stores vending percussion equipment are almost invariably operated by musicians who have had performance experience. The proprietor has firsthand knowledge of the kinds of equipment drummers need and can also help with maintenance. As will be mentioned later about music retailers in general, percussion merchants usually offer lessons on the premises to amateurs and beginning professionals. And sometimes, it's the best place in town to hear word of auditions and potential jobs.

Keyboards

A well-rounded keyboard department or store will offer a full line of vertical and grand **acoustic** pianos, to accommodate the full gamut of musicians, from the professional who needs a 9-foot concert grand to the student first learning to play. This store will also make vertical, student-grade pianos available through

Photo courtesy of NAMM (International Music Products Association).

rent-to-own arrangements. Some keyboard retailers have found a lucrative market in long-term piano rentals to people who have no intention of buying, an innovation in piano operations that has special appeal for commercial **venues**,
such as hotel lobbies and cocktail lounges.

The newest entry into this marketplace is the electronic keyboard, which
comes in a range of models from grand piano configuration to small, easily portable instruments. They offer a wide variety of sound combinations to the player.

The development of the electronic organ has made it possible for the music
merchant to be the major player in the church organ market. Pipe organs have
priced themselves out of all but a small market, and they are fragile, vulnerable to
many ills, and take constant maintenance. The Allen & Rogers instruments have
become very acceptable instruments for serious concert and church performances. In much of the United States, the potential for church organ sales to new
or renovated churches within a 100-mile radius of a keyboard store is estimated
to be in the hundreds of thousands of dollars.

Home organs were thought to be a dead market for many years, after a first
lively period in the 1950s and 1960s, but this market has gotten healthy again, the
best buyers being the elderly. Stores offering these instruments offer free lessons
for life and lifetime warranties for the instruments, which has resulted in many
customers upgrading their organs several times in a period of a few years.

Competent repair service and technicians are a must in supporting keyboard
sales. Acoustic pianos must be kept in tune. Electronic church organs must be
ready for church services; to meet this need, some stores ensure repair within 12
hours of a problem turning up.

Band and Orchestra Instruments

The market for band and orchestra instruments and equipment is made up of
three groups of customers, the smallest being the professional musicians. The
next largest group includes the amateurs, the individual music hobbyists—children and adults. The largest part—at least 75%—involves schools and colleges,
which host some 100,000 school ensembles. These ensembles have an aggregate
membership of several million young musicians (it has been estimated that 1 in
10 elementary school students joins a school band or orchestra). Their instruments, equipment, and music are acquired by individual musicians' families and
by the schools themselves. We'll look at this segment of the market more closely.

In a full-line store, the section selling band and orchestra instruments is referred to in the industry as BI. The literal translation is *band instruments*, but it includes orchestral strings, too. The success of BI merchants depends on developing strong and loyal business relationships with the school band and orchestra directors in the area.

Flutes, clarinets, trumpets, alto and tenor saxes, trombones, and violins and violas are instruments normally purchased or rented by students and families, often through rent-to-own (or lease-to-own) options where the rent or lease money can be used toward purchase, in whole or part. BI merchants sometimes build up very large rental businesses. It's important for them to keep an eye on the balance of rentals and sales, however, to maintain both a decent cash flow and the confidence of bankers.

Many BI instruments are manufactured in three levels of quality and price that roughly correspond to the three groups of purchasers: student-beginner level, step-up or midlevel, and professional. The least expensive models are recommended to beginners and parents, since it's uncertain whether the youngsters will continue their musical activities. These instruments are ruggedly constructed, provide acceptable intonation, and are the type normally used for rentals. Some firms manufacture instruments and equipment "privately labeled," as well as their own name brands. A typical example would be a "Sears" clarinet actually manufactured by C. G. Conn Ltd., now owned by UMI (United Musical Instruments).

The harmony instruments (tuba, string bass, cello, baritone sax, French horn, euphonium, English horn, bassoon, the lower-voiced clarinets, and often, oboe and piccolo), along with the entire percussion section, are owned by the schools.

Service to school accounts must be a high priority for this market and should include frequent, regular visits to the schools by a store rep. The rep picks up and returns instruments for repair and should carry along a good stock of accessory items, such as reeds, mouthpieces, **ligatures,** and valve grease. As in the keyboard and MI areas, competent repair service for all customers, school based or otherwise, is critical. Free repair loaners should be available. And anyone working in this end of the business must know instrument nomenclature, such as "undercut tone holes," "diaphragmatic sound boards," and "draw knob combination preset action," for instance.

As students make progress, some will trade in their beginning instruments for middle-grade or professional ones. The top level of merchandise is made up of the first-line instruments required by the professionals. This equipment costs at least twice as much as the economy student models. Instruments of this quality are often sold in specialty shops run by owner-operators who are expert craftsmen.

Music School

It's smart, and sometimes critical, for a retail music store to give lessons to help their customers enjoy their instruments. For pianos and organs, it's usual for 6 months of lessons to be included in a rent-to-own contract. Along with teaching the customers to enjoy their purchases, the music school generates traffic inside the store, a vital ingredient for any retail store to keep its doors open. While customers are waiting for their lessons, they often spot other items they want to buy, especially if the store has a good musical boutique offering things like pencils and sweatshirts.

Consumer Audio Equipment

There are three levels of audio equipment: professional, semiprofessional, and for home use. Most sound systems purchased for the home are sold through audio specialty stores, because they can show the great variety of products on the **market**. Local department stores have a small share of this market but usually for low-end products, not state-of-the-art equipment.

Increasingly sophisticated technology continues to generate improvements in all kinds of audio recording/reproducing equipment, including miniaturization of amplifiers and speaker systems. Fortunately for the stereo merchants, audiophiles never seem quite satisfied with last year's equipment. As ever-new components appear on the market, consumers step up to spend their money.

Price cutting among audio hardware merchants is endemic, even epidemic. Big chains periodically cut their prices in apparent attempts to wipe out smaller competitors. Sometimes they succeed. The mass buying available to chain stores makes a retail pricing policy possible that the mom-and-pop stores cannot match.

Stereo stores rarely sell professional audio equipment, the kind required for theaters and arenas. Professional systems of this kind are sold, installed, and serviced by *sound companies* specializing in this kind of business.

Print Music

Two types of retail outlets generally sell **print**. One is the music store that concentrates on instrument sales, and stocks print as a service to their customers. A full-line store will stock pop folios, piano music to support serious piano study, and pedagogical vocal music, such as the Schirmer Library editions. This kind of retailer usually doesn't delve into the school and church music market.

The second type is the **institutional print** dealer. Institutional print is music used by schools and churches, for bands, **choruses** and choirs, and orchestras. The leaders in this field are Wingert-Jones in Kansas City, Missouri, and J.W. Pepper in Valley Forge, Pennsylvania. J.W. Pepper has satellite stores throughout the United States. The great majority of institutional print—85% to 90%—is sold by phone, mail, or computer. The two leaders have taken very different approaches to providing service to their customers, and both are effective. Merrill Jones, founder of Wingert-Jones, often said that the "print music business is the Woolworth's of the music [products] business." The profit margins are comparable to other parts of the industry, but it takes a lot more $25 and $50 sales to net the kind of profit generated by the sale of one Steinway piano.

The biggest challenge for the institutional print retailer is how to make the buyers aware of new music. This is done in a number of ways: new-materials reading sessions, arranged through retail stores; direct-mail efforts of recordings of new material; descriptions in retail catalogs; and through people talking to people.

What to buy, when to buy it, and how many copies to stock is a challenge to any print retailer. At best, it can only be an educated guess, but it better be a well-educated one; the publisher won't want the product back, and there's nothing as dull as last year's top seller, whether it be a pop music folio or institutional print.

Again, service is the key to operating a successful print business. Some stores pride themselves by claiming that if an order is received by noon, it will be shipped by 3:00 p.m. the same day. If the item is not in stock and it's a real emergency, the retailer will call the publisher and have the product drop-shipped directly to the customer. Most print music retailers have a "memo-bill" system in place to let customers receive the music they need immediately, without having to wait the 30 to 60 days needed for the purchase order system to grind along.

Pricing. Some merchants who are primarily instrument retailers or full-line store operators have adopted a policy that print is a necessary evil for them to service their customers. They offer discounted prices and operate the print music division on a break-even basis. This is financially dangerous. All retailers are entitled to a good gross profit from every sale. The entire concept of discounting comes down to simple arithmetic. If a piece of print bought for $5 wholesale is priced at $10, and 20% discount is taken off, there's a gross profit of $3—not a good margin unless volume is huge.

Books, Magazines, and Trade Journals

Music Books. The biggest market for books on music is in the elementary education field. Huge quantities are sold to schools every year, and some publishers specialize in just this one field. Perhaps the next biggest sellers are the popular accounts of the life and times of rock stars. The next largest market share is in music appreciation and music theory books. Jazz history books also sell well. The increase in record industry technology courses has generated a sizable market for textbooks in that field. Another popular type targets the amateur songwriter. Interest in textbooks in the music business is also growing. There are also certain scholarly books on music, of interest to musicologists and college students working on graduate degrees. W. W. Norton is the leading publisher in this field.

The merchandising of these products covers a broad range of outlets. Textbooks are naturally marketed through the bookstores of colleges offering pertinent courses. Some instrument stores carry books that might be interesting to their customers (e.g., some drum shops carry biographies of famous drummers and histories of particular kinds of drums). Bookstores market the more general-interest titles if their communities respond, and the Internet provides access to practically any title, no matter how esoteric.

Music Magazines and Trade Journals. The publication and sale of music-related magazines and trade journals are important facets of the music business. Musicians who write well can often find employment in this field as reporters, reviewers, or critics.

There are two basic categories of music magazines: popular and professional. *Music Trades* and *Music, Inc.* are the two primary journals for music product sellers. The *Instrumentalist* is another big one. Trade journals are generally merchandised by direct mail to businesses and through trade shows.

Billboard and *Radio and Records* are the two major recording industry publications. *Billboard* calls itself "the international newsweekly of music and home entertainment." It is almost required reading for professionals. *Billboard's* charts, although often criticized, have great influence in the record and broadcast industries. *Radio and Records's* **airplay charts** are followed avidly by most radio programmers and recording industry people. A trade magazine of lesser influence and circulation is *Cash Box,* which began its career focusing, as its title suggests, on the jukebox industry.

Several magazines focus on recording technology; they attract a professional readership of audio technicians and record producers as well as persons aspiring to careers in these fields. The most widely read publication of this kind is *Mix* magazine. Certain publications, overlapping fields, might be classified among the trades: *Broadcasting & Cable, Amusement Business, Advertising Age,* and many others. These magazines are most generally available through individual subscriptions and in a few record stores on the two coasts.

Outside the professional trades are the "popular" music magazines. Their goal is broad circulation. Probably the best known are *Rolling Stone, Spin,* and *Down Beat. Musician,* owned by the publisher of *Billboard,* attracts a sizable following of serious fans, as well as amateur and professional songwriters and performers. Hard rock/heavy metal publications such as *Circus* and *Hit Parader* target young males, many of whom play guitar, drums, or keyboards. These magazines are available by subscription and also through well-stocked news and magazine vendors.

Established professional musicians receive *International Musician* each month if they are members of the American Federation of Musicians (AFM). Members of the International Association of Jazz Educators (IAJE) receive copies of the *Jazz Educators Journal* with their membership. Arts administrators value the American Symphony Orchestra League's *Symphony* magazine. Another publication, *Campus Activities Programming,* is the journal for college concert promoters and talent agents. Two scholarly music journals should be mentioned: *Notes,* read by music librarians, and the *Journal of the American Musicological Society.*

As is true for publishing in general, these products are each merchandised by their publishers and targeted to reach their intended readers as directly as possible. For a more complete listing of the leading music magazines, see Selected Readings at the end of this book.

PROMOTION

The proprietor who has invested money in a music store is not really alone financially. The investment is backed up by the far larger resources of manufacturers of the lines sold. Manufacturers invest huge sums every year, not only in production but also in sales promotion and advertising. They know that their prosperity, their very survival, is dependent on their retailers. Musical instrument and accessory manufacturers do all they can to presell the retail customer. They try to implant their brand name in the customer's mind before shopping begins. Many customers are presold through national advertising campaigns shouting the merits of particular products.

One sales promotion device is the *cooperative ad:* The manufacturer and the merchant share the cost. Another cooperative effort develops when the manufacturer supplies point-of-sale items for the merchant to display, such as signs, banners, streamers, show cards, special display racks, and window dressings. Some stores festoon their premises with these point-of-sale stimuli.

Local instrument merchants supplement national promotions with their own advertising. Well-established retailers set annual ad budgets. Larger advertisers often employ advertising agencies to write and place ads; small stores will advertise when they can find the working capital. Merchants had best study advertising, if only to learn if their money is being wisely spent.

Since school and college musical directors are among the biggest buyers of background instruments and equipment, manufacturers display these wares at professional educators' meetings and conventions. Manufacturers often employ well-known performers as goodwill ambassadors to attend conventions and music clinics, representing themselves as users of the firm's instruments, as is sometimes true. Some firms supply the services of these professionals to schools for benefit concerts with school bands or orchestras, further developing goodwill for the firm and its products.

Blending distribution and promotion, acoustic and electronic piano manufacturers have linked up with retailers to offer instrument loaner programs for colleges and universities. The retailer buys the instruments, loans them to the school (usually for the school year), offers them at sale prices at the end of the year, and then pays the manufacturer for them. In this kind of creative alliance, everyone benefits: The school has enough instruments for its students, the students have good instruments to learn and practice on, and the manufacturer and retailer have good opportunities to sell the instruments.

Music store sales promotion is often most effective through direct contact with potential customers. Retailers seeking sales to schools regularly dispatch field salespersons to call on educators. In smaller communities, it is the store owner who gets out and around the county drumming up business with schools and colleges. The objective is not only to sell to the schools but to create awareness among students that a particular store handles good merchandise and treats customers well.

Even more direct contact with potential customers occurs on the floor of the store when a family walks into the shop. The youngster of the family may have dropped in to get something repaired and left with a new Selmer alto sax. Many large sales develop through a store's offering music accessories, including instrument cases and equipment designed to enhance the performance of the musical instrument. Accessories offer high markup, draw a variety of customers into the store, and then cause them to return, since most accessories are expendable and need replacement.

Although some merchants cater to young musicians and schools, most retailers also seek the business of professional musicians. They not only buy the higher-priced professional instruments and equipment, but they can be an effective sales force for the store—nearly all professionals, even semiprofessionals, have pupils who need recommendations on where to shop. Professionals who frequent music stores also use them for communication centers ("I need a drummer for Saturday night. Know anyone who can do the **gig**?"; "John Doe's rehearsal band is meeting Tuesday night this week. Will you help pass the word?").

TRADE ASSOCIATIONS

The music retail business has a number of trade associations that are active, vital, and dedicated to members of the industry. Among these associations are the International Music Products Association (formerly the National Association of Music Merchants and still known by its original acronym, NAMM), the National Association of Band Instrument Merchandisers (NABIM), and the Guitar & Accessories Marketing Association (GAMA).

The most representative trade association for people selling instruments, equipment, and accessories is NAMM. It is composed worldwide of more than 6,000 music retailers, manufacturers and their representatives, wholesalers, and distributors. NAMM helps its members increase their business by providing

NAMM International Music Market. Photo courtesy of NAMM
(International Music Products Association).

training programs, supporting private and public music education, and by generally promoting the benefits of music making.

The NAMM trade shows, held twice yearly, showcase music instruments, professional audio equipment, and the latest in music electronics and software. NAMM provides educational sessions, sales and management seminars, industry publications, and market research studies to its members. NAMM's annual statistical review of the music products industry, *Music USA*, is the most comprehensive summary available of market sales and trends in the musical instrument field.

Though not exactly a trade association, NAMM'S education arm, NAMBI, is another organization worth mentioning. Its goal is to encourage college students to consider music merchandising as a career choice.

American Music Conference is another important organization closely allied to the trade. It's a national, nonprofit educational association that promotes the benefits of music, music making, and music education to the general public. One of its undertakings is the dissemination of information about ongoing research, gathered by the University of California at Irvine, on the relationship between music training and mental development.

FINANCIAL MANAGEMENT

As with many kinds of businesses, music stores can find financial management to be more critical than sales development. Large numbers of merchants enter the field with inadequate backgrounds in money management and accounting. Frequently, a merchant will appear to be doing good business but may in fact be losing money and not even know it. The financial record keeping was inadequate—or the entrepreneur had the information but did not know how to interpret it. This is probably the number one reason so many businesses fail.

Stores, large and small, have cash registers that double as computer input terminals. The salesperson punches up the transaction, and all the merchant's record keeping is recorded instantaneously—daily journal, ledger, and inventory. This information is vital in planning future purchases, as well as in controlling the finances of the business.

The small merchant, new to the game, may tend to mix personal finances with those of the business. This is unacceptable to auditors and tax collectors. The store requires its own separate bank account and accounting procedures, including a separate checkbook. All receipts should be recorded and deposited daily. All stores employing two or more persons are required to maintain complete payroll records. Forms appropriate for this are available in stationery stores, although an outside payroll service is often preferred.

Just as critical to complete record keeping are the merchant's balance sheets and P/L (profit and loss) statements. The balance sheet shows the financial condition of the store at a given time, usually at the close of business on the last day of each month and the last day of each year. It lists the assets and liabilities of the business and the *owner's equity* (sometimes called *proprietorship*).

A P/L statement summarizes the store's operation over a given period and shows how much profit or loss resulted. It shows how much merchandise was purchased and sold, the cost of the goods sold, the gross margin, various types of expense, any income other than that from sales, and the profit or loss for the period. Merchants do not need to be CPAs, but they do need to know how to interpret P/L statements, for they tell the proprietor whether the business is currently making money.

One of the most critical issues facing a music store—or any retailer—is inventory turnover. A merchant must know how fast the inventory is moving. Few expenses can be more costly than wasting floor space on dormant stock. Inventory turnover is a clear indicator of merchandising efficiency: The faster the turnover, the less capital is required in proportion to sales. Less money must be borrowed, and new merchandise can be acquired and sold more quickly.

For further information on financial management, contact NAMM regarding its "Cost of Doing Business" survey.

There are more entry-level job opportunities in retailing music products than in any other part of the industry, especially if people are willing to travel to the places where the jobs are waiting. Through NAMM and its education affiliate NAMBI, formal music business curricula have been developed at the college and university level to train young people for careers in the music products industry. The industry has often found that a fine musician who knows nothing about business is often not successful as a music merchant, just like the businessperson who knows nothing about music.

In stores of all sizes, successful music merchants are visible in their communities. They had best be on good terms not only with their bankers but also with other individuals and institutions in their area who help make the community a better place to live. The motivation may be altruistic—the result could mean good business.

See the Starting Your Own Business section in Chapter 25 ("Career Options") for more information.

13 ARTS ADMINISTRATION

THE SERIOUS MUSIC MARKET

It is difficult to set forth precise definitions for such general terms as popular, classical, **art music,** and serious music. The confusion prevailed long before the 1924 premiere of George Gershwin's symphonic jazz composition *Rhapsody in Blue,* and disputes about the correct way to classify music will continue. But to provide a framework for this chapter, the terms *serious music, classical music,* and *art music* are used interchangeably and include the repertoire generally associated with the symphony orchestra, opera, ballet, recital, modern dance, choral music, chamber music, and church music.

Even though the pop field gets most of the publicity, a great many people are involved in the serious music field, and its production and consumption are big business.

The production and purveyance of serious music has traditionally been separate from pop. Though the artists and administrators often come from different backgrounds and pursue different goals, they are, more often than not, engaged in very similar kinds of work. "Crossing the line"is an everyday occurrence. Individuals qualified to function in the world of "art music" often end up in "commercial music"; some who start their careers in one of the pop fields may find themselves working for a symphony orchestra or perhaps in church music.

It is customary to distinguish between pop and serious music by describing the former as commercial or profit oriented and the latter as nonprofit, since the large performing groups, such as orchestras, ballet companies, and the like, are legally formed as not-for-profit organizations. But here, profit and nonprofit intersect, because many individuals in the serious music business make a very fine living from performing or producing serious music; for example, it isn't unusual

← © Eric Kamp/Phototake/PNI.

for starting wages for symphony orchestra musicians to be in the neighborhood of $80,000 per annum. To keep things simple, this chapter uses the customary terms *nonprofit* or *not-for-profit* in discussing arts administration.

PERSPECTIVE

The quarter century from the early 1960s to the mid-1980s saw an unprecedented growth in the arts in America. The number of professional symphony orchestras and opera or music theater companies nearly doubled in the 1960s, and in the 15 years preceding 1985, ballet and modern dance companies burgeoned from 30 to more than 150. In those 15 years, there was also a dramatic increase in arts performances, employment of artists and arts administrators, and attendance at arts events.

But that encouraging picture was changing by the end of the 1980s, though performing arts organizations had continued to proliferate—there were nearly 300 opera companies, many of which had high operating budgets, as well as 98 more middle-level symphony orchestras than two decades earlier. In the early 1990s, a number of orchestras experienced severe financial problems, some to the point of canceling seasons or declaring bankruptcy. These travails were largely due to fund-raising difficulties—caused in part by government and foundation cutbacks—and a new toughness in contract negotiations between orchestra musicians and management.

Arts organizations, especially orchestras, began aggressive marketing campaigns to increase audiences. Their major targets have been the **baby boomers,** perceived to have larger discretionary incomes than other segments of the population. Marketing techniques have included more emphasis on contemporary programming, special-interest concert and opera events, informal preconcert lectures, and performances incorporating film and other visual and electronic media. The now-common use of English supertitles for operas has made that art form more accessible to audiences of all ages. Programs undertaken by local symphony and chamber orchestras, such as active outreach to schools and instrument classes offered by orchestra musicians under the aegis of the orchestra, have made the organizations more visible in their communities, building broader bases of support.

The exposure afforded by increased television viewing of the arts, particularly through the Public Broadcasting Service (PBS) and the Corporation for Public Broadcasting (CPB), has fueled the growth of interest in the symphony, opera, and dance. There have been sponsored weekly radio broadcasts of the Metropolitan Opera for decades, as well as of symphony orchestras (San Francisco, Seattle, Los Angeles, Chicago, among others). Telecasts of the Boston Pops and Boston Symphony have drawn audiences of millions. Imaginative producers such as Emmy Award winner Allan Miller have found ways to make symphonic music look interesting on film and TV. Cable, too, has gotten into the act, with such channels as Arts & Entertainment, Bravo, and the Arts Channel.

This widely expanded exposure of serious music via radio and television has increased the sale of recorded symphonic, opera, and ballet music. Royalties from sales constitute a significant segment of the annual incomes of major orchestras, such as Cleveland, Boston, New York, Chicago, and Los Angeles. The once-familiar claim that recording companies must continue to record only European orchestras to make a profit is not necessarily true. The skill of American orchestras often makes possible the completion of master takes in less time than with many European orchestras. Thus, companies can still meet the much higher union rates in the United States.

Some serious music recordings, particularly the repertoire called *contemporary serious music,* often have difficulty making a profit. An important group of recordings of this repertoire is found on the CRI (Composers Recordings Inc.) label. CRI limits its releases exclusively to contemporary serious music. A nonprofit corporation, CRI sells its recordings by direct mail, distributes to retail accounts, and through its subscription program, sells to university and municipal libraries across the United States.

Innovative marketing methods have greatly expanded the sale of classical music. For example, the Metropolitan Opera Guild now uses a direct mail approach that offers opera videos, recordings on the Met's label, books, and opera-related gifts through its catalog, the *Metropolitan Opera Companion.*

In the past, classical music recordings have not generally been big sellers. In the 1960s, Stravinsky complained that sales of records of works he had written after 1920 rarely exceeded 5,000 copies. These pieces—even by the world-famous composer—lost money. But in 1977, when RCA released a record of Stravinsky's *Firebird* ballet suite (premiered in 1910), the label was able to sell 100,000 copies. Sales of serious music at this level were unheard of until the 1970s, when RCA and many other labels learned how to promote and package releases appealing to buyers who formerly limited their purchases to pop music. The **crossover recording** in the classical field now reaches expanded markets worldwide, as evidenced by the phenomenal success of *Chant* in the mid-1990s, a recording of traditional Gregorian chant brilliantly marketed to the pop audience. As pointed out in coverage of the recording industry, one of the strongest markets for crossover records is with movie music; sound track music appeals to both classical and pop music fans here and abroad.

REPRESENTATIVE ORGANIZATIONS

The world of serious music and arts administration includes a number of important organizations that represent the special interests of professionals in the field (see Chapter 7 on the unions and **guilds** representing artists in the classical field). A number of other important organizations—not necessarily "guilds," despite some of their names—are listed below.

Organists—including students, professional organists, choir directors, teachers, organ builders, technicians, suppliers, amateur musicians, and dedicated supporters—are represented by the American Guild of Organists. The special interests of composers in the classical field have been served, since 1937, by the American Composers Alliance (ACA). Its American Composers Edition serves as a music publisher for its members, making scores and parts available through loans, rentals, and sales. One of ACA's member services is registering works with BMI. For many years, American composers have been active in the U.S. Section of the International Society for Contemporary Music (ISCM), founded in 1922 and formerly called the League of Composers. Founded by Aaron Copland and other distinguished American composers, this group has fostered public acceptance of contemporary serious music by offering concerts, goodwill, and publicity. The ISCM is active in 30 countries and sponsors annual World Music Days.

Another organization devoted to the promotion of contemporary music is the American Music Center, which provides composers and performers with assistance and information on career development, funding, performance and study opportunities, and numerous other concerns. It maintains a library of scores and recordings available for circulation worldwide and sponsors an American Music Week each year. The center pioneered one of the first music sites on the World Wide Web in the early 1990s.

The professional organization most representative of opera is Opera America. It assists opera companies with various informational, technical, educational, and administrative resources and, through its Next Stage program, has assisted with the production of underperformed American operas. It also offers a Fellowship Program in opera administration. Professional music critics have formed the Music Critics' Association of North America, which includes a large number of major critics in its membership. The organization Americans for the Arts (formerly Associated Councils for the Arts and the American Council for the Arts) forms a useful clearinghouse for information and ideas relating to state and regional arts council activities. The country's only national, all-arts advocacy organization, Americans for the Arts, publishes useful pamphlets and books on arts administration.

Arts administrators have organized the Association of Performing Arts Presenters (formerly Association of College, University and Community Arts Administrators). Educators in that field are represented by the Association of Arts Administration Educators.

An umbrella organization of broad scope is the National Music Council (NMC), chartered by Congress in 1956 to serve the interests of commercial and noncommercial music associations throughout the United States. It has some 50 member organizations that represent, in turn, an aggregate membership of some 1.5 million members. A partial list of its member organizations indicates the scope of NMC: AFM, AGMA, AMC, ASCAP, ASOL, BMI, CMA, IAJE, IAWM, MEIEA, MENC, MPA, NMPA, RIAA, and SESAC. The National Music Council has been designated the official U.S. representative to the International Music Council, a UNESCO-sponsored organization of national and international music committees. It holds a biennial general assembly and World Congress to discuss issues of musical importance. It began International Music Days, and it initiates a multitude of projects, including research into new media and technologies.

SYMPHONIC MUSIC

American Symphony Orchestra League

In the field of serious music, the largest audience is for symphonic music. About 1,800 symphony orchestras are found in the United States. Nearly half of these are banded together in the American Symphony Orchestra League (ASOL).

Founded in 1942 and chartered by Congress in 1962, ASOL is the national nonprofit service and educational organization dedicated to strengthening symphony and chamber orchestras. ASOL's annual conventions draw enthusiastic delegates from all over the country. Its strong professional staff provides artistic, organizational, and financial leadership and service to the music directors, musicians, direct service and governance volunteers, managers, and staff who make up its member orchestras. Its work is made possible by grants from private and public institutions, contributions from individuals, and from members' dues; for member orchestras, these are scaled according to the size of the orchestra's annual budget. ASOL is research oriented and serves as a data gathering and distribution agency for its members, who are interested in arts administration, audience building, and fund-raising.

One of the most useful services provided by ASOL is educational. Each year, the league staffs and sponsors regional workshops. Professional managers, symphony board members, conductors, and volunteer workers attend these meetings to learn from experts how to function more effectively in their own communities. ASOL devotes attention to the needs of orchestra conductors and trustees. It offers annual workshops and symposia with leading conductors. Its Resource Center provides updated literature on governance. ASOL also sponsors orchestra management seminars where current and aspiring orchestra managers attend classes for several days of intensive study on how to run a professional symphony orchestra. One of the most significant programs for people interested in this field is the Orchestra Management Fellowship Program, which offers opportunities for prospective orchestra managers to serve for a year in three residencies with professional orchestras of different budget sizes, as well as exposure to community orchestras and the for-profit music industry. ASOL receives partial support of its educational activities from the National Endowment for the Arts.

ASOL offers an Employment Search and Referral Service to help match conductors and administrators with orchestras; its Professional Affiliates receive regular announcements, either by mail or e-mail, listing available positions at symphony orchestras and other music and arts organizations. The league's magazine, *Symphony*, provides information to professionals and amateurs interested in the life and times of symphony orchestras and the music they perform.

One of the important components of ASOL is its Volunteer Council. The Volunteer Council publishes *The Gold Book* each year, a collection of information on how volunteers can raise money, sell tickets, and organize educational and community projects.

Salary Arrangements

The most highly budgeted orchestras—generally, those with annual budgets greater than $1 million—provide their 75 to 110 contract musicians with their primary source of income. Among these orchestras are those in New York,

Worcester Symphony Orchestra, Mechanic's Hall, Worcester, MA. © Richard Pasley/Stock, Boston/PNI. ➔

TABLE 13.1   Symphony Orchestras With Budgets Greater Than $1 Million

American Symphony Orchestra League
1998-1999 Member Orchestras

Alabama
  Alabama Symphony Orchestra
  Huntsville Symphony Orchestra
Arizona
  Phoenix Symphony Orchestra
  Tucson Symphony Orchestra
Arkansas
  Arkansas Symphony Orchestra
California
  California Symphony
  Fresno Philharmonic Orchestra
  Long Beach Symphony Orchestra
  Los Angeles Chamber Orchestra
  Los Angeles Philharmonic
  Monterey Symphony
  New West Symphony
  Pacific Symphony Orchestra
  Pasadena Symphony Orchestra
  Philharmonia Baroque Orchestra
  San Francisco Symphony
  San Jose Symphony
  Santa Barbara Symphony Orchestra
  Santa Rosa Symphony
Colorado
  Boulder Philharmonic Orchestra
  Colorado Music Festival
  Colorado Springs Symphony
  Colorado Symphony
Connecticut
  Hartford Symphony Orchestra
  New Haven Symphony Orchestra
  Stamford Symphony Orchestra
Delaware
  Delaware Symphony Orchestra
District of Columbia
  National Symphony Orchestra
  Washington Chamber Symphony
Florida
  Florida Orchestra
  Florida Philharmonic Orchestra
  Florida Symphonic Pops (Boca Pops)

  Florida West Coast Symphony Orchestra
  Jacksonville Symphony Orchestra
  The Naples Philharmonic
  New World Symphony
  Palm Beach Pops
Georgia
  Atlanta Symphony Orchestra
  Savannah Symphony
Hawaii
  Honolulu Symphony Society
Illinois
  Chicago Sinfonietta
  Chicago Symphony Orchestra
  Elgin Symphony Orchestra
  Grant Park Symphony Orchestra
  Lake Forest Symphony
  Music of the Baroque
Indiana
  Evansville Philharmonic Orchestra
  Fort Wayne Philharmonic
  Indianapolis Symphony Orchestra
  South Bend Symphony Orchestra
Iowa
  Cedar Rapids Symphony Orchestra
  Des Moines Symphony Orchestra
  Quad City Symphony Orchestra
Kansas
  Wichita Symphony Orchestra
Kentucky
  The Louisville Orchestra
Louisiana
  Baton Rouge Symphony
  Louisiana Philharmonic Orchestra
  Shreveport Symphony Orchestra
Maine
  Portland Symphony Orchestra
Maryland
  Baltimore Symphony Orchestra
Massachusetts
  Boston Symphony Orchestra
  Springfield Symphony Orchestra

Michigan
  Grand Rapids Symphony
  Kalamazoo Symphony Orchestra
Minnesota
  Duluth-Superior Symphony Orchestra
  The Minnesota Orchestra
  Saint Paul Chamber Orchestra
Mississippi
  Mississippi Symphony Orchestra
Missouri
  Kansas City Symphony
  Saint Louis Symphony Orchestra
Nebraska
  Omaha Symphony
New Jersey
  New Jersey Symphony Orchestra
New Mexico
  New Mexico Symphony Orchestra
New York
  American Composers Orchestra
  American Symphony Orchestra
  Brooklyn Philharmonic Orchestra
  Buffalo Philharmonic Orchestra
  Long Island Philharmonic
  New York Chamber Symphony
  New York Philharmonic
  The New York Pops
  Queens Symphony Orchestra
  Rochester Philharmonic Orchestra
  Syracuse Philharmonic Orchestra
  Westchester Philharmonic
North Carolina
  Charlotte Symphony Orchestra
  Greensboro Symphony Orchestra
  The North Carolina Symphony
  Winston-Salem Piedmont Triad Symphony
Ohio
  Akron Symphony Orchestra
  Canton Symphony Orchestra
  Cincinnati Symphony Orchestra
  The Cleveland Orchestra
  The Columbus Symphony Orchestra
  Dayton Philharmonic Orchestra
  Ohio Chamber Orchestra
  Toledo Symphony Orchestra
  Youngstown Symphony Orchestra

Oklahoma
  Oklahoma City Philharmonic
  Tulsa Philharmonic
Oregon
  Oregon Symphony
Pennsylvania
  Erie Philharmonic Orchestra
  Harrisburg Symphony Orchestra
  Northeastern Pennsylvania Philharmonic
  Pittsburgh Symphony Orchestra
  Reading Symphony Orchestra
Rhode Island
  Rhode Island Philharmonic Orchestra
South Carolina
  Charleston Symphony Orchestra
  Greenville Symphony Orchestra
Tennessee
  Chattanooga Symphony & Opera Association
  Knoxville Symphony Orchestra
  Memphis Symphony Orchestra
  Nashville Symphony
Texas
  Amarillo Symphony
  Austin Symphony Orchestra
  Dallas Symphony Orchestra
  Fort Worth Symphony Orchestra
  Houston Symphony
  San Antonio Symphony Orchestra
Utah
  Utah Symphony Orchestra
Vermont
  Vermont Symphony Orchestra
Virginia
  Fairfax Symphony Orchestra
  Richmond Symphony
  Roanoke Symphony Orchestra & Chorus
  The Virginia Symphony
Washington
  Seattle Symphony
  Spokane Symphony Orchestra
West Virginia
  West Virginia Symphony Orchestra
  Wheeling Symphony
Wisconsin
  Madison Symphony Orchestra
  Milwaukee Symphony Orchestra

SOURCE: *Symphony*, January-February, 1999. Used with permission of American Symphony Orchestra League.

Boston, Baltimore, the District of Columbia, Chicago, Cleveland, Cincinnati, Los Angeles, Dallas, and Minnesota (see Table 13.1).

Orchestras unable to offer their musicians a sufficient annual salary vie with each other for the best available players. To attract the best musicians to orchestras with smaller budgets, some communities offer full- or part-time musical work or extra-musical jobs in order to aggregate a respectable annual income for the musicians. For example, a small community might line up a full-time job for a good bassoonist who would work during the week as a piano salesperson and would be available for evening rehearsals and weekend concerts with the community orchestra—which might be unable to pay anything at all for those musical skills. Another community might be able to pay an imported bassoonist $5,000 a year as a musician, then line up a job for that person with local industry. These package deals may not have been the artistic goal of a conservatory graduate, but they are more attractive than abandoning professional music altogether. It is not unusual for colleges and universities to attract top-notch studio teachers with the additional incentive of the opportunity to perform in the local symphony. Among orchestras in smaller communities, it is these kinds of arrangements that make possible professional and semiprofessional ensembles of genuine quality.

FUNDING THE ARTS

The hard fact is that even the best-managed arts organization cannot expect to break even at the box office. All symphonies and opera and ballet companies, no matter how efficiently run, are unable to earn sufficient income to cover their expenses. Simply stated, all real arts organizations are dependent on outside funding for survival. This has been true at various times throughout history. Among the earliest patrons of the arts were the church and the nobility. Concurrent with patronage of this kind, artists occasionally earned part of their livelihood from municipal and national governments. When public theaters and concert halls increased in number in the 17th and 18th centuries, money generated by ticket sales to the middle class helped support musicians, as did persons with private wealth. In modern times, "arts societies" were formed by patrons to organize financial backing for orchestras and opera companies. For generations, U.S. arts organizations have enjoyed large gifts from wealthy individuals. But when the federal tax laws changed and limited unrestricted giving to arts organizations, our orchestras and opera companies began to experience serious financial difficulties. Today, the tax laws are such that large gifts from wealthy individuals are less frequent.

Performing arts organizations earn anywhere between 30% and 65% of their costs of operation by ticket sales. This means that they must raise the complementary 35% to 70% of their budgets from sources other than the box office. If ticket prices were raised to cover all overhead, the Business Committee for the Arts estimates that prices would then be out of the range of most patrons.

Offering more performances each season is not the answer either—for two reasons. First, most of our performing groups are already scheduled to capacity. Second, when an arts group adds a performance, it increases its operating indebtedness. Here is a classic Catch-22 situation: The greater the number of services provided, the greater the financial loss.

In Europe, symphonies and opera companies have long enjoyed governmental subsidies. This is such a strong tradition that music lovers there have some assurance that their symphonies and opera companies will survive from year to year. In contrast, governmental support of the arts in the United States has been near zero throughout most of our history, but in the late 1960s it increased measurably and continued to rise through the 1970s. In the early 1980s, federal funding for the arts was reduced, but there was an upswing in state funding in the mid-1990s. It is likely that governmental support for the arts, either directly through grants or indirectly through tax benefits for donors, will continue to ebb and flow, and arts organizations will continue to creatively seek their needed funds.

National Endowment for the Arts

The federal agency most directly concerned with helping the creative and performing arts in this country is the National Endowment for the Arts (NEA). In 1965, Congress established the National Foundation for the Arts and Humanities. Within the foundation were established two agencies: the NEA and the National Endowment for the Humanities (NEH). In 1966, Congress appropriated $5 million for these agencies to "foster the arts." The enabling legislation provided that NEA funds were to be allocated upon the advice of the National Council on the Arts, a group of 14 private citizens appointed by the president and 6 (nonvoting) members of Congress to oversee the affairs of the NEA and NEH. Currently, the NEA receives several thousand applications a year, with between a quarter and a third of them receiving grants. Several hundred orchestras and about 200 opera companies are eligible. To apply, they must have a sizable minimum annual expenditure level, an established history, and a paid professional staff. On average, applications take 9 to 12 months to process.

The NEA provides financial assistance in three ways:

1. Matching grants to nonprofit, tax-exempt organizations, such as opera companies, symphonies, and ballet companies. This means that the applicant must match the Endowment award at least dollar for dollar with nonfederal contributions and that no more than half of the cost of the project can be covered by federal funds.
2. Matching grants to state and local arts agencies, tribal communities, arts service organizations, and regional arts groups.
3. Nonmatching fellowships to American artists of exceptional talent.

Funding from the NEA has many categories and includes awards to or for

1. Individuals of exceptional talent; these fellowships include several for jazz.
2. A wide range of performing ensembles, including chamber and jazz groups, **choruses,** and opera companies, as well as orchestras.
3. Various types of services, including music festivals, resident composers, and some types of advanced training for musicians.
4. American music not previously recorded or no longer available in any catalogs.

Early on, NEA leaders were aware that the financial difficulties of arts organizations were due, in part, to inept management, and it has traditionally given support to local groups attempting to improve their planning, management, and control of finances. To assist arts groups in acquiring more sound management, NEA grants have gone to universities to support graduate study in arts administration. Federal money has also been available to help finance professional apprenticeship programs in arts management (e.g., the ASOL Orchestra Management Fellowship Program).

In 1985, the NEA and the U.S. Information Agency launched a joint initiative to increase American representation at international performing arts events; the

Rockefeller Foundation began contributing to the project 3 years later, and by 1998, the Pew Charitable Trust also was a contributor. Called the Fund for U.S. Artists at International Festivals and Exhibitions, the program improves and increases the role of American artists in international visual arts exhibitions and performing arts festivals throughout the world.

STATE ARTS COUNCILS

According to the NEA, the number of community, regional, and state arts councils has been on the increase. Federal law requires the NEA to assign 40% of its programming funds to state and regional arts agencies.

Some state legislatures began support of the arts with great reluctance. Pressure on politicians from their constituents changed that. Many states assign tax dollars to help support artists and arts organizations, beyond those monies from the NEA. For instance, in the late 1990s, Minnesota, Hawaii, and Washington all increased their arts funding dramatically.

New York began to appropriate far more (total) dollars for the arts than any other state years ago, after a wide-scale study of cultural and economic impact of the arts on the state. The study showed that the great majority of the electorate favored generous support of cultural enterprises from tax money and that money spent in these ways served to benefit the state's economy.

Arts enthusiasts in other states have used similar evidence to demonstrate the favorable economic impact of dollars paid out for symphonies, opera, and ballet companies. For example, the millions spent each year for the Boston Symphony Orchestra exert a strong influence on the economy of the Boston area. About one half of that huge budget will be spent around Boston through the wages paid the orchestra's artists and staff people. Other millions of that budget will be fed back into the local economy for transportation, utilities, advertising, and equipment. And hundreds of thousands of concertgoers further feed the Boston-area economy for such things as dinners out, taxicabs, even baby-sitting.

Ticket Sales. Performing arts administrators and volunteers expend tremendous energy raising money. An administrator's first concern is to sell tickets. The most successful efforts of this kind focus on generating subscription sales. Tickets may sometimes be more easily sold for individual performances, but most major symphonies and opera and dance companies now understand their energies are best spent seeking sales of a full series of performances. Patrons who buy season tickets not only commit themselves to more money, they are much more loyal and enthusiastic than those who attend only occasionally. The subscriber feels like a patron of the arts, a supporter of the performing group who takes pride in its health and progress.

Arts groups have, in recent years, adopted some of the ticket-selling techniques of professional sports. It is becoming standard practice for symphonies and opera companies to attempt to sell blocks of seats to large companies. Executives are attracted to buying boxes or even larger sections of seats for the season, not only for themselves but to give to their customers and potential customers. Corporations are also attracted to creating images in their communities of being involved in good works and cultural affairs.

Donations and Gifts. Recent tax laws have made large gifts to arts groups less attractive now than they once were. Consequently, fund-raising efforts for the arts concentrate less on the size of gifts and more on their quantity. Armies of volunteers are active each spring and summer drumming up small donations from persons of modest means but who are interested in helping out the local performing groups. The standard method is to sell "memberships" in the sponsoring society for annual dues of, say, $20. The money usually goes to help support performing artists, not to run the society or club. Those giving more than the minimum dues are listed in the programs as "donors" or "benefactors" or "sponsors," depending on the size of their contributions. These appeals to individual involvement (and vanity) produce millions of dollars each season for the arts.

There are special techniques in seeking individual gifts. One was mentioned in an interview with the president of New York's Lincoln Center: He said he never expends energy seeking unrestricted gifts for Lincoln Center. Rather, he identifies the particular enthusiasm of a potential patron. For example, when he learns someone with money is an opera enthusiast, he'll ask for money for the Metropolitan Opera and not even mention the other performing groups connected with Lincoln Center. He finds that gifts come from particular arts lovers who will often extend themselves to support their personal favorites.

Foundations, Corporate Giving

Foundations have been a major arts funding source; they still are, but of diminishing significance. When the difficult economic period of the early 1970s hit

Los Angeles Music Center. Photo by Donna Carroll.

such organizations as the Ford and Rockefeller foundations, their assets dropped in value, and grants were cut accordingly or remained level. But hundreds of foundations still make important grants to the arts. Everyone in the field knows this, and these organizations spend much of their time receiving and processing pleas for money. Many of them are now contributors to the Foundation Center, a valuable and extensive clearinghouse for information about foundations and the grants they award. The Foundation Center publishes *Foundation Fundamentals: A Guide for Grantseekers*, which includes recommended procedures for locating information on foundations in specific areas and identifying their particular interests. Among its many targeted publications, it publishes the *National Guide to Foundation Funding in Arts and Culture*.

Many businesses are interested and eager to support their local arts organizations. When arts groups complain about their lack of support from big corporations, the problem may not be lack of interest from the corporations as much as the absence of solicitation. Some of the big companies have never been asked.

And most of them will not give money until someone steps forth and helps them understand why they should.

In most communities, well-organized, comprehensive canvassing of corporations of all sizes generally turns out to be successful. This is particularly true if businesses are asked to contribute to local rather than national groups. These businesses are more likely to fund arts groups that have a direct impact on their own communities, which, in turn, may offer to give lunchtime or holiday-season performances on-site for employees.

The Business Committee for the Arts, Inc. (BCA), founded in 1967 by David Rockefeller and other prominent business leaders, is a national, not-for-profit organization that encourages businesses to support the arts and provides the resources necessary to develop effective business-arts alliances. BCA's approximately 100 member companies have long-term commitments to developing partnerships with the arts that benefit business, the arts, and society.

Volunteer Support

Performing arts groups that are financially vibrant are the ones that have developed the support of volunteers who know how to ask for money. One standard procedure is to nominate wealthy executives in the community to serve on the board of directors, then persuade them to contact their wealthy friends personally for donations. A symphony board member might never have heard of Bartok but may have landed that prestigious spot on the board because it was assumed that the member knew how to contact money sources.

Another way of raising money, mentioned earlier, is universally employed by art groups: They enlist large numbers of socially conscious citizens to get out in the community and seek donations, large and small. Symphony, dance, and opera companies that can organize several dozen committees to get on the telephone and follow up with mail solicitations generally find that this group of people becomes an irresistible force. The most effective campaigns of this kind are not only carefully timed and organized, but each solicitor undergoes training—how to talk to people, what to say, how to "close the sale."

In addition to their effective work in selling subscriptions, volunteer committees take on a great variety of fund-raising projects. Typical of such undertakings are radio and TV marathon broadcasts, fashion shows, antique sales, and auctions. These projects raise millions for the arts. And to hear the volunteer workers

tell it, taking part is also a lot of fun. No arts enterprise anywhere could function without the generous and enthusiastic efforts of its volunteer workers.

Funding sources for the arts also include the American Federation of Musicians (AFM) Music Performance Trust Funds (see Chapter 16). Each year, hundreds of communities receive funding from this source for live music performances ranging from soloists in hospital wards to cosponsorship of Handel's *Messiah.* The AFM provides money not only for union musicians' wages but also for such things as publicity and hall rentals.

Any account of subsidies for the arts should include recognition of the generous contributions of the artists themselves—composers, **copyists,** conductors, performers. In every community in the land, these individuals subsidize the arts by either working without fee or for fees below professional levels. They donate their artistry to the cause because their love for music exceeds their desire for financial reward. Without these generous gifts of time and talent, the production and performance of the arts would suffer greatly.

ADMINISTRATION

The Need

Training. Leading U.S. arts administrators define their work as "the art of losing money gracefully." Until recent years, their profession was unknown. The people who had the responsibility of managing an orchestra or opera company learned on the job and muddled through. This pattern still prevails too often today in hundreds of arts organizations, which may be one reason many of them experience serious financial trouble.

Probably the first organized movement to offer education for arts administrators occurred in 1969 when the NEA gave UCLA's Graduate School of Business $10,000 to organize two conferences to examine the problem of how to prepare people to function as arts administrators. Today, approximately 35 quality educational programs in colleges and universities offer master's degrees in arts administration. The Association of Arts Administration Educators keeps updated information available on current programs and how to contact it on its Web page.

Although a few thousand graduates of various arts management training programs are currently employed in the field, there still is a shortage of individuals fully qualified to manage the affairs of arts groups, many of which have operating budgets in the millions. ASOL states that there is an acute shortage of persons qualified to fill the job openings in this country for symphony orchestra management. William Dawson, former executive director of the Association of Performing Arts Presenters, has stated that jobs await individuals possessing "professional skills" in the field. And fortunately, more and more resources are becoming available to hone the skills needed for success (see the Selected Readings list for some of these).

One way to gain a perspective on the need for professional arts administrators is to look at the staff of a major symphony orchestra. An organization with an annual budget in the range of $2 million to $6 million will have these professionals at work 50 weeks a year:

General Manager or Executive Director
Assistant Manager
Director of Development
Assistant Director of Development
Special Projects Coordinator
Two to four additional professional money raisers
Director of Public Relations or Director of Press Relations
Assistant Public Relations Director
Publications Director
Art Director
Advertising Manager
Development Manager
Personnel Director
Road Manager or Stage Director
Assistant Stage Director
Property Manager
Head Librarian
Assistant Librarian
Controller or Accountant
Two to four assistants to the Controller (bookkeepers, etc.)
Ticket Sales Manager
Assistant Ticket Manager
Volunteer Activities Coordinator

Office Manager
Secretaries, Assistants

Responsibilities. It is the responsibility of the general manager to ensure that the other individuals understand their responsibilities and discharge them properly. If the manager's associates function properly, this allows the manager time to operate at a higher level—thinking, planning, budgeting, promoting, following directives from the board, raising money, handling finances, and creating an environment for the symphony that makes possible ever-finer artistic achievements, the reason this effort is expended in the first place.

Management, too, is an art, as Mozart's father once said. First of all, it is the art of working with people effectively. Arts organizations are remarkable in that they involve professionals and volunteers working side by side. The smooth cooperation of professionals and amateurs is not achieved easily, and some arts administrators never really get the hang of it. When an individual works for free, it isn't a good idea for the professional manager to push that person around. Armies of volunteers, essential to all arts organizations, just won't work unless they believe wholeheartedly in the artistic goals and the management of the ensembles and know that they are appreciated and important to the success of their organizations.

In addition to possessing the ability to organize and motivate large numbers of volunteer committees, the arts administrator must be responsive to the policies of and instructions from the board of directors. ASOL's Ralph Black was fond of saying that the number one problem of professional symphony orchestras is not money but weak boards. Helen M. Thompson, former staff head of ASOL, directed a study some years ago that showed that truly successful symphony orchestras enjoy the support of board members who really work at it. The second finding of the ASOL research demonstrated that the really well-run orchestras "had etched out a sound basic philosophy of the value of the orchestra as a permanent institution in the life of the community."

Assuming the manager and the board see eye to eye, the administrative head has these responsibilities:

1. Supervise the work of the staff. Hire and fire.
2. Organize and supervise volunteers.
3. Direct long-range planning.

4. Raise money. This is a large part of the board's responsibility, but it needs direction and a lot of help.

5. Prepare budgets, including debt management, endowment funds, retirement plans, campaign funds, and operations budgets.

6. Work with the artistic director in the conception and implementation of programs—including casting, scheduling.

7. Negotiate contracts for professional services. The most difficult may be with the AFM, whose contracts normally run for 2 to 3 years. Dozens of contracts must also be negotiated with guest conductors and guest soloists. The manager who spends too much leads the organization deeper into debt. If too little is spent, artistic standards may drop.

8. Supervise technical matters relative to performances, the daily moving of artists and equipment; staging and lighting; and booking transportation, hotels, and meals for more than 100 artists. (Many of these duties will generally be handled by other staff members, but the director carries the ultimate responsibility for them.)

9. Handle press relations and public relations; keep the volunteers happy, the press happy, the politicians happy, the schoolchildren and their teachers happy, the National Endowment happy, the board happy, and above all, keep the audience happy.

Because no one individual knows how or has time and energy to accomplish all these things directly, it might be more instructive to list the specific skills and attributes required of a successful arts administrator.

The administrator:

▶ Doesn't just like music, *loves* it

▶ Has great energy and enthusiasm—the kind that makes others want to work, too

▶ Uses energy and time efficiently and knows how to organize the energies of others

▶ Knows how to run a meeting: starts on time, announces a specific agenda, manages the flow of conversation, prohibits digressions, encourages all points of view, summarizes decisions made, and adjourns on time

▶ Keeps in mind long-range goals but knows the most important thing to do on Monday morning

▶ Can prepare a sensible budget, present it clearly, and stay within it; although not a CPA, can count and doesn't throw other people's money around

Financial Management

Management of arts organizations is difficult because there will never be enough money, so the administrators may limp along, improvising each day some kind of quick fix against impending disaster. Arts groups that survive must manage their finances astutely, starting with a well-conceived financial plan. This is a minimum requirement in avoiding serious fiscal difficulties but not an easy one. An arts organization's financial plan is not like a plan for a commercial business operation, because a symphony, opera, or dance company has no easy way of calculating what accountants like to call *cost-benefit ratios.* This is a way of asking, "If we spend $1,000 here, what benefits will that money produce?" Because arts groups are not-for-profit in nature, the decision about that $1,000 outlay must be calculated not on what profit it might yield but by what it might produce artistically—and artistic achievements cannot be listed on profit-and-loss statements. So the arts administrator must make many important financial decisions intuitively.

In many communities, experts in financial management, insurance, advertising, printing, graphic arts, and public relations volunteer their assistance without cost to arts organizations. These are significant contributions and help keep costs low. CPAs often tell arts administrators that their money problems don't particularly stem from a need for more frugality. Indeed, many arts groups can teach commercial concerns how to get things done at minimum cost. Rather, the accountants and other financial experts observe that lack of financial planning by boards and arts administrators for income, expense, and debt management is at the heart of many arts administration problems.

If an arts organization can learn good financial management, the other essential component leading to success is an infusion of love. Money and love: a powerful combination.

Part IV

THE RECORDING INDUSTRY

SCOPE OF THE RECORDING INDUSTRY

I have learned from experience that it is easier to make a businessman out of a musician than a musician out of a businessman.

—Goddard Lieberson

The recording[1] industry overwhelmingly dominates the art and business of music today. Once a piece of music is composed, not much of importance can happen to it in the marketplace until it is recorded. The lives and fortunes of composers, performers, publishers, agents, and merchants rise and fall with the sale of recorded music. If CDs and tapes sell well, all other sectors of the business prosper. When they flop, everyone hurts.

For an understanding of how the recording industry functions today, some historical background will be helpful (see Table 14.1).

PERSPECTIVE

Well over a thousand recognized recording companies operate in the United States, with releases on more than 3,000 different **labels.** Probably the best way to gain a true picture of the record business is to analyze it in terms of *major* versus *independent* labels. It is probably best to define a major label as any label that is owned and/or distributed by one of the handful of major distribution companies. Conversely, an independent label is any label lacking an affiliation with a major.

An understanding of this structure is important because the majors dominate the sales of records in the United states. Even though independents account for

← The Capitol Records building in Hollywood. Photo courtesy of Capitol Records. The Capitol Tower is a trademark of Capitol Records, Inc. All rights reserved.

TABLE 14.1   Historical Background

1877:	Edison invents the cylinder phonograph.
1894:	The first commercial disc recordings appear in the U.S. market.
1900s:	The Victor Talking Machine Co. is incorporated in 1901, develops 10,000 dealers. At first, opera repertoire dominates. Then dance music begins to sell well (on Victor and Columbia labels).
1917:	The first jazz record is released.
1920s:	By 1921, 100 million records are produced in the United States. Large impetus from "commercial" jazz.
1924:	Bell Laboratories develops an electrical process for recording, increasing audible range over the earlier acoustical recordings to 100-5,000 Hz. Bass instruments can now be heard. Meteoric rise of radio popularity puts recording industry into a tailspin.
1929:	Stock market crash.
1930s:	The Great Depression hurts all business, particularly the record industry. Sales of discs and phonographs drop 90% compared to the 1927 peak year (total retail sales in 1933: $5.5 million).
	Jukebox industry grows large, helping salvage the record business. By the late 1930s, the jukebox operators were buying 13 million discs to serve their machines.
	Decca starts marketing low-cost (35 cents) singles featuring artists such as Bing Crosby, the Mills Brothers, the Dorsey Brothers, Guy Lombardo; sells 19 million records in 1939.
	Dealers sell record players near cost to encourage record sales.
	First albums appear by mid-1930s, each single 78-rpm disc within the binder selling for 50 cents.
	Department stores introduce record and phonograph departments.
1940s:	Weekly volume of new records released in the early 1940s: 10 to 20 singles (78 rpm); by the end of the decade, 40 to 100 per week, depending on the season.
	American Federation of Musicians (AFM) strike against record companies paralyzes the industry 1942-1945, damages popularity of big band recordings, which, in turn, accelerates sales of records featuring pop singers.
	Airplay not yet a major promotion factor except big band remote broadcasts. Jukeboxes help break new hits, particularly in race music (as it was then called) and country fields.
Late 1940s:	*One-stops* (distributors handling all labels) come into being, mainly to accommodate jukebox operators. Rise of independent record labels, which begin to dominate the rhythm and blues (R&B) field. Proliferation of distributors into smaller markets. Average dealer markup: 38%.
1948:	Columbia introduces the 33⅓-rpm LP, retailing for $5.79.
	Race records, country and western (C&W) diverge from pop records.
1950s:	Television rises rapidly, grabs a large share of the radio audience. Radio loses advertising revenue. To economize, stations drop most live music and turn to recorded music. Increasing popularity of TV also sharply reduces record sales from 1949 to 1954.
	R&B and C&W markets become dominated by independent labels.
	Interest in high-fidelity sound increases buyers of middle-of-the-road records.
	Rock and roll craze begins in the mid-1950s. "Cover record" concept initiated.

1955:	Record clubs begin. Columbia starts, soon followed by RCA and Capitol.
1957:	Rack jobbing begins.
1958:	Stereo is introduced.
	Record retailing changes. Proliferation of labels and products burdens retailers with huge inventories. Space demands forced abandonment of listening booths. Record supermarkets begin concurrently with proliferation of the small-rack setups. Record retailing in chaos amid price cutting and expanding sales.
1959:	Classical music's first million-seller: Van Cliburn's performance of Tchaikovsky's *Concerto for Piano and Orchestra*.
1960s:	Social turmoil of the decade finds its "voice" in popular music, influences large sales increases of rock, R&B, soul, country records. Rock becomes the catalyst for Woodstock-type mass concerts.
	National Association of Recording Merchandisers (NARM) formed in early 1960s by record wholesalers.
	Rack jobbers cut heavily into "mom-and-pop" retailing and become dominant in the market; record clubs cut further into conventional retailing.
	Beatles craze accelerates worldwide interest in pop-rock music; sales boom ensues.
	Record supermarkets and retail chains proliferate in response to decreasing profit margins, growing inventories.
	Major labels recapture some markets lost earlier to independents.
1970s:	Independent record producers rise to greater importance.
	Singer-songwriters become the superstars. Crossover records become the superhits.
	Sophistication of technology increases: 16- and 24-track consoles; synthesizers, computer-assisted mixing, digital recording.
	Sophistication of music increases: rock softens, classical influences on polyphony, texture, instrumentation, form.
1980s:	Technological change advances sophistication of recording/reproducing equipment. inexpensive keyboards and samplers enable a new generation of young producers to make records.
	Compact discs gain market share.
	Video clips change record promotion methods, break new acts.
	Long-form videos develop as take-home consumer software.
1990s:	New technologies further erode protection of intellectual property.
	New technologies make high-quality home recording possible.
	Sophisticated in-store sampling units provide new vehicles for exposure and trial. DAT (digital audiotape) hardware is approved for consumer use in the United States.
	Electronic delivery of music arrives, in addition to traditional sales at "record" stores.
	Recorded music finds new means of exploitation through the use of multimedia and interactive media.
2000	Government clamps down on label co-op ad rates, lowering CD prices.
	Web technologies such as MP3 and Napster scare labels with threat of piracy.

the overwhelming majority of the many thousands of different records *released* each year, majors typically account for between 80% to 90% of the total number of records *sold.* Looking at the radio **charts,** video playlists, sales charts, and so forth, at any time, it would be hard to find an independent release. This is because the majors are well funded, and this gives them a tremendous advantage over the independents.

MAJOR LABELS

The major distribution companies are owned by some of the larger multinational corporations in the world. The competitive advantage of being well financed manifests itself in myriad ways. The record business requires a tremendous investment in the areas of production, distribution, and marketing. The majors can afford to sign more artists and offer more money to sign the best artists. A commonly quoted industry statistic is that only one out of five records earns its money back. By being well financed, the major labels can ride out the frequent losses and wait for the big score. Moreover, artists are attracted to the large advances and the prestige of being associated with a label such as Sony or Mercury, the security of knowing there are sufficient funds for marketing, and the stability of an established company in a business where one of the greatest difficulties is getting paid. The major labels can also afford to fund more elaborate recordings with the best producers, musicians, and studios. And they usually have their own duplication facilities and can manufacture more units at a lower unit cost. More money also means the majors can put a lot more records into the marketplace and can afford the losses associated with excess inventory.

The advantages in distribution are also profound. The majors operate according to a branch system, with regional offices functioning in coordination with one another to penetrate the marketplace much more thoroughly than independents can—they can get many more records into many more stores. Another advantage major labels have is in promotion: When a big firm releases a new recording, it can assign its entire field force and merchandising personnel to that particular project. They can bring to bear 200 or more individuals actively working a particular release. Although major labels rarely assign their full energies to just one release, they can shift their field personnel whenever they find it necessary to push particular products. Because they sell more records, they can put much greater pressure on retailers to accept a lot of product, particularly from new artists. And major labels offer stability and longevity. This can mean that they are more likely to maintain inventories and continue distribution of recordings long after their first release. Smaller labels may find it impossible to offer such ongoing service.

In contrast, independent labels are usually forced to find a patchwork of different independent distributors throughout the country. Just like artists, independent labels have trouble getting paid. Independent distributors and retailers frequently have difficulty paying their bills, and it is not unusual for even the largest of them to go out of business. Independent labels are the last to get paid, and if an account is large enough to an independent label, the bankruptcy of a distributor can result in the failure of the label as well.

Last, the majors have a clear advantage in the costly marketing of records. Again, the structure of the majors allows many individuals to work together on distribution and marketing. It's a severe disadvantage for independent labels that independent distributors do not perform any marketing functions.

Radio promotion can cost $100,000 or more per single. Video production costs can range from $50,000 to the millions for one song. Retail placement and promotion can easily run into seven figures for a single album release. Add to this amount the cost of advertising, tour support, publicity, and the overhead for staff.

The national impact of this force can put over even a weak recording. This issue is strongly disputed, some arguing that even heavily concentrated promotion cannot persuade the public to buy music that doesn't actually have it "in the grooves." But certainly, the powerful promotional forces of the major labels have much greater success with weak material than the smaller firms. Prominent artists are attracted to major labels primarily because of their powerful promotion departments and well-organized distribution networks. Artists are also attracted by the prestige of being signed by a major label. They would rather be known as "an MCA artist" than as "a Smith artist."

INDEPENDENT LABELS

Fortunately for the independents, the sheer size of the majors has built-in disadvantages. First, they are conservative companies that tend to be out of touch with consumers and are slow to catch up with changes in musical tastes. Most important developments in music have started at the independent level: Rock and roll in the '50s and '60s; punk and modern rock in the '70s and '80s. Alternative and "grunge" rock as well as rap and hip hop in the '80s and '90s. Independent labels have been described by knowledgeable music industry professionals as the "lifeblood of the business." To discover "the next big thing" in music, you need only look to the independents. Of course, the natural evolution and goal of some independents is to become so successful that they are ultimately bought out and absorbed by the majors for many millions of dollars.

Many of today's biggest major labels started out as independents. Many small firms have lived through high-risk periods to develop into very profitable companies. Three English labels that started very small and grew very rich before being bought out by major labels are Island, Chrysalis, and Virgin. Three U.S. labels that did the same thing are Arista, Geffen, and Sire. From the outset, these companies exhibited creative leadership and determination—a winning combination.

The majors are set up so that they must concentrate their efforts on the most popular music with the best sales potential. This leaves many of the more modest-selling genres and artists to the independents. Independent labels can also develop brand name awareness and consumer loyalty that is rare among the majors. Music fans will often purchase records from labels such as Alligator, Sup-Pop, Rounder, and so on, on the basis of their trust in that label's taste.

Another fertile area for an independent label is at the local or regional level. An independent can make necessary connections with the radio stations, publicity outlets, and retailers in a limited geographical area. Relationships are the backbone of this industry, and if a group can earn the good favor of a few regional program directors, editors, and store managers, a modest success can begin and grow from there, especially if the acts can play in the area. In fact, many groups start their own labels, and if they have a local following, they might make more money doing it themselves than if they signed with a major label.

Developments in technology may benefit the independents. The affordability of recording equipment and proliferation of studios have brought the cost of recording down considerably. The refinements of CD manufacturing and the number of duplication facilities have brought the cost down to under $1 per unit. The Internet has made it possible for anyone to promote and distribute their recordings to the entire world.

SPECIALTY LABELS

Some of the most successful independents are specialty labels, and a number of these are in the **classical music** field, for instance, Nonesuch, Deutche Grammaphon, Westminster, Odyssey, and Angel. The classics have been and are still being recorded by the world's greatest artists, and classical labels are largely concerned with selling from existing inventories. Larger classical labels such as Columbia will, from time to time, tape what some people call "new music," the works of "serious" contemporary composers.

Some specialty labels, particularly in the field of contemporary classical music, release their records "privately." They bypass more conventional distribution channels and seek to locate buyers of their sometimes esoteric product through the mail, addressed particularly to colleges and universities.

Other specialty labels limit their activities to certain demographic markets. They find ways to reach cultural enclaves or ethnic groups in particular parts of the country and work directly with retail outlets in those communities. Another kind of specialty label is Folkways, which offers a variety of folk, blues, ethnic, and jazz music, selling mostly by mail to schools and libraries.

One of the most successful types of specialty label sells gospel music. Some people refer to this repertoire as contemporary Christian music. Among the most effective promotional methods used by gospel record companies are the many personal appearances of their contract artists. Touring gospel singers draw large audiences and sell lots of tapes and CDs.

Once again, these labels are successful because they do not compete directly with the mainstream music concentrated on by the majors and because they do not rely as heavily on traditional and expensive forms of promotion, such as radio and video.

RECORD COMPANY STRUCTURE

Record companies range in size from the multinational major to the modest, one-person operation, and their structures vary accordingly. But whatever their structure, they must handle the kinds of tasks described, and certain generalizations can be made about how production, distribution, and marketing are organized and administered. Figure 14.1 gives an example of a typical record company structure.

Chief Executive Officer (CEO)

The CEO or president is often a strong entrepreneur who started the label and who had the vision it reflects. CEOs come from a variety of backgrounds, but two stand out. Lawyers often assume this position because the record business relies

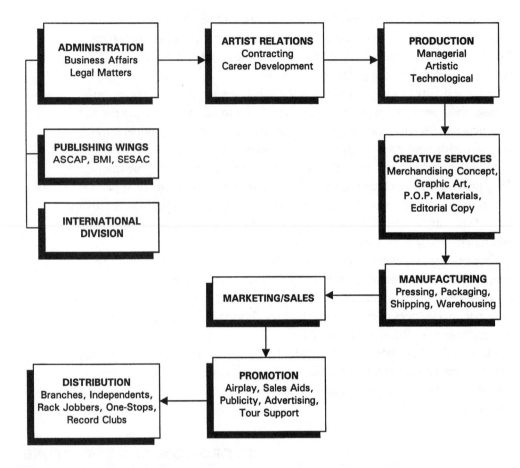

Figure 14.1   Record Company Organization: From Song to Street
NOTE: P.O.P. = point-of-purchase.

in large part on contracts and copyrights. Producers are also quite often in charge of labels because they know the music. This is particularly true in country music and urban music. Whether or not CEOs are lawyers or producers, they must have their respective abilities: They must know the "art of the deal" to negotiate favorable business arrangements, and they must have good "ears" to determine commercial recordings. They are often strong leaders, like David Geffen, Clive Davis, and Ahmet Ertegun.

Artist and Repertoire (A&R)

The A&R department is concerned first and foremost with finding and signing new talent. The staff needs to keep informed, through a network of contacts, submitted **demo** tapes, the independent music scene, industry publications, and/or going to clubs to hear new music. After an act has been signed, the A&R department remains involved on a number of different levels, including assisting artists in developing a particular project and/or their careers; administering the many production, budgetary, and other details of an album; or just acting as liaison between the artist and the label. If the label is large enough, separate departments may be established to handle these specific tasks, such as Artist Development, A&R Administration, Artist Relations, and Production on both the audio and video side.

Business and Legal Affairs

Since this industry revolves around contracts and copyrights, record companies usually have legal departments to negotiate and draft agreements. These range from artist recording agreements to licenses issued by and to the record company for the use of copyrighted materials. This department must also do its best to minimize the frequent litigation that occurs in this industry. Some larger companies have a separate department for business and legal affairs or smaller departments to handle specific tasks, such as licensing or copyright departments.

Accounting

Record companies require a large and sophisticated accounting department to handle the incoming and outgoing royalties. Accounting may also be heavily involved in the development and administration of recording budgets, inventory, and manufacturing, with separate departments designed for each, such as operations and finance departments.

Distribution/Sales

Whether a record company is a major or independent, it must have personnel who either oversee or are directly involved with convincing retailers to buy its records. Maximizing sales and controlling inventory are absolutely necessary to a label's success.

Marketing

While sales and marketing are often linked, the marketing role is so important and so distinct that it usually functions separately and is divided into several areas of specialization.

Radio Promotion. This is the very heart of the marketing of most records in most genres. The radio promotion department is in charge of getting radio airplay and charting; there is little chance of success without them. Some large labels subdivide this department by genre of music.

Video Promotion. This department attempts to get video airplay for artists.

Publicity. In-house publicists manage media exposure through TV appearances, magazine articles, newspaper reviews, and the like. Many labels are concentrating more and more on publicity since it is so much less expensive than promotion.

Advertising. This department arranges the advertising for a label and may be part of or work closely with the distribution/sales department since much of the advertising cost is shared between label and retailer (co-op advertising).

Creative Services. The creative services department is responsible for designing and producing any materials necessary to execute a marketing campaign such as posters, point-of-purchase materials, album artwork, and window displays.

Product Management. Found in most medium and large record companies, product managers coordinate and oversee all aspects of a current release, including packaging, advertising, tours, publicity, promotion, and sales activities. This entails close liaison with personnel from other label activities, for instance, A&R, sales, and creative services.

International Department

The global nature of the record business is such that most record companies now have international departments to oversee foreign sales and ensure effective communication between domestic and foreign affiliates. For some companies and some genres, foreign sales can equal or exceed domestic sales.

Publishing Affiliates

All record labels own or control at least two **publishing** companies—one connected with the American Society of Composers, Authors and Publishers (ASCAP) and one signed with Broadcast Music Inc. (BMI). Labels with aggressive publishing wings may seek to persuade their contract artists to grant them publishing rights to the music the artist records for the label. Although a publishing company may be owned by the same parent company as its affiliated record company, the publishing company is expected to show profit from its own operations and may sign many artists who are not on the recording company's roster. An exception may be found with publishing companies that are affiliated with very small labels. These companies may exist primarily to handle the publishing of that label.

PIRACY, COUNTERFEITING, BOOTLEGGING

Since the 1960s, the piracy, counterfeiting, and bootlegging of recordings has been a worldwide problem of overwhelming proportions. Some observers fear that copyright abuses of this kind may run some legitimate companies out of business. *Piracy* is the sale of the unauthorized duplication of prerecorded product. *Counterfeiting* is the unauthorized manufacture and distribution of copies of prerecorded product that are packaged to look like the original product. *Bootlegging* is the sale of product created from the unauthorized recording of live or broadcast performances.

Probably the most comprehensive international studies of the problem are made by the World Intellectual Property Organization (WIPO), headquartered in Geneva. WIPO's research shows that the worldwide sale of pirated, counterfeited, and bootlegged merchandise has a retail value of billions of dollars. The seriousness of illegal record copying varies widely from country to country. In some parts of the world, no copyright laws exist; in other regions, the laws may be there but are not enforced.

In the United States, progress has been made toward reducing, if not controlling, record piracy and counterfeiting. But most recent reports of the Recording Industry Association of America (RIAA) stress that the problem is far from solved in this country. At every recording industry meeting, leaders prod each other to reduce this problem that hurts everybody in the legitimate business, particularly copyright owners.

But progress in the right direction continues: A variety of package-marking or coding devices has been developed to protect against counterfeit merchandise. In 1984, an amendment was passed affecting the Generalized System of Preferences (GSP), which provides preferential tariffs and duty-free treatment to Third World nations, where many of these abuses occur. The amended law provides that a nation that refuses to cooperate with the United States in crackdowns of pirating and bootleg operations will be denied, at the president's discretion, future preferential treatment under the GSP. This law helps induce Third World countries, out of self-interest, to cooperate more fully with efforts to control copyright abuses of this kind.

In a further effort to address the problem, in 1992 the U.S. Congress enacted the Audio Home Recording Act, which amended the 1976 Copyright Act by allowing home audiotaping and by implementing a royalty payment system and Serial Copy Management Systems for digital audio recordings. As a result of this amendment, royalty payments must be made by any person who imports, distributes, or manufactures digital hardware and software. (Some other countries also require compensatory royalties on the sale of blank tape and/or recording equipment.)

Challenges Presented by New Technologies

The problems of piracy, counterfeiting, bootlegging, and home taping have been exacerbated by digital technologies. It is now possible to have access to almost any and all music through the Internet. There are many sites that offer the opportunity for anyone with a computer to download music illegally through technologies such as MP3. These transactions deprive the copyright holders, artists, and songwriters of any compensation for their work. RIAA and other industry coalitions are working to ensure that the laws are sufficient to prohibit this activity.

For example, in 1997 the Net Act was enacted to address criminal copyright issues that have to do with the Internet, especially pirate bulletin board systems and Web sites, defining the "willfulness" element needed to establish criminal liability: when a person intended to violate copyright law. This act deals only with criminal liability, however, and has no impact on civil liability for copyright infringement. And the Digital Millennium Copyright Act implements two global treaties designed to protect creative works in the digital era. It prohibits the manufacture and distribution of devices used to circumvent technology that protects sound recordings and other copyrighted material. This prohibition provides a mechanism for securing copyrighted music online.

The more pressing and difficult concern, however, is to police the illegal practices. This is accomplished by monitoring the Internet and finding and prosecuting the criminal providers and consumers of this illegal material. An equally vigorous effort is being made to design and integrate these technologies into the record business so that they operate to the benefit of the record companies, the artists, and the consumers. It may be the most challenging issue confronting the industry.

NATIONAL ACADEMY OF RECORDING ARTS & SCIENCES

The National Academy of Recording Arts & Sciences (NARAS) is known to the public through annual telecasts of its Grammy Awards. NARAS's regular membership is limited to persons professionally active in the artistic, creative, or technical side of the industry (composers, performers, producers, **engineers,** etc.). Associate membership is open to those in the recording field who are only indirectly involved in record production. Some of NARAS's associate members are students planning professional careers in recording. Applications are accepted at NARAS regional offices, located in major cities.

Grammy Award classifications and voting procedures change from time to time, and information on current practices is announced in the trades and, occasionally, in the general press. Receipt of a Grammy Award is prized, not only for the prestige but because the attendant national publicity often helps boost recording sales.

NOTE

1. The terms *record, album,* and *single* have become generic—a compact disc or an audiocassette of an artist's music is still often referred to as a "record."

Grammy Award ® © NARAS. Photo used with permission of the
National Academy of Recording Arts & Sciences, Inc.

RECORD MARKETS

RESEARCH DEVELOPMENT

A record company must know its customers—those who are currently buying and those who might be persuaded to buy in the future—as well as their musical tastes. The industry is fiercely competitive. The companies with access to the best market research hope that this information will allow them to lead the pack.

Musical tastes and trends change rapidly. Companies that move too slowly and cautiously may find themselves out of touch with their customers. Of all the "research" used in the recording business down through the years, the **charts** were among the most suspect. Until the 1990s, research of record "sales" data was generally imprecise and too often failed to make clear the distinctions between the figures for merchandise actually sold as compared to the huge amounts of unsold stock returned by dealers. Data collection services such as **SoundScan** and **BDS** (Broadcast Data Systems)—and later, **Mediabase 24/7**—produced much more accurate sales information than had been available in the past.

THE CHARTS

Everyone in the recording business who enjoys eating regularly follows the charts in the industry's trade journals. Profits soar or plunge, careers flourish or collapse—in direct ratio to the relative altitude certain recordings reach on these weekly sales reports.

Billboard publishes the most widely quoted charts and employs a large staff in its Charts and Research Department. Every category of music has its own chart, some more than one. Even foreign sales are listed. Some charts indicate only **airplay**; others list only estimates of sales. Some charts combine these data and formulate overall rankings. In 1991, *Billboard* also began producing Catalog Title charts featuring older music that is still available for purchase.

Broadcast Data System

Billboard's Broadcast Data System (BDS) enables computers in major and secondary markets to "listen" to radio stations 24 hours a day. The BDS technology monitors broadcasts and recognizes songs and/or commercials aired by radio and TV stations. Records and commercials must first be played into the system's computer, which, in turn, creates a digital "fingerprint" of that material. The fingerprint is downloaded to BDS monitors in each market. Those monitors can recognize that fingerprint or "pattern" when the song or commercial is broadcast on one of the monitored stations. Once a song pattern has been recognized by the remote computer, it updates its records, identifying the exact time, date, and station. Each evening, the pattern library is updated and the day's detection history is transmitted from the remote sites to the BDS central operations facility where the equipment spews out relative chart positions for the recordings that particular week.

Mediabase 24/7

By blending technology and people, Mediabase 24/7 provides data very quickly. Both music and programming data are gathered by computers within 15 minutes of being aired; the audio is identified, the data are proofed and posted within 2 hours of the final broadcast hour. Like BDS, Mediabase monitors music on hundreds of stations; unlike BDS, Mediabase is able to take into account broadcast anomalies such as obscure oldies, in-studio performances, and mix shows. In addition to the usual statistics available to music and program directors, Mediabase also provides monitoring of a host of other programming elements—promotions, contests, and morning show components, for example—that go beyond the identification capabilities of computer-based-only airplay monitoring.

SoundScan

Whereas BDS monitors airplay, SoundScan tabulates sales of recorded product. SoundScan's sales tabulations are generated by a computer network linked to retail outlets, **rack jobbers,** and the Internet, representing more than 65% of the nation's record sales. Previously, record companies were forced to estimate sales based on the number of records they manufactured and shipped to retailers. Even approximately accurate sales figures were not available until the retailer had shipped unsold product back to the label. Known as *returns,* this product wasn't received by a label until sometimes months after the initial shipment. SoundScan's sales data are used to compile the *Billboard* 200 and all other *Billboard* retail speciality charts, including all Singles Sales Charts.

For 30 years before it became associated with SoundScan in 1991, *Billboard* had relied on sales rankings provided each week by selected retailers. Stores provided no exact sales figures, only a listing of the top sellers in an approximate order and amount. Some retailers neglected to include country, rhythm and blues, and other genre product in their lists of the top 200 albums sold, relegating those releases to specialty charts even though they were outselling more mainstream titles. What's more, the old system was subject to manipulation by recording companies that targeted certain stores for extra promotion and by bribable store managers and radio programmers. SoundScan eliminated much of the potential for inaccuracies in reporting. SoundScan data are used by *Billboard, Rolling Stone,* and the *Wall Street Journal.*

Experienced chart watchers note the entry level of new releases. If they first appear relatively high, that may indicate they will climb rapidly through the ranks. Recordings with the largest increases in chart position, those with the largest increases in sales and/or airplay, and those with the biggest percentage growth are indicated on *Billboard's* many charts.

Album Cuts

Singles, nowadays rarely profitable in themselves, are used primarily to turn people on to buying follow-up albums; only albums can generate significant profits. Album charts must be determined largely by unit sales, because album airplay is difficult to identify. Some trades offer charts, such as *Billboard's Air Play Monitor,* that identify songs that get the most airplay whether they are from singles or album cuts. These kinds of data are useful, of course, to radio programmers who broadcast a mix of singles and album cuts.

Comparison of the Charts

Many people compare rankings of recordings among *Billboard* and one or more "inside" publications, for example, *Radio and Records,* which charts only airplay and not sales figures, or *The Gavin Report,* which has a reputation for being objective. Then they may compare these data with *tip sheets,* which vary greatly in quality.

Major stations employ people to call up local record stores and inquire which CDs and cassettes are selling well. These stations believe localized information will be far more useful to them in local programming than any data reflecting tastes of national audiences.

RECORDING INDUSTRY ASSOCIATION OF AMERICA

The most comprehensive market research in the recording industry is carried on (or commissioned) by the Recording Industry Association of America (RIAA). RIAA is the most representative trade association in the record manufacturing business and includes companies accounting for about 90% of all recordings sold in the United States. All major labels are members of RIAA. The organization is well financed, deriving its funding from members' dues, which are calculated based on gross revenues/market share.

RIAA is best known to the public through its certification of recordings as "gold," "platinum," "multi-platinum," or "diamond." When a label believes its sales justify such a certification, RIAA has an independent audit conducted (even non-RIAA members may request such an audit). RIAA awards are based on manufacturers' unit shipments and dollar value, net after returns.

Gold album status is awarded at 500,000 units. As record sales have increased over the years, RIAA has continued to add distinctions for recordings that sell far more than the amounts qualifying them for gold status. Thus, the platinum record was established, and that status is certified when a single or album sells 1 million copies. An album or single previously certified platinum is eligible for RIAA's multi-platinum award: 2 million or more units sold. The diamond award honors artists with releases that have sold 10 million units or more.

One kind of research RIAA has commissioned concerns estimates of how many copies of a recording must be sold to break even. Results from these studies have produced data that are depressing to anyone in the music business. Although the figures change from year to year, most RIAA members report that about 85% of their releases fail to return their investments. Yet some companies claim their track records are much better. Whatever the proportion of hits to flops, recording companies that survive do so because their hits yield sufficient profits to compensate for the flops. Another of the important services RIAA performs for the industry is the commitment of its resources to fighting record counterfeiting and piracy.

RECORD CATEGORIZATION

There is little agreement on the categorization of different styles of music. This lack of consensus on classification makes it difficult, sometimes impossible, for one person in the field to know what the other person is really talking about. This is particularly apparent in understanding record charts. When categorizing an album, a primary genre is initially assumed, and the music is placed on the corresponding chart. This is done so that radio stations playing that particular type of music can feel ownership of the album. However, if the album gains popularity on stations featuring other genres, the album is then "crossed over" to one or more additional charts.

If a recording is crossing over from one audience to another, it might rank number 5 on the Hot 100 chart, number 10 on Adult Contemporary, and perhaps number 40 on the Country chart.

Regardless of the category selected for a particular song or recording, one thing is certain: The public does not really care. For many years, the record-buying public has repeatedly demonstrated that it is attracted by the sound of the music, not its type, and the clearest evidence of the public's disinterest in categories is the **crossover recording,** mentioned above. Nearly all superhits today are crossover—or *multiformat*—recordings, achieving multimillion-selling status by picking up listeners crossing traditional lines.

RIAA offers the following list of musical genres:

Rock	Classical
Country	Jazz
R & B	Oldies
Rap	Soundtracks

> Pop   New Age
>
> Gospel   Children's
>
> Other (includes ethnic, standards, big band, swing, Hispanic,
>   electronic, instrumental, comedy, humor, spoken word, exercise,
>   language, folk, and holiday music)

New categories of recordings are always finding new markets to exploit. A good example of this would be children's recordings, which used to be one of the smaller markets but has grown to be very important.

STYLISTIC PREFERENCES

Because pop music is in a state of constant development and change, acts—particularly in the rock and rap fields—can go from star to has-been status, sometimes within the same year. Artists who attach themselves to musical trends (or who are marketed that way by their recording companies) are often washed up once the public tires of the trend.

The classic rock format has been embraced by former album-oriented rock (AOR) radio stations that have found nostalgic programming to be an effective vehicle for delivering demographically desirable listeners to their advertisers. Ironically, the format found success with many younger listeners, not even born when most of the 1960s and 1970s music was originally released. Acts such as the Beatles and the Rolling Stones created music that has lasted for decades. More recent artists such as Bruce Springsteen, Bonnie Raitt, Sarah McLaughlin, and Whitney Houston further contributed to rock's legacy.

How a hit becomes a hit is the subject of enduring debate. On one hand, it is argued that a hit can be "created" through promotion. On the other hand, it is argued that a hit cannot be created: "It's got to be in the grooves." However, if it is true that in the past poor recordings have obtained high chart rankings solely through the cleverness of promoters, this would prove a much rarer phenomenon today: Not only have listeners become more sophisticated, they are also more inclined to buy what they like, rather than what they are told they should like. Hence, a poor recording that does happen to make it to the top today will quickly disappear from the "hit" category if the music is not good.

Public taste in music is more constant outside the rock genre. Some performers have remained top favorites for decades—Tony Bennett, Frank Sinatra, Johnny Cash, Ella Fitzgerald, the Boston Pops.

Reaching the Buyer

How does a music lover find out which recordings to buy? Most research shows that the strongest influence on potential buyers of popular music is broadcasting—radio and video. Browsing through record stores and word of mouth are probably next in effectiveness in spreading the word. TV exposure is most effective with younger buyers, as is radio. Record buyers in their mid-20s appear influenced somewhat by newspaper ads and articles. This age group (and some older persons) is also turned on by the music they dance to in clubs. Enthusiasts of college radio believe that medium can break recordings and, if subsequently picked up by other media, can turn them into big sellers.

Configurations

Changes in technology and lifestyle have led to an ever-changing parade of audio media. In the 1980s, cassettes were the leading format; in the 1990s, compact discs took center stage, followed by the rise of audio streaming on the Internet. Whether in tape or disc formats, digital playback media and newer "electronic delivery" of music have pushed the older analog technologies into the recesses of entertainment history.

DEMOGRAPHICS

Studies of stylistic preference provide only one part of the information available to recording companies from research. Some companies use demographics such as the record buyer's age, income level, place of residence, and cultural and ethnic background. They use this information to predict which configuration or format is most likely to be successful, which genre of music has experienced the largest growth, and which market outlets have been the most popular.

Percentage of U.S. Dollar Volume

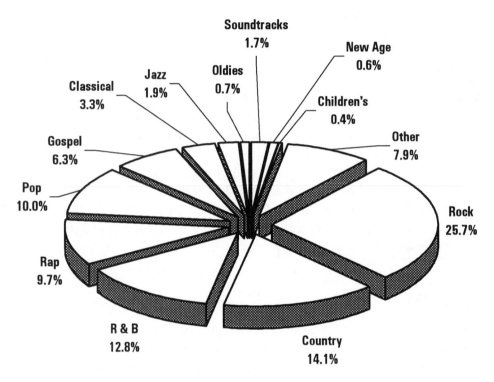

Figure 15.1   Recorded Music Buyers' Preferences
SOURCE: Recording Industry Association of America, 1998.
NOTE: Does not add to 100% because of "Don't know/no answer" responses.

However, other recording companies adhere to the "if you produce it (a good recording), they will buy" theory. These companies use more of a "commonsense" approach: Be as scientific as you can, but don't forget it's entertainment. *Billboard's* Director of Charts, Geoff Mayfield, explains this theory more specifically: (a) Make a good recording; (b) don't screw it up.

Percentage of U.S. Dollar Volume

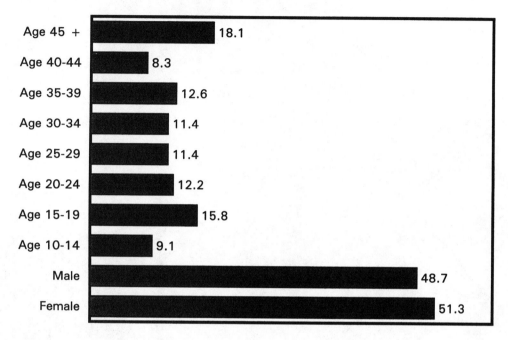

Figure 15.2   Recorded Music Purchases by Age and Gender
SOURCE: Recording Industry Association of America, 1998.

Percentage of U.S. Dollar Volume

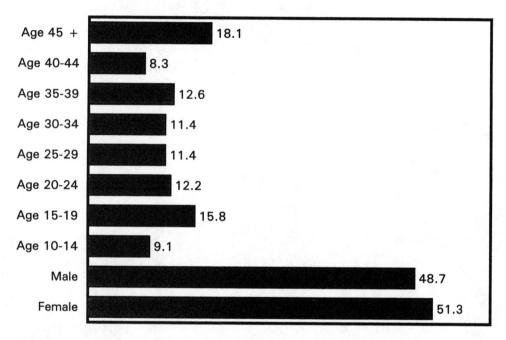

Figure 15.2   Recorded Music Purchases by Age and Gender
SOURCE: Recording Industry Association of America, 1998.

ARTISTS' RECORDING CONTRACTS

Almost all recognized, nationally distributed recording labels enter into a labor contract with the American Federation of Television and Radio Artists (AFTRA) for the services of singers. This agreement, known as the AFTRA National Code of Fair Practice for Sound Recordings, covers all singers from featured singers to backup vocalists, soloists to full choirs. The present contract covers essential concerns of AFTRA with respect to wage **scales, overdubbing,** working conditions, **reuse** payments, and labels' contributions to AFTRA's Health & Retirement Funds.

Vocal Contractors

Where recording involves three or more AFTRA members, AFTRA requires a union **contractor.** That individual is usually a singing member of the group. The AFTRA code defines contractors as "those artists who perform any additional services, such as contracting singers, prerehearsing, coaching singers, arranging for sessions or rehearsals, or any other similar or supervisory duties, including assisting with and preparation of production memoranda." AFTRA makes no distinction in this respect between a vocal contractor and a vocal director. The AFTRA contractor is required to be present at all recording sessions in order to supervise the adherence of the record producer to the terms of the AFTRA code. An AFTRA contractor is also required when the recording of a Broadway show

← Music industry crossroads at Sunset and Vine, Hollywood. Dozens of music industry companies are housed in the two buildings shown here (Motown building is at left). Photo © Leigh Wiener.

involves a group of three or more singers. In addition to a fee as one of the group singers, the contractor receives compensation per hour or per **side** of recording, whichever is higher.

One of the contractor's important responsibilities is to keep track of overdubbing, or reuse of a taped performance of voices. Voices are overdubbed either "live on tape" or through electronic means, such as tape delays. These techniques are sometimes used to change the **timbre,** resonance, or intensity of voices. Sometimes the mixing engineer can cause one to four voices to sound like many more singers are performing. The practice is called **tracking.**

Because most tracking results in a net loss of employment for singers, and more work for the singers involved, AFTRA attempts to control its use through assessing extra charges for such services when singers record additional tracks. The practice of tracking is almost universal today, and it is the task of the AFTRA contractor to log these events, then charge the producer for them. AFTRA requires that when its singers record additional tracks, they are to be paid for the session "as if each **overtracking** were an additional side." Producers sometimes find that extensive overdubbing can run their costs higher than they would have been if additional singers had been engaged in the first place.

For all sessions involving AFTRA-member singing groups, the contractors, the producers, or the singers render AFTRA's Phonograph Record Sessions Report and P&W Report, which cites the record producer's name, hours of recording, the names of AFTRA members involved, and wages due them. The contractor has the producer sign this form, then turns it in to the AFTRA office.

Although lobbying efforts on behalf of recording artists continue, Congress has yet to require that performance royalties be paid to those singers whose recordings are broadcast (except for digital transmission of performances, which require licenses in limited circumstances). Performers enjoy more protection in this matter in Europe than they do in the United States, where stronger broadcasting lobbies exert formidable influence.

Scales

A royalty artist may be paid by advance or recording fund rather than by the session, but also receives royalties based on the number of recordings sold. With respect to self-contained acts and all other royalty artists, the maximum wage required to be paid by the company per recording side (not counting royalties) is three times the minimum AFTRA scale, irrespective of the number and length of the sessions required for that side.

The AFTRA code sets forth in detail its requirements regarding minimum wages. A producer or contractor should consult an AFTRA representative for current details. There are several common classifications of employment and wages. For example, AFTRA classifies its singer members as:

1. Soloists or duos
2. Group singers
3. Soloists who "step out" of a group
4. Singers who record original cast albums (Broadway shows, etc.)
5. Choral singers recording or broadcasting classical or religious music

It wasn't until 1974 that AFTRA managed to negotiate a contract incorporating the minimum royalty concept—a significant breakthrough in how extra wages were to be calculated for singers. AFTRA singers who do not receive a royalty started receiving additional wages based on recordings sold. In the past, artists other than royalty artists enjoyed no such additional rewards, no matter how successful a particular recording became. When these extra payments were agreed on, they became known as **contingent scale payments.** Here are typical payments under the current contract:

1. When an album reaches a sales plateau of 157,500, nonroyalty AFTRA singers on that album receive a payment equal to 50% of their original scale for those particular sessions. There are 11 contingent scale plateaus, totaling an additional 550% of scale.
2. When a single recording attains sales of one-half million, nonroyalty singers receive 33.33% of scale. There are 6 contingent scale plateaus for singles, totaling an additional 200% of scale.
3. Singers recording original cast albums receive 40% of scale when sales of 320,000 are reached. There are 4 contingent scale plateaus for cast albums, totaling an additional 130% of scale.

A recording is considered for these payments for a period of 10 years following its initial release. Payments are limited to sales in the United States that occur through normal retail channels. Sales through record clubs, premiums, and mail orders are excluded. Also excluded from these calculations are recordings distributed for promotional purposes. In determining which releases are subject to these payments, only the initial release of a record side in album form is included, not any subsequent inclusions of that side in albums. As for singles, only the initial release is eligible for these payments, but a single later included in an album is also eligible. A side first released in an album is eligible when it first reappears as a single.

With respect to the AFTRA Health & Retirement Funds, recording companies are required to pay on behalf of AFTRA recording artists about 11% (the rate may vary) of their gross compensation for the recording. The term *gross compensation* is defined by the AFTRA code in this respect as including royalties paid AFTRA members by the recording company. Payment into the fund is limited to the first $110,000 of gross compensation paid to the artist by the recording company in any calendar year. The payment into these funds is also required with respect to the contingent scale payments described above.

Acquired Masters

When a singer records for one of its signatory labels, AFTRA has little difficulty controlling minimum wages and working conditions. But many recordings are made by very small companies and by independent record producers who then later attempt to sell or lease their master tapes to a third party. This practice is widespread in the music business, and full union control is difficult, often impossible. AFTRA and the American Federation of Musicians (AFM) do what they can, however, to protect their members from unfair practices.

The rights of performers are often abused when a producer transfers rights in a master tape to another person. The first producer may have met all the provisions of the AFTRA contract, but royalties and contingent scale obligations on the first producer's recording may continue to accrue and yet not be paid. The third party acquiring rights to the master (and possibly including an inventory of merchandise unsold) is required to continue payment of singers' royalties and contingent scale and other contractual obligations on all sales the third party generates.

A more complicated situation arises when the original master was not recorded under the AFTRA code. In anticipation of this kind of situation (not uncommon), the AFTRA code requires that if a signatory record company produces a sound recording from a master from an outside nonsignatory source, the total cost to that outside source must have been at least equal to what the cost would have been under the AFTRA sound recordings code that was in effect at the time the recording was produced. The purpose of this requirement is to ensure that no producer will be economically motivated to have a sound recording produced by a nonsignatory.

When a third party acquires interest in or ownership of a master recording, the obligations for payment of royalties and contingent payments are spelled out by AFTRA. But the courts have occasionally been unpredictable in their rulings on these matters. In an attempt to dispel all ambiguities, the AFTRA code specifies that the responsibility to pay AFTRA obligations devolves upon the transferee and, in turn, any subsequent transferee, for sales made under such transferees or their licensees.

Artists' unions do all they can to protect the interests of their members when master tapes recorded for one medium are licensed for use in another medium. Perhaps the most common occurrence of this kind involves a tape prepared for a commercial recording and then transferred for use on television, where the on-camera artist lip-synchs the performance. Whatever kind of secondary use is made of a recording (called a **new use** or reuse), AFTRA requires the record company to get a warranty from the new user guaranteeing that the singers will receive no less than the appropriate scale payment for the new use. With respect to the music video field, AFTRA has a separate agreement with the producers.

Nonunion Recording

Even though AFTRA has more than 75,000 members and agreements with all the major labels, the practice of nonunion recording is widespread. Aspiring young performers, eager to get their professional careers off to a quick start, often do not take time to learn established professional practices. Some artists never do discover the advantages of collectivism, the concept of all union activity.

A young performer who fails to convince a recognized recording label to sign a contract may produce a master, perhaps even press a few hundred records, and attempt to place them on the market. Rarely do such entrepreneurs adhere to AFTRA or AFM regulations or scales. Many "self-produced" performers, at the start of their careers, are not even aware of the artists' unions and their traditions. Occasionally, the performer-producer-distributor-merchant experiences initial success in a limited geographic area. Some one-person recording companies manage later to sell or lease their masters to an established label with national distribution. At that point, either the original entrepreneur or the lessee must meet the AFTRA obligations described above. Thus, the original entrepreneur saves no money in the long run by initially circumventing AFTRA and the AFM, for their members must ultimately be paid for any recording to take off in the national market.

It is important to remember that there is typically a pronounced disparity of bargaining power between any one artist and an entertainment conglomerate. Unions, therefore, remain key players in the entertainment business, providing an important source of artists' rights protection.

AFM AGREEMENTS

Phonograph Record Labor Agreement

Most record companies that distribute their products nationally have a contract with the AFM for the services of instrumentalists, directors, arrangers, orchestrators, and **copyists**. Every 3 years, the AFM, under the supervision of the AFM president, establishes a committee to negotiate a successor agreement with recording industry representatives. The current contract is known as the Phonograph Record Labor Agreement. It governs wages, benefits, and working conditions for all services of musicians working in the recording industry in the United States and Canada. The Phonograph Record Labor Agreement provides that only the services of members in good standing of the American Federation of Musicians of the United States and Canada shall be used for the performance of all instrumental music, and in copying, orchestrating, or arranging of such music; in recording phonograph records; and, in the employment of persons eligible for membership in the federation, only such persons as shall be members thereof in good standing shall be so employed.

In addition to wages paid for musicians' services, the contract also requires the employer to pay a fixed amount into the AFM Health and Welfare Fund (AFM H&W) to locals that have established them or directly to musicians, absent such a plan, and up to 10% of gross (scale) wages into the AFM-EP, the AFM Employers Pension Fund.

The contract provides 200% of **sideman's** pay for the leader (musical director). Where a session calls for 12 or more musicians, an AFM contractor is required and receives double sideman's wages. Musicians doubling on a second instrument are paid, with some exceptions, 20% extra for the first **double,** then 15% for each additional double. The agreement contains many other details covering rest periods, meal breaks, and surcharges for work performed after midnight and on holidays, as well as special rates and conditions for work performed on electronic instruments. Even cartage fees for heavy instruments are stipulated.

The Phonograph Record Labor Agreement requires that all music "prepared" for recording must be handled exclusively by arrangers, orchestrators, and copyists who are members of the AFM. Because the AFM claims no jurisdiction over the work of songwriters and other kinds of composers, the agreement does not cover their services.

Enforcement of the scales and working conditions stipulated in the agreement can be generally managed with the well-established, recognized labels when they produce their own masters. But, as noted above, the practice is widespread in the industry for recording companies to lease or buy "outside" masters. The agreement deals with this problem in detail (Paragraph 18), but policing of these transactions is difficult, sometimes impossible. Record manufacturers are prohibited from using acquired masters unless the music was recorded under the AFM contract and the scale wages it required were paid, or the musicians have been paid equivalent wages and the required contribution to the AFM Pension Fund has been made. The company may satisfy its obligation in respect to acquiring masters by securing a "representation of warranty" from the seller or licensor that the requirements of the AFM have been satisfied.

Special Payments Fund

Phonograph Records. When a recording company signs the AFM Phonograph Record Labor Agreement, it must also simultaneously execute a Phonograph Record Manufacturers Special Payments Fund Agreement.

Record companies make payments into the Special Payments Fund twice each year, based on the aggregate sale of recordings in the company's catalog. The "royalty" due the fund is less than 1% (each contract tends to vary the rate) of the suggested retail price of each recording sold. Record companies are allowed discounts for packaging (up to 15%) and for free promotional copies distributed (up to 20%) and for recordings sold through record clubs (up to 50%). Companies must pay these royalties for a period of 10 years dating from the initial release of a recording.

All these royalties are paid by the recording companies to the Administrator of the Fund. After administrative expenses are deducted, all funds are then paid to the musicians who, during the preceding 5-year period, performed on any of the recordings covered by the Special Payments Fund Agreement. The amount paid to each musician is based on the musician's earnings in the phonograph field. Payments are based on overall record sales, not on the sale of particular recordings. Musicians who earned the same scale payments from work on audio recordings will receive the same amount from the Special Payments Fund, even if one musician worked on a multi-platinum album and the other worked on an album that sold only 5,000 copies. About a half-dozen AFM members receive checks of $40,000 or more. Some 400 recording musicians receive checks of $10,000 and up.

Motion Pictures. The Motion Picture Special Payments Fund is collected from film companies and paid to musicians who have worked on sound tracks of films. Unlike the Phonograph Special Payments, the Motion Picture Special Payments reflect the relative success of each project. A musician who worked on a picture that made a lot of money will receive more than a musician who spent the same amount of time working on a picture that was not a commercial success. In both cases, musicians are also paid for the hours they actually spend in the studio.

The Special Payments Fund Agreement recognizes that, during the 10 years royalties must be paid, the ownership and control of a recording may change. In anticipation of these changes, the agreement provides that any such purchaser, assignee, lessee, licensee, transferee, or user shall become an additional first party hereto, meaning that such persons must assume the obligations to the AFM of the company first producing the masters or records. Because of the extensive changes in the recording industry—companies and ownership come and go—the control and collection of these funds by the AFM is difficult and cannot always be accomplished.

Music Performance Trust Funds

The MPTF, or Music Performance Trust Funds, was established to help keep live music available to the public. From the beginning, the AFM recognized that the increasing impact of recording technology was devastating to the music profession except, of course, for the AFM members who, each year, earn at least part of their livelihood from recording. Knowing that nothing could prevent the rapid technological growth in the recording industry, the AFM managed to negotiate agreements with the recording companies that return to union musicians at least a fraction of the income lost through the reduction of jobs performing music live. Recording companies must enter into a Trust Fund Agreement with the AFM. Payments are made to the fund's trustee and are based on record sales. The Trust Fund Agreement provides that the trustee is obligated to use all monies collected, except for operational expenses, to set up performances of live music performed by AFM members. In actual practice, administration of these monies is shared by each of the AFM locals that parcel out jobs to their members, irrespective of whether the members are recording musicians, and pay them prevailing local union scales. AFM locals may use some of the money for these live performances to hire halls, finance publicity, print tickets, and so on. Cosponsors of concerts are generally required. The intent of the Trust Fund is to foster public understanding and appreciation for live music; most performances are for schools, hospitals, religious organizations, cultural events, and patriotic celebrations. If no admission is charged, the live performances may be broadcast. Established cultural organizations, such as symphony orchestras, opera, and ballet companies, often call on the Trust Fund to finance or partially finance live music performances.

Recent contracts call for sharply reduced contributions by the recording manufacturers to the AFM's Trust Fund Agreement and Special Payments Fund. Each succeeding contract negotiation finds the union fighting to keep these programs alive.

Nonunion Recording

AFM and AFTRA have been trying to maintain strict **union shops** in the recording studios for decades, with uneven results. Following enactment of the Taft-Hartley Act and **right-to-work laws** in various states, establishment and maintenance of a strict union shop concept has been difficult. All professional symphony orchestra recording in the United States is under the AFM, as is most pop-type recording in the major recording centers. Union control is less strong in the rock, soul, and country fields. Particularly with younger rock bands, quantities of master tapes are produced every year, sometimes recorded by fly-by-night producers and managers who promise the kids they'll get rich quick. Many of these operators disappear shortly after sundown. The AFM, from time to time, activates a PR campaign to attract very young players ("Young Sounds of the

AFM") with reduced fees and dues. As young musicians gain professional experience, they usually discover that working under the protection of AFM membership offers greater long-term rewards than a fast dollar picked up in nonunion sessions.

Another kind of nonunion recording, somewhat more legitimate, is the **spec** session. Producers will hire some musicians, pay them perhaps $50 per hour, then promise to make full payment later, "when the recording sells," in an amount equal to AFM scale. Still other producers pay the musicians (union or nonunion) nothing up front, promising to pay full union scale later when the producer can raise the money. Both these kinds of spec recording are disapproved of by the AFM, which does have a lower "demo" scale than its regular recording scale.

The most effective point of control is found with the independent producer when attempting to lease or sell masters to a recording company. But if that record company is not a signatory to the AFM recording agreements, or is a signatory but fails to adhere to those agreements, nonunion masters can get produced and sold. But engaging in this kind of fly-by-night activity is short-lived and rarely profitable. This follows because, should a nonunion recording company experience temporary success, it will want to sign other artists, and all the established ones are AFM members recording under AFM contracts. The nonunion company will be unsuccessful in such attempts. Furthermore, if the nonunion artist starts to experience success on a nonunion label, that artist will want to sign subsequently with a more stable company that can offer much better long-range opportunities.

One of the union's most effective means of controlling nonunion recording is to penalize its own members. Some locals assess union rulebreakers fines of $1,000, $2,500, even as much as $5,000 for second- and third-time offenses. In addition to heavy fines, most locals' bylaws permit the union to expel a member who fails to follow AFM rules governing recording services.

ROYALTY ARTIST CONTRACTS

Every performer thinks that a really prosperous career is largely dependent on obtaining a recording contract. Therein lies the big money, the international reputation. Until a performer becomes recognized as a recording artist, it is almost impossible to attract enough notice to draw employment offers from concert promoters, major booking agencies, television, and film producers. Of course, an artist can develop a satisfactory career in one area—for example, on Broadway—and never establish a career on records. But most performers would not pass up the chance for the prestige and potential income gained through recording.

Although the AFM and AFTRA contracts control wages and working conditions for backup artists, the individuals and groups whose names and sounds are used to sell recordings negotiate contracts for their services, not through an artists' union, but in direct negotiations with a recording company. Such performers are known as *royalty artists.* The AFM defines such a performer as a musician

> who records pursuant to a phonograph record contract which provides for a royalty payable at a basic rate of at least three percent of the suggested retail list price of records sold (less deductions usual and customary in the trade), or a substantially equivalent royalty, or who plays as a member of (and not as a sideman with) a recognized **self-contained group** . . . [which is] two or more persons who perform together in fields other than phonograph records under a group name (whether fictional or otherwise); and . . . the members of which are recording pursuant to a phonograph record contract which provides for a royalty payable with respect to the group at a basic rate of at least three percent . . . and all of the musicians of which are or become members of the American Federation of Musicians as provided in this Agreement.

The AFM position has been codified with the AFM Phonograph Labor Agreements so that royalty artists receive one session payment for each song recorded on an album. The session payment may be part of recording costs that are recouped from artist royalties.

Types of Deals

In earlier times it was simple: A record company signed an artist, instructed one of its house A&R (artist and repertoire) people to produce the records, and that was that. Today, that simple formula still applies at times. More often, though, the record company and the artist have a number of other options in working out a contract. These different kinds of recording deals exist because of the presence, sometimes dominance, in the business of the independent producer.

Here are the most common types of deals being made today in placing an artist under contract:

1. The label signs the artist, then has one of its producers handle the project **in-house.** The artist gets royalties, the staff producer receives a salary, perhaps a royalty override. The label pays all costs pursuant to a budget and may or may not pay advances to the artist.

2. The label already has the artist under contract, then retains an independent producer (or production company) to deliver a master tape. The recording company assigns a production budget to the producer, possibly pays a production "fee" up front, usually an advance on royalties, and negotiates a royalty for the producer of 2% to 5% based on the retail list price of recordings sold by the artist.

3. The independent producer and an independent artist strike a deal, create a master tape, then try to induce a recording company to buy it. The label accepting the master pays the parties royalties based on recording units sold (the artist and the producer had worked out beforehand how they would share these royalties).

4. In a master lease deal, the artist or production company pays all recording costs and leases the master to the label in exchange for a royalty. The label may or may not pay an advance in the nature of reimbursement of recording costs. Since the artist or production company as licensor assumes the risk of recording, the record company normally does not obtain ownership but merely the right to distribute for a limited time in a limited territory. The licensor leases the master to the label on a royalty basis.

5. An artist forms a production company to deliver a master tape to a label. The producer on the project might be on the production company's payroll or might be engaged freelance just for this particular project. The label pays the artist's company a royalty. The artist then pays the producer a share of those royalties.

6. A corporation has an employment agreement with the artist, then agrees to loan out the artist's services to a recording company. The label pays royalties directly to the corporation. The corporation, in turn, pays the artist a salary, possibly a royalty override. This arrangement could provide a tax shelter for the artist, who might also receive from the corporation certain additional benefits, such as a retirement plan.

Negotiations

Most recording companies are very selective today in determining the talent they want to sign. Unlike earlier times when a label would sign artists on a speculative basis to test public reaction, current practice is to limit signings to artists the label is reasonably certain will find strong public acceptance. Today's conservative signing policies result largely from the prohibitive costs of "breaking" new pop artists, which could start in the range of $250,000 to $500,000 or more for production and initial promotional and marketing expenses.

The label will invite the artist and management and lawyers to begin discussions about a possible contract. Following at least one exploratory meeting where deal terms are proposed and negotiated, lawyers would meet to hammer out the fine print of the agreement. This scenario typically develops after an artist with shrewd management has created a "stir" among industry insiders. In the most desirable situation (from the artist's point of view), several companies will bid competitively for a contract with the artist.

If the artist lacks management and legal counsel, established labels will insist the artist be represented by an attorney. Onerous contracts have been set aside by courts when it was learned that the artist had no attorney. The negotiations for the label would be handled by a senior executive and the company's legal counsel. Sometimes a company's vice president for "business affairs" or the A&R head is empowered to negotiate an artist's contract.

Both parties look upon the negotiations as an opportunity to maximize self-interests. The prevailing party will almost always turn out to be the one with the strongest negotiating position: in a word, clout. Compromise, however, is usually the key to an enduring, long-term relationship. Take, for example, one chief negotiating point—the advance. A large signing advance or recording budget might improve an artist's state of mind but substantially increase the record company's risk. An effective negotiation might satisfy both parties by providing royalty rate adjustments or bonuses as certain sales levels (sometimes called plateaus) are reached.

The Issues

Properly drawn recording contracts will cover the following issues:

Term. Until recently, the standard length of an artist's recording contract would be 1 year, with a given number of 1-year options for the company to extend.

More common today, at least with important artists, is a period without a time limit, but with the length of the contract tied to the timing of master deliveries and recording release requirements. Experienced lawyers often attempt to negotiate contracts on a per-album basis—for example, a three-album contract. If the first album does not sell well, the parties are bound to each other for two follow-up releases that afford them an opportunity to test the effectiveness of their alliance. A per-album deal often provides for delivery of an album every 6 to 9 months, with the contract terminating after delivery of the third album unless there are options. But the parties could, of course, subsequently negotiate a new contract to extend their relationship.

In a three-album contract, should the label decline to release all three albums, the contract should provide a penalty, normally a sum of money ("liquidated damages") payable to the artist. Well-drawn contracts provide guarantees of artist's delivery by a certain date and the company's release of the recordings. Experienced lawyers try to get the label to guarantee release within 90 to 120 days following delivery of the master to the company.

The holiday period of November-December is always excluded from these date specifications. During downturn periods in the recording business, or if the artist is unknown, companies sometimes commit to singles and "EP (extended play) deals." EPs usually include five or six songs, and record companies may prefer to limit their risk and incur initial recording expenses of, say, $5,000 per side or less rather than the much larger amount it might take to turn out a full album. This sort of deal occurs frequently in the urban and alternative music genres where there are many small indie labels.

Exclusivity. Almost all recording contracts require the artist to record, during the term of the contract, only for the label that has the artist under contract. But if the artist also records from time to time in a capacity other than as a solo artist or featured group, for instance, as a **session musician** or sideman on a jazz recording, the artist's lawyer will want the contract to permit such outside services to enable the contract artist to maximize income.

Royalties, Advances. Depending on how badly the label wants to sign the artist, the royalty offer will be in the range of 10% to 12% of the retail price, with perhaps 3 points of that amount going to the producer. Major stars have been known to get as high as 18% to 22% of retail. Sometimes a label will try to hold the initial royalty below 10%, then escalate the rate as sales rise. For example, the artist might receive 9% on the first 100,000 sales, 10% on the next 100,000, then something like 12% if the recording goes gold. Lawyers might persuade a label to start the initial royalty rate higher on a second album, should sales of the first album turn out to be satisfactory.

There is no standard policy among record companies on royalty advances. Record companies generally hold back about 25% or more of the royalties in a "reserve account," in anticipation that some records "sold" will be returned by dealers for credit. The contract should limit this reserve account and specify the maximum time period such royalties can be held back.

Production Budget Minimums. Major recording artists can negotiate a big-budget commitment from a label to cover recording production costs. Less prominent recording artists would not be able to impose such a demand. But a promising new artist would be well advised, if negotiating with a label of limited resources, to demand a minimum budget commitment or risk being caught in a low-quality project that could hurt a developing career.

A recording budget is an estimate of the cost of the album production. If actual production or recording expenses are less than the amount in the budget, the recording company generally doesn't pay any more than actual recording expenses unless the contract provides for a recording fund rather than a recording budget. In that case, an agreed-on sum is set aside for a fund, with one third to perhaps one half of the amount being released to the artist (or the producer) at the commencement of recording. The balance is released from the fund following completion and satisfactory delivery of the master tape. Should the production expense total an amount smaller than the recording fund, some contracts allow the artist (or producer) to keep the difference, with the understanding that the entire sum is recoupable by the label from royalties accrued from sales of the record.

Creative Control. Recording stars often demand, and usually receive, control over such issues as the selection of songs to be recorded, the selection of a producer, and album graphic art. Less important artists will probably have to accept the judgments of the company in such matters. The parties usually compromise on the question of who selects the record producer: It is usually by mutual consent. The label will typically want a new artist to collaborate with a producer who has a proven track record, thus reducing some of the many uncertainties in developing a new act. As for the selection of songs, although it is rare for a record company to give up its power to make the ultimate selection of which songs go on a record, few labels would force a recording artist to record material or work with a producer with whom the artist could not perform comfortably.

Commitment to Promote. A strong-selling recording artist will probably be able to demand that the label commit sufficient money and personnel to fully **exploit** the recordings released. Most artists, including the big stars, regularly complain that the label is not providing adequate promotion. This promotion issue is the one that causes most recording contracts to break down. If the CDs or tapes don't sell, the label blames the artist; the artist insists the sales would have been just fine if the firm had done an adequate promotion job. Specifically, the artist or the artist's manager should seek label commitment for tour support, press coverage, interviews, independent radio promotion, retail in-store promotion, and TV, trade, and consumer magazine and newspaper ads.

Charge-Backs. Royalty contracts routinely include the stipulation that the recording company does not have to pay the artist any royalties, except for advances that are negotiated, until the label has recovered, through a recoupment from the artist's royalties, its out-of-pocket production costs and advances. Production expenses that are considered legitimate to charge back include studio rentals, the cost of blank tape, union wages to AFM and AFTRA members, and music arranging and copying expense. Such costs can easily total $200,000 and more for a pop album. When a royalty artist completes a project, all the artist gets are advances or the overage on the fund, if there is one. No more money comes to the artist until the recording company has recouped its recording costs. It is evident the records will have to sell well just for the artist to break even.

Advances to artists are not returnable although they are almost always recoupable. When trying to determine how many albums must be sold before an artist has recouped advances, many attorneys use an estimate of 1 percentage point at retail being worth roughly 10 cents of royalty income to the artist per album sold. Therefore, 10 points would equal $1.00 per album sold. To recoup $100,000, the recording company would have to sell 100,000 albums.

Obviously, recoupment of an artist's recording account is not always necessary for the recording company to realize a satisfactory return on an artist's recordings. Although it is true that it would take 100,000 sales to recoup $100,000, the average wholesale price of a CD is close to $10.00, and so that same 100,000 sales will generate $1 million in gross income. Of course, there are costs involved with

those sales, but many attorneys argue that the recording company in this situation sees profits long before the artist's royalty account is recouped.

It is not unusual for an artist to have fulfilled all recording obligations under a contract, have some recordings that sold well, but still not receive any royalties. Even with successful albums, the artist's overall royalty account may remain in an unrecouped position. Almost all recording companies include a clause in the contract making costs accrued on all recordings recoupable out of royalties on all recordings (see the Royalty Discounts section, below). This language, called cross-collateralization, makes it difficult for the artist's royalty account to ever be recouped or "in the black."

Ownership of Masters. Initially, the recording company owns all rights. But when a contract is terminated, artists' attorneys often will try to negotiate transfer of ownership to their clients. Recording companies are rarely willing to give up ownership of masters. Master recordings of established artists have considerable residual value, particularly when a firm repackages and/or reissues old records. Master tapes are often sold or leased to secondary labels for this purpose.

Reissues of old recordings in new formats have contributed significantly to album sales. Most large recording companies now have separate departments dedicated solely to reissues of their back catalogs. Only true superstars might be able to negotiate some eventual return of masters but the general rule is that if a label pays to record a master, the label will own it in perpetuity.

Publishing Rights, Controlled Compositions. Where the artist composes original songs, many recording companies will try to persuade the artist to place all of those songs with a publishing company owned by or affiliated with the label. When this happens, the artist-writer may receive additional advances. If the label's publishing wing cannot obtain full publishing rights, it will probably attempt to "split" the copyrights in some way, sharing the publishing revenue with the composer-performer in what is known as a copublishing arrangement. If the label or production company cannot share "in the publishing," it will almost always demand a reduced mechanical rate, commonly 25% below the current statutory rate, for all works owned or controlled by the recording artist. Such language is called controlled composition language, and the artist refusing to accept this language may not get signed.

Controlled composition language usually specifies that the label will pay a rate equal to 75% rate of the minimum statutory rate. Controlled composition language also provides that the maximum album rate for all compositions, controlled and noncontrolled, cannot exceed 10 times the per-composition rate. This can lead to disastrous results when the artist records both controlled and noncontrolled compositions. The publishers of the noncontrolled compositions are, of course, not going to abide by the 75% language and will demand full rate, which, in the case of longer works such as jazz recordings, could exceed the minimum rate applicable to works of 5 minutes or less. Since there is an album cap of $10 \times 75\%$ of the minimum, the artist's own rate will be reduced below 75% and in extreme cases could go to zero or even be negative, so the artist could actually owe the label money. The statutory rate used in such calculations is the minimum rate in effect at the time the album was delivered or supposed to have been delivered. These sections of record contracts can rarely be avoided except by major stars.

Video Rights. Most recording contracts today include consideration of music video. In the early period of music video history, labels and artists did not know how significant the genre would become, so they negotiated "wait and see" clauses. These clauses stated the parties would come to terms later, if and when videos became important. When it was discovered that videos could help sell records and even sell in cassette form for home entertainment, the recording labels hastened to replace the ambiguous language of the earlier contracts.

Many labels demand the exclusive services of their contract artists for any and all performances on videos (clips, compilations, and long forms such as concerts), offering to share any of the potential income from distributors. They also charge to the artist's recording royalty account all video production costs.

A typical negotiated recording contract will include agreement on the following issues relating to videos:

1. Videos must be defined as "promotional" or "commercial." Promotional clips, compilations, and video "albums" (or "long-form" videos) are defined according to their lengths in order to clarify further the distinctions between promotional and commercial videos.
2. The label generally pays for production costs of the video. Video costs are recouped first from royalties on video sales. To the extent video sales are

insufficient for the recoupment of these costs, most recording contracts provide for recoupment of the balance of those costs from the artist's general audio royalty account. Contracts vary as to what percentage of video costs are recoupable from this account. Most labels insist initially on recouping 100%, but this point is negotiable, and some labels will agree to limit video cost recoupment under the audio account to 50%.

3. If the artist owns or controls any of the music used on a video, the artist will be expected to waive licensing fees and royalties on that material, provided the video is only for promotional purposes. But if the video is nonpromotional in nature, the artist-composer can argue for synchronization fees and mechanical royalties.

4. The artist should seek reasonable control over the selection of video directors, other production personnel, the budget, and storyline.

5. If the label refuses to produce a video, the artist may try to reserve the right to produce the video at the artist's own expense.

Foreign Releases. The artist's lawyer should try to persuade the recording company to specify the foreign territories in which the recording will be released. This is essential, in that most records sold worldwide are sold outside the United States and Canada. In addition to getting the label to list specific foreign territories, the artist should try to get the label to effect these releases simultaneously with or shortly after the American release, to maximize the effectiveness of a promotion campaign and minimize the damage of imports into a territory like Japan, where cheaper records imported from Europe and the United States compete with the expensive domestic version. All major labels have their own foreign affiliates, but there are smaller labels that work through licensees.

The artist will want to negotiate carefully how royalties are earned on sales in foreign territories. Many labels pay only 50% of the domestic rate. This can usually be increased through negotiation. When a sale takes place outside the United States, the artist is entitled to an accounting only after the licensee accounts to the U.S. label.

Overseas, recordings are rarely sold on consignment. In Europe, a sale is a sale; you get paid for what is purchased. This makes accounting simpler and obviates the need for the foreign licensee to hold back royalty reserves. The U.S. label might still take a reserve on foreign sales since they would not differentiate these sales in terms of general reserve policies.

Assignment. Contracts normally specify the terms under which a label may assign a contract to another entity. Recording companies, particularly the smaller ones, change ownership, leadership, or direction. Under such circumstances, the label may assign its contract rights.

The artist's attorney should try to limit the right of the company to assign the artist's contract only as part of a sale of the company's total business or assets. The distinction is made between the right to sell existing masters, which is almost always permitted, and the right to require the artist to record for another company, which usually can be restricted to an affiliated entity.

Right to Audit. Royalty statements are rendered to the artist semiannually. The parties usually agree that the artist may, upon proper written notice, audit the books of the label. In most states, a right to audit would be inferred by a court even if it weren't in the contract; therefore, labels write in a very restricted audit clause to avoid a much broader one being defined by a court.

Audits for major stars are expensive, since most experienced auditors work by the hour rather than for a percentage of the recovery. The artist's lawyer should seek a provision in the recording contract that requires the recording company to pay the entire cost of the examination if the amount found to be owing exceeds 10% of the amount actually paid. Although audits rarely reveal that the company has deliberately cheated an artist, discovery of royalties owed is a regular occurrence.

Default, Cure. If the parties have a serious disagreement, certain remedies are available to either side.

Suppose the artist is scheduled to deliver an album but decides to take a 6-month vacation. If the label believes the artist is not meeting contractual obligations, it can suspend the term of the agreement and its obligation to pay royalties or it can terminate the agreement and possibly sue for damages.

Because recording contracts involve personal services, few courts will tell an artist to perform such services against the artist's will. If the recording company enjoins the artist from recording for a competing firm during a period of dispute, the artist has three options: (a) to give up the battle and not record at all; (b) to attempt to renegotiate the contract; (c) to admit defeat and continue recording for the first company.

When a recording company and an artist have a serious disagreement over a contract, sometimes the label will agree to renegotiate. Neither party can prosper in the long run when compelled to work under a contract viewed as inequitable or unfair. That would be a poor climate for making music.

Royalty Discounts. Record companies try to reduce the price on which royalties are calculated as much as possible despite protests from knowledgeable artists' lawyers. Here are commonly seen limitations on the royalty base:

1. *Breakage allowance.* Some labels still offer royalties based on 85% or 90% of sales, a practice once justified, in that about 10% of the old 78-rpm records would become damaged in transit. Although this proportion of damage is no longer the case, the practice of paying royalties on less than 100% of sales remains.

2. *Packaging discount.* Labels deduct up to 25% of the price to cover costs of tape or CD packaging materials. These materials do not cost this much anymore, but the charge is assessed anyway, universally 25% of retail on CDs and other digital formats and 20% on tapes.

3. *Free goods.* Companies usually discount royalties for free goods given to distributors and retailers as incentives and quantity discounts (e.g., "Buy 10 and we'll give you 12"). The royalty-based price is always reduced at least 15% to reflect this policy. Some labels believe they must give away nearly one half of their singles to sell the other half. Artists receive no royalties on these "free goods" or promo copies.

4. *CD rate discounts.* Profits are supposedly lower on CDs than on tapes, and labels try to pay a lower royalty on them, usually 15% to 20%, which means that if the tape rate is 10%, the CD rate will be 75% to 80% of that.

5. *Record club sales.* Labels usually pay a tiny royalty on their net receipts from sales through record clubs, which in turn pay a very low royalty to the label.

6. *Merchandising.* Some recording companies acquire these rights and make merchandising deals on behalf of the artist. Artists' attorneys should seek to retain artists' rights in this area unless the label is really in the merchandising business, which is rarely the case.

7. *Cross-collateralization.* All recording companies seek the right to **cross-collateralize** an artist's royalties. If one recording sells well, royalties from it are discounted to the extent necessary for the label to recoup its production costs on the artist's other recordings that may not have sold as well. In

addition, as previously stated, recording companies will charge to the artist's royalties all the label's out-of-pocket costs in producing videos for the artist. Another cross-collateralization privilege is sought when the label still has a loss under an earlier contract: While negotiating for a contract extension or revision, the label will attempt to encumber the new recording agreement by charging against royalties earned in order to recoup unrecovered charges under the old contract.

In most cases of contract negotiation with new artists, the recording company bargains from a position of strength, creating a contract that is essentially one-sided and most likely will not yield significant royalties to the artist. As an artist's success grows, advances, recording budgets, and royalties go up and the balance of power begins to even out to some degree. When an artist achieves superstar status, the recording company really acts more as a distributor, working for a relatively small "participation" to recoup an enormous investment of production, promotion, and distribution costs.

RECORD PRODUCTION

Just as it is said that movie making is "the director's art," so one may say that creating sound recordings is "the producer's art." It is rare to hear a successful recording today that does not reveal the sure hand of a competent producer. Even if the song is great and the performance outstanding, these elements must be brought together and presented to the ear as one artistic whole.

The record producer's number one challenge is matching artist to repertoire, seeking a union of the performer and the material. An imaginative producer goes beyond this to contrive ways of producing a good master tape even with material that is less than great, with an artist who may not always shake the earth.

PRODUCING TALENTS

Different kinds of producers exist, and their modes of working vary from superbly organized to seat-of-the-pants. Some producers blazed ahead as the best in their class of music majors at school; others cannot read music. Whatever their level of formal education, most working producers fit into one of the descriptions below:

The Complete Producer. The complete producer, one who is qualified to handle all the important elements that make up record production—artistic, managerial, and technological—is rare. Talents of this magnitude often operate their own production company or recording company or head a creative department for a major label.

The Engineer-Producer. An engineer-producer is basically an engineer (audio **mixer**) engaged to run sessions for an **executive producer** or **creative director.** The engineer-producer excels at "getting sounds"from the console, but may lack many of the other talents and skills possessed by the more versatile producer.

The Artist-Producer. An artist-producer is probably a self-producing artist or writer who may also produce the songs and performances of other artists. This producer may lack technological skills and depend wholly on the audio mixer for engineering judgments and may have to rely on others to handle the managerial aspects of production, such as contracts or budgeting.

The Executive Producer. Executive producers make it as "producers" due to their abilities to raise money. The money acts as a catalyst, drawing together diverse talents—artists, writers, mixers, among others. Master tapes get laid down here through a kind of committee action, though a good executive producer might well possess the musical sensitivity and know-how in the studio that earns the respect of the other pros involved.

The Coproducer. A coproducer shares the responsibilities—either musical, technological, or managerial—with other persons. Some are identified as coproducers who are performers on the sessions and assume a leadership role during taping and mixdown.

The Independent Producer

Over the years, employment practices concerning producers have varied widely. Until the advent of rock and roll, recording companies maintained a staff of full-time **house producers,** who had strong control over who was recorded and precisely what material the chosen few were to record. In the 1960s, large numbers of rock stars composed their own songs and attempted to control the selection of material. They achieved this either by sheer weight of their influence or by insisting they "produce themselves" or bring in their own producers from outside. Since that time, most firms, large and small, have used a mix of in-house and independent producers.

An independent producer today may be a one-person company. One musician adept at keyboard synthesis can handle every facet of composition, arranging, performing, mixing, editing, and production of everything up to tape **mastering,** thanks to MIDI (musical instrument digital interface). The advanced technology of MIDI enables the patching together of several pieces of equipment for recording or performance.

Many independent producers keep one to four associates on the company payroll whose collective talents are sufficient to attract jobs from recording labels. Between assignments, the independent producer or production company helps pay the bills by engaging in related enterprises such as artist management, music publishing, perhaps even video production.

Getting Started as an Independent Producer. If you plan to develop a career as a record producer, you will need determination, talent, and luck. Before you get too far along with your plan, ask these questions:

1. Have you got the will? Can you hang in there?
2. Are you gifted in locating artists with star potential? Neither you nor your acts will make a dime unless that potential is there. Can you persuade strong acts to sign exclusively with you?
3. Do you have a talent for picking songs with hit potential? If not, align yourself with people who do.
4. Can you evaluate the combined impact of the material, artist's delivery, and production sound?
5. Do you have access to lots of money? Do you know how to present a convincing plan to potential investors?
6. Do you know how to present your artists to potential buyers of master tapes? You have three ways to do this: present live showcases, present **demo** tapes (audio, perhaps video), or present master tapes.

If you lack any of these abilities, you must locate associates who are strong in areas where you may be deficient. Translation: Form an independent production company. Few individuals are talented or fortunate enough to go it alone.

If All Else Fails. If an independent producer can't sell the master tapes, the next thought is likely to be, "I'll show the big shots. I'll set up my own label!" This is an option if the producer has sufficient funds for manufacture, production, promotion, and distribution of recorded music and the knowledge to operate such a

Warner Bros. Records in Burbank, California. Photo courtesy of Warner Bros.

diverse enterprise. Or, if the producer is successful in some phase of the industry, can line up investors, then get strong acts under contract, there is some chance of setting up a new label and making a go of it.

Another way to go is underground: Read Diane Sward Rapaport's book (see the Selected Readings section in the Appendix) on how unknown acts, unheard-of producers, and small investors can sometimes successfully launch small independent labels.

PRODUCTION DEALS

Record producers are employed in various ways. Here are the most frequent working arrangements:

1. A record company engages a producer as a full-time employee, provides a weekly salary, perhaps a royalty override. The label's head of A&R

(artist and repertoire) assigns projects to the producer, who may have little to say about which artists or what music is recorded for the company.

2. The producer works as an independent **contractor**—as an entrepreneur or for a production company. Labels that employ the producer assign a budget, "deliver" the artist, and expect completion of a master. The producer, who gets a production fee, often recoupable by the label from royalties, will receive an advance on royalties, as will the artist.

3. The producer delivers the artist and a master. The two invest their time and money on the project, then set about trying to sell the master to an established label. If they succeed, the parties negotiate a **master purchase agreement** that will provide the recoupment of all or part of the production costs as well as a royalty that is shared by the producer and the artist.

4. The producer's services are delivered by the artist, who has the producer under contract. This is sometimes called an "all-in" deal: Artist's representatives negotiate a package that involves a royalty and an advance on royalties. The artist then shares the advance and the royalties with the producer.

Established producers rely heavily on their attorneys in drawing up production agreements. The producer will require legal counsel knowledgeable in this special area, because production agreements can be more complicated than artists' royalty contracts.

Royalties, Fees

Except on work turned out by a label's staff producers, all independent production agreements today provide a royalty for the producer. In this sector of the business, people often refer to a producer's *points*, a term synonymous in this context with percentages. One point equals 1% (e.g., 1 point may equal 1% of retail). A point may also equal a percentage of a percentage (e.g., 1 point may equal 1% of retail of 90% of recordings sold). How many points can a producer extract from a company? It is always the same story when negotiating a contract: The party with clout prevails. A young producer just breaking in may get only 1 point. Most producers receive 2 to 4 points. A few superstar producers ask for and receive 5% and 6% on sales.

Some contracts treat the producer better than the featured artist, who must wait for royalties until the label has recouped its production costs. The artist will normally receive a royalty 2 to 5 times higher than the producer's, but the producer may have a contract that requires royalties from sale number one. If this kind of immediate payment is agreed on, it is likely the record company talked the producer into fewer points.

In addition to royalties, it is standard practice for the label to pay a production fee. Some producers are fortunate to get a few thousand dollars in front as their fee, one half of which is normally paid before the first session begins, the other half upon delivery of the master. Some fees are not extra payments, but advances on the producer's royalties. Major producers can get tens of thousands of dollars in production fees, usually nonrecoupable by the label from royalties.

The Three Phases of Production

The complicated and expensive process of professional record production can be most clearly understood by examining its three phases: preproduction (planning), work in the studio, and postproduction activity (see Table 17.1).

PRODUCTION BUDGETING

The responsibility of developing and controlling budgets will be a part of the producer's job, whether the work is for a label or freelance.

Preparing a production budget with precision is difficult because many of the expenses can be only roughly estimated. At budget-writing time, the producer may not even know in which city the recording will take place. Perhaps a rhythm section must be flown in from Nashville. Will some of the songs on the album require an expensive complement of string players? All the budget-maker can do at the outset is identify expense parameters. After assembling all available data, costs must be specified in detail.

Budget Control

Well-organized producers work up budgets on some kind of summary sheet. Table 17.2 shows one kind of budget sheet, which may be used as is or tailored to a specific situation.

A budget control sheet must reflect careful research of current studio costs and the latest union wage scales and surcharges. Experienced producers often call in

TABLE 17.1   The Three Phases of Record Production

Preproduction phase

1. Create the concept
2. Prepare a budget, raise the money
3. Locate and sign an artist
4. Select the songs
5. Negotiate mechanical licenses
6. Engage the musical director, union contractors
7. Book time in a studio
8. Engage an engineer, test studio equipment, acoustics
9. Confirm availability of any special equipment and instruments needed
10. Reconfirm all of the above
11. Rehearse the music

In the studio

1. Lay down basic tracks, vocals
2. Add sweetener tracks
3. Prepare final mixdown to 2-track stereo
4. Obtain W-4 and I-9 forms and copies of identification from all employees
5. Sequence A and B sides
6. Pull out possible singles
7. Make cassette copies as needed
8. Prepare union contracts for musicians and vocalists

Postproduction

1. Locate a mastering studio
2. Supervise mastering
3. Obtain clearances from graphic artist, photographer, liner notes writer
4. Turn over signed mechanical licenses to the company
5. Deliver W-4 and I-9 forms, copies of identification, and union contracts to the company
6. Deliver lyric sheets and technical credit sheets to the company
7. Identify samples/interpolations and hire a sample clearinghouse
8. Deliver information on any samples/interpolations to the company
9. Confirm graphic art, liner notes are being prepared
10. Confirm all bills have been paid
11. Reconfirm everything
12. Deliver master tape

RECORDING BUDGET

Artist/Group _____   Date _____

Producer _____   Studio _____

Label/Client _____   Project No. _____

Contact _____   Engineer _____

	Cost Per Unit	No. of Units	Total Unit Cost	Subtotal	Extension
STUDIO					
Basic Rate					
Outboard Equipment					
Set up/Strike					
Basic Tracks					
Overdubs					
Vocals					
Mixing/Editing					
Tape Duplicating					
Tape					
Tax					
ENGINEERS					
1st engineer					
2nd engineer					

ARRANGING/COPYING						
Music title	*Arranging*	*Copying*				
1.						
2.						
3.						
4.						
5.						
6.						
7.						
8.						
9.						
10.						
Union surcharges						

ARTISTS	*Instrumentalists*	*Singers*	*Soloists*				
Rehearsals							
Basic Tracks							
Sweetening							
Union Surcharges							

EQUIPMENT					
Rentals					
Cartage					
Tax					

MISCELLANEOUS (Payroll, tax, etc.) _____

UNFORESEEN EXPENSE (15% of total) _____

TOTAL PRODUCTION COST

their American Federation of Musicians (AFM) and American Federation of Television and Radio Artists (AFTRA) contractors to help them pull together accurate figures.

Budgeting costs for taping singles is difficult enough, but when it comes to calculating the expense of recording an album, the producer enters an arena of high finance and maximum risk. Out-of-pocket expense of recording a quality master for an album today will start in the six-figure range.

Producers of rock albums often budget 10 to 20 hours of studio time per song. Some rock albums may clock 300 hours or more, including mixing, editing, and mastering. Producers and other recording executives worried about exorbitant recording costs should compare their figures with the studio time required by **session musicians.** These superb artists sight-read the **charts** and are able to perform an acceptable take on the second or third reading. Jazz album producers may let the machines roll and catch great performances the first time, entirely unrehearsed—improvised.

An even more impressive comparison of recording time for rock can be made with the classical field. A professional symphony orchestra of the second or third rank can record a 15- to 25-minute work, such as Stravinsky's *Rite of Spring,* in 6 to 9 hours! Of course, the orchestra would have learned the piece a few seasons back—but such an achievement is still remarkable. If new rock performers were to record as efficiently—as, of course, some do—their take-home royalties could increase significantly per release.

High recording costs often result for one of these reasons:

1. The group is poorly prepared; it uses the recording studio for rehearsal, even for composition.
2. The performers can't read music or can't blend or can't come up with the right style.
3. The producer can't decide what is needed.
4. The engineer can't come up with the right sounds.
5. One or more of the participants is not qualified for the job; the talent or the experience to compete professionally is lacking.

Recording expenses that are paid for by the label will be considered an advance against future earnings. Sometimes, these expenses are paid for out of a recording budget. If the recording costs less than anticipated, the excess money is returned to the record company. In other situations, anticipated recording expenses come out of a recording fund. As explained in Chapter 16, if the master is produced for an amount less than the fund, some contracts provide that the balance can be retained (by the artist or the producer, depending on their contract with each other) as an advance from the label against royalties.

Recording funds and budgets are more often overspent than underspent. Unforeseen events, or just bad luck, cause many projects to become more expensive than planned. If the producer exceeds the budget by no more than 10%, there will probably be no complaint from the employer. When a project is nearing completion and has developed momentum, most labels will permit reasonable budget overruns.

Whether the production money is transferred or kept in-house, the label will assign some individual to keep track of this money flow on a day-to-day basis. The producer will be asked to keep this budget monitor informed whenever expense is incurred.

CREATIVE CONTROL

Creative control refers to the right of the producer to make artistic judgments. The artist may have such high stature that creative control is relinquished to no one. More likely, the producer and the featured artist will share decision making of this kind.

Probably the most controversial "call"in matters relating to producing recordings is the selection of material. If the artist composes songs, the producer will want to hear everything the artist has in mind for the album. The producer and the recording artist will be constantly pressured by professional associates and friends, not to mention complete strangers, to accept songs "that will be just terrific for the date. Can't miss!"Selecting repertoire is too serious a business to be influenced by this kind of favoritism.

With rock bands in particular, the producer will have the group run through all the material it has available. The producer has the difficult task of selecting the best material and rejecting the weakest, without offending the writers in the process. Many groups are insensitive to audience endurance. The producer must persuade the musicians that material of interminable length probably won't get on the air.

The Professional Relationship

Unless the producer is new to the field and hard up for work, selectivity in assignments is important. A producer desperate to get a new career off the ground won't fly very far unless there is a mutual respect shared with the recording artist, and they discover early on that they can work together comfortably.

The experienced producer will meet with the act before signing up for the project. Preliminary meetings are critical with a new artist or group, in that the artists probably have only a dim view of what lies ahead, are fearful of the outcome, and tend to look upon the producer as the only person in the world who can lead them to the promised land.

Producers say they find that at least one half of their time must be spent as resident psychologists, appraising the personality traits of the individuals, learning whom they can pressure when necessary, who withdraws for hours when reproached. Producers skillful in human relationships also search for the group's resident comedian. Usually the funny man in the group can be counted on to relieve tensions all around when it is 3 o'clock in the morning and everyone is getting surly.

After the producer and the act have selected the material, they must lay out how each song is to be treated. Does this need strings? Is some of the material going to be most effective when presented with complete simplicity? And so on.

When these kinds of decisions have been made, the producer engages arrangers to score the charts. Producers with strong musical backgrounds will probably work with arrangers in sketching out the arrangements, to increase the likelihood that the producer's conception will be implemented.

If the act and the producer have reached a working understanding on how the material is to be treated, rehearsals normally follow, to make sure the music is prepared before going into the studio. Organized groups rehearse for free, of course. But if the charts call for added instruments such as horns and strings, established session musicians will expect to be paid, often at straight recording scale, just for rehearsals.

If the charts call for outside singers, the producer needs to know which AFTRA contractors can deliver the required session singers.

Selecting the Studio

There is an oversupply of good recording studios, many of which are going broke and are actively searching for producers with money to spend. The pro-

Recording in progress. © Lori Grinker/Contact Press Images/PNI.

ducer of long experience will know the costs and available facilities of most major recording studios in the United States and will also have developed a good working relationship with studio owners and engineers.

The producer has another important decision to make besides the cost of studio rentals: contracting for facilities where the artist wants to record. No seasoned producer will ever insist on recording in a room where the artist either does not feel comfortable or has had unpleasant dealings with studio personnel.

In addition to the need for congenial atmosphere, the producer will select a studio in which a good sound can be achieved and where the maintenance of the hardware is reliable. If a particular studio has a staff engineer who can meet those needs, that facility may be favored over one with more sophisticated equipment. The producer who brings in a freelance engineer can expect an experienced mixer to adapt quickly to a new console.

A producer who is particular about equalization and **timbre** will usually go into a studio a day or two early with the engineer to check out the console, the monitoring system, and the acoustics. One who goes to this effort (not uncommon among top pros) will bring in a familiar recording. If the playback does not sound exactly as it should, time will be spent with the engineer and a house engineer to adjust equalization of speakers and amplifiers. It is important to know precisely what sounds are coming over the monitors.

Seasoned producers are usually prepared for at least one disaster every 24 hours. One of their biggest problems is **downtime** in the studio. When the machines are not working properly, the loss is not so much in dollars as in momentum; the recording artists may be unable to regain what they had going prior to the equipment failure.

The Recording Process

The producer just getting started in the field will learn early on that success is largely dependent on working well with studio personnel. As one successful producer put it, "Those people can help you or they can kill you."

Practices vary, but most producers keep a written record of what is laid down on each **track**; this record is referred to as a *tracking sheet.* Tracking sheets cite the artist, the date, the studio, song titles, "take" numbers, timings, and footage counts for the start and end of takes. Of course, if the recording process is digital with search-and-find capability, location and level settings are readily recalled with the push of a button.

As the recording process goes forward, the producer will be challenged from all sides. Although the first concern will be the music, the producer is supposed to know enough about recording technology to work effectively with the engineer. The self-confident producer will encourage the engineer to contribute creatively to the recording process. When the producer cannot come up with a solution to a problem, perhaps the engineer can save the day. Usually, the most successful producers take all the creative input they can find, whatever the source.

Master Delivery Requirements

Even when the producer has survived production of the master, the job is far from over. If the producer has been retained by a recording company, the firm now imposes specific delivery requirements, for example,

1. The master tape, multitrack or two-inch, must be mixed down to two-channel stereo, 2-track or half-inch tape, and formatted for sides 1 and 2 of an album. The label will probably also expect the producer to pull out several tracks for possible release as singles. If so, the singles must be edited to appropriate lengths (usually under 4 minutes).

2. Letters of consent must be obtained from all individuals involved in the project, allowing the label to use their names and photographs in promoting the music. Release letters must also state that the artists are unencumbered by conflicting recording agreements with any other firm.

3. The producer must deliver letters of consent from all photographers and graphic artists for the use of their works.

4. The producer must furnish evidence that all copyrights are clear and the owners have granted **mechanical licenses** for each cut on the album.

5. Lyric sheets must be submitted. Labels want to see in writing whether the song texts are acceptable for radio broadcast.

6. A technical credits summary sheet is required setting forth such details as the names of the engineers, where the master was recorded, who the arrangers and musical director were, the names of the union contractors, who mastered the tapes, and identities of artists' personal managers and booking agents.

7. A sign-off statement is required from the producer providing evidence that the bills have been paid and there are no liens or encumbrances that might prevent the label from releasing the recording.

8. The producer must collect W-4 forms, I-9 forms, and union contracts for every individual involved on the project to whom wages were paid.

The smart producer won't mail in the master, but will want to make an appointment with the person who set the job up, then walk in with the master and present it personally. At the same time, at least two or three cassette transfer copies should be delivered, so that the A&R people and other executives in the firm can hear the producer's work.

Assuming the label accepts the master, the producer will then be paid the other half of the production fee or advance on royalties. All of the responsibilities under the production agreement have been met, but the seasoned producer will want to take part in controlling mastering of the tape. It is customary for the record company to pay for mastering and all subsequent steps leading to manufacture of the recordings. But some companies will try to charge mastering to the artist's and producer's royalties.

Some conscientious producers continue their postproduction services up to and including the checking of test pressings, to make sure all the effort invested in the project will be reflected in the ultimate sound of the music.

CMA Award. Photo courtesy of Country Music Association.

RECORD PROMOTION, DISTRIBUTION, AND RETAILING

THE MARKETING PLAN

Recording companies will go to extreme lengths to get the best possible sounds on tape. But up to this point, all they really have is debt. The only way they can begin to recover their production expense is to get the word out—try to get people interested enough to buy the recording. It should be easy; millions of music lovers purchase music every week. For many people, recorded music is their first choice for entertainment. If the audience has the desire and the buying habit, why do recording companies go through such agony trying to get people to buy?

Agony it is, because everyone knows that the stakes are high. If you win, you win very big. If you lose, you can drop a million dollars on one campaign. Worse yet, contract artists will complain and look for an excuse to defect if your sales and marketing people cannot move a lot of units.

To understand how recorded music is promoted, it is important to remember the point made earlier: This is a mass market business. Sales must be developed, not only nationally but also all over the world. Because of astronomical production and promotion costs, a label often has to sell several hundred thousand records—quickly. Many labels think they are holding their own if 20% of their releases are profitable.

Personnel

With some labels, promotion efforts are supervised by a top officer of the company holding a title such as "Vice President, Promotion." Beyond that, little

345

agreement exists on distinctions among such terms as *promotion, marketing, merchandising, publicity,* and *sales promotion.* In practice, some of these terms are used interchangeably. Whatever the name a company attaches to a particular department, whatever job titles are used, everyone active in this general area has the same objective: to get people to buy recordings. Large labels might include in their marketing department the following personnel:

▶ *Merchandisers,* who conceive, then execute, sales campaigns and provide sales aids to distributors and retailers.

▶ *Promoters,* who are located in the home office and in regional offices. Main task: Get play on the radio.

▶ *Publicists,* who work mostly out of Los Angeles and New York City, trying to plant stories and "news"releases with print and broadcast media.

▶ *Advertising managers,* who conceive, produce, and place ads in print and broadcast media. (The role of product manager often combines merchandising and advertising functions.)

The Concept

A unique marketing plan is a useful way to attract attention with a new recording, but a large, multinational label can release more than 200 albums a month. Such a demand for fresh marketing ideas challenges the most creative staffs. Many companies enlist market researchers to help identify target markets, thereby enabling them to cater to specific demographic audiences. Armed with this information, a recording company attempts to put together a marketing campaign that ties in with the nature of the music and the style of performance.

Conscientious merchandising people usually start their thinking by listening to the music they are going to try to sell. At this early stage, the company's marketing people try to come up with a **hook.** Those invited to help conceive the marketing plan might include the artist's manager, producer, head of merchandising, the art director, and the heads of promotion and publicity for the label.

Once this group invents the marketing concept, the art department renders sketches; a photographer or other artist is engaged; the copy is written and the **mechanical** (assembled graphic elements) is rendered.

Meanwhile, other merchandising people are trying to implement the marketing plan in the form of P.O.P.—industry shorthand for point-of-purchase materials. P.O.P. might include posters, banners, stand-ups, special display racks, window displays, flags and streamers, and perhaps souvenir items the record merchant can give away to shoppers. Each of these P.O.P. items carries out the basic merchandising idea. P.O.P. is very costly to produce, but recording companies believe the investment in these sales stimuli pays off.

While the packaging art and P.O.P. are being produced, the firm's advertising department is inventing print ads, perhaps broadcast spots, too.

RECORD PROMOTION

Targets

Radio. Even though radio is no longer the sole influence on record sales, it is still a heavyweight medium for record promotion. A promoter does not have to twist arms to persuade stations to go with a new release of a superstar. Such product is largely presold, and program directors will add a new release from an artist of international stature even before receiving word that other stations are also going with the recording. But new releases of a performer below superstar status require promoters to hustle, because competition for airplay is fierce. There is space on many playlists for only two or three new artists at a time because stations don't want too much unfamiliar music on the air.

Large recording companies employ a staff of full-time people to handle promotion in-house. Outside promoters, known as independent promoters, are also used routinely. Independent promoters are retained by the label, usually on a record-by-record basis, for the sole purpose of obtaining or increasing radio airplay. This type of promotion is so expensive that recording companies may negotiate recoupment of some or all of independent promotion expenses from artist royalties.

Promoters always have a difficult time "breaking" new artists. Although discovering and establishing new talent does remain an art form, the promoter's job has been made somewhat easier by the proliferation of format-specific stations.

Reporting Stations. Knowledgeable promoters focus nearly all their attention on reporting stations. A reporting station is one that the trade papers and tip sheet publishers monitor to learn which recordings have been programmed. This is the information that causes a particular recording to land on the charts—

or fall off and disappear. Program directors are asked by the chart makers not only what records (singles, album cuts) are on their playlists but also their *rotation*—how often particular records are scheduled in a 24-hour period. Reporting stations are also asked which records are "playlist adds"for the week and which ones are being dropped. This method of information gathering is used for recordings that may not be ranked by electronic systems such as the Broadcast Data System (see Chapter 15).

Although rare with new artists, if a new release can gain airplay on influential radio stations, it may land a position on the charts. If that first chart appearance should occur, say, in the midrange of a national chart, the promotion people more often than not have a hit on their hands. At this point, most recording companies accelerate their efforts, instructing their label's regional promotion staff to intensify their campaigns. The promotion staff is now in a position to prove the claim that the new release, which is starting to break nationally, has strong hit potential. At this point, radio station programmers who were too timid weeks ago to take a chance on the new release may now be persuaded to jump on this potential hit. As the singles promotion campaign continues to snowball with strong national airplay, a hit is born.

Sometimes there is a catch to this. Occasionally, we have "turntable hits": A recording manages to get good airplay but people just don't walk into the stores and buy it. No one has come up with a satisfactory explanation for the turntable hit phenomenon.

To gain the confidence of radio program directors (PDs), promoters must establish a reputation for credibility. What the PD needs most is useful information—research, not fast talk. The station needs to know whether a new release fits its programming and whether it is gaining airplay elsewhere. It also wants to know a release's overall ranking with the rest of the records getting researched; it wants to know the release's "burn factor"—do people really want to hear it more?

If a promoter cannot provide these assurances to the station, there is one other hope: The music might appeal to the personal tastes of the PD or musical director. Occasionally, these decision makers will program a new release just because they like it, but few stations permit personal tastes to have too much influence on these important decisions. That influence is now even more limited with the advent of the Group PD—a single PD responsible for a network of stations spread geographically.

Video. The promotion of recordings is inextricably bound to TV-related transmissions of music, including conventional TV, cable, and direct satellites. Recording labels learned years ago that sales could be increased by linking music to visual entertainment, whether the medium was a movie musical, a TV broadcast, or a music video. Broadcasters and cable companies transmit dozens of video shows, and their impact on record sales is clear: Videos not only can increase record sales, they can break new acts, even prolong the chart life of new recordings. Production of music videos has reached a level of sophistication that often requires large budgets, gifted directors, choreographers, and production specialists.

Record promoters today are busier than ever trying to get their videos produced and aired. Just as with radio, when they can't get playlist adds by networks and major market stations, they work secondary, even tertiary, stations in smaller markets for video exposure.

The music video field is discussed further in Chapter 22.

Mailings, Telephone Follow-Ups. Because only a small number of stations can be reached by personal contacts, promoters mail free promotional copies to a larger number of outlets. Mailing out this many free recordings is extremely expensive, so experienced promoters use a very select mailing list, one that includes mostly influential stations or stations where the promoter has personal contacts.

Mail campaigns need to be followed up by telephone calls ("Hello, Frank. Did my stuff come in? How'd you like it? What did you find time to listen to? What have you added? No? How about next week? So-and-so is breaking big in Toledo; you won't want to miss out on it. How can I help you . . ." and so on). The success of this kind of telephone call follow-up depends not only on the suitability of the recordings mailed but also on the rapport between the caller and the station programmer.

Club Promotions. Dance clubs have sometimes been effective places to test new recordings. Prior to commercial release, recording labels may remix to make long versions of singles, favored by dancers, then get them into clubs to test patrons' reactions. If the clubs report strong response, the label will be encouraged to go into a general commercial release. Most labels supply clubs through companies that are in the business of setting up record "pools" of new releases for their clients.

If strong word of mouth develops through dance clubs, and if the same release gains good airplay in that region, the single may be headed for the charts.

Another way dance clubs contribute to record promotion is by showing music videos of new releases. Clubs obtain most of their tapes through video distribution companies that act as liaisons between recording companies and clubs. Dancers who become literally surrounded by the club's multiple screens and overpowering sound systems may be stimulated later to walk into a store and pick up a copy (audio or video) to continue enjoying the music at home.

Campaign Management. Most labels assign one individual to manage a promotional campaign. That manager receives a budget from the company's promotion director and is expected to develop regional, then national, airplay. The manager may also have the responsibility of assigning promotion personnel to certain geographic areas and of coordinating the efforts of staff promoters working out of the label's branch offices. The director of national promotion will put out the word on timing of the campaign and how much attention and emphasis it is to receive.

This "campaign manager" is sometimes called a **tracker** because the job's responsibilities include keeping track of which radio and TV stations are adding or dropping the new release. If the tracker observes good airplay developing in a particular geographic area, the tracker may double efforts there in an attempt to develop a regional hit, which can sometimes be built into a national one.

The tracker or project director also has the task of following the progress of a new release on the trade charts. The entry, rise, and fall of a recording on the charts provides guidance on how to spend (or withdraw) the money available for a campaign.

Publicity

Many recording companies have publicity departments separate from their promotion operation; others combine these two activities under a marketing division. Some recording companies handle their publicity activities in-house; others have only a small resident staff and engage publicists and PR firms to help out. A small label may depend totally on an outside firm for PR.

Even the most imaginative publicist cannot catch public attention unless the public can be persuaded that something is happening—a new recording is released, the artist is on tour, or a TV appearance is scheduled. When the publicist has no story, one might be invented. The job centers around the task of getting the artist and the songs talked about. Many merchants believe the most effective sales force is word of mouth. Record buyers who hear the talk and catch the music on the radio just might enter a store and make a purchase.

Advertising

Print, broadcast, point-of-sale, and direct mail advertising can be important components of record promotion. All advertising seems to help sales, but the difficulty is measuring whether the resulting sales justify the expense. With this mass consumer product, large labels find it profitable, from time to time, to place ads in mass print media—magazines and newspapers.

Most advertising is **institutional**—for example, a print page or media buy that doesn't mention a store, or **cooperative**, in which the retailer benefits. Co-op advertising funds are paid to the retailer by the label from a co-op budget determined by the retailer's volume of purchases from the label. Such advertising not only helps get the message to the consumer, but it also helps the retailer make money, which in turn can be used as a supplement to gain "price and position" for the record company. In other words, the label gets prime merchandising location and good retail pricing.

In 2000 major labels were forced to loosen a restrictive policy known as "M.A.P." (minimum advertised pricing). M.A.P. had been used by the labels to restrict large discount retailers from undercutting smaller merchants.

International Promotion

Multinational recording companies may spend more money and effort promoting releases abroad than they do in this country, since foreign sales can contribute more than one half of world sales.

Increasing numbers of artists are becoming international stars. They have had the good fortune of being with a recording company that has a worldwide promotion setup, or one that licenses its foreign releases to others. A multinational entertainment conglomerate must determine, each time out, whether to have foreign releases occur simultaneously with the U.S. release, or whether to test the recording here before promoting it abroad.

Sometimes the recording company does not have the option of delaying foreign releases: The star's contract may specify not only that the label release the recordings abroad simultaneously but also the countries where they are to be made available.

The big recording companies have large, fully staffed affiliates in foreign territories that have the responsibility of releasing and promoting the firm's product. Among the strongest European markets for breaking new U.S. recordings are the Netherlands, the United Kingdom, Germany, and France. Firms with international operations know the special promotional techniques that are most effective in these countries.

Foreign promotions cannot be handled like those in this country. In all these territories, fewer radio stations are available for record exposure. The stations that do exist may be state controlled and allow no advertising; time buys may be unavailable.

RECORD DISTRIBUTION

If the promotion people have created interest in a new recording, the manufacturer must find a way to get the product to potential customers—wherever they may be, at the right time and in sufficient quantities. This is a very difficult thing to do well, because the market is unpredictable and widely dispersed. After many years of trial and error, even major labels are still trying to figure out a better distribution system. As for small labels, the lack of effective distribution has caused many to fail in the marketplace.

Periodically, record retailing has been plagued by price wars among merchants, which has a direct effect on the distributors (those who provide product to retailers). Merchants fighting to remain afloat amid irrational retail pricing competition appeal to their distributors for better discounts to help them survive the competition. Distributors can respond to these appeals most often when they can sell at high volume. But when a merchant becomes too aggressive in buying and becomes burdened with expensive inventory, the distributor will soon hear a plea for lenient "return privileges."

Distributors try to strike a balance between overselling their accounts or offering an undersupply. With the former, both parties suffer the inconvenience and expense of "returns"; only the shipping industry profits with returns. But when a distributor's customers buy too conservatively and a recording hits suddenly, both parties miss out on sales when the merchandise is not available to the buying public.

Major Label Distribution

Large record companies handle distribution through the branch offices of their affiliated distribution companies located in major cities across the country. Although most distribute only product of their own labels, some large firms also contract to distribute products of independent record companies.

Major distributor branch offices normally have two divisions. One handles regional promotion, the other concerns itself with distribution and sales. The distributor's promotion staff coordinates its activities with the promotion staff of each distributed label. Major labels may have more than one distributing subsidiary, each of which has different strengths and expertise.

Branch offices of large recording companies employ salespeople, too. Some companies call them "merchandisers" or "route men." Their task is to call on retailers, try to sell them, perhaps deliver the actual recordings, help set up promotional displays, and do what they can to help the retailer attract customers. Record route people work on salary or commission, or a salary plus an override. These are not the most glamorous jobs in the music business, but a number of ambitious merchandisers have graduated to management positions and gone on up the corporate ladder.

Independent Distribution; Association for Independent Music

A handful of major multinationals handle the preponderant share of record distribution in the United States. But they don't do it all. A share of the business is in the hands of independent distributors, who provide services for hundreds of independent labels.

Independent distributors usually provide promotion services as well. Most have a staff of enterprising salespeople and merchandisers who call on record stores, deliver merchandise, and set up displays, for instance, much like the major label branch offices do.

There are regional independent distributors as well as national independent distributors, some of which have evolved through a merger or confederation of regional distributors. Large independent distributors are confronted with pleas from new labels to take on yet another line. If they consider adding new labels, management must determine whether it has the capacity to handle the increased inventory and the will to tie up additional working capital on unproven suppliers. If they stocked every recording that appears promising, they would soon go broke. But if they fail to stock new product that suddenly bursts wide open at the retail level, their local accounts will sometimes bypass the local distributor and buy directly from the record manufacturer.

The interests of these independent companies are represented by the Association for Independent Music (AFIM), formerly NAIRD, the National Association of Independent Record Distributors. The association promotes the independent recording industry by presenting a unified voice in the industry for small labels and independent distributors. Its national conventions provide small labels a convenient place for the exchange of information and for the forming of distribution arrangements for companies not affiliated with the major labels and their distribution networks.

One-Stops. One-stops are a special kind of distributor. They came into being in the 1940s mainly to accommodate the needs of jukebox operators. A one-stop is a distributor that handles all labels, including the majors. One-stops are set up to service not only jukebox operators but also small rack jobbers and mom-and-pop retailers. Most of these customers place small orders. Because major distributors have minimum-order requirements that are too high for most mom-and-pop retailers, and because one-stops must purchase records from distributors, one-stops cannot offer as good a discount as a major distributor. But their customers pay the higher prices because they appreciate the convenience of a one-stop operation and may have nowhere else to go. One-stops sell more labels, in lower quantities but at a higher price, than the traditional independent distributors.

Music Clubs. In 1955, Columbia got the idea that records could be sold directly through the mail. It was right: The Columbia House Record Club (initially owned by CBS) has been running well ever since. Shortly after CBS got started in the field, RCA (now BMG) and then Capitol Records followed in establishing record clubs (Capitol has since discontinued this kind of promotion). When record clubs began, retailers threatened court action, arguing that a big company pushing sales of only its own label through the mail constituted unfair competi-

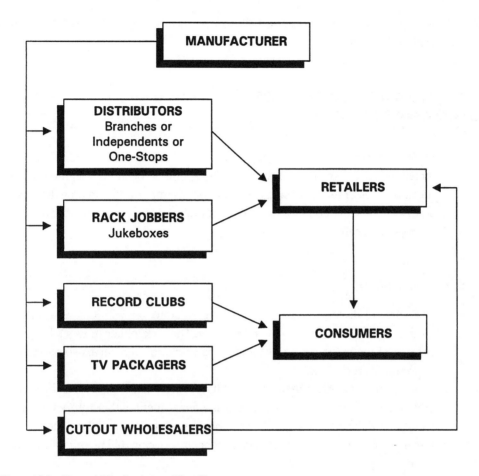

Figure 18.1 Record Distribution and Retailing

tion and restraint of trade. Columbia responded by expanding its club offerings to include products from other labels. Clubs now offer for sale any album that proves sufficiently popular to earn a listing in their advertisements.

Club memberships are developed through TV, magazine, direct mail, and Internet ads offering a starter supply of CDs or tapes below cost, together with a commitment from the "member" to purchase several more within a specified time at the regular price.

In recent years, struggling clubs rethought their selling strategies and tapped the growing power of the Internet as a sales tool. Clubs are reluctant to disclose their grosses, but retailers still believe that record clubs cut heavily into their walk-in business.

MERCHANDISING AUDIOCASSETTES AND COMPACT DISCS

From the distributor or label warehouse, the goods flow to retailers. The retail merchandising of recorded music constitutes one of the largest segments of the music business. Merchandising success depends importantly on how the retailer assesses buyer preferences, both as to configuration (tape vs. disc) and genre (jazz vs. classical).

Rack Jobbers

Before we discuss the conventional record store, we will look at a different kind of supplier-merchant—the rack jobber. The rack jobber moves a large percentage of the audio recordings and tapes sold and even serves some kinds of conventional record stores.

A customer walking into a large multiline retailer cannot know just by looking around whether that record selling area is a department of the store, whether it is space leased to an outside firm, or whether it is serviced by a jobber who supplies the racks and bins. Chances are, a rack jobber is servicing that record selling operation.

Jobbers work out various kinds of contracts with the store that supplies the retail space. Among the most common are the following:

1. The jobber rents space for racks and bins from the retailer for a flat monthly fee. The jobber offers complete servicing of the area and retains all the money collected from sales.
2. The jobber pays the host store a percentage of sales.
3. The jobber and store management work out a minimum lease fee, then if sales exceed an agreed-on figure in any given month, the jobber pays the store a percentage of the overage.

Percentage of U.S. Dollars

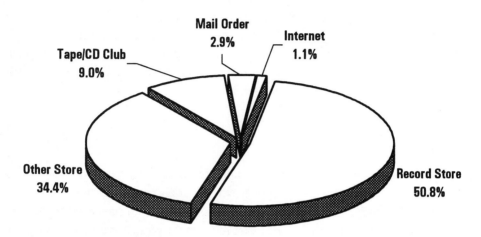

Figure 18.2   Recorded Music Sales by Type of Outlet
SOURCE: Recording Industry Association of America, 1998.

Retailers like record racks on their premises because they can often make more profit per square foot of floor space from this kind of merchandise than they can from other lines. Merchants also benefit from increased shopper traffic generated by the high volume of record buyers.

When a rack jobber sets up a large number of racks and bins, the jobber needs clerks to assist customers and restock supplies daily. Where a rack setup of this size is in operation, it is practically indistinguishable from a "leased department." When a jobber leases enough space for this kind of operation, the jobber has a major commitment of capital and will probably have a dedicated checkout counter and handle money separately. Leased departments are common in department stores and discount chains. Large retailers can demand hefty lease payments from the record merchant/jobber and, at the same time, are spared all responsibility of running the record sales department.

Large retailers and chains, observing the success on their premises of these record sales operations, will, from time to time, decide to take over the same space, install their own record department management, then pocket the percentage formerly kept by the rack jobber. Rack jobbers try to anticipate this kind of temptation by offering the store trouble-free, profitable operations, sparing retailers the problem of trying to run a kind of retailing they do not really understand.

Companies that started out as rack jobbers or distributors are now also heavily involved in operating "stand-alone" retail outlets. The lines between record distribution, jobbing, and retailing are now blurred; some of the most successful merchants operate in all three areas. This blending of record selling operations was originally accelerated by the need of merchants to buy products at ever-higher discounts through volume purchasing.

Retail Stores

Retailing today is much more complicated than in the past. Even retail operations of medium size are expected to stock not only current releases but also past hits. The stock should cover all major styles, from pop to classical. The video explosion has dictated that many major retailers carry music video titles and theatrical film releases. Customers will also expect to find blank cassettes and a full line of accessories. Stocking, controlling, and merchandising such a diverse inventory demands much more working capital than in simpler times. Music retailing today is big business.

On the whole, the small record stores are disappearing. One reason is that they cannot buy enough stock to receive an adequate discount from distributors. In turn, this means they cannot discount their retail prices to compete with larger stores. Another reason the small store rarely survives today is that many customers want to browse through endless bins of merchandise. Tastes are more diverse now; a customer may favor country music, but might stumble on something interesting to take home in adult contemporary or jazz. Only a retailer with a large inventory of diverse styles can attract this kind of customer.

One type of relatively small record store does well when it is well managed: the proprietor who locates in a special neighborhood, earns the confidence of a small but loyal clientele, and stocks the particular kind of music that appeals to that community. For example, one such operation does a strong business in Boston selling polka records.

Another kind of specialized record store is found in the inner city, where entrepreneurs catering to urban music tastes find a ready market. Yet another kind of specialized record store is often found in shopping communities adjoining a large university where the market for classical music is strong. When staffed by knowledgeable clerks, such stores may do well.

Prices, Discounts. When a merchant manages to pull together enough working capital to set up a retailing operation, the problems have just begun. One of the greatest challenges is determining at what price the merchant can afford to buy—and then what kind of discounts can be offered customers.

Distributors will try to influence the retailer with all kinds of discount offers, seeking to encourage greater and greater volume. But if the merchant is persuaded to buy 100 CDs at special discount on one release, the pool of money (called "open-to-buy") available to buy other merchandise shrinks in proportion. When the retailer reduces cash through heavy purchasing, the next recourse is to persuade the banker to loan just a little more, then a little more. Credit at the bank and with distributors can soon become overextended, and the aggressive merchant might have done better going into the fish business.

By federal law, major label distributors cannot give individual direct accounts special discounts. All must get the same discount offer. Labels can, however, offer more co-op advertising money. Additionally, to help maintain the precarious balance retailers hold between overstocking and not having enough product on hand, labels have established fairly liberal return policies and extended terms for payment.

Retail Chain Stores

As music software retailing becomes a business of increasing risk, the smaller entrepreneur becomes easy prey for sale to a retail chain. The growth of record chain operations results from the same economic pressures already cited: To make a profit, the merchants must find ever new ways to buy cheaper, and the mass merchandiser is certainly in a better position to do this than mom and pop. Another advantage is that chain store advertising is far more cost-effective than a mom-and-pop campaign—which can rarely include such an important medium as TV. Chain store operators provide an additional advantage to their component units: When one store overbuys and gets stuck with inventory, it can often shift some of this product to another unit in the chain that may have run short. Chain store locations help each other balance their inventories.

However, one disadvantage chain stores have is the inability to pinpoint local tastes. Because the chain buys for stores nationwide, some stores will inevitably run out of stock on products that are popular in their areas.

Returns

Distributors regularly pressure dealers to buy more stock than dealers believe they can move. This pressure assumes various forms. Record companies or distributors will often offer merchants liberal merchandise return privileges. At one time, practically all records and tapes in this country were sold on consignment: If you can't sell the merchandise, return it for full credit. The practice now is often one that requires the merchant to return the stock within a prescribed time limit and to return only a prescribed percentage of goods ordered.

Cutouts, Repackaging

Recording manufacturers find it difficult to estimate how many records to press. If they underestimate demand, customers cannot be accommodated. If they overestimate demand, they will find their warehouses stocked with dead merchandise. Once the demand drops sharply, the manufacturer will stop production. The inventory remaining is known as **cutouts**. Retail outlets cannot move this stock at normal prices, and the manufacturer finds it prudent to unload this merchandise at cost or below cost on buyers who specialize in cutouts. These cutout merchants buy up quantities, warehouse the units, then vend them to rack jobbers and other retailers at a very low price. Their customers, in turn, offer these cutouts at extremely low prices. Both parties usually turn a profit, and the retail customer gets a bargain—but artists do not generally receive royalties on cutouts.

Some music stores find that their profit margin from cutouts is better than from conventional sales. Some cutout companies buy or lease old masters, then rerelease fallen stars who still have loyal fans ready to gobble up ancient hits at bargain prices. For example, for years cutout merchants and repackagers have been able to sell "rereleases" or "new" releases of the big name band hits of the 1940s. Another perennial repertoire comes from the early rock and roll hits. Reissues of country music also continue to sell, through "new" releases, new packages, or cutouts.

Perhaps the most successful merchandising of old repackaged hits is seen on television. Companies buy up or lease masters from recording companies holding the rights to old hits, then repackage them under their own labels. These repackagers favor such titles as "Sinatra's Greatest Hits" or "The Best of Country Music." They produce low-cost, hard-sell TV spots, obtain time on TV and cable, and provide a mailing address and toll-free telephone number for viewers to place their orders.

National Association of Recording Merchandisers

The National Association of Recording Merchandisers (NARM) is the international trade association that represents the recorded music distribution industry.

More than 1,100 companies are NARM members. Individuals automatically become members when their companies join. The two categories of company membership are:

1. General members: This category includes retailers and direct mailers as well as wholesalers such as rack jobbers, one-stops, and independent distributors.
2. Associate members: This category includes entertainment software suppliers such as manufacturers and suppliers of music, video, and other forms of recorded entertainment, as well as suppliers of related products and services such as accessories, display fixtures, advertising, printing, packaging, security systems, and computer hardware and software.

All companies who join NARM pay annual dues based on their yearly sales volume. Member benefits include:

Annual convention—a trade show for new products and services, and a forum for recording merchandisers and manufacturers to network and discuss mutual opportunities and concerns.

Merchandising campaigns—NARM supplies point-of-purchase materials free to its members, as well as educational videos on merchandising.

NARM schedules additional conferences and meetings for its members, and it lobbies to represent members' interest in local, state, and federal legislative matters.

NARM's loss prevention initiatives spearheaded the effort to adopt a universal technology for electronic article surveillance (EAS) at the point of manufacture. NARM's Annual Survey and *Sounding Board* newsletter provide useful information to its members.

HOME VIDEO RETAILING

When music video channels started to broadcast video promo clips, no one anticipated the activity would break new acts, increase music sales, influence movie-making styles, and incidentally, revolutionize the entertainment industry. And when producers started linking videos together and packaging "long-form" videos, it was discovered, again almost by accident, that viewers might want to take them home and see them again and again.

Music videos were, at the start, largely limited to one musical style—rock—because MTV would not program much else. But MTV, VH1, and those that followed learned that other audiences could be attracted to video entertainments featuring pop music, adult contemporary artists, urban, jazz, and even classical music.

NARM has argued that the record merchants are most knowledgeable and experienced in marketing home entertainment software and should lead the pack in video retailing. But because music has failed to dominate prerecorded video to the degree it has dominated prerecorded audio, another type of retailer has emerged to merchandise video product. Hedging its bets in the early 1980s, NARM's leadership nurtured the creation of a sister organization representing retailers primarily involved with video, the Video Software Dealers Association.

Although the thousands of video specialty stores have been effective de facto rental libraries for videocassettes, mass merchants including Blockbuster Video and some of the huge record chains sell the most home videos. Unlike video specialty stores, these retail giants can buy in sufficiently large quantities to attain the maximum volume discounts. Sometimes mass merchants use big video titles to entice customers into their stores where they will, presumably, make other purchases as well. Smaller market shares are held by various kinds of merchandisers, including supermarkets, drugstores, bookstores. Most of these retailers also sell blank tape and accessories.

As with audio, video merchandising is hit driven. The rule of thumb is that 20% of a store's inventory generates 80% of its business. But trimming the number of titles stocked can depress sales because customers expect a good selection. With both audio and video, the retailer's ongoing challenge is to stock enough of the hits while at the same time keeping a variety of slower moving "catalog" product always available—and always, keep open-to-buy inventory and sales levels in balance. It's not an easy job.

FUTURE OF RETAILING

As entertainment delivery systems evolve, merchandising is adapting and changing. The following are among the trends analysts see in the crystal ball:

► Retailers are continuing to specialize. Hardware will usually be merchandised separately from its corresponding software.

► Chain stores will continue to gobble up smaller and less efficient competitors.

► Retailing will be changed by competitors promising to deliver similar entertainments by purely electronic means.

► Existing label systems and retailing will be threatened by—and find new ways to exploit—Internet retailing and electronic streaming.

► A whole new generation of electronic devices will merge computers with audio, video, data, and graphics.

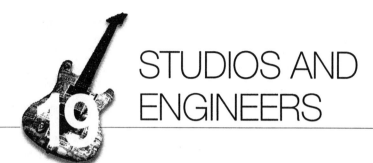

STUDIOS AND ENGINEERS

O ne of the most important areas of the recording industry involves the operation of recording studios, only a small portion of which are owned by record manufacturers. Except to industry insiders, the operation of recording studios is largely a hidden industry, most of the best of them remaining unknown to the public. But with thousands of recordings being laid down each year just in the United States, it is reasonable to estimate that the recording studio business grosses several hundred million dollars a year.

Although the industry is primarily based in New York, Los Angeles, Nashville, and to some extent, Chicago, professional studios are found in other areas of the country, with affiliates around the world and creative resources everywhere. Thousands of people are employed full-time in this unique industry, which requires cooperation between entrepreneurs, technicians, engineers, designers, acousticians, managers, and musicians. Here, art and technology must find accommodation.

Although some sound recording studios limit their services to audio recording, in the major music centers many studios are also expected to offer film and television producers complete audio services for synchronizing sound with picture. Because the various modes of video entertainment are rapidly expanding, increasing numbers of sound facilities in New York, Los Angeles, and Nashville find it necessary (and quite profitable!) to offer a complete range of recording services, even sometimes including Web pages. In fact, in some full-production studios, audio is but one component of the operation. There are facilities that provide recording and processing for digital computer animation and "visual synthesis." Musicians, audio **mixers,** and video producers work side by side in these studios.

SEMIPROFESSIONAL RECORDING

Recording occurs in every conceivable kind of environment, from the semiprofessional setup in a residential garage to the 96-**track** monster studios now found in dozens of cities in this country and abroad. As equipment has become more sophisticated, professional studios have had to raise their rates to amortize their investments, and their prices are now out of reach for many potential users. In recent years, such increases, along with the availability of good software programs for only a few thousand dollars, have led to an escalation in the home recording business with amateur equipment and a proliferation of what we can call semiprofessional recording. When a producer begins spending thousands of dollars weekly for recording studio bills, the decision may be made to halt that expenditure and divert funds into a personal recording operation.

To accommodate the individuals who are attempting to do this, and to serve the investor who requires something better than consumer-quality equipment, manufacturers now market an array of hardware known as semiprofessional equipment. Most of this hardware is superior to the best home-type machines and is beginning to approach the performance and durability found in fully professional equipment. The machinery we are discussing here fills that middle gap and is priced well below fully professional hardware.

This kind of equipment serves those who have no need for 16-, 24-, 48-, or 96-track studios with their high hourly fees.

Semipro setups are frequently used by songwriters, publishers, performers, and independent producers. Many of these individuals manage to amortize their investments after a year or so of recording their own material.

Semiprofessional recording has its own problems, however. The American Federation of Musicians (AFM) doesn't like it, because that union has no way of policing these operations. Sometimes the investors regret having entered the field, because they cannot or do not want to continually replace equipment that rapidly becomes obsolete. Semiprofessional recording is increasing, however, because of the rising rental costs of conventional studios and because it meets the needs of so many individuals so effectively.

DEMO STUDIOS

One notch above the converted garage is the studio that specializes in demo recordings. Nearly all of them offer 4- to 8-track equipment and room enough for a small ensemble. Because demo studios can offer hourly rates far lower than full commercial studios, they service the bulk of demo recording needs of writers and publishers.

Well-managed demo studios can make a profit; however, financial difficulties may occur as the small operator attempts to keep up by purchasing all the latest expensive equipment. When demo studio operators make the giant leap from, say, a modest 4-track facility to 16-track with all its attendant gadgetry, they may soon find their fancy hardware in the hands of the bank, awaiting auction.

Some demo studios live long and prosper by becoming headquarters for small production companies, small labels, beginning publishers, even artists' managers and agents trying to get established. Whether or not these people share ownership or management, those involved often find it mutually advantageous to work together, sharing expertise and contacts.

Another kind of recording operation, which might be called the **in-house** studio, has become increasingly popular with publishers and even advertising agencies. These are private operations, rarely open to the public, and are intended to serve the host company and its business associates. They range in size from 8- to 16-track and provide in-house production for everything from simple demos to master tapes.

INDEPENDENT STUDIOS

The step above the demo studio is the full-line independent studio, which has at least 24-track recorders with multi-input consoles, and other **outboard equipment** sufficient to compete with plants operated by the major record labels.

To attract knowledgeable producers, the independent studio must have a lot going for it. It must be heavily capitalized in order to acquire adequate space, buy the latest equipment, and have enough cash to carry it over lean times when bookings are light. To compete today, an entrepreneur setting up a full-service independent recording studio, including sound-to-picture for video, should have at least $1,000,000 to $1,500,000 for a two-room setup, in start-up financing, with more under the mattress readily available.

A full-service independent studio will normally have one or two rooms capable of handling a studio orchestra or smaller groups, mixdown and editing, full MIDI (musical instrument digital interface) capabilities, equipment rack rooms, and possibly a maintenance shop, traffic control office, and lockers for equipment storage.

Small Independent Studios

Small independent studios often produce recordings released on independent record labels. These studios are well above the demo studios in quality of product, design, and equipment. They usually have capital investments in the range of $200,000 to $500,000, depending on the number of rooms, and are located in the more remote sections of the country.

LABEL-OWNED STUDIOS

Most of the large recording companies own and operate their own studios in Los Angeles and Nashville, and several continue to operate studios in New York. In the early days of the industry there were no independent studios, and record companies had to build their own. The practice continues today with the older, larger companies.

The company's traffic office reserves time first for the label's own producers and artists, and if any studio time remains open, it is usually made available to outsiders. Physical facilities and equipment are generally equal to, sometimes superior to, that found in major independent studios.

STUDIO ACOUSTICS, DESIGN, AND AMBIANCE

A studio with the latest hardware is in trouble if it lacks good acoustics in two critical areas: the control rooms and the studios themselves. The science of acoustics has now advanced to the stage where qualified engineers can predict how sounds will behave in a given space. Unfortunately, investors continue to throw money away on bad designs. What's more, even where the designs are right, the construction may be faulty. When the elaborate RCA studios opened in Hollywood, they were replicas of RCA's outstanding facilities in Rome. But when RCA's Hollywood Studio A first opened, a blanket had to be hung on the wall behind the mixing console. The acoustician had not properly designed that surface to diffuse the sounds bouncing around behind the mixing console.

Modern control rooms are difficult to design because the proper balance of stereo is largely dependent on where the mixer sits in the room—and the producer, perhaps only 3 feet away from the mixer, hears a different balance. Now, home-theater-type sound systems compound this problem, as sound is derived from six locations rather than two, putting a different spin on the entire process. Further compounding these problems, engineers and producers forget sometimes that many music lovers cannot afford the more expensive systems and that the programs professionals monitor over elaborate speakers only slightly resemble what the music lover hears on an inexpensive radio. Increasingly, formal training is becoming necessary, such as that offered at the University of Miami, and a good sense of "hearing" sound must also be accompanied by a good understanding of mathematics.

Studios often sink or swim on whether the performing musicians feel comfortable in them. One essential acoustical requirement for orchestras and ensembles is sound diffusion, which allows performers to hear a fair amount of the sounds occurring around them. However, the precise opposite occurs in tracking: Performers want very short reverberation times when using earphones, because they want to hear only themselves and the program coming over the phones.

Regardless of what the studio offers in equipment and acoustics, many artists and producers patronize facilities with a comfortable atmosphere featuring a congenial staff and low or no pressure. In fact, numerous small-city studios prosper because many artists feel more relaxed recording outside of the larger cities. Anyone recording in the easygoing environment of Nashville favors the atmosphere of a more comfortable venue over the pressure cookers of New York City and Los Angeles.

Although a studio may be well equipped and comfortable, its success may depend merely on superstition, as many producers and recording artists refuse to book time in a studio that has not produced hit records. They suspect that because hits are really just "sounds," they must use studios with a track record for producing *hit* sounds.

STUDIO OPERATION

Label-owned studios and the larger independent studios maintain a full-time staff of perhaps 20 to 50 or more, including a business manager, who is responsible for collecting delinquent accounts and determining to whom credit should be extended. A studio's staff also includes traffic managers, who book studio time. These individuals are sometimes pressured by producers who seem to believe that, if they can't get into the studios in 10 days, the world will end. Traffic managers must sometimes schedule week-long sessions months in advance, booking time for acts, for example, who will be coming off the road and who are determined to lay down an album at a specific time of the year. Besides these long-range booking problems, the studio traffic department must be adept at estimating when a session may run overtime.

Studio profit depends on how closely contiguous hours can be booked. When sessions fail to begin and end on schedule, both the studio and producer may experience serious financial losses. Major accounts planning to record an album often "block book" studio time. The producer estimates how many days or weeks are needed to lay down 10 or more songs, then persuades the studio to reserve a particular room exclusively for that project. In block booking, the artists can leave equipment in place and not waste time trying to reinvent the setup that worked so well the previous day. Also, studios that block off a room for several days or weeks will offer the producer a much lower total price for the project than would have been charged on a per-hour basis.

In addition to the traffic manager and business manager, the staff comprising a full-line studio includes a chief engineer, a staff of house engineers, mixers, editors, **mastering** engineers/technicians, perhaps a video/film projectionist/technician, maintenance personnel, and people handling setups and the equipment movement. An office crew completes the staff of a full-line studio.

Few recording studios have sales departments or promotion people. Management finds that business comes or goes based largely on the word-of-mouth reputation of a studio. Ads do not help much.

CHANGING TECHNOLOGY

Although recording studios continually struggle to keep abreast of changing technology, this is almost an impossible dream. Some clients want **digital recording**; others insist on an analog sound. Only heavily capitalized studios can keep up with every innovation. Studios often start out by leasing leading-edge gear, because of the lower capital outlay—and because they want to trade in outdated equipment as more sophisticated hardware becomes available.

Some so-called digital recordings are not wholly digital; the recording machine may employ digital technology, but it is usually hooked up to analog microphones and consoles.

Many studios use "automated" consoles that are interfaced with computers, and these consoles are used as a mixing and remixing aid. The computers "remember" previous sound settings, leaving the engineer free to perform other tasks. Recording technology schools understand that their graduates must now be at least somewhat computer literate to work in today's studios. They must understand how a database operates across a network and be familiar with a multitude of computer applications, including sequencing programs, word processors, and spreadsheets.

Recording studios are also challenged by increasingly complicated multi-timbral synthesizers as well as digital and multimedia techniques. As is widely known, keyboard players often play several electronic instruments simultaneously. Because they are accustomed to doing so live, when they walk into a studio they expect the engineer to accommodate their recording needs. This task is often facilitated by use of the MIDI system, which allows electronic instruments and studio gear to communicate and interact. The MIDI controller sends electronic MIDI performance information, and a MIDI recording device, such as a computer or hardware sequencer, permits playback of that information.

Engineers must also understand how to properly record synthesized percussion, various portable keyboards, and experimental instruments that defy classification.

THE ART AND SCIENCE OF MIXING

Whatever the technology used in the recording process, much more important to the final musical result is the mixer, or "engineer." Until recently, these audio engineers were usually handymen technologists, most of whom lacked formal training. They learned mixing hit-or-miss, on the job, and some learned more about mixing through experience, than most electrical engineers could ever hope to know. They combine the talents of a competent technician with an intuitive ear for music. Still others in audio engineering come, not from the radio and TV repair shop fraternity, but from the musical world. Some of the musician-mixers do a better job at the console than anyone else, for they may bring to the task a university-trained background in orchestration, arranging, and perfor-

Grammy Award-winning producer/engineer Val Garay conducts
mixing session at Berklee College of Music, Boston. Photo © Kimberly Grant.

mance. These musicians then hang around enough recording scenes to learn how to mix and master.

Studios have had difficulty finding mixers and engineers who are thoroughly qualified and sufficiently versatile because, until recent years, there has been no place for them to obtain adequate preparation. The difficulty is obvious: This group of professionals is expected to be fully educated in two different disciplines—electrical engineering and music.

The mixers most in demand are those with "magic ears." They may not understand how to trace a short in an amp or adjust the azimuth on a recording head, but they do know how to lay down good tracks. They ride those **faders** with a sure touch, pulling from the console much more interesting sounds than the microphones deliver to it. In short, the top mixers are sensitive to sound and music, and work their electronic wizardry like sound sorcerers—which they are. They have a good feel for the impact that a sound or musical sequence will have on the listener.

Besides the ability to ride a console with sensitivity and creativity, these artists have one additional attribute without which they would run screaming from the control room: Their temperament seems immune to high stress and tension. Consider this scenario: This one individual controls over a million dollars' worth of equipment, the act on the other side of the glass is getting paid $100,000 a night to perform, and the recording company plans to spend $500,000 to produce and $500,000 to promote the recording the engineer is mixing. The mixer bears great responsibility for the final result. The top mixers feel the pressure, but they can handle it.

Although the industry is saturated with mixers, the musician-engineer who has "the ears" and a cool temperament is the individual most likely to find regular employment and high income. These musician-artist-engineers are not in over-supply: They should be guarded by the Secret Service as national treasures.

Those less adept at mixing or who prefer to work under less pressure may find work if they are thoroughly qualified to maintain audio equipment. Now that equipment is becoming increasingly sophisticated, particularly the interface with computer technology, jobs available in audio engineering will be filled more and more by graduate electrical engineers and computer scientists, not by talented fix-it people. Those with these kinds of backgrounds are needed, not only to keep the hardware operating but also to design new equipment and installations. Electrical engineers engaged in studio design will be working with scientists specializing in electroacoustics, even psychoacoustics.

PROFESSIONAL ASSOCIATIONS

Individuals who are serious about getting into sound recording should be active in the professional associations serving this sector of the industry. The Audio Engineering Society (AES), for example, holds annual conventions that feature seminars, technical paper presentation, and workshops on new recording technologies and displays of equipment manufacturers' latest audio products. AES has a committee dealing with the educational aspects of recording technology and career opportunities in audio.

SPARS, the Society of Professional Audio Recording Services, also concerns itself with educational standards for training audio technicians. Its programs include placement of interns, business conferences, educational seminars, regional meetings, networking, and consulting. SPARS membership includes postproduction recording studios, individual engineers and producers, production houses, postproduction facilities, manufacturers of professional audio recording equipment, schools, colleges, studio designers, leasing companies, and those who serve the audio recording industry. Individuals believing they may want to work in the audio departments of TV and film studios can learn more about this field from SMPTE, the Society of Motion Picture and Television Engineers (see Chapter 24).

# 20 BUSINESS MUSIC

A substantial portion of music produced today is not really meant for active listening. Rather, it is intended to remain on the edge of consciousness, providing an "extramusical" service, affecting people's moods and energy levels. Background music murmurs on, as we all know, just about everywhere people can be found: in many places of business, including restaurants, malls, supermarkets, airports, elevators, sometimes even in rest rooms—and during "hold" time on the phone.

There are two basic kinds of business music—foreground and background. *Foreground* music is designed specifically for the business in which it is used and is played for very particular purposes, such as drawing in targeted customers and keeping them in stores, entertaining telephone callers on hold so they will be less likely to hang up, or helping airline passengers stay calm and relaxed. Though as carefully designed for its particular setting, *background* music is intended to go largely unnoticed in a conscious way, an unobtrusive accompaniment to work, shopping, conversation, dining, and relaxation. It's plugged as being effective in reducing stress and even in making the hearers more likely to stay healthy.

The music that **underscores** films, videos, and television can be either foreground or background or both. This kind of music is discussed in Chapter 24. Here, we discuss Muzak-type foreground and background music, which is sometimes referred to as *wired music service* or *business music.*

Research in music effects has demonstrated that the controlled application of music can modify mood, energy level, and behavior. Studies of manufacturing plants, for example, have shown that workers exposed to music are more productive and happier than when working in silence or with nothing but the drone of machines in the background. Psychologists and music therapists consult with companies offering wired music service so that the compositions heard are programmed to fit specific environments. Hospitals use it to help doctors as well as patients. Many studies have shown that music has an unusual power to help a patient's recovery from physical or mental trauma.

SERVICE COMPANIES

The business music industry in the United States is dominated by two companies, both based in Seattle, Washington: Muzak, Inc., the largest and oldest firm, founded in 1934, and AEI Music Networks, Inc., formerly Audio Environments, Inc., which has found its own considerable niche in this field. They provide their services to around 300,000 businesses worldwide, large and small. These companies not only offer the music, they also design, install, and service the sound systems to deliver it, including interactive video-music packages.

Muzak contracts services to franchised dealers, offering contracts running several years with an option to renew. Local franchise operators are, in effect, distributors, who put salespersons in the field to line up users of the service. AEI contracts with businesses directly and through regional offices. Local, independently owned companies can also affiliate with Muzak or AEI, thus being able to offer what the big companies have, as well as services specifically tailored to their own communities.

Transmission. The major companies currently beam their signals all over the world using broadcast satellites as well as FM **multiplex** transmissions, where the signal is broadcast on the low end of the FM band through local radio stations. Muzak's main transmission center is located in Raleigh, North Carolina, where CD jukeboxes are sent for use with special software designed to choose the appropriate program and transmit it via satellite to the client. When sending music to businesses, the company may use special 2-track tapes. Because the speed differs from the standard cassette player, the tapes must be played back on a special machine, which the company provides. This prevents tape piracy.

Companies that contract with Muzak and AEI have a broad choice of channels, such as

Easy listening music

Adult contemporary music using original artists

Top 40 music

Light **classical music** from the romantic style period

Contemporary jazz flavors

Country currents

Up-tempo adult contemporary

Jukebox gold: 1960s through 1980s rock

Contemporary instrumental

Expressions: supermarket music with a little country, a little easy listening music, a little adult contemporary, and contemporary jazz

Holiday music: current holiday pop

Latin styles

East/West Coast **easy listening**

Environmental: Sounds from nature

Musical Production. Muzak and AEI do not generally hire songwriters or other kinds of composers. Material is drawn from music already published, mostly standards and near-standards. But they don't use **canned tracks** from a library. If a particular song is needed, musicians are hired to record it. Some of these recordings are made in the United States and some are made in Europe. European musicians are sometimes willing to work for lower rates than AFM (American Federation of Musicians) scale in the United States.

Companies often engage the arranger-director as a producer to handle the project as a package. The packager, or producer, is given a lump sum, then pays for music copying, studio time, tape, and musicians' wages. If any money is left, the packager may be paid for time spent writing arrangements and directing the session. Arranger-directors work with great efficiency, for every half hour of time saved means more money left for themselves. To effect maximum cost savings, many of the masters have been recorded as they were read: The "rehearsal" becomes the take. Quite often, the only delays in the procedure have been caused by mistakes in the copied parts, not by the inability of the musicians to sight-read them.

Licensing and Copy Protection. Much foreground music uses original artists performing the same music heard on the radio. To do this, the company must purchase a **new use** license, because the music, originally designed to be played by the private consumer or on the radio, will now be broadcast in a business.

Airline Music. One specialized field within this already specialized field is supplying music to airlines for the in-flight entertainment of travelers. More than a dozen companies compete for this market nationally and internationally. (Muzak has never been involved in this area; AEI has been active from its early days.) Airlines can choose up to 20 music channels featuring formats such as classical, opera, pop, jazz, rock, New Age, easy listening, country, children's, Broadway, sound tracks, showcase, and regional music. The length of the transcriptions is chosen by the airline and ranges from 60 to 120 minutes. Each airline also chooses how often to change the programs; 2 months is usual. As with other business music, the programs are designed to enhance the airline's image—and also to ensure that the passengers recognize a majority of the selections on their chosen channels.

PRODUCTION MUSIC LIBRARIES

Production music libraries offer music and sound effects that are original, rather than covers of already existing songs and music. Musicians record original music that is then sold for specific use, such as theme music for a news broadcast. Before 1980, the AFM and AFTRA (American Federation of Television and Radio Artists) required that musicians who recorded production music be paid each time the music was used, so production libraries and music users bought their music from Great Britain, Germany, and France, where such **reuse** payments were not required. In the 1980s, AFTRA and AFM were unable to maintain this stance, so U.S. production music libraries began to gain prominence in this field.

Killer Tracks, a production music library that opened its doors in 1990, serves as a good example of a successful, modern music production company. Its library, divided into 23 categories and genres, has been a source for music used in feature films, commercials, and corporate productions and by TV shows, networks, cable stations, and CD-ROM producers. The service is inexpensive and music users don't have to worry about getting a license, because the license is supplied as part of the fee paid. Material is licensed for use within a specific amount of time, for

example, within 1 year or on a per-project basis. Each type of music usage requires a separate fee. If a music user purchased music for a 30-second use as
background music in a newscast, a separate fee would be required if the licensee
wanted to use that same music in a 30-second ad spot.

Production music libraries offer a basic library of CDs of diverse categories and
musical styles. Some CDs feature compositions in 30- and 60-second lengths.
Others contain full-length cuts, in addition to 30-, 60-, and a variety of 10- and
15-second lengths. Each cut may feature a variety of mixes, such as "full," "narration," and "alternate." The narration version deletes the lead or melody instrument so as not to compete with a narrator's voice. The alternate version may offer
additional instrumentation, a "lite" rhythm mix, or something unexpected. Also,
many compositions feature live vocal effects. Software is available that allows the
user to retrieve, sort, cross-reference, and log use of the music that has been chosen. Digitally recorded libraries of thousands of sound effects are available. Production music libraries offer employment for experienced musicians as well as
newer composers, who can use this experience as a springboard for work in films
and television.

Part V

MUSIC IN BROADCASTING AND FILM

MUSIC IN RADIO

From the beginning of commercial broadcasting, radio has had an enormous influence on the business and profession of music. The early radio broadcasts were all live, of course, often featuring opera stars and other artists in the classical field. The audio quality was poor and the broadcast signals were filled with static, but audiences loved the novelty of radio and rushed out to buy the new crystal sets to receive the broadcasts in their homes.

The first commercially licensed station went on the air in 1920. Entrepreneurs saw the potential of the medium, and within 3 years, more than 500 stations were licensed and the first radio network had been formed. Radio grew as did the popularity of phonograph records, and these two industries formed the first mass media for sound. Music could now be delivered to audiences of millions—at the speed of light. The art and business of music was never again to be the same. As the radio audience grew within a few years from dozens to millions, it was inevitable that business firms would step forth to sponsor programs if they could get their names mentioned on the air.

By the late 1920s, a wide variety of programming had developed. For instance, a Boston station brought listeners news (supplied by the *Boston Herald*), concerts, lectures, and sports, in addition to special broadcasts of the Boston Symphony Orchestra. In the 1930s, programming was similar to that of television stations in a later era: Most of the larger stations boasted network affiliation, and a host of serials, variety programs, and live entertainment shows found national audiences.

← Photo © Mark C. Burnett/Stock, Boston Inc./PNI.

In the early 1940s, the *Make Believe Ballroom* made its appearance and attracted a big following—it was the first radio show to use only recorded music. Stations throughout the country quickly followed suit, spurred by the realization that they didn't need live orchestras to attract listeners.

By 1950, with the growing popularity of TV, radio hit a major stumbling block. Serials and variety shows moved quickly to the new medium, and millions of listeners went with them. But rock and roll and other new forms of popular music were emerging, and radio picked up on the opportunity and became the way to hear the new styles, new artists, and new songs.

Although radio had developed an audience of millions, it was not yet known that within the "popular audience" was the potential for many smaller audiences with specialized tastes and identifiable buying habits.

Since World War II, the influence of radio over the music business has been so powerful that successful exposure via this medium can now "make" a song, a recording, or an artist. Although publishers, recording companies, and performers recognize the promotional power of music videos, most new recording releases must also have radio exposure to go to the top of the charts—so radio affects just about everyone in the music business. To get a picture of how the phenomenon has developed historically, see Table 21.1.

TYPES OF STATIONS

One way to classify stations is by their *carrier waves.* AM stands for amplitude modulation, where the power or amplitude of the carrier wave varies but the wave frequency remains constant. FM stands for frequency modulation, where the carrier wave frequency varies but its amplitude remains constant. In the beginning, AM stations dominated radio broadcasting. Although FM stations have been around since the 1940s, it was in the early 1970s that they increased their share of the audience dramatically. And the strong growth of FM in the number of stations and audience size has continued.

Network Radio

Another way of classifying stations is by whether they are individual stations or part of a network. The original concept of a radio network as defined by the Federal Communications Act—linked stations broadcasting the same programs simultaneously—dominated the industry until about 1950. At that time, the na-

TABLE 21.1   Historical Development

1864:	The basic theory of electromagnetism is set down by British scientist James C. Maxwell.
1865:	Italian inventor Guglielmo Marconi develops the first radio.
1920:	The first commercially licensed radio station goes on the air (KDKA, Pittsburgh), broadcasting the presidential election returns (Harding vs. Cox). At this time, only three stations are on the air.
1922:	The novelty of radio quickly attracts larger audiences. Sixty stations are on the air (though not all will survive to 1930).
1923:	Radio broadcasting booms. AT&T inaugurates the first radio network.
1926:	Radio rapidly becomes "show business." Stars of the Metropolitan Opera and other classical artists are featured. Vaudeville headliners begin to be programmed.
1930s:	Over 600 stations are on the air by 1931. In 1934, the Federal Communications Commission (FCC) is set up by the Federal Communications Act. Broadcasting is turned over to "free enterprise" with minimum federal control. During the Great Depression, when people cannot afford to buy records or tickets to the movies, radio offers "free" entertainment to mass audiences. Network shows feature vaudeville headliners, movie stars, and name bands. Advertising revenue soars.
1941:	The FCC authorizes commercial FM stations, but development is delayed until after World War II.
1945:	By the end of World War II, 950 AM stations are on the air.
1946:	The postwar boom is on—many additional stations, AM and FM, go on the air.
1950s:	The rapid growth of television nearly kills network radio, quickly wiping out most live music and radio staff orchestras. As network programming fades, local stations take over, programming newly developing pop music through "electrical transcriptions" and other kinds of recorded music. The disc jockey begins to dominate. Payola scandals bring national attention to the way music is selected for airplay.
1960s:	The FCC authorizes multiplex broadcasting. The record business booms, largely due to the promotional medium of radio. FM stations increase in number and begin to attract special audiences.
1970s:	FM stations turn more toward the "middle" audience in quest of a larger market share. Most AM and FM programming becomes predictable, with few programmers risking innovation. But the medium continues to earn good money.
1980s:	The FCC relaxes controls over programming. FM stations gain larger audiences. Stations continue their search for that magic music format that will beat the competition. Radio's once-dominant power to influence record sales is now shared by music video.
1990s:	Formats split into tighter niches. Digital audio reaches radio stations in the form of digital workstations in production rooms and control rooms. Number of stations individual owner can hold increases, radically changing management and staffing patterns and greatly speeding up duplication of successful formats.

tional networks were NBC, CBS, ABC, and MBS. Today, the term is also used to describe the radio chain in which a parent firm owns several stations.

In 1996, the signing of the Telecommunications Act revolutionized the business of radio. Companies were no longer limited in the number of stations they could own nationwide. Instead, ownership was restructured into four basic market tiers, with limits placed on the number of stations that could be owned by one party, based on how many radio signals were operating in a particular market. For instance, in markets with 45 or more radio signals, one owner may own, operate, or control as many as eight stations. Major mergers immediately occurred, leaving a handful of broadcasters in control of the majority of radio stations in the United States.

AUDIENCE IDENTIFICATION AND MARKET RESEARCH

Most radio stations adopt a supremely simple programming philosophy: To attract a particular segment of the radio audience, broadcast its favorite music. The trouble comes in keeping close tabs on what that favorite music is. For many years now, many broadcasters have held the view that the characteristics of radio audiences can be identified and classified with considerable precision. In the past, demographic research was able to help stations predict the types of audiences their programs would attract. But today, although radio is more research oriented, so many different tastes are being appealed to and the pace at which those tastes are changing is so rapid that such forecasts are no longer as successful.

Paralleling the broadcasters' dependence on information about listeners' musical tastes, advertisers also have had great faith in the value of market research. Because broadcasting is a dominant advertising medium, radio and television markets are more intensively researched than any other. Radio stations are busily engaged in trying to figure out what people like to hear. If a station can manage to count and diagnose its potential audience accurately, it will probably make money. A station that is unable to do so will have difficulty surviving.

Demography. Audience research is based on demographic studies. Demography can be defined as the statistical science dealing with the distribution, density, and vital statistics of populations. Stations and their advertisers are interested in the location, ages, gender, education, economic status, and races of their potential audience—and above all, how many people listen to the station at various times during the day.

When talking with a retailer of motorcycles, a station salesperson needs to be able to convince that merchant that at 5 p.m. on weekdays, the station can "deliver" 100,000 listeners who are 18 to 24 years of age, of medium income, prefer rock music, and seem to be the kind of folks that like motorcycles. The salesperson asks the merchant to spend $10 per thousand to broadcast a sales message to those 100,000 potential customers. If that sounds reasonable to the merchant, the salesperson will write $1,000 worth of radio spot announcements concerning the merchant's motorcycles. If the salesperson lacked this kind of specific demographic research data, the sales approach would be much less convincing.

Research Methods. Radio market research largely depends on polling samples of its audience or potential audience. It is much like political polling, where a candidate for national office may spend vast sums to try to figure out reactions of the electorate. Nearly all polls are based on sampling. Most samples are tiny (perhaps .01% of the total), and it can appear absurd that a poll of less than .01% of a total potential radio audience could in any way provide accurate information on the makeup of the other 99.99%. The validity of this kind of market research rests on the quality of the sample. When the sampling is accumulated with careful scientific controls, data yielded from the research can be remarkably accurate.

Companies sampling broadcast audiences assert that their figures are in the 3% to 5% accuracy range. But not all market research is this good or this useful to broadcasters and their advertisers. Research methods range from casual to scientific. The most trustworthy, systematic methods used for broadcasters attempt to determine three basic sets of statistics:

- ▶ *Station rating.* This is determined by counting the percentage of the audience that is listening to a particular station at a particular time. For example, if a station has a rating of 15.2 at noon on weekdays, that means that out of every 100 households contacted, 15.2 were listening to that station at noon on a weekday.
- ▶ *Sets in use.* This is a count of the actual number of sets turned on in the homes sampled. For example, a 62.4 sets-in-use figure indicates that of 100 homes sampled, 62.4 had their radios turned on.

▶ *Audience share.* This is a statistic indicating the comparative popularity of a program being broadcast at a particular time. For example, if a show has a 10.1 share, that means that, of the homes that had their sets turned on, 10.1% were listening to that particular program at that particular time. The audience share is obtained by dividing the station (program) rating by the number of sets in use.

Individual stations generally call on independent research companies for studies that compare the performance of a number of stations in a given market. Several dozen firms offer this kind of service. Some function regionally, others nationally. The most widely used firm that operates nationally is the Arbitron Company. Four times a year, Arbitron surveys radio listeners at random in more than 250 markets, the smallest being Casper, Wyoming. The process is fairly simple and tends to provide the most accurate assessment of listeners' radio-listening habits. Arbitron provides data for regional and local markets and uses controlled samples of listeners, who are asked to maintain weekly diaries of the stations they listen to. These diaries are periodically collected and analyzed, and the results are mailed to subscriber stations. Aside from listener trends and estimates for each rated radio station, an Arbtitron report also provides qualitative data on the listeners useful to the stations, such as lifestyle groups, population, income and employment rates, car registrations, sales data, and magazine and newspaper readership.

Trade Charts. Most stations read the trade paper charts each week to learn what music appears to be gaining or falling in national popularity. Less well known to the public but influential with radio management are certain tip sheets—"The Gavin Report," for instance. Stations do not agree on the usefulness of music charts in determining playlists. There is also disagreement on the objectivity of some of the trade charts. Charts may purport to show the extent of airplay recordings receive, the number distributed and sold, the rate of rise or fall of individual recordings, and the geographic location where they may be breaking or fading from popularity. Stations lacking their own research resources tend to rely heavily on their favorite charts. Stations with their own research departments tend to use national charts in combination with their own local research. National charts are becoming more accurate based on actual airplay monitors, such as Broadcast Data Systems.

In addition to data bought from independent research companies, individual stations conduct their own data gathering, as their budgets permit. One of the popular ways of determining what gets played and how often is the auditorium test. A station will invite its "P1" listeners, those who choose their station more than any other, to a session where the listeners gather in an auditorium and rate a number of songs on a scale of 1 to 5, 5 being the most favored. From these data, a station will determine what types of music it will play. Local sales estimates for particular songs and albums are also extremely important in determining what gets on the air.

Stations get additional information on their audience size and preferences through incoming telephone calls. Disc jockeys sometimes encourage listeners to call in to express their views. Another audience information source comes from fan mail. Caution needs to be used in interpreting incoming calls and fan mail, however, because they may not be reliable indicators of overall audience opinion.

Data Interpretation

It is one thing to accumulate research data. It is quite another matter to interpret their meaning. The accuracy and usefulness of audience research information is widely disputed. Questions commonly raised are the following:

1. How good was the sample? Did it typify the market?
2. How weak, how strong was the program preceding/following the program being measured?
3. How strong, how clear was the station's signal at the time the sampled audience was listening?
4. How strong were the competing programs?
5. What was the influence of publicity?
6. What was it that most attracted listeners (the music, the disc jockey, the talk show host, a prize contest)?

Data must be interpreted with great care. Programmers and sales personnel must know what they are talking about if the station is going to accumulate a profitable share of the market.

Influence on Music Sales. There is abundant evidence that radio exposure helps sell recordings. But it's also true that a radio station's audience size for a particular kind of music programming does not necessarily translate into sales of recordings. For example, "adult" radio listeners often favor adult contemporary, but they do not buy as much music in this style as the size of their radio audience would suggest.

SPECTRUM OF FORMATS

Commercial broadcasters have one common goal: making money. Although most early stations served in the public's interest and offered a wide variety of information and entertainment, stations survived on how well the programming attracted advertisers—and that remains the bedrock of this business. The development of specific formats is a direct result of a wider variety of musical choices coupled with the broadcaster's desire to reach a large audience. If a station gains listeners, it can attract new advertisers, adjust rates accordingly, and make a hefty profit. Formats that can capture the greatest number of listeners in the 25- to 54-year age range, the majority of them women, are likely to earn the most money.

Looking to fill a particular niche in a given market, stations specialize or **narrowcast** a particular sound for their audiences. There are many more choices of music formats than there were just a few years ago. Broad descriptions follow of some of the popular ones—but keep in mind that the lines between many musical genres have become fuzzy, as have the exact ages of people who listen to them. Consequently, new formats are constantly being tried, to increase the station's audience and encourage its loyalty. Station consolidation has meant that formats found to be successful in one city can be spread to other sister stations in short order—lots of rapid change for the listeners.

Youth Market

Today's market is 13- to 19-year-olds. Differences in taste are frequently cited for males and females. Between 75% and 85% of their programming is dominated by heavy metal, alternative music, and rap. For this market, "personality-type" disc jockeys seek a rapport with the listeners that is both impersonal (straight broadcast) and personal (e.g., contests to "meet the DJ"). Commercials emphasize concerts, contests, and other music-related events of interest to this group.

Adult Contemporary

Adult contemporary (A/C) is a broad category containing subgroupings such as hot A/C (new hot releases), Adult Top 40, and mainstream and modern rock tracks. It also draws on oldies—hits from the past four decades.

Country

Country music stations initially programmed the type of popular music traditionally associated with Nashville, what old-timers like to call real country. This repertoire is still widely loved and broadcast to some degree, but the balance has shifted to pop country, country rock, LA country, and other stylistic mutations. Broadcasters who go after this market will program a great variety of music, ranging from Nashville to pop.

Because country music audiences are diverse geographically and musically, the format is found in markets all over the nation in all categories of stations, AM and FM, commercial and noncommercial, and the number of country music stations has increased dramatically over the past several decades.

Urban Contemporary

Some stations seek a predominantly black, inner-city audience. The genres of music are primarily rhythm and blues, and rap, with target audiences varying by geographical distribution. Some stations in this group focus on gospel music and prefer the label "gospel station."

Alternative

The alternative genre is made up of all kinds of music that do not appear to fit elsewhere, such as world music, reggae, some kinds of fusion rock, punk, "grunge," and techno styles. Perhaps the next decades will see the alternative moniker split into various new niches. When asked to define *alternative*, one record executive gave a wry look and said, "Anything that sells less than 50,000 units."

Classical

Many people in the music industry think of classical music as a money loser. Sometimes it is but certainly not always. And the term *classical* can be confusing, since it's used to refer to the general kind of music as well as to a particular era within it.

There are classical stations and "classical" stations. The "purist" stations eschew even the "light classics." Others are more permissive, define the term more loosely, and include even Broadway show music. Stations holding to strictly classical fare may program the repertoire roughly in this proportion:

▶ Music to 1800 (early music, Classical period, and Baroque period)—30%

▶ Music from 1800 to 1900 (romantic period)—65%

▶ 20th-century classical music—5%

Audiences are relatively small, and advertising rates are correspondingly low. Demographic studies show that these audiences are predominantly well educated, affluent, middle-aged, and just as snobbish in their preferences as devotees of other styles of music. Announcers are usually well informed, educated in the classical music repertoire, and able to chat with their audiences about composers, works, artists, and stylistic periods. Classical music stations find it to their benefit to associate themselves with the cultural life of their communities and with educational institutions, which contributes to building loyal audiences. The number of listeners being small, however, these stations struggle to stay profitable. In some major cities, as well as most small and medium-sized towns, the "classical music station" is supported by listeners and funded with grants from the Corporation for Public Broadcasting.

Others

Christian Stations. Many stations addressing an audience attracted by music oriented toward religious faith and church activities are located in the Bible Belt and its bordering states. Most of these stations have no difficulty holding almost exclusively to the great supply of recordings available in this style.

Spanish-Language Stations (and other foreign languages). Over the past several decades, the number of Spanish-language stations has grown enormously, covering markets from Los Angeles to Miami to Chicago to New York, and offering five or six distinct formats. And in areas with large enough populations speaking other languages, particularly Asian communities, radio stations have emerged to serve them, as well. The key word for this market is growth.

National Public Radio. The Federal Communications Commission (FCC) sets aside a segment of the FM broadcast band (88 to 92 megahertz) for schools, colleges, civic entities, and others who devote all or part of their programming to education, the arts, and other kinds of nonprofit enterprise. Most public radio stations are low powered, 10 watts or less. They each address a limited geographic area and they do not accept commercial advertising. Their audiences are generally smaller than those of commercial stations.

Stations located on college campuses are often connected with one or more campus departments, such as music, broadcasting, or theater. These stations are usually operated by students of the college, with or without faculty supervision. Programming tends to lean to the personal tastes of the current group of station managers. Alternative music and lesser-known recording artists are sometimes featured. Promoters and agents for the artists are well received by campus stations, and promoters from recording companies say that pushing alternative discs to the college radio stations has had a major impact on sales.

Most public radio stations are receptive to special programming that might include chamber music, opera, electronic music, avant garde, ethnic and world music, campus recitals, and concerts featuring faculty and students. These stations also sometimes broadcast educational music programs, such as "Music Appreciation" or "Understanding Jazz."

Many public radio stations are affiliated with National Public Radio (NPR), the equivalent of TV's Public Broadcasting System. NPR was incorporated in 1970. The network and its affiliates receive financial support from the Corporation for Public Broadcasting, the National Endowment for the Arts, cities, state arts councils, and private donations. Some public radio stations receive support from American Federation of Musicians (AFM) locals, which use this medium to foster "live" broadcasts of music and musicians. NPR has a long-standing agreement with the AFM, not only to pay union wages but also to protect AFM members from unauthorized new uses of music originally cleared only for NPR broadcasts.

HOW COMMERCIAL RADIO STATIONS WORK

Operations

As a result of the 1996 Telecommunications Act and the consolidation of ownership of the stations, the management structure of the majority of commercial stations has changed, as well. Where it had been common to see one general manager, program director, and marketing and promotions director for one or two radio stations, it soon became clear that a company that owned eight stations in one market could manage them all with one manager. It's now common to find one market manager running six stations in a given city, a promotions manager in charge of those six, and one sales manager selling them, either individually or in combination. Program directors (PDs) and engineers often perform their functions for several sister stations, as well.

Photo © Robert Brenner/PhotoEdit/PNI.

Personnel

Market Manager. This is the person who is ultimately responsible for the smooth running of the station or stations in every aspect, with particular responsibility for

> The stations' FCC licenses and periodic renewals
>
> Office management and accounting
>
> Personnel
>
> Finance
>
> Audience research (also a programming and sales function)
>
> Relationships with advertising agencies and their clients
>
> Music licenses with ASCAP, BMI, and SESAC
>
> Union negotiations and contracts
>
> Legal matters
>
> Community relations
>
> Equal Employment Opportunity programs and FCC reporting

Sales Personnel. These folks have the crucial responsibility of selling airtime to local and national advertisers. Rates are determined on a cost-per-thousand basis. This information is shared with advertising agencies, clients, and prospective clients on a *rate card*. Besides just selling airtime, salespeople may develop advertising concepts for sponsors. They also become involved, when needed, in the actual production of advertisements and complete broadcast campaigns.

Program Director. Generally, making up the playlist is the PD's principal concern, together with the selection and scheduling of any on-the-air personalities.

Music Director. Most music directors have the responsibility for either meeting music promoters in person or taking their telephone calls. The music director also shares responsibility for listening to new releases, reading the trade magazines and tip sheets to keep up with national trends, calling retailers about sales, and tracking the station's own research (if it conducts any). All of this research is then pulled together and brought to a meeting to decide the playlist for the coming week.

Engineers. The engineering department has the following responsibilities:

1. Process the audio signals for transmission. Historically, these signals were sent to the transmitter via leased telephone lines. Today, these signals are generally sent via microwave.
2. Maintain the equipment in the studio and at the transmitter. Evaluate, purchase, and install equipment as needed.
3. Operate the transmitter station. Monitor and control the broadcast signal per FCC regulations.
4. Assist in recording and rerecording program components—music, commercials, other announcements—and produce composite tapes for broadcast.
5. Monitor computers that receive music transmitted via satellite. Station computers can also be programmed to play particular sets of songs in a specific order. (Usually, comments of a live disc jockey or one broadcast via satellite can be interspersed with songs and commercial spots.)

Disc Jockeys. These are the on-air personalities, to whom listeners can get very attached and who are a major element of a station's particular sound. With the prevalence of station consolidation and syndication, these may be coming to the listeners from locations across the country.

Program Consultants. Though not strictly station personnel, independent programming consultants can be called in by management to advise how to increase audience share. Sometimes a program consultant will have a greater influence on establishing a station's format than the station's own staff.

The Economics of Commercial Radio

The traditional major source of a commercial radio station's income is its sale of airtime for commercial ads—both national and local accounts. Generally speaking, if a station gains listeners, it can attract new advertisers, adjust rates accordingly, and make a profit. No matter how popular a format a station develops, if it doesn't also attract advertisers, it won't be able to survive in that form. A growing stream of revenue hinges on the Internet and involves nontraditional income sources.

Like any other business, a radio station's income must cover its overhead costs, including salaries and equipment upkeep. Beyond this, significant portions of a station's budget go to music licensing fees and to its various research and promotion efforts. The station must spend money to make sure it's delivering what listeners want and to continue attracting its listeners, new and ongoing. From commercials to billboards to contests to megaconcerts, a radio station must keep itself in the listening public's eyes and ears—the more creatively, the better.

Programming

Once a station has settled on a format, there's the ongoing work of putting together the week's playlist, the day-to-day programming, including what new songs to fold into the current playlist and what older ones to drop. Although it can't be said that the consolidation of radio stations has made it more difficult for songs to make it on the air, it has meant that the decisions about what gets aired rests in the hands of a lot fewer people. For many years, songs landed on a station's playlist based on three criteria: local sales figures, requests, and the music director's gut instinct. Today, it's a bit more complicated; for one thing, requests are generally made by just 2% of a station's listeners.

Record companies spend lots of money promoting their artists, from magazine ads promoting a new single or album, to visits to radio stations, to billboard campaigns. They know that as important as it is to promote their new wares directly to the public, it's getting them airtime that will make the difference.

Until the late 1950s, most of the records that got on the air were selected by the disc jockeys, who were prime targets for the blandishments and bribes of music business promoters, which led to **payola** scandals that hit the national news. Since then, stations have kept a careful eye out to prevent them happening again. Yet record promoters remain a necessary and powerful force in the business, and business arrangements between them and station management are a fact of life. Sometimes, a fine line has to be walked.

In most cases, songs end up on the air in the most democratic of ways: the music meeting. At stations large and small, the program director and music director will meet with other staff members (or sometimes just the two of them) and sift through the many records that have arrived during the past week. Sometimes, a shorter list of "possibles" to choose from comes from top management. Hooks, the most catchy portion of a song, are played one after the other; in most cases, songs are judged on their hooks. In a typical week, 10 to 15 songs may be up for consideration as "adds" of new songs for the station's playlist. However, usually only three will be chosen for the choice spots.

Program Content

Most music radio stations devote 75% to 85% of their broadcast time to music. Practically all music broadcast is prerecorded. Most of it derives from commercially released recordings originally licensed for private use in the home.

Reverse Programming. Most radio stations have discovered that radio audiences tend to leave a particular station on provided they don't hear a song they dislike. Many listeners will explore the radio dial, not for a particular station but for a style of music they like. Studies repeatedly show that the listener will not move off a station unless a record comes on that is different in musical style, inconsistent with the other music the station typically programs. When the listener notices the station is playing a song different from what is familiar or pleasing, that listener may then punch out and search for another station that is more consistent, less disturbing. Radio programmers therefore do everything they can to avoid upsetting their audience, which has led to what's known as "the blanding of radio."

Song Clustering, Pacing. Whatever the dominant type of music programmed, stations often cluster their songs, then cluster their commercials. Some studies show that this pattern of grouping tends to hold an audience more effectively than a pattern of announcement-song-commercial, announcement-song-commercial, and so on. A typical example of clustering is the playing of *sets*, such as six songs in a row or 30 minutes of nonstop music.

There are different views on how to pace recordings. Some believe that in a three-song cluster, audiences will favor a sequence of tempos, say, slow-medium-fast. Others prefer to alternate solo artists with groups.

Stations using cluster programming and **back-announcing** allow for a span of airtime for the disc jockey to speak continuously for a while, thus affording an opportunity to chat and invest some personality into the reading of commercial copy or in recommending a particular advertiser whose products we should not do without. This kind of "personality radio" seems to appeal to many listeners. With all the music being canned, about the only element of personality a station can provide is through the disc jockeys.

Commercial Loading, Day Parting. Stations must pay attention to what is often termed *commercial load,* the proportion of their broadcast time given to spot announcements. Too many spots turn off listeners; too few reduce income. Broadcasters search for a winning balance.

Some programming consultants recommend a station show consistency of programming style throughout each 24-hour period. Other programmers believe more in **day parting,** a kind of programming that divides the broadcast day into such segments as "morning drive," "midday," "evening drive," and so forth. The reasoning is that particular DJs and particular musical styles are best suited for listeners as they drive to and from work, traditionally the most valuable parts of the broadcast day.

Syndication

Independent production companies package complete programs, then license or sell them to stations. Such programs are said to be in syndication; their packagers are called syndicators. The producer of syndicated programs determines a format for a show or series of shows, engages the announcers, then lays in the elements—music tracks, interviews, whatever is to go into the programs.

A radio station or a radio chain can order prepackaged programs delivered on digital audiotape, CDs, phone line, the Internet, or by satellite transmission. The shows provide time for insertion or addition of commercial messages by the local station. Syndicated program material can range in length from 30 seconds to several hours. It can be an individual, one-time program or a series.

For many years, syndicated programs were mainly once-a-week countdown programs, say, of the Top 40 pop or country songs, and talk shows. In the early 1990s, a few companies such as Westwood One began to take talent from a wide variety of successful radio stations and offer their shows to stations in other markets, no matter what size they were. Soon, Howard Stern could be heard every morning in Las Vegas, Albany, San Jose, and Miami. Rush Limbaugh and Dr. Laura Schlessinger became national talk superstars, airing in just about every city in the United States. This success led many companies to increase their syndicated fare, and many options are available. Many programs air at different times, depending on the needs of the stations. Other companies offer syndicated day part personalities, enabling stations to import morning, midday, or evening talent.

One of the consequences of syndication has been that the air talent displaced by syndicated shows has grown in number, and opportunities have greatly diminished for up-and-coming talent to land positions in smaller markets and hone their skill before moving up to the larger markets—the traditional route that disc jockeys in the past took to become high-profile, well-paid successes.

Satellite-Delivered Formats

Today, most networks use satellites to deliver their programming. Some companies send a 24-hour-a-day format, complete with a live announcer, music, mini features, and commercials (as well as commercial availabilities for the local station), which may be broadcast simultaneously on hundreds of stations.

This method of delivery allows the on-air sound to seem incredibly local. A device used involves the "network announcer" recording tapes that deliver the local stations' call letters and slogans. These tapes are then inserted (via an inaudible tone system) locally and, when heard in total, appear to have the national announcer sitting right there in "Anytown, USA!"

Alternatives to listening to the radio have slowly eroded audience shares over the past three decades, though radio is still a very strong industry. The Internet's development of audio-streaming channels has enabled radio stations around the globe to place their stations on the World Wide Web, allowing listeners anywhere to tune them in, an alternative to conventional radio that has added to the decline in audience shares. Satellite-to-car radio also promises a multitude of niche formats, many of which may not be available on conventional stations in the local markets.

MUSIC IN TELEVISION

22

Have you seen Michael's new song?

—Excited young fan

For a full understanding of the present chapter, review Chapters 5 and 6 (video copyright and licensing), Chapter 16 (video issues in recording contracts), and Chapter 18 (promotion, distribution, and retailing). This summary chapter focuses on jobs in TV music, delivery systems, and video production.

MUSIC AND VIDEO

The music business has been entwined with the television industry from the beginning. In the 1950s, the "music variety show" was popular and offered jobs for instrumentalists, singers, arrangers, and directors. But that kind of program lost its audience with the increased interest in dramatic shows and sitcoms. Today's "variety shows" are primarily the award shows, such as the Grammy telecast and the Country Music Awards, and occasionally a "special," such as a tribute to a famous composer like Stephen Sondheim or Andrew Lloyd Webber. The steadiest employment for musicians in TV has been in scoring commercials and underscoring dramatic action and animation (see Chapters 23 and 24).

← Emmy Award. Photo Courtesy of ATAS/NATAS.

In the 1980s, record labels and independent producers developed a relatively new style of music dramatization: music videos. When music videos first began, they lost a lot of money. Not only did it take a while for the public to appreciate their value, but management and record companies were concerned about the artist whose "image" might not be theatrical enough. Intellectuals, scholars, psychologists, and others felt that the freedom of the listener to use imagination would be severely limited, and the music would then have only one interpretation. All the concerns were well grounded; yet today, music video is important both financially and artistically. It is hard to imagine the industry without it.

In 1981, Warner Amex suggested that a cable channel be created showing music videos 24 hours a day. It was called MTV. Most of the early videos were based on rock-and-roll records, and the visual entertainments invented to accompany the sounds reflected the energy, craziness, and creativity of the music. Music fans took to the rock videos enthusiastically. Music videos became so popular that their fast-paced, sometimes spectacular style was borrowed for TV commercials and theatrical movies.

After MTV gained large audiences of rock fans, some **videocasters** discovered the medium could also attract viewers preferring other musical styles, from folk to classical. The recording companies made similar observations: A medium initially used only to promote rock recordings could be effective in generating sales of other musical styles. An entertainment form born of cable TV burst out of its original territory and is now seen, as we all know, in supermarkets, at theme parks, in movie theaters, on airplanes, in sports arenas, and in concert halls. As if that weren't enough, videos increased their sales in the form of home video software.

STATIONS AND NETWORKS

Ninety-eight percent of American homes own at least one TV set, most of them color sets. Four major commercial networks dominate conventional broadcasting, and the more frequently viewed conventional TV stations tend to be affiliated with one of them.

The incredible success of commercial television can be attributed to two factors. One is that it delivers a variety of entertainment and information into homes 24 hours a day, seemingly without cost to the viewer. But the more fundamental reason is that *TV is a magic selling machine.* Ultimately, the function of the enter-

Television station control room. Photo © Bob Cunningham.

tainment segments of the programs is to lure the viewer to watch the commercials. Advertising rates for TV are determined by the size and demographic makeup of audiences, which are influenced heavily by the time period in which the **spots** air. Audience measurement techniques for TV are more sophisticated and probably much more accurate than those available for radio. Advertisers can know before they spend their money what their "cost-per-thousand" will be to deliver a commercial message. Early in the 1950s, many advertisers learned that selling via TV was generally more effective than print media.

Commercial TV stations and networks take in about $45 billion a year in time sales. Many more dollars are spent each year to produce the commercials and program material filling these time slots. A sizable chunk of this production money goes to musicians, entertainers, their managers, and agents.

Station Organization

Most television stations lead two lives. One is the station's local existence in its own community. Its second level of existence is as a network affiliate. Another bifurcation can be observed in a station's sales department. The vice president for sales assigns salespersons to either local advertising or **national accounts** (some personnel function at both levels). A large station will have at least a half-dozen salespersons calling on prospective local advertisers and negotiating with advertising agency **media buyers.** Others in the sales department will handle national sales accounts, usually brought to the station by national advertising agencies, which buy time and assist in scheduling broadcast campaigns. Stations affiliated with networks periodically negotiate the amount of airtime to share with the network and how much should be withheld for local advertisers. The station determines what portion of this nonnetwork time should be used for national spot advertisers whose ad agencies buy time directly from local stations or their representatives.

Station sales departments sometimes get involved in conceiving, even producing, ad campaigns for sponsors. When production begins to get elaborate, however, the salespeople leave such problems to an agency or to the station's programming personnel.

Television programming departments are headed by a director of programming in larger stations. But in most stations, the great bulk of station-generated program production occurs in the news department. Now that most people favor broadcast journalism over print media as their news source, audiences have grown large enough to allow most news shows to turn a profit. Other than news, local station program production is normally limited to low-budget children's programs, audience game shows, talk shows, perhaps an occasional local talent show, and public service shows. The use of music in local station programming is minimal. Orchestras larger than quartets are rarely hired. If music is needed in connection with locally produced shows, library music tracks are most often used.

The engineering department of a TV station functions somewhat like its counterpart in radio, except the task in television is more than twice as complex—the engineering department must have experts in both audio and video. The engineers must know how to operate and maintain complicated electronic tools that generate, manipulate, record, and play back images and sound. Engineers also assist in inserting local material into network feeds. Anyone who has witnessed the master control room of a large station, with its elaborate mixing consoles, equipment racks, multiple screens, and supporting hardware, can well appreciate that engineers perform complicated tasks to keep the station on the air.

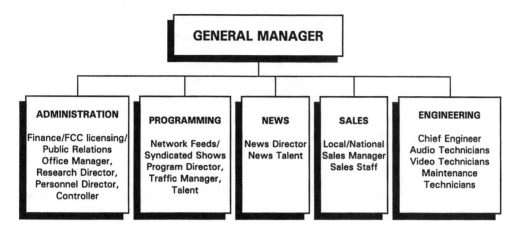

Figure 22.1   Television Station Organization

The office operation of a television station is comparable to that of a large radio station or other business concern that must find efficient ways to handle such departments as personnel, accounting, research, legal affairs, and community relations. Figure 22.1 gives a picture of a TV station's organization.

CABLE TELEVISION

Cable TV has grown in popularity because it offers more than 100 channels and caters to smaller audiences of select tastes. This kind of programming is sometimes referred to as **narrowcasting**. Cable TV programmers have reduced conventional TV watching, but narrowcasting has not been a panacea. Most people spend relatively little time watching channels of narrow interest. Cable operators also try to attract about the same mass audience that is accustomed to conventional TV. The larger cable operators already have corporate ties with TV broadcasters and program production companies. These interlocking relationships allow cable operators to fill much of their program needs within their own "families."

Just as cable TV eroded the market share of traditional broadcasting, a variety of newer media threaten to splinter the marketplace further:

▶ Prerecorded video has stolen some viewing hours—certainly slowing the growth of **pay-TV** during home video's growth phase in the 1980s.

▶ Pay-per-view programming, a variation on traditional pay-TV, delivers a specific program for a separate fee. Although initially slow to catch on, this potentially lucrative medium has offered everything from live concerts to movies not yet seen on any other form of television.

▶ Cable TV is further threatened by the development of direct broadcast satellites, which bypass cable in delivering entertainment directly to the home.

▶ Services and delivery capabilities of telephone companies (*telcos*) compete with cable delivery of entertainment.

Cable companies and telcos are constantly upgrading and replacing equipment and technology to stay ahead of their competitors. They seek new innovations using multimedia, the integration of information types for presentation on a television, desktop computer screen, personal information manager, or other computer-driven device with a screen **interface.** Multimedia information can include text, still graphics, animation, audio, full-motion video, or still photos.

Twenty of the most successful cable networks in the United States are listed in Table 22.1 along with their original programming formats. The year of first broadcast is shown in parentheses.

PRODUCING TV MUSICAL SPECIALS

Take a careful look at Figure 22.2. It represents graphically how musicians and other personnel work together in this sector of the **telecommunications** field. This flowchart shows a huge payroll; productions on this scale are economically feasible only for network shows and cable TV specials. It is probable that part of the cost of such productions is borne through exploitation of **aftermarkets**—home videos, theatrical showings, or foreign exhibitions, for instance.

The Production Line. A program of this kind requires the services of a large number of talented artists and businesspeople. Here is a typical sequence of activity, which we might call the music production line:

TABLE 22.1   Twenty of the Most Successful U.S. Cable Networks and Their Original Programming

Cable Network (year of first broadcast)	Programming (24 hr/day, except as noted)
A&E (1984)	Biographies, mysteries, dramatic adaptations, and investigative documentaries
AMC (1984)	Classic films from 1930s to 1980s, original documentaries, specials, and series
CNBC (1989)	Business news and analysis, interviews
CNN (1980)	News
CNN Headline News (1982)	News
C-Span (1979)	Government and public affairs
Discovery (1985)	Science and technology (18 hr/day)
ESPN (1979)	Sports
FOX Family Channel (1977)	Original and acquired series, specials, and movies
The Learning Channel (1980)	Mix of science, history, and how-to shows (21 hr/weekdays; 18 hr/weekends)
Lifetime Television (1984)	Entertainment and information for women
MTV (1981)	Music video, entertainment, and news aimed at young adults
Nickelodeon/Nick at Night (1979/1985)	Animated and live action, comedy, adventure, music and magazine shows for children 2-15 years/Classic television (15 hr/day; 9 hr/day)
QVC (1986)	Shop at home
TBS Superstation (1976)	Movies, original shows, sports, and special events
TNN the Nashville Network (1983)	Country music, news, and lifestyle; sports (18 hr/day)
TNT (1983)	Classic and original films, children's shows, sports, and special events
USA Network (1980)	Original and acquired series, movies, specials, and sports
VH1 (1985)	Music videos, concerts, and music-based news and movies for viewers 25-44 years
Weather (1982)	Local, regional, national, and international weather

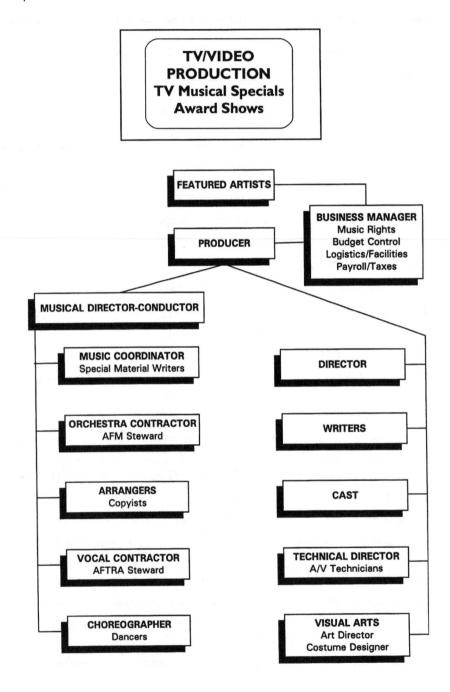

Figure 22.2   TV and Video Production

1. The producer contracts with the director, writers, and performers.

2. The producer schedules a series of meetings to decide what music is to be programmed and who is to perform it. These decisions are made by the individuals invited to the production meetings: musical director, writers, choreographer, featured performers, and art director. Star performers will probably bring along their own personal musical directors, perhaps their personal managers.

3. The musical director meets with the **special material** writers, **music coordinator,** and featured artists to set music routines—style, key, sequence, length, and so forth. The music is then sketched for full scoring later.

4. The music coordinator, often doubling as the rehearsal pianist, will rehearse the featured performers, using musical sketches, confirming keys, routines, and more.

5. The musical director hires arrangers to score the music for the orchestra, often from sketches or ideas for routines.

6. If background singers are to be used, the musical director will probably hire a choral director to prepare the music for the singers, hire the singers, and rehearse them separately from the orchestra.

7. The arrangers hire copyists or a music preparation company to extract the individual parts for the instrumentalists and singers, run off multiple copies as needed, bind the scores, set up the books, and deliver them to the studio for rehearsal and recording. The **supervising copyist** will attend the recording sessions, serve as music librarian, and almost certainly be called on to correct mistakes in the parts, even reorchestrate a passage if need be.

8. Meanwhile, the musical director has hired an AFM (American Federation of Musicians) contractor to engage the individual musicians who are to constitute the studio orchestra. The contractor and supervising copyist develop a list of **doublers**—the musicians in the orchestra who will be required to play more than one instrument. The contractor then notifies the doublers what additional instruments to bring to the sessions. This is particularly critical for woodwind players and percussionists.

9. The orchestra will prerecord most, if not all, of the show. Prerecording may be done to provide accompanying music for dancers. Featured singers might prerecord their voices, too, particularly if they are called on to dance when they sing.

Television station equipment room. Photo © Bob Cunningham.

10. After preliminary rehearsal, the background singers join the orchestra to record their tracks. Meanwhile, the audio engineers have been busy recording the best possible orchestra-choral sounds and coordinating live recording with prerecorded tracks. They are assisted in this effort by music cutters or editors. Final master tapes are produced that now include music, dialogue, and sound effects as well.

Jobs in TV Musical Specials

Creation of TV musical specials requires a large number of artists and production personnel. Among the most important are these people:

Executive Producer. The executive producer is the individual in charge of the whole undertaking, delegating some responsibilities to associates. An executive producer might well be the person who has the financial backing for the program or the network support, or may control a star who is to be featured.

Producer. The day-to-day management often falls to the producer, perhaps the most ambiguous title because it can apply to a senior decision maker, who handles many of the decisions relating to concept, budget, casting, writing, and filming, as well as to a more minor functionary.

Associate Producers. Musical specials have two to six individuals who execute the decisions of the producer and often make important decisions on their own in respect to such matters as minor casting, stage direction, scheduling, equipment rentals, filming of remotes, rerecording, rehearsals, liaison with contractors—and anything else needed to keep the producer from going crazy. These helpers are called associate producers or production assistants. Some associate producers are merely gofers; others wield important responsibility.

Production Manager. Most TV musical specials employ production managers. These individuals handle business affairs, budget control, logistics, facilities and equipment rentals, accounting, payroll taxes, and insurance.

Line Producer. Many of the line producer's functions overlap those of the production manager, although the line producer is generally the producer's representative in the studio or on location or wherever the tape is being shot.

Director. The director must possess strong administrative skills and talent for creating imaginative "visuals." Videos now lead movies in visual production values, the pace being set by short-form promotional clips. Besides skillfully moving performers and cameras, the video director uses a variety of mechanical and optical effects, multiple images, jump-cut editing, and perhaps computer-generated graphics.

Featured Performers. Singers, instrumentalists, actors, and dancers who are cast as featured artists are engaged by the producer. The individual doing the hiring first signs the stars, then contracts for the supporting cast.

Musical Director. The musical director shares with the producer and the director the task of selecting material for the production, such as songs, dance music, underscoring, and special material. The musical director also engages arrangers, retains an orchestra contractor, conducts the orchestra, and confers with the audio technicians. If background singers are used, this person will engage a vocal contractor.

Special Material Writers. Many shows engage composers and lyricists to prepare special numbers for featured artists using original music or newly composed versions of existing music. Quite often, these writers will prepare elaborate medleys, portions of which may include new music, new lyrics, bridges, and patter. These writers are hired by the producer or director or musical director. Many writers of this kind of special material learn their craft through experience on Broadway.

Music Coordinator. Music coordinators assist the musical director in setting up music routines for featured artists. Sometimes, they help in locating obscure copyrights. They may assist communication between the musical director, arrangers, and the orchestra contractor. Most music coordinators have backgrounds as rehearsal pianists. If they do, they are called on to help featured performers learn the charts. They may have participated in, for instance, laying out sketches for the arrangers, setting keys, and reprises.

Music Editor. Music editors, sometimes referred to as **music cutters,** are required whenever prerecorded music is intercut with live music or newly recorded tracks. They work with the other sound technicians in mixing music with dialogue and sound effects.

Students producing music and sound effects for video production.
Photo courtesy of Trebas Institute.

Arrangers. Most of the scoring is done by freelance arrangers hired by the musical director. All arrangers working on network shows are AFM members. Most of them work for AFM scale. The busiest arrangers can handle a variety of styles, and they survive in this competitive field by being able to do quality work under deadline. Instrumentation, style, keys, and overall length of charts are usually determined "by committee." This decision-making group will often include, besides the arranger, the music director, music coordinator, the star, and perhaps the star's own musical director.

Copyists. Major shows use a great quantity of music, nearly all of which is in score form. The musical director or the arrangers hire copyists to extract the individual parts. Because of the volume of work and pressure of time, arrangers usually engage a supervising copyist, who in turn hires other copyists to assist in meeting deadlines. All network TV shows use AFM members exclusively for copying, proofreading, and library work. Much of this work is assigned to music preparation services, firms that assume the full responsibility of getting the music ready for performance.

Orchestra Contractor. An orchestra contractor is hired by the musical director to engage the individual musicians making up the studio orchestra. The contractor is the AFM union steward and is responsible for seeing to it that the terms of the contract between the producer and the AFM members are carried out. In addition to engaging each instrumentalist (only AFM members are used) and supervising adherence to AFM work rules, the contractor is responsible for making out the payroll, calculating wages, deductions, and benefits. Finally, this individual must see to it that paychecks are available when due. The contractor also assists the union in collecting AFM fees for its members for reuse and new use of music recorded for the show.

Orchestra Musicians. Orchestra musicians are hired by the orchestra contractor with the advice and consent of the musical director. These musicians are drawn from a select pool of artists who can play nearly any style, at sight, without mistakes. First readings often sound as good as actual takes. Most delays are to correct errors in the score or parts and to make adjustments suggested by the sound engineers.

Vocal Group Director. When background singers are used, the musical director hires a vocal group director to engage the individual singers. This person is usually one of the singers in the group. The vocal director may also be the vocal arranger, cooperating with the orchestra arrangers in perfecting the arrangements for the singers. In addition to directing the group, this person doubles as the AFTRA (American Federation of Television and Radio Artists) union steward, and in that capacity performs tasks for AFTRA like those performed by the AFM counterpart: seeing to it that the singers are paid, fringe benefits are covered, work rules are followed, and fees for reuse or new use are paid to the AFTRA members.

Background Singers. The vocal contractor hires singers from a select pool of artists who are able to sing, almost at sight, any style from Renaissance to blues. Most of them have studied voice extensively and probably started acquiring their skills in ensemble performance at an early age in school and church choirs.

Background singers for TV can be classified in two groups. "Off-camera"singers can perform as described above but may not have the physical appearance required by the producer to sing and move on camera. These singers are heard, not seen. The second group might be called "camera-ready"singers. Besides possessing the musical talents described above, these artists have the physical appearance acceptable for on-camera exposure. They understand stage movement and can respond quickly to instructions from the director or choreographer. A select number of this group are also trained as dancers, the performers who are known affectionately on Broadway as "the kids in the show." Some of these "kids," Broadway alumni, are pushing 50 but they maintain an appearance acceptable to the producer. These versatile artists are the first to be called and the highest paid of their kind.

Choreographer and Dancers. Most of the top choreographers and dancers used to come from Broadway. In recent years, colleges have been developing musical theater programs, and trade schools have increased in number, so that prospective television artists can get excellent training.

Audio Technicians. Two or more audio technicians are used on TV musical specials to supervise microphone movement, mixing, remixing, equalization, and all the other maneuvers understood by the individuals in this elite fraternity. Some of the audio technicians possess strong musical backgrounds. Others have strengths, perhaps even university degrees, in electrical engineering. Producers put together a combination of such talents to get the sounds they want.

Musical productions of this scale also require the expert services of many other artists and technicians that relate only indirectly to music: scene designers, lighting directors, and costume designers, for example.

PRODUCING SHORT-FORM VIDEOS

Producing short-form videos calls for many of the same skills and processes involved with TV music specials, though they're most often produced by record companies. Most recording companies do not have **in-house** video directors and engage independent directors and production companies. Once a label decides to produce a video, the next step is to propose a budget, then form a committee to come up with a concept for the visual entertainment. Although situations vary, it is common for a large recording company to have an executive heading up the label's video production. Smart executives know their limitations and gather around them several individuals to help create ideas for visualizing the master audiotape.

Video production decisions are often shared among the aforementioned label executives, the A&R (artist and repertoire) department, the artist and/or artist's management, and most important, the outside video director. The director will probably dominate this production committee and help those involved settle on the concept for the production. Most directors have backgrounds directing films and/or TV commercials. The recording artists hope that the director cares about the music and is sensitive to how the sounds might be most artistically fused with the visual events. All concerned hope, or should hope, that the final result manages to avoid the many clichés and excesses that so often plague the medium.

The organization most representative of short-form video producers is the Music Video Production Association (MVPA). MVPA claims its major goals are to exchange technical information, standardize production bidding procedures, and formulate guidelines for fees and payment schedules.

The video director will want to engage, early on, a writer, a production designer, and possibly a choreographer. A video **storyboard** is created, similar to the storyboards created for TV commercials (see Chapter 23), and a shooting schedule is set. Table 22.2 shows the three phases characterizing most short-form video production.

Budgeting. Even low-cost videos incur expenses more diverse than those for turning out an audio master. Typical budget items are fees for the director, production designer, writer, choreographer, **production manager**; wages for grips, **gaffers,** electricians, carpenters, sound operator, special effects personnel, video **mixers**/editors, and talent (actors, dancers, extras); and expenses of set construction, costume design and construction, equipment cartage and rental, location rental, soundstage rental, audio/video film/tape lab costs, postproduction editing, processing, insurance, and transportation.

Artistic Control. Differences may arise over "artistic control." The director may want one thing, the artist something else. The artist's recording contract, when properly drawn, will articulate who decides how the videos are to be handled, particularly in respect to style, content, and choice of director. Smart artists will usually defer to the judgments of directors of proven ability.

TABLE 22.2   Short-Form Video Production: The Three Phases

Preproduction phase

1. Audio master tape is completed. Record company negotiates a synchronization license with the music publisher for the video.
2. Label determines a production budget, negotiates with the artist for possible sharing of costs.
3. Budget is set, and label engages a freelance video director.
4. Director, label, and artist develop a concept for the video.
5. Director engages a writer, production manager, possibly a choreographer, supporting cast, director of photography.
6. Director, writer, and production designer lay out a storyboard.
7. Sets are designed, then constructed or rented; costumes are designed, then executed or rented.
8. Soundstage is booked; production manager engages production personnel (gaffers, stagehands, etc.).
9. Production manager rents equipment as needed (cameras, lights, dollies).
10. Director orders audio click tracks to aid rehearsals.
11. Production manager takes out accident, health, and liability insurance.
12. All of the foregoing are reconfirmed.

On the soundstage

1. Director rehearses the performers' lip-synching, stage movements. Choreographer rehearses dancers.
2. Director rehearses camera movements, approves lighting, plans special effects.
3. The production is shot.

Postproduction phase

1. Production manager orders return of all rented equipment, sets, costumes; orders sets struck, soundstage cleared.
2. Director supervises all postproduction work, including editing, processing of visual effects, computer graphics, opticals; edits final master, orders copies made.
3. Production manager (a) obtains releases from all performers, artists, and creative personnel; (b) gets signed W-4 forms from all personnel; (c) satisfies all union contractors; and (d) authorizes payments to all personnel.
4. Director delivers video master to the recording company.
5. Director and production manager confirm all bills have been paid.
6. Director and production manager reconfirm everything.
7. All concerned look for their next job!

Record company seeks airplay, attempts to recoup production costs through nonvideocast performances and from sales/rentals of home video products.

MUSIC IN ADVERTISING

One of the first memorable uses of "commercial music" was the radio **jingle,** "Pepsi-Cola hits the spot/Twelve full ounces/That's a lot." The early jingles jangled, and the "jingle" label is still used by the American Federation of Musicians (AFM) and first-generation advertisers who created the monotonous commercials in the early days of broadcasting. The public simply calls them commercials, of course. Advertising agencies and broadcasters call them **spots.**

As pointed out in the chapters on radio and television, it would be difficult to exaggerate the importance of broadcast commercials in the field of advertising. With radio, it is sounds, creating a "theater of the mind," that sell. In TV, it is pictures and sounds that move the goods and services, and musical sounds can often be more effective sellers than verbal ones.

Advertisers continue to experiment with different kinds of spots. One season, "testimonials" are in high fashion. Another season, comedy spots are in vogue, or perhaps animals. Whatever the changing fashion, one type continues to hold favor over the years—the commercial with music.

Ad copy that is sung is easier to remember than copy that is spoken. Yet another advantage of the musical spot is that audiences learn an advertiser's theme music and remember the tune and the association long after the broadcast is over. The best commercial is one in which the music stays in the listener's mind and becomes associated with the product. Music also enhances the pictures and acts as a "**clutter**-breaker" to sort out the jumble of spots. Advertisers continue to pay for music in commercials, knowing that it is money well spent.

← Stephen Frisch/Stock, Boston/PNI.

Influences on Style

Ad agencies and their clients expect the musicians they hire to be capable of playing or singing in current styles. The most effective spots often copy the music trend that is selling well in record stores, especially if that music is receiving a lot of airplay. However, the decision to use a certain type of music should spring, ideally, from the concept that shapes the particular spot. Many television commercials employ the visual effects pioneered by music videos. These kinds of high-energy, fast-paced production styles hold viewers' attention, especially in this day and age when society, itself, is fast-paced. However, a slower-paced spot sometimes makes a very effective contrast.

Now that so many TV shows are recorded in the home for later viewing, viewers tend to use their remote controls to bypass commercials. Advertisers experiment with shaky handheld camerawork and flashing visuals to grab the attention of viewers who may fast-forward through a block of commercials. Black-and-white spots are also used to gain viewer attention, and this technique works particularly well when the target market is of an age that grew up with black-and-white television. One advertising agency executive said that his clients are searching for unusual sounds to put in their spots that will "rivet the ear and stop the zap." In fact, he said, the line between music and sound effects has blurred, so that sounds made by musical instruments are now being combined with those made by nonmusical instruments. In response to this new emphasis on unusual sounds, "sound design boutiques" employing "sound specialists" have sprung up in creative centers across the country for advertisers who want a distinctive sound to go with their pictures. Today, to capture the public's attention, sound must go beyond reality.

Another problem for advertisers is clutter, that is, the crowding together by broadcasters of many short spots (some, only 7 seconds) during a commercial break. Studies show that viewers tend to forget the commercials that run in the middle of a long string, thereby limiting the effectiveness of those spots. In smaller markets where small budgets may dictate that "talent" is composed of the local radio or television personnel, the wise advertiser will spend a few more dollars and use an "outside" voice, someone different than local station personnel.

Jobs

Writing music and lyrics for commercials is an exciting combination of composition and commerce and, in the larger markets, is one of the most lucrative forms of music employment available; the competition for jobs is therefore ferocious. At the national level, advertisers and agencies are willing to pay fees large enough to attract hit songwriters and alumni from Broadway. Commercials were a starting point for such successful musicians as Barry Manilow and Paul Williams.

In addition, the spot field at the local level affords good opportunities for talented but unknown writers to break into the commercial field.

MUSIC USES

In the musical commercial, the composer's goal is to form in the listener's mind a memorable association of the melody with the product. When the melody includes words identifying the product name, it is even more memorable, often inseparable in the listener's mind. Advertisers call this phenomenon "product identification." A good musical theme and underscoring will establish immediate identity with the product whether the listener is in the room in which the commercial is playing or just passing by.

Another use of music with commercials involves underscoring dramatic action in a manner similar to the way films are scored. Many commercials are conceived as little plays, and music is used to help create the appropriate mood or perhaps to **punch up** action. If the minidrama is comedic, the music may be scored in a style associated with movie cartoons or even television situation comedies, because the theme songs from these shows are already familiar to the audience.

Sometimes commercials will simply borrow music from another source. The melody may already be familiar to the listener, but the original words are discarded and new language is written to convey the advertising message. If the producer wants to borrow a copyrighted melody, permission must be obtained from the copyright owner to alter the material and use it for advertising purposes.

Another type of musical commercial might be called "star based." A well-known person offers, by acting or singing or dancing, a "testimonial" for the advertiser. The advertiser assumes the audience will be persuaded to buy the same product the star "uses." Original music is composed for the star, but if the artist has a pop, rock, or country hit, that recognizable tune might be sung with modified lyrics, as mentioned above. Although audiences today are more sophisticated, and therefore less likely to purchase products just because a celebrity endorses them, the technique still works with many artists. One classic example is

Detail, Capitol Records mural. Photo by Donna Carroll.

Ray Charles's ad for Diet Pepsi, one of the most memorable examples of this type of ad.

Budgets

Music budgets range from $2,000 to $5,000 for a local spot to the high six figures and sometimes even seven with licensing and performance rights included (for well-known celebrity music) for an elaborate national campaign with a multiple-year contract. One of the reasons the spot business is so good for musicians is that even hometown, local advertisers like to promote their products by purchasing their own theme music or product **logo.** Many composer-directors of limited experience break into the music spot business through low-budget advertising jobs financed by the local furniture store or car dealership.

The small-budget TV advertiser may try to save money by using music from a stock **music house** that supplies radio, TV, and films with **canned tracks.** If an advertiser also uses local radio spots, portions of the audio tracks may be **lifted** and transferred to video use, thus drawing extra mileage from the money originally invested in custom music for the radio campaign.

Nearly all local broadcast spots have limited budgets for music. National campaigns, however, often spend huge sums for custom music. Not long ago, the majority of network campaigns were produced in New York, where most national advertising agencies had their headquarters; these giant firms controlled most advertising in this country. Now, though, the creative thrust has shifted, and the hot creative centers include San Francisco, Los Angeles, Minneapolis, Seattle, Chicago, Atlanta, and Nashville.

Station Logos

One of the most widely used types of musical commercial is the **station logo** or ID. Most radio and television stations hire an independent production company to create a musical "trademark" or fragment of sound that is used whenever the station announces (or shows on the screen) its call letters. Many station logos feature a small vocal ensemble. Electronically synthesized sounds are primarily used (at a cost far less than a full orchestra) and are often supplemented by "real" or acoustic instruments (live drums, guitar, flute, saxophone, or strings). Logos are often 10 seconds long but vary in length from a few seconds to thematic types of extended duration. The latter, sometimes called "image-type" logos, function more as theme songs and can be broadcast full-up or in the background for **voice-over** announcements. Wealthy stations often use a whole series of musical IDs, played frequently enough for the listener to learn to associate the music with the station and its call letters.

THE AGENCY ROLE

Most advertising is handled through advertising agencies. These firms range in size from one-person, office-in-your-hat operations to such supergiants as BBDO Worldwide, whose annual billings in broadcast and production media alone total in the billions of dollars. Most advertisers prefer to place their radio and TV spots through ad agencies because, theoretically, the service doesn't cost them anything. Except for an agency fee for production services, the advertiser does not normally pay its ad agency to service the account and place its business—the ad agency receives nearly all of its fees not from the client/advertiser, but from the medium in which it places its client's advertising.

Agency fees are actually called commissions, and they vary by client from a set fee to a percentage upwards to 20%. For example, if the rate is 15% and the ad agency places $1 million worth of business with CBS-TV, the network discounts the billing to the agency $150,000. When an ad agency undertakes to produce for its client a series of commercials, it will be billed, say, $100,000 in production costs for such items as studio rental, actors, composers, and the like. The agency, in turn, bills its client for that $100,000 and adds 17.65% (17.65% of the net cost is equal to 15% of the gross cost) for its commission. The advertiser and the agency may agree, before starting a relationship, that certain kinds of services are noncommissionable. The traditional 15% figure has become negotiable in the face of competition from "creative boutiques"and from media buying companies, which sell many of the services offered by a large agency but without the high overhead costs.

In recent years, many of the financial arrangements between agencies and clients have been negotiated contractually on a case-by-case basis. Clients use different agency departments à la carte. An advertiser/client may choose to hire only the media buying department, or only the creative people from a particular agency, to cut costs. The more high profile or desirable the client is in terms of name recognition, the more flexible an agency may be in order to attract the business.

Advertisers retain ad agencies on the theory that companies that specialize in marketing know more about how to sell things than the advertisers. Many small and medium-sized advertisers maintain in-house "advertising agencies" where their own employees conceive, produce, and place the company's advertising. But even in-house "agencies" will often retain an external agency to assist it in spot production and media buying.

An advertising agency—a competent one, that is—offers important services to the advertiser who wants to use broadcast media. Probably the most valuable of these is creativity, meaning that the advertiser leans heavily on its ad agency to invent ideas to sell things. People in music and advertising often use the word **hook** or concept to describe an advertising approach or selling angle. Most ad campaigns seek some unifying ingredient or premise.

An advertiser determines what can be spent in 1 year for advertising, then retains an ad agency to offer advice on what part of that ad pie should be sliced for broadcast commercials. Once the radio and TV ad budget is agreed on, the agency uses that money to implement the campaign. If the ad agency is very large, it will have on its staff a radio/TV production department and its own in-house staff of writers. Large agencies also often have their own small recording studios in-house. Although it is rare that even the largest agencies will attempt to record masters involving music in-house, they will often use their own facilities to produce **demos** and voice tracks.

The ad agency's next task is to farm out what it cannot handle in-house. This would normally include rental of production studios, set design, acting, music, and editing. Even the largest agencies will normally go outside their own shops for music. Many agencies do retain on their creative staffs individuals with some competence in music, particularly in the composition of lyrics and other kinds of copy intended for musical setting.

After the production work is completed, the agency has the responsibility of recommending to its client how and when the spots should be placed. Once the client and the agency agree on these matters, the agency instructs its **media buyer** to purchase the time, and the spots go on the air. If the campaign appears to be selling effectively, the advertiser will be advised to stay with whatever happens to be working. If the results of the broadcasting campaign are disappointing, the advertiser may change the commercials—or it may fire the agency. Alliances in advertising survive only as long as the advertiser is satisfied with the results.

In addition to serving their advertising clients in traditional ways, some large agencies are involved in outside work—for example, the production of music videos for recording companies. Because videos have reenergized commercial TV music, they offer a fertile field for ad agencies' creative talent to explore. Some agencies are doing "infomercials" of various lengths from 5 minutes to 1 hour.

SPOT PRODUCTION

All advertising is concerned with persuasion. Because many TV spots are now 30 seconds or less in length, skill is required to make the "sale"—fast!

Writing Copy

Top writers make these recommendations:

1. Mention the advertiser's name as often as you dare.
2. Be economical with words. In radio, let the music say it; in TV, let the pictures "talk."

3. Use simple language.

4. Express one idea—again and again.

Another school of thought, born of this age of clutter, is that the body of the commercial should interest the viewer and pique curiosity, while the name of the advertiser is shown or mentioned only once at the end of the spot. In other words, sometimes less is more.

One of the things done least well by advertising agencies is writing copy to be set to music. It is astonishing how often even **national accounts** will accept music that is almost halted in its flow by the awkwardness of the words being sung. In preparing ad copy or lyrics for singers, the minimum requirement is to come up with language that permits a natural rhythm.

Scoring Music

If the copywriter submits lyrically conceived texts, the melodic rhythm almost sings itself. Too often, agency copywriters lack musical sensitivity, and the composer must adjust the text to permit a rhythm that not only makes musical sense but is naturally singable. Before starting to invent a melody, the composer must first scan the text to discover its natural speech accents. This should be accomplished by speaking the text aloud and observing on what syllables the speech accents in a phrase naturally occur. For example:

All texts for musical setting should be scanned in this manner to make sure they can be sung naturally.

A number of additional guidelines will be found useful by composers trying to get established in the commercial field. For example, words ending with consonants require tones of short duration:

Words ending on vowels can have tones of long duration:

$$
\begin{array}{c|c|c}
\frac{4}{4} & \text{It's} \ \big| \ \text{all} \ ---\text{for} & \big| \ \text{you} \ --- \\
\end{array}
$$

$$
\begin{array}{c|c}
\frac{4}{4} & \text{Try} \ ---\text{our} \ \big| \ \text{co-la} \ --- \\
\end{array}
$$

When creating music for commercials, the most successful composers in the field appear to follow these guidelines:

1. Melody should be simple, singable, and memorable.
2. Harmony should progress, give a feeling of drawing the music forward. Stylistic consistency is essential.
3. Rhythm should be conceived in the musical style the producer ordered.
4. Spoken accents should be matched by metric accents in the music.

Clients are not always articulate when it comes to musical sounds. The smart composer will arrive for a briefing session armed with examples, usually actual sample **tracks,** either original or taken from current on-air notables.

Instrumentation was once determined largely by budget constraints. With the rise of electronically synthesized music, however, choices have become more flexible, more open to a broad range of styles, sounds, and effects. Unlike much popular music making, just about everything for commercials is written out. Improvisation is limited to appropriate liberties taken by the rhythm section. The arranger's main goal is to have the **front line** stay out of the way of the singers. The advertiser wants to hear the text, not the background. The cardinal rule for all arrangers scoring backgrounds for singers is: Stay out of their way. Modern technology helps, because each vocal line is often recorded on a different tape track. During the process known as mixing, when the final sounds are selected, the main track is mixed farther forward (made to sound much louder) than the background vocals, allowing the listener to hear the words. The important rule for arrangers is to score background vocals in a vocal range different from the main vocal line.

Melodies appropriate for commercials have a limited range, usually one octave to an octave and a fifth. The key for the singers must be very carefully determined. All else is sacrificed to provide the most comfortable, effortless **tessitura** for the lead singer. The following is an easy working range for singing groups in the commercial field:

Production Companies

Although commercial production companies once specialized in either radio or television, such specialization has become rare. Today, production companies tend to produce spots for all media for their clients. Total production costs for national spots using music run from tens to hundreds of thousands of dollars. These firms are typically staffed by a producer (or producer-director), a director (or director-cameraperson), office personnel, and sales staff. The production company will sometimes contract for audio and video technicians through a technical production house. An art director and perhaps a graphic artist will be engaged freelance, as will musicians.

Television production companies lease or own their own studios, which must provide room for at least single-camera film, sophisticated lighting, scenery/prop/graphics production, and film and tape recording facilities. Almost all commercials today are edited on videotape at a video postproduction facility. Wages and rental of facilities run to hundreds, sometimes thousands, of dollars per day, depending on the extent to which the production company farms out part of the work.

Companies outside of New York, Chicago, and Los Angeles are typically smaller operations that serve local, regional, and occasionally, national accounts. They would probably have, in-house, a staff of two to five persons. Companies with small staffs may have modest TV filming studios, or more likely, they will rent shooting stages. Audio is usually recorded in recording studios, then later synchronized with tape or film.

Production companies specializing in radio commercials operate in dozens of cities, because their accounts are usually local and regional, not national. Radio spot firms range in size from 1-person operations to an in-house staff of up to 10. Many have their own recording studios or ally with a recording studio by sharing offices and staff. These firms often have studios big enough to handle small choral/instrumental sessions. When an advertiser wants something on a grander scale, producers rent independent recording studios. In smaller markets, there is often a close relationship between the local radio stations and production companies. In fact, very often the local radio station is the production studio for local producers.

Firms involved in production often offer their clients complete programming services in whatever musical format the station wants—CHR (contemporary hit radio), adult contemporary, country, rap, and so on. They write original music tracks for the client. In addition, full-production houses also offer their clients music **library services** that include "commercial **beds.**"These are 30- or 60-second music tracks that are arranged for use with whatever ad copy the station or advertiser wants. For example, the library would contain solid, dignified-sounding music for such sponsors as banks and insurance companies. When a station needs music background for a store advertising clothing for teenagers, it can select from the library any number of CHR-type beds. The necessity of keeping music beds up to date with changing musical styles opens up another avenue for employment opportunities in music. Most of this updating takes place in major production areas, however, such as New York City.

Library services also include a selection of "neutral" tracks for advertisers not seeking a particular musical trademark or association. These commercial beds are often arranged in three segments: A 60-second bed would open with perhaps a 20-second front that establishes the tone of the commercial. A **bridge** follows, where the music is less full in orchestration and less active in texture. This provides a musical background (bed) that makes it easier for the listener to understand the ad copy. This copy can be read live by the disc jockey or it can be prerecorded. Following this middle section, the remaining time, perhaps 10 seconds, is where the bed rises up, so to speak, offering a musical reprise of the front. This end section is often called the tag, a term borrowed from vaudeville. Tags return to the **"up full"** sound of the front.

Production companies can be engaged to add singers and custom copy to the front and tag sections of canned tracks of this kind. This radio commercial format was widely used in the 1950s and beyond. Because the format became so predictable, more imaginative producers and advertisers now prefer a less pat format and have experimented with a variety of sequences of copy, music, reprises, **cold copy**, and musical trademarks.

Commercial producers, whether supplying custom spots or library services, regularly offer their clients **lifts**. These are usually 10-second extrapolations from 60-second spots that were initially scored in anticipation of a short section being lifted from the full-length commercial. These lifts provide the sponsor with the option of buying 10-second time segments and having available spots of the appropriate length—with minimal additional production cost.

Artists and Fees

Advertisers and agencies are accustomed to paying **creative fees** for music and texts. Although some composers charge no creative fee—only for their arranging, copying, and conducting—it is not uncommon for a spot composer to get paid a creative fee (for one piece of material) of $500 or more for a local campaign. At the national level, creative fees vary widely, from $2,000 to tens of thousands (or even more) if using a "star" composer.

Composers generally work for ad agencies on a buyout basis: As employees performing "work for hire," they give up all copyrights in their work. For a while, increasing numbers of agencies had contracts with their creative people that provided that the composer retained copyright in the music and assigned rights for use into perpetuity to the agency or the advertiser for advertising purposes only. This kind of contract left the composer free to seek exploitation of the material in other media, particularly the pop song field. But agencies have begun to realize that there is gold in publishing and are now trying to procure the publishing rights to music. The composer with enough clout doesn't let them do that. The lesser-known composer has no choice. Some ad agencies that "buy out" a composer's copyright may still allow the composer to collect the writer's share of performance income.

Fees are paid in a number of ways. There is usually a partial payment when the contract is signed and final payment when the material is completed. Sometimes, however, the creative fee is paid up front, then the commercial is written. If the spot is approved by the client, the rest of the fee is then paid upon the completion of the project after everything (orchestration, recording, etc.) is finished.

Returning for a moment to budgets for small markets, advertisers will often seek **package deals**. A composer-arranger scratches around for an assignment and discovers a prospective client who has, say, $3,500 for a musical spot. The musician agrees to take on the complete package for that fee and composes the music, perhaps the text too, scores the arrangement, extracts the parts, rents the studio, engages the performers—and delivers the master tape to the client. If this packager could get away with using just one singer and a three-piece band, or better yet, one synthesist who sounds like a three-piece band, there might be a few hundred dollars left for the 2 weeks of labor. Or if the job was budgeted carelessly and ran overtime in the studio, the packager could end up in the hole. In national campaigns, package deals are less common. But here, instead of one individual taking on the whole project, an ad agency will engage a music production house for a flat fee. This kind of company often figures its budgets on two levels: **above-the-line** costs (creative fees, "talent") and **below-the-line** costs (expenses such as studio rentals, scale payments to union artists, music copying, tape).

Some music production firms are owned or partly owned by the composer. Such houses will offer a client, for one lump fee, composition, text, arranging, orchestration, and musical direction. Such fees for national accounts are in the tens of thousands of dollars.

A producer or agency may locate a naturally gifted songwriter to do the creative work for a campaign. Some of these individuals may have attracted the attention of producers through their songwriting success on pop records. Some are musical illiterates and are helpless without the aid of competent arrangers. They will often sing their tunes into a tape recorder, then hire an arranger to pull the music off the tape and render it in correct music notation. The **leadsheet** thus produced is then turned over to the arranger-orchestrator-director who is hired to score the music for the recording session.

Artists' Contracts

Singers, instrumentalists, arrangers, and **copyists** employed on national spots are members of their respective unions. The total dollars earned by AFM members working in the spot field rivals the amount earned by union musicians scoring TV movies and theatrical motion pictures. The national contract covering AFM members in this field covers employment in radio and TV commercials, as well as their use on commercials for in-store videos and movie theaters.

The contract also governs the employment of AFM instrumentalists, leaders, **contractors,** orchestrators, music librarians, and copyists. As with certain other AFM contracts, "leaders" receive double scale. A leader may be a conductor or an instrumentalist who has some extra responsibility during a recording session. Instrument **doublers** make 30% extra for the first double, then 15% for additional doubles. If the orchestra contractor is an individual other than the leader, the pay is double scale.

The use of synthesizers is treated, not as instrument doubling, but as **overdubbing**: The musician charges scale for each of the different parts that are played, although the number of parts for which a synthesist will be paid will probably be negotiated up front, before the session begins.

If the employer and employees are all signatories to the AFM contract, they all agree to abide by the terms of that contract. The employer (who may be the advertising agency or the spot producer) must also pay into the AFM-EP (Employers Pension Fund). Some union locals add surcharges for the benefit of their members working in the spot field.

The AFM contract stipulates that the employer is responsible for additional payments to the musicians for uses of the music following the initial 13-week period covered by the basic fees. For such **extended use** (starting with the 14th week) or for each spot dubbed into a new commercial or used in a new medium, each AFM member who was employed on the original project receives an additional payment per 13-week cycle. National advertising agencies and their clients are accustomed to paying these extended use (or **new use**) payments, and musicians lucky enough to land this kind of work make big money over the years. But at the local and regional levels, circumvention of extended use and **reuse** payments is common when nonunion parties are involved. Many local spots are straight buyouts by the advertiser or the ad agency for all services creative and artistic. This is convenient for all concerned, but it yields far less income in the long run for the musicians. Although the employer is obligated to file an initial-use date, thereby placing the spot on record, some AFM locals simply fail to police and enforce their contracts; many just look the other way when their members record local spots.

The American Federation of Television and Radio Artists (AFTRA) claims jurisdiction over professional singers on radio, and the Screen Actors Guild (SAG) has jurisdiction for television. Signatory agencies and advertisers are obligated to adhere carefully to union scales for national campaigns and most regional campaigns.

As with standard recordings prepared for commercial release to the public, AFTRA and SAG have set, in the spot business, special scales for solo, duo, and group (three or more) singers.

One of AFTRA's important tasks is obtaining payments for each use of its members' recorded work. Rates for singers are per use of the singer's recorded work: Each use requires a new payment. On the other hand, AFM members are paid per 13-week cycle for all use, not for each use. Responsibility for payment of fees may rest with different people, depending on the terms of the initial contract for the union artists—and sometimes upon who can be located to meet their obligations to the union. As with the AFM, AFTRA artists may well receive more income via reuse payments than they do from the initial recording sessions. When singers receive conflicting calls for jobs, they will opt for the work that appears most likely to stay on the air beyond 13 weeks. Top jingle singers in the major production centers can earn huge incomes through extended-use payments across multiple commercials just at AFTRA and SAG scale.

The singers who get hired to record national spots are usually drawn from a select pool of vocal artists. In addition to being able to sing almost any style and sight-read like demons, spot singers must excel at clear diction. The advertiser's first concern is not an "operatic" voice quality—**bel canto**—but clarity of language. The composer may have scored music comparable to the "Hallelujah Chorus," but the **account executive** may demand it be discarded in favor of a **unison** jingle if the listener can't make out the words.

Production Sequence

The process of producing a broadcast commercial is very involved. Here is how the events might fall in place for a network television commercial where the budget for music is large. Events in the sequence below might occur in a different order than the one listed. Also, we will assume the advertising agency retains a production company to assist.

1. The advertiser instructs its advertising agency to come up with a TV campaign for a new soap.
2. The agency head notifies the agency's **creative director** of the assignment. These two call a staff meeting to discuss the objectives of the campaign and search for ideas for a hook on which the campaign might be hung.
3. The agency decides on a concept and calls a production meeting. Agency staff attending are the creative director (chairperson), writers, TV producer, art director, and account executive.

Storyboard for TV commercial: "First Day." Courtesy of Rubin Postaer and Associates.

4. The creative department creates a **storyboard** for the advertiser's approval. A TV storyboard is a visual representation, measuring perhaps 24" × 36", that shows rough drawings of the sequence of events scheduled to occur on the screen. That is the visual component. The aural components (dialogue, music) are indicated below each picture on the storyboard as captions, enabling the viewer to perceive an approximation of how the eyes and ears are engaged in the 30-second spot.

5. The advertiser likes the storyboard and accepts the advertising concept for the campaign. Music is often presented with the storyboard, although the music may be changed again before actual production of the spot.

6. The agency develops a detailed budget to cover the cost of production. The sponsor says it's too high.

7. The agency's creative director or **house producer** contacts two or three **music houses** (production companies) and/or recognized commercial music composers and invites them to submit appropriate music. Composers and houses will compose soap-selling music—good, clean sounds—on a demo tape, on **spec.** This means they may even pay for out-of-pocket expenses of recording the demo. Some ad agencies will pay for costs of demo production, although the demo is usually paid for by the advertiser. The agency creative group selects its favorite from the spec demos submitted.

8. The agency contacts a casting agent or casting director, who may issue what is known in the trade as a **cattle call** for actors and actresses, according to the specifications that the agency supplies. Or the agent may simply

select from casting books half a dozen 8″ × 10″ glossies of actors and actresses who might look right for the cast. Calls will be made to the agents representing the artists, asking them to send videotapes of their client's work or inviting the prospects to a casting session, which some members of the agency's creative department may attend. If a casting session is held, it is videotaped. The agency's creative department, some other agency personnel, and sometimes even the advertiser will either review the individual casting tapes provided by the artists' agents or watch the recorded casting session and make their talent selections.

9. The producer negotiates with the agents for acceptable fees, then gets the advertiser's approval of casting.

10. Meanwhile, back at the agency the creative department has rejected five versions of the script. The creative director gives final approval to the script recommended by his staff.

11. The producer notifies the music house/composer that the advertiser and agency people liked Track 3 on the demo best, and they settle on a creative fee for music. The music house/composer accepts the fee and asks to retain all publishing rights exclusive of the advertiser's uses of the music. The agency, well aware of the value of holding on to music publishing rights, balks on this point. The composer, who has an established track record for innovative work, remains adamant. The agency eventually agrees on a contract price that is high enough to convince the composer to give up the publishing rights.

12. The producer tells the music director or business manager of the music house that there is a production budget for a 20-piece orchestra and five singers, and a recording date is set.

13. The composer reserves a studio for the recording and is guaranteed a favorite engineer.

14. The business manager/musical director calls up an AFM and a SAG contractor to engage the performers, telling the AFM contractor that the two percussionists on the date will be expected to bring every instrument they can think of short of the cannon traditionally fired in the *1812 Overture.* Agreed.

15. Before the recording date, the music director calls the **music preparation** service to pick up the score and deliver it, all parts copied, to Studio A for the orchestral recording session at 9 a.m., and the vocal recording session

at 10:00 a.m. in Studio B. Any questions? Just one: Does the composer understand that AFM copying scale is double after midnight? Understood, and the music preparation service can bill the producer accordingly.

16. Our musical director-composer retires for 4 hours of sleep.

17. The morning of the date, the orchestra starts reading through the chart. The only delay is to correct some wrong notes. After the engineer gets an acceptable balance of the instruments, the musicians record **Take** 1. Takes continue for the 1 hour budgeted.

18. As the orchestra is finishing the final takes, the singers arrive. The AFTRA contractor-vocal director rehearses the singers. For the rest of the hour budgeted, the artists record takes with the prerecorded orchestral music, then leave for their next session down the street.

19. The final mix, attended by the producer and the music director, may be done that day or another day.

20. The musical director, producer, and account executive select the best take and instruct the studio to deliver three **DATs** to the agency by 5 p.m. that same day.

21. The producer meanwhile has filmed all the visuals, processed the **opticals,** created a final edit, then proceeded to lip-synch the actors with the musical track. Following adjustments in the picture transfer, the complete commercial is ready for duplication and distribution to broadcasters.

22. The agency's media buyer has secured airtime for broadcast of the campaign on all the major commercial networks. For this big-budget campaign, the agency buys most of its exposure in prime time.

23. The agency files work reports with all the unions representing the singers and musicians. The agency, working through a talent payroll service familiar with all the current rates, issues the payroll checks for distribution.

24. The campaign was a success, and the agency picks it up for an additional 13 weeks of national exposure. Knowing that this now entitles the singers and musicians to reuse payments to cover this extension, the agency contacts the talent payment service and sends them the information about the media buy (where and when the spots will play and for how long). The talent payment service issues the checks.

Postscript. In rare instances, the wise and/or powerful composer who has been able to retain publishing rights to the music (limiting the advertiser's music rights to use in advertising) finds a lyricist to set new words to the music, then submits it to a publisher. A publisher accepts the song in the hope that it can get a free ride based on the current popularity of the music generated by the broadcast campaign. Everyone is happy, even the advertiser, who now enjoys additional identity through the popularity of the pop song version of the theme music.

DRAMATIC SCORING FOR MOTION PICTURES AND TV

M any musicians consider film scoring their ultimate professional goal, maybe because of the so-called glamour traditionally associated with Hollywood. The term *film* includes not just movies but also TV shows on film or videotape.

Business, educational, training, and documentary films and videos also usually require film scoring. Under the term *scoring,* we include composition, orchestration, copying, and recording. Professionals use the expression *film scoring* in reference to the preparation and recording of **dramatic music** intended to synchronize with and augment the action on the screen.

According to one American Society of Composers, Authors and Publishers (ASCAP) source, "The musical score is the glue that holds much of [a] movie together." Music evokes human emotional response. The action on screen can be intensified, made humorous, or relaxed (or trivialized) by what happens in the musical score. Sometimes, it functions as background; other times, the music is definitely in the conscious foreground. Film composers have saved many a weak scene. The artistic contributions of our best movie composers often surpass those of the actors observed on the screen. As for public acceptance, it is not unusual for a movie sound track album to turn a bigger profit than the film itself, and some of the music scored for TV dramas will probably be remembered longer than the programs.

BACKGROUND

From the very first days, music has been an integral part of the movie experience. Silent films were accompanied by small orchestras, or if that was too expensive,

← Composer/conductor Henry Mancini at work. Photo © Archive Photos/PNI.

by piano players or in the big movie palaces, organists, who improvised to suit the action (at least, the first time they saw a film).

The first music heard by the public on a movie sound track occurred in 1927, when vaudevillian Al Jolson broke into song in the middle of a film titled *The Jazz Singer*. The public loved it, and very quickly producers began adding music and audible dialogue to their movies. At first, they simply borrowed music from other sources—Broadway, Beethoven, Liszt, **Tin Pan Alley.** But soon, producers turned to classical composers to score original music. These included many prestigious composers of the early 20th century: Satie, Milhaud, Honegger, Hindemith, Shostakovich, Stravinsky, Schoenberg, Prokofiev, Castelnuovo-Tedesco, Thomson, Vaughan Williams, Toch, Copland, and Bernstein. These composers scored films only sporadically; most movies have been scored by composers who work in the field full-time.

The period of the 1930s and 1940s is known to film music buffs as the Golden Age. All the major studios in Hollywood—MGM, 20th Century Fox, Paramount, Columbia, Universal, Disney, Warner Bros., and RKO—had composers on salary full-time. Each major studio had a staff orchestra of almost symphonic proportions, required because the preferred musical style was **neo-romantic.** Producers would explain that they wanted music that sounded like Tchaikovsky, Rachmaninoff, or Debussy. Leaders in the neo-romantic style were Alfred Newman, Franz Waxman, Bronislau Kaper, and Miklos Rozsa (although the latter broke 19th-century bonds with such period pictures as *Ben Hur*). These scores sounded European because most of these composers were either from Europe or trained in European styles.

Changing Styles

Tastes began to change after World War II. In the 1950s, a number of first-rate film composers began to abandon the musical clichés in order to experiment with more contemporary American sounds. The leaders in this break from European romanticism included Hugo Friedhofer, David Raksin, Jerome Morros, and later, Bernard Herrmann, Alex North, and Henry Mancini.

Composers were influenced, until the 1960s, by techniques used for movie cartoons, such as Popeye the Sailor and Mortimer (later changed to Mickey) Mouse. Producers wanted their composers to **catch the action:** If Mickey Mouse slipped on a banana peel, the composer was expected to **underscore** the action with a trombone **glissando.** When the Good Guy discovered the Bad Guy lurking in the shadows, the orchestra was expected to play what is still known in the business as a **stinger**, a **sforzando** chord. Remnants of the old Mickey Mouse style remain here and there, but a film composer using it today can sound silly, because audiences have long since memorized these clichés.

In many of the early comedies, the entire movie was underscored with a popular song droning in the background, even under dialogue. Of a higher artistic order was the practice in the 1930s of hiring Broadway and Tin Pan Alley composers to write songs for feature films. Some of these early Hollywood musicals spawned a fair share of the standards we know today.

The discovery by film producers of the value of a good popular song occurred in 1949, when the main theme from *The Third Man* film, featuring a zither, hit the pop record **charts.** The message was not lost on other film producers, who searched for film composers who could turn out hits that could be incorporated into their feature films. Many of these songs had nothing to do with the film itself. Nevertheless, producers continue to include seemingly pointless songs in their films in the hope that if the movie bombs at the box office, they might recover some of their production losses with a pop sound track recording. They are often right.

By the 1950s, movie composers could be classified into one of two categories: (a) those able to underscore drama on film, and (b) the pop songwriters, most of whom were unfamiliar with techniques for writing for sound tracks or background music. By the 1960s, a third group had emerged, artists who could not only underscore film drama appropriately but could also invent attractive melodies that could be pulled from a sound track and popularized on hit records and sheet music. This kind of versatility was new to the movies but hardly unknown in traditional music—Mozart, Verdi, Bizet, and many other theater music composers knew how to underscore drama, then follow with a popular-type song as the occasion might demand.

Jazz found its place in the movie-scoring business, too, and was given further impetus from television. In 1959, film composer Henry Mancini wrote the score for the television mystery series *Peter Gunn.* It was agreed that Mancini would use a "big band" playing driving jazz. It was particularly appropriate for this series, because the big-city chase scenes seemed to call for the frenetic energy of jazz. It worked so well it became one of the great classics of TV scoring. A new generation of film composers emerged who could do both dramatic, classical-based underscoring and contemporary jazz. Some left concert touring with name bands and found new homes (big ones) in Hollywood. Lalo Schifrin, European trained but very creative in jazz styles, could not only handle dramatic underscoring but would occasionally score an entire film using improvised jazz, such as in *The World of Insects.* For this film, he brought to the scoring stage just some sketches, tone clusters, and 12-tone rows, then instructed his small chamber orchestra to improvise freely on these fragments.

After some experimentation with synthesizers when they first hit the scene, the industry has turned again to late-19th-century neo-romantic music with full orchestra as the basic foundation for film music, even the thrillers. Into this, themes, styles, and instrumentation from the whole world of music are integrated, in the service of enhancing the films. For films with a strong ethnic element, native instruments are folded into more standard orchestration, and musical clichés and phony ethnic music are carefully avoided. Moviegoers (and directors) have developed sophisticated ears!

Emergence of Sound Tracks

Including potential hit songs in sound tracks has evolved to the point where **song scores** are now quite prominent. Many of these songs and sound track albums have been gigantic hits, netting tremendous profits for the films' producers and the composers (see Table 24.1 for an example).

THE CRAFT

Those who underscore films use many of the techniques employed for centuries by opera composers, and most film composers are classically trained and fluent in many musical dialects. But the unique time-lapse illusions in cinema art challenge the creative powers of film composers well beyond the more familiar techniques of scoring music for the theater.

The Process

The film is first shot completely and taken through at least one edit and often more. At this point, a temp score, a mock-up of the score to come, is put together by a music editor (also called a **cutter**) gleaning from existing music. Sometimes, the temp score is so excellent, the director prefers it to the finished score, but it can't be used—the royalties tangle prohibits it.

TABLE 24.1   Example of Income for a Successful Movie Song

Synchronization and video buy-out fee	$25,000
U.S. radio and television royalties for a hit single	275,000
"A" side single U.S. CD/tape sales (1 million copies)	69,500
U.S. album sales	139,000
Foreign theatrical performances	7,500
Academy Awards Show performance in "Best Song" category	4,000
Grammy Awards Show performance in "Best Song" category	4,000
Sheet music and folios	20,000
Initial TV broadcasts of the film on pay and network television	7,000
Advertising commercial	110,000
Foreign "A" side single CD/tape sales	53,500
Foreign album sales	85,000
Foreign radio and TV performance royalties for a hit single	250,000
Miscellaneous royalties	15,000
Total writer and publisher royalties	1,064,500

SOURCE: URL http://www.ascap.com/artcommerce/movies-part5.html, November 1998.

Spotting the Film

The first time the composer views the movie, it is usually in the company of the producer, director, film editor, and music editor. The director and composer watch the film roll by and **spot** the film, identifying the turning points, the changes in mood. Just as important, they also discuss where music should *not* be used. The music editor listens to this conversation and makes notes and comments on what the other two have decided. When the spotting is complete, the composer generally receives the first part of the agreed-on fee.

Spotting Notes. The music editor gives the composer **spotting notes,** which specify where each cue will happen when in the movie. An example of the shorthand follows:

1M1	(reel #1, Music, location of cue on reel #1)
02:40:20:00	(SMPTE time code—see next paragraph)
393 + 12	(film footage of start)
:46	(timing or length of cue)

Scene Break Downs. Music editors use video/SMPTE (Society of Motion Picture and Television Engineers) technology to gather the timing information needed to write scene break downs for each reel of film. Most contain the name of each scene calling for music, net film footage, and timings to 1/10 (or even 1/100) of a second. Another column provides space for indication of **click tracks.** The "click" is simply a steady beat that can be made to go faster or slower, depending on the needs of the picture. The click track enables the composer to sync music to film with mathematical precision.

Theatrical film moves through the projector at a rate of 24 frames per second, or 1,440 frames per minute; video moves at approximately 30 frames per second. To create a film music *tempo,* the editor or composer divides the metronome (M.M.) tempo into 1,440; the result is known as a *frame-click tempo.* Let's say the tempo is M.M. 144; dividing 1,440 by 144 gives 10, which means the cutter must prepare a 10-frame click track. Click tracks are generated by computer, and they can even determine clicks for *rubato* (speeding up/slowing down) passages. This is called a *variable click track,* and it can identify those split seconds in the score when the music must catch the action precisely. During recording sessions, the sound of the clicks will be conveyed to the conductor and musicians in the orchestra via headsets.

Composers on major films will usually want to view a picture several times before starting to score it, and they use videocassette recorders to do so. A music-editing system is used almost universally to transfer the film to videotape, using a synchronization scheme that transfers film feet and frames to the standard SMPTE time code. The picture is electronically synchronized with multitrack recorders. The videotape copy of the film normally has a sequencing program, a time code, and a feet and/or frames reference for film footage conversion burned into the picture; in addition, the tape is "striped" with SMPTE code so that the code numbers can be read on a synchronizer/SMPTE code reader. This time code provides precise reference points to the composer for critical timings. The code appears this way: "00:10:23:18" and translates as follows: 0 hours, 10 minutes, 23 seconds, and 18 frames.

Composition

So, having become familiar with the film, the composer composes the new score. When the score is complete, another part of the fee is paid. Many contracts for full-length feature films provide that the composer shall write the music and get it on tape in 10 weeks. In actual practice, the producer is more likely to give the composer 3 to 4 weeks to complete the job. Some composers work under 6-week deadlines, which may or may not include recording. In Europe, the composer has traditionally been expected to present a completed score to the copyists. In the United States, film composers may compose orchestral sketches, perhaps three to eight staves per system (*system* being a grouping of staves), then give the sketch, with indications for instrumentation, to an **orchestrator** to render the full score. This practice developed because producers were always in a hurry—and still are. They have been willing to pay the extra costs of dividing the writing of movie scores between two persons. A few unschooled but highly gifted composers also hire orchestrators to write out their scores.

Film scoring today is done electronically as well as acoustically, and often, both are used for the same project. A number of computer synchronization methods are now available, as well as service companies that can aid composers in laying out whole movie scores with appropriate clicks, meters, bars, and tempos.

Recording to Film

Then it's time to record the music; when that's accomplished, the final part of the fee is paid. Whether a film composer uses an optical click-track system or computer methods, it should be pointed out that many composers prefer to conduct to film by free timing, using a system of "streamers and punches" as timing guideposts. A *streamer* is a straight line that takes 2 seconds to traverse the screen from left to right, and a *punch* is the flash of light produced by punching a hole in the film, usually every three frames. Such composer-conductors leave precise synchronizations to the ingenuity of their music cutters.

Many films combine synthesizers, samplers, and orchestra and require multitrack recording and **mixing.** Feature films are commonly recorded all at once, "live," with the full orchestra present, often including an extensive arsenal of electronic (MIDI, or musical instrument digital interface) instruments as a significant section of the big studio orchestra. Most feature films are recorded on movie "scoring stages." These facilities are huge. Besides a half-acre of musicians, soundstages are attended during recording sessions by scoring **mixers,** a music librarian, the music editor, the composer's agent, and the head copyist.

Occasionally, a film director will throw out a complete score, fire the composer, and engage another one to redo the job. But these instances are rare. However, producers and/or directors often require music changes on the scoring stage,

Photo © Michael Newman/PhotoEdit/PNI.

placing everyone under tremendous pressure. Usually, this high-tension environment proceeds with efficiency—because the stage is inhabited by pros. As a rule, the only delays in scoring movies are similar to the ones afflicting most other recording sessions—mistakes in the orchestra parts or equipment malfunction.

The Final Mix

Following the music recording sessions, which last for several days on major films, the music tapes are combined with dialogue and sound effects in *dubbing* sessions. This final phase of sound synchronization, called *rerecording*, is mostly concerned with setting relative sound levels and making final choices regarding the music and sound, including whether some segments need to be recut. These dubbing sessions are attended by the composer, music cutter, sound effects person, and one to three engineers or mixers. At elaborate dubbing facilities, the remixing setup may call for up to seven mixers at a huge console. Film directors attend these sessions to make sure the sounds they require are sufficiently prominent. Not infrequently, the composer approaches despair when music gets lost behind shouting dialogue or screaming sirens.

MUSIC SCORING FOR TV

Movies produced for television employ the same stylistic approach as for feature films, but the time frame is much faster, and the person who makes the music decisions is the producer of the show, not the director. Composers often work in both media.

TV drama series (including soap operas and sitcoms) also use original music along with their libraries of prerecorded themes and melodic fragments. The amount of music varies from show to show—one might record new music three times a week; another, once every 2 or 3 years. Composers for new shows often compose 2 or 3 weeks' worth of new material to establish the "feel"; for later shows, the music editors cut the bits they want from the show's library, which has been created from the new music. Styles incorporate the same wide range as feature films; one multiple Emmy Award winner, for instance, orchestrated a Beethoven string quartet to underscore a chase scene! It has been the task of the music cutter over the years to take the various musical sources and lay them in as appropriately as possible in subsequent shows in a series, trying to make them fit not only new timings but different dramatic situations. A TV series' composer is sometimes required to become, literally, a one-person band—composing, conducting, and playing the music, perhaps joined by a few other instrumentalists. The composer usually has one or two assistants, along with a music engineer, and occasionally may assign orchestration to nonstaff personnel.

An organization to be aware of is the Society of Composers and Lyricists, whose members work exclusively in TV and films.

LIBRARY MUSIC

Beyond the glitter of Hollywood, thousands of educational films, documentaries, and movies are produced for business and industry every year, and practically all of them use only library music tracks. The reason is simple: low cost. Purchase of music from a library for prerecorded music includes all necessary clearances and licenses for use of the music. A producer can underscore complete productions with **cues** (or **bridges**) lifted from the music library.

Library services classify cues in predictable ways (you can buy the whole catalog or pay for individual **needle drops**). Even "neutral" bridges are available. The lengths of these fragments are rarely critical. The director can instruct the mixer to fade out the music whenever necessary. Library-type material is often prepared by composers with MIDI studios. See Chapter 20 for more information about production music libraries.

HIRING PRACTICES

AFM Contracts

The musicians' union does not set scales for composition, leaving that issue to be negotiated between the composer and the producer. But the American Federation of Musicians (AFM) does set minimums for other persons engaged in **music preparation**—arrangers, orchestrators, conductors, copyists, proofreaders, and librarians. Union musicians earn premium rates for services performed after 8 p.m. and on holidays, and music preparation people earn the same fringe benefits as instrumentalists.

Musicians working in film receive additional income once a year from the AFM Theatrical and Television Motion Picture Special Payments Fund. This fund derives its income from producers and movie studios that sell exhibition rights to their movies in additional marketplaces.

Package Deals

In the film scoring field, producers and directors require the services of composers, orchestrators, arrangers, music editors, supervisors, copyists, librarians, and instrumentalists, as well as recording and mixing engineers. At one time, all of these services could be provided by the major film studios, which retained these artists and technicians on staff, most of them full-time. But after 1957, when the staff musicians were let go by the film studios, producers had to engage all their musicians on a freelance basis. To make this situation manageable, producers would often negotiate **package deals** with independent **contractors.** This practice prevails today in many aspects of the field. For instance, almost all TV shows are packaged. Some composers of electronic scores agree to package deals because their compositional skills combined with their computer skills allow them to function as the composer, orchestrator, copyist, instrumentalist, and scoring mixer.

Producers like package deals because the system transfers their financial risk to the independent contractor. The production company usually budgets a set figure for music. That money must cover all music production costs—composition, orchestration, arranging, copying, proofreading, library services, conducting, instrumentalists, instrument cartage, studio or soundstage rental, tape, mixing, and editing. The producer will contract with a composer to assume all these responsibilities and expenses for a lump sum.

Many composers learn how to budget their time and expenses and come out well on these deals. Many manage to pay full AFM scale and have enough left over for themselves to compensate for several grueling weeks of composition and orchestration. Recognizing that some independent pictures are produced for a total cost that's less than the music budget for a blockbuster, the AFM has come up with a two-tier scale for motion picture work. Producers of music for low-budget films are allowed to hire musicians at a significantly lower scale than that required for a high-budget film.

Composers

In the field of underscoring movies and TV drama, there are many employment opportunities for the fully qualified professional. Although some feature films are still recorded in New York, most American-made movies are recorded in Los Angeles. Well-known composers say they get their picture assignments because of their reputations; their agents do not actually find them jobs but assist in drawing up contracts with producers and help in keeping their business affairs in order. Producers are accustomed to negotiating with composers' agents.

For many years, a small handful of agents has dominated the scene, and the young composer often finds it extremely difficult to acquire the services of an established agent. The composer must thus function as the agent and contact directors, producers, and anyone else who might be a potential employer. A composer has a better chance of securing an agent after achieving several scoring credits. Some composers rely on building and maintaining good relationships with particular filmmakers to land their projects and use the services of **lawyers** for the contract negotiation rather than agents.

Top film composers sometimes get so busy they find it necessary to call in helpers to meet deadlines. These assistants include not only arrangers, orchestrators, and copyists but composers as well. Under pressure of time, or possibly because the producer has provided funds to pay for orchestration in addition to composition, studio composers will entrust completion of their sketches to arrangers and orchestrators who understand how the composer wants the music to sound. All arrangers and orchestrators used in these secondary capacities are selected by the composer, never by the producer or director.

The use of orchestrators is much more common in feature film work than in television. They are paid by the musician whose name goes on the screen credits. Purists may be bothered by the **ghost-writing** phenomenon, but this is the route many hopefuls have found for breaking into TV and film scoring. Yet another way of cracking these high-paying media is to be an advanced student of a busy composer. Not infrequently, teachers farm out some of their work to their best students, who later begin to locate scoring jobs in their own names. Sometimes, composers take on composer assistants, a form of apprenticeship of benefit to both parties.

Of interest to aspiring film composers is a fascinating and invaluable book by Robert Faulkner titled *Music on Demand: Composers and Careers in the Hollywood Film Industry* (see Selected Readings in the Appendix). Faulkner examines in depth the career paths taken by various Hollywood film composers. Several excellent books have been written about music in the movies. Fred Karlin's *Listening to Movies: The Film Lover's Guide to Film Music* is an authoritative and readable survey of movie music.

Music Supervisors

With the rise to prominence of song scores, many film producers now hire a music supervisor. In some situations, this individual finds songs and music to support and enhance the video or film image. Such responsibilities are much like those of a record producer or an A&R (artist and repertoire) executive with a recording company. Sometimes, the music supervisor is responsible for putting together only the songs used in the sound track but in other instances is in charge of every facet of the score, including hiring a composer for dramatic scoring.

Music supervisors may have various duties, depending on the type of production and the amount of budget of a film or video project. A music supervisor may be asked to

1. Make up a budget, make deals, and act as a music department for an independent film company.
2. Place existing songs in appropriate spots of the movie. (This person would need a strong recording company background and contacts.)
3. Oversee a musical movie, picking songs from a certain period or place to match the action and plot of the movie.
4. Be in the studio when a performer from the movie is recording a song that will be used in the movie.
5. Prepare people for the set, deciding on those who can do their own vocals and those who will need to lip-synch over someone else's singing voice.
6. Assist the director and choreographer in designing shots that will work with the music. This can be very creative work, much like directing.
7. Explain "score design" to investors and other interested parties. Some investors in film properties are quite knowledgeable, but others are new to the business or lack the experience necessary to make responsible budgetary decisions during the making of the movie. These investors often want to see evidence of progress during the movie-making process, so music supervisors make the temp tracks available for a showing of a movie preview.

The music supervisor may also help make the transition from the temp track to the music track that is eventually composed for the movie.

Copyists

Copyists are engaged by the composer or sometimes by the orchestrator. In the film and TV fields, it has been traditional to schedule composition and recording sessions within a time frame calculated to produce a maximum level of panic in all concerned. Last-minute recording sessions are the rule. Also standard in the business is the tendency for composers to begin their assignments several hours beyond the last possible minute. Thus, the copyists consistently work under intolerable time pressures. Because many scores cannot be copied by an individual in the time available, it is common practice for head copyists to turn over some or all of the work to a music preparation service. Although some copyists still manually write notes in musical parts, others are adept at using the various computer programs that exist for this purpose, such as Finale. Most computer music programs allow the copyist or arranger to make instant changes of key and time signature if such changes are required to suit the picture.

When television shows or films are being recorded, the **supervising copyist** is expected to attend the sessions to serve as music librarian and, more important, to be available to correct errors in the extracted parts during the recording.

Orchestra Musicians

Instrumentalists hired to play film and video scores produced in the United States are most often members of the AFM. The number of movies produced in the United States that are scored and recorded by nonunion musicians has increased through the application of MIDI studios and computer one-person bands. When large groups of musicians are called for, they are engaged by the orchestra contractor. The contractor and the composer together prepare a first-call list of players, with a supplemental list of second- and third-choice players, should their favorite musicians not be available. Many composers conduct as well, but some prefer to hire conductors so they themselves can be on the spot in the sound booth, conferring with the mixer and the film's producer or director.

In New York and Los Angeles since the 1930s, the artists getting this high-paying work have been selected from a relatively small pool of musicians. These musicians have earned reputations over the years for being able to play almost anything placed before them perfectly at sight, and they often make the music sound better than it is.

Musicians who play in major symphony orchestras have successfully completed a series of demanding and highly competitive auditions, but musicians who work in recording studios have rarely auditioned for those jobs. Instead, they prove their worth and bring themselves to the favorable attention of music contractors by a variety of other methods.

Musicians who want to break into the studios are rarely accepted before they've spent the time necessary to prove their abilities to the inside pool of players. When a new player earns credentials by establishing a good reputation, not just with contractors or conductors but with the players themselves, there will be a much better chance of being recommended for recording sessions. The inside players are always alert to evaluate the newcomers.

Another pipeline to the inside is through players who are also teachers. Musicians too busy to accept all the offers they receive may recommend their most advanced students for studio and symphony jobs.

String players, almost without exception, are current members or alumni of symphony orchestras. A high percentage of them are former **concertmasters** or **first-desk** players. Besides competence in standard orchestral playing, these string players must understand jazz phrasing and the kind of style that is sometimes called "the Hollywood sound"—beautiful tone, romantically expressive, perfect intonation, entirely relaxed. As for double bass, many studio players have, in addition to extensive traditional backgrounds, the ability to play jazz—and often the electric bass. But when a really hot bass line is required, specialists in the rock or rhythm and blues fields are added.

Brass players making it in the studios originally came from theater orchestras and symphonies. In the 1940 to 1960 period, many brass players came off the road from name bands. In more recent years, some brass players have come from the nation's leading university concert bands. All brass players, whatever their backgrounds, are expected to handle not only **legit** music but any other style, from country to rock. When brass players take their chairs in the studio or on the scoring stage, they already know who is expected to play lead; which chair, if any, is "the jazz chair"; what horn player will play the lyrical solos. Even among this prestigious clique of superb artists, some players enjoy a special additional prestige. Most trumpet players are expected to play trumpets in B, C, or perhaps even the piccolo trumpet in D. Most **double** on fluegelhorn. Trombone and French horn players are sometimes called upon in big film scores to double on Wagner tuba, euphonium, or tenor tuba, even contrabass trombone.

Many studio woodwind players have backgrounds in professional symphony orchestras, and many are graduates of university concert bands and orchestras.

It is generally known that woodwind and saxophone players are expected to be competent doublers on clarinet and flute, perhaps even double reeds. But this demand for doubling is less common for feature films and TV movies, where the composers may prefer to engage specialists on each instrument.

Many woodwind and brass players now double on MIDI controllers. Composers are asking for these instruments more and more because of their versatility and the seemingly infinite number of colors and effects that are possible. They are particularly popular in TV scoring.

Studio percussionists usually come from wide backgrounds that would include extensive study and experience in styles ranging from jazz and Latin to symphonic and rock. When a particularly authentic rock or "urban" sound is wanted, sometimes specialists are brought in. The use of electronic drum sets and MIDI percussion has become widespread, and most working commercial drummers now own electronic setups. If the timpani work is extensive, many contractors will engage a player with solid experience in symphony work. Even though nearly all studio percussionists play mallet instruments, contractors will sometimes hire special artists to handle elaborate solos.

Keyboard players are expected to be able to play traditional and current styles, sight-read, and improvise. The use of MIDI keyboard controllers has become so prevalent that it is now rare to find a working studio keyboard player who does not own an extensive collection of synthesizers, samplers, and related gear.

Guitarists must be competent in several musical styles. Not only are they expected to be excellent sight readers, they must also be able to improvise, to play music by ear, or even to compose music on the spot, to suit the style of music being recorded.

Music Editors

Music editing can make or break a film's score. The editor often must make copies of cues in order to use pieces of them again in the film and cut down existing cues when the picture is recut after it has been scored. Many low-budget films provide no budget at all for music cutters and expect composers to deliver a fully synchronous score, whatever system is used for timing music to picture. Composers just breaking into the profession must often function as the music editor on their projects.

The job of the music editor is to make sure the music is cued to exactly the right spots in the action. An understanding of SMPTE code, click tracks, and Pro Tools—a digital editing software program—is essential. The music editor must be completely literate and fluent in music.

Until recently, film music editors have acquired their skills on the job. Some started out as film editors who then turned to music cutting. Others had been composers or orchestrators, then switched to music editing. The best music cutters are amazingly versatile, possessing great musical sensitivity, a keen ear for balance, and an awareness of how music can make or break a scene, all combined with a knowledge of the special technology used in synchronizing music tracks to film or tape. Fortunately, some schools now have excellent courses in film music editing.

Society of Motion Picture and Television Engineers

Technicians wanting to inform themselves about recording techniques in film and TV often participate in the Society of Motion Picture and Television Engineers (SMPTE). In addition to serving as an information exchange, SMPTE attempts to standardize recording and synchronization techniques to enable its members to move comfortably to jobs in either medium. SMPTE has its headquarters in White Plains, New York.

Part VI

CAREER PLANNING AND DEVELOPMENT

25 CAREER OPTIONS

Hope is the thing with feathers, that perches in the soul, and sings the tune without the words, and never stops at all.

—*Emily Dickinson*

Students, parents, teachers, and counselors sometimes hold distorted views of the career options in the music industry. Their information may be inaccurate and out of date. The goal of this chapter is to provide a comprehensive account of music career options and set forth precisely how aspirants may qualify for a career in music.

The U.S. Department of Labor lists more than 20,000 different occupational titles. Its Bureau of Labor Statistics publishes yearly the *Occupational Outlook Handbook,* which predicts the jobs that might be in demand in future years. Although some parts of the field are tremendously overcrowded, there is a shortage of qualified people in other areas.

When the music industry is regarded as part of the larger entertainment industry, a complete inventory of music-related occupations reveals an astonishing diversity. Most successful people in the business have a strong spirit of entrepreneurship. They stay alert to trends and try to predict new areas of interest in the marketplace. The individual searching for employment in music will discover a very large number of career options. To provide a perspective, we group them as follows:

Creative Careers	Teaching Careers
Producing/Directing Careers	Music-Related Careers
Performing Careers	

← Bruce Springsteen. Photo © Barbara Y. Pyle/Contact Press Images/PNI.

TABLE 25.1   Career Planning and Development

Discovering yourself
  Self-appraisal of temperament, talent
  Professional assessment of your temperament, talent

Defining goals
  Personal needs, preferences
  Investigation of career options
  Short-term employment objectives
  Long-term career goals

Getting prepared
  Education, training
  Apprenticeship, work experience
  Diplomas, degrees, licenses, union affiliations

Finding work
  Surveying the job market: current, potential
  Predicting entry: time, place, pay, status
  Breaking in: auditions, demos, letters, résumés, interviews
  Self-employment options

Climbing the ladder
  Planning advancement: status, income, power
  Vertical vs. horizontal job change
  Quitting vs. hanging on
  Attainment of career goals
  Realization of personal goals
  Periodic reassessment of goals

Retirement
  When, how
  Estimated financial requirements

Choosing the right career can be one of the most important decisions in a person's life. Before proceeding to examine the options available, look at the summary in Table 25.1, which outlines the stages the prudent individual could go through in planning and developing a career.

CREATIVE CAREERS

Professional Songwriter
Lyricist
Composer of Show Music
Composer of Dramatic Music
Composer of Educational Materials

Composer of Children's Music
Composer of Classical Music
Arranger/Orchestrator
Music Editor
Music Copyist

Professional Songwriter

Career Description. The professional songwriter spends about half the time composing, focusing creative energy on one market: the record business. The other half of the songwriter's workweek is usually spent promoting—trying to persuade performers and producers to record the material. Most songwriters have difficulty gaining acceptance and find it necessary to support themselves with other kinds of employment that may or may not relate to music. Genuinely talented songwriters, once they obtain initial acceptance, usually discontinue moonlighting and devote their full attention to writing and promoting their songs. When this happens, they often find themselves increasingly involved in such related activities as music publishing, record production, perhaps even artist management or show production.

Professional songwriters generally find it helpful to live and work in a major recording center where they can make direct personal contacts with publishers, record producers, and recording artists. The real pros write not just dozens of songs but hundreds, knowing that prolific activity is required to sustain a full-time songwriter career. As for working conditions, they are ideal: the songwriter sets the hours and vacation periods, usually writes at home, and can limit professional contacts to the kinds of individuals desirable to be around—musicians and show people. Unlike most other professionals, the writer need not clutter the workweek with "the public," amateurs, groupies, salespersons, or sponsors' spouses.

Qualifications and Preparation. Because the publishing/recording business requires hundreds of new songs every week, even untalented, poorly prepared songwriters often get heard—initially. But such individuals experience only brief acceptance and are soon displaced by those who are genuinely qualified. Aspiring songwriters can usually discover whether or not they possess genuine creative talent by offering songs to performers and producers over a period of time. They should learn, with persistent effort, whether song users judge them as really talented. If aspirants find no acceptance after 2 or 3 years' effort of this kind, the message becomes clear: They do not have what song users want.

Assuming for the moment that the aspirant has demonstrable creative talent, a key requirement is to learn the craft. Chapter 3 treats this topic at length.

If the aspirant is talented and competent, professional success will also depend on the right kind of temperament. Unless the aspirant is so creatively gifted that song users beat a path to the door, certain personal traits will be required to survive in the field. The essential personal attribute is determination. The writer must be strongly motivated to write songs and then more songs and then get out on the street and push the material unrelentingly, day after day. Even established pros rarely enjoy the luxury of sitting at home waiting for the telephone to ring. Songwriters learn that the world must be continuously reminded that they are still alive, still producing. Another desirable personality trait is infinite patience. Some top writers waited years for recognition. A less patient temperament might have given up.

Most of the pros exhibit these personality traits and work habits:

1. They are self-assured and confident in their music. They can handle unkindness, insult, disappointment, without caving in.
2. They just won't give up. They persevere until they gain acceptance.
3. They have a strong sense of curiosity. They may start out ignorant of both their craft and their profession, but they study, observe, and ask questions.

Employment Prospects. If the aspirant is genuinely talented, is professionally competent, has the temperament described, and is persistent, the chances of experiencing professional success are good. But if there's a shortfall in even one of these areas, the songwriter should forget the first-choice career plan and turn to something else.

Songwriters are employed almost exclusively by publishers. If a publisher believes in a writer, the publisher will normally contract for the writer's services for a year or more on an exclusive basis, meaning that the individual can write only for that particular publisher. Most such writers receive a weekly salary, but this may be treated as an advance on future royalties earned by the writer. The standard contract provides that all royalty advances and salaries based on potential royalties are fully recoupable by the publisher from royalties the writer earns under the agreement.

Employers often prefer to contract for writers' services on a work-made-for-hire basis. Review Chapter 5 for information on these contracts.

Lyricist

Individuals who are talented in expressing themselves lyrically can develop careers writing words to songs. It is not possible to describe a typical career for a lyricist because no two are alike. The first difficulty in attempting to make it as a lyricist is the same one confronting the pop singer: Almost all of us think we can do it. This conceit among songwriters, particularly lyricists, is reinforced every day by the quick popularity gained by songs lacking even basic craftsmanship, let alone any artistic quality. Employment prospects of lyricists aspiring to full-time careers are not promising for anyone lacking a distinctive creative talent with words. Unless writers are richly endowed, their careers may continue to support them only if they become active also as composers or in some other music-related work, such as publishing, producing, or artist management.

Lyricists who want to write for the musical theater must have a genuine sense of theater and a love for what takes place there. They will probably associate themselves with other composers and creative talents of similar tastes and professional goals. This often occurs, as it did with Cole Porter, Richard Rodgers, and others, when the writer is still in college, where student-written shows provide vehicles for novices to learn their craft.

When a writer has a feeling for how a song can contribute to the progress of the drama on stage, the writer will probably take the next step and become involved in collaborating with others in writing the **book** for shows, a term used on Broadway for the text of a musical play. Among the most distinguished (and wealthy) lyricists who also wrote (or helped write) books for successful Broadway shows were Ira Gershwin, Oscar Hammerstein II, and Alan Jay Lerner. The field of writing for the professional musical theater is very difficult to break into, but the rewards, artistic and financial, can be rich indeed.

Composer of Show Music

Career Description. A small group of professional composers devotes most of its creative efforts to writing music for shows. Years ago, this would have meant only the kind of creative work involved in mounting a Broadway production. Today, additional show-writing opportunities can be found off-Broadway and "off-off-Broadway"—in regional theaters, dinner theaters, children's theater, and industrial shows.

Composer George Gershwin. Photo © N/A/Archive Photos/PNI.

Show music composers work differently from pop songwriters. The latter are free to invent whatever material they think might appeal to record producers. But show music composers normally start work only after a producer or writer has presented them with a script defining the nature of the show, the scenario, dialogue, and early on, the book for the production. The composer works sometimes on a daily basis with the show writers and producers, searching for music and lyrics that enhance the show and move it forward. Show music composers often work steadily on a project for several months, even a year or more, shaping and reshaping the music to fit the script—which is also probably undergoing constant rewriting. Completed, polished songs may have to be thrown out and new ones hastily inserted. Casting may change, and the composer may have to rethink the type of material that will best suit the new performer. Show music composers may be handed a lyric and be asked to come up with the music in 2 or 3 days, even overnight. Some great standards that were composed overnight have emerged from Broadway hits; Stephen Sondheim wrote the music and lyrics to

Send in the Clowns in just one evening! On the other hand, Rodgers and Hammerstein (*Oklahoma!, South Pacific, Carousel, The Sound of Music,* etc.) were known for working and reworking music and lyrics on just a handful of songs for a year or more until they attained their artistic goal. Composers and lyricists of stature are almost always called on to serve as consultants to the producer in such matters as casting, dialogue, staging, and orchestrations. Show music composers/ lyricists are, then, men and women "of the theater," and their work starts and ends with what works on stage.

Some show music composers are occasionally called on to write not just show songs, but also instrumental music, dance music, even dramatic music to underscore stage action. For example, the master show music composer, Richard Rodgers, was called on to compose dramatic ballet music, *Slaughter on Tenth Avenue,* for one of his Broadway shows. A composer able to handle diverse assignments of these kinds rises above the ranks of "songwriter" and becomes a "composer's composer." It is more common in most shows, however, to expect the composer-lyricists working on the project to be engaged only for songs, not dramatic music.

Qualifications and Preparation. Show music composers must possess the same qualifications cited for songwriters plus a sense of theater. Show composers are often expected to work well with collaborators, particularly lyricists. Although Broadway has had a few masters who could write words and music— Cole Porter, Irving Berlin, Stephen Sondheim, for example—most shows are created by a kind of committee involving composers, lyricists, playwrights, and directors. Choreographers and lighting directors also have their say. The creative artist who is comfortable only when working alone is better off staying away from the theater.

How does a person prepare for this level of composition? Unless gifted with bountiful natural talent and polished with private instruction, such a composer would have to spend at least 4 to 6 years beyond high school studying music, probably in a university. The aspirant might major in composition and minor in theater—getting experience in campus or local productions, as did Stephen Sondheim, Oscar Hammerstein, Cole Porter, Richard Rodgers, and many others. The "complete" show music composer would not only become immersed in the Broadway repertoire but also study the great "show music" composed by earlier masters, such as Mozart and Wagner, not to mention Stravinsky and Copland in the 20th century.

What kind of temperament must a composer have to work professionally in the theater? Already mentioned was the need for an ability to collaborate artistically; a "loner" cannot make it in this environment. Also, the show music composer must be able to endure the sudden rejection of material without experiencing total collapse of ego. The aspirant must have unlimited patience—be willing to work on one project for a year or two, then see the show fold after one performance and be willing to go through the whole process again. The person must also possess sufficient aggressiveness to search for show backers and producers. Creative musicians working in the theater must hustle their own financial support and convince investors that the project is as good as the composers believe it is. In this aspect of a theater composer's career, there is little room for modesty. Self-confidence and drive are as important to professional success as the musician's creative prowess.

Employment Prospects. There is no such thing as an "employer" or a "job" for show music composers. Rather, they work on projects, perhaps for long periods without compensation, in the hope that they can locate a financial backer along the way. Despite the hit-flop ratio of musical shows, every season **angels** emerge, money in hand, ready to sink up to several million dollars into an untried, unproved musical dream. A show composer may struggle for years and never find financial backing or a receptive producer. Still, writers new and old continue to make their way in the theater.

Elsewhere in this volume are described potential income sources for show music. Because royalties for show music from records and print media can be huge, it is this pot of gold that every year attracts still more show music composers determined to follow the rainbow. Because the rewards are great, composers always seem willing to endure long periods of starvation waiting for that hit. Individuals engaged in this long-odds game must have outside income of some kind. Fortunately for those who love good musical theater, there seems to be an unending supply of creative artists who are willing to keep knocking at the stage door.

Composer of Dramatic Music

Career Description. Large numbers of musicians develop full-time careers composing background music for television and movies. These composers see the film, then sit with the film director (or producer in television) and music cutter to determine where music should be underscored and just what kind of music would be appropriate for the dramatic situation. Background music composers must write at top speed. Producers may demand a score for a 30-minute TV episode, even a 1-hour show, in 1 week or less. Movie producers may require the music score be written and recorded for a feature film within 4 to 6 weeks. Even well-established composers in this field experience feast and famine; they may make weekly visits to the unemployment office for a while, then suddenly be called on to turn out a 13-week TV series in 3 months and work on a film score concurrently. Hot and cold, rich and poor, that is the pattern.

Generally, TV and film composers must locate in Los Angeles, New York, or a major foreign production center to find work in TV and the movies. Within the field, there is an array of specialization. Some composers specialize in writing musical themes for films and TV series. Others find opportunities writing mood music for music libraries.

Some composers who prefer to write for the live theater and other dramatic media focus on writing ballets and operas. Professional work of this kind is almost invariably performed on commission, and the composer can live anywhere. But many dramatic music composers are employed as teachers by universities.

Qualifications and Preparation. The musician aspiring to a professional career scoring dramatic music must possess outstanding creative talent. The aspirant must also be highly sensitive to dramatic values, tone painting, and how music can enhance theatrical experience. Today's film and TV composers must have strong backgrounds in symphonic music, and be able to draw from all styles available.

Successful film composers today use electronic instruments and computers in all phases of their work, from demos for directors to the final recording itself.

Employment Prospects. The most readily employable composers of dramatic music today are those adept at scoring for electronic instruments as well as acoustic instruments. One way composers can break into the film world is by first working as orchestrators or apprentices for established composers. For additional kinds of employment prospects in underscoring drama, review Chapter 24.

Composer of Educational Materials

Career Description. When schools and colleges accelerated their music education programs following World War II, publishers became increasingly involved in attempting to supply the print music needs of school bands, orchestras, and choruses, as well as the requirements of the individual student in search of learning materials. This print music market expanded in the 1960s to involve several hundred composers-arrangers-editors in the publication of music education materials. Nearly all professional composers in this field come from the teaching profession. Most of these pros write music only part-time and continue to hold their teaching jobs 9 months a year.

This division of professional activity has developed for two reasons. First, few educational field composers can earn enough at it to support themselves; it may yield very respectable royalties but usually not enough to justify quitting a teaching post. Second, their jobs in schools and colleges keep them aware of the changing market for educational music. Furthermore, these composers are able to maintain their contacts with potential customers through educational organizations, clinics, and conventions.

The most successful composers of educational materials usually concentrate on the particular medium that they know best: Band directors tend to compose mostly band pieces; choral directors tend mostly to create choral repertoire. Our best educational field composers do not limit their creative work to the educational market but are active in the general field of serious music, with performances of their compositions given by professional symphony orchestras and ballet and opera companies.

How do most educational field composers function? Simply by scoring what they believe is their best work, making a demo tape with a school group, forwarding the score and demo to a publisher—then crossing their fingers. Publishers usually have knowledgeable chief editors who are adept at determining if a particular score shows promise. Some composers receive advances on royalties. The standard royalty in this field is usually 10% of sales at the retail price. The largest markets are in the school band and choir fields.

Qualifications and Preparation. An individual who wants to become a professional composer specializing in the educational field will almost certainly major in music in college—and probably go on to graduate school for a master's degree, perhaps a D.M.A. (Doctor of Musical Arts) degree. The aspirant should have several years of experience with school ensembles as a director. Also important is familiarity with the repertoire of the past and present that has been found suitable for educational purposes. The aspirant would, in the course of ongoing study and directing experience, become thoroughly familiar with the performance capabilities of amateur musicians at various grade levels, then score music to accommodate the needs of particular segments of the market. Besides understanding the craft, let us hope that the aspirant is also creative, capable of composing music of substance and meaning.

Employment Prospects. If a composer heading for specialization in the educational field is really talented, creative, knows the craft, and can produce acceptable demo tapes, publishers will be receptive: that is, if the composer follows certain procedures. The first step is to address a specific market (such as high school bands) and medium. The next step is to inquire about submission guidelines from publishers active in that area. Publishers are much more receptive to scores that come in conforming to their requirements. A letter accompanying submission of the full score and parts should offer a description of the piece and state for whom it is intended, together with any other information pertinent to the composition that the publisher might need to know, such as whether the copyright claim for the piece is already registered.

All educators complain they have difficulty locating a sufficient number of high-quality works for students to study, so the field is open to persons with real talent in this area.

Composer of Children's Music

Career Description. When mass production of printed and recorded music accelerated after World War II, one of the new markets discovered was in the area of music addressed to children. The Walt Disney people led the way in marketing special music of this kind, eventually discovering that sound tracks and videos are extremely lucrative reminders of a pleasant viewing experience.

A composer seeking a professional career writing children's music must understand how to score ideas in a simple style, yet avoid the simplistic. Competition in the field is strong, and even the simplest songs should reveal at least a hint of charm, if not originality. Song texts are essential to most music appealing to children. If not adept at composing lyrics, the composer will need to locate someone who knows how to handle song texts without sounding totally vacuous. Also, the aspiring composer in this field needs to know how limited in range melodies must be for young voices.

One aspect of composing music for kids spills over into the educational field, particularly through children's television programming. This market includes material that helps young children learn to count, to spell, to recognize the names of animals, and so forth, sometimes correlated to music books with sound recordings. Composers interested in this kind of writing and production are involved not just in entertainment but in education as well.

Qualifications and Preparation. Aspirants may find work in this field with the qualifications cited above for writers of popular songs—natural creative gifts. An arranger can always be called in to bail out the illiterate composer who is not informed in the craft. But it is more likely that publishers and record producers, given a choice, will prefer to look at the music submitted by musicians who know how to score what they create. Serious children's writers also need a good grasp of children's age-level characteristics and would be well advised to enroll in child development courses.

Employment Prospects. Most income in this field derives from recordings and printed music that follow the release of a successful musical film or TV program. Some of this work is rendered by songwriters hired by the film producers. Music publishers and recording companies then follow up the film with special editions. The composer aspiring to work in the children's music field, once qualified, should contact publishers who address this market. The quickest route to discovering who these publishers are is to examine the children's section of a music store. Music discovered there will not compete with Beethoven's *Ninth Symphony*, but the royalties it generates for composers will certainly help pay the rent.

Composer of Classical Music

Career Description. Musicians who aspire to professional careers as composers of classical music generally view themselves as functioning outside the music "business," believing they can spare themselves confrontation with the commercial world. But most composers in the field bump up against the rude realities of the marketplace just like their counterparts in popular music. If gifted with both abundant talent and the right temperament for such a career, the serious music composer should become acquainted with the professional lives of Bach, Handel, or Chopin—not to mention Schoenberg and Bartok. Each of these composers discovered that he had to devote much of his time to hustling for jobs, commissions, and students. Nowadays, only a handful of composers devote their full workweek to composing. Either through choice or financial necessity, nearly all composers divide their time among composing, teaching, performing—and job hustling.

Practically all serious music composers find that about the only place they can find steady employment is on the teaching staff of a conservatory or university (in recent decades, Schoenberg, Bartok, Harris, Piston, Hindemith, Persichetti, Crumb, Foss, Schuller).

Once a composer starts to acquire a good reputation, commissions follow. Sometimes a commission looks large, but if it does not include copying and re-production of the parts, the composer may pay out more for these services than the fee received for composing the music. A composer of national and interna-tional reputation could live fully off commissions alone, for musicians of this stat-ure receive more requests to compose than they can accept. But the composer as-piring to this high station may have to wait a lifetime to reach these heights.

Composers of even modest reputation enter composing contests. These come along all the time, and an energetic composer can often earn several modest sums a year this way. Certain contests of this kind can lead to a national reputa-tion; through them composers can receive commission offers, even teaching jobs.

Qualifications and Preparation. To find employment, the aspirant must be highly motivated and determined. Let us hope for talent as well. But how can the first-rate serious music composer be identified today? There is no consensus on this question. Critics, musicologists, and audiences do not agree at all on pre-cisely which composers are outstanding and which just hide their limitations behind compositional systems and bleeping oscillators.

As it turns out, the composers who manage to achieve more than regional reputations are those who discover how to attract attention. Sometimes this at-tention is generated by using outlandish tricks (quartet for strings and cement mixer)—or "composing" pieces that are silent musically (John Cage). Or a com-poser may attract attention through tricking critics (garnering rave reviews for a piece that was deliberately performed backwards).

Other serious music composers get their music played because they appear as soloists or conductors. If they are really good at either, they give the impression of being first-rate at anything musical.

How does a serious music composer prepare for a career? Practically all of them today who get teaching jobs must have an earned terminal degree from an accredited university. Of these, the most useful is the Doctor of Musical Arts (D.M.A.) in composition, the degree now most often awarded to musicians planning professional careers as composer-teachers. Some colleges and universities award the Doctor of Music, Doctor of Philosophy, or Master of Music as the terminal degree, also with a specialization in composition. Most advanced-degree candidates serve as teaching assistants to the faculty under which they are studying or teach music in a school to support themselves financially during the arduous period of graduate study. Whatever the work/study combination the degree candidate can set up, advanced study focuses on developing the student's craft—through extensive exercises, performances, and study of master works.

Employment Prospects. The musician aspiring to employment as a composer of serious music cannot expect to earn a living scoring masterpieces. The aspirant will almost certainly find work, early on, primarily as a teacher of theory and composition in a college or university. As a potential pedagogue, the aspirant should know that the supply of qualified, certified teachers has often exceeded demand. Still, those who are sufficiently motivated will continue their quest for employment as serious composer-teachers.

How does the aspiring composer-teacher land the first job? In these ways: (a) developing a good reputation with influential musician-teachers; (b) joining the College Music Society and following up its job-opening notices; (c) registering with the alma mater's placement bureau; (d) attending professional meetings and getting acquainted, setting up performances of new work, seeking publicity; (e) registering with teacher employment services; and (f) persevering for at least 5 years.

Arranger-Orchestrator

Career Description. Many creative musicians earn most of their incomes as arrangers. They take music written by someone else and arrange or add voices to suit the needs of the artist or film company. They accomplish this in diverse ways, ranging from writing leadsheets to scoring motion pictures. Hundreds of arrangers make their living working for songwriters and publishers, turning out leadsheets and song copies. The American Federation of Musicians (AFM) has scales covering this kind of work, but they are often ignored because the union has few opportunities to police this kind of employment.

Publishers engage arrangers to score various editions particularly for the educational field. Astute publishers hire only specialists for this kind of work—choral arrangers for vocal editions, jazz specialists for jazz charts, and so on.

The largest number of professional arrangers work for performers. Most professional performers use custom arrangements exclusively. Nearly all arrangers are employed freelance; few are retained on regular salaries. Their services are considered, under copyright law, as work done for hire; they receive one flat fee, up front, and do not receive royalties on copies or recordings sold.

Orchestrators take music that has been written by someone else and write or score the music for instruments. Arrangers and orchestrators usually work under tight deadlines, largely because composers and producers are also working under tight deadlines. It is a very high-pressure field. Panic-type time schedules are regularly relieved, however, with intermittent periods of idleness. But musicians attracted to the arranging field appear to love their work and manage to survive careers that are a mix of great artistic satisfaction and trips to the unemployment office.

Many musicians work as part-time arrangers, dividing their professional efforts among such related fields as composition, directing, producing, and performing. Others are working at least part-time in such fields as publishing and management.

Qualifications and Preparation. To qualify as a professional arranger, the individual should have thorough training in music theory, sight-singing, and ear training.

An arranger's ear must be as finely tuned as that of a composer, and many professional arrangers qualify as composers, too. An arranger is expected to work quickly and be able to knock out a score overnight when necessary.

Besides schooling in music theory, the best training for aspirants is to write—and write and write—then hear the score in rehearsal. Then rewrite. Then rehearse the revision—and on and on over several years of experimentation, trial and error. All good writers, whether they create prose, poetry, or music, recommend two basic activities: Read a lot and write constantly.

Employment Prospects. The aspiring professional arranger need not starve throughout the learning experience. All arrangers who eventually make it as pros begin to pick up small jobs early on—first for free, then maybe for a few dollars for one of their charts—if they'll copy off the parts and run the rehearsal.

Really talented arrangers attract attention quickly, and they begin receiving requests for their work, often from those not able to pay much. But outstanding talents can break in. Employment prospects for them are generally good, provided they are prepared, at least early in their careers, to fill out their workweeks with other jobs. Top arrangers working in the recording field for stars or busy record producers earn big money. If they manage to keep abreast of ever-changing musical styles, their careers can last longer than those of the artists for whom they write.

Music Editor

Career Description. There are several kinds of music editors. (The professional who lays music tracks to film is identified as either a music editor or music cutter, as explained in Chapter 24. Career opportunities for this kind of professional are described later in this chapter in the Music-Related Careers section, as are career opportunities for writers about music—critics and journalists, for instance.) Here we discuss only the kind of music editor who prepares music manuscripts for publication.

All publishers of printed music require professional editors, because even skilled composers and arrangers are rarely knowledgeable concerning precisely how scores and parts must be edited before the music is printed. In the popular field, most publishers contract with one of the major printing houses to handle their music editing and paper publishing.

Music print publishers of classical music engage editors to rewrite the composers' or arrangers' scores so that they conform in content and style to the standards this country inherited centuries ago from master European engravers and printers. Most modern printed versions of musical notation are produced on computers and then printed in quantity. Prospective music editors are advised to gain substantial knowledge of music-editing traditions as well as computer skills.

The music editor must first correct and proofread music that has been submitted to the publisher. Part of their work can involve actual rescoring, arranging, and even original composition. The music editors who are most in demand are almost always qualified as composers and arrangers, too. Many editors specialize in just one field, such as choral music or piano music.

Editorial staff often contribute to judgment on acquisitions in respect to musical quality, style, and market suitability. Publishing decisions will be based on those judgments.

Qualifications and Preparation. To qualify for a job as a music editor, the individual should undertake a complete musical education in theory, history, literature, and performance practices. This broad background is most readily available in universities with strong music departments.

Employment Prospects. For many musicians, particularly composers and arrangers with good educational backgrounds, music editing is a fallback position; they enter the field as a second career choice, or more commonly, as one component of a combination career.

Nearly all freelance editors earn part of their incomes from composing, arranging, copying, performing, or teaching.

Music Copyist

Career Description. Many musicians break into the composing and arranging fields as music copyists. Other musicians develop satisfying, well-paying careers in the copying field itself. There is an actual shortage of fully qualified musicians who have the knowledge and skill required of professional copyists who must be highly skilled in notation and transposition, have music theory training, and be extremely accurate.

Qualifications and Preparation. Many professional copyists are also arrangers, for the two professions have much in common. The aspiring copyist will also learn from the ease with which musicians read the completed work. The critical issue with music copying is accuracy. Professional copyists are expected to make no mistakes, and they are also expected to correct the errors in the scores they work on. The experienced professional copyist may not be able to reach the composer-arranger to answer questions about illegible notes or incomplete sections. The copyist must then have sufficient skill and knowledge to correct, then complete the score without guidance.

Employment Prospects. Computer-generated scores and parts are commonplace. The aspiring music calligrapher must become proficient in using these tools.

Copying jobs exist everywhere. But the aspirant must sniff them out and make the service known to every composer-arranger who can be located. Most copyists supplement their income in other branches of music. Combination careers can often yield satisfactory incomes.

PRODUCING/DIRECTING CAREERS

Music Director-Conductor	Theatrical Producer-Director
Record Producer	Video/Film Producer-Director

Music Director-Conductor

Career Description. Most musical performers require musical direction of some sort.

The conductors best known by the public are those engaged as music directors of symphony orchestras and opera companies. Some are called "artistic director." It is customary for musicians holding these posts to assist management in selecting, then contracting guest conductors and guest soloists, selecting programs, working with orchestra managers in planning operating budgets, and hiring and firing musicians.

Artistic directors also become involved with the major orchestras in negotiating recording contracts for their ensembles. Because of the heavy responsibilities assumed by these kinds of musical directors, they require at least one assistant conductor. Some of the major orchestras have two or more assistant conductors who help the artistic director by conducting performances for school children and pop concerts.

Musicians who serve time as assistant conductors often graduate to roles of principal conductors and music directors of orchestras and opera companies.

Music directors and assistant directors have such heavy responsibilities that they rarely find time for any other professional employment, save for the guest conducting of other symphony orchestras. In addition to their directing, they must meet with the various committees charged with the responsibility of raising money for operations. An important part of this aspect of the work is fostering goodwill among the individuals and corporations and foundations who pledge money to support the artistic goals of the ensemble.

Some music directors are engaged by arts centers and community centers as artistic directors. They not only may conduct rehearsals and performances, but are also likely to function as organizers and supervisors of artistic and educational programs for these entities.

Thousands of music directors are employed by churches. These professionals may be organists or other performers, many of whom serve double duty as choir directors. Large churches sometimes call their music directors "ministers of music." A person serving in such a capacity may direct choral and other musical groups for the institution. While the largest churches pay their music directors full-time salaries, smaller institutions do not, expecting them to fill out their incomes through other activities.

Music directors for movies and TV can be hired first as composer-arrangers and be expected to conduct their own music when their scores are recorded. This same pattern prevails in the field of music library services: Music directors usually serve the producers as triple-threat artists, composers-arrangers-directors.

In the pop field, the individual serving as music director may not be a conductor but simply a performer in the group who assumes a leadership role. Musical direction of groups of this kind is sometimes shared, but dividing this important responsibility usually leads to difficulties. As for soloists, when an artist reaches star status, the artist usually finds it necessary to employ a music director, at least for appearances on tour. These individuals are almost invariably rehearsal pianists-accompanists who assist the artist by selecting material, arranging it, conducting rehearsals and live performances. Many of these pianist-conductors are not trained baton twirlers but manage to make sufficient hand gestures from their position at the piano keyboard to cue the musicians.

Some jobs for music directors in the pop field are found in major cities, conducting shows. Other musical directing jobs are available in the field of industrial shows. Broadway, off-Broadway, and regional theaters employ music directors.

Qualifications and Preparation. All successful music directors share a common attribute: a commanding presence. They know how to lead, either intuitively or through training. This leadership quality is not limited to musical matters but extends to relationships with the variety of human personalities they work with in rehearsal and performance.

Nearly all successful music directors have had extensive schooling, often a combination of formal education and private instruction. Because music directors must be well informed on all aspects of music, their education, at least through the baccalaureate degree level, will be broad. Postbaccalaureate study may include emphasis in performance, composition, or conducting.

In the pop field, directors are often performers, and they are usually involved in composition and arranging, perhaps rehearsing and directing performances of the music they themselves have scored.

The best environment for an aspiring music director is a first-rate university with a strong faculty and a variety of performance groups. In addition, most conductors start early, usually while still in college, to direct a church choir or jazz band or pop chorus or whatever group they can get their hands on; some major cities, such as Los Angeles and New York, also have youth or training orchestras that can offer the talented novice conductor opportunities to practice the craft.

Employment Prospects. Job prospects for music directors can be compared with those found in other aspects of the arts and business: Work is available for top people. Symphony and opera conductors of repute often hold down at least two conducting posts. Other fine musicians prefer to serve smaller communities where the salaries are lower, but so are the pressures.

Music directors in the popular field rise or fall less on their abilities as conductors or leaders than on their abilities to please their employers as writers. A music director who is a really competent composer and arranger can usually find work—and the ability to rehearse and conduct groups is a minor consideration. Employers tolerate incompetent leadership qualities and baton techniques when the music director is a whiz at writing music.

In the pop field, young music directors usually start out earning no more than the other performers in the group they direct. When the group goes union, AFM scales generally call for the leader to receive double sideman's scale. When a record producer or music library service (syndicator) production house hires a music director, the director will probably be paid AFM scale (double sideman's wages), then be paid again for any arranging.

Record Producer

Career Description. The work of the various kinds of record producers is described in more detail earlier in this book. Individuals employed as record producers function at a level and in a manner that reflects their particular competence. Some producers are successful largely because they are very good at locating the right musical material, then matching it to the right artists. This is why the old label for these practitioners was "artist and repertoire producers."

Photo courtesy of Trebas Institute. Photo by Malcolm P. Gibson.

Some producers are masters of the control room. Others know how to raise money, then hire outside experts to arrange the music, mix the sound, and supervise postproduction. Still other producers are master musicians who make it in the field because they are creative and capture artistic performances on tape.

Most record producers don't have "careers." They just get jobs. More than half of the work is performed freelance. The nearest thing approaching steady employment is found with major labels, which hire staff producers and place them on full-time salaries. Producers float from job to job pretty much like recording artists; they get return engagements when their music sells. If they produce a string of flops, their telephones stop ringing. Greater employment continuity is found among staff producers, but even here a label won't retain a house producer beyond a year or so unless sales from the producer's output are sufficient to at least justify the salary.

Independent producers often own their own production companies, and they stay in the field as long as they can turn out at least occasional hits. One good hit may keep them afloat for a year or so. But without periodic successes in the marketplace, independent producers are forced to change directions or fold.

Qualifications and Preparation. An individual aspiring to a career in record production should not expect to follow an orderly path. Nearly all producers who make it discover that they must first become recognized in an allied field—such as songwriting, arranging, sound mixing, or musical direction. In addition to competence in one or more of these facets of music, the record producer usually possesses some kind of leadership ability and a temperament that mixes well with artists, technicians, and executives. The producer must remain stable when others on the project are disintegrating through frustration or fatigue; the role requires handling the job in a manner that elicits cooperation from co-workers.

The producer has the additional worry of staying within budget. Budget panics are endemic with record production, and the individual in charge is responsible for keeping costs under control. So the record producer must be a kind of miracle person, possessing strong musical ability, technological know-how, business sense, magic ears, and the stability to remain rational under great pressures—all the while serving as referee in conflicts of ego that threaten working relationships.

Employment Prospects. Because no one possesses all these talents, those who come close find themselves in high demand. Investors, labels, and artists are always searching for record producers who can pull all the elements together, get them on tape and on the charts. Producers possessing the essentials of the art and craft will work and prosper.

Because of the absence of employment continuity, nearly all record producers have other irons in the fire, just as most musicians do. They may write songs, own part of a publishing company, manage artists, function as agents, write arrangements, produce shows—whatever works.

Staff producers earn regular salaries; some of them also have contracts providing royalties based on sales. Some contracts provide that although royalties are earned on all of the producer's recordings, royalties are not actually paid until they exceed the amount of the accumulated salary. Some producers do not start receiving royalties until the label has recovered its out-of-pocket production costs. Some independent producers are given all their production expenses by a recording label and receive a flat production fee plus royalties, or possibly no fee, just royalty income.

The producer of classical music must possess many of the same qualifications as the pop record producer, plus a few more. This professional has to be as good a score reader as the conductor and know details of the score being recorded. Ideally, the producer in the booth should be the twin of the conductor on the podium, so close must they understand each other and the musical interpretation the literature requires.

To qualify to produce classical music recordings, the musician must have training identical to the kind described for classical music conductors. In addition, the producer must have knowledge of technology, perhaps even acoustics, sufficient to give direction to the mixing and mastering technicians. Few record producers possess all these talents. Those who come closest are the ones the major labels call for repeatedly in this highly specialized work.

Theatrical Producer-Director

Career Description. The theatrical producer-director is one of several types of individuals whose talents may cover multiple disciplines, including everything from writing scripts and music to turning out complete productions. Such "hyphenates" are active on Broadway and in music video.

Theatrical producer-directors usually work freelance or get hired through an independent production company. On Broadway, they spend most of their time searching for *properties,* show-biz talk for a script or, more commonly, a book or play on which a script might be based. Simultaneously, theatrical producers are searching for money to stage their properties. On Broadway, the hit-to-flop ratio is at least as bad as 1:10. But each year, enterprising producer-directors find angels anxious to spend their millions and get into show business.

Qualifications and Preparation. Producer-directors who have located what they think is a strong property and willing backers will be actively searching for "bankable" stars whose marquee value will help sell tickets. Many successful producer-directors have emerged from the field of choreography and dance; their names alone attract investors and star performers. Some producer-directors of high achievement started their careers as songwriters—for example, Rodgers and Hammerstein.

Producer-directors in the movie field work much like their brothers and sisters on Broadway: They must find properties, investors, and strong performers. The music video medium draws its producers from Broadway, Hollywood, commercials, college and community theaters, and left field.

With a little luck, the producer-director turning out musical productions and videos will have some competence in music. Because no producer-director can know it all, the smart ones engage specialists to cover all the bases.

Employment Prospects. Beyond what has been stated above, it is not possible to generalize about job openings in this field. About all that can be said is that an individual who approximates the kind of versatility the field demands will attract the attention of employers. Only a few producer-directors are hired on yearly contracts with predictable salaries. Producers and directors don't get jobs. Rather, they take on projects; most of the time they have to invent their employment. Even established professionals in the musical theater experience feast and famine.

As with the field of recording, the musical theater continues to draw artists and investors because of the possibility that they might share in a hit. Whether or not a producer or producer-director has invested in a show, this key person invariably shares in the royalties that accrue from a successful production.

Video/Film Producer-Director

Career Description. Versatile artists who aspire to direct videos or filmed musicals will have spent years in related activities such as songwriting, live musicals, record production, and commercials. Many directors, of course, may have little direct knowledge of music. They pick up what musical knowledge they have as they go along—and are smart enough to rely on specialists to fill in the gaps.

Qualifications and Preparation. A good way to learn the craft is directing low-budget videos. Developing a respectable track record in this arena may lead to opportunities for more elaborate projects.

Good preparation can come from college film/TV programs. Directors sometimes come from the ranks of editors as well as writers. Work on low-budget commercials in local markets could be training for videos, which in turn can lead to a longer form work.

Employment Prospects. Although supply exceeds demand, there is always room for a hustling, talented director in tune with contemporary tastes.

PERFORMING CAREERS

Singer   Instrumentalist

Singer

Career Description. In the field of popular music, singers find careers not only as soloists and recording artists but also as group singers, background vocalists on commercials, and "production" singers, singing actors or singing dancers. As most singers have already discovered, a career often starts at school, college, or local clubs where the individual can learn quite early whether audiences respond well. In the pop field, these amateur and semiprofessional beginnings are often combined with instrumental performance or songwriting, sometimes both.

Steady employment in the singing field depends on the performer's skill, and it is common for performers to be constantly on the move. Professional singers rarely stay very long in one city; their lives are filled with almost incessant travel. The longest engagements occur when an artist remains in one location for a month or two to complete recording an album. Stars who play Las Vegas may be booked in for a few weeks, but most other singing jobs in the pop field are strings of one-nighters or weeklong engagements.

Successful singing careers invariably involve a mix of live appearances and recordings. Established recording stars also appear on television, sometimes in commercials and films. Few experiences are more exhausting than constant traveling, and a professional singer's first concern, under these strains, is to stay healthy. The second concern is, or should be, finding a competent personal manager. Third priority is the ongoing search for good material.

Even singers who write most of their own songs must somehow find outside sources to feed their acts. Nonwriting singers never stop searching for good songs. Writers and publishers know this and follow singers around, leadsheets in hand, trying to persuade them they have just what the artist is seeking. Successful singers are also plagued with enthusiastic, even overbearing fans who want to get to them. These multiple pressures can debilitate a performer, and only the hardy can survive. But those attracted to the field seem to sustain themselves on the applause and adulation of their audiences—not to mention their money.

Even singers with competent managers must give some attention every few days to business affairs. Also, singers must work constantly with arrangers and musical directors to ensure that their performances are presented in the most effective way. Major artists must also find time for costume fittings, makeup jobs, and lighting tests. All touring artists find it difficult to locate edible meals while traveling and must guard their health against junk food and too many calories.

Qualifications and Preparation. To qualify for a successful career as a professional singer, it is helpful for the aspirant to be able to sing. But any audit of the field will reveal that dozens of nonsingers manage to make a living as "singers." Individuals with no recognizable musical talent sometimes win an audience. This usually occurs when the public becomes attracted to a performer, not for singing ability, but because of the individual's personality or acting ability.

Those performers who have made a successful career for themselves do, however, share some important characteristics: some musical talent, charisma, self-discipline, physical stamina, versatility, creative ability, and poise.

In classical music, most artists who qualify for work have spent several years studying voice in college or with outside teachers. College music majors often pursue the master's degree, majoring in voice or perhaps choral music.

Should the "legitimate" singer aspire to opera, the performer may opt for a music conservatory diploma rather than a university degree. The former provides concentrated training in performance. Opera students must acquire facility in several foreign languages, with French, Italian, and German being the most important.

Employment Prospects. The job outlook for singers ranges from grim to excellent. Naturally, the fewest opportunities lie in the musical arenas that attract the smallest audiences and, therefore, bring in the least amount of money. These would include the solo recital and concert fields, especially for singers with only classical training. Some employment is available with symphony orchestras and in community concert series, but these engagements are mainly seasonal.

In the field of opera, artist managers arrange some engagements; other artists are in such demand, they book themselves—opera companies outbid each other for their services. Unfortunately, only a few trained singers qualify for leading roles with good companies. Thousands of university graduates aspiring to careers in their fields are disappointed each year, and turn to Broadway, schoolteaching, voice coaching, or church choir jobs.

Churches offer many jobs to trained singers who can also direct choirs. Some singers who are unable to develop the performing careers they had planned turn to schoolteaching, then pick up singing jobs at weddings and funerals. Practically all of this work is nonunion.

Musical theater sometimes offers an employment option for trained singers, particularly if the auditioners are young, of the right physical size and shape, and able to act and/or dance. Although New York producers audition and hire many new singing actors each season, more extensive job opportunities are found in regional and dinner theaters, theme parks, and cruise lines. Aspiring singers sometimes begin their professional careers as supporting players, then graduate to leading roles.

Another source of fairly steady employment can be found by crackerjack singers willing to locate near centers of commercial and film music production. These versatile singers need to be expert sight readers in any musical genre and be able to perform with minimal rehearsal.

When it comes to job prospects for pop singers, there is yet another set of conditions. The difficulty here, as pointed out, is that large segments of the public fail to distinguish between the truly gifted singer and the nonsinger who gets by just on personality—or sex appeal or publicity.

A pop singer wastes an important opportunity by bypassing a test in the local community. It is risky to ignore local receptivity, make a fancy demo, then descend on big-city record producers. Producers don't need the aspiring singer who has not yet proved something with the hometown audience. If the home folks don't respond, who will?

A pop singer today has one other way to break in that beats them all: composing songs. Since the Beatles in the mid-1960s, the preponderant number of new singing artists breaking big in the business have been performing composers. These artists may not be either great singers or top composers, but the combination enchants audiences, and these versatile artists sell a lot of music.

Instrumentalist

Career Description. The working hours of a full-time instrumentalist may average only 3 hours a day, but most musicians are busy at least 40 hours a week.

Jazz trombonist J. J. Johnson greets music
business students at Indiana State University, Terre Haute.

Practically all professional instrumentalists do at least some teaching. These accomplished musicians often have more students waiting for openings than they
can accept. Student fees not only offer income to supplement playing jobs, but
they can often provide at least minimum sustenance during periods when musicians cannot find playing jobs. Besides setting hours aside for teaching, professionals usually engage in regular daily practice, continuing throughout their careers to polish their skills and expand their repertoire.

In addition to these musical activities, a large percentage of professional instrumentalists are actively employed outside of music. From choice or necessity,
many pros moonlight (more often, daylight) at jobs with flexible hours, thus providing release time for them to accept whatever music jobs come along.

Many professional musicians manage a different kind of moonlighting: They
accept every attractive playing job that comes along, then fill in the balance of
their workweek in music-related employment such as composition, arranging,
copying, perhaps artist management or record production. Many professional

musicians work fairly regularly as instrumentalists, while filling their daytime hours as music merchants—selling instruments, equipment, and so forth.

An important consideration for those planning careers as performers is the matter of travel. Most musicians must move around a lot—which can be fun when they are young, but becomes intolerable after several years of the gypsy life. Another important concern is the seasonal aspect of most performing careers. Many symphony, opera, and dance company musicians are laid off in the summer months. Broadway pit musicians know only seasonal employment, which generally means the life of a particular show. Instrumentalists working clubs on so-called steady engagements are delighted when a job extends beyond a few weeks.

Qualifications and Preparation. The young instrumentalist who has ambitions for a full-time, fully professional playing career must be endowed with outstanding musical talent. Instrumental study should begin in childhood and continue throughout the career.

To qualify for the concert and symphonic field, students today will usually complete at least the master's degree, often the doctorate, in performance (some graduates complete a "diploma" program). Whatever amount of formal training the musician might undergo, the working professional must be familiar with performance practices of both classical and popular music. Practically all symphony orchestras have a pops series where traveling artists bring in charts ranging in style from blues to country. And musicians in the theater and recording fields are expected to be able to perform any musical idiom in the correct style. The old days of the "classical" and "jazz" musician are nearly gone. Almost all pros now must cross the line.

The great majority of full-time professional instrumentalists are expected to be musically literate and read at sight what is placed before them. Some nonreaders are financially and artistically successful, but their success is often based more on their personality, composing, or strong natural talent.

Besides having a personality that works well with others, the real pro must be willing to work very hard for long years and persevere during periods of disappointment. Just "liking music" is not enough. Most truly accomplished professional artists reach their goal through a love, even a passion, for music making.

Yet another personal attribute is essential for the instrumentalist who strives for the highest paying fields, particularly symphony and studio work: strong nerves. Young musicians shooting for the big time are generally unaware of the working atmosphere in the recording field particularly, which is one not just of high tension but of sheer terror. Those jobs demand perfection in performance. There is minimum tolerance for error and none whatever for carelessness. A top studio player is allowed an occasional flub but is subject to being quickly displaced, sometimes forever, by a competitor who can demonstrate even greater reliability. Nerves of steel come in handy, but before the faint-of-heart abandon their dreams of the big time, it should be reassuring to remember that artists of international stature—musicians, dancers, actors—have told us that controlled tension aids artistic performance.

Employment Prospects. Even though there are thousands of unemployed and underemployed instrumentalists, the truth is that there is a scarcity in some areas. Employment prospects depend on the particular instrument as well as the musician's talent and training.

Keyboard Players. There is a daunting oversupply of first-rate concert pianists and recitalists. Conservatories and colleges continue to turn out thousands of these artists, but their employment prospects are poor. There is also an oversupply of piano teachers in most communities, except those who have acquired the pedagogical techniques of group instruction. Most communities have an abundance of restaurant, club, and lounge pianists.

In the theater music field, there is a shortage in most communities of keyboard artists who can sight-read a traveling Broadway show book, handle the written-out parts, and also play **comp** style. In the recording field, there are brilliant keyboard artists, but an actual shortage in most cities of musicians who can handle such diverse styles as jazz, pop, and rock. Even more scarce are those pianists who can handle these styles and Mozart or Chopin or Gershwin's concert pieces. If a keyboard artist seeks work in the recording field (and even in pit orchestras), employability will be increased by facility in performance synthesizers. Many keyboard players specialize in the electronic realm.

Finally, keyboardists can often find employment as accompanists. Some pianists consider accompanying second-class employment, but truly competent performers are often in demand.

Guitarists. There is a huge oversupply of amateur and semiprofessional guitarists who want to become full-time professionals. Many of these individuals do not understand the difference between an amateur and a truly professional performing artist.

Any guitarist who is a good reader and who can perform artistically in the basic idioms of jazz, blues, rock, and country will probably need a telephone answering service to handle the job offers. This kind of competence and versatility is in demand everywhere.

Percussionists. Even before rock and roll, the world was oversupplied with drummers. Nevertheless, in most communities today there is an undersupply of fully competent, versatile percussionists. Directors and contractors can rarely find a drummer/percussionist who can really read well and who can handle not only conventional percussion but also mallet instruments and timpani. Many drummers play great jazz or rock or Latin rhythms, but don't really know how to play concert or show music.

Few percussionists take the time to study seriously the art of timpani tuning and playing or to learn much about non-Western music. Percussionists who can do most or all of the basic musical styles well, and are good readers, are rare in most areas and in high demand. Percussionists in the next most active group are those who come close to the prowess and versatility of the "complete professional percussionist." Drummers who are unwilling to undertake this level of training will continue to compete with thousands of other drummers of comparable skill. Competition among "average" musicians will always be great.

Wind Instrument Players. The school band programs of recent decades have produced a large supply of good wind instrument performers. There is even an oversupply of fully qualified wind players with master's, even doctoral, degrees. When an opening is advertised by a professional symphony orchestra on, say, clarinet or trumpet, it is not unusual to see several hundred applicants. A respectable percentage of that group would have professional experience that would qualify them for serious consideration. In the recording studios, there is a great abundance of wind players scrapping for those high-paying jobs. Extensive woodwind doubling is expected in the show music field and in recording. Because it takes a lifetime to master even one instrument, it is understandable why top doublers are so scarce. Those that come closest to really playing several winds get a lot of work—and when they do, they earn, through their doubling ability, 20% to 100% above basic scale.

In any discussion of career opportunities for wind players, mention must be made of the hundreds of jobs open for them in military bands. For current enlistment information, inquire at your local military recruitment offices.

String Players. Hundreds of string players find full- to part-time employment in America's many symphony orchestras. For details, review Chapter 13. Performers heading for careers as soloists in the classical field will find it difficult to break in without the aid of an agent or manager. The most active concert agents and management companies are listed in the annual directory of *Musical America*, which also includes the names and addresses of symphony orchestras and opera companies here and in Europe.

The most direct route for an instrumentalist in any field to find work is through establishing a reputation for being able to handle whatever opportunities come along—and a reputation for being better qualified than the competition. An instrumentalist of genuine ability becomes known throughout the musical community very quickly. That person is almost immediately conspicuous—and other players, directors, and contractors mark that musician as the one to call. Jobs can be scarce, but when they come along the really good players are in demand.

A musical reputation can work even more quickly the other way around: Less talented performers, weak readers, and undependable musicians earn overnight reputations, too. They may never learn why the telephone does not ring, for who wants to tell an individual that he or she can't cut it?

TEACHING CAREERS

Studio Teacher   College Music Instructor
School Music Educator   Music Therapist

Every musician is a teacher. Composers, performers, directors—all who make music are involved, directly or indirectly, in teaching others to do what they do. No other sector of the music profession includes within its ranks so diverse a group of individuals.

Studio Teacher

Career Description. A studio teacher is a private instructor who gives individualized or group lessons. Some are contracted by music stores and may work at the store, but most operate out of their own homes or offices, setting their own fees and developing their own lesson plans. The studio teacher most in demand is the real pro who is an active performer engaged in teaching as a sideline. Practically all active professionals teach at least part-time. The best of them fill every vacant hour in 40- to 60-hour workweeks and experience excellent income. Others, unable to stand an unending stream of kids passing through their studios, will accept only a limited number of pupils.

Fully professional teachers are able to demonstrate artistic performance to their students, with teacher and student often performing side by side during the lesson.

Qualifications and Preparation. Genuinely qualified music teachers have completed 4 to 8 years of college-level music study, are competent performers themselves, possess sound pedagogical techniques, and know how to motivate students. Persons so qualified have no difficulty finding students.

Employment Prospects. How does a qualified musician build up a student clientele? By building a strong reputation in the community, first, as a musician, and second, as a teacher. Students will find such a person with careful searching, as will school music educators, who will make recommendations to their pupils.

School Music Educator

Career Description. Music educators work in public, private, or parochial schools. Duties vary depending on the ages taught and the guidelines often set by state or district supervisors. Music teachers employed in Grades K (kindergarten) through 6 have responsibilities different from those working in junior and senior high schools. Most school districts try to finance a sufficient number of general music teachers for the lower grades to provide at least some music listening and participation for every child: singing, movement to music, and improvised performance on simple rhythm instruments and toys.

Teachers in junior and senior high schools are usually hired for specific duties. At this level, one teacher may teach music appreciation and music reading while another may give instrumental lessons on one or more instruments. One director may be in charge of brass, wind, and string ensembles while another has responsibilities for the choral groups; either of these—or both—may be involved in the production of musical plays. The number of teachers and the division of responsibilities are usually determined by the size and financial commitment of the school.

Bands seem to dominate music education, and most senior high schools have an assortment: concert band, marching band, pep band, stage band. From August through November, high school band directors' lives are generally consumed by rehearsing their football bands. During these frantic weeks, music educators often feel they are not so much musical directors as drill sergeants, arrangers, copyists, and entertainment directors for the school's athletic department. Following football season, these teachers must hastily prepare a holiday program, then springtime music festivals involving their concert bands and stage bands. When summer vacation finally arrives, they usually spend some of their time off trying to get equipment repaired and shows planned for the fall football season. High school music educators are accustomed to 60-hour workweeks, but many appear to thrive on their heavy loads.

Music Education Supervisor. Most school districts employ at least one "music supervisor" to direct and coordinate activities of all vocal and instrumental music teachers. The role of the supervisor is to guide formulation of educational policy, assist school principals in hiring new teachers, fight for and control music budgets, and offer pedagogical guidance to the music educators employed in their districts. Music supervisors also administer acquisition and circulation of central music lending libraries for their districts. These individuals are also involved in organizing music festivals, reading clinics, and contests. Many also teach. Some supervisors are employed, not for the school year, but on 12-month contracts.

Qualifications and Preparation. Except for the field of music therapy, school music teaching is the only kind of employment where applicants are required to have a college degree in music. School music teachers (Grades K through 12) in practically all states are also required to have a teaching certificate or teaching credential. Some states will automatically certify a teacher in a particular music teaching field if the teacher holds a baccalaureate degree in music from a state-accredited college or university. Other states require that college graduates in music also successfully pass a state-administered certifying examination. Types of teaching certificates vary from state to state.

In addition to a college degree and teaching license, those who do most of the music teacher hiring (school principals, usually) look for one or more of these qualifications or attributes: a good reputation as a teacher, high grades in college and on the certifying examination, and an outgoing personality.

Employment Prospects. For many years, a reasonably talented college student majoring in music education could expect to find a full-time teaching position upon graduation. But more recently, the employment prospects for school music teachers have diminished. Top universities with distinguished track records of turning out fine teachers continue to place most of their graduates. But decreasing employment opportunities for individuals seeking teaching jobs in music and the other arts in most cities will probably continue due to pressure on school budgets.

College Music Instructor

Career Description. Before describing careers in college and university music teaching, the junior colleges should be discussed. Most junior or community colleges offer such courses as music appreciation, music theory, class piano, perhaps class guitar, band, and stage band. Junior colleges that offer a 2-year associate in arts degree in music may also offer such courses as music arranging, music history—and music business courses. Individuals aspiring to employment in one of these junior colleges are usually required to teach about 20 hours a week, almost double the teaching load of music instructors in 4-year colleges and universities. Because of this extremely burdensome schedule, few junior college music teachers have adequate time to prepare for their classes as well as for rehearsals, and they are among the most overworked teachers in the music education field.

Quite a different kind of employment is found at 4-year colleges and universities, where full-time music faculty members usually teach between 12 and 16 hours a week. Practically all music instructors at this level specialize in one particular aspect of music, and most, if not all, of their teaching and directing responsibilities relate to that specialty, for example, theory, choral music, instrumental music, applied music instruction, music history, perhaps jazz education. They may teach only three or four different classes or ensembles a week, but their "off time" is filled with preparation for their hours in the classroom or rehearsal hall. Most university-level music teachers claim to have a workweek that averages well above 48 hours. Teachers who have attained higher academic rank, such as associate or full professor, are normally assigned somewhat lighter teaching loads. But the senior professors may be even busier than their colleagues of lower academic rank—engaged in research and other creative activities such as writing music, articles, and books.

Qualifications and Preparation. Practically all states require that their junior college teachers have not only a master's degree in music from an accredited in-

Dr. Janet Nepkie instructs music business students at
State University of New York, College at Oneonta. Photo by Lilly Smith.

stitution but, in addition, a junior college teaching certificate. Musicians applying for "the choral job" or "the band job" at a particular junior college are expected to have established reputations in their field of specialization. Such
reputations are usually acquired first at the high school level before the aspirant
is considered for a faculty position in a junior college. Prospective faculty members are normally hired by the junior college president, upon recommendation
of the resident music faculty.

Four-year colleges and universities normally hire only those individuals who
have earned a terminal degree in music—D.M.A., D.M., or Ph.D., for example.
Some prestigious schools occasionally hire faculty members who lack a terminal
degree but whose reputations as performers, composers, or scholars are equal in
prestige to a doctoral degree. Many colleges and universities will not consider
prospective faculty who lack publications; either music compositions/arrange-
ments or writings about music or music-related topics are considered "publica-

tions." These same institutions tend to waive this requirement when they are evaluating prospective members for their "applied music" faculty.

Employment Prospects. In some colleges and universities, funding for new faculty positions has been difficult to find. The number of music majors in American colleges has been influenced by the increasing awareness that many college-level music studies appeared to lead to no job. But the individual aspiring to college-level music teaching would be mistaken to conclude that no career opportunities exist. Although we are oversupplied with aspirants holding even doctoral degrees in theory, history, musicology, piano, and choral directing, some colleges and universities have difficulty finding fully qualified instructors (with doctorates) in certain specialties. The areas of specialization that are least crowded include ethnomusicology, music therapy, jazz education, electronic music, pop choral music, improvisation, sound synthesis, recording, and the music business.

Music Therapist

Career Description. Music therapy is the prescribed use of music by a qualified person to effect positive changes in the psychological, physical, cognitive, or social functioning of individuals with health or educational problems.

Music therapists assess the emotional well-being, physical health, social functioning, communication abilities, and cognitive skills of their clients through musical responses. They then design music sessions using techniques such as music improvisation, receptive music listening, songwriting, lyric discussion, music and imagery, music performance, and learning through music. Music therapists participate in interdisciplinary treatment for people with developmental and learning disabilities, mental health needs, Alzheimer's disease and other aging-related conditions, and brain injuries, among others.

Qualifications and Preparation. To qualify as a professional music therapist, the aspirant must graduate from an approved college degree program, which requires completion of a clinical internship with a 6-month minimum. These individuals are then eligible to sit for the national examination offered by the Certification Board for Music Therapists. Music therapists who successfully complete the independently administered examination hold the music therapist-board certified credential (MT-BC). The curricula offer a thorough study of music, along with coursework in psychology and in biological, social, and behavioral sciences. Graduate degrees are offered at several universities in music therapy and related disciplines.

Employment Prospects. Music therapists are finding employment in record numbers in psychiatric hospitals, rehabilitative facilities, medical hospitals, outpatient clinics, day care treatment centers, agencies serving developmentally disabled persons, community mental health centers, drug and alcohol programs, senior centers, nursing homes, hospice programs, correctional facilities, halfway houses, schools, and private practice. The job outlook looks promising, especially in terms of job opportunities related to our aging population and interest in alternative forms of treatment.

MUSIC-RELATED CAREERS

Critic/Journalist/Editor	Broadcasting/Advertising
Music Services	Business/Merchandising
Science and Technology	Legal Services
Managerial/Executive	Arts/Graphics

Some of the careers listed here relate directly to music, others only indirectly (see Table 25.2). Some are open to trained musicians, others offer employment opportunities to nonmusicians. The more prevalent music-related careers are discussed in the following pages.

Critic/Journalist/Editor

Some of history's most distinguished musicians have used their creative energies not just for composing but also to write about music. Though few musicians have managed to perform these two tasks as well as Richard Wagner, today hundreds of creative persons have fashioned rewarding careers as music critics, journalists, and editors. Those who follow these paths find that their work schedules are filled with attending concerts about 8 nights a week, their workdays occupied in reviewing endless stacks of new recordings and books on music. The most conscientious critics attempt to study new scores before attending premiere performances; some try to attend rehearsals and recording sessions to inform them-

TABLE 25.2   A Sampling of Music-Related Careers

Words and music
  Composer
  Historian
  Librettist
  Lyricist
  Critic/Journalist
  Playwright
  Publisher
  Writer/Editor
Music services
  Music Coordinator
  Music Copyist
  Music Cutter/Editor
  Music Librarian
  Music Therapist
  Talent Coordinator
  Transcriber
Managerial/executive
  Advance Person
  Artist and Repertoire Administrator/
      Coordinator
  Agent (Talent Agent)
  Arts Administrator
  Artists' Union Officer
  Audience Research Director
  Broadcasting Executive
  Business Manager
  Company Manager (TV, Theater)
  Concert Promoter
  Development Director (Arts)
  Educational Director
  Entertainment Director
  Market Research Director
  Nightclub Manager
  Orchestra Manager
  Personal Manager
  Personnel Director
  Product Manager (Recordings)
  Production Manager
  Professional Manager
  Program Director
  Programming Consultant
  Project Director
  Recording Company Executive

Recording Studio Manager
Road Manager
Stage Manager
Studio Manager
Talent Agency Manager
Talent Coordinator
Tour Coordinator
Traffic Manager
Broadcasting/advertising
  Account Executive
  Consumer Researcher
  Creative Director
  Disc Jockey
  Jingle Writer
  Musical Director
  Program Supervisor
  Promotional Staffer
  Research Director
  Spot Producer/Director
Business/merchandising
  Broadcasting Station Broker
  Concert Promoter
  Music Merchant/Salesperson
  Music Rights Manager
  Music Wholesaler/Distributor
  Publicist
  Salesperson
  Ticket Sales Manager/Agent
Music production (theater, film, TV)
  Arranger
  Audio Technician/Engineer
  Choreographer/Dancer
  Conductor
  Church Music Director
  Costume Designer
  Director/Supervisor
  Floor Manager
  Instrumentalist
  Lighting Designer
  Music Coordinator
  Orchestra Contractor
  Producer/Executive Producer
  Property Master
  Scenic Designer

(continued)

TABLE 25.2   Continued

Singer/Actor	Mastering Technician
Special Material Writer	Multimedia Developer
Stage Director	Music/Rerecording Mixer
Stage Manager	Piano Tuner/Technician
Studio Musician	Recording Engineer
Synthesis Specialist	Sound Engineer/Technician
Talent Coordinator	Studio Designer/Acoustician
Technical Director	Legal services
Theme Specialist	Copyright Researcher
Variety Artist	Copyright Lawyer
Visual Synthesist	Entertainment Business Lawyer
Science and technology	Paralegal
Audio Engineer/Technician	Arts/graphics
Computer Music Programmer	Commercial Artist
Digital Audio Editor	Graphic Artist
Digital Remastering Engineer	Scenic Designer
Equipment Designer	Music Calligrapher
Equipment Maintenance Technician	Music Engraver
Instrument Designer/Manufacturer/Repairer	

selves on how creative and interpretive artists prepare new works or rework old pieces.

To qualify as a music critic in the classical field, an individual should have a thorough musical education acquired through formalized university-level study or individual effort. Our most distinguished critics have grown into their work after long years of observation and study. They not only develop penetrating insights on compositions and performances but manage to write in a style that communicates effectively with a broad general readership.

But many professional critics lack these qualifications and inflict their incompetence on ignorant editors and a gullible public. It is not unusual for a newspaper to ask a general-assignment news reporter to cover concerts and review recordings. The smartest among this group are those who avoid writing about the music itself and focus on the composers' or performers' personalities or personal habits. Other music critics, not qualified to write about music or perhaps more interested in its personalities rather than technical aspects, tend to focus on the words to songs, for if they have any right at all to comment about a performance, it might be that they may know something about language. Critics of this stripe are more accurately described as journalists or reporters, and they are particularly active in the pop-rock and jazz fields. Some of these reporters are very good writers, and they accommodate the interests of music lovers who enjoy reading about the performers' personalities and the show-biz aspects of music.

What about careers in writing about music? Major newspapers and popular general-interest magazines may employ one or more critics or music journalists. There is a shortage of fully qualified, versatile music critics who can write well. Those aspiring to the field will probably have to begin their efforts to break into full-time professional writing by volunteering occasional reviews for neighborhood newspapers, perhaps college newspapers, or small magazines. Really good writers about music will probably attract a responsive readership and perhaps graduate to more prestigious, better-paying media.

Only the major papers and magazines offer really top salaries. The great majority of critics and music reporters are rather poorly paid and earn salaries comparable to most other journalists, which are not high. Some "stringers" work for freelance fees. Critics and music reporters, even if employed full-time, often find it necessary to moonlight in other fields, such as teaching. Some are college students who get started in the field by reviewing concerts and records for their campus newspaper.

An individual more interested in journalism than music criticism may be able to land a job on a newspaper in an editorial capacity. Some of these jobs carry the title "music editor." Most newspapers receive dozens of publicity releases every week from publicity chairpersons of performing groups, and most newspapers assign their "entertainment editor" or music editor to select the pieces most deserving of publication. This gatekeeper is also expected to serve some time in humble tasks such as rewriting other writers' work. A small salary is partially compensated when the music writer is granted a by-line—but it's hard to eat modest notoriety for breakfast.

Individuals wishing to pursue the various kinds of employment available in writing about music can obtain further information from the Music Critics Association of North America.

Music Services

Music Editor/Music Cutter. Full-time careers can be developed in the field of music editing. Music editors are often called music cutters, referring to the days when an editor's job included splicing pieces of audiotape or film together. As explained in the chapter on film scoring, music editors are the individuals who are responsible for selection, timing, and synchronization of music tapes to TV or movie film. Editors also work with music for radio and TV commercials, and music videos. Although many videos hold entirely to the audio master tape, others call for music editors to change the sound tracks to fit the action called for in the script.

Those qualified to work as music cutters have usually acquired their craft and art as apprentices, working alongside other, more experienced, cutters who themselves learned in a master-apprentice relationship over many years. Many good cutters are expert musicians. Others are simply very sensitive to how music can enhance dramatic events and do expert work without having acquired formal musical training. The individual seeking a career as a music editor should expect to follow the time-honored apprenticeship training, perhaps getting started on amateur movies, or educational or sales films.

For further information on music editing careers, contact the Motion Picture Editors Guild.

Music Librarian. Librarians are employed in a variety of settings. The most familiar are individuals working in college and public libraries as music specialists. Some of these jobs involve little more than clerking. At the other end of the scale are the trained music catalogers and researchers who apply knowledgeable judgments and perform sophisticated, occasionally even scholarly tasks. All but the smallest libraries employ paraprofessionals and professionals. For the former, college degrees are sometimes required. Individuals aspiring to careers as fully professional music librarians should plan to acquire a baccalaureate degree in music, preferably with a concentration in music history and literature. Then they should plan to go on to a master's degree in library science, preferably from a university with a well-respected curriculum. Few libraries will consider applicants lacking these credentials.

Another kind of music librarian is employed by production music libraries. For these jobs, the qualifications are a solid and broad knowledge of musical styles, both contemporary and historical; a terrific musical memory; and an affinity for detail work. No degree is required, but people with degrees in musicology may have a edge.

Radio Station Music Director. The station's music director now does much of the work that a music librarian once did—and more. The music director is often responsible for listening to weekly releases from recording companies, talking with record promoters, conducting research about listener preferences in music, and cataloging the station's musical offerings for airplay. The music director and program director together make the decision about the station's playlist. Often, a station's on-air personality fills this slot, too (see *Disc Jockey*, page 508).

To qualify for a job as a radio station music director, the aspirant should be knowledgeable about recorded music, recording artists, demographic research methods, and the vagaries of public taste, as well as be computer literate. Aspirants possessing some of these qualities may perform in the job quite well without any special music training. The individuals who accept these jobs should have one additional personal attribute: the ability to handle continuous pressure from record promoters.

Music Preparation. Another kind of music service that offers some career opportunities is in the field of music preparation. This is the appellation commonly used in reference to the companies that offer mass-produced music copying, music duplication, music-writing supplies, and music library services, including delivery of scores and parts to customers. Music preparation companies are located in all major recording centers and employ copyists, proofreaders, arrangers, orchestrators, and clerical help. Proprietors of these service companies are the supervising copyists, and invoices to their clients (arrangers, composers, producers) include a surcharge for supervision, amounting to at least the AFM minimum (usually 25%). Persons seeking a career in the music service field will normally start out as freelance copyists, develop a reputation for dependability and good work, then get hired by an established company. Most are employed, however, on a piece-work basis—being called in when outside help is needed to meet deadlines. Many individuals in this field also work freelance elsewhere in music or music-related fields.

Science and Technology

Sound Engineer/Technician. Individuals employed in the technical aspects of sound reinforcement, recording, and broadcasting are generally referred to as *engineers*. Many in the field are more accurately called *technicians*. The appellation *audio engineer* is more accurately reserved for university graduates who hold degrees in electrical engineering or, perhaps, physics, audiology, acoustics, or computer science. These engineers engage in such work as research and development of audio equipment, studio and equipment design, record mastering, equipment maintenance, and sound mixing. Most of these engineers are employed full-time by equipment manufacturers, sound reinforcement companies, recording studios, radio and TV stations, and film studios. Some engineers are assigned only one type of work, such as design or maintenance or audio mixing. In smaller firms, audio engineers perform a variety of tasks.

Employers also hire audio technicians, who may or may not have a university-level education. Many audio technicians and mixers are simply talented, self-taught handypersons who, through years of apprenticeship, earn job assignments that involve sophisticated technology. Most engineers and technicians are attracted to these music-related jobs by their love for music, and some of them hold college degrees in music or have studied music informally. The art of sound mixing demands considerable musical knowledge and the ability to make sensitive aural judgments.

To qualify for employment as a sound engineer, university degrees in both electrical engineering and music would be ideal, but few professionals are so prepared. With the increasing sophistication of audio equipment, employers more and more require not just audio technicians but sound engineers and computer scientists as well. Engineers believing they may find employment in broadcasting will usually have to qualify for an FCC (Federal Communications Commission) operator's license.

Individuals who want to go to the top in recording technology and sound engineering should not only study as much music as they can, but they should go on to at least some studies in acoustics. Such persons might be called on to design and build state-of-the-art recording studios. The professionals who can claim this kind of preparation will be in high demand and enjoy good earnings.

Instrument Design/Maintenance. From early times, the inventors and designers of musical instruments have held a distinguished place in the history of the art. Though the basic design of most acoustic musical instruments was set centuries ago, scientists and technicians continue not only to improve instruments but also to invent new ones. Persons interested in the physics of sound, acoustics, and electronics manage to develop music-related careers. It cannot be said that there is a big demand for instrument designers, but positions can be found for qualified persons with manufacturing companies, particularly those involved in developing ever-new electronic instruments.

As for careers in the field of instrument maintenance, there is a shortage in most communities of competent instrument repair technicians. It is simply impossible to find sufficient numbers of real craftsmen. Qualified repair technicians can just about choose where they want to live, then knock on the door of the nearest instrument repair shop and go to work the same day.

Other jobs await qualified maintenance personnel in school systems, colleges, and universities, not to mention the armed services. Persons aspiring to such careers can acquire their training in some junior colleges and some universities. It is more common, however, for aspirants to learn their craft as apprentices to masters.

Repair technicians often specialize in keyboard instruments. Many communities lack fully qualified piano technicians/tuners. The best of them have been factory trained or learned their craft as apprentices. Fortunately, piano tuners today do not even have to have a true sense of pitch. Tuning can be accurately handled with the use of electronic pitch-measuring machines that are readily available with piano repair kits. Piano technicians are almost always independent contractors working out of their homes; they set their own hours and vacation periods. The competent ones are in demand and make a good living.

There is also a shortage of electronic keyboard maintenance personnel. Those who acquire competence in repairing electronic keyboard instruments will be able to find steady employment at good pay. And those with musical backgrounds will, on most jobs, be able to do a better job than just straight technicians.

With the proliferation of lower-cost electronic musical equipment of all kinds, it is safe to predict that steady employment at good pay will be available to those who take the time to educate themselves in electronics and music. This is clearly a growth area of employment.

Managerial/Executive

Individuals not involved directly in music making can develop successful careers in the business and managerial sectors of the arts and entertainment industry. Dozens of options await them. The simple truth is, the music business has never had an adequate supply of people who are qualified to run things.

It is not possible to predict career patterns in music and arts management. The person who aspires to become an artists' manager may start out in music publishing and end up in record production. The individual who initially wants to run a talent agency may experience greater success as a TV executive. Rapid change is so pervasive in the music business, it is rarely possible, or even desirable, for a manager or executive-type person to hold with one job throughout a career. Fast learners who are quick on their feet will seize career opportunities as they develop. The most creative executives won't wait for job offers; they will create their own opportunities.

Qualifications and Preparation. The college or university graduate who has gone through an educational program that integrates music and business and the recording arts has the advantage in breaking into the field. These graduates often have experience with college radio stations or college concert boards. Dozens of colleges and universities in the United States and Canada now offer these kinds of curricula, and their graduates are finding their places in the arts and entertainment industry.

A profession directly related to music business management is arts administration. Educational institutions with degree programs leading to professional employment in that area include the University of California, Los Angeles; the University of Wisconsin–Madison; Yale University; and New York University.

How does one qualify as an arts administrator? A master's degree will probably help. For a fuller answer to this question, review Chapter 13. Of all the music-related career options available, arts administration may present one of the greatest challenges to an individual's versatility and imagination.

Employment Prospects. Those who take the time to prepare themselves in business and music will be among the most sought-after executives. A clear indication of this is the track record of schools offering music business studies. The good ones are placing an impressive percentage of their graduates in beginning and middle management positions.

Broadcasting/Advertising

The fields of broadcasting and advertising in the United States are so closely allied that they will be considered here as inseparable. A person aspiring to a career in either of these fields will very likely become professionally involved with the other. Even so-called public broadcasting, although nonprofit, is dependent on large corporations that grant money to PBS and local nonprofit stations in the form of **institutional ads**: prominent corporate name identification at the beginning and end of programs.

In broadcasting, the most accessible entry-level employment is found in radio, as an "air personality." Translation: disc jockey.

Disc Jockey. The individual who masters the ceremony of getting recordings identified and on the air is a key figure in radio broadcasting. As explained in Chapter 21, disc jockeys in major markets are often confined to introducing recordings and making commercial announcements, these proceedings interrupted by ad-lib comments by the jock about the entertainment, the performers, or most anything that might engage the listeners.

In addition to time on the air, the DJ is usually occupied in a variety of tasks related to the operation of the station. Most station managers try to increase community visibility by encouraging their air personalities to become involved in such activities as being master of ceremonies (**MC**) for shopping center openings and judging beauty contests. Many jocks are involved in promoting, even sometimes acting as MC for, rock concerts. Some DJs assist their station's PR activities by involving themselves in charities and other public services.

Disc jockeys in smaller markets are often called on to perform every conceivable task at their stations, from making up playlists to sweeping out the studio. In many markets, jocks assist in writing and producing commercials and may even sell spots. A station with a limited budget will also require its DJs to run the audio engineering board concurrently with physically handing the discs and tapes.

Qualifications and Preparation. Some disc jockeys get started with little or no professional training. Some self-taught air personalities (or on-the-job apprentices) rise to the top of their profession. But the life expectancy of a disc jockey can be short, comparable to that of a professional athlete or ballet dancer. DJs may tend to lose touch with their listeners, stations often make changes in search of bigger audiences, and the best air personalities sometimes move up to become program directors, even station managers.

Although it is not difficult to get some kind of modest start as a disc jockey, individuals planning a career in broadcasting should take time out to earn a college degree or two in broadcasting, communication, or an allied field such as music, theater, perhaps even journalism. Those who qualify themselves with a good education will almost certainly rise faster in their broadcasting careers than others whose backgrounds may limit their potential for leadership roles.

Employment Prospects. Most DJ jobs are landed through the submission of airchecks accompanied by the individual's résumé. A home tape recording won't do: A station manager wants to hear how the individual sounds on the air during an actual broadcast. Airchecks submitted for audition should have most of the music edited out, retaining only a few seconds to enable the auditor to hear how the performer gets in and out of the music.

Those seeking their first job and those changing jobs can learn of available openings by word of mouth and through trade magazines.

Jocks often change jobs as frequently as musicians do. The disc jockey just starting may find opportunities in very small stations for some kind of tryout, partly because such stations (even some larger ones) pay their inexperienced DJs only minimal wages. Of course, top DJs in major markets (and syndicates or networks) can earn celebrity incomes.

Broadcast Producers/Directors. Career opportunities in radio and television for producers and directors are so diverse, they defy generalization. The easiest to describe is the radio program director (PD); that job is covered in Chapter 21. Many radio PDs gain their background as DJs, and may continue as on-the-air personalities with reduced schedules. In consultation with the station's general manager, they hire and fire disc jockeys, and on some stations, the PD may also participate in engaging and disengaging other on-the-air types such as news reporters.

Radio PDs can perform their jobs well without strong musical backgrounds, depending on their musical intuition to help them come up with playlists appropriate for their markets. PDs who demonstrate strong leadership qualities may eventually grow into the role of group PD or radio station general manager.

Musicians who aspire to leadership roles in television will discover a variety of opportunities. Individuals with imagination may find their entrée via involvement with music videos. Low-budget videos offer entry-level positions for producers, writers, and directors who can figure out how to turn out low-cost masters that look like a million dollars.

Producers and directors in radio and television often gain middle and upper management positions following success in sales. Employers appear attracted to persons who have proven their abilities in the business side of the industry.

Jobs for energetic producers and directors occur with radio stations and networks, program syndicators, record label video departments, and independent production companies.

Business/Merchandising

Thousands of careers in the music business are available for individuals who prefer to involve themselves in the marketing of goods and services relating to the industry. Even live music is a "product" that must be advertised, packaged, and sold. Music merchandising is a multibillion-dollar enterprise, and talented

Warner Paige (left), Past Chairman of the Board of NAMM, being
honored with the Indiana State University Distinguished Alumni
Citation by James F. Slutz, Director of Music Business at Indiana State,
and Michelle Snyder, President of the Music Industry Association.
Photo courtesy James F. Slutz.

persons will probably be able to develop full-time careers in it—if they apply
their energies in the right places. See Chapter 12 for a discussion of this field.

Career patterns cannot be described here, because products and markets
change overnight. Jobs come and go; merchants sink or swim. Even in periods of
economic depression, employers will always take on an employee who can sell—
if not on salary, at least on commission. The music industry requires peddlers as
well as top executives.

Most music merchants, whether working as employer or employee, enjoy satisfactory careers because they know how to hustle; they do not wait for the telephone to ring. They are out on the street, ever searching for something to buy or

sell. The strongest operatives survive, because ever-new opportunities come along.

Qualifications and Preparation. Until recent years, a music merchant or talent salesperson did not require a university degree to succeed in the music business. Such a person could often make it, at least for a while, just being "street smart." But as the music business tends more and more toward large corporations, even international conglomerates, the person who wants to rise to the top may find an acute need for a strong academic background. Corporate boards no longer want to entrust the buying and selling of merchandise and musicians to mom and pop. The small community will still need the small businessperson, but the big-money prizes are now going to the merchants and agents and promoters who are informed in such fields as market research, advertising, accounting, and finance.

Employment Prospects. Individuals who are fully prepared and motivated for work in contemporary business will find good career opportunities. Particularly employable today are persons with strong university training in music and business. Those who go on to earn the M.B.A. degree start at high salaries, particularly if they graduate from a prestigious school of business such as those at Stanford and Harvard.

Whatever the educational background, a musician-merchant's ultimate achievements will probably be governed more by imagination and drive. Armed with these two attributes, the aspirant will create "luck." As more than one person of achievement has expressed it, "The harder I work, the luckier I get."

Legal Services

Each year, the music business requires the services of more and more legal experts, because nearly every aspect of the industry involves copyright law and the negotiation of contracts. Even though all law schools train their students in contracts, it is often impossible for an attorney in general practice to be sufficiently well informed to handle certain kinds of music business contracts. In the field of copyright, the attorney lacking expertise often gets in too deep and is unable to counsel clients adequately. For these reasons, increasing numbers of lawyers now specialize in entertainment law and copyright.

Music business specialists are often hard-pressed to keep abreast of the complexities of the industry. In the copyright field, lawyers, clients, and adversaries continue to do battle over the meaning of the fine print. Law students who believe that they will want to practice entertainment law should focus their studies on intellectual property including copyright, patent and trademark, contract, and agency law, and unfair competition, privacy, and publicity rights.

What are the employment prospects? The brightest, best-informed entertainment attorneys have plenty of clients and high incomes. Those of considerable experience often get full-time positions as legal counsel for such firms as publishers, recording companies, and film studios. Others go into artist management. But our law schools turn out about twice as many lawyers as we can accommodate. Attorneys of lesser talents (or ambition or luck) may find it necessary to go into some field other than law.

The individual who is attracted to the law might not be able to gain admission to a good law school or might lack sufficient funds to complete the education. Such a person can often find employment as a copyright researcher, music rights agent, or paralegal. Still others may already be working in some aspect of the music business, attending law school concurrently. Upon admission to the bar, persons with this kind of background would probably find themselves more readily employable than their competitors.

For an extensive treatment of the role of lawyers in the music business, review Chapter 8.

Arts/Graphics

Creative persons in the aural and visual arts have often worked in close alliance. Some have been talented in both fields. For example, Schoenberg and Gershwin were good painters; Stravinsky worked closely with Picasso in stage design and costuming. Today, musical performers must be attractively staged and costumed. Music merchandise must be packaged to sell. These circumstances create many career opportunities for talented individuals interested in graphics and other visual arts. Recording companies alone require the services of hundreds of graphic artists, whom they employ on staff or freelance. Printers and commercial art companies employ artists who have a feeling for music and how visual impressions—packaging and displays—can move people to buy music.

In the video field alone, many graphic and scenic artists find challenging employment as production designers. Artists who bring a musical sensitivity to these assignments may develop the most successful careers in this part of the industry.

STARTING YOUR OWN BUSINESS

Many persons of independent mind choose not to work as an employee, preferring to "go it alone." They become entrepreneurs of one kind or another. If you can't find a job, create your own! Now, you may not be able to set up your own TV network or movie studio, but it is possible, with a limited amount of capital, to start your own music-oriented company, such as a production firm, concert promotion organization, management company, or publishing business.

Structuring the Business

Music and nonmusic business enterprises are operated according to the way they have been structured financially. In the United States, a business enterprise is generally organized in one of three ways: (a) sole proprietorship, (b) partnership, or (c) corporation.

Each of these forms of ownership has certain advantages, as well as certain disadvantages.

Sole Proprietorship. The principal advantage of a sole proprietorship is that it is easy to set up and get under way. All the entrepreneur really needs is some money (personal or borrowed funds) and a great amount of energy—and a lot of nerve. The sole proprietor who wants to get out fast can do that, too; there is no need to call a meeting of the board to make decisions. An entrepreneur may venture forth largely because of a dislike of working for someone else as well as a satisfaction in being the boss. The proprietor runs the show and enjoys the advantage of all the profits; no need to share them with anyone.

That's the good news. Now for the bad news: The sole proprietor is personally responsible for all financial losses the business may experience. If our Horatio Alger runs out of money, the creditors can take possession of all personal property, including a home—whatever there is of value. The sole proprietorship has the omnipresent problem of limited capital. Even if the business is going well, the single operator may find it difficult to raise enough money to expand the business. A proprietor may employ many others, although typically the team is small.

TABLE 25.3   Types of Business Ownership

Sole Proprietorship	Partnership	Corporation
Advantages		
1. You are the boss	1. Simple to organize	1. Limited personal liability
2. Easy to form, easy to dissolve	2. Complementary management skills	2. Maximum capitalization
3. You retain all profits	3. Expanded capitalization per unit of doing business	3. Lower cost per unit of doing business
Disadvantages		
1. Very hard work	1. Unlimited financial responsibility	1. Expensive, complicated to form
2. Unlimited financial liability	2. Potential conflicts of authority	2. Legal restrictions
3. Management deficiencies	3. Potential personality conflicts	3. Double taxation
4. Limited working capital		4. Impersonal, insensitive
5. Potential lack of continuity of operation		

The one-person operation will be deficient in some management capabilities; no one person can do everything well. For example, a whirlwind salesperson-manager can pull the company under if unable to understand basic accounting principles. Finally, the sole proprietorship may have to cease operations suddenly if the owner-manager becomes physically or mentally disabled, gets divorced, or moves away.

Partnership. Partnerships are another form of business ownership. They are defined by the Uniform Partnership Act as "associations of two or more persons who operate a business as co-owners by voluntary legal agreement." General partnerships are established when all partners involved carry on the business as co-owners. Limited partnerships (not permitted in some states) are composed of one or more general partners and one or more limited partners. A limited partner is one whose liability to the company is limited to the amount that person has invested in it. Joint ventures are a third type of partnership and are popular with investors who join together temporarily to undertake a short-term business enterprise, such as producing a show.

Partnerships offer certain advantages of ownership. First of all, they are easy to form. The partners should negotiate, at the outset, a written agreement that defines shares of ownership and spells out each partner's responsibilities to the firm. Partnerships are also likely to have, in the beginning, more working capital than sole proprietorships. It is also likely that a firm where two or more individuals are active in management will have people with complementary skills. For example, one partner may be tops in sales, another may be adept at accounting.

The principal disadvantage of this form of organization is that the partners may disagree on how to run the business. Add to this the possibility that the partners may develop personality conflicts. And if the partners reach an impasse, it is difficult for them to dissolve the company; disputes may arise over disposition of inventory and how outstanding debts are going to be paid.

Corporation. Sole proprietors and partners are people, whereas a corporation is an entity. The impersonal aspect of a corporation was set forth in 1819 by U.S. Chief Justice John Marshall, who observed that a corporation is "an artificial being, invisible, intangible, and existing only in contemplation of law." The most obvious advantage of a corporation is that management may have more money with which to work, particularly if the corporation is public, meaning its ownership shares may be sold through a mechanism such as a stock market. Corporations may also have a diversity of managerial talents and the financial capability to buy in large quantities, thus reducing costs per unit of doing business. Also, a shareholder knows that personal liability to the corporation is limited to the value of the stock the shareholder owns. Even if the company folds, shareholders' personal property is not usually vulnerable to claims against the corporation.

Of the three types of business organization, the corporate structure is the most difficult to set up and the slowest and most expensive to get into operation. Each state charters corporations according to its own laws, and state and federal regulatory agencies can burden management with costly paperwork.

Another disadvantage for investors in corporations is that they experience double taxation: Not only do they pay corporate taxes, they also pay personal income taxes on dividends received from the corporation.

Starting a Music Publishing Company

One of the music businesses that is easiest to get started and least expensive to finance is publishing. This fact is reconfirmed all the time by hundreds of new firms being set up, usually by songwriters frustrated after repeated turn-downs of their material by others. They decide to strike out on their own.

Here is a step-by-step approach to setting up a publishing company in the popular music field.

1. **Research.** Study this book and publications concerning business management found in most libraries.

2. **Acquisitions.** You have to acquire *properties* (property interests in musical compositions) before you can start publishing. The easiest way to acquire copyrights is to write your own music. In addition to your own copyrights, search out other qualified writers and gain their confidence and assistance in your publishing plans. Retain a lawyer to assist in drawing up contracts. Use the guidelines listed in Chapter 4.

3. **Structure your financing and business entity.** You have three basic options in structuring your company and its capitalization. Once you have determined whether you will be organized as a sole proprietorship, partnership, or corporation, you know what working capital you will have and you can now tentatively select a firm name.

4. **Contact ASCAP, BMI, or SESAC.** Choose a company name and ask whether it is already being used by someone else. The licensing organization may ask you to supply your first choice as well as alternate choices for your firm name. The organization will not accept into membership a firm with a name identical to or similar to an established publishing company. If the name is cleared, request an application for affiliation as a publisher. At this point, a prudent move might be to initiate a trademark search to see whether your name is being used anywhere else in the United States (see Chapter 5).

   Affiliate with one of these organizations (requirements are explained in Chapter 6).

5. **Register your firm name.**

   a. If your company is a sole proprietorship or partnership, call on your county clerk and recorder's office and search the records to learn if your choice of firm name has been previously registered in the county. Duplications will not be accepted. Unless you identify the company with your own full, legal name, you will be required to register a fictitious firm name (some counties use the term *trade name*). For example, if your name is John Doe, the county will record your firm as "John Doe dba Hit Publishing Company" ("dba" is the abbreviation for "doing business as"). The county clerk will also require this filing to be published in a legal newspaper in the county. Procedures and applicable fees vary from county to county.

b. If your firm is to be a corporation, you must meet the requirements for incorporation of the state in which you are doing business.

6. **Establish your company bank account.** Your bank will not open your account until your firm name has been published as described above. Do not commingle personal funds with your company account, even if you are the sole proprietor. Commingled accounts make difficult problems in accounting and tax matters.

7. **Business license.** If you limit your firm's activities just to publishing, you will not need a business license. But if your company should branch out into artists' agency work, most states would consider that as a kind of employment agency, and nearly all states license and regulate employment agencies.

8. **Arrange outside services.** Because most new publishing companies start on a shoestring, proprietors generally do not attempt, at the outset, to handle everything themselves. Many small publishers in New York, Nashville, and Hollywood share a small office (perhaps three to six firms) along with the costs of rent, a secretary, and so forth. Outside companies are available to handle just about any service a business needs—mail handling, telephone answering, secretarial, bookkeeping, accounting, and more.

9. **Prepare your materials.** A songwriter sometimes manages with leadsheets and demos prepared by amateurs. But now that you are a publisher trying to exploit your properties, everything you present to a producer or artist for consideration must be suitably prepared.

10. **Your first success.** The essence of the publishing business in the pop field is getting material recorded and released. The first release of any recording requires the manufacturer to receive a mechanical license from the

publisher. Many publishers use their own mechanical license forms and negotiate directly with the recording companies, settling on mutually agreeable terms. If your first recorded song hits, you may want to publish it in printed form. You will probably license a music printing company to handle this for you (see Chapter 4). Also, reread in Chapter 4 how to set up subpublishing deals abroad through licensing agreements with firms active internationally.

11. **Forms, contracts.** Copyright forms are readily available, without cost, from the U.S. Copyright Office (lcweb.loc.gov/copyright). When you negotiate writers' publishing contracts, retain a qualified music business attorney—or use the draft contract discussed in Chapter 4 as a basis for your discussions with an attorney less experienced in the music field.

12. **Your second company.** Just as soon as your first company gets under way, establish a second one so that you can accommodate properties from writers affiliated with either ASCAP or BMI. Except for the preliminaries outlined here, the procedures for setting up a second firm are the same as for your first venture.

13. **Persistence and continued success.** Once your new firm starts to get its copyrights licensed and recorded here and abroad, don't sit waiting for royalty checks. Real profitability comes along when a firm can achieve continuity year to year, building catalogs of hundreds, eventually thousands, of songs and exploiting those copyrights. So the search for new writers and new properties goes on and on. That is the publishing business.

CAREER
DEVELOPMENT

Eighty percent of success is showing up.

—*Woody Allen*

Recent studies reveal that involvement in some aspect of music is one of the most frequently named career goals. Millions of young people are drawn to music and want somehow to become part of the profession. But many of these dreams are poorly defined. Aspirants can be attracted by the "glamour" and big money of the music and entertainment fields but have no clear idea of how they might break in.

The world of music and entertainment has always had a certain mystique. The most visible people in these fields seem to be rich and famous. Producing and selling music can be enjoyable and profitable, but there's another whole world concerned with what goes on backstage, off-camera. Here we uncover thousands of individuals no one has ever heard of, most of them employed quite regularly, earning respectable incomes—and probably enjoying what they are doing.

Landing a Job Versus Building a Career. It is important to distinguish between a "job" and a "career." To borrow from Gertrude Stein, a job is a job (is a job). But a career, properly defined, is more likely an ongoing series of related jobs that add up to an employment sequence that has continuity and development.

← The Beatles. Photo © John Launois/Black Star/PNI.

Recording studio, University of Miami School of Music, Florida.

Using Counselors. Although employment counselors may not be able to address everything a person may need, they are probably the most competent persons in the community to offer professional help, what can be called structured intervention. Most counselors have information concerning career options and statistical projections of employment prospects. One of the useful services a qualified counselor can offer is assisting aspirants in finding out who they are. Counselors can offer a battery of aptitude tests, interest measurements, and temperament tests. The objectivity and value of these tests and measurements remain in dispute, but they are almost always somewhat helpful, and career seekers should avail themselves of every possible opportunity to find out where they may excel and just what makes them tick.

For people out of high school and college, counselors are available through state employment services. In larger communities, professional career counselors, independent of government, are available, with payment of a fee. People who are still in high school or college can, of course, generally avail themselves of well-trained advisers and career placement and development staff.

Discovering Yourself. Concurrently with defining career goals, you should try to define *yourself*—analyze not only your interests but also your particular temperament and personality. Along with this personal discovery should come measurement of aptitudes and talents. In addition to doing all you can to discover who and what you are, you should obtain outside appraisals from qualified professionals.

A large part of the workforce is probably miscast. Whole lifetimes can be spent in frustration and failure. Although many different reasons may be identified for these unsuccessful lives, very often they got started off wrong, before they knew who they were or measured their talents or considered whether they could meet the competition. Well-planned careers do not always work out. But if you proceed sensibly, with all available information, at the very least you will have reduced the probability of failing in a chosen field.

Many students have used the "Discovering Yourself" form (see Table 26.1), devised particularly for people interested in careers in the arts and the music business. There is no "passing" or "failing" score. Rather, the answers should be interpreted and evaluated in light of the information set forth in these pages concerning music-related careers and the kinds of talents and personalities that have been found appropriate in pursuing certain careers. For example, if your answers show a dislike for travel and fear of not always having a steady job, you might be unhappy and unsuccessful in attempting to build a career as a performing musician. On the other hand, if your highest priority is being free to create and there is little concern about job security, you might be a strong candidate for building a career as a composer or record producer.

Besides seeking to understand your own interests and value system, it is equally important at this early stage to conduct an inventory of personal strengths, weaknesses, and talents. The accompanying form (Table 26.2) can assist you in these assessments; to be useful, they must be rendered as objectively as possible.

Inaccurate talent appraisals are readily available. For example, a musician who works every Saturday night at the local American Legion Hall can offer a "professional" opinion but may have no idea what level of talent or what type of specific musical skill is required in the recording studios. The local singing teacher may hold an advanced degree in music but not know what would be expected of voice students seeking work in broadcast commercials. Many of our university professors of music composition do not know the level of talent (and craft) demanded of film composers. Seek the opinion of such people because they have valuable

TABLE 26.I   Discovering Yourself

Effective career planning should begin with careful self-appraisal. What is important to you? What makes you most effective? What kinds of talents do you have? Place a number from 1 to 10 in the appropriate spaces below. Think of the number 1 as "low," "little," or "poor," depending on the nature of the category. Use the number 5 for "average." Number 10 means "high," "a lot," or "very important." After you have indicated your own appraisals, seek an outside professional opinion to learn if others view you as you see yourself.

MY VALUE SYSTEM

	ESTIMATE	OUTSIDE ESTIMATE
Need for respect from others		
Need for prestige, status		
Need for audience approval		
Desire for peace of mind		
Need to be liked		
Desire to be loved		
Need for artistic freedom		
Concern for health		
Desire for leisure time		
Desire to have children		
Importance of artistic achievement		
Importance of job security		
Importance of money		
Tolerance for jobs demanding travel		
Desire for personal development		
Desire for artistic development		

TABLE 26.2   My Strengths, Weaknesses, Talents

This form can be revealing for both musicians and people in business. Use the 1-10 numbering system described for Table 26.1.

	Today		When Fully Developed	
	My Estimate	Outside Estimate	My Estimate	Outside Estimate
Motivation, ambition				
Self-confidence				
Creative talent				
Performing ability				
Musical knowledge				
Business sense				
Effectiveness as an oral communicator				
Effectiveness in written communication				
Ability as an organizer				
General leadership ability				
Musical leadership ability				
Capacity to accept direction				
Ability to work with others				
Understanding of the music profession				
Understanding of the music business				
Emotional stability, health				
Intelligence				
Capacity for musical growth				
Capacity for personal growth				
Personal habits				
Ability to adjust to change				

My strongest personal attribute _____

_____

My strongest talent _____

_____

_____

knowledge, but also seek the advice, when possible, of people who have achieved some level of success in the specific career in which you are interested.

If, through systematic appraisal of temperament and talent, the aspiring musician discovers a love of music but no desire to perform, there still are scores of career options in music-related fields. Many musicians are surprised to find that they can be successful in the business world. Many of the same qualities that make a good musician are also important to a music business person: perseverance, a willingness to work as much time as it takes to get the job done well, and a strong belief in one's own abilities. Of course, it is also helpful to have a "good ear" and to love music.

CLIMBING THE LADDER

No two people hold the same views on just what constitutes "success." To many, the professional who earns a good living has achieved success. But in the arts, many individuals place a higher value on personal fulfillment, artistic idealism. They refuse to be seduced by the dollar; they won't "go commercial," preferring to hold to their conception of artistic integrity, whatever the consequences. Psychologists would describe this kind of idealist as one who is more concerned with "psychic rewards" than financial security.

How many people in the working world are happy with what they do for a living? Many surveys have been made; most of them indicate that *more than half* of those interviewed stated they were unhappy with their jobs. Unhappiness over low pay was rarely the number one concern. Those interviewed have most often complained they felt trapped in their jobs and that they had little confidence they had a chance to "get ahead." A majority of those asked stated that, if they had the opportunity, they would change their line of work. Those planning a career related to the arts have to know at the outset that they are engaging in a high-risk enterprise. But even though careers in the arts, particularly music, often provide only minimum security, many aspirants would not give up the personal rewards the field offers in exchange for more stable employment.

For those who contemplate climbing the music career ladder, it will be helpful to be aware of the following:

1. Most music-related careers are combination careers. For example, many performers also teach music students in schools or in private studios.

2. Most people experience serial careers; they move from job to job, not necessarily because they quit or get fired but because of the nature of the profession. A typical example is a person who starts out as a gofer; then begins to get a few music copying jobs; and may then progress to arranging, composing, perhaps get into the publishing business; and eventually becomes involved in artist management and record production. Each job helps the individual prepare for the next step up the ladder.

3. The music business offers decreasing opportunities for the poorly prepared. The jobs offering the best potential for advancement go more and more to well-educated, genuinely competent individuals.

4. Men still dominate the business. Women, with some notable exceptions, are underrecognized, underutilized, and underpaid, at some levels of the business.

5. Young people tend to dominate the creative and performing aspects of popular music. Persons of more mature years tend to dominate the field of serious music, music teaching, and the business and managerial facets of both popular and serious music.

6. All professions, all fields, are characterized by rapid change. But in music, career opportunities change every day. New jobs and new opportunities keep coming along.

FINDING WORK

Career counselors and research experts declare that at any given moment in the United States, there are at least 1 million job openings of all kinds. The person pounding the pavement searching for work scoffs at such a figure when unable to discover even one opening. The 1-million figure, although a rough estimate, can be understood in part by polling several hundred music and entertainment industry employers. Most complain they cannot find really qualified employees and insist the openings are there for individuals of demonstrated ability. Surveys show that many companies would either offer jobs or create new positions for people who could produce more, sell more, write better, work harder, or manage more efficiently.

Networking. Most career counselors urge job hunters to develop what is often called a "network" of personal and professional contacts. It takes time to develop a strong supportive group of people who will speak well of you, but nothing could be more valuable in building a career. An effective network need not be limited to persons of high influence; the best contact could turn out to be a casual acquaintance in a laundromat who mentions that so-and-so's band is looking for new people.

Most jobs in the music business are never advertised or made known to outsiders. In this field, there is often no need to place ads in the trades for help. Applicants line up immediately when word hits the street that some job may be coming up. So who gets the call? As with most fields of endeavor, what really counts in the music business is word of mouth. In short, "Who do you know who could cut it? Who might be ready for this job?" The individual who is prepared has built a good reputation and has a network of supportive contacts—that person wins in the end. Of course, once your network has helped you to get an interview or a job, you also need the specific skills or knowledge required for that job. If you are able to get a job without these skills, you'll still have a chance to succeed if you have a good, basic knowledge of the business you're entering so that you can build on the understanding you already have. When you become part of the music business, you'll still need to build on what you've learned through classes and texts like this one, but you'll have a good foundation on which to build.

Internships. Many college music industry programs require or strongly recommend that the student serve an internship as part of the degree requirements. Internships can provide valuable, practical examples of concepts learned in school. They can also help in two other very important ways:

1. They can give you actual experience in the industry. This experience can look very good on your résumé.
2. They can help you build your network of contacts. If you do good work during your internship, the professionals with whom you have worked are more likely to offer you a job or help you find employment after you've graduated. They may also give you permission to use their names as references. A successful intern understands that the internship can act as an audition for a job and will show up early for work and stay late, looking for ways to be useful and things to learn.

Personality, Work Habits. Another major influence on career development is the matter of human personality. Many jobs are won or lost not so much on intelligence and skill but on such personal considerations as dependability, flexibility, and congeniality. Research in the field of counseling has revealed that career problems are usually "people problems." Can you be counted on? Can you work effectively with others, or does your network of contacts report back that you are difficult to get along with, that you are not always dependable? It is people, then—their word about you—that can thrust you forward or hold you back.

The Value of Research. If your network of contacts is working for you, not against you, job opportunities are bound to come up. Before trying to get an interview, carefully research your prospective employer. Focus your fact-finding on trying to discover what the employer needs most. Present yourself as a solution to the problem. An employer, perhaps having just fired your predecessor, is really searching for a replacement who will solve problems the other person left behind. For example, your chances of getting hired might hinge largely on your perceived ability to follow through—filling the shoes of the person fired whose most annoying shortcoming, perhaps, was never finishing an assignment. Individuals who get hired, get promoted, and earn the most generally appear to have their egos under control and expend their energies trying to make the boss look good.

The Résumé. Job hunters automatically assume that they must mail out a lot of résumés to gain the interest of prospective employers. But the usefulness of circulating dozens, perhaps hundreds, of résumés is very limited: Many studies show that only a tiny share of jobs are landed through the submission of such documents. Dozens of books on the subject are readily available, and one of the best of them is Richard Bolles's *What Color Is Your Parachute?*

Résumé-writing techniques are covered in other books, so here, information on that subject is limited to what might be especially useful in seeking music business-related employment.

Gaining Interviews. All résumés should be accompanied by a cover letter requesting an interview or audition. Again, you must "translate" your aspirations to solving your potential employer's perceived needs:

1. Address your résumé and letter only to the individual with the authority to hire you.

2. Everything you put in the documents should focus on one thing: helping attain the reader's goals.

3. Keep in mind that all the résumé and letter can really do is describe your past. The reader must guess what your past might indicate for your future and your usefulness to the company tomorrow.

4. Cite no negatives; don't use such words as "fired," "didn't like my boss."

5. Use colorful terms to describe jobs you have performed. If you ran errands, don't say you were a "gofer." Try "production assistant."

6. Don't list references, but be sure to state they are available.

7. Emphasize "you," not "I." The first sentence in your letter, or at least one in your first paragraph, should state precisely what you can do to help fulfill the employer's needs.

8. The résumé and letter should be perfectly typed, with correct spelling, grammar, and punctuation.

9. Your résumé and cover letter should each be only one page. The reader is too busy to read your life story.

10. The final sentence should specify just what next step you want the reader to take.

If your résumé and cover letter hit the prospective employer right, you may be invited for an interview. In that case, intensify your research on what the company is looking for and what you might expect from the particular interviewer. Don't go in cold. The best books on how to handle yourself in job interviews generally agree on the following:

1. Dress appropriately, in line with other employees at the firm working at levels near the one you might be assigned.

2. Your interviewer may not know how to conduct a job interview properly. Be helpful; raise appropriate questions, if necessary, to deliver useful information about yourself and what you might do for the firm.

3. Don't get too cozy, too breezy—or too formal. Be respectful yet congenial.

4. Learn what the job normally pays, then ask for a little more (not a lot more).

5. Focus on how you believe you can help solve the interviewer's needs.

6. Immediately following the interview—the same day—mail a thank-you letter to the interviewer for the opportunity provided for you to learn more about the firm. Your competition probably won't think of doing this. Your thoughtfulness might favorably impress the interviewer.

7. Attend as many job interviews as you can; such experiences often tend to reduce nervousness and increase effectiveness.

Applying these suggestions should be helpful, but successful interviews often depend on intangibles. For example, if the conversation affords you an opportunity to suggest a new idea for the company (usually hard to do), that one contribution might yield a job offer. Or if you and the prospective employer get into discussing a mutual acquaintance, a personal consideration of this kind might help create an atmosphere of trust. A job offer could follow.

It makes little difference in the music business at just what level of entry the newcomer breaks into the field. Associates will quickly assess competence, and that person's career will rise or fall accordingly. As has been stressed time and again here, artistic and financial success in the music business are possible, even likely, when you, the aspirant, can present this package to the world:

- ▶ You have genuine talent.
- ▶ You have the right temperament.
- ▶ You get the important information.
- ▶ You work with qualified associates.
- ▶ You have the will to win.

Hang in there.

Part VII

CANADIAN MUSIC INDUSTRY AND INTERNATIONAL COPYRIGHT

The Beatles are commemorated by replicas of their equipment cases in front of the Liverpool Institute for the Performing Arts. Seated are David Leonard, President, Trebas; and David Price, Director of Learning, LIPA. Standing right is George Hood, Director, Trebas. Photo courtesy of Trebas Institute.

WHAT YOU NEED TO KNOW ABOUT CANADA'S MUSIC SCENE

Richard Flohil

S ummarizing a whole nation's involvement with the music industry is a daunting task. Where to begin? What about a bunch of quick facts and some basic geography and history:

- ▶ Canada is the United States' largest single trading partner.
- ▶ The east-west border between Canada and the United States is 3,223 miles long.
- ▶ The population of Canada is roughly 10% that of the United States.
- ▶ Almost 80% of all Canadians live within 200 miles of the American border.
- ▶ Canada remains a member of the British Commonwealth of Nations.
- ▶ Canada has 10 provinces (and the Northwest Territories), compared to the 50 states in the United States.
- ▶ One quarter of all Canadians speak French as their mother tongue.
- ▶ The largest cities in Canada are Toronto (4.41 million), Montreal (3.37 million), and Vancouver (1.89 million). The capital is Ottawa (1.04 million).
- ▶ In recent years, the Canadian dollar has been worth considerably less than the American dollar.

All these factors affect Canada's music industry and affect the way U.S. Americans approach it. But most of all, Americans have to understand Canadian attitudes—particularly those involving our relationship to the United States.

Canadians know far more about the United States than Americans know about Canada. We live, after all, in the lap of the United States; we read American books and magazines, we watch American television, we go to see American movies, and we avidly consume American music. In contrast, in Mississippi recently, on my way to the SXSW convention in Austin, I was asked by a waitress whether I was from Canada.

"So," she said, "are you guys Communists up there, or are you free?" My response was a muttered: "Well, we're free to be Communists if we want to. So far, we haven't wanted to."

This story, apart from illustrating an ignorance about Canada, indicates a somewhat more relaxed attitude about the role of government than may be the norm in the United States, but the political landscape has considerably affected the music industry.

Most Canadians express their nationality in terms of what we are not rather than in terms of what we are. We tend to have a greater degree of government involvement in our lives than do Americans; we tend to be less assertive and more reflective than Americans; we have a strongly negative response to handguns, capital punishment, urban decay, and other things we see as symptomatic of American life.

We hate being taken for granted, and we figure that Americans do that to us all the time, and we are very proud of ourselves. And at the same time, Canadian achievements are usually seen in the light of American approval of them. (A musical case in point: The Canadian band Barenaked Ladies was seen as washed up in Canada until American record buyers catapulted their album to double-platinum status in the late 1990s, whereupon they became instantly hip all over again at home.)

WOULD YOU BELIEVE A GOVERNMENT THAT MAKES POP MUSIC A PRIORITY?

Canada's federal government starts from the position that it is desirable to support the Canadian "cultural industries" (including the domestic music industry), which it sees necessary in view of the fact that we are in danger of total domination by foreign (i.e., U.S.) culture. With this in mind, the regulatory body that parallels the Federal Communications Commission (FCC), the Canadian Radio-Television and Telecommunications Commission (CRTC), instituted the "Canadian content" (CanCon) regulations. Starting in 1970, Canadian radio stations were required to ensure that 30% (as of 1999, 35%) of all music played was either written or performed by Canadians and produced in Canada. Thus, the components of each musical piece were broken down: Music, Artist, Production, Lyrics (the acronym MAPL neatly indicates the maple leaf, Canada's national symbol). Two or more of those four elements were enough to gain a piece status as "Canadian."

Decades later, the subject of the CanCon regulations still starts heated arguments. However, the regulations kickstarted a domestic music industry in Canada on every level. Back in 1970, there were few Canadian artists, and denied radio play, it was difficult to build anything like a national hit. Most bands performed in their immediate home markets, with word of mouth building a sufficient fan base to support local gigs. Because there was no radio play, and therefore no hits, there also were no facilities in which to make good records.

The CanCon regulations were bitterly opposed by the radio industry, which wanted to stick to the status quo, claiming there was insufficient quality Canadian material for them to broadcast. And to be honest, it was easier for broadcasters to work from a *Billboard* playlist than to create their own, factoring in Canadian records. Many broadcasters feared they would lose listeners to U.S. stations across the borders—but this, in fact, did not happen, and today it seems apparent that Canadians are listening to Canadian radio in part *because* of the Canadian content.

But almost overnight, the regulations began to work. The major multinational companies operating in Canada decided to produce Canadian artists; quality recording studios were built, equipped, and opened; and independent record companies surged into business.

Naturally, there were problems getting started. Some of the brand-new studios were found wanting, many of the records made in them sounded awful, and many of the new artists simply didn't have what it takes to compete. For their part, the broadcasters, even given an initial phase-in period, fudged the figures and seriously overplayed the handful of successful early artists (Neil Young, Joni Mitchell, Gordon Lightfoot, Anne Murray, the Guess Who). Records by many of the newer artists were consigned to what became known as "beaver hour" programming. Named after the industrious little animals that are something of a national symbol in Canada, these programs were aired at midnight or 6 in the morning, and filled the letter of the content requirements but hardly their spirit.

Despite these difficulties, the regulations did work. Canadian songwriters began to earn a significantly larger share of performing rights income. More and more Canadian artists discovered that they could perform outside their own cities and towns; one booking agency estimated that, prior to the regulations, it had half a dozen acts on its books that could tour across the country; 2 years later, there were more than 50. Canadian exposure gave more artists access to American and European markets—and performing rights income from abroad for Canadian songwriters and publishers skyrocketed from some $100,000 (Canadian) in 1970 to well over $20 million today.

Generally speaking, the success of the regulations is taken for granted today. But Canadian broadcasters still—off the record—despise the CRTC for initiating them in the first place, are unhappy with revised rules that demand that CanCon music has to be evenly distributed throughout the playday, and are livid that the quotas have been increased to 35%. The rules, however, are here to stay—and perhaps the only thing that will unseat them is foreign pressure.

Canada and the United States have, for many years, had a free trade agreement, which means—with various exceptions and qualifications—that goods and services flow back and forth across that 3,223-mile border. Canada, however, specifically exempted cultural elements from this agreement. This does not sit well with elements of the American music industry—specifically, the Recording Industry Association of America (RIAA)—who understand the economic impact of American music and are well aware that in Canada, much of it cannot earn an income because it is not played on Canadian radio.

On the other hand, the idea of domestic music quotas, pioneered in Canada, has spread to a number of other territories, including Australia and France. American music interests will continue to oppose these quotas, but at least in the short haul, it appears likely that they will continue to put up with them.

In Canada, government support for the arts—including popular music—is expressed in a number of other ways. The country's senior arts funding body, the Canada Council, supplies grants that help individual artists, provides financial support for tours, and supports programming initiatives at festivals and theater venues. The various provincial governments, too, offer a variety of support programs, as do some of the larger municipalities. Other music industry associations, largely funded by provincial governments, can also be accessed by local artists and music companies.

The music industry earns considerable financial support—some $6 million a year—from FACTOR, the Foundation to Assist Canadian Talent on Records. Funded by the federal government, and to a lesser extent by radio stations, which are required to contribute under the terms of the licenses they earn from the CRTC, FACTOR distributes this money through grants or loans to individual musicians, bands, or record labels. Canadian artists can apply for tour support in foreign countries (yes, that includes the United States), and for half the costs of foreign showcases such as SXSW in Austin, CMJ in New York, MIDEM in the south of France, or Music in the City in the UK. Since 1982, FACTOR has distributed some $25 million in loans and outright grants.

THE RECORD INDUSTRY IN CANADA

The Canadian record industry is dominated by the same big players that rule the roost in the United States.

All these companies have a number of Canadian artists on their rosters, and the spate of mergers that have consolidated the industry into a handful of large companies has encouraged companies to make a commitment to Canadian artists—in part because the Canadian government, in agreeing to approve mergers and consolidations, has informally asked the companies to do so as a condition of their agreement.

Any artist who signs with a major label in Canada is required, in effect, to sign with that company for the world; this looks good in a press release that claims "a world-wide record deal" but is difficult when the rest of the world—particularly the United States—shows little interest in the artist. The biggest single band in Canada during the late 1990s, the Tragically Hip, routinely sold hundreds of thousands of albums at home and sold out summer tours in 50,000+ venues, but had serious trouble filling medium-sized clubs south of the border.

Therefore, many Canadian artists, knowing that the U.S. market alone is 10 times the size of the domestic one, usually prefer to sign with the company in the United States. This way, they figure there will be an American commitment that may be missing if they sign to the Canadian branch.

Independent Record Companies

In addition to the major companies, there are a handful of independents, almost all of which are headquartered in Toronto. The largest is Attic, with a large back catalog of Canadian artists and an even bigger roster of foreign artists (mostly from Europe) that the label has built through extensive international contacts.

Most independent record companies, however, are related to specific artists. For example, Nettwerk, based in Vancouver, has succeeded by its savvy build-up of Sarah McLachlan and the ground-breaking Lilith Fair tour.

There are a handful of "niche" labels releasing a variety of specific genres such as blues and folk music.

And as in the United States, there are literally hundreds of small, artist-owned labels, usually formed because the artists could not get interest from the majors or the established indies (independents) and had to have "product" if for no other reason than to leverage their careers forward and have something to sell off-stage.

The overwhelming role of the majors, however, extends to the distribution of the independents as well; many smaller labels are distributed by them to retailers. There are, however, a number of smaller distribution companies that handle a variety of Canadian, U.S., and European labels and are able to secure reasonable placement in stores across the country.

Thanks in part to the help available to Canadian artists, it is probably easier to make and market a record in Canada than in most other countries. And while a great deal of less-than-sterling records die on the vine, the independent do-it-yourself system is, in effect, an informal farm team for the larger indies and the major labels.

Record retailing in Canada is dominated by a handful of retailing giants. "Big box" retailers such as Wal-Mart have cut into the market share of traditional record stores. More recently, bookstore chains have begun to cater to an older, more affluent audience, which finds normal record stores noisy, distracting, and unpleasantly teenaged.

Total retail record sales in Canada totaled $730,000,000 (Canadian) in the late 1990s. Total sales of CDs, cassettes, singles, and music videos in 1997 added up to well over 69 million units.

As a result of the competition between the major chains, record prices in Canada are among the lowest in the world. Only imported product is more costly, when the low cost of the Canadian dollar works against the buyer. The largest chains, in particular, are extremely hospitable to Canadian independent product and not only regularly stock it but front-rack it as well. This, of course, puts further pressure on the diminishing number of independent retail stores, most of them specialist outlets that, like their counterparts in the United States, survive in part because of their trade in second-hand CDs and discounted cut-outs.

MUSIC PROMOTION OPPORTUNITIES IN CANADA

Canada may be a small market and one complicated by its geography, but there are plenty of channels to promote music. The country boasts two trade publications, *The Record* and *RPM*. *The Record* is considered the most influential, while *RPM*—established in the 1960s—maintains its old-guard constituency.

Canada now has three music television channels, which parallel MTV, VH1, and CMT in the United States. MuchMusic is skewed to younger audiences, particularly since MuchMoreMusic (M3), an adult contemporary channel, went on air in 1998. CMT Canada is quite different from its U.S. parent and goes out of its way to showcase Canadian artists—whom it pays on a per-play basis, up to a maximum of $15,000, thus ensuring that they are able to make new videos.

Much and M3 operate VideoFACT, which provides funding for a variety of pop videos, and the Canadian version of Bravo! offers money for the creation of jazz and classical music videos.

Once again, there is a Canadian content requirement on Canadian television and cable channels, although the average Canadian can also see a host of channels from across the border. Most Canadians—the most "cabled" television audience on earth—have between 50 and 60 channels to choose from.

Both of Canada's major TV networks, CBC and CTV, have spotty records as producers of music specials. But the public network, CBC, has usually had one major prime-time musical variety series up and running and broadcasts the annual Juno Awards (Canada's equivalent of the Grammys), and CTV traditionally aired the Canadian Country Music Association's annual award shows. Both of these shows get audiences of between 1.2 and 1.8 million viewers.

Canada also has a variety of music publications aimed at broader audiences than the trade mags; the longest running is *Canadian Musician*, more recently joined by a plethora of magazines and fanzines aimed at individual segments of the music market.

Almost all of Canada's daily newspapers, like those in the United States, cover pop music on a continuing basis, and the national news agency, Canadian Press (and its broadcasting arm, Broadcast News), provides extensive coverage. The country's largest chain of daily newspapers, Southam, also covers the music scene with news, commentary, and feature articles.

To touch back on Canadian radio, there are slightly fewer than 500 stations in the country, including CBC radio outlets in all major markets. Two CBC radio channels provide a wide variety of regional and national music programs, including thoughtful, well-crafted specialist shows covering classical, blues, jazz, and alternative pop/rock. In addition, the CBC succeeds in topping a 60% CanCon level, although it is legally not required to exceed the current 35%.

QUEBEC: VIVE LA DIFFÉRENCE

For slightly under one out of every four Canadians, French is the mother tongue, and nowhere else in the world (and that includes France) is the language more promoted and protected than in Quebec. In addition to Canadian content rules, broadcasters in the province with French-language licenses must play 65% French-language music.

Although Montreal, the province's capital, is thoroughly bilingual, there are still people surviving in the city whose knowledge of French is less than that of an average grade-school child in Omaha. Traditionally, Montreal, a sophisticated, European-style city, has acted as a breaking-in point for many international acts—Pink Floyd and Dire Straits among them—in North America.

For all that, the rest of this part of Canada remains an island of "francophonie" in an English-speaking continent, and as a result, the music scene in Quebec is dramatically different.

Demographically, Quebecers buy more records than anyone else in North America, and they also buy records far longer into their life cycles. English-speaking North Americans, as a rule, stop being major record purchasers when they have acquired spouses, homes, cars, and children—but this isn't the case in Quebec, where people go on buying records well into their 50s and later.

The results of this demographic quirk is that Quebec has an entirely separate French-speaking music industry, with dozens of artists at any given time who may sell platinum (100,000 copies) or more and yet who are unknowns only 350 miles down the highway in Toronto and as a result never venture near the place. Superstar artists in Quebec tend to see Europe, rather than the rest of Canada or the United States, as the logical market to expand into.

LIVE MUSIC IN CANADA: A MATTER OF GEOGRAPHY, TAXES, AND BORDER FEES

The leader of the Downchild Blues Band, for three decades Canada's best known band in the idiom, struck a chord with musicians when he explained his band's success: "Once we made a record," he said, "it was just a matter of geography."

And the geography will certainly challenge any U.S. musician who's used to working in the population-rich areas of the stateside music scene. There are, basically, three major urban centers in Canada. From east to west, there is Montreal (with its own peculiarities), Toronto (the music business capital of the country), and Vancouver, some 2,370 miles to the west. Domestic air fares within Canada are high, gas is expensive, and the distances are brutal. Touring in Canada is not for the faint-hearted or for those without deep pockets.

Distance keeps U.S. touring musicians from other centers in the Maritimes—Halifax, Moncton, Charlottetown—although a few bands make the trek when they're in northern Maine. Moving west, hitting Quebec City and Montreal is possible from upstate Vermont, while the southern Ontario markets—primarily Toronto, but including Kingston, Ottawa, London, Kitchener-Waterloo, and Windsor—are all easily accessible via Buffalo or Detroit.

Working one's way north over the top of Lake Superior is a long and not very profitable haul into Winnipeg—a decent enough market, but one best approached out of Minneapolis-St.Paul. Other markets within a long day's drive of Winnipeg are Regina and Saskatoon, and then you've another long day before you hit Calgary and Edmonton.

Still heading west, it's time to cross the Rockies into Vancouver, although most bands who play that market see it as a logical extension of the Seattle/Portland markets and the top end of a West Coast tour.

Geography aside, touring in Canada is not helped by the Department of Manpower and Immigration, which levies an exorbitant fee for musicians (and other entertainers, from strippers to opera singers) to cross the border in the first place.

With contracts in hand—and there's no way you're getting in without one—you will be charged (as of 1999) $150.00 (Canadian) if you're an individual performer, and $450.00 if you're in a group of between 2 and 14 members, if you cross at the same border point at the same time. If, by chance, there are more than 15 of you, you'll enter Canada free of charge—basically because the hockey, basketball, football, and baseball teams have greater lobbying power than musicians. Of course, this is discriminatory—Elton John can perform in Canada for a million dollars (and he does) and take away all but 15% percent (which he must leave behind for federal income tax); a baby band making its first foray into the bar scene will probably earn $400 for a gig, less 15%, and less the border fee.

On your arrival, you'd better have—in addition to your contracts—passport (or at worst, picture ID), cash to pay duties on merchandise you may be bringing in to sell in Canada, and a list of all your instruments and gear (including the original cost and the serial numbers).

Add to all of this the value of the Canadian dollar, and the lesson is obvious: Performing in Canada, for foreign artists, is something only for the rich or for those with rich record companies behind them!

For complete data on working in Canada, check with the Canadian consulate nearest you; there's an excellent chapter on crossing the border in Jeri Goldstein's valuable 1999 book *How to Be Your Own Booking Agent* (New Music Times, Box 1105, Charlottesville, VA 22902).

ROYALTY COLLECTION IN CANADA

Canada manages its royalty collection process quite differently from the United States. Performing rights are handled by a single organization rather than the three that operate in the United States. SOCAN (Society of Composers, Authors and Music Publishers of Canada) is based in Toronto, with major offices in Montreal and Vancouver and regional offices in Edmonton and Halifax. It is the result of the merger of two organizations, one of which was initially founded by ASCAP and PRS, the British society, and the other, which was originally a branch of BMI.

Songwriters and publishers in Canada join SOCAN and may then elect which of the three U.S. organizations (ASCAP, BMI, or SESAC) will represent them in the United States. If they do not make a choice, ASCAP will collect their royalties and pass them to SOCAN for distribution. Meanwhile, SOCAN administers performing rights in Canada for all the members of all three American organizations plus, of course, the members of all other foreign societies.

In Canada, performing rights income on a per capita basis is considerably higher than it is in the United States (partly because the overhead of running a single society is considerably less than the cost of running three organizations). A total of 2.5% of all concert revenues is payable to SOCAN—and royalties are payable to the composers of the music performed, regardless of which society they are members of.

Radio revenues to SOCAN equal 3.2% of gross revenues, slightly higher than U.S. stations' pay to the three organizations. But overall revenues, based on the income of 500-odd radio stations (compared to some 15,000 in the United States), are obviously much smaller.

Total SOCAN revenues now exceed $100 million (Canadian) per year, with some 55% delivered to performing rights organizations outside the country (the overhead is some 16%, and the remainder is distributed to Canadian members).

Mechanical royalties and synchronization rights in Canada are administered by CMRRA (Canadian Musical Reproduction Rights Agency), owned and operated by the Canadian Music Publishers Association, which operates parallel to the Harry Fox organization.

COPYRIGHTS

In a couple of copyright areas, Canada is leading the way in North America. Legally, revisions to the Copyright Act allow for the collection of a levy on blank recordable media (cassettes, CD-Rs, and any other copying methods to come), with the revenues passed to the music industry. At the same time, the act officially legalizes personal copying.

Uncertainty surrounds aspects of the Copyright Act pertaining to *neighboring rights* and to the levy on recordable media. Long a familiar part of the music industry in Europe, neighboring rights allow a payment for radio play of recordings to the artist (as opposed to composers and publishers, who at present receive earnings via SOCAN). Radio stations, of course, bitterly oppose the imposition of additional tariffs.

At the turn of the century, Canada's Copyright Board, the three-person judicial panel, still had to decide such issues as (a) what the tariff would be, (b) exactly what collective would administer the revenue stream, and (c) who would receive the income and in what proportion among the artist, the record company, the producer, and the session musicians. Such decisions are expected to be ironed out early in the new millennium.

One more point must be made: Foreign record companies, composers, and musicians cannot expect to see any revenue from either neighboring rights or a tape levy unless they have similar laws and agree to reciprocal arrangements. And the chances of the United States applying either of these extensions of copyright law are remote.

CANADA: A HOTHOUSE FOR TALENT— AND A CHALLENGE FOR U.S. MUSICIANS

Canadian talent has become so ubiquitous on the international scene that most people simply don't know (or probably care) whether Shania Twain, Alanis Morissette, Céline Dion, the Barenaked Ladies, Bryan Adams, Sarah McLachlan, the Moffats, Crash Test Dummies, David Foster, Deborah Cox, Dan Ayckroyd of Blues Brothers fame, or the Wilkinsons are Canadian or not. That's not all, of course. Canadian pioneers go back all the way to Guy Lombardo, if you want to go back that far.

But whether or not the idea of government involvement in the arts makes sense to you—and it remains a discussion starter at any Canadian event where more than two or three musicians or businesspeople are gathered together— there is little doubt that the system seems to work. Ambitious, focused, dedicated artists with a unique sound and good songs do rise, like cream, to the top, and Canada's current crop of star-bright talent, as the new millennium begins, is stronger than it has ever been.

At the same time, Canada remains a tiny market for U.S. artists to tackle, as well as one that presents considerable hurdles.

For all that, audiences north of the border have always extended a warm welcome and encouraging applause to artists from around the world, with a particular regard for our friends from the United States.

Richard Flohil is a Toronto-based music industry veteran, who works as a writer, concert promoter, and publicist. He is a founding editor of *The Record*, one of Canada's two music business trade publications, and worked with SOCAN for almost 25 years.

TABLE I   Twenty-One People to Help You Access the Canadian Music Business

David Basskin, General Manager, Canadian Musical Reproduction Rights Agency (CMRRA), roughly equivalent to the Harry Fox Agency. Ph: (416) 926-1966
    E-mail: inquiries@cmrra.ca, URL http://www.cmrra.ca

Rob Bennett, Vice President, Universal Concerts, Canada's largest concert and club promoter.
Ph: (416) 260-5700
    E-mail: rob.bennett@umusic.com, URL http://www.universalconcerts.ca

Daniel Caudeiron, Black Music Association Canada (BMAC). Ph: (416) 463-8880

Brian Chater, President, Canadian Independent Record Production Association (CIRPA). This organization represents independent music organizations. Ph: (416) 485-3152
    E-mail: cirpa@cirpa.ca, URL http://www.cirpa.ca

Brad Clark, Executive Director, Songwriters Association of Canada (SAC). Ph: (905) 681-5320
    E-mail: sac@goodmedia.com, URL http://www.goodmedia.com/sac

Gary Cristall, Sound Recording Grants Coordinator, Canada Council for the Arts. Ph: 1-800-263-5588
    E-mail gary.cristall@canadacouncil.ca, URL http://www.canadacouncil.ca

Neill Dixon, General Manager, Canadian Music Week. (Canada's major industry gathering, trade show, and showcase series, held annually in March.) Ph: (416) 695-2553
    E-mail: cmw@ican.net, URL http://www.cmw.net

Daisy Falle, President, Canadian Academy of Recording Arts & Sciences (CARAS). (CARAS organizes the Juno Awards, Canada's equivalent of the Grammys.) (416) 485-3135
    E-mail: caras@juno-awards.ca, URL http://www.juno-awards.ca

David Farrell, Publisher, *The Record,* Canada's major music industry publication, available online at www.therecord.com. Ph: (416) 322-5777
    E-mail: record@ican.net

Sam Feldman, CEO, S.L. Feldman & Associates, Ltd. (the largest agency in the country handling pop and rock acts). Ph: (604) 734-5945
    E-mail: feldman@slfa.com, URL http://www.slfa.com

Andrew Flynn, pop columnist, Canadian Press Wire Service, the major newspaper wire service.
Ph: (416) 507-2145
    E-mail: aflynn@cp.org, URL http://www.cp.org

Sheila Hamilton, Executive Director, Canadian Country Music Association (CCMA), equivalent of Country Music Association.
Ph: (905) 850-1144
    E-mail: country@ccma.org, URL http://www.ccma.org

(continued)

Ralph James, Jack Ross, The Agency Group, Canadian branch of U.K.-based agency; handles rock, blues, and pop acts. Ph: (416) 368-5599
E-mail: agency@direct.com

Andy McLean, General Manager, NXNE. (Another major showcase opportunity, this event parallels Austin's famed SXSW.) Ph: (416) 469-0986
E-mail: inquiries@nxne.com, URL http://www.nxne.com

Heather Ostertag, Executive Director, Foundation to Assist Canadian Talent on Records (FACTOR), provides funding for Canadian recording initiatives. Ph: (416) 368-8678
E-mail: factor@factor.ca, URL http://www.factor.ca

Gilles Paquin, Paquin Entertainment Agency, handles adult contemporary and family artists.
Ph: (204) 697-0650
E-mail: info@paquinentertainment.com, URL http://www.paquinentertainment.com

Robert Pilon, Association québecoise de l'industrie du disque, du spectacle, et de la vidéo (ADISQ). This group represents all aspects of music in Quebec. Ph: (514) 842-5147
E-mail: adisq@mlink.net, URL http://www.adisq.com

Brian Robertson, President, Canadian Recording Industry Association (CRIA), the Canadian equivalent of RIAA. Ph: (416) 967-7272
E-mail: cria@interlog.com

Michael Rock, General Manager, Society of Composers, Authors and Music Publishers of Canada (SOCAN), the Canadian equivalent of ASCAP, BMI, SESAC. Ph: (416) 445-8700
E-mail: socan@socan.ca, URL http://www.socan.ca

Ed Skira, Publisher, *The Chart*, the country's best alternative music publication. Ph: (416) 363-3101
E-mail: chart@chartnet.com, URL http://www.chartnet.com

Joan Walters, Bureau Chief, Southam Press. Ph: (416) 202-6800
E-mail: jwalters@stb.southam.ca

INTERNATIONAL COPYRIGHT: The World Market Outside the United States

Phil Hardy
Dave Laing

The increasing integration of the global economy has meant that many of the issues facing the music business elsewhere in the world are similar to those faced by the U.S. music industry. In particular, the growing importance of the Internet as a means of communication and commerce presents the music industry everywhere with new problems and challenges. Indeed, the early evidence of both "hybrid" Internet commerce—ordering goods from a Web site, which are then posted to the consumer—and the full digital delivery of products, such as music, is that Internet commerce knows no national frontiers.

Nevertheless, there remain important cultural and legal differences between the music industries of the United States and other countries. For example, performing rights for all sections of the industry tend to be more strongly developed in Europe where the royalties collected from broadcasters, concert promoters, and other music users are greater per capita than in the United States. At the same time, representatives of U.S. composers and publishers have become increasingly critical of the high level of deductions made by copyright societies in Europe for spending on cultural activities and, less defensibly, welfare payments to their own members. Bodies such as ASCAP and BMI point out that a large proportion of these deductions come from royalties earned by American music in Europe but that U.S. songwriters do not benefit from the resulting cultural spending. In response, the European societies point out that it is only because they make such cultural subsidies that they have the ear of their governments and are able to ensure that composers, including U.S. authors and composers, are fully rewarded for their efforts.

Another important contrast is that record companies and recording artists outside the United States have performance rights that enable them to collect copyright fees from radio and television stations. The strength of the broadcasting lobby in the United States has so far meant that such rights have not been introduced there.

Over the past 50 years, foreign markets have become increasingly more important to the U.S. music industry for two reasons: (a) Since the 1950s, American pop music has found bigger and bigger audiences around the globe; (b) since the 1960s, the proportion of world record sales by the U.S. music industry has been slowly falling as the music industries first of Europe and then of Asia and Latin America have grown to maturity. Sales of sound recordings of U.S. repertoire are particularly strong in Europe and Australasia, where they represent between 25% and 50% of the market. In fact, some American artists sell more albums overseas than at home. Similarly, a growing proportion of the royalties collected by ASCAP, BMI, and SESAC, the U.S. performance rights organizations, comes from abroad. These organizations receive monies for the use of American music overseas through bilateral contracts with other national societies.

U.S. copyright owners have benefited in recent years from the proliferation of new music radio and television stations in most parts of the world. In many countries, this is the result of the abolition of state-owned broadcasting monopolies, while the spread of satellite and digital technologies has encouraged the launch of regional music stations and channels in Asia, Europe, and Latin America by MTV and other companies. The growth in the quantity of music on the world's airwaves has increased the amount of performance royalties collected by national copyright societies. In 1996, broadcasting provided $1.5 billion out of the $6.2 billion global revenues of the music publishing industry, according to figures published by the National Music Publishers Association.

In the 1970s, record sales in the United States accounted for half the world market by value. By the late 1990s, this had fallen to 32%. Nevertheless, the United States remains the largest national **soundcarrier** market by far. The next largest is Japan, followed by Germany, the United Kingdom, and France. Outside Japan and Western Europe, the most important foreign markets are those of Brazil, Canada, and Australia.

TABLE 1   Recorded Music: Top 10 Territories by 1997 Share of World Market

	Millions (in U.S. $)	% Share
United States	11,906.0	31.3
Japan	6,261.7	16.4
Germany	2,836.8	7.4
United Kingdom	2,729.7	7.2
France	2,199.5	5.8
Brazil	1,199.1	3.1
Canada	977.5	2.6
Australia	739.1	1.9
Netherlands	600.1	1.6
Spain	599.9	1.6

SOURCE: International Federation of the Phonographic Industry (IFPI).

TABLE 2   Music Publishing: Top 10 Territories by 1996 Share of World Market

	Millions (in U.S. $)	% Share
United States	1,423.63	22.9
Germany	931.96	15.0
Japan	728.81	11.7
France	655.19	10.5
United Kingdom	521.18	8.4
Italy	387.40	6.2
Netherlands	302.53	4.9
Austria	145.61	2.3
Spain	143.83	2.3
Canada	114.65	1.8

SOURCE: National Music Publishers Association (NMPA).

Within Europe, the European Union (EU) forms a single market for trading purposes. Although most major recording companies maintain national offices for A&R (artist and repertoire), promotion, and marketing purposes, European manufacturing and production is increasingly centralized. The five largest recording companies also route much of their mechanical royalty payments through central licensing agreements covering several or all European nations.

The fastest-growing markets in the 1990s were those of Southeast Asia. Sales of CDs and cassettes there grew by more than 50% between 1992 and 1997, although this growth was subsequently affected by the general economic problems in the region. Nevertheless, the increasing demand for pop music in such countries as Singapore, Taiwan, and Thailand, plus the decline in the amount of cassette piracy in the region, have made them important targets for U.S. recording companies and artists. Many of these countries are now included in the world tours of top performers; in some cases, separate marketing campaigns have been developed for Asia. Mainly because of language differences, U.S. music takes a smaller share of Asian markets than of European ones. The most important pan-Asian language for pop music is Chinese, in both its Cantonese and Mandarin versions. The largest potential market is mainland China itself, which is slowly emerging from a long period of centralized state control and widespread piracy of both cassettes and CDs.

The market in counterfeit and pirate copies of foreign as well as local recordings has been the biggest barrier to the formation of successful music industries in many parts of the world. A 1998 report from the International Intellectual Property Association (a U.S.-based lobbying coalition of American copyright-based industry groups) detailed some $10.8 billion in alleged losses to U.S. companies from "copyright piracy." Of this, almost half came from unauthorized copying of computer software. Pirated music accounted for about 15% of the total, or $1.6 billion. The piracy problem remains particularly acute in Africa where low levels of disposable income and political instability in many countries mean that the legitimate music industry has established itself in only a half-dozen nations. The situation is better in Latin America, notably in Brazil, Argentina, and Chile, although inflation and other economic problems have negatively affected the music industry in most other countries in the region.

The sheer size of the U.S. music market has made it a target for foreign pop and rock acts ever since the Beatles spearheaded the "British Invasion" of the 1960s. Although overseas artists account for only about 10% of U.S. soundcarrier sales, in dollar value this amount is greater than most domestic markets elsewhere in the world. However, only a small percentage of successful acts from abroad achieve success in the United States—due partly to differences in national musical tastes and partly to the very different methods of marketing and promotion found in North America compared with Europe or Australia. Foreign artists are therefore highly dependent on the local knowledge of their U.S. labels and promoters; it follows that independent labels in Europe and elsewhere are keen to work with individuals familiar with the U.S. industry. Graduates of music business programs might possibly find employment abroad in this capacity.

INTERNATIONAL COPYRIGHT AGREEMENTS

There are two kinds of international copyright agreements. First, there is a series of *copyright conventions* whose membership is open to all nations willing to accept their terms. The conventions (or treaties) are administered by United Nations' organizations, principally WIPO (World Intellectual Property Organization). Second, there are *bilateral* or *multilateral agreements* on levels of copyright protection among groups of countries that are trading partners.

Copyright Conventions

Copyright owners are affected by four important international conventions. Two (the Berne Convention and the International Copyright Convention) concern the rights of authors and composers, and two (the Geneva or Phonograms Convention and the Rome Convention) are concerned with the interests of *neighboring rights* owners such as performers, record producers, and broadcasters. The United States is also a member of a regional agreement, the Buenos Aires Convention.

Berne Convention

The oldest of these four is the Berne Convention for the Protection of Literary and Artistic Works, signed in 1886 and amended six times since. The main purpose of the amendments has been to enable authors' rights to keep pace with new uses of their works brought about by technological change. The Berlin revision of 1908 incorporated references to photography, cinema film, and sound recording. The Rome Act of the convention in 1928 extended authors' control of their work to sound broadcasting, and television was brought within the scope of the convention at Brussels in 1948.

The concept of an author's *moral rights* was first included in 1928. Later revisions in Stockholm (1967) and Paris (1971) concentrated on such issues as the *compulsory licensing* of films and possible exemptions from parts of the convention for Third World countries. The most recent addition to Berne is the Copyright Treaty Agreement of 1996, which provides for copyright protection in relation to the Internet and other digital platforms.

Nine countries signed the original Berne document, seven of them European. By the end of the 20th century, there were over 130 signatories to the convention. By acceding to the convention, each signatory agreed in principle to incorporate the provisions of the convention into its national law. But there are significant limits to this process and to the protection a Berne signatory can provide for works of citizens of other Berne states.

Berne provides minimum standards of protection that may be increased in national law. A number of its provisions are optional—for example, the granting of "moral rights" (such as the right of an author to be properly identified and to insist that any editing of a work preserves its integrity). When the United States finally joined the Berne Convention in 1989, pressure from film industry interests ensured that the country did not accede to the moral rights part of the treaty.

Reciprocal Treatment. Although the purpose of the Berne Convention is that each country should provide protection for foreign authors within its own copyright law, these rights can be adopted into national law in two distinct ways. *National treatment* for foreign authors means simply that these copyright owners will receive the same level of protection as domestic authors. But a Berne Convention member can also decide to grant *reciprocal treatment.* This means that foreign authors will get only the level of protection that is granted in their own country. The most prominent example of reciprocal treatment for authors concerns the private copying or home-taping levies that exist in a number of European countries. The only foreign composers entitled to share in the distribution of these levies are those from countries that also have a blank tape levy in place.

Broadcasting Right Options. Another crucial "opt-out" for national governments was written into the Berne Convention's broadcasting clause. The general rights of authors granted by the convention gave them the power to "authorize or prohibit" the use of their work. By the late 1920s, the radio industry had itself become a powerful force in Europe, and music was one of its most important sources of program material.

When the issue of broadcasting rights for composers was considered by the Berne Convention nations, a strong lobby favored substituting a compulsory license for the prohibition right. Under this system, the copyright owner is compelled by law to allow works to be used, subject to appropriate payment from the music user. Rather than making this substitution, the Berne Convention countries decided to allow each national government to opt for one or the other in relation to broadcasting. By allowing countries to operate a compulsory license procedure, the Berne Convention ensured a constant supply of music for radio, even when there was a dispute over royalty payments. Songwriters and publishers were obliged to permit broadcasters' use of their work, subject only to the payment by radio stations of equitable remuneration. The ultimate decision on what constitutes equitable remuneration is made in most countries by a government-appointed tribunal or special court.

Film Authorship. The definition of *authorship* itself came into question in 1928 when the nature of cinematographic works was under discussion. Prior to this, the Berne Convention had accepted that an author of a book, play, or song was a single individual or a partnership of named individuals. The author had a separate existence from the publisher,whose role was to put the work into circulation. The collaborative nature of filmmaking made it more difficult, however, to locate a single individual as author; it was decided that the definition of the author of a film should be a matter for decision by each member of the convention.

Buenos Aires Convention

At the start, the Berne Convention was almost exclusively a union of European countries. Subsequent to its adoption, several attempts were made by countries in the Americas to conclude a similar copyright agreement. These concluded in the Buenos Aires Convention of 1910. Its members included the United States, Argentina, Brazil, Chile, Colombia, Costa Rica, the Dominican Republic, Ecuador, Guatemala, Haiti, Honduras, Nicaragua, the Republic of Panama, Paraguay, Peru, and Uruguay. Under this convention, compliance with the copyright law of the country of first publication qualifies the work for protection in the other member countries. In addition, each work must carry a notice indicating that the property rights in the work are reserved. This requirement has traditionally been satisfied by American nations with the inclusion of the words "all rights reserved"as part of the copyright notice.

Universal Copyright Convention

Although the Buenos Aires Convention governs U.S. copyright relations with most American nations, the treaty is unlikely to attract additional members because of the establishment of the Universal Copyright Convention (UCC). The United States was a founding member of the UCC in 1955.

Because the sponsor of the UCC, the United Nations, wished to attract a maximum number of adherents, the number of exclusive rights granted under this convention are held to a minimum level of "adequate and effective protection." According to the UCC, such protection includes "basic rights ensuring the author's economic interests, including the exclusive right to authorize reproduction by any means, public performance and broadcasting." Formal notification of copyright protections should be indicated by having all relevant copies bear the copyright symbol (©), the name of the copyright proprietor, and the year of first publication—in such a manner as to provide reasonable notice of claim to copyright.

One of the goals of the UCC was to avoid competition with other prevailing international copyright agreements, particularly Berne and Buenos Aires. Where provisions differ, the UCC provides that "the most recently formulated convention" shall prevail.

Rome Convention

The 1961 Rome Convention for the Protection of Performers, Producers of Phonograms and Broadcasting Organizations put record producers (i.e., recording companies) and performers on the international map as rights *owners* as opposed to rights *users*.

The Rome Convention confirmed the rights of both performers of music and record producers to control the reproduction of their work and its public performance. It set a minimum period of copyright protection at 20 years. Today, most national laws protect sound recordings for 50 years, and this figure was included in the 1996 Performances and Phonograms Treaty agreed by a committee of WIPO. The 1996 treaty also extended protection for neighboring right owners in relation to the Internet and other digital platforms.

Broadcasting Rights. On broadcasting, the Rome Convention followed Berne and provided for a compulsory license with equitable remuneration. Both the compulsory license and the 20-year minimum represented a concession to broadcasters who wished to see recordings fall into the **public domain** and therefore become free of copyright royalties as quickly as possible. Signatories to the Rome Convention could also opt out of granting broadcasting rights to producers and performers altogether. Monaco and Luxembourg, two small European countries, have exercised this option; the result is that they have powerful music radio stations broadcasting to neighboring countries. The Rome Convention left to national laws the basis on which broadcasting royalties should be shared between record producers and performers.

Membership. In the first 45 years of its existence, the Rome Convention was joined by some 60 states, less than half the membership of Berne after 100 years. The relationship between "contracting" and "noncontracting" states is complex, notably in relation to broadcasting royalties. As with Berne, Rome provides a fundamental national treatment for performers, producers, and broadcasters of other contracting states.

Rights owners from noncontracting states may also share in royalties if the recording in question received "simultaneous publication" in the contracting state. *Simultaneous* is defined here as within 30 days of the recording being released in its country of origin. Any contracting country may, however, drop the criterion of "publication" of a recording and replace it with one of *first fixation*. This term refers to the geographical location of the studio where the recording was created. To adopt this criterion means to exclude all recordings from noncontracting countries from the share-out of royalties.

At the time of writing, the United States is not a member of the Rome Convention.

To adopt the criterion of first fixation, as such countries as Finland, Sweden, France, and Italy have done, means that performers and producers of U.S. recordings cannot benefit from airplay of their works in those countries—though under the Berne Convention, royalties must of course be paid to U.S. songwriters.

Geneva Phonograms Convention

The Rome Convention provided broad protection against copyright infringement; however, it was drafted at a period when the piracy of sound recordings was still a relatively minor problem for the music industry. Although unauthorized copies of vinyl records had been produced in earlier decades, it was the arrival of the compact tape cassette in 1963 that provided the technology for music piracy to become big business. By the end of the 1960s, it was clear that the piracy and counterfeiting of prerecorded cassettes were becoming endemic, and pressure grew from the music industry and some governments for a new international treaty specifically designed to deal with piracy.

The result was the 1971 Convention for the Protection of Producers of Phonograms Against Unauthorized Duplication of Their Phonograms, known more briefly as the Phonograms Convention. This treaty added new import and distribution rights to those already granted in the Rome Convention. Record producers could now stop illegal imports and take action against wholesalers and retailers as well as those who manufactured illegal copies. The Phonograms Convention gained the adherence of 36 countries by 1983 and 47 by 1998.

Multilateral and Bilateral Agreements

The recognition by governments of the economic importance of the music business and other copyright-based industries has meant that copyright protection is now frequently a consideration in trade agreements between nations. The most far-reaching of these agreements is TRIPS (Trade Related Aspects of Intellectual Property Rights, Including Trade in Counterfeit Goods). This is one chapter of the treaty agreed to by more than 120 countries at the conclusion of the Uruguay Round of the General Agreement on Tariffs and Trade (GATT) in 1993. First negotiated in 1948, GATT is an international treaty designed to promote and police free trade on a worldwide basis. The GATT treaty is renegotiated about every 10 years; the 1986 Uruguay round of discussions, named after the country in which the discussions started, incorporated trade in intellectual property for the first time.

Many of the TRIPS treaty's 73 clauses echoed the Berne and Rome Conventions in providing fundamental rights for authors, performers, and producers. TRIPS includes detailed provisions on the role of customs services and courts in dealing with piracy. The treaty makes allowances for the difficulties of developing countries by permitting them to phase in the TRIPS provisions over 5 or 10 years. Broadly, the treaty pleased Western copyright owners by opening up Third World markets in a more comprehensive way than before.

A second forum for international copyright treaties has been within the context of the growing number of free trade areas embracing several nation states. Here, the principle is that each country that is a member of a free trade area or "single market" must apply the same standards of copyright protection as its fellow members. The most important examples of the single-market systems are the North American Free Trade Agreement (NAFTA) and the EU. NAFTA's members are the United States, Canada, and Mexico; the EU includes an increasing number of the countries of Western and Northern Europe. The intent of NAFTA is to end trade barriers between Mexico, the United States, and Canada. Under NAFTA, the three countries will give national treatment to each other's copyright owners. NAFTA, however, specifically permits the continuation of the Canadian government's program of state support for the arts, which includes an airtime quota for Canadian music.

The EU program for a single market dates from the late 1980s. It includes a scheme to **harmonize** the copyright laws of its 15 member countries and the two countries (Norway and Switzerland) associated with the EU in the European Economic Area. The harmonization scheme consisted of a number of directives that, once agreed on, would be incorporated into each country's national law. Those of direct interest to the music industry included directives on rental, private copying, the transborder aspects of cable and satellite broadcasting, and the equalization of the duration of copyright protection at 70 years for authors and 50 years from publication for neighboring rights owners. The launch of the Euro marked a further stage of the integration of the EU as a single market. In 1999, 11 countries (Austria, Belgium, Finland, France, Germany, Ireland, Italy, Luxembourg, the Netherlands, Portugal, and Spain) linked their currencies to the Euro as a means of creating a single currency zone. A further 20 countries, including Russia, Poland, and Hungary, have applied to join the EU, and they are required to harmonize their copyright laws with those of the EU as a condition of membership.

Bilateral Treaties

Another method of improving copyright protection internationally is the use of bilateral treaties. The United States has made the greatest use of this strategy through the Special 301 provision of the 1988 Omnibus Trade and Competitiveness Act. This permits the United States Trade Representative (USTR) to nominate "Priority Foreign Countries" whose trading practices are alleged to be harmful to U.S. industries, including those like music that are dependent on the protection of intellectual property. Once designated, nations can be subject to trade sanctions if they fail to improve their commercial and trading rules.

As a preliminary stage of its activities, in 1989 the USTR set up a Watch List and a Priority Watch List of countries felt to be unfair trading partners of the United States. Two years later, three countries—Thailand, China, and India—

were the first to become Priority Foreign Countries for their failure to protect U.S. copyright material adequately. An intensive 6-month period of negotiation and investigation followed. Afterward, the governments of China and India announced plans to improve copyright protection. China joined the Berne Convention in 1992, and the Indian government agreed to ease restrictions on the operations of foreign companies. In subsequent years, the Special 301 Priority Foreign Countries list was lengthened to include such countries as Argentina, Bulgaria, Taiwan, and South Korea.

INTERGOVERNMENTAL BODIES AND INTERNATIONAL INDUSTRY ORGANIZATIONS

World Intellectual Property Organization

The World Intellectual Property Organization (WIPO) is an organ of the United Nations, with headquarters in Geneva, Switzerland. WIPO is the body responsible for administering the Berne and Rome Conventions as well as other conventions dealing with patents, trademarks, semiconductor varieties, and plant varieties and seeds. WIPO's meetings provide a forum for discussions about the updating or redrafting of copyright conventions in response to technological developments such as those that have taken place in the recording, duplication, and distribution of music since the arrival of digital technology. In the light of such technologies, in 1991 a WIPO committee met to consider the feasibility of a "protocol" to the Berne Convention. The result was the publication in 1996 of two new international treaties, one on copyright and one on performance and phonograms. After ratification by 30 national governments, these treaties added new rights to those already guaranteed by the Berne and Rome Conventions.

World Trade Organization

The task of implementing and policing the GATT and TRIPS agreements has been entrusted to the World Trade Organization (WTO), which is a successor body to the former GATT secretariat. The similarity between the TRIPS agreement on enforcement and that proposed by WIPO is an indication of the convergence of the international trade organization and the international copyright bodies.

In relation to the TRIPS agreement, the WTO is responsible for resolving disputes or complaints concerning noncompliance made by one country against another. The WTO must also ensure that developing countries upgrade their copyright laws to TRIPS standards within the time limits allowed to them.

International Confederation of Societies of Authors and Composers

The International Confederation of Societies of Authors and Composers (CISAC) groups together organizations from more than 60 countries. CISAC has a small secretariat based in Paris; the confederation is run by an executive board composed of representatives from many affiliated societies. In addition to convening a world congress every 2 years, CISAC's main role is to encourage cooperation among its members and to help form new authors' societies, particularly in developing countries and in the former communist nations.

The key issues for CISAC include evolving a common policy for protecting copyright in the face of advancing technologies and the rationalization of documentation, so that musical works can be more easily identified worldwide and payments can be allocated more efficiently.

To help new societies, CISAC maintains a regional office in Singapore that in recent years has worked closely with composers in Vietnam, Indonesia, and the People's Republic of China. There is also a "twinning" scheme whereby established authors' societies undertake to advise and train officials of newly established ones.

Bureau international des sociétés gérant les droits d'enregistrement et de reproduction mécanique

Founded in 1929, the Bureau international des sociétés gérant les droits d'enregistrement et de reproduction mécanique (BIEM) is another grouping that represents the interests of composers and music publishers. In regular negotiations with the IFPI (International Federation of the Phonographic Industry, the global recording industry body), BIEM sets the standard rate at which mechanical royalties are paid in most of Europe and Latin America. The BIEM-IFPI rate does not apply in the United States, Canada, or the United Kingdom.

(text continues on p. 566)

TABLE 3   Foreign Affiliates of the Harry Fox Agency, Inc., as of January 1, 1999

Society/Agency	Territories
ACUM Authors, Composers, and Music Publishers Association (Tel Aviv, Israel)	Israel
AEPI Hellenic Society for the Protection of Intellectual Property S.A. (Athens, Greece)	Greece
AMCOS Australasian Mechanical Copyright Owners Society, Ltd. (St. Leonards, Australia)	Australia Fiji New Zealand Pacific Island Territories Papua New Guinea
ARTISJUS Magyar Szerzoi Jogvedo Iroda Egyesulet (Budapest, Hungary)	Hungary
AUSTRO MECHANA[a] (Vienna, Austria)	Austria
CASH Composers and Authors Society of Hong Kong, Ltd. (Central, Hong Kong)	Hong Kong Macau
FILSCAP Filipino Society of Composers, Authors, and Publishers, Inc. (Manila, the Philippines)	Republic of the Philippines
GEMA Gesellschaft Für Musikalische Aufführungs und Mechanische Vervielfältigungsrechte (Munich, Germany)	Bulgaria Germany Poland Romania Turkey
HDS Croatian Composers' Society (Zagreb, Hrvatska [Croatia])	Croatia

JASRAC
Japanese Society for Rights of Authors, Composers & Publishers   Japan
(Tokyo, Japan)

KCI
Yayasan Karya Cipta Indonesia   Republic of Indonesia
(Jakarta, Indonesia)

KOMKA
Korea Music Copyright Association   Republic of Korea
(Seoul, Korea)

MCPS/The Music Alliance
Mechanical Copyright Protection Society, Ltd.   United Kingdom and
(London, United Kingdom)   Northern Ireland
Bahamas
Bermuda
British Virgin Islands
India
Ireland (Eire)
Jamaica
Kenya
Nigeria
Uganda
Zimbabwe[b]

MCSC
Music Copyright Society of China   People's Republic of China
(Beijing, People's Republic of China)

NCB
Nordisk Copyright Bureau   Denmark
(Copenhagen, Denmark)   Finland
Iceland
Norway
Sweden

OSA
Ochranny Svaz Autorsky   Czech Republic
(Czech Republic)

SABAM
Société Belge des auteurs, compositeurs et editeurs   Belgium
(Brussels, Belgium)

SADAIC
La Sociedad Argentina de Autores & Compositores de Musica   Argentina
(Buenos Aires, Argentina)

SARRAL
South African Recording Rights Association, Ltd.   South Africa
(Braamfontein, Republic of South Africa)   Botswana
          Lesotho
          Swaziland

SDRM/SACEM
Société pour l'administration du droit de reproduction mécanique   Andorra
des auteurs, compositeurs et editeurs de musique   Benin
(Neuilly, France)   Burkina Faso
          Cameroon
          Central African Republic
          Chad
          Congo (Brazzaville)
          Côte d'Ivoire
          Djibouti
          Egypt
          Republic of France
          Gabon
          Gambia
          Guinea
          Lebanon
          Luxembourg
          Madagascar
          Mali
          Mauritania
          Monaco
          Morocco
          Niger
          Senegal
          Togo
          Tunisia
          Zaire

SGAE
Sociedad General de Autores de España   Spain
(Madrid, Spain)

SIAE
    Societa Italiana degli Autori ed Editori
    (Rome, Italy)

                    Italy
                    San Marino
                    Vatican City

SOZA
    Slovensky Ochranny Zvav Autorsky
    (Bratislava, Slovak Republic)

                    Slovak Republic

SPA
    Sociedade Portuguesa de Autores
    (Lisbon, Portugal)

                    Azores
                    Madeira
                    Portugal

STEMRA
    (Amsterdam, the Netherlands)

                    Aruba
                    Dutch Antilles
                    Irian Barat
                    The Netherlands
                    Surinam

SUISA
Schweizerische Gesellschaft für die Rechte der Urheber
    Musikalisher Werke
    (Zurich, Switzerland)

                    Liechtenstein
                    Switzerland

In addition to its relations with the foreign affiliates listed above, the Harry Fox Agency (HFA) also coordinates representation in certain foreign territories through its wholly owned subsidiary, the Fox Agency International, Inc., as follows:

Fox Agency International

                    Hong Kong
                    Indonesia
                    Malaysia
                    The Philippines
                    People's Republic of China
                    Singapore
                    South Korea
                    Taiwan
                    Thailand

a. Although the Austro-Mechana repertoire is represented in the United States by HFA, the HFA repertoire is represented in Austria by GEMA.

b. In addition to this list are other selected British Commonwealth and/or former Commonwealth countries, where reasonably practicable.

For the period 1997 to 1999, the BIEM-IFPI contract stipulated a standard rate of 9.1% of the "published price to dealers" of all disc and tape formats. The standard figure is subject to slight variations at national levels, based on local agreements about packaging deductions, including television-advertised albums, the number of tracks on an album, and other factors. Nevertheless, through the BIEM-IFPI contract the level of mechanical royalties paid to songwriters and composers throughout much of the world market is virtually identical.

International Federation of the Phonographic Industry

The need to find a common position in relation to BIEM was the major motivation for the 1933 formation of an international organization to represent recording companies. This was the International Federation of the Phonographic Industry (IFPI), whose first congress in Rome was attended by representatives of national trade organizations from Germany, France, Italy, and the United Kingdom. The federation's statutes defined its objects as

> the defense in the international domain of the interests of the members by preserving their existing rights, statutory or otherwise, and the promotion of new legislation to extend such rights or to create them in those countries where they do not already exist. In general IFPI is concerned to safeguard the present and future welfare of members by means of representation as a federated body in negotiations with and representations to governments and other interested and representative bodies.

Over subsequent years, IFPI has become one of the most skilled lobbyists for copyright reform at the international level. It has NGO (nongovernmental organization) status with the International Labor Organization, UNESCO, and WIPO. IFPI has also established itself as a consultative body with the European Commission.

IFPI now has more than 1,400 member companies in 50 countries. In more than 30 countries, there is a trade organization that constitutes an IFPI National Group. The Recording Industry Association of America (RIAA) is a U.S. affiliate of IFPI.

The policy-making bodies of IFPI are four regional boards in Europe, the Pacific Rim, Latin America, and North America. Each board has representatives from the major international recording companies as well as the leading local independent labels. The secretariat of IFPI is based in London. It provides the industry's official statistics for world disc and tape sales and for global piracy. It also coordinates lobbying for copyright reform and provides logistical support for the negotiations on mechanical royalties with BIEM.

International Federation of Musicians and International Federation of Actors

The two international unions of performers, the International Federation of Musicians (FIM) and the International Federation of Actors (FIA), also have NGO status with WIPO and with the International Labor Office (ILO), another United Nations body. The American Federation of Musicians is a member of FIM; Actors' Equity is a member of FIA.

The principal impact of FIM and FIA on the world music business is through their long-standing agreement with IFPI on the distribution of broadcasting royalties between neighboring rights owners. Under this agreement, the two parties agree to divide equally any broadcasting royalties collected on their joint behalf. In most European countries as well as in Japan, a single collecting society for performers and producers is in operation.

Phil Hardy is Editor and **Dave Laing** is Associate Editor of *Financial Times Music & Copyright*, London.

Part VIII

APPENDIX

APPENDIX

ASCAP Membership Agreement

Agreement made between the Undersigned (for brevity called "*Owner*") and the AMERICAN SOCIETY OF COMPOSERS, AUTHORS AND PUBLISHERS (for brevity called "*Society*"), in consideration of the premises and of the mutual covenants hereinafter contained, as follows:

1. The *Owner* grants to the *Society* for the term hereof, the right to license non-dramatic public performances (as hereinafter defined), of each musical work:

Of which the *Owner* is a copyright proprietor; or

Which the *Owner*, alone, or jointly, or in collaboration with others, wrote, composed, published, acquired or owned; or

In which the *Owner* now has any right, title, interest or control whatsoever, in whole or in part; or

Which hereafter, during the term hereof, may be written, composed, acquired, owned, published or copyrighted by the *Owner*, alone, jointly or in collaboration with others; or

In which the *Owner* may hereafter, during the term hereof, have any right, title, interest or control, whatsoever, in whole or in part.

The right to license the public performance of every such musical work shall be deemed granted to the *Society* by this instrument for the term hereof, immediately upon the work being written, composed, acquired, owned, published or copyrighted.

The rights hereby granted shall include:

(a) All the rights and remedies for enforcing the copyright or copyrights of such musical works, whether such copyrights are in the name of the *Owner* and/or others, as well as the right to sue under such copyrights in the name of the *Society* and/or in the name of the *Owner* and/or others, to the end that the *Society* may effectively protect and be assured of all the rights hereby granted.

(b) The non-exclusive right of public performance of the separate numbers, songs, fragments or arrangements, melodies or selections forming part or parts of musical plays and dramatico-musical compositions, the *Owner* reserving and excepting from this grant the right of performance of musical plays and dramatico-musical compositions in their entirety, or any part of such plays or dramatico-musical compositions on the legitimate stage.

(c) The non-exclusive right of public performance by means of radio broadcasting, telephony, "wired wireless," all forms of synchronism with motion pictures, and/or any method of transmitting sound other than television broadcasting.

(d) The non-exclusive right of public performance by television broadcasting; provided, however, that:

(i) This grant does not extend to or include the right to license the public performance by television broadcasting or otherwise of any rendition or performance of (a) any opera, operetta, musical comedy, play or like production, as such, in whole or in part, or (b) any composition from any opera, operetta, musical comedy, play or like production (whether or not such opera, operetta, musical comedy, play or like production was presented on the stage or in motion picture form) in a manner which recreates the performance of such composition with substantially such distinctive scenery or costume as was used in the presentation of such opera, operetta, musical comedy, play or like production (whether or not such opera, operetta, musical comedy, play or like production was presented on the stage or in motion picture form): provided, how-

ever, that the rights hereby granted shall be deemed to include a grant of the right to license non-dramatic performances of compositions by television broadcasting of a motion picture containing such composition if the rights in such motion picture other than those granted hereby have been obtained from the parties in interest.

(ii) Nothing herein contained shall be deemed to grant the right to license the public performance by television broadcasting of dramatic performances. Any performance of a separate musical composition which is not a dramatic performance, as defined herein, shall be deemed to be a non-dramatic performance. For the purposes of this agreement, a dramatic performance shall mean a performance of a musical composition on a television program in which there is a definite plot depicted by action and where the performance of the musical composition is woven into and carries forward the plot and its accompanying action. The use of dialogue to establish a mere program format or the use of any non-dramatic device merely to introduce a performance of a composition shall not be deemed to make such performances dramatic.

(iii) The definition of the terms "dramatic" and "non-dramatic" performances contained herein are purely for the purposes of this agreement and for the term thereof and shall not be binding upon or prejudicial to any position taken by either of us subsequent to the term hereof or for any purpose other than this agreement.

(e) The *Owner* may at any time and from time to time, in good faith, restrict the radio or television broadcasting of compositions from musical comedies, operas, operettas and motion pictures, or any other composition being excessively broadcast, only for the purpose of preventing harmful effect upon such musical comedies, operas, operettas, motion pictures or compositions, in respect of other interest under the copyrights thereof; provided, however, that the right to grant limited licenses will be given, upon application, as to restricted compositions, if and when the *Owner* is unable to show reasonable hazards to his or its major interests likely to result from such radio or television broadcasting; and provided further that such right to restrict any such composition shall not be exercised for the purpose of permitting the fixing or regulating of fees for the recording or transcribing of such composition, and provided further that in no case shall any charges, "free plugs," or other consideration be required in respect of any permission granted to perform a restricted composition; and provided further that in no event shall any composition, after the initial radio or television broadcast thereof, be restricted for the purpose of confining further radio or television broadcasts thereof to a particular artist, station, network or program. The *Owner* may also at anytime and from time to time, in good faith, restrict the radio or television broadcasting of any composition, as to which any suit has been brought or threatened on a claim that such composition infringes a composition not contained in the repertory of *Society* or on a claim by a non-member of *Society* that *Society* does not have the right to license the public performance of such composition by radio or television broadcasting.

2. The term of this *Agreement* shall be for a period commencing on the date hereof and continuing indefinitely thereafter unless terminated by either party in accordance with the Articles of Association.

3. The *Society* agrees, during the term hereof, in good faith to use its best endeavors to promote and carry out the objects for which it was organized, and to hold and apply all royalties, profits, benefits and advantages arising from the exploitation of the rights assigned to it by its several members, including the *Owner*, to the uses and purposes as

provided in its Articles of Association (which are hereby incorporated by reference), as now in force or as hereafter amended.

4. The *Owner* hereby irrevocably, during the term hereof, authorizes, empowers and vests in the *Society* the right to enforce and protect such rights of public performance under any and all copyrights, whether standing in the name of the *Owner* and/or others, in any and all works copyrighted by the *Owner*, and/or by others; to prevent the infringement thereof, to litigate, collect and receipt for damages arising from infringement, and in its sole judgment to join the *Owner* and/or others in whose names the copyright may stand, as parties plaintiff or defendants in suits or proceedings; to bring suit in the name of the *Owner* and/or in the name of the *Society*, or others in whose name the copyright may stand, or otherwise, and to release, compromise, or refer to arbitration any actions, in the same manner and to the same extent and to all intents and purposes as the *Owner* might or could do, had this instrument not been made.

5. The *Owner* hereby makes, constitutes and appoints the *Society*, or its successor, the *Owner*'s true and lawful attorney, irrevocably during the term hereof, and in the name of the *Society* or its successor, or in the name of the *Owner*, or otherwise, to do all acts, take all proceedings, execute, acknowledge and deliver any and all instruments, papers, documents, process and pleadings that may be necessary, proper or expedient to restrain infringements and recover damages in respect to or for the infringement or other violation of the rights of public performance in such works, and to discontinue, compromise of refer to arbitration any such proceedings or actions, or to make any other disposition of the differences in relation to the premises.

6. The *Owner* agrees from time to time, to execute, acknowledge and deliver to the *Society*, such assurances, powers of attorney or other authorizations or instruments as the *Society* may deem necessary or expedient to enable it to exercise, enjoy and enforce, in its own name or otherwise, all rights and remedies aforesaid.

7. It is mutually agreed that during the term hereof the Board of Directors of the *Society* shall be composed of an equal number of writers and publishers respectively, and that the royalties distributed by the Board of Directors shall be divided into two (2) equal sums, and one (1) each of such sums credited respectively to and for division amongst (a) the writer members, and (b) the publisher members, in accordance with the system of apportionment and distribution of royalties as determined by the Board of Directors in accordance with the Articles of Association as they may be amended from time to time.

8. The *Owner* agrees that the apportionment and distribution of royalties by the *Society* as determined from time to time by the Board of Directors of the *Society*, in case of appeal by him, shall be final, conclusive and binding upon him.

The *Society* shall have the right to transfer the right of review of any apportionment and distribution of royalties from the Board of Directors to any other agency or instrumentality that in its discretion and good judgment it deems best adapted to assuring to the *Society*'s membership a just, fair, equitable and accurate apportionment and distribution of royalties.

The *Society* shall have the right to adopt from time to time such systems, means, methods and formulae for the establishment of a member's apportionment and distribution of royalties as will assure a fair, just and equitable distribution of royalties among the membership.

9. **"Public Performance" Defined**. The term "*public performance*" shall be construed to mean vocal, instrumental and/or mechanical renditions and representations in any manner or by any method whatsoever, including transmissions by radio and television broadcasting stations, transmission by telephony and/or "wired wireless"; and/or reproductions of performances and renditions by means of devices for reproducing sound recorded in synchronism or timed relation with the taking of motion pictures.

10. **"Musical Works" Defined**. The phrase "*musical works*" shall be construed to mean musical compositions and dramatico-musical compositions, the words and music thereof, and the respective arrangements thereof, and the selections therefrom.

11. The powers, rights, authorities and privileges by this instrument vested in the *Society*, are deemed to include the World, provided, however, that such grant of rights for foreign countries shall be subject to any agreements now in effect, a list of which are noted on the reverse side hereof.

12. The grant made herein by the owner is modified by and subject to the provisions of (a) the Amended Final Judgment (Civil Action No. 13-95) dated March 14, 1950 in *U.S.A. v. ASCAP* as further amended by Order dated January 7, 1960, (b) the Final Judgment (Civil Action No. 42-245) in *U.S.A. v. ASCAP*, dated March 14, 1950, and (c) the provisions of the Articles of Association and resolutions of the Board of Directors adopted pursuant to such judgments and order.

SIGNED, SEALED AND DELIVERED, on this ———— of ——————————— , ——————— .
                                        day   month   year

Owner { ————————————————————————————————————
          Sign your name here
          ————————————————————————————————————

Society { AMERICAN SOCIETY OF COMPOSERS, AUTHORS AND PUBLISHERS,

            By————————————————————————————————
                    President and Chairman of the Board

ASCAP Membership Agreement

FOREIGN AGREEMENTS AT THIS DATE IN EFFECT
(See paragraph 11 of within agreement)

COUNTRY	WITH (Name of Firm)	EXPIRES	REMARKS

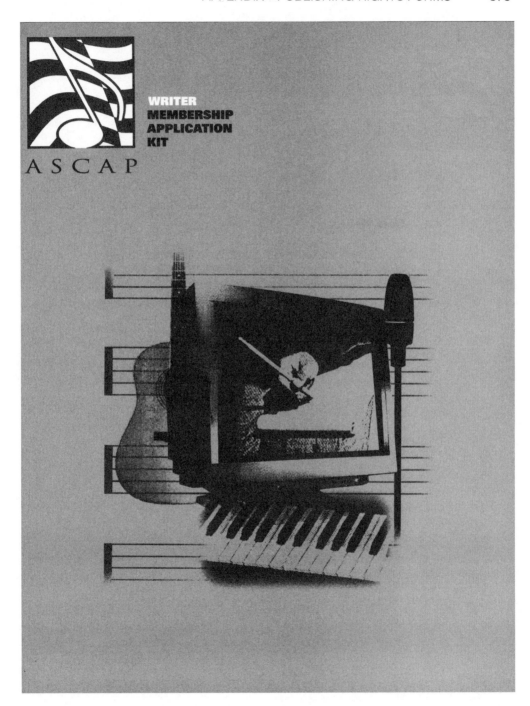

Dear Writer:

Hello and welcome to ASCAP. By applying, you are joining not only a tradition of quality representation, but a global family that includes the top composers, lyricists and publishers in the world of music.

In this package, you will find everything you'll need to become a member of ASCAP. Alongside the application form, there are useful step-by-step instructions to guide you through the application. Also included are ASCAP's Articles of Association, which outline ASCAP's governance procedures, as well as some other descriptive material to keep for your reference.

I hope that this will be the beginning of a long and prosperous association in your career.

Best regards,

Marilyn Bergman
PRESIDENT and CHAIRMAN OF THE BOARD

**INSTRUCTIONS
FOR COMPLETING
WRITER
APPLICATION
(cont'd)**

◄ For 11:

There are two types of ASCAP writer membership: (a) Full Membership and (b) Associate Membership Associate members are writers who do not yet qualify for full membership and, therefore, cannot receive royalties. You may only apply in one category, not both.

◄ (a) Full Membership

You must submit one of the following with your completed application forms in order to substantiate your membership:

- A commercial recording (e.g., a 45, LP, CD, cassette or a copy of the label copy) listing your name as a writer or co-writer of at least one work. Test pressings or homemade tapes are not sufficient.
- Evidence of a performance in ASCAP-licensed media (e.g., a radio or television station, a cable television service/system, or a nightclub or similar establishment) such as a letter from the station or establishment. The letter should include: title of work, writer, publisher, name of establishment, and date of performance, and must be signed by a representative from the station or establishment.
- A concert program listing the performance in a hall or university.
- For commercials, jingles, ads, promos and public service announcements: any evidence of the broadcast of that work (for example, a media schedule or written confirmation from the broadcaster or ad agency).
- A cue sheet prepared by a TV station or the producer of a TV/cable program or feature film, if your application is based on the performance of a composition (including underscoring) on TV/cable or in a feature film. At least one work on the cue sheet must list you as a writer or co-writer.
- For a concert work: confirmation of a published work (e.g., letter from the publisher or a copy of a catalog showing price or rental fee).
- Commercially available printed sheet music listing your name as a writer or co-writer of the work.

(b) Associate Membership

To be elected to associate membership, you must submit a copy of the PA or the SR Copyright registration certificate (indicating words and music) filed with the Copyright Office and bearing the Copyright registration number. PA certificates indicating lyrics only will not be accepted.

You can get a supply of PA or SR forms from the United States Copyright Office, Library of Congress, Washington D.C. 20559, or by telephone request at (202) 707-3000. Associate membership is limited to a three year period from the date of election.

PLEASE REMEMBER TO ADVISE ASCAP AS SOON AS YOU BECOME ELIGIBLE TO CHANGE YOUR STATUS FROM ASSOCIATE TO FULL MEMBERSHIP.

◄ For 13:

This item is here to help ASCAP better identify and serve the needs of its membership. Please do not check most or all of the boxes, even if you write occasionally in all categories we are interested in the one or two areas in which you really concentrate.

◄ For 14:

If you have been a member of or affiliated with any other performing right licensing organization, you must enclose a copy of your release from that organization. In this way, we can make sure our own information is up to date, and be certain that other past or present affiliations will not prevent your election to ASCAP.

◄ For 15:

The signature at the end of this application must be your written, not printed, signature. Please be sure all of the signatures in your application materials are consistent on all documents submitted to ASCAP.

Please use the attached checklist to ensure that the proper forms and materials necessary to become a writer member are returned to ASCAP. For your convenience, a return envelope is provided. After your election, you will receive more specific information about ASCAP, including instructions on how to properly register your compositions with us. We look forward to welcoming you to the Society.

The following is a list of all the materials you need to become a writer member of ASCAP. To see the entire application and instructions, please unfold this booklet completely.

If you have any questions, please feel free to contact the Membership Office nearest you. Our addresses, telephone and fax numbers are on the reverse side.

There is no fee for application. Annual membership dues of $10 for full writer members will either be billed to you or deducted from your royalties. Do not send money with this application.

WE CANNOT PROCESS YOUR APPLICATION IF WE DO NOT RECEIVE ALL OF THE INFORMATION AND MATERIALS REQUESTED. THANK YOU.

Application

Please complete the attached application in its entirety. A set of line-by-line instructions is attached to guide you through this form.

Substantiation

This is material that confirms that:

1. You have had at least one public performance (if you are applying for full membership); or

2. You have had one work registered with the U.S. Copyright Office (if you are applying for associate membership).

See application instructions. #11 for more information about substantiation materials.

Membership Agreements

This application kit contains TWO unsigned copies of the Membership Agreement. BOTH agreements must be signed and returned with your application.

1. Please do not write on the front page.

2. Please turn to the inside page of the Agreement. Fill in the date, which should be the same date as the one on your application. As an example, if the date was March 12, 1997, you would complete the line so it would read as follows:

SIGNED, SEALED, DELIVERED, on this 12th day of March, 1997.

3. Sign your name on the top line next to the word "Owner". This signature should match your signature on the application. Print or type your name on the line underneath that. If you are under the age of 18, a parent's or guardian's signature is required on the Agreement, as well as on the application.

DO NOT ENTER ANYTHING IN THE LOWER LEFT HAND CORNER ABOVE THE LINE THAT READS "PRESIDENT AND CHAIRMAN OF THE BOARD".

4. Complete the second blank Agreement in the same way as the first, and return both copies. One fully executed Agreement, countersigned by ASCAP, will be returned to you following your election.

Digital Audio Royalty Form & Fact Sheet

Please complete and return this form with your application if you authorize ASCAP to collect royalties which may be due you based on the Audio Home Recording Act of 1992.

Name Clearance Form

If you plan to publish or co-publish your own works, you must join ASCAP separately as a publisher member. Before requesting a publisher application, you must use this form to make sure the name you wish to use is available for your exclusive use.

1. Please list three names in order of preference.

2. Return the form to the Membership Office nearest you. You will receive written notification about your name choice in approximately ten (10) business days.

REMINDER: CLEARED NAMES ARE ONLY HELD ON RESERVE FOR YOU FOR SIX MONTHS.

W-9 Form (Request for Taxpayer Identification Number and Certificate)

The IRS requires that ASCAP maintain on file accurate tax information (on form W-9) for all members who are U.S. citizens or resident aliens. If you are not a U.S. citizen or resident alien, please contact us at (212) 621-6240 for further information.

ASCAP CANNOT PROCESS THIS APPLICATION IF THE W-9 FORM, WHERE REQUIRED, IS NOT INCLUDED OR IS INCOMPLETE.

Your name and Social Security Number (SS#) must match the name and number as they appear on your Social Security card.

INSTRUCTIONS FOR COMPLETING WRITER APPLICATION

For 1: ▶

To qualify for full writer membership, an applicant must have at least one musical work commercially recorded, sheet music for a work commercially printed, or a performance of at least one work in an ASCAP-licensed medium or venue.

To qualify for associate membership, an applicant must have a musical work registered with the Copyright Office. Associate members are not qualified for full membership and cannot receive royalties.

Please check only one box. See #11 for more information.

For 2: ▶

Identifying yourself as only a "composer" or only an "author" does not affect your membership in any way; it simply provides the Society with information about the makeup of its membership.

For 3: ▶

Your legal name is your name as it would appear on your driver's license or Social Security card. You must use your legal name on the application even if you use another name professionally.

For 4: ▶

"Pseudonyms" include any name or names you may be using professionally that are different from the legal name listed in Item #3. Please also list any name which includes a middle initial.

For instance, if your legal name is James Smith, but you use the name "Jimmy Smith" for writing or performing purposes, then you should list Jimmy Smith in Item #4. (This will enable us to link the name Jimmy Smith to you if you use this name on a title registration or on other materials submitted to ASCAP.)

For 6, 7A and 7B: ▶

If you would like correspondence (letters, meeting notices, magazines, etc.) sent to you at home, but would like your royalties and performance statements sent to a different address (for example, your accountant, attorney or manager) please indicate here. If neither is checked, all mailings from ASCAP will be sent to your home address.

PLEASE BE SURE TO NOTIFY THE SOCIETY WHEN YOUR ADDRESS CHANGES.

(continued on back)

(PLEASE TYPE OR PRINT IN BLOCK LETTERS)

1. I AM APPLYING FOR   ❑ **FULL**   ❑ **ASSOCIATE**   **WRITER MEMBERSHIP**

2. I AM APPLYING AS: ❑ **COMPOSER** (music)   ❑ **AUTHOR** (lyrics)   ❑ **BOTH**

3. PLEASE PRINT YOUR LEGAL NAME ON LINE BELOW
(E.G., THE NAME OF YOUR DRIVER'S LICENSE OR SOCIAL SECURITY CARD):
Check one: ❑ **Mr.**   ❑ **Ms.**   ❑ **Miss**   ❑ **Mrs.**   ❑ **Dr.**   ❑ **Other:** _____

(FIRST)   (MIDDLE NAME OR INITIAL)   (LAST)

4. PLEASE PRINT ANY PSEUDONYMS OR PROFESSIONAL NAMES YOU ARE USING, IF DIFFERENT FROM YOUR LEGAL NAME (DO NOT LIST BAND OR GROUP NAME):

          A   B   C

5. HOME ADDRESS:

STREET   APT. OR SUITE # (IF APPLICABLE)

CITY   STATE   ZIP CODE

Telephone number: (_____) _____   FAX number (if applicable): (_____) _____

6. ALTERNATE ADDRESS (if applicable):

C/O

STREET   APT. OR SUITE # (IF APPLICABLE)

CITY   STATE   ZIP CODE

Telephone number: (_____) _____   FAX number (if applicable): (_____) _____

7A. WHERE SHOULD WE SEND YOUR CORRESPONDENCE? (CHECK ONE) ❑ **Home**   ❑ **Alternate**

7B. WHERE SHOULD WE SEND YOUR ROYALTIES? (CHECK ONE) ❑ **Home**   ❑ **Alternate**

8. DATE OF BIRTH: MONTH _____ DAY _____ YEAR _____

9. ARE YOU A RESIDENT OF THE UNITED STATES? ❑ **YES**   ❑ **NO**

IF "NO", WHAT IS YOUR COUNTRY OF PERMANENT RESIDENCE? _____

10. SOCIAL SECURITY NUMBER OR TAXPAYER IDENTIFICATION NUMBER (TIN): _____

(continued on back)

11. I AM APPLYING FOR: (a) FULL MEMBERSHIP OR (b) ASSOCIATE MEMBERSHIP BASED ON THE FOLLOWING <u>SONG</u> TITLE WRITTEN OR CO-WRITTEN BY ME:

TITLE

If **(a)**, submit substantiation with this application (see Instruction sheet, #11, for acceptable forms of substantiation).

If **(b)**, enclose copy or either PA or SR Copyright Registration Form from the Copyright Office.

PLEASE SUBMIT SUBSTANTIATING MATERIAL WITH THIS APPLICATION (SEE #11 ON INSTRUCTION SHEET FOR ACCEPTABLE FORMS OF SUBSTANTIATION). APPLICATIONS WITHOUT SUBSTANTIATION, OR SUBMITTED WITH INCOMPLETE OR INACCURATE SUBSTANTIATION, CANNOT BE PROCESSED.

YOUR APPLICATION DOES NOT REGISTER THIS WORK FOR PURPOSES OF RECEIVING ROYALTIES FROM ASCAP. REGISTRATION MATERIALS WILL BE SENT TO YOU AFTER YOUR ELECTION TO MEMBERSHIP.

12. I HAVE PAID A RECORD OR PUBLISHING COMPANY TO HAVE THE TITLE LISTED IN #11 ABOVE RECORDED OR PUBLISHED: ❏ YES ❏ NO

If YES, please indicate the company to which payment was made:

COMPANY

13. I MAINLY WRITE (check no more than three items):

❏ Adult Contemporary   ❏ Country   ❏ Jazz   ❏ Reggae   ❏ Symphonic & Concert
❏ Alternative   ❏ Dance/Club   ❏ Latin   ❏ Rock
❏ Blues   ❏ Film   ❏ Library Music ❏ Standards
❏ Cabaret   ❏ Folk   ❏ New Age   ❏ World Music
❏ Commercials/Promos/Jingles ❏ Gospel   ❏ Pop   ❏ TV
❏ Contemporary Christian ❏ Hip Hop/Rap   ❏ R&B   ❏ Theater   ❏ Other

14. I AM CURRENTLY (or) I HAVE BEEN A MEMBER OR AFFILIATE OF:

❏ ASCAP   ❏ BMI*   ❏ SESAC*   ❏ OTHER*

AS: ❏ A WRITER   ❏ AND/OR A PUBLISHER

If affiliated as a publisher, please list company's name above:

*PLEASE ATTACH A COPY OF YOUR RELEASE FROM THIS ORGANIZATION. APPLICATIONS WITHOUT NECESSARY RELEASES CANNOT BE PROCESSED.

IF YOU PLAN TO PUBLISH OR CO-PUBLISH YOUR OWN WORKS, YOU MUST JOIN ASCAP SEPARATELY AS A PUBLISHER MEMBER. PLEASE USE THE ENCLOSED REQUEST FOR NAME CLEARANCE FORM TO RESERVE A NAME FOR YOUR COMPANY. AFTER CLEARING AND RESERVING A NAME FOR YOUR PUBLISHING COMPANY, YOU MUST COMPLETE AND RETURN AN APPLICATION FOR PUBLISHER MEMBERSHIP USING THAT NAME WITHIN SIX MONTHS.

15. WARRANTIES & REPRESENTATIONS

A. I represent that there are no existing assignments or licenses, direct or indirect, of non-dramatic performing rights in or to the musical work listed in #11 above, except to or with the publisher(s) of this work. If there are assignments or licenses other than with publishers, I have attached copies of such assignments or licenses.

B. I have read the Society's Articles of Association and agree to be bound by them, as now in effect, and as they may be amended, and I agree to execute agreements in such form and for such periods as the Board of Directors shall have required and shall hereafter require for all members.

C. I warrant and represent that all of the information furnished in this application is true. I acknowledge that any agreement entered into between ASCAP and me will be in reliance upon the representations contained in this application, and that my membership will be subject to termination if the information contained in this application is not complete and accurate.

PLEASE SIGN YOUR LEGAL NAME AS IT APPEARS IN ITEM #3

SIGNATURE   DATE

SIGNATURE OF PARENT OR GUARDIAN IF APPLICANT IS UNDER 18   DATE

NEW YORK
ONE LINCOLN PLAZA
NEW YORK, NY 10023
PHONE: (212) 621 - 6000
FAX: (212) 724 - 9064

CHICAGO
1608 W. BELMONT AVENUE
SUITE 200
CHICAGO, IL 60657
PHONE: (773) 472 - 1157
FAX: (773) 472 - 1158

LOS ANGELES
7920 SUNSET BOULEVARD
SUITE 300
LOS ANGELES, CA 90046
PHONE: (323) 883 - 1000
FAX: (323) 883 - 1049

LONDON
#8 CORK STREET
LONDON W1X 1PB
GREAT BRITAIN
PHONE: 011 - 44 - 171 - 439 - 0909
FAX: 011 - 44 - 171 - 434 - 0073

NASHVILLE
TWO MUSIC SQUARE WEST
NASHVILLE, TN 37203
PHONE: (615) 742 - 5000
FAX: (615) 742 - 5020

ATLANTA
541-400 10TH STREET NW
ATLANTA, GA 30318
PHONE: (404) 753 - 4679
FAX: (404) 755 - 4373

MIAMI
844 ALTON ROAD
SUITE 1
MIAMI BEACH, FL 33139
PHONE: (305) 673 - 3446
FAX: (305) 673 - 2446

PUERTO RICO
PHONE: (800) 244 - 3087

PUBLISHER APPLICATION

We are delighted that you have expressed interest in affiliation as a BMI publisher. We should like to bring to your attention the fact that affiliation with BMI is likely to be of practical financial benefit to you only if you currently have some musical compositions which are being performed or are likely to be performed either publicly or on broadcast or cable media or over the internet. If you have no such composition, please do not submit the application at this time.

PLEASE NOTE:
ALL QUESTIONS MUST BE ANSWERED.
APPLICATION MUST BE SIGNED ON LAST PAGE AND RETURNED TO THE APPROPRIATE BMI OFFICE WITH A CHECK OR MONEY ORDER FOR $150 FOR INDIVIDUALLY OWNED PUBLISHING COMPANIES AND $250 FOR PARTNERSHIPS, CORPORATIONS AND LIMITED LIABILITY COMPANIES FOR THE ADMINISTRATION FEE MADE PAYABLE TO BMI. (NOTE: THIS AMOUNT IS NOT REFUNDABLE)

1. NAME OF YOUR PROPOSED PUBLISHING COMPANY:
   (In order to eliminate confusion it is necessary to reject any name identical with, or similar to, that of an established publishing company)

   1st Choice: _____

   2nd Choice: _____

   3rd Choice: _____

   4th Choice: _____

   5th Choice: _____

   NOTE: Once affiliation is completed, a $75.00 administration fee is required in order to process either a change of the name of your publishing company, or for a change in ownership.

2. BUSINESS ADDRESS: _____

   _____

3. BUSINESS TELEPHONE: _____ FAX: _____
                          Area Code   Area Code
4. E-MAIL ADDRESS: _____

Complete and return to BMI the enclosed W-9 form, which is used to report your Social Security Number and/or Federal tax account number for tax purposes. Non-resident aliens should request Form 1001 from BMI for completion.

PLEASE TURN PAGE

FOR INTERNAL USE ONLY	REQUEST NAME CLEARANCE:	ENTERED
☐ RETURNED	(DATE)	BY: _____
☐ RE-RECEIVED	FOR: _____	VERIFIED: _____
	NAME RESERVED: _____	
	VIA MEMO/TELEX: _____	JINGLES 1
☐ CHECK		TV 2
☐ CASHIER'S CHECK	CODE NO: _____	THEATRE 3
☐ MONEY ORDER		CONCERT 4
TO ACCTG: _____	D. OF C. _____	JAZZ 5
	PERIOD: _____	

BMI Publisher Application

5. BUSINESS STRUCTURE (Please check one box only)

    A. ☐ Individually owned   B. ☐ Formally organized corporation   C. ☐ Partnership   D. ☐ Formally organized limited liability company

FILL OUT ONLY THE SECTION BELOW (A, B, C, OR D) THAT CORRESPONDS TO THE BOX CHECKED ABOVE

    A. <u>INDIVIDUALLY OWNED:</u>

Name of Individual _____ Soc. Sec. No. _____

Home Address _____

If you are now or have ever been a writer-member or writer-affiliate of BMI, ASCAP, SESAC or any foreign performing rights licensing organization, state below the name of the organization and the period during which you were a member or affiliate.

Name of Organization _____ Period of Affiliation _____

CAE # _____

    B. <u>FORMALLY ORGANIZED CORPORATION</u> State of Incorporation _____
    (Complete only if corporation is now in existence)

Fed. Tax Acct. No. _____ (If not available, request form S.S. #4 from I.R.S.)

**PHOTOCOPY OF CERTIFICATE OF
INCORPORATION MUST BE SUBMITTED
WITH THIS APPLICATION**

List All Stockholders (If more than four, attach extra sheet)

Name	Home Address & Zip Code	Soc. Sec. No. or Fed. Tax Acct. No.	Percentage Of Ownership

List All Officers (If more than four, attach extra sheet)

Name	Home Address & Zip Code	Soc. Sec. No. or Fed. Tax Acct. No.	Office Held	Does he/she have authority to sign agreements and otherwise act on behalf of company?

    C. <u>PARTNERSHIP</u> (If more than four, attach extra sheet)

Fed. Tax Acct. No. _____
(If not available, request form S.S. #4 from I.R.S.)

(If not supplied, IRS requires BMI to withhold 31 percent of your earnings.

Names of Partners	Home Address & Zip Code	Soc. Sec. No. or Fed. Tax Acct. No.	Percentage Of Ownership	Does he/she have authority to sign agreements and otherwise act on behalf of company?

D. <u>FORMALLY ORGANIZED LIMITED LIABILITY COMPANY</u>   State where organized _____
(Complete only if company is now in existence)

Fed. Tax Acct. No. _____ (If not available, request form S.S. #4 from I.R.S.)

PHOTOCOPY OF ARTICLES OF ORGANIZATION
MUST BE SUBMITTED
WITH THIS APPLICATION

<u>List All Members</u> (If more than four, attach extra sheet)

Name	Home Address & Zip Code	Soc. Sec. No. or Fed. Tax Acct. No.	Percentage Of Ownership

<u>List Manager(s) Authorized Under Articles of Organization, If Any</u>

Name	Home Address & Zip Code	Soc. Sec. No. or Fed. Tax Acct. No.	Does he/she have authority to sign agreements and otherwise act on behalf of company?

6. LIST ALL EXECUTIVE EMPLOYEES OTHER THAN OFFICERS
(for example, professional manager, general manager, etc.):

Name	Home Address & Zip Code	Soc. Sec. No. or Fed. Tax Acct. No.	Position Held

7. If any owner, stockholder, officer or executive employee has been or is connected with any record company, publishing company, songwriters' agency or any organization engaged in the solicitation, publication or exploitation of music, please give the following information:

Name of Individual	Name of Company	If Publishing Co. is it BMI?	Position Held	Years of Association From To

COMPLETE THE ENCLOSED CLEARANCE FORM listing one composition owned by your publishing company that has been commercially recorded, is likely to be broadcast, performed in concerts or otherwise publicly performed, and return it with the application. Please refer to the backside of the clearance form for instructions and additional information.

8. BMI Repertoire Song Title Database Publisher Contact Information
Complete the section below only if you wish to have BMI add your contact information to BMI's website.

Publisher Name: _____

Contact Name: _____ Title: _____

Phone: _____ Fax: _____

Address: _____

City: _____ State: _____ Zip: _____

Email: _____

Web Page Address (URL): _____

NOTICE

IT IS ACKNOWLEDGED THAT ANY CONTRACT CONSUMMATED BETWEEN APPLICANT AND BMI WILL
BE ENTERED INTO IN RELIANCE UPON THE REPRESENTATIONS CONTAINED IN THIS APPLICATION AND THE REP-
RESENTATION THAT THE OWNERS, INCLUDING PARTNERS, ARE OVER THE AGE OF EIGHTEEN. THE CONTRACT
WILL BE SUBJECT TO CANCELLATION IF ANY QUESTION HEREIN CONTAINED IS NOT ANSWERED FULLY AND
ACCURATELY OR IF THE TRUE NAME OF EACH OWNER, STOCKHOLDER, OFFICER AND/OR EXECUTIVE EMPLOYEE
IS NOT REPORTED IN QUESTION 4, 5 AND 6 HEREOF.

Date _____ Signature _____

_____
(Please print name and title of person signing)

Is your Publishing Company currently being administered by another publishing company? ☐ Yes ☐ No

_____
Name of Administrator (please print)

_____
Contact Person (please print)

_____
Address

SIGNING THE AGREEMENTS:

BOTH COPIES of the agreement should be signed on the back page, bottom line, by an owner, partner, officer or member/manager of the publishing company exactly as signed on the application. BMI will enter the date, your company name and address and the period of the contract in Paragraph FIRST. The contract will be effective at the beginning of the calendar quarter in which we received your documents in acceptable form.

RETURNING THE PROPER DOCUMENTS (see map below):

YOU MUST RETURN THE FOLLOWING DOCUMENTS TO THE APPROPRIAT E BMI OFFICE
(An envelope is enclosed for your convenience):
1. THE COMPLETED APPLICATION
2. BOTH COPIES OF THE SIGNED AGREEMENT
3. THE COMPLETED CLEARANCE FORM
4. CASHIER'S CHECK, MONEY ORDER OR PERSONAL CHECK PAYABLE TO BMI FOR $150 FOR INDIVIDUALLY OWNED PUBLISHING COMPANIES, or $250 FOR PARTNERSHIPS, CORPORATIONS AND LIMITED LIABILITY COMPANIES
5. THE COMPLETED W-9 FORM OR FORM 1001 FOR NON-RESIDENT ALIENS
6. ARTICLES OF INCORPORATION OR ARTICLES OF ORGANIZATION, IF APPLICABLE.

Upon receipt of the properly completed documents, there will be a delay of four to six weeks before you receive your copy of the fully executed agreement.

Proper forms, instructions and additional clearance forms for reporting your works to BMI's Clearance Department will be mailed with your fully executed agreement. Please DO NOT SUBMIT ANY SONGS or additional clearance forms for registration to BMI, EXCEPT THE SONG LISTED ON THE CLEARANCE FORM AND RETURNED WITH YOUR APPLICA TION, until you have received additional forms and instructions.

We suggest that you keep the enclosed payment schedule and brochures for your own reference. If you have any questions with respect to the application or agreement, please contact the Publisher Relations Department of the BMI office in whose territory your state is located.

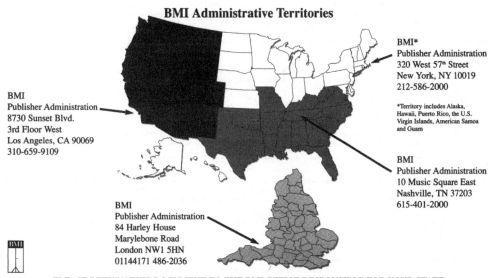

BMI Administrative Territories

BMI*
Publisher Administration
320 West 57th Street
New York, NY 10019
212-586-2000

*Territory includes Alaska, Hawaii, Puerto Rico, the U.S. Virgin Islands, American Samoa and Guam

BMI
Publisher Administration
8730 Sunset Blvd.
3rd Floor West
Los Angeles, CA 90069
310-659-9109

BMI
Publisher Administration
10 Music Square East
Nashville, TN 37203
615-401-2000

BMI
Publisher Administration
84 Harley House
Marylebone Road
London NW1 5HN
01144171 486-2036

PLEASE RETURN THIS DOCUMENT TO THE BMI OFFICE RESPONSIBLE FOR YOUR STATE
ATTENTION: PUBLISHER ADMINISTRATION

WRITER APPLICATION

APPLICATION WILL NOT BE ACCEPTED UNLESS ALL QUESTIONS ARE ANSWERED

PLEASE PRINT OR TYPE

1. FULL LEGAL NAME: Mr.
                      Ms. _____
                         (First Name)   (Middle Name or Initial)   (Last Name)

2. ADDRESS: (number, street, and apt. or suite no.) _____

3. CITY, STATE and ZIP CODE: _____
                              (City)   (State)   (ZIP Code)

4. PHONE NUMBER: (_____) _____ - _____   5. FAX NUMBER (_____) _____ - _____
                 (Area Code)   (Area Code)

6. DATE OF BIRTH: _____ /_____ / _____   7. CITIZENSHIP: _____   8. RESIDENCE: _____
                 (Month) (Day) (Year)   (Country)   (Country)

9. LIST ALL OTHER NAMES THAT YOU HAVE USED OR WILL USE AS A WRITER:

10. Are you now or have you ever been a writer-member or writer-affiliate of BMI, ASCAP, SESAC or any foreign performing rights licensing organization? If so, state name of organization and the period during which you were a member or affiliate:

11. SUBSTITUTE W-9 FOR AN INDIVIDUAL

Name
(First Name)   (Middle Name or Initial)   (Last Name)
Please check appropriate box: ☐ Individual/Sole Proprietor   ☐ Corporation

TAXPAYER Identification Number (TIN)
Enter your TIN in the appropriate box. For individuals, this is your social security number (SSN).

Social Security Number		or	Employer Identification Number	

CERTIFICATION
Under penalties of perjury, I certify that:
A. The number shown on this form is my correct taxpayer identification number (or I am waiting for a number to be issued to me), and
B. I am not subject to backup withholding because: (a) I am exempt from backup withholding, or (b) I have not been notified by the Internal Revenue Service that I am subject to backup withholding as a result of a failure to report all interest or dividends, or (c) the IRS has notified me that I am no longer subject to backup withholding.

Certification Instructions: You must cross out item B above if you have been notified by the IRS that you are currently subject to backup withholding.

12. I warrant and represent that all of the information on this application is true. I acknowledge that any contracts between me and BMI will be entered into in reliance upon the representations contained in this application, and that the contract will be subject to cancellation if any question herein is not answered fully or accurately.

Sign Here	
Signature:	Date:

Non-resident aliens should request
Form 1001 from BMI for completion

If applicant is under 18 years of age, the parent or legal guardian must sign below and on both copies of the agreement.)

Guardian Signature: _____

FOR INTERNAL USE ONLY

CODE NO.:	CKD DATA BASE: _____	DATE RECEIVED: _____
	DATE:	JINGLES 1
	STATUS:	TV 2
D. OF C.:		THEATRE 3
	ENTERED	CONCERT 4
	BY: _____	JAZZ 5
PERIOD:	VERIFIED: _____	CKD CAE: _____

<u>SIGNING THE AGREEMENTS:</u>

The two copies of the writer contracts accompanying this application must be signed by you under the words "ACCEPTED AND AGREED TO" with your full legal name as indicated on line 1 of this application. We will type the date, your name and address and the period of the contract in Paragraph 1.

<u>RETURNING THE PROPER DOCUMENTS</u> (see map below):

YOU MUST RETURN THE FOLLOWING DOCUMENTS TO THE APPROPRIATE BMI OFFICE
(an envelope is enclosed for your convenience):

1. THE COMPLETED APPLICATION
2. BOTH COPIES OF THE SIGNED AGREEMENT

Change of address forms, instructions and clearance forms for reporting your new works to BMI's Clearance Department will be mailed with your fully executed agreement. Please DO NOT SUBMIT ANY SONGS for registration to BMI until you have received the appropriate forms and instructions.

We suggest that you keep the enclosed payment schedule and brochures for your own reference.

If you have any questions with respect to the application or agreement, please contact the Writer Relations Department of the BMI office in whose territory your state is located.

BMI Administrative Territories

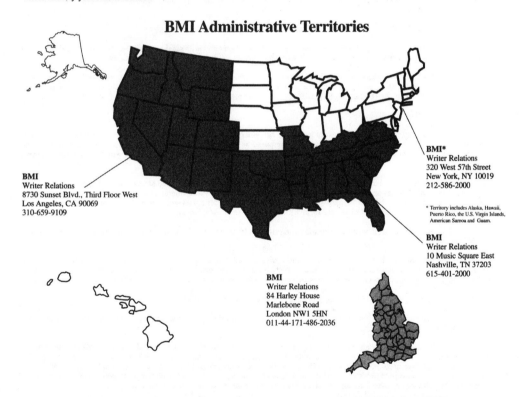

BMI*
Writer Relations
320 West 57th Street
New York, NY 10019
212-586-2000

* Territory includes Alaska, Hawaii,
Puerto Rico, the U.S. Virgin Islands,
American Samoa and Guam.

BMI
Writer Relations
10 Music Square East
Nashville, TN 37203
615-401-2000

BMI
Writer Relations
8730 Sunset Blvd., Third Floor West
Los Angeles, CA 90069
310-659-9109

BMI
Writer Relations
84 Harley House
Marlebone Road
London NW1 5HN
011-44-171-486-2036

PLEASE RETURN ALL DOCUMENTS TO THE BMI OFFICE RESPONSIBLE FOR YOUR STATE

11/15/98

BMI • 320 West 57th Street, New York, NY 10019-3790 • 212-586-2000 • FAX 212-245-8986

Date

Dear

The following shall constitute the agreement between us:

1. As used in this agreement:

(a) The word "Period" shall mean the term from   to   ,
and continuing thereafter for additional terms of two years each unless terminated by either party at the end of said initial term
or any additional term, upon notice by registered or certified mail not more than six (6) months or less than three (3) months prior
to the end of any such term.

(b) The words "Work" or "Works" shall mean:

(i) All musical compositions (including the musical segments and individual compositions written for a dramatic or
dramatico-musical work) composed by you alone or with one or more co-writers during the Period; and

(ii) All musical compositions (including the musical segments and individual compositions written for a dramatic or
dramatico-musical work) composed by you alone or with one or more co-writers prior to the Period, except those in which there
is an outstanding grant of the right of public performance to a person other than a publisher affiliated with BMI.

2. You agree that:

(a) Within ten (10) days after the execution of this agreement you will furnish to us a completed clearance form available
in blank from us with respect to each Work heretofore composed by you which has been published in printed copies or recorded
commercially or synchronized commercially with film or tape or which is being currently performed or which you consider as likely
to be performed.

(b) In each instance that a Work for which a clearance form has not been submitted to us pursuant to sub-paragraph 2(a)
is published in printed copies or recorded commercially or in synchronization with film or tape or is considered by you as likely
to be performed, whether such Work is composed prior to the execution of this agreement or hereafter during the Period, you will
promptly furnish to us a completed clearance form with respect to each such Work.

(c) If requested by us in writing, you will promptly furnish to us a legible lead sheet or other written or printed copy
of a Work.

3. The submission of each clearance form pursuant to paragraph 2 shall constitute a warranty and representation by you that
all of the information contained thereon is true and correct and that no performing rights in such Work have been granted to or
reserved by others except as specifically set forth therein in connection with Works heretofore written or co-written by you.

4. Except as otherwise provided herein, you hereby grant to us for the Period:

(a) All the rights that you own or acquire publicly to perform, and to license others to perform, anywhere in the world,
any part or all of the Works.

(b) The non-exclusive right to record, and to license others to record, any part or all of any of the Works on electrical
transcriptions, wire, tape, film or otherwise, but only for the purpose of performing such Work publicly by means of radio and
television or for archive or audition purposes. This right does not include recording for the purpose of sale to the public or for
the purpose of synchronization (i) with motion pictures intended primarily for theatrical exhibition or (ii) with programs distributed
by means of syndication to broadcasting stations, cable systems or other similar distribution outlets.

(c) The non-exclusive right to adapt or arrange any part or all of any of the Works for performance purposes, and to
license others to do so.

5. Notwithstanding the provisions of sub-paragraph 4(a):

(a) The rights granted to us by sub-paragraph 4(a) shall not include the right to perform or license the performance of
more than one song or aria from a dramatic or dramatico-musical work which is an opera, operetta or musical show or more than

five (5) minutes from a dramatic or dramatico-musical work which is a ballet, if such performance is accompanied by the dramatic action, costumes or scenery of that dramatic or dramatico-musical work.

(b) You, together with all the publishers and your co-writers, if any, shall have the right jointly, by written notice to us, to exclude from the grant made by sub-paragraph 4(a) performances of Works comprising more than thirty (30) minutes of a dramatic or dramatico-musical work, but this right shall not apply to such performances from (i) a score originally written for or performed as part of a theatrical or television film, (ii) a score originally written for or performed as part of a radio or television program, or (iii) the original cast, sound track or similar album of a dramatic or dramatico-musical work.

(c) You, the publishers and/or your co-writers, if any, retain the right to issue non-exclusive licenses for performances of a Work or Works in the United States, its territories and possessions (other than to another performing rights licensing organization), provided that within ten (10) days of the issuance of such license we are given written notice thereof and a copy of the license is supplied to us.

6.   (a) As full consideration for all rights granted to us hereunder and as security therefor, we agree to pay to you, with respect to each of the Works in which we obtain and retain performing rights during the Period:

(i) For radio and television performances of a Work in the United States, its territories and possessions, amounts calculated pursuant to our then current standard practices upon the basis of the then current performance rates generally paid by us to our affiliated writers for similar performances of similar compositions. The number of performances for which you shall be entitled to payment shall be estimated by us in accordance with our then current system of computing the number of such performances.

You acknowledge that we license performances of the Works of our affiliates by means other than on radio and television, but that unless and until such time as methods are adopted for tabulation of such performances, payment will be based solely on performances in those media and locations then currently surveyed. In the event that during the Period we shall establish a system of separate payment for performances by means other than radio and television, we shall pay you upon the basis of the then current performance rates generally paid by us to our other affiliated writers for similar performances of similar compositions.

(ii) In the case of a Work composed by you with one or more co-writers, the sum payable to you hereunder shall be a pro rata share, determined on the basis of the number of co-writers, unless you shall have transmitted to us a copy of an agreement between you and your co-writers providing for a different division of payment.

(iii) Monies received by us from any performing rights licensing organization outside of the United States, its territories and possessions, which are designated by such performing rights licensing organization as the author's share of foreign performance royalties earned by your Works after the deduction of our then current handling charge applicable to our affiliated writers and in accordance with our then current standard practices of payment for such performances.

(b) Notwithstanding the provisions of sub-paragraph 6(a), we shall have no obligation to make payment hereunder with respect to (i) any performance of a Work which occurs prior to the date on which we have received from you all of the information and material with respect to such Work which is referred to in paragraphs 2 and 3, or (ii) any performance of a Work as to which a direct license as described in sub-paragraph 5(c) has been granted by you, your co-writers, if any, or the publishers, or (iii) any performance for which no license fee shall be collected by us, or (iv) any performance of a Work which you claim was either omitted from or miscalculated on a royalty statement and for which we shall not have received written notice from you of such claimed omission or miscalculation within nine (9) months of the date of such statement.

7.   In accordance with our then current standard practices, we will furnish periodic statements to you during each year of the Period showing the monies due pursuant to sub-paragraph 6(a). Each such statement shall be accompanied by payment of the sum thereby shown to be due you, subject to all proper deductions, if any, for taxes, advances or amounts due BMI from you.

8.   (a) Nothing in this agreement requires us to continue to license the Works subsequent to the termination of this agreement. In the event that we continue to license your interest in any Work, however, we shall continue to make payments to you for such Work for so long as you do not make or purport to make directly or indirectly any grant of performing rights in such Work to any other licensing organization. The amounts of such payments shall be calculated pursuant to our then current standard practices upon the basis of the then current performance rates generally paid by us to our affiliated writers for similar performances of similar compositions. You agree to notify us by registered or certified mail of any grant or purported grant by you directly or indirectly of performing rights to any other performing rights organization within ten (10) days from the making of such grant or purported grant and if you fail so to inform us thereof and we make payments to you for any period after the making of any such grant or purported grant, you agree to repay to us all amounts so paid by us promptly with or without demand by us. In addition, if we inquire of you by registered or certified mail, addressed to your last known address, whether you have made any such grant or purported grant and you fail to confirm to us by registered or certified mail within thirty (30) days of the mailing of such inquiry that you have not made any such grant or purported grant, we may, from and after such date, discontinue making any payments to you.

(b) Our obligation to continue payment to you after the termination of this agreement for performances outside of the United States, its territories and possessions, of Works which BMI continues to license after such termination shall be dependent upon our receipt in the United States of payments designated by foreign performing rights organizations as the author's share of foreign performance royalties earned by your Works. Payment of such foreign royalties shall be subject to deduction of our then current handling charge applicable to our affiliated writers and shall be in accordance with our then current standard practices of payment for such performances.

(c) In the event that we have reason to believe that you will receive, are entitled to receive, or are receiving payment from a performing rights licensing organization other than BMI for or based on United States performances of one or more of your Works during a period when such Works were licensed by us pursuant to this agreement, we shall have the right to withhold payment for such performances from you until receipt of evidence satisfactory to us that you were not or will not be so paid by such other organization. In the event that you were or will be so paid or do not supply such evidence within eighteen (18) months from the date of our request therefor, we shall be under no obligation to make any payment to you for performances of such Works during such period.

9.   In the event that this agreement shall terminate at a time when, after crediting all earnings reflected by statements rendered to you prior to the effective date of such termination, there remains an unearned balance of advances paid to you by us, such termination shall not be effective until the close of the calendar quarterly period during which (a) you shall repay such unearned balance of advances, or (b) you shall notify us by registered or certified mail that you have received a statement rendered by us at our normal accounting time showing that such unearned balance of advances has been fully recouped by us.

10.   You warrant and represent that you have the right to enter into this agreement; that you are not bound by any prior commitments which conflict with your commitments hereunder; that each of the Works, composed by you alone or with one or more co-writers, is original; and that exercise of the rights granted by you herein will not constitute an infringement of copyright or violation of any other right of, or unfair competition with, any person, firm or corporation. You agree to indemnify and hold harmless us, our licensees, the advertisers of our licensees and their respective agents, servants and employees from and against any and all loss or damage resulting from any claim of whatever nature arising from or in connection with the exercise of any of the rights granted by you in this agreement. Upon notification to us or any of the other parties herein indemnified of a claim with respect to any of the Works, we shall have the right to exclude such Work from this agreement and/or to withhold payment of all sums which become due pursuant to this agreement or any modification thereof until receipt of satisfactory written evidence that such claim has been withdrawn, settled or adjudicated.

11.   (a) We shall have the right, upon written notice to you, to exclude from this agreement, at any time, any Work which in our opinion is similar to a previously existing composition and might constitute a copyright infringement, or has a title or music or lyric similar to that of a previously existing composition and might lead to a claim of unfair competition.

(b) In the case of Works which in our opinion are based on compositions in the public domain, we shall have the right, upon written notice to you, either (i) to exclude any such Work from this agreement, or (ii) to classify any such Work as entitled to receive only a fraction of the full credit that would otherwise be given for performances thereof.

(c) In the event that any Work is excluded from this agreement pursuant to paragraph 10 or sub-paragraph 11(a) or (b), all rights in such Work shall automatically revert to you ten (10) days after the date of our notice to you of such exclusion. In the event that a Work is classified for less than full credit under sub-paragraph 11(b)(ii), you shall have the right, by giving notice to us, within ten (10) days after the date of our notice advising you of the credit allocated to the Work, to terminate our rights therein, and all rights in such Work shall thereupon revert to you.

12.   In each instance that you write, or are employed or commissioned by a motion picture producer to write, during the Period, all or part of the score of a motion picture intended primarily for exhibition in theaters, or by the producer of a musical show or revue for the legitimate stage to write, during the Period, all or part of the musical compositions contained therein, we agree, on request, to advise the producer of the film that such part of the score as is written by you may be performed as part of the exhibition of said film in theaters in the United States, its territories and possessions, without compensation to us, or to the producer of the musical show or revue that your compositions embodied therein may be performed on the stage with living artists as part of such musical show or revue, without compensation to us. In the event that we notify you that we have established a system for the collection of royalties for performance of the scores of motion picture films in theaters in the United States, its territories and possessions, we shall no longer be obligated to take such action with respect to motion picture scores.

13.   You make, constitute and appoint us, or our nominee, your true and lawful attorney, irrevocably during the Period, in our name or that of our nominee, or in your name, or otherwise, in our sole judgment, to do all acts, take all proceedings, execute, acknowledge and deliver any and all instruments, papers, documents, process or pleadings that, in our sole judgment, may be necessary, proper or expedient to restrain infringement of and/or to enforce and protect the rights granted by you hereunder, and to recover damages in respect to or for the infringement or other violation of said rights, and in our sole judgment to join you and/or others in whose names the copyrights to any of the Works may stand; to discontinue, compromise or refer to arbitration, any such actions or proceedings or to make any other disposition of the disputes in relation to the Works, provided that any action or proceeding commenced by us pursuant to the provisions of this paragraph shall be at our sole expense and for our sole benefit. Notwithstanding the foregoing, nothing in this paragraph 13 requires us to take any proceeding or other action against any person, firm, partnership or other entity or any writer or publisher, whether or not affiliated with us, who you claim may be infringing your Works or otherwise violating the rights granted by you hereunder. In addition, you understand and agree that the licensing by us of any musical compositions which you claim may be infringing your Works or otherwise violating the rights granted by you hereunder, shall not constitute an infringement of your Works on our part.

14.   BMI shall have the right, in its sole discretion, to terminate this agreement on at least thirty (30) days' notice by registered or certified mail if you, your agents, employees or representatives, directly or indirectly, solicit or accept payment from writers for composing music for lyrics or writing lyrics to music or for reviewing, publishing, promoting, recording or rendering other services connected with the exploitation of any composition, or permit use of your name or your affiliation with us in connection with any of the foregoing. In the event of such termination no payments shall be due to you pursuant to paragraph 8.

15.   No monies due or to become due to you shall be assignable, whether by way of assignment, sale or power granted to an attorney-in-fact, without our prior written consent. If any assignment of such monies is made by you without such prior written consent, no rights of any kind against us will be acquired by the assignee, purchaser or attorney-in-fact.

16. In the event that during the Period (a) mail addressed to you at the last address furnished by you pursuant to paragraph 20 shall be returned by the post office, or (b) monies shall not have been earned by you pursuant to paragraph 6 for a period of two consecutive years or more, or (c) you shall die, BMI shall have the right to terminate this agreement on at least thirty (30) days' notice by registered or certified mail addressed to the last address furnished by you pursuant to paragraph 20 and, in the case of your death, to the representative of your estate, if known to BMI. In the event of such termination no payments shall be due to you pursuant to paragraph 8.

17. You acknowledge that the rights obtained by you pursuant to this agreement constitute rights to payment of money and that during the Period we shall hold title to the performing rights granted to us hereunder. In the event that during the Period you shall file a petition in bankruptcy, such a petition shall be filed against you, you shall make an assignment for the benefit of creditors, you shall consent to the appointment of a receiver or trustee for all or part of your property, or you shall institute or shall have instituted against you any other insolvency proceeding under the United States bankruptcy laws or any other applicable law, we shall retain title to the performing rights in all Works the rights to which are granted to us hereunder and shall subrogate your trustee in bankruptcy or receiver and any subsequent purchasers from them to your right to payment of money for said Works in accordance with the terms and conditions of this agreement.

18. (a) You hereby authorize us to negotiate for and collect royalties or monies to which you may become entitled as a writer pursuant to the Audio Home Recording Act of 1992 and/or any amendments thereto or substitutions therefor and, to the extent possible, collect for and distribute to you royalties arising from or as compensation for home recording in countries outside the United States, its territories and possessions. This authorization with respect to royalties and monies under the Audio Home Recording Act of 1992 may be revoked by you at the end of any calendar year on prior written notice by you to us by registered or certified mail. Such revocation shall be effective beginning with the calendar year subsequent to the time of notice and shall in no way affect the Period of this agreement with respect to any of the other rights granted to BMI by you hereunder.

(b) We agree to distribute to you royalties and monies collected by us pursuant to the authorization granted in sub-paragraph 18(a), pursuant to our then prevailing practices, including deduction of our expenses therefor.

19. All disputes of any kind, nature or description arising in connection with the terms and conditions of this agreement shall be submitted to the American Arbitration Association in New York, New York, for arbitration under its then prevailing rules, the arbitrator(s) to be selected as follows: Each of us shall, by written notice to the other, have the right to appoint one arbitrator. If, within ten (10) days following the giving of such notice by one of us, the other shall not, by written notice, appoint another arbitrator, the first arbitrator shall be the sole arbitrator. If two arbitrators are so appointed, they shall appoint a third arbitrator. If ten (10) days elapse after the appointment of the second arbitrator and the two arbitrators are unable to agree upon the third arbitrator, then either of us may, in writing, request the American Arbitration Association to appoint the third arbitrator. The award made in the arbitration shall be binding and conclusive on both of us and shall include the fixing of the costs, expenses and reasonable attorneys' fees of arbitration, which shall be borne by the unsuccessful party. Judgment may be entered in New York State Supreme Court or any other court having jurisdiction.

20. You agree to notify our Department of Writer/Publisher Administration promptly in writing of any change in your address. Any notice sent to you pursuant to the terms of this agreement shall be valid if addressed to you at the last address so furnished by you.

21. This agreement constitutes the entire agreement between you and us, cannot be changed except in a writing signed by you and us and shall be governed and construed pursuant to the laws of the State of New York.

22. In the event that any part or parts of this agreement are found to be void by a court of competent jurisdiction, the remaining part or parts shall nevertheless be binding with the same force and effect as if the void part or parts were deleted from this agreement.

Very truly yours,

BROADCAST MUSIC, INC.

ACCEPTED AND AGREED TO:

By..
                                                                    Vice President

....

4/94

BMI

AGREEMENT made on .... between BROADCAST MUSIC, INC. ("BMI"), a

New York corporation, whose address is 320 West 57th Street, New York, N.Y. 10019-3790 and ....

....

a .... doing business as ....

.... ("Publisher"), whose address is ....

....

W I T N E S S E T H :

FIRST: The term of this agreement shall be the period from ....

to ...., and continuing thereafter for additional periods of five (5) years each unless terminated by either party at the end of such initial period or any additional period, upon notice by registered or certified mail not more than six (6) months or less than three (3) months prior to the end of any such period.

SECOND: As used in this agreement, the word "Work" or "Works" shall mean:

    A.   All musical compositions (including the musical segments and individual compositions written for a dramatic or dramatico-musical work) whether published or unpublished, now owned or copyrighted by Publisher or in which Publisher owns or controls performing rights, and

    B.   All musical compositions (including the musical segments and individual compositions written for a dramatic or dramatico-musical work) whether published or unpublished, in which hereafter during the term Publisher acquires ownership of copyright or ownership or control of the performing rights, from and after the date of the acquisition by Publisher of such ownership or control.

THIRD: Except as otherwise provided herein, Publisher hereby sells, assigns and transfers to BMI, its successors or assigns, for the term of this agreement:

    A.   All the rights which Publisher owns or acquires publicly to perform, and to license others to perform, anywhere in the world, any part or all the Works.

    B.   The non-exclusive right to record, and to license others to record, any part or all of any of the Works on electrical transcriptions, wire, tape, film or otherwise, but only for the purpose of performing such Work publicly by means of radio and television or for archive or audition purposes. This right does not include recording for the purpose of sale to the public or for the purpose of synchronization (1) with motion pictures intended primarily for theatrical exhibition or (2) with programs distributed by means of syndication to broadcasting stations, cable systems or other similar distribution outlets.

    C.   The non-exclusive right to adapt or arrange any part or all of any of the Works for performance purposes, and to license others to do so.

FOURTH: Notwithstanding the provisions of subparagraph A of paragraph THIRD hereof:

    A.   The rights granted to BMI by said subparagraph A shall not include the right to perform or license the performance of more than one song or aria from a dramatic or dramatico-musical work which is an opera, operetta or musical show or more than five (5) minutes from a dramatic or dramatico-musical work which is a ballet, if such performance is accompanied by the dramatic action, costumes or scenery of that dramatic or dramatico-musical work.

    B.   Publisher, together with all the writers and co-publishers, if any, shall have the right jointly, by written notice to BMI, to exclude from the grant made by subparagraph A of paragraph THIRD hereof performances of Works comprising more than thirty (30) minutes of a dramatic or dramatico-musical work, but this right shall not apply to such performances from (1) a score originally written for or performed as part of a theatrical or television film, (2) a score originally written for or performed as part of a radio or television program, or (3) the original cast, sound track or similar album of a dramatic or dramatico-musical work.

    C.   Publisher, the writers and/or co-publishers, if any, retain the right to issue non-exclusive licenses for performances of a Work or Works in the United States, its territories and possessions (other than to another performing rights licensing organization), provided that within ten (10) days of the issuance of such license BMI is given written notice thereof and a copy of the license is supplied to BMI.

FIFTH:

    A.   As full consideration for all rights granted to BMI hereunder and as security therefor, BMI agrees to make the following payments to Publisher with respect to each of the Works in which BMI has performing rights:

        (1)   For radio and television performances of Works in the United States, its territories and possessions, BMI will pay amounts calculated pursuant to BMI's then standard practices upon the basis of the then current performance rates generally paid by BMI to its affiliated publishers for similar performances of similar compositions. The number of performances for which Publisher shall be entitled to payment shall be estimated by BMI in accordance with its then current system of computing the number of such performances.

        Publisher acknowledges that BMI licenses performances of the Works of its affiliates by means other than on radio and television, but that unless and until such time as methods are adopted for tabulation of and payment for such performances, payment will be based solely on performances in those media and locations then currently surveyed. In the event that during the term of this agreement BMI shall establish a system of separate payment for performances by means other than radio and television, BMI shall pay Publisher upon the basis of the then current performance rates generally paid by BMI to its other affiliated publishers for similar performances of similar compositions.

        (2)   For performances of Works outside of the United States, its territories and possessions, BMI will pay to Publisher monies received by BMI in the United States from any performing rights licensing organization which are designated by such organization as the publisher's share of foreign performance royalties earned by any of the Works after the deduction of BMI's then current handling charge applicable to its affiliated publishers and in accordance with BMI's then standard practices of payment for such performances.

        (3)   In the case of Works which, or rights in which, are owned by Publisher jointly with one or more other publishers, the sum payable to Publisher under this subparagraph A shall be a pro rata share determined on the basis of the number of publishers, unless BMI shall have received from Publisher a copy of an agreement or other document signed by all of the publishers providing for a different division of payment.

    B.   Notwithstanding the provisions of subparagraph A of this paragraph FIFTH, BMI shall have no obligation to make payment hereunder with respect to (1) any performance of a Work which occurs prior to the date on which BMI shall have received from

BMI Writer Agreement

Publisher of all the material ·with respect to such Work referred to in subparagraph A of paragraph TENTH hereof, and in the case of foreign performances, the information referred to in subparagraph B of paragraph FOURTEENTH hereof, or (2) any performance of a Work as to which a direct license as described in subparagraph C of paragraph FOURTH hereof has been granted by Publisher, its co-publishers or the writers, or (3) any performance for which no license fees shall be collected by BMI, or (4) any performance of a Work which Publisher claims was either omitted from or miscalculated on a royalty statement and for which BMI shall not have received written notice from Publisher of such claimed omission or miscalculation within nine (9) months of the date of such statement.

SIXTH: In accordance with BMI's then current standard practices, BMI will furnish periodic statements to Publisher during each year of the term showing the monies due pursuant to subparagraph A of paragraph FIFTH hereof. Each such statement shall be accompanied by payment of the sum thereby shown to be due to Publisher, subject to all proper deductions, if any, for taxes, advances or amounts due to BMI from Publisher.

SEVENTH:

A. Nothing in this agreement requires BMI to continue to license the Works subsequent to the termination of this agreement. In the event that BMI continues to license Publisher's interest in any Work, however, BMI shall continue to make payments to Publisher for such Work for so long as Publisher does not make or purport to make directly or indirectly any grant of performing rights in such Work to any other licensing organization. The amounts of such payments shall be calculated pursuant to BMI's then current standard practices upon the basis of the then current performance rates generally paid by BMI to its affiliated publishers for similar performances of similar compositions. Publisher agrees to notify BMI by registered or certified mail of any grant or purported grant by Publisher directly or indirectly of performing rights to any other performing rights organization within ten (10) days from the making of such grant or purported grant and if Publisher fails so to inform BMI thereof and BMI makes payments to Publisher for any period after the making of any such grant or purported grant, Publisher agrees to repay to BMI all amounts so paid by BMI promptly with or without demand by BMI. In addition, if BMI inquires of Publisher by registered or certified mail, addressed to Publisher's last known address, whether Publisher has made any such grant or purported grant and Publisher fails to confirm to BMI by registered or certified mail within thirty (30) days of the mailing of such inquiry that Publisher has not made any such grant or purported grant, BMI may, from and after such date, discontinue making any payments to Publisher.

B. BMI's obligation to continue payment to Publisher after the termination of this agreement for performances outside of the United States, its territories and possessions, of Works which BMI continues to license after such termination shall be dependent upon BMI's receipt in the United States of payments designated by foreign performing rights licensing organizations as the publisher's share of foreign performance royalties earned by the Works. Payment of such foreign royalties shall be subject to deduction of BMI's then current handling charge applicable to its affiliated publishers and shall be in accordance with BMI's then standard practices of payment for such performances.

C. In the event that BMI has reason to believe that Publisher will receive, or is entitled to receive, or is receiving payment from a performing rights licensing organization other than BMI for or based on United States performances of one or more of the Works during a period when such Works were licensed by BMI pursuant to this agreement, BMI shall have the right to withhold payment for such performances from Publisher until receipt of evidence satisfactory to BMI that Publisher was not or will not be so paid by such other organization. In the event that Publisher was or will be so paid or does not supply such evidence within eighteen (18) months from the date of BMI's request therefor, BMI shall be under no obligation to make any payment to Publisher for performances of such Works during such period.

EIGHTH: In the event that this agreement shall terminate at a time when, after crediting all earnings reflected by statements rendered to Publisher prior to the effective date of such termination, there remains an unearned balance of advances paid to Publisher by BMI, such termination shall not be effective until the close of the calendar quarterly period during which (A) Publisher shall repay such unearned balance of advances, or (B) Publisher shall notify BMI by registered or certified mail that Publisher has received a statement rendered by BMI at its normal accounting time showing that such unearned balance of advances has been fully recouped by BMI.

NINTH:

A. BMI shall have the right, upon written notice to Publisher, to exclude from this agreement, at any time, any Work which in BMI's opinion is similar to a previously existing composition and might constitute a copyright infringement, or has a title or music or lyric similar to that of a previously existing composition and might lead to a claim of unfair competition.

B. In the case of Works which in the opinion of BMI are based on compositions in the public domain, BMI shall have the right, at any time, upon written notice to Publisher, either (1) to exclude any such Work from this agreement, or (2) to classify any such Work as entitled to receive only a stated fraction of the full credit that would otherwise be given for performances thereof.

C. In the event that any Work is excluded from this agreement pursuant to subparagraph A or B of this paragraph NINTH, or pursuant to subparagraph C of paragraph TWELFTH hereof, all rights of BMI in such Work shall automatically revert to Publisher ten (10) days after the date of the notice of such exclusion given by BMI to Publisher. In the event that a Work is classified for less than full credit under subparagraph B(2) of this paragraph NINTH, Publisher shall have the right, by giving notice to BMI within ten (10) days after the date of BMI's notice to Publisher of the credit allocated to such Work, to terminate all rights in such Work granted to BMI herein and all such rights of BMI in such Work shall thereupon revert to Publisher.

TENTH:

A. With respect to each of the Works which has been or shall be published or recorded commercially or synchronized with motion picture or television film or tape or which Publisher considers likely to be performed, Publisher agrees to furnish to BMI:

(1) A completed clearance form available in blank from BMI, unless a cue sheet with respect to such Work is furnished pursuant to subparagraph A(3) of this paragraph TENTH.

(2) If such Work is based on a composition in the public domain, a legible lead sheet or other written or printed copy of such Work setting forth the lyrics, if any, and music correctly metered; provided that with respect to all other Works, such copy need be furnished only if requested by BMI pursuant to subsection (b) of subparagraph D(2) of this paragraph TENTH.

(3) If such Work has been or shall be synchronized with or otherwise used in connection with motion picture or television film or tape, a cue sheet showing the title, writers, publisher and nature and duration of the use of the Work in such film or tape.

B. Publisher shall submit the material described in subparagraph A of this paragraph TENTH with respect to Works heretofore published, recorded or synchronized within ten (10) days after the execution of this agreement and with respect to any of the Works hereafter so published, recorded, synchronized or likely to be performed prior to the date of publication or release of the recording, film or tape or anticipated performance.

C. The submission of each clearance form or cue sheet shall constitute a warranty and representation by Publisher that all of the information contained thereon is true and correct and that no performing rights in any of the Works listed thereon have been granted to or reserved by others except as specifically set forth therein.

D. Publisher agrees:

(1) To secure and maintain copyright protection of the Works pursuant to the Copyright Law of the United States and pursuant to the laws of such other nations of the world where such protection is afforded; and to give BMI, upon request, prompt written notice of the date and number of copyright registration and/or renewal of each Work registered in the United States Copyright Office.

(2) At BMI's request:

(a) To register each unpublished and published Work in the United States Copyright Office pursuant to the Copyright Law of the United States.

(b) To obtain and deliver to BMI copies of: unpublished and published Works; copyright registration and/or renewal certificates issued by the United States Copyright Office; any agreements, assignments, instruments or documents of any kind by which Publisher obtained the right to publicly perform and/or the right to publish, co-publish or sub-publish any of the Works.

E. Publisher agrees to give BMI prompt notice by registered or certified mail in each instance when, pursuant to the Copyright Law of the United States, (1) the rights granted to BMI by Publisher in any Work shall revert to the writer or the writer's representative, or (2) copyright protection of any Work shall terminate.

ELEVENTH: Publisher warrants and represents that:

A. Publisher has the right to enter into this agreement; Publisher is not bound by any prior commitments which conflict with its undertakings herein; the rights granted by Publisher to BMI herein are the sole and exclusive property of Publisher and are free from all adverse encumbrances and claims; and exercise of such rights will not constitute infringement of copyright or violation of any right of, or unfair competition with, any person, firm, corporation or association.

B. Except with respect to Works in which the possession of performing rights by another person, firm, corporation or association is specifically set forth on a clearance form or cue sheet submitted to BMI pursuant to subparagraph A of paragraph TENTH hereof, Publisher has performing rights in each of the Works by virtue of written grants thereof to Publisher signed by the authors and composers or other owners of such Work.

TWELFTH:

A. Publisher agrees to defend, indemnify, save and hold BMI, its licensees, the advertisers of its licensees and their respective agents, servants and employees, free and harmless from and against any and all demands, loss, damage, suits, judgments, recoveries and costs, including counsel fees, resulting from any claim of whatever nature arising from or in connection with the exercise of any of the rights granted by Publisher in this agreement; provided, however, that the obligations of Publisher under this paragraph TWELFTH shall not apply to any matter added to, or changes made in, any Work by BMI or its licensees.

B. Upon the receipt by BMI or any of the other parties herein indemnified of any notice, demand, process, papers, writ or pleading, by which any such claim, demand, suit or proceeding is made or commenced against them, or any of them, which Publisher shall be obliged to defend hereunder, BMI shall, as soon as may be practicable, give Publisher notice thereof and deliver to Publisher such papers or true copies thereof, and BMI shall have the right to participate and direct such defense on behalf of BMI and/or its licensees by counsel of its own choice, at its own expense. Publisher agrees to cooperate with BMI in all such matters.

C. In the event of such notification of claim or service of process on any of the parties herein indemnified, BMI shall have the right, from the date thereof, to exclude the Work with respect to which a claim is made from this agreement and/or to withhold payment of all sums which may become due pursuant to this agreement or any modification thereof until receipt of satisfactory written evidence that such claim has been withdrawn, settled or adjudicated.

THIRTEENTH: Publisher makes, constitutes and appoints BMI, or its nominee, Publisher's true and lawful attorney, irrevocably during the term hereof, in the name of BMI or that of its nominee, or in Publisher's name, or otherwise, in BMI's sole judgment, to do all acts, take all proceedings, and execute, acknowledge and deliver any and all instruments, papers, documents, process or pleadings that, in BMI's sole judgment, may be necessary, proper or expedient to restrain infringement of and/or to enforce and protect the rights granted by Publisher hereunder, and to recover damages in respect of or for the infringement or other violation of said rights, and in BMI's sole judgment to join Publisher and/or others in whose names the copyrights to any of the Works may stand, and to discontinue, compromise or refer to arbitration, any such actions or proceedings or to make any other disposition of the disputes in relation to the Works; provided that any action or proceeding commenced by BMI pursuant to the provisions of this paragraph THIRTEENTH shall be at its sole expense and for its sole benefit. Notwithstanding the foregoing, nothing in this paragraph THIRTEENTH requires BMI to take any proceeding or other action against any person, firm, partnership or other entity or any writer or publisher, whether or not affiliated with BMI, who Publisher claims may be infringing Publisher's Works or otherwise violating the rights granted by Publisher hereunder. In addition, Publisher understands and agrees that the licensing by BMI of any musical compositions which Publisher claims may be infringing Publisher's Works or otherwise violating the rights granted by Publisher hereunder, shall not constitute an infringement of Publisher's Works on BMI's part.

FOURTEENTH:

A. It is acknowledged that BMI has heretofore entered into, and may during the term of this agreement enter into, contracts with performing rights licensing organizations for the licensing of public performing rights controlled by BMI in territories outside of the United States, its territories and possessions (herein called "Foreign Territories"). Upon Publisher's written request, BMI agrees to permit Publisher to grant performing rights in any or all of the Works for any Foreign Territory for which, at the time such request is received, BMI has not entered into any such contract with a performing rights licensing organization; provided, however, that any such grant of performing rights by Publisher shall terminate at such time when BMI shall have entered into such a contract with a performing rights licensing organization covering such Foreign Territory and shall have notified Publisher thereof. Nothing herein contained, however, shall be deemed to restrict Publisher from assigning to its foreign publisher or representative the right to collect a part or all of the publishers' performance royalties earned by any or all of the Works in any Foreign Territory as part of an agreement for the publication, exploitation or representation of such Works in such territory, whether or not BMI has entered into such a contract with a performing rights licensing organization covering such territory.

B. Publisher agrees to notify BMI promptly in writing in each instance when publication, exploitation or other rights in any or all of the Works are granted for any Foreign Territory. Such notice shall set forth the title of the Work, the Foreign Territory or Territories involved, the period of such grant, the name of the person, firm, corporation or association entitled to collect performance royalties earned in the Foreign Territory and the amount of such share. Within ten (10) days after the execution of this agreement Publisher agrees to submit to BMI, in writing, a list of all Works as to which BMI has, prior to the effective date of this agreement, granted to any person, firm, corporation or association performing rights and/or the right to collect publisher performance royalties earned in any Foreign Territory.

FIFTEENTH: BMI shall have the right, in its sole discretion, to terminate this agreement if:

A. Publisher, its agents, employees, representatives or affiliated companies, directly or indirectly during the term of this agreement:

(1) Solicits or accepts payment from or on behalf of authors for composing music for lyrics, or from or on behalf of composers for writing lyrics to music.

(2) Solicits or accepts music and/or lyrics from composers or authors in consideration of any payments to be made by or on behalf of such composers or authors for reviewing, arranging, promotion, publication, recording or any other services connected with the exploitation of any composition.

(3)   Permits Publisher's name, or the fact of its affiliation with BMI, to be used by any other person, firm, corporation or association engaged in any of the practices described in subparagraphs A(1) and A(2) of this paragraph FIFTEENTH.

(4)   Submits to BMI, as one of the Works to come within this agreement, any musical composition with respect to which any payments described in subparagraphs A(1) and A(2) of this paragraph FIFTEENTH have been made by or on behalf of a composer or author to any person, firm, corporation or association.

B.   Publisher, its agents, employees or representatives directly or indirectly during the term of this agreement makes any effort to ascertain from, or offers any inducement or consideration to, anyone, including but not limited to any radio or television licensee of BMI or to the agents, employees or representatives of BMI or of any such licensee, for information regarding the time or times when any such BMI licensee is to report its performances to BMI, or to attempt in any way to manipulate performances or affect the representative character or accuracy of BMI's system of sampling or logging performances.

C.   Publisher fails to notify BMI's Department of Writer/Publisher Administration promptly in writing of any change of firm name, ownership or address of Publisher.

In the event BMI exercises its right to terminate this agreement pursuant to the provisions of subparagraphs A, B or C of this paragraph FIFTEENTH, BMI shall give Publisher at least thirty (30) days' notice by registered or certified mail of such termination. In the event of such termination, no payments shall be due to Publisher pursuant to paragraph SEVENTH hereof.

SIXTEENTH: In the event that during the term of this agreement (1) monies shall not have been earned by Publisher pursuant to paragraph FIFTH hereof for a period of two consecutive years or more, or (2) the proprietor, if Publisher is a sole proprietorship, shall die, BMI shall have the right to terminate this agreement on at least thirty (30) days' notice by registered or certified mail addressed to the last address furnished by Publisher in writing to BMI's Department of Writer/Publisher Administration and, in the case of the death of a sole proprietor, to the representative of said proprietor's estate, if known to BMI. In the event of such termination, no payments shall be due Publisher pursuant to paragraph SEVENTH hereof.

SEVENTEENTH: Publisher acknowledges that the rights obtained by it pursuant to this agreement constitute rights to payment of money and that during the term BMI shall hold title to the performing rights granted to BMI hereunder. In the event that during the term Publisher shall file a petition in bankruptcy, such a petition shall be filed against Publisher, Publisher shall make an assignment for the benefit of creditors, Publisher shall consent to the appointment of a receiver or trustee for all or part of its property, Publisher shall file a petition for corporate reorganization or arrangement under the United States bankruptcy laws, or Publisher shall institute or shall have instituted against it any other insolvency proceeding under the United States bankruptcy laws or any other applicable law, or, in the event Publisher is a partnership, all of the general partners of said partnership shall be adjudged bankrupts, BMI shall retain title to the performing rights in all Works the rights to which are granted to BMI hereunder and shall subrogate Publisher's trustee in bankruptcy or receiver and any subsequent purchasers from them to Publisher's right to payment of money for said Works in accordance with the terms and conditions of this agreement.

EIGHTEENTH: All disputes of any kind, nature or description arising in connection with the terms and conditions of this agreement shall be submitted to the American Arbitration Association in New York, New York, for arbitration under its then prevailing rules, the arbitrator(s) to be selected as follows:

Each of the parties shall, by written notice to the other, have the right to appoint one arbitrator. If, within ten (10) days following the giving of such notice by one party, the other shall not, by written notice, appoint another arbitrator, the first arbitrator shall be the sole arbitrator. If two arbitrators are so appointed, they shall appoint a third arbitrator. If ten (10) days elapse after the appointment of the second arbitrator and the two arbitrators are unable to agree upon the third arbitrator, then either party may, in writing, request the American Arbitration Association to appoint the third arbitrator. The award made in the arbitration shall be binding and conclusive on the parties and shall include the fixing of the costs, expenses and reasonable attorneys' fees of arbitration, which shall be borne by the unsuccessful party. Judgement may be entered in New York State Supreme Court or any other court having jurisdiction.

NINETEENTH: Publisher agrees that it shall not, without the written consent of BMI, assign any of its rights hereunder. No rights of any kind against BMI will be acquired by the assignee if any such purported assignment is made by Publisher without such written consent.

TWENTIETH: Any notice sent to Publisher pursuant to the terms of this agreement shall be valid if addressed to Publisher at the last address furnished in writing by Publisher to BMI's Department of Writer/Publisher Administration.

TWENTY-FIRST: This agreement constitutes the entire agreement between BMI and Publisher, cannot be changed except in a writing signed by BMI and Publisher and shall be governed and construed pursuant to the laws of the State of New York.

TWENTY-SECOND: In the event that any part or parts of this agreement are found to be void by a court of competent jurisdiction, the remaining part or parts shall nevertheless be binding with the same force and effect as if the void part or parts were deleted from this agreement.

IN WITNESS WHEREOF, the parties hereto have caused this agreement to be duly executed as of the day and year first above written.

BROADCAST MUSIC, INC.

By...

Vice President

....

By...

(Title of Signer)...................................

FORM PA

For a Work of the Performing Arts
UNITED STATES COPYRIGHT OFFICE

REGISTRATION NUMBER

PA   PAU

EFFECTIVE DATE OF REGISTRATION

Month   Day   Year

DO NOT WRITE ABOVE THIS LINE. IF YOU NEED MORE SPACE, USE A SEPARATE CONTINUATION SHEET.

1

TITLE OF THIS WORK ▼

PREVIOUS OR ALTERNATIVE TITLES ▼

NATURE OF THIS WORK ▼ See instructions

2

a

NAME OF AUTHOR ▼

DATES OF BIRTH AND DEATH
Year Born ▼   Year Died ▼

Was this contribution to the work a "work made for hire"?
☐ Yes
☐ No

AUTHOR'S NATIONALITY OR DOMICILE
Name of Country
OR { Citizen of ▶
Domiciled in ▶

WAS THIS AUTHOR'S CONTRIBUTION TO THE WORK
Anonymous? ☐ Yes ☐ No
Pseudonymous? ☐ Yes ☐ No
If the answer to either of these questions is "Yes," see detailed instructions.

NATURE OF AUTHORSHIP Briefly describe nature of material created by this author in which copyright is claimed. ▼

NOTE

Under the law, the "author" of a "work made for hire" is generally the employer, not the employee (see instructions). For any part of this work that was "made for hire" check "Yes" in the space provided, give the employer (or other person for whom the work was prepared) as "Author" of that part, and leave the space for dates of birth and death blank.

b

NAME OF AUTHOR ▼

DATES OF BIRTH AND DEATH
Year Born ▼   Year Died ▼

Was this contribution to the work a "work made for hire"?
☐ Yes
☐ No

AUTHOR'S NATIONALITY OR DOMICILE
Name of Country
OR { Citizen of ▶
Domiciled in ▶

WAS THIS AUTHOR'S CONTRIBUTION TO THE WORK
Anonymous? ☐ Yes ☐ No
Pseudonymous? ☐ Yes ☐ No
If the answer to either of these questions is "Yes," see detailed instructions.

NATURE OF AUTHORSHIP Briefly describe nature of material created by this author in which copyright is claimed. ▼

c

NAME OF AUTHOR ▼

DATES OF BIRTH AND DEATH
Year Born ▼   Year Died ▼

Was this contribution to the work a "work made for hire"?
☐ Yes
☐ No

AUTHOR'S NATIONALITY OR DOMICILE
Name of Country
OR { Citizen of ▶
Domiciled in ▶

WAS THIS AUTHOR'S CONTRIBUTION TO THE WORK
Anonymous? ☐ Yes ☐ No
Pseudonymous? ☐ Yes ☐ No
If the answer to either of these questions is "Yes," see detailed instructions.

NATURE OF AUTHORSHIP Briefly describe nature of material created by this author in which copyright is claimed. ▼

3

a **YEAR IN WHICH CREATION OF THIS WORK WAS COMPLETED** This information must be given ◀Year in all cases.

b **DATE AND NATION OF FIRST PUBLICATION OF THIS PARTICULAR WORK**
Complete this information ONLY if this work has been published.
Month ▶   Day ▶   Year ▶   ◀ Nation

4

See instructions before completing this space.

COPYRIGHT CLAIMANT(S) Name and address must be given even if the claimant is the same as the author given in space 2. ▼

TRANSFER If the claimant(s) named here in space 4 is (are) different from the author(s) named in space 2, give a brief statement of how the claimant(s) obtained ownership of the copyright. ▼

APPLICATION RECEIVED

ONE DEPOSIT RECEIVED

TWO DEPOSITS RECEIVED

FUNDS RECEIVED

DO NOT WRITE HERE
OFFICE USE ONLY

MORE ON BACK ▶ • Complete all applicable spaces (numbers 5-9) on the reverse side of this page.
• See detailed instructions.   • Sign the form at line 8.

DO NOT WRITE HERE
Page 1 of _____ pages

✏ Application Form PA ✏

Detach and read these instructions before completing this form.
Make sure all applicable spaces have been filled in before you return this form.

BASIC INFORMATION

When to Use This Form: Use Form PA for registration of published or unpublished works of the performing arts. This class includes works prepared for the purpose of being "performed" directly before an audience or indirectly "by means of any device or process." Works of the performing arts include: (1) musical works, including any accompanying words; (2) dramatic works, including any accompanying music; (3) pantomimes and choreographic works; and (4) motion pictures and other audiovisual works.

Deposit to Accompany Application: An application for copyright registration must be accompanied by a deposit consisting of copies or phonorecords representing the entire work for which registration is made. The following are the general deposit requirements as set forth in the statute:
Unpublished Work: Deposit one complete copy (or phonorecord).
Published Work: Deposit two complete copies (or one phonorecord) of the best edition.
Work First Published Outside the United States: Deposit one complete copy (or phonorecord) of the first foreign edition.
Contribution to a Collective Work: Deposit one complete copy (or phonorecord) of the best edition of the collective work.
Motion Pictures: Deposit *both* of the following: (1) a separate written description of the contents of the motion picture; and (2) for a published work, one complete copy of the best edition of the motion picture; or, for an unpublished work, one complete copy of the motion picture or identifying material. Identifying material may be either an audiorecording of the entire soundtrack or one frame enlargement or similar visual print from each 10-minute segment.

The Copyright Notice: Before March 1, 1989, the use of copyright notice was mandatory on all published works, and any work first published before that date should have carried a notice. For works first published on and after March 1, 1989, use of the copyright notice is optional. For more information about copyright notice, see Circular 3, "Copyright Notice."

For Further Information: To speak to an information specialist, call (202) 707-3000 (TTY: (202) 707-6737). Recorded information is available 24 hours a day. Order forms and other publications from the address in space 9 or call the Forms and Publications Hotline at (202) 707-9100. Most circulars (but not forms) are available via fax. Call (202) 707-2600 from a touchtone phone. Access and download circulars, forms, and other information from the Copyright Office Website at www.loc.gov/copyright.

> **PRIVACY ACT ADVISORY STATEMENT Required by the Privacy Act of 1974 (P.L. 93-579)**
> The authority for requesting this information is title 17, U.S.C., secs. 409 and 410. Furnishing the requested information is voluntary. But if the information is not furnished, it may be necessary to delay or refuse registration and you may not be entitled to certain relief, remedies, and benefits provided in chapters 4 and 5 of title 17, U.S.C.
> The principal uses of the requested information are the establishment and maintenance of a public record and the examination of the application for compliance with the registration requirements of the copyright code.
> Other routine uses include public inspection and copying, preparation of public indexes, preparation of public catalogs of copyright registrations, and preparation of search reports upon request.
> NOTE: No other advisory statement will be given in connection with this application. Please keep this statement and refer to it if we communicate with you regarding this application.

LINE-BY-LINE INSTRUCTIONS

Please type or print using black ink. The form is used to produce the certificate.

1 SPACE 1: Title

Title of This Work: Every work submitted for copyright registration must be given a title to identify that particular work. If the copies or phonorecords of the work bear a title (or an identifying phrase that could serve as a title), transcribe that wording *completely* and *exactly* on the application. Indexing of the registration and future identification of the work will depend on the information you give here. If the work you are registering is an entire "collective work" (such as a collection of plays or songs), give the overall title of the collection. If you are registering one or more individual contributions to a collective work, give the title of each contribution, followed by the title of the collection. For an unpublished collection, you may give the titles of the individual works after the collection title.

Previous or Alternative Titles: Complete this space if there are any additional titles for the work under which someone searching for the registration might be likely to look, or under which a document pertaining to the work might be recorded.

Nature of This Work: Briefly describe the general nature or character of the work being registered for copyright. Examples: "Music"; "Song Lyrics"; "Words and Music"; "Drama"; "Musical Play"; "Choreography"; "Pantomime"; "Motion Picture"; "Audiovisual Work."

2 SPACE 2: Author(s)

General Instructions: After reading these instructions, decide who are the "authors" of this work for copyright purposes. Then, unless the work is a "collective work," give the requested information about every "author" who contributed any appreciable amount of copyrightable matter to this version of the work. If you need further space, request additional Continuation Sheets. In the case of a collective work such as a songbook or a collection of plays, give information about the author of the collective work as a whole.

Name of Author: The fullest form of the author's name should be given. Unless the work was "made for hire," the individual who actually created the work is its "author." In the case of a work made for hire, the statute provides that "the employer or other person for whom the work was prepared is considered the author."

What is a "Work Made for Hire"? A "work made for hire" is defined as: (1) "a work prepared by an employee within the scope of his or her employment"; or (2) "a work specially ordered or commissioned for use as a contribution to a collective work, as a part of a motion picture or other audiovisual work, as a translation, as a

supplementary work, as a compilation, as an instructional text, as a test, as answer material for a test, or as an atlas, if the parties expressly agree in a written instrument signed by them that the work shall be considered a work made for hire." If you have checked "Yes" to indicate that the work was "made for hire," you must give the full legal name of the employer (or other person for whom the work was prepared). You may also include the name of the employee along with the name of the employer (for example: "Elster Music Co., employer for hire of John Ferguson").

"Anonymous" or "Pseudonymous" Work: An author's contribution to a work is "anonymous" if that author is not identified on the copies or phonorecords of the work. An author's contribution to a work is "pseudonymous" if that author is identified on the copies or phonorecords under a fictitious name. If the work is "anonymous" you may: (1) leave the line blank; or (2) state "anonymous" on the line; or (3) reveal the author's identity. If the work is "pseudonymous" you may: (1) leave the line blank; or (2) give the pseudonym and identify it as such (example: "Huntley Haverstock, pseudonym"); or (3) reveal the author's name, making clear which is the real name and which is the pseudonym (for example: "Judith Barton, whose pseudonym is Madeline Elster"). However, the citizenship or domicile of the author must be given in all cases.

Dates of Birth and Death: If the author is dead, the statute requires that the year of death be included in the application unless the work is anonymous or pseudonymous. The author's birth date is optional, but is useful as a form of identification. Leave this space blank if the author's contribution was a "work made for hire."

Author's Nationality or Domicile: Give the country of which the author is a citizen, or the country in which the author is domiciled. Nationality or domicile must be given in all cases.

Nature of Authorship: Give a brief general statement of the nature of this particular author's contribution to the work. Examples: "Words"; "Coauthor of Music"; "Words and Music"; "Arrangement"; "Coauthor of Book and Lyrics"; "Dramatization"; "Screen Play"; "Compilation and English Translation"; "Editorial Revisions."

3 SPACE 3: Creation and Publication

General Instructions: Do not confuse "creation" with "publication." Every application for copyright registration must state "the year in which creation of the work was completed." Give the date and nation of first publication only if the work has been published.

Creation: Under the statute, a work is "created" when it is fixed in a copy or phonorecord for the first time. Where a work has been prepared over a period of time, the part of the work existing in fixed form on a particular date constitutes the created work on that date. The date you give here should be the year in which the author completed the particular version for which registration is now being sought, even if other versions exist or if further changes or additions are planned.

Publication: The statute defines "publication" as "the distribution of copies or phonorecords of a work to the public by sale or other transfer of ownership, or by rental, lease, or lending"; a work is also "published" if there has been an "offering to distribute copies or phonorecords to a group of persons for purposes of further distribution, public performance, or public display." Give the full date (month, date, year) when, and the country where, publication first occurred. If first publication took place simultaneously in the United States and other countries, it is sufficient to state "U.S.A."

4 SPACE 4: Claimant(s)

Name(s) and Address(es) of Copyright Claimant(s): Give the name(s) and address(es) of the copyright claimant(s) in the work even if the claimant is the same as the author. Copyright in a work belongs initially to the author of the work (including, in the case of a work made for hire, the employer or other person for whom the work was prepared). The copyright claimant is either the author of the work or a person or organization to whom the copyright initially belonging to the author has been transferred.

Transfer: The statute provides that, if the copyright claimant is not the author, the application for registration must contain "a brief statement of how the claimant obtained ownership of the copyright." If any copyright claimant named in space 4a is not an author named in space 2, give a brief statement explaining how the claimant(s) obtained ownership of the copyright. Examples: "By written contract"; "Transfer of all rights by author"; "Assignment"; "By will." Do not attach transfer documents or other attachments or riders.

5 SPACE 5: Previous Registration

General Instructions: The questions in space 5 are intended to show whether an earlier registration has been made for this work and, if so, whether there is any basis for a new registration. As a rule, only one basic copyright registration can be made for the same version of a particular work.

Same Version: If this version is substantially the same as the work covered by a previous registration, a second registration is not generally possible unless: (1) the work has been registered in unpublished form and a second registration is now being sought to cover this first published edition; or (2) someone other than the author is identified as copyright claimant in the earlier registration and the author is now seeking registration in his or her own name. If either of these two exceptions applies, check the appropriate box and give the earlier registration number and date. Otherwise, do not submit Form SR. Instead, write the Copyright Office for information about supplementary registration or recordation of transfers of copyright ownership.

Changed Version: If the work has been changed and you are now seeking registration to cover the additions or revisions, check the last box in space 5, give the earlier registration number and date, and complete both parts of space 6 in accordance with the instructions below.

Previous Registration Number and Date: If more than one previous registration has been made for the work, give the number and date of the latest registration.

6 SPACE 6: Derivative Work or Compilation

General Instructions: Complete space 6 if this work is a "changed version," "compilation," or "derivative work," and if it incorporates one or more earlier works that have already been published or registered for copyright, or that have fallen into the public domain, or sound recordings that were fixed before February 15, 1972. A "compilation" is defined as "a work formed by the collection and assembling of preexisting materials or of data that are selected, coordinated, or arranged in such a way that the resulting work as a whole constitutes an original work of authorship." A "derivative work" is "a work based on one or more preexisting works." Examples of derivative works include recordings reissued with substantial editorial revisions or abridgments of the recorded sounds, and recordings republished with new recorded material, or "any other form in which a work may be recast, transformed, or adapted." Derivative works also include works "consisting of editorial revisions, annotations, or other modifications" if these changes, as a whole, represent an original work of authorship.

Preexisting Material (space 6a): Complete this space and space 6b for derivative works. In this space identify the preexisting work that has been recast, transformed, or adapted. The preexisting work may be material that has been previously published, previously registered, or that is in the public domain. For example, the preexisting material might be: "1970 recording by Sperryville Symphony of Bach Double Concerto."

Material Added to This Work (space 6b): Give a brief, general statement of the additional new material covered by the copyright claim for which registration is sought. In the case of a derivative work, identify this new material. Examples: "Recorded performances on bands 1 and 3"; "Remixed sounds from original multitrack sound sources"; "New words, arrangement, and additional sounds." If the work is a compilation, give a brief, general statement describing both the material that has been compiled and the compilation itself. Example: "Compilation of 1938 Recordings by various swing bands."

7, 8, 9 SPACE 7, 8, 9: Fee, Correspondence, Certification, Return Address

Deposit Account: If you maintain a Deposit Account in the Copyright Office, identify it in space 7a. Otherwise, leave the space blank and send the filing fee of $30 (effective through June 30, 2002) with your application and deposit. (See space 8 on form.)

Correspondence (space 7b): This space should contain the name, address, area code, telephone number, fax number, and email address (if available) of the person to be consulted if correspondence about this application becomes necessary.

Certification (space 8): This application cannot be accepted unless it bears the date and the **handwritten signature** of the author or other copyright claimant, or of the owner of exclusive right(s), or of the duly authorized agent of the author, claimant, or owner of exclusive right(s).

Address for Return of Certificate (space 9): The address box must be completed legibly since the certificate will be returned in a window envelope.

MORE INFORMATION

"Works": "Works" are the basic subject matter of copyright; they are what authors create and copyright protects. The statute draws a sharp distinction between the "work" and "any material object in which the work is embodied."

"Copies" and "Phonorecords": These are the two types of material objects in which "works" are embodied. In general, **"copies"** are objects from which a work can be read or visually perceived, directly or with the aid of a machine or device, such as manuscripts, books, sheet music, film, and videotape. **"Phonorecords"** are objects embodying fixations of sounds, such as audio tapes and phonograph disks. For example, a song (the "work") can be reproduced in sheet music ("copies") or phonograph disks ("phonorecords"), or both.

"Sound Recordings": These are "works," not "copies" or "phonorecords." "Sound recordings" are "works that result from the fixation of a series of musical, spoken, or other sounds, but not including the sounds accompanying a motion picture or other audiovisual work." Example: When a record company issues a new release, the release will typically involve two distinct "works": the "musical work" that has been recorded, and the "sound recording" as a separate work in itself. The material objects that the record company sends out are "phonorecords": physical reproductions of both the "musical work" and the "sound recording."

Should You File More Than One Application? If your work consists of a recorded musical, dramatic, or literary work and if both that "work" and the sound recording as a separate "work" are eligible for registration, the application form you should file depends on the following:

File Only Form SR If: The copyright claimant is the same for both the musical, dramatic, or literary work and for the sound recording, and you are seeking a single registration to cover both of these "works."

File Only Form PA (or Form TX) If: You are seeking to register only the musical, dramatic, or literary work, not the sound recording. Form PA is appropriate for works of the performing arts; Form TX is for nondramatic literary works.

Separate Applications Should Be Filed on Form PA (or Form TX) and on Form SR If: (1) The copyright claimant for the musical, dramatic, or literary work is different from the copyright claimant for the sound recording; or (2) You prefer to have separate registrations for the musical, dramatic, or literary work and for the sound recording.

EXAMINED BY	FORM PA
CHECKED BY	
☐ CORRESPONDENCE Yes	FOR COPYRIGHT OFFICE USE ONLY

DO NOT WRITE ABOVE THIS LINE. IF YOU NEED MORE SPACE, USE A SEPARATE CONTINUATION SHEET.

PREVIOUS REGISTRATION Has registration for this work, or for an earlier version of this work, already been made in the Copyright Office?

☐ Yes ☐ No If your answer is "Yes," why is another registration being sought? (Check appropriate box.) ▼ If your answer is "no," go to space 7.

a. ☐ This is the first published edition of a work previously registered in unpublished form.

b. ☐ This is the first application submitted by this author as copyright claimant.

c. ☐ This is a changed version of the work, as shown by space 6 on this application.

If your answer is "Yes," give: **Previous Registration Number** ▼   **Year of Registration** ▼

5

DERIVATIVE WORK OR COMPILATION Complete both space 6a and 6b for a derivative work; complete only 6b for a compilation.

Preexisting Material Identify any preexisting work or works that this work is based on or incorporates. ▼

Material Added to This Work Give a brief, general statement of the material that has been added to this work and in which copyright is claimed. ▼

a

6

See instructions before completing this space.

b

DEPOSIT ACCOUNT If the registration fee is to be charged to a Deposit Account established in the Copyright Office, give name and number of Account.

Name ▼   **Account Number** ▼

a

7

CORRESPONDENCE Give name and address to which correspondence about this application should be sent.   Name/Address/Apt/City/State/ZIP ▼

b

Area code and daytime telephone number ▶ (   )   Fax number ▶ (   )

Email ▶

CERTIFICATION* I, the undersigned, hereby certify that I am the

Check only one ▶ { ☐ author
☐ other copyright claimant
☐ owner of exclusive right(s)
☐ authorized agent of _____

Name of author or other copyright claimant, or owner of exclusive right(s) ▲

of the work identified in this application and that the statements made by me in this application are correct to the best of my knowledge.

8

Typed or printed name and date ▼ If this application gives a date of publication in space 3, do not sign and submit it before that date.

Date ▶

Handwritten signature (X) ▼

☞ X _____

Certificate will be mailed in window envelope to this address:

Name ▼
Number/Street/Apt ▼
City/State/ZIP ▼

YOU MUST:
• Complete all necessary spaces
• Sign your application in space 8

SEND ALL ELEMENTS IN THE SAME PACKAGE:
1. Application form
2. Nonrefundable filing fee in check or money order payable to *Register of Copyrights*
3. Deposit material

As of July 1, 1999, the filing fee for Form PA is $30.

MAIL TO:
Library of Congress
Copyright Office
101 Independence Avenue, S.E.
Washington, D.C. 20559-6000

9

*17 U.S.C. § 506(e): Any person who knowingly makes a false representation of a material fact in the application for copyright registration provided for by section 409, or in any written statement filed in connection with the application, shall be fined not more than $2,500.

June 1999—200,000
WEB REV: June 1999

♻ PRINTED ON RECYCLED PAPER   ☆U.S. GOVERNMENT PRINTING OFFICE: 1999-454-879/68

☺ **Application Form SR** ☺

Detach and read these instructions before completing this form.
Make sure all applicable spaces have been filled in before you return this form.

BASIC INFORMATION

When to Use This Form: Use Form SR for registration of published or unpublished sound recordings. It should be used when the copyright claim is limited to the sound recording itself, and it may also be used where the same copyright claimant is seeking simultaneous registration of the underlying musical, dramatic, or literary work embodied in the phonorecord.

With one exception, "sound recordings" are works that result from the fixation of a series of musical, spoken, or other sounds. The exception is for the audio portions of audiovisual works, such as a motion picture soundtrack or an audio cassette accompanying a filmstrip. These are considered a part of the audiovisual work as a whole.

Deposit to Accompany Application: An application for copyright registration must be accompanied by a deposit consisting of phonorecords representing the entire work for which registration is to be made.

Unpublished Work: Deposit one complete phonorecord.

Published Work: Deposit two complete phonorecords of the best edition, together with "any printed or other visually perceptible material" published with the phono-records.

Work First Published Outside the United States: Deposit one complete phonorecord of the first foreign edition.

Contribution to a Collective Work: Deposit one complete phonorecord of the best edition of the collective work.

The Copyright Notice: Before March 1, 1989, the use of copyright notice was mandatory on all published works, and any work first published before that date should have carried a notice. For works first published on and after March 1, 1989, use of the copyright notice is optional. For more information about copyright notice, see Circular 3, "Copyright Notices."

For Further Information: To speak to an information specialist, call (202) 707-3000 (TTY: (202) 707-6737). Recorded information is available 24 hours a day. Order forms and other publications from Library of Congress, Copyright Office, 101 Independence Avenue, S.E., Washington, D.C. 20559-6000 or call the Forms and Publications Hotline at (202) 707-9100. Most circulars (but not forms) are available via fax. Call (202) 707-2600 from a touchtone phone. Access and download circulars, forms, and other information from the Copyright Office Website at www.loc.gov/copyright.

LINE-BY-LINE INSTRUCTIONS

Please type or print neatly using black ink. The form is used to produce the certificate.

1 SPACE 1: Title

Title of This Work: Every work submitted for copyright registration must be given a title to identify that particular work. If the phonorecords or any accompanying printed material bears a title (or an identifying phrase that could serve as a title), transcribe that wording completely and exactly on the application. Indexing of the registration and future identification of the work may depend on the information you give here.

Previous, Alternative, or Contents Titles: Complete this space if there are any previous or alternative titles for the work under which someone searching for the registration might be likely to look, or under which a document pertaining to the work might be recorded. You may also give the individual contents titles, if any, in this space or you may use a Continuation Sheet. Circle the term that describes the titles given.

2 SPACE 2: Author(s)

General Instructions: After reading these instructions, decide who are the "authors" of this work for copyright purposes. Then, unless the work is a "collective work," give the requested information about every "author" who contributed any appreciable amount of copyrightable matter to this version of the work. If you need further space, request additional Continuation Sheets. In the case of a collective work such as a collection of previously published or registered sound recordings, give information about the author of the collective work as a whole. If you are submitting this Form SR to cover the recorded musical, dramatic, or literary work as well as the sound recording itself, it is important for space 2 to include full information about the various authors of all of the material covered by the copyright claim, making clear the nature of each author's contribution.

Name of Author: The fullest form of the author's name should be given. Unless the work was "made for hire," the individual who actually created the work is its "author." In the case of a work made for hire, the statute provides that "the employer or other person for whom the work was prepared is considered the author."

What Is a "Work Made for Hire"? A "work made for hire" is defined as: (1) "a work prepared by an employee within the scope of his or her employment"; or (2)

"a work specially ordered or commissioned for use as a contribution to a collective work, as a part of a motion picture or other audiovisual work, as a translation, as a supplementary work, as a compilation, as an instructional text, as a test, as answer material for a test, or as an atlas, if the parties expressly agree in a written instrument signed by them that the work shall be considered a work made for hire." If you have checked "Yes" to indicate that the work was "made for hire," you must give the full legal name of the employer (or other person for whom the work was prepared). You may also include the name of the employee along with the name of the employer (for example: "Elster Record Co., employer for hire of John Ferguson").

"Anonymous" or "Pseudonymous" Work: An author's contribution to a work is "anonymous" if that author is not identified on the copies or phonorecords of the work. An author's contribution to a work is "pseudonymous" if that author is identified on the copies or phonorecords under a fictitious name. If the work is "anonymous" you may: (1) leave the line blank; or (2) state "anonymous" on the line; or (3) reveal the author's identity. If the work is "pseudonymous" you may: (1) leave the line blank; or (2) give the pseudonym and identify it as such (for example: "Huntley Haverstock, pseudonym"); or (3) reveal the author's name, making clear which is the real name and which is the pseudonym (for example: "Judith Barton, whose pseudonym is Madeline Elster"). However, the citizenship or domicile of the author **must** be given in all cases.

Dates of Birth and Death: If the author is dead, the statute requires that the year of death be included in the application unless the work is anonymous or pseudonymous. The author's birth date is optional, but is useful as a form of identification. Leave this space blank if the author's contribution was a "work made for hire."

Author's Nationality or Domicile: Give the country in which the author is a citizen, or the country in which the author is domiciled. Nationality or domicile **must** be given in all cases.

Nature of Authorship: Sound recording authorship is the performance, sound production, or both, that is fixed in the recording deposited for registration. Describe this authorship in space 2 as "sound recording." If the claim also covers the underlying work(s), include the appropriate authorship terms for each author, for example, "words," "music," "arrangement of music," or "text."

Generally, for the claim to cover both the sound recording and the underlying work(s), every author should have contributed to both the sound recording and the underlying work(s). If the claim includes artwork or photographs, include the appropriate term in the statement of authorship.

3 SPACE 3: Creation and Publication

General Instructions: Do not confuse "creation" with "publication." Every application for copyright registration must state "the year in which creation of the work was completed." Give the date and nation of first publication only if the work has been published.

Creation: Under the statute, a work is "created" when it is fixed in a copy or phonorecord for the first time. Where a work has been prepared over a period of time, the part of the work existing in fixed form on a particular date constitutes the created work on that date. The date you give here should be the year in which the author completed the particular version for which registration is now being sought, even if other versions exist or if further changes or additions are planned.

Publication: The statute defines "publication" as "the distribution of copies or phonorecords of a work to the public by sale or other transfer of ownership, or by rental, lease, or lending"; a work is also "published" if there has been an "offering to distribute copies or phonorecords to a group of persons for purposes of further distribution, public performance, or public display." Give the full date (month, date, year) when, and the country where, publication first occurred. If first publication took place simultaneously in the United States and other countries, it is sufficient to state "U.S.A."

4 SPACE 4: Claimant(s)

Name(s) and Address(es) of Copyright Claimant(s): Give the name(s) and address(es) of the copyright claimant(s) in the work even if the claimant is the same as the author. Copyright in a work belongs initially to the author of the work (including, in the case of a work made for hire, the employer or other person for whom the work was prepared). The copyright claimant is either the author of the work or a person or organization to whom the copyright initially belonging to the author has been transferred.

Transfer: The statute provides that, if the copyright claimant is not the author, the application for registration must contain "a brief statement of how the claimant obtained ownership of the copyright." If any copyright claimant named in space 4a is not an author named in space 2, give a brief statement explaining how the claimant(s) obtained ownership of the copyright. Examples: "By written contract"; "Transfer of all rights by author"; "Assignment"; "By will." Do not attach transfer documents or other attachments or riders.

5 SPACE 5: Previous Registration

General Instructions: The questions in space 5 are intended to show whether an earlier registration has been made for this work and, if so, whether there is any basis for a new registration. As a rule, only one basic copyright registration can be made for the same version of a particular work.

Same Version: If this version is substantially the same as the work covered by a previous registration, a second registration is not generally possible unless: (1) the work has been registered in unpublished form and a second registration is now being sought to cover this first published edition; or (2) someone other than the author is identified as copyright claimant in the earlier registration and the author is now seeking registration in his or her own name. If either of these two exceptions applies, check the appropriate box and give the earlier registration number and date. Otherwise, do not submit Form SR. Instead, write the Copyright Office for information about supplementary registration or recordation of transfers of copyright ownership.

Changed Version: If the work has been changed and you are now seeking registration to cover the additions or revisions, check the last box in space 5, give the earlier registration number and date, and complete both parts of space 6 in accordance with the instructions below.

Previous Registration Number and Date: If more than one previous registration has been made for the work, give the number and date of the latest registration.

6 SPACE 6: Derivative Work or Compilation

General Instructions: Complete space 6 if this work is a "changed version," "compilation," or "derivative work," and if it incorporates one or more earlier works that have already been published or registered for copyright, or that have fallen into the public domain, or sound recordings that were fixed before February 15, 1972. A "compilation" is defined as "a work formed by the collection and assembling of preexisting materials or of data that are selected, coordinated, or arranged in such a way that the resulting work as a whole constitutes an original work of authorship. A "derivative work" is "a work based on one or more preexisting works." Examples of derivative works include recordings reissued with substantial editorial revisions or abridgments of the recorded sounds, and recordings republished with new recorded material, or "any other form in which a work may be recast, transformed, or adapted." Derivative works also include works "consisting of editorial revisions, annotations, or other modifications" if these changes, as a whole, represent an original work of authorship.

Preexisting Material (space 6a): Complete this space and space 6b for derivative works. In this space identify the preexisting work that has been recast, transformed, or adapted. The preexisting work may be material that has been previously published, previously registered, or that is in the public domain. For example, the preexisting material might be: "1970 recording by Sperryville Symphony of Bach Double Concerto."

Material Added to This Work (space 6b): Give a brief, general statement of the additional new material covered by the copyright claim for which registration is sought. In the case of a derivative work, identify this new material. Examples: "Recorded performances on bands 1 and 3"; "Remixed sounds from original multitrack sound sources"; "New words, arrangement, and additional sounds." If the work is a compilation, give a brief, general statement describing both the material that has been compiled and the compilation itself. Example: "Compilation of 1938 Recordings by various swing bands."

7,8,9 SPACE 7,8,9: Fee, Correspondence, Certification, Return Address

Deposit Account: If you maintain a Deposit Account in the Copyright Office, identify it in space 7a. Otherwise, leave the space blank and send the filing fee of $30 (effective through June 30, 2002) with your application and deposit. (See space 8 on form.)

Correspondence (space 7b): This space should contain the name, address, area code, telephone number, fax number, and email address (if available) of the person to be consulted if correspondence about this application becomes necessary.

Certification (space 8): This application cannot be accepted unless it bears the date and the **handwritten signature** of the author or other copyright claimant, or of the owner of exclusive right(s), or of the duly authorized agent of the author, claimant, or owner of exclusive right(s).

Address for Return of Certificate (space 9): The address box must be completed legibly since the certificate will be returned in a window envelope.

MORE INFORMATION

"Works": "Works" are the basic subject matter of copyright; they are what authors create and copyright protects. The statute draws a sharp distinction between the "work" and "any material object in which the work is embodied."

"Copies" and "Phonorecords": These are the two types of material objects in which "works" are embodied. In general, "copies" are objects from which a work can be read or visually perceived, directly or with the aid of a machine or device, such as manuscripts, books, sheet music, film, and videotape. "Phonorecords" are objects embodying fixations of sounds, such as audio tapes and phonograph disks. For example, a song (the "work") can be reproduced in sheet music ("copies") or phonograph disks ("phonorecords"), or both.

"Sound Recordings": These are "works," not "copies" or "phonorecords." "Sound recordings" are "works that result from the fixation of a series of musical, spoken, or other sounds, but not including the sounds accompanying a motion picture or other audiovisual work." Example: When a record company issues a new release, the release will typically involve two distinct "works": the "musical work" that has been recorded, and the "sound recording" as a separate work in itself. The material objects that the record company sends out are "phonorecords": physical reproductions of both the "musical work" and the "sound recording."

Should You File More Than One Application? If your work consists of a recorded musical, dramatic, or literary work and if both that "work" and the sound recording as a separate "work" are eligible for registration, the application form you should file depends on the following:

File Only Form SR if: The copyright claimant is the same for both the musical, dramatic, or literary work and for the sound recording, and you are seeking a single registration to cover both of these "works."

File Only Form PA (or Form TX) if: You are seeking to register only the musical, dramatic, or literary work, not the sound recording. Form PA is appropriate for works of the performing arts; Form TX is for nondramatic literary works.

Separate Applications Should Be Filed on Form PA (or Form TX) and on Form SR if: (1) The copyright claimant for the musical, dramatic, or literary work is different from the copyright claimant for the sound recording; or (2) You prefer to have separate registrations for the musical, dramatic, or literary work and for the sound recording.

Fees are effective through June 30, 2002.
After that date, check the Copyright Office
Website at www.loc.gov/copyright or call
(202) 707-3000 for current fee information.

FORM SR
For a Sound Recording
UNITED STATES COPYRIGHT OFFICE

REGISTRATION NUMBER

_____

SR   SRU

EFFECTIVE DATE OF REGISTRATION

_____

Month   Day   Year

DO NOT WRITE ABOVE THIS LINE. IF YOU NEED MORE SPACE, USE A SEPARATE CONTINUATION SHEET.

1

TITLE OF THIS WORK ▼

_____

PREVIOUS, ALTERNATIVE, OR CONTENTS TITLES (CIRCLE ONE) ▼

2

a

NAME OF AUTHOR ▼

DATES OF BIRTH AND DEATH
Year Born ▼   Year Died ▼

Was this contribution to the work a "work made for hire"?
☐ Yes
☐ No

AUTHOR'S NATIONALITY OR DOMICILE
Name of Country
OR { Citizen of ▶_____
{ Domiciled in ▶_____

WAS THIS AUTHOR'S CONTRIBUTION TO THE WORK
Anonymous?   ☐ Yes ☐ No
Pseudonymous? ☐ Yes ☐ No
If the answer to either of these questions is "Yes," see detailed instructions.

NATURE OF AUTHORSHIP Briefly describe nature of material created by this author in which copyright is claimed. ▼

NOTE

Under the law, the "author" of a "work made for hire" is generally the employer, not the employee (see instructions). For any part of this work that was "made for hire," check "Yes" in the space provided, give the employer (or other person for whom the work was prepared) as "Author" of that part, and leave the space for dates of birth and death blank.

b

NAME OF AUTHOR ▼

DATES OF BIRTH AND DEATH
Year Born ▼   Year Died ▼

Was this contribution to the work a "work made for hire"?
☐ Yes
☐ No

AUTHOR'S NATIONALITY OR DOMICILE
Name of Country
OR { Citizen of ▶_____
{ Domiciled in ▶_____

WAS THIS AUTHOR'S CONTRIBUTION TO THE WORK
Anonymous?   ☐ Yes ☐ No
Pseudonymous? ☐ Yes ☐ No
If the answer to either of these questions is "Yes," see detailed instructions.

NATURE OF AUTHORSHIP Briefly describe nature of material created by this author in which copyright is claimed. ▼

c

NAME OF AUTHOR ▼

DATES OF BIRTH AND DEATH
Year Born ▼   Year Died ▼

Was this contribution to the work a "work made for hire"?
☐ Yes
☐ No

AUTHOR'S NATIONALITY OR DOMICILE
Name of Country
OR { Citizen of ▶_____
{ Domiciled in ▶_____

WAS THIS AUTHOR'S CONTRIBUTION TO THE WORK
Anonymous?   ☐ Yes ☐ No
Pseudonymous? ☐ Yes ☐ No
If the answer to either of these questions is "Yes," see detailed instructions.

NATURE OF AUTHORSHIP Briefly describe nature of material created by this author in which copyright is claimed. ▼

3

a

YEAR IN WHICH CREATION OF THIS WORK WAS COMPLETED
_____ ◀ Year
This information must be given in all cases.

b

DATE AND NATION OF FIRST PUBLICATION OF THIS PARTICULAR WORK
Complete this information ONLY if this work has been published.
Month ▶_____ Day ▶_____ Year ▶_____
_____ ◀ Nation

4

a

COPYRIGHT CLAIMANT(S) Name and address must be given even if the claimant is the same as the author given in space 2. ▼

See instructions before completing this space.

b

TRANSFER If the claimant(s) named here in space 4 is (are) different from the author(s) named in space 2, give a brief statement of how the claimant(s) obtained ownership of the copyright. ▼

APPLICATION RECEIVED
_____

ONE DEPOSIT RECEIVED
_____

TWO DEPOSITS RECEIVED
_____

FUNDS RECEIVED
_____

DO NOT WRITE HERE
OFFICE USE ONLY

MORE ON BACK ▶ • Complete all applicable spaces (numbers 5-9) on the reverse side of this page.
• See detailed instructions.   • Sign the form at line 8.

DO NOT WRITE HERE
Page 1 of _____ pages

EXAMINED BY	FORM SR
CHECKED BY	
CORRESPONDENCE ☐ Yes	FOR COPYRIGHT OFFICE USE ONLY

DO NOT WRITE ABOVE THIS LINE. IF YOU NEED MORE SPACE, USE A SEPARATE CONTINUATION SHEET.

PREVIOUS REGISTRATION Has registration for this work, or for an earlier version of this work, already been made in the Copyright Office?

☐ Yes ☐ No If your answer is "Yes," why is another registration being sought? (Check appropriate box) ▼

a. ☐ This work was previously registered in unpublished form and now has been published for the first time.

b. ☐ This is the first application submitted by this author as copyright claimant.

c. ☐ This is a changed version of the work, as shown by space 6 on this application.

If your answer is "Yes," give: **Previous Registration Number ▼**   **Year of Registration ▼**

5

DERIVATIVE WORK OR COMPILATION
Preexisting Material Identify any preexisting work or works that this work is based on or incorporates. ▼

a

Material Added to This Work Give a brief, general statement of the material that has been added to this work and in which copyright is claimed. ▼

b

6

See instructions
before completing
this space.

DEPOSIT ACCOUNT If the registration fee is to be charged to a Deposit Account established in the Copyright Office, give name and number of Account.
Name ▼   **Account Number ▼**

a

CORRESPONDENCE Give name and address to which correspondence about this application should be sent.   Name/Address/Apt/City/State/ZIP ▼

b

Area code and daytime telephone number ▶   Fax number ▶
Email ▶

7

CERTIFICATION* I, the undersigned, hereby certify that I am the

Check only one ▼

☐ author

☐ other copyright claimant

☐ owner of exclusive right(s)

☐ authorized agent of _____
Name of author or other copyright claimant, or owner of exclusive right(s) ▲

of the work identified in this application and that the statements made by me in this application are correct to the best of my knowledge.

Typed or printed name and date ▼ If this application gives a date of publication in space 3, do not sign and submit it before that date.

_____   Date▶ _____

Handwritten signature (x) ▼

X _

8

Certificate will be mailed in window envelope to this address	Name ▼
	Number/Street/Apt ▼
	City/State/ZIP ▼

YOU MUST
• Complete all necessary spaces
• Sign your application in space 8

SEND ALL 3 ELEMENTS IN THE SAME PACKAGE
1. Application form
2. Nonrefundable filing fee in check or money order payable to *Register of Copyrights*
3. Deposit material

MAIL TO
Library of Congress
Copyright Office
101 Independence Avenue, S.E.
Washington, D.C. 20559-6000

As of
July 1, 1999,
the filing fee
for Form SR
is $30.

9

*17 U.S.C. § 506(e): Any person who knowingly makes a false representation of a material fact in the application for copyright registration provided for by section 409, or in any written statement filed in connection with the application, shall be fined not more than $2,500.

June 1999—50,000
WEB REV: June 1999

PRINTED ON RECYCLED PAPER

☆U.S. GOVERNMENT PRINTING OFFICE: 1999-454-879/48

BOOKS

American Symphony Orchestra League Staff. *The Gold Book: A Sourcebook of Successful Fund-Raising, Education, Ticket Sales, and Service Projects.* American Symphony Orchestra League. [Annual]

Barrow, T. *Inside the Music Business.* New York: Chapman & Hall, 1995.

Billboard Staff. *Billboard International Buyers Guide 1999.* New York: Watson-Guptill, 1998. [Annual]

Black, Henry C., et al. *Black's Law Dictionary.* 6th ed. St. Paul, MN: West, 1993.

Bolles, Richard Nelson. *The 1999 What Color Is Your Parachute? A Practical Manual for Job-Hunters & Career Changers.* Rev. ed. Berkeley, CA: Ten Speed, 1998.

Brabec, Jeffrey, and Brabec, Todd. *Music, Money, and Success: The Insider's Guide to the Music Industry.* New York: Schirmer, 1994.

Cardinal Business Media Staff. *Recording Industry Sourcebook, 1999.* 10th ed. Emeryville, CA: Cardinal Business Media, Music & Entertainment Group, 1999. [Annual]

Consumer Electronics Annual Review. Arlington, VA: Consumer Electronics Manufacturers Association, annual.

Counseling Clients in the Entertainment Industry 1999: Film & Television; Sound Recordings; Ethics, Business Management & The Development of an Entertainment Law Practice; Music Publishing & Personal Management. 2 vols. New York: Practising Law Institute, 1998. [Annual]

Dannen, Fredric. *Hit Men: Power Brokers & Fast Money Inside the Music Business.* New York: Random House, 1991.

Denisoff, R. Serge. *Inside MTV.* New Brunswick, NJ: Transaction, 1990.

Eargle, John M. *Handbook of Recording Engineering.* 3rd ed. New York: Chapman & Hall, 1996.

Eargle, John M. *Music, Sound and Technology.* 2nd ed. New York: Van Nostrand Reinhold, 1995.

Elias, Stephen, and Levinkind, Susan. *Legal Research: How to Find & Understand the Law.* 6th ed. Berkeley, CA: Nolo, 1998.

Eliot, Marc. *Rockonomics: The Money Behind the Music.* Secaucus, NJ: Carol Publishing Group, 1993.

Entertainment Law Institute. [Various titles and authors]. Los Angeles: University of Southern California. [Annual]

Faulkner, Robert R. *Hollywood Studio Musicians: Their Work and Careers in the Recording Industry.* Lanham, MD: University Press of America, 1985.

Faulkner, Robert R. *Music on Demand: Composers and Careers in the Hollywood Film Industry.* New Brunswick, NJ: Transaction, 1982.

Feist, Leonard. *Popular Music Publishing in America.* New York: National Music Publishers Association, 1980.

Fink, Michael. *Inside the Music Industry: Creativity, Process, and Business.* 2nd ed. New York: Schirmer, 1996.

Frascogna, Xavier M., and Hetherington, H. Lee. *Successful Artist Management.* Enl. rev. ed. New York: Watson-Guptill, 1990.

Friedman Group Staff. *No Thanks, I'm Just Looking: Professional Retail Sales Techniques for Turning Shoppers Into Buyers.* Dubuque, IA: Kendall/Hunt, 1995.

Gaar, Gillian G. *She's a Rebel: The History of Women in Rock & Roll.* Seattle, WA: Seal, 1992.

Goldstein, Jeri. *How to Be Your Own Booking Agent and Save Thousands of Dollars: A Performing Artist's Guide to a Successful Touring Career.* Charlottesville, VA: New Music Times, 1998.

Halloran, Mark, ed. and comp. *The Musicians Business and Legal Guide.* 2nd rev. ed. Paramus, NJ: Prentice Hall, 1996.

Johnson, Pattie, ed. *Foundation Fundamentals: A Guide for Grantseekers.* Rev. 6th ed. New York: Foundation Center, 1999.

Karlin, Fred. *Listening to Movies: The Film Lover's Guide to Film Music.* New York: Schirmer, 1994.

Karlin, Fred, and Wright, Rayburn. *On the Track: A Guide to Contemporary Film Scoring.* New York: Schirmer, 1990.

Karmen, Steve. *Through the Jingle Jungle.* New York: Billboard Books, 1989.

Kohn, Al, and Kohn, Bob. *Kohn on Music Licensing.* 2nd ed. New York: Aspen Law & Business, 1996. [Also periodic supplements]

Koontz, Harold D., and Weihrich, Heinz. *Essentials of Management.* 5th ed. New York: McGraw-Hill, 1990.

Krasilovsky, M. William, and Shemel, Sidney. *More About This Business of Music.* 5th enl. rev. ed. New York: Watson-Guptill, 1994.

Krasilovsky, M. William, and Shemel, Sidney. *This Business of Music: A Practical Guide to the Music Industry for Publishers, Writers, Record Companies, Producers, Artists, Agents.* 7th rev. ed. New York: Watson-Guptill, 1995.

Lathrop, Tad, and Pettigrew, Jim, Jr. *This Business of Music Marketing and Promotion.* New York: Billboard Books, 1999.

Leikin, Molly-Ann. *How to Make a Good Song a Hit Song: Rewriting and Marketing Your Lyrics and Music.* Milwaukee, WI: Hal Leonard, 1996.

Lindey, Alexander. *Lindey on Entertainment, Publishing and the Arts: Agreement and the Law.* 2nd ed. 4 vols. Deerfield, IL: Clark Boardman Callaghan, 1980-1982.

Mandell, Jim. *The Studio Business Book.* Jewett, Andy, ed. Emeryville, CA: Cardinal Business Media, Music & Entertainment Group, 1995.

Marcone, Stephen. *Managing Your Band: Artist Management: The Ultimate Responsibility.* Wayne, NJ: HiMarks, 1995.

Martin, George, and Hornsby, Jeremy. *All You Need Is Ears.* New York: St. Martin's, 1994.

McPherson, Brian. *Get It in Writing.* Milwaukee, WI: Hal Leonard, 1999.

Music USA 1998. Carlsbad, CA: NAMM, 1998. [Annual]

Nimmer, Melville B. *Nimmer on Copyright.* 5 vols. New York: Matthew Bender, 1978. [Updates]

Passman, Donald S. *All You Need to Know About the Music Business.* Rev. ed. New York: Simon & Schuster, 1997.

Pettigrew, Jim, Jr. *The Billboard Guide to Music Publicity.* New York: Watson-Guptill, 1997.

Pleasants, Henry. *Serious Music—And All That Jazz.* New York: Simon & Schuster, 1969.

Rachlin, Harvey. *The TV and Movie Business: An Encyclopedia of Careers, Technologies, and Practices.* New York: Crown, 1991.

Rapaport, Diane S. *How to Make and Sell Your Own Recording: The Complete Guide to Independent Recording.* 5th ed. Paramus, NJ: Prentice Hall, 1999.

Sanjek, Russell, and Sanjek, David. *Pennies From Heaven: The American Popular Music Business in the Twentieth Century.* New York: Da Capo, 1996.

Scheider, Therese, ed. *Musical America 1999: International Directory of the Performing Arts.* Hightstown, NJ: K-III Directory, 1998. [Annual]

Scott, Michael D. *Multimedia: Law & Practice.* Englewood Cliffs, NJ: Prentice Hall Law & Business, 1993.

Siegel, Alan H. *Breaking Into the Music Business.* Rev. ed. New York: Simon & Schuster, 1990.

So You Want to Open a Music Store. Rev. ed. Carlsbad, CA: NAMM, 2000.

Steinberg, Irwin, and Greenblatt, Harmon. *Understanding the Music Business: A Comprehensive View.* Needham Heights, MA: Simon & Schuster, 1998.

Stim, Richard. *Music Law: How to Run Your Band's Business.* Berkeley, CA: Nolo, 1998.

Taubman, Joseph. *In Tune With the Music Business.* New York: Law-Arts, 1980. [Out of print]

Thorne, Robert, and Viera, John David, eds. *Entertainment, Publishing and the Arts Handbook, 1999.* Eagan, MN: West Group, 1998. [Annual]

Vogel, Harold L. *Entertainment Industry Economics: A Guide for Financial Analysts.* 4th ed. New York: Cambridge University Press, 1998.

Wadhams, Wayne. *Dictionary of Music Production and Engineering Terminology.* New York: Schirmer, 1988.

Wadhams, Wayne. *Sound Advice: The Musician's Guide to the Record Industry.* New York: Schirmer, 1990.

Weissman, Dick. *Making a Living in Your Local Music Market: How to Survive and Prosper.* Milwaukee, WI: Hal Leonard, 1990.

Whitsett, Tim. *The Dictionary of Music Business Terms.* Emeryville, CA: MixBooks, 1999.

Wilder, Alec. *American Popular Song: The Great Innovators, 1900-1950.* New York: Oxford University Press, 1972.

Woram, John, and Kefauver, Alan P. *The New Recording Studio Handbook.* Rev. ed. New York: Elar, 1989.

JOURNALS, MAGAZINES, NEWSPAPERS, NEWSLETTERS

Advertising Age	Weekly trade publication covering agency, media and advertising, news and trends
Amusement Business	Weekly trade newspaper covering mass entertainment management including events, attendance, and spending
Billboard	Professional international news weekly for members of music and video and home entertainment industries and related fields
Broadcast Engineering	Technical monthly covering digital television technology, systems, installation, management, and maintenance
Broadcasting & Cable	Weekly business publication for broadcast and cable TV, radio, satellite, and interactive multimedia industries
Campus Activities Programming Magazine	Trade magazine covering college campus programming for the student and professional
Cash Box	Weekly magazine for members of the phonograph record and music industries
Circus Magazine	Monthly consumer magazine about rock and roll
College Music Symposium	Interdisciplinary quarterly
Columbia-VLA Journal of Law & the Arts	Scholarly quarterly with articles concerning timely art law topics
Copyright Law Reports	Monthly with articles about today's rules, new and proposed regulations, current case law activity, and views of the regulators
Country Music	Bimonthly consumer magazine covering country music artists and the recording industry
Daily Variety	Daily tabloid newspaper of the entertainment industry
DJ Times	Business monthly with the latest technology, trends, music, and business information for DJs
Down Beat	Monthly consumer magazine covering contemporary music and aimed at seriously involved player and listener

Electronic Musician	Monthly business magazine covering electronics and computers in the creation and recording of music
Entertainment Law Reporter	Business monthly covering legal developments and matters of importance to lawyers and executives in the entertainment industry
Facilities	Monthly trade magazine for the public assembly industry
Film Score Monthly	Publication providing film music reviews and composer interviews
Gavin	Business weekly magazine for the record industry
Hit Parader	Consumer monthly with news of the heavy metal music industry
Hollywood Reporter	Daily business news and reviews of all phases of the entertainment, theatrical, and communications fields
Instrumentalist	Business monthly with practical, professional information for school band and orchestra directors
International Musician	Monthly journal for members of the American Federation of Musicians
Jazz Educators Journal	Quarterly covering news and events related to jazz and popular music in education
Journal of the American Musicological Society	Scholarly articles on diversified branches of musicology, published three times a year
Journal of the Copyright Society of the U.S.A.	Quarterly dealing with domestic and foreign copyright laws, revisions, and court decisions
Journal of Music Therapy	Research-oriented quarterly for practitioners and others
Mix, the Recording Industry Magazine	Monthly business magazine focusing on contemporary music arts and audio and video music production
Modern Drummer	Monthly for the student, semipro, and pro drummer
Music & Copyright	Publication providing global reporting on the commercial aspects of the music industry, published semimonthly by the *Financial Times*

Music & Sound Retailer	Monthly serving owners, managers, and sales personnel in retail musical instrument and sound product dealerships
Music Business International	European bimonthly publication dealing with law, talent, technology, and broadcast and retail issues for music industry managers
Music Educators Journal	Bimonthly dealing with all facets of study and teaching methods at all levels
Music Inc.	Business monthly providing newest trends in merchandising, new products, industry news, and dealer and manufacturer profiles
Music Trades	Business monthly for music stores selling instruments, accessories, music, and electronic music and home equipment
Musician	Consumer monthly providing interviews and business essentials for active musicians
NARAS Journal	Publication addressing the needs of the membership of the National Academy of Recording Arts & Sciences
Notes	Quarterly journal covering developments in music librarianship and activities of the Music Library Association
Overture	Monthly trade union paper
Performance Magazine	Weekly publication covering all aspects of the live entertainment concert touring industry
Post	Monthly serving the field of TV, film, and video production and postproduction
Producer Report	Biweekly newsletter covering record producer activity
Radio and Records	Weekly trade newspaper providing news, sales, marketing innovations, and airplay data
Radio Business Report	Semiweekly publication covering business issues, inside news on people, and company controversies
Recording	Consumer monthly focusing on all aspects of home and small studio recording

Rolling Stone Magazine	Biweekly coverage of American culture
Sound and Communications	Business monthly for sound contractors, engineers, consultants, and system managers
Sounding Board	Monthly publication with news, events, views, and industry data for members of NARM
Soundtrack!	Quarterly magazine covering film music
Spin Magazine	Consumer monthly covering trendsetters in music world and other entertainment personalities
Stereo Review	Monthly service magazine offering guidance to buyers of all types of audio equipment and the discs and tapes to be played with it
Symphony Magazine	Bimonthly publication with news and articles for symphony orchestra managers, trustees, volunteers, and musicians
Variety	Consumer weekly reporting on the entertainment industry worldwide
Wall Street Journal	Daily business newspaper focusing on the business and investment communities

PROFESSIONAL ORGANIZATIONS

Acoustical Society of America (ASA)
2 Huntington Quadrangle, Ste. 1NO1, Melville, NY 11747-4502
(516) 576-2360   URL http://asa.aip.org

Actors' Equity Association (AEA)
165 West 46th St., 15th Fl., New York, NY 10036
(212) 869-8530   URL http://www.actorsequity.org

Alliance of Motion Picture and Television Producers (AMPTA)
15503 Ventura Blvd., Encino, CA 91436-3140
(818) 995-3600

American Choral Directors Association (ACDA)
502 SW 38th St., Lawton, OK 73505
(580) 355-8161   URL http://www.acdaonline.org

American Composers Alliance (ACA)
170 W. 74th St., New York, NY 10023
(212) 362-8900   URL http://www.composers.com

American Federation of Labor and Congress of Industrial Organizations (AFL-CIO)
815 16th St., NW, Washington, DC 20006
(202) 637-5000   URL http://www.aflcio.org

American Federation of Musicians of the United States and Canada (AFM)
1501 Broadway, Ste. 600, New York, NY 10036
(212) 869-1330   URL http://www.afm.org

American Federation of Television and Radio Artists (AFTRA)
260 Madison Ave., New York, NY 10016-2402
(212) 532-0800
5757 Wilshire Blvd., 9th Fl., Los Angeles, CA 90036-3689
(323) 634-8100   URL http://www.aftra.com

American Guild of Musical Artists (AGMA)
1727 Broadway, New York, NY 10019
(212) 265-3687   URL http://agmanatl.com

American Guild of Organists
475 Riverside Dr., Ste. 1260, New York, NY 10115
(212) 870-2310   URL http://www.agohq.org

American Guild of Variety Artists (AGVA)
184 5th Ave., 6th Fl., New York, NY 10010
(212) 675-1003

American Mechanical Rights Agency, Inc. (AMRA)
  (formerly American Mechanical Rights Association)
1888 Century Park East, Ste. 222, Los Angeles, CA 90067
(310) 785-1600   URL http://www.amermechrights.com

American Music Center (AMC)
30 W. 26th St., Ste. 1001, New York, NY 10010-2011
(212) 366-5260   URL http://www.amc.net

American Music Conference (AMC)
5790 Armada Dr., Carlsbad, CA 92008
(619) 431-9124   URL http://www.amc-music.com

American Music Therapy Association, Inc. (AMTA) (formerly American
  Association for Music Therapy/National Association for Music Therapy)
8455 Colesville Rd., Ste. 1000, Silver Spring, MD 20910
(301) 589-3300   URL http://www.musictherapy.org

American Musicological Society (AMS)
201 S. 34th St., Philadelphia, PA 19104-6313
(215) 898-8698/(888) 611-4267   URL http://musdra.ucdavis.edu/documents/ams/
  ams.html

American Society of Composers, Authors and Publishers (ASCAP)
1 Lincoln Plaza, New York, NY 10023
(212) 621-6000   URL http://www.ascap.com

American Symphony Orchestra League
33 W. 60th St., 5th Fl., New York, NY 10023
(212) 262-5161   URL http://www.symphony.org

American Theatre Wing
250 W. 57th St., Ste. 519, New York, NY 10107-0599
(212) 765-0606   URL http://www.tonys.org

American Women in Radio and Television (AWRT)
The Emma L. Bowen Foundation for Minority Interests in Media
825 Seventh Ave., 2nd Fl., New York, NY 10019
(212) 456-1992   URL http://www.awrt.org

Americans for the Arts (formerly American Council for the Arts)
1000 Vermont Ave., NW, 12th Fl., Washington, DC 20005
(202) 371-2830   URL http://www.artusa.org

Amusement and Music Operators Association (AMOA)
401 N. Michigan Ave., Chicago, IL 60611
(312) 245-1021   URL http://www.amoa.com

Archive of Contemporary Music
54 White St., New York, NY 10013
(212) 226-6967   URL http://www.arcmusic.org

Associated Actors and Artistes of America (4As)
165 W. 46th St., Ste. 500, New York, NY 10036-2501
(212) 869-0358

Association for Independent Music (AFIM) (formerly National Association
    of Independent Record Distributors and Manufacturers/NAIRD)
P.O. Box 988, 147 East Main St., Whitesburg, KY 41858
(606) 633-0946/(800) 767-6526   URL http://www.afim.org

Association of Arts Administration Educators (AAAE)
Professor Joan Jeffri, Program in Arts Administration, Dept. of the
    Arts and Humanities, Box 78, Teachers College, Columbia University,
    525 West 120th St., New York, NY 10027
(212) 678-3271   URL http://www.artsnet.org/aaae

Association of Independent Music Publishers (AIMP)
120 E. 56th St., Ste. 1150, New York, NY 10022
(212) 758-6157

Association of Performing Arts Presenters
1112 16th St. NW, Ste. 400, Washington, DC 20036
(202) 833-2787   URL http://www.artspresenters.org

Audio Engineering Society, Inc. (AES)
60 E. 42nd St., Rm. 2520, New York, NY 10165-2520
(212) 661-8528   URL http://www.aes.org

Authors Guild (AG)
330 W. 42nd St., 29th Fl., New York, NY 10036
(212) 563-5904   URL http://www.authorsguild.org

Authors League of America, Inc. (ALA)
330 W. 42nd St., 29th Fl., New York, NY 10036-6902
(212) 564-8350

Broadcast Music Inc. (BMI)
320 W. 57th St., New York, NY 10019-3790
(212) 586-2000   URL http://www.bmi.com

Bureau international des sociétés gérant les droits d'enregistrement et de
    reproduction mécanique (BIEM)
14 rue Lincoln, 75008 Paris, France
(33) 1 53 93 67 00   URL http://ourworld.compuserve.com/homepages/biem

Business Committee for the Arts, Inc. (BCA)
1775 Broadway, Ste. 510, New York, NY 10019-1942
(212) 664-0600   URL http://www.bcainc.org

California Copyright Conference (CCC)
P.O. Box 1291, Burbank, CA 91507
(818) 848-6783

Chamber Music America (CMA)
305 Seventh Ave., New York, NY 10001
(212) 244-2022   URL http://www.chamber-music.org

College Music Society (CMS)
202 W. Spruce, Missoula, MT 59802
(406) 721-9616   URL http://www.music.org

Copyright Management International (CMI) (formerly Copyright Management, Inc.)
1625 Broadway, Ste. 400, Nashville, TN 37203
(615) 327-1517

Copyright Society of the U.S.A. (CSUSA)
1133 Avenue of the Americas, New York, NY 10036
(212) 354-6401   URL http://www.csusa.org

Country Music Association (CMA)
1 Music Circle S., Nashville, TN 37203
(615) 244-2840   URL http://www.cmaworld.com

Country Music Foundation (CMF)
4 Music Square E., Nashville, TN 37203
(615) 256-1639   URL http://www.countrymusichalloffame.com

Directors Guild of America (DGA)
7920 Sunset Blvd., Los Angeles, CA 90046
(310) 289-2000   URL http://www.dga.org

Dramatists Guild of America
1501 Broadway, Ste. 701, New York, NY 10036
(212) 398-9366   URL http://www.dramaguild.com

Early Music America
11421½ Bellflower Rd., Cleveland, OH 44106
(216) 229-1685   URL http://www.cwru.edu/affil/ema

Electronic Industries Alliance (EIA) (formerly Electronic Industries Association)
2500 Wilson Blvd., Arlington, VA 22201-3834
(703) 907-7500   URL http://www.eia.org

Entertainment Services and Technology Association (ESTA)
875 Sixth Ave., Ste. 2302, New York, NY 10001
(212) 244-1505   URL http://www.esta.org

Foundation Center
79 Fifth Ave./16th St., New York, NY 10003-3076
(212) 620-4230   URL http://fdncenter.org

Gospel Music Association (GMA)
1205 Division St., Nashville, TN 37203
(615) 242-0303   URL http://www.gospelmusic.org

Guild of Italian-American Actors (GIAA) (formerly Italian Actors Union)
352 W. 44th St., New York, NY 10036
(212) 262-7300   URL http://www.angelfire.com/ny/giaa

Guitar and Accessories Marketing Association
38-44 W. 21st St., Rm. 1106, New York, NY 10010-6906
(212) 924-9175

Harry Fox Agency, Inc.
711 Third Ave., New York, NY 10017
(212) 370-5330   URL http://www.nmpa.org/hfa.html

Hebrew Actors Union
31 E. 7th St., New York, NY 10003
(212) 674-1923

Interactive Digital Software Association (IDSA)
1775 Eye St., NW, Washington, DC 20006
(202) 833-4372   URL http://www.idsa.com

International Alliance for Women in Music (IAWM)
Kristine H. Bucks, IAWM Membership Director, Florida International University,
    School of Music, University Park, Miami, FL 33199
(305) 348-2219/385-9517   URL http://music.acu.edu/www/iawm/home.html

International Alliance of Theatrical Stage Employes, Moving Picture Technicians,
    Artists and Allied Crafts of the United States, Its Territories and Canada (IATSE)
1515 Broadway, Ste. 601, New York, NY 10036-5741
(212) 730-1770   URL http:www.iatse.lm.com

International Association of Assembly Managers (IAAM)
    (formerly International Association of Auditorium Managers)
4425 W. Airport Fwy., Ste. 590, Irving, TX 75062-5835
(972) 255-8020/(800) 935-4226   URL http://www.iaam.org

International Association of Jazz Educators (IAJE) (formerly National Association of
    Jazz Educators)
Box 724, 2803 Claflin Rd., Manhattan, KS 66505
(785) 776-8744   URL http://www.iaje.org

International Confederation of Societies of Authors and Composers (CISAC)
11, rue Kepler 75116 Paris, France
(33) 1 53 57 34 00   URL http://www.cisac.org

International Federation of Actors (FIA)
Mrs. Katherine Sand, Secretary General, Guild House, Upper St. Martin's Lane,
    London WC2H 9EG, United Kingdom
(44) 020 7 379 0900

International Federation of Musicians (FIM)
Mr. Jean Vincent, Secretary General, 21 bis, rue Victor Massé, 75009 Paris, France
(33) 1 45 26 31 23

International Federation of the Phonographic Industry (IFPI)
IFPI Secretariat, 54 Regent St., London W1R 5PJ, United Kingdom
(44) 020 7 878 7900   URL http://www.ifpi.org

International Music Products Association (NAMM) (formerly National Association of Mu-
    sic Merchants)
5790 Armada Dr., Carlsbad, CA 92008
(760) 438-8001/(800) 767-6266   URL http://www.namm.com

International Rhythm and Blues Association (IRBA)
P.O. Box 16215, Chicago, IL 60616
(312) 326-5270

ITA, International Recording Media Association
182 Nassau St., Ste. 204, Princeton, NJ 08542-7005
(609) 279-1700   URL http://www.recordingmedia.org

League of American Theatres and Producers, Inc.
226 W. 47th St., New York, NY 10036
(212) 764-1122   URL http://www.broadway.org

League of Resident Theatres (LORT)
c/o Harry Weintraub, Glick and Weintraub, 1501 Broadway, Ste. 2401, New York, NY 10036
(212) 944-1501

Los Angeles Copyright Society (LACS)
Amanda Seward, c/o Warner Brothers Feature Animation, 15303 Ventura Blvd.,
    Sherman Oaks, CA 91403
(818) 977-7667   URL http://www.lacopyright.org

Metropolitan Opera Guild (MOG)
70 Lincoln Center Plaza, 6th Fl., New York, NY 10023
(212) 769-7000   URL http://www.metopera.org/guild

Motion Picture Association of America (MPAA)
1600 I St. NW, Washington, DC 20006
(202) 293-1966   URL http://www.mpaa.org

Motion Picture Editors Guild
7715 Sunset Blvd., Ste. 200, Hollywood, CA 90046
(323) 876-4770   URL http://www.editorsguild.com

Mu Phi Epsilon (International Music Fraternity)
International Executive Office, 4202 Atlantic Ave., Ste. 202, Long Beach, CA 90807-2826
(562) 424-9799/(888) 259-1471   URL http://home.muphiepsilon.org

Music and Entertainment Industry Educators Association (MEIEA)
Dr. Steve Widenhofer, MEIEA Public Relations, School of Music, Millikin University,
    Decatur, IL 62522
(217) 424-6305   URL http://www.meiea.org

Music Critics Association of North America (MCA) (formerly Music Critics Association)
7 Pine Ct., Westfield, NJ 07090-3444
(908) 233-8468

Music Educators National Conference (MENC)
1806 Robert Fulton Dr., Reston, VA 20191
(703) 860-4000/(800) 336-3768   URL http://www.menc.org

Music Library Association, Inc. (MLA)
P.O. Box 487, Canton, MA 02021
(781) 828-8450   URL http://www.musiclibraryassoc.org

Music Performance Trust Funds, the Recording Industries (MPTF)
1501 Broadway, Ste. 202, New York, NY 10036-5501
(212) 391-3950   URL http://www.mptf.org

Music Publishers' Association of the United States (MPA)
c/o NMPA/HFA, 711 Third Ave., New York, NY 10017   URL http://host.mpa.org

Music Teachers National Association (MTNA)
441 Vine St., Ste. 505, Cincinnati, OH 45202-2814
(513) 421-1420   URL http://www.mtna.org

Music Video Production Association (MVPA)
1553 N. Commonwealth Ave., Los Angeles, CA 90027
(323) 469-9494   URL http://www.mvpa.com

NAMM Affiliated Music Business Institutions (NAMBI)
Professor Keith Mann, President, NAMBI, Red Deer College, Box 5005, Red Deer,
    AB T4N 5H5, Canada
(403) 342-3216/(800) 767-6266   URL http://www.ecnet.net/users/mimusba/nambi

Nashville entertainment Association (NeA) (formerly Nashville Music Association)
P.O. Box 121948, 1105 16th Ave. South, Ste. C, Nashville, TN 37212
(615) 327-4308   URL http://nea.net

Nashville Songwriters Association International (NSAI)
1701 West End Ave., Third Fl., Nashville, TN 37203
(800) 321-6008   URL http://nashvillesongwriters.com

National Academy of Popular Music (NAPM)/Songwriters Hall of Fame
330 West 58th St., Ste. 411, New York, NY 10019
(212) 957-9230   URL http://www.songwritershalloffame.org/napm

National Academy of Recording Arts & Sciences, Inc. (NARAS)
3402 Pico Blvd., Santa Monica, CA 90405
(310) 392-3777   URL http://www.grammy.org

National Academy of Songwriters (NAS)
6255 Sunset Blvd., Ste. 1023, Hollywood, CA 90028
(323) 463-7178/(800)826-7287   URL http://www.nassong.org

National Academy of Television Arts & Sciences (NATAS)
111 W. 57th St., Ste. 1050, New York, NY 10019
(212) 586-8424   URL http://www.internetgroup.com/natas

National Alliance for Musical Theatre
330 W. 45th St., Lobby B, New York, NY 10036
(212) 265-5376   URL http://www.bway.net/namt

National Assembly of State Arts Agencies
1029 Vermont Ave. NW, 2nd Fl., Washington, DC 20005
(202) 347-6352   URL http://www.nasaa-arts.org

National Association for Campus Activities (NACA)
13 Harbison Way, Columbia, SC 29212-3401
(803) 732-6222   URL http://www.naca.org

National Association of Band Instrument Manufacturers (NABIM)
38-44 W. 21st St., Rm. 1106, New York, NY 10010-6906
(212) 924-9175

National Association of Broadcast Employees and Technicians–Communications
    Workers of America (NABET-CWA)
501 3rd St. NW, 8th Fl., Washington, DC 20001
(202) 434-1254   URL http://nabetcwa.org

National Association of Broadcasters (NAB)
1771 N St. NW, Washington, DC 20036
(202) 429-5300   URL http://www.nab.org

National Association of Negro Musicians, Inc. (NANM)
Mrs. Fredericka F. Hurley, Membership Chairperson, 3799 Wisteria Ln.,
    S.W., Atlanta, GA 30318
(404) 696-1894   URL http://edtech.morehouse.edu/cgrimes

National Association of Recording Merchandisers (NARM)
9 Eves Dr., Ste. 120, Marlton, NJ 08053
(856) 596-2221   URL http://www.narm.com

National Association of Schools of Music (NASM)
11250 Roger Bacon Dr., Ste. 21, Reston, VA 20190
(703)437-0700   URL http://www.arts-accredit.org/nasm/nasm.htm

National Association of Teachers of Singing
JU Station, 2800 University Blvd. N, Jacksonville, FL 32211
(904) 744-9022   URL http://www.nats.org

National Conference of Personal Managers (NCOPM)
964 Second Ave., New York, NY 10022
(212) 421-2670   URL http://www.cybershowbiz.com/ncopm

National Endowment for the Arts (NEA)
1100 Pennsylvania Ave., NW, Washington, DC 20506
(202) 682-5400   URL http://arts.endow.gov

National Federation of Music Clubs (NFMC)
1336 N. Delaware St., Indianapolis, IN 46202-2481
(317) 638-4003   URL http://www.nfmc-music.org

National Music Council (NMC)
425 Park St., Upper Montclair, NJ 07043
(973) 655-7974   URL http://www.musiccouncil.org

National Music Publishers' Association (NMPA)
711 Third Ave., New York, NY 10017
(212) 370-5330   URL http://www.nmpa.org

National Music Theatre Network (also known as Broadway Dozen)
1697 Broadway, Ste. 902, New York, NY 10019
(212) 664-0979   URL http://www.broadwayusa.org

National Opera Association (NOA)
Arvid Knutsen, Executive Secretary, 6805 Tennyson Dr., McLean, VA 22101
(703) 790-3393   URL http://www.noa.org

Opera America (absorbed Central Opera Service)
1156 15th St. NW, Ste. 810, Washington, DC 20005
(202) 293-4466   URL http://www.operaam.org

Phi Mu Alpha-Sinfonia Fraternity of America, Inc.
10600 Old State Rd., Evansville, IN 47711-1399
(812) 867-2433/(800) 473-2649   URL http://www.sinfonia.org

Piano Technicians Guild (PTG)
3930 Washington, Kansas City, MO 64111-2963
(816) 753-7747   URL http://ptg.org

Producers Guild of America (PGA)
400 S. Beverly Dr., Ste. 211, Beverly Hills, CA 90212
(310) 557-0807   URL http://www.producersguildonline.com

Recording Industry Association of America, Inc. (RIAA)
1330 Connecticut Ave., NW, Ste. 300, Washington, DC 20036
(202) 775-0101   URL http://www.riaa.com

Recording Musicians Association
817 Vine St., Los Angeles, CA 90038-3715
(328) 462-4762   URL http://www.rmaweb.org

Screen Actors Guild (SAG)
5757 Wilshire Blvd., Los Angeles, CA 90036-3600
(323) 954-1600   URL http://www.sag.org

SESAC, Inc.
55 Music Square East, Nashville, TN 37203
(800) 826-9996   URL http://www.sesac.com

Society of Composers, Inc.
P.O. Box 296, Old Chelsea Station, New York, NY 10113-0296
(212) 989-6764   URL http://www.utexas.edu/cofa/music/ems/sci

Society of Motion Picture and Television Engineers, Inc. (SMPTE)
595 W. Hartsdale Ave., White Plains, NY 10607
(914) 761-1100   URL http://www.smpte.org

Society of Professional Audio Recording Services (SPARS)
    (formerly Society of Professional Audio Recording Studios)
4300 10th Ave. N., Lake Worth, FL 33461-2313
(561) 641-6648/(800) 771-7727   URL http://www.spars.com

Society of Singers, Inc.
8242 W. 3rd St., Ste. 250, Los Angeles, CA 90048
(323) 651-1696/(888) 570-1318   URL http://www.singers.org

Society of Stage Directors and Choreographers (SSDC)
1501 Broadway, Ste. 1701, New York, NY 10036-5653
(212) 391-1070   URL http://www.ssdc.org

Songwriters Guild of America (SGA)
1500 Harbor Blvd., Weehawken, NJ 07087-6732
(201) 867-7603   URL http://www.songwriters.org

United Scenic Artists, Local 829
16 W. 61st St., New York, NY 10023
(212) 581-0300   URL http://frontpage1.shadow.net/usa829fl

Video Software Dealers Association (VSDA)
16530 Ventura Blvd., Ste. 400, Encino, CA 91436-4551
(818) 385-1500   URL http://www.vsda.org

Volunteer Lawyers for the Arts (VLA)
1 E. 53rd St., 6th Fl., New York, NY 10022-4200
(212) 319-2787   URL http://www.vlaa.org

Women in Film (WIF)
6464 Sunset Blvd., Ste. 1080, Hollywood, CA 90028
(323) 463-6040   URL http://www.wif.org

World Intellectual Property Organization (WIPO)
34, chemin des Colombettes, P.O. Box 18, CH-1211 Geneva 20, Switzerland
(41) 22 338 91 11   URL http://www.wipo.int

World Trade Organization
154 rue de Lausanne, 1211 Geneva 21, Switzerland
(41) 22 739 51 11   URL http://www.wto.org

Writers Guild of America, East, Inc.
555 W. 57th St., New York, NY 10019
(212) 767-7800   URL http://www.wgaeast.org

Writers Guild of America, Inc. (west)
7000 W. Third St., Los Angeles, CA 90048
(323) 782-4532   URL http://www.wga.org

Young Audiences, Inc. (YA)
115 E. 92nd St., New York, NY 10128-1688
(212) 831-8110   URL http://www.ya.org

GLOSSARY

A

A&R producer.   Artist and repertoire (record) producer.

Above-the-line (expense).   Special production expenses, e.g., salaries for featured artists, creative fees, above-scale wages. Contrasts with below-the-line expense.

Accessory.   Item used to enhance the musical effect of an instrument or musical experience.

Account executive.   Liaison person between an advertising agency and one of its clients; salesperson.

Acoustic instrument.   An instrument that is not electronic and is not amplified.

Adult contemporary music.   Broad music genre made up of mainstream and modern rock and classic hits from the past.

Aftermarket.   Income sources available for exploitation following first exposure of a tape or film.

Airplay.   Radio broadcast of a commercially released music recording.

Alternative music.   Youth-based, active music incorporating new wave, punk, "grunge," and techno styles.

AM station.   Radio station using an amplitude modulation signal.

Angel.   Financial backer of a Broadway show.

Annual billing.   Amount invoiced time buyers for the calendar year by broadcasters.

AOR.   Album-oriented rock.

Arbitration clause.   Provision in a contract requiring the parties to submit disputes to an impartial arbiter, usually the American Arbitration Association.

Arbitron.   (1) The Arbitron Company, supplier of radio and television ratings research. (2) Electronic device attached to a home TV set to inform researcher what stations are turned on at a particular time.

Arm's length.   (1) A relationship between two parties not on close terms. (2) A relationship other than one between, e.g., a lawyer and client or between a person and a trustee; other than a fiduciary relationship.

Art music.   Repertoire associated with opera, ballet, symphony, and chamber music. Often used interchangeably with *classical music* or *serious music.*

Assignment.   Turning over of a contract or copyright to another person's control or ownership.

Atonality.   Absence of key or tonal center.

Attorney-at-law.   "An advocate, counsel, or official agent employed in preparing, managing, and trying cases in the courts" (*Black's Law Dictionary*).

Attorney-in-fact.   "A private attorney authorized by another to act in his place and stead, either for some particular purpose, as to do a particular act, or for the transaction of business in general, not of a legal character" (*Black's Law Dictionary*).

Audience share.   Comparative popularity of broadcast program, determined by dividing the program rating by the number of sets in use at a particular time.

Audiovisual work.   Work that consists of a series of related images intended to be shown by the use of projectors, viewers, or electronic equipment, together with accompanying sounds, if any.

Automated radio.   Station whose programming is almost entirely on prerecorded tapes, the tapes being controlled for broadcast by a sophisticated transport system that requires minimum attention from an operator.

B

Baby boomers.   Americans born between 1946 and 1965, courted by entertainment media and advertisers because of their large discretionary incomes.

Back-announce.   In radio broadcasting, the accumulation of a group of announcements following several uninterrupted playings of recorded music.

BDS.   Broadcast Data Systems. A data collection service whose technology monitors broadcasts and recognizes songs and/or commercials aired by radio and TV stations.

Bed.   Advertising: Musical background for a commercial announcement.

Bel canto.   Fine singing; the Italian tradition of classical vocal production.

Below-the-line (expense).   Costs in production budgeting, such as union scale, wages for technicians, equipment and facilities rentals. Contrasts with above-the-line expense.

Belt.   To sing a pop song or show tune with gusto, using chest-tone resonance.

Best edition.   For purposes of copyright: The edition of a work that the Library of Congress determines to be the most suitable for its purposes.

Beta (Betamax).   A type of videocassette recorder-reproducer, obsolete in consumer market.

Bio.   Biography—a written summary of an individual's professional background.

Blackout.   A turning off of stage lighting.

Board.   Recording console.

Boilerplate.   Time-tested language that may be found in most contracts but does not require a great deal of negotiation.

Book.   In a musical play, the scenario and dialogue for a production.

Breach.   "The breaking or violating of a law, right, or duty, either by commission or omission" (*Black's Law Dictionary*).

Breach of contract.   "Failure, without legal excuse, to perform any promise which forms the whole or part of a contract" (*Black's Law Dictionary*).

Bridge.   Musical phrase in a song following the hook, sometimes called "release" or "B phrase."

Bundle of rights.   The six exclusive rights in copyright ownership vested initially and exclusively in the author of a work.

Buyout.   The purchase of rights in a property (usually for a lump sum), rather than the payment of royalties for the use of the property.

C

Camcorder.   One-piece video camera/recording machine.

Canned.   Prerecorded or filmed, in contrast to live.

Canned release.   Copy written for the press.

Canned spot.   A prerecorded broadcast commercial.

Canned track.   A prerecorded segment of music that has not been written for the particular work for which it may be used.

CARP.   Copyright Arbitration Royalty Panel (the successor to Copyright Royalty Tribunal) appointed by the Librarian of Congress to conduct hearings, set and adjust royalty rates, and distribute royalties deposited with the Copyright Office to copyright owners.

Catch action.   Compose a musical cue to synchronize with specific action on the screen.

Cattle call.   Producer's announcement of open auditions.

CATV.   Community Antenna Television, or cable television.

CD.   Compact audio disc.

CD, Enhanced.   Compact audio disc that is compatible with both audio CD players and multimedia ROMs. Along with recorded music, it can include video clips, still pictures, and other information.

CD-R.   A blank disc that can be loaded with sound recordings by means of a personal computer.

Channel.   (1) The frequency of transmission for a broadcaster. (2) A program service feeding programming to one or more stations, cable systems, satellite services or Web sites. (3) A mode of product distribution, e.g., rack jobber channel.

Charge-back.   An expense assessed by a recording company against an artist's royalties.

Chart.   (1) Musical arrangement. (2) Trade paper list of recordings currently most popular on radio or in record stores.

Chorus.   (1) The refrain section of a song that includes a phrase repeated at intervals. (2) a group of persons singing or speaking something simultaneously.

Clam.   Wrong note in the copied parts or a note performed incorrectly.

Classic jazz.   The "pure," traditional jazz sound: predominantly instrumental, rarely vocal, largely improvised rather than arranged, performed primarily on acoustic, not electronic, instruments.

Classic rock.   The enduring music of such rock-and-roll trendsetters as Elvis Presley and the Beatles, originating in the 1950s and 1960s and still popular today.

Classical music.   The repertoire associated with symphony, opera, ballet, chamber, and some choral music.

Click track.   Audible guide used by musicians scoring music to aid synchronization with film.

Close-miking.   Recording with a microphone close to the sound source.

Cluster programming.   Radio broadcast of several recordings uninterrupted by announcements.

Clutter.   The airing in rapid succession of many short spots during a television commercial break.

Cold.   In advertising, copy read without musical introduction or background.

Collective bargaining.   Negotiation between an employer or group of employers and representatives of union employees in order to reach agreement on terms of employment such as wages, work hours, and conditions.

Collective work.   For purposes of copyright: A work, such as a periodical issue, anthology, or encyclopedia, in which a number of contributions, constituting separate and independent works in themselves, are assembled into a collective whole.

Commercial bed.   *See* Bed.

Commercial load.   The proportion of a radio station's broadcast time that is given to spot announcements.

Common law.   A body of law, written or unwritten, that originated in England and that derives its authority from tradition or from judgments and decrees of the courts recognizing such tradition.

Comp style.   An improvised piano accompaniment often characterized by syncopated, block chords.

Competent party.   Of sound mind and body; not demented or otherwise unable to act responsibly.

Compilation.   For purposes of copyright: A work formed by the collection and assembling of preexisting materials or of data that are selected, coordinated, or arranged in such a way that the resulting work as a whole constitutes an original work of authorship. The term *compilation* includes collective works.

Compressor.   Electronic sound device that limits the dynamic response to create a more constant, even dynamic level.

Compulsory license.   In copyright law, the provision that copyright owners of nondramatic music have complete control over recording rights of their properties until they license the material for the first recording. But after this first recording is distributed to the public, they are compelled by law to license any other person to produce and distribute recordings of the copyrighted music in exchange for a fixed statutory royalty.

Concertmaster.   Leader of the first violin section of an orchestra who has special authority and consults with the conductor about musical matters more than other musicians do.

Consideration.   "The inducement to a contract, the cause, motive, price, or impelling influence which induces a contracting party to enter into a contract. The reason or material cause of a contract" (*Black's Law Dictionary*).

Contingent fee, contingency fee.   A fee that is a percentage of the money received from a certain contract. An attorney, for example, might charge a fee of 5% of the money received by his or her client as a result of a contract negotiated by the attorney.

Contingent scale payment.   Royalties on sales of recordings paid to certain AFTRA members.

Contractor.   In unions, the steward who hires performers, supervises their working conditions, and confirms they are properly paid.

Cooperative advertising.   Form of advertising placed by the retailer, but funded in whole or in part by the manufacturer.

Copublishing.   Act of two or more entities sharing publishing income but not necessarily the publishing responsibilities.

Copyist.   A person who copies music or parts of a musical score.

Copyright.   The legal right to reproduce, adapt, distribute, perform publicly, and display a work of intellectual property.

Copyright proprietor.   Same as copyright owner.

Cost-per-thousand.   The fee for delivering a commercial message to 1,000 readers, listeners, or viewers.

Coterminous.   Two or more contracts that end on the same date.

Country.   Music genre traditionally associated with Nashville, now ranging from country/western and bluegrass to pop-flavored styles.

Cover, cover record.   Song that has been rerecorded by other artists after a first recording by the artist who introduced it.

CPB.   Corporation for Public Broadcasting.

Creative director.   (1) In an advertising agency, the individual in charge of creative advertising concepts; supervises writers, graphic artists, and audio-video producers. (2) For a production company or recording label, the person in charge of creative services.

Creative fee.   Money paid a composer or copywriter by an advertising agency, producer, or production company.

Creative services.   Division of a recording company that provides marketing concepts, graphic art, sales aids, editorial services, and advertising materials.

Cross-collateralize.   Shift of royalties earned by one property to the credit or debit of another property, resulting in a net total of royalties earned by all of them.

Crossover recording.   A recording focused on one market segment that achieves sales in one or more additional markets.

Cue.   Short musical passage composed to accompany dramatic action or underscore dialogue.

Cure.   Satisfy a complaint or resolve a dispute concerning a contract.

Cut-in.   Owner of a property shares ownership.

Cutouts.   Surplus recording inventory sold at bargain prices.

Cutter.   Film (or tape) editor of music recorded for synchronization with film or videotape.

D

DAT.   Digital audiotape.

Day parting.   Radio programming that divides the broadcast day into segments, such as "morning drive," "midday," and so forth.

DBS.   Direct broadcast satellite.

Deal breaker.   Issue that, if not settled, terminates contract negotiations.

Decay.   Diminution of sound pressure (audible volume).

Default.   Failure to perform under a legal contract.

Demo.   Demonstration recording.

Demography.   The statistical method used in researching the characteristics of populations.

Derivative work.   For purposes of copyright: A work based on one or more preexisting works, such as a translation, musical arrangement, dramatization, fictionalization, motion picture version, sound recording, art reproduction, abridgment, condensation, or any other form in which a work may be recast, transformed, or adapted.

Digital recording.   Audio or video recording made with the aid of digital computer technology (as contrasted with analog).

Digital transmission.   The transfer of music encoded as digital data. This transfer occurs by means of the Internet, satellites, cables, phone lines, or other means.

Discharge.   To void a contract, cause it to be nonbinding.

Display.   To show a copy of a work.

Distributor.   Wholesale source of a retailer's goods, often an intermediary between the manufacturer and the retailer.

Double.   The second (sometimes third) instrument a musician is called upon to play. For example, a flute is a common double required of saxophonists.

Doubling.   Act of playing more than one instrument in a performance.

Downtime.   A period when recording or filming equipment is not functioning properly, thus unusable.

Dramatic music, dramatico-musical.   Music closely related to drama or a scenario, particularly opera, a musical play, ballet, narration.

Drop ship.   Fulfillment of a customer's order by shipment from an entity other than the one from which the customer ordered.

E

Easy listening.   Primarily instrumental music genre, gentler in sound than adult contemporary.

Electronic publishing.   Communications system delivering information to computer terminals and TV screens.

Engineer.   An audio mixer or sound technician.

EP.   (1) Employers Pension Fund of the AFM. (2) Extended-play record.

EQ.   Equalization.

Equity.   Actors' Equity Association.

Executive producer.   Top administrator and/or financier of a production.

Executory, executory provision.   A requirement of performance to be rendered following disengagement from (termination of) a contract.

Exploit.   In the entertainment field, to promote, advertise, publicize, display, distribute, and advance an artist or a property.

Extended use.   A prerecorded tape or film used for a period longer than the one initially paid for.

F

Fader.   A recording console control used to effect changes in sound level.

Fair use doctrine.   Legal defense to a copyright infringement claim, allowing minimal takings of copyrighted material for purposes such as scholarship, research, and news reporting.

FCC.   Federal Communications Commission.

Fiduciary.   (1) A person who manages money or other things of value for another person and in whom the second party has a right to place trust. (2) A situation or relationship between persons where one acts for another in a position of trust. Example: a lawyer or agent acting on behalf of an artist.

Find.   To decide and declare.

Finding.   "The result of the deliberations of a jury or a court" (*Black's Law Dictionary*).

First-call musician.   Performer a contractor prefers to hire above others available.

First desk/first chair.   The lead instrumentalist in a section of an orchestra.

Flack.   A publicist.

Flat.   A natural sound, without coloration or alteration of highs and lows.

FM radio.   Radio broadcasting using a frequency modulation signal.

Four-walling.   Producer rents a performance facility where the landlord offers only the venue—no stagehands, ushers, or box office help.

Franchised agent.   A talent agent or booker licensed by an artists' union or guild.

Front line.   Melodic instruments in a band or orchestra, as opposed to the rhythm section.

G

Gaffer.   Lighting technician on a video, television, or motion picture set.

Ghost writer.   A writer or composer who does work for hire under the name of another writer or composer.

Gig.   Job; engagement of a musician or entertainer for a specified time.

Glissando.   The musical effect produced by playing a series of instrumental notes in quick succession without performing each individually.

Gofer.   An assistant who may run errands and "goes for" whatever is requested.

Grand right.   Performance right in dramatic music.

Graphic equalizer.   A sound control that provides adjustment of a signal over a broad range of frequencies.

Guild.   An association of professional persons with similar interests (sometimes used synonymously with *trade union*).

H

Harmonize.   To rewrite or amend statutes or regulations so that they are in agreement or accordance with other statutes or treaties.

Harmonizer.   A signal-processing device that creates delay effects and changes the pitch of a sound without affecting its tempo.

Head.   Start of a tape or film reel.

Headset.   Earphones.

Hook.   (1) Song: Memorable melodic (or lyrical) phrase. (2) Advertising: Campaign slogan or concept.

House agency.   Advertising department within a company.

House producer.   One of the company's salaried staff production employees.

H&W Fund.   AFM's Health and Welfare Fund.

Hyphenate.   Artist providing multiple services, e.g., producer-director, singer-songwriter.

I

ID.   Station: *See* Station logo.

Immaterial.   "Not material, essential, or necessary; not important or pertinent" (*Black's Law Dictionary*).

In-house.   Done within a company itself; not hired out.

Institutional ad (or spot).   Promotion intended to impress the public with a firm's or organization's merit (as opposed to that of a specific product).

Institutional print.   Music that is used by schools and churches for bands, choruses, choirs, and orchestras.

Intellectual property.   Ideas translated from people's minds to tangible creations such as songs, writing, and other forms of communication.

Interactive TV.   Permits viewer to change the picture or add to it.

Interface.   To connect by means of a machine or specific software protocol.

I.p.s.   Inches per second, referring to tape-reel speed.

J

Jingle.   Original term for a broadcast commercial containing music. More common today is the use of the terms *commercial* or *spot;* music in the spot.

Joint venture.   A business partnership of limited duration set up for a limited purpose.

K

Key man clause.   Contractual provision that if an artist's business representative or record producer leaves a particular company, the artist may follow that individual without legal or financial reprisals.

L

Label.   A brand of commercial recordings, usually issued under a trademarked name.

Lawyer.   "A person learned in the law; as an attorney, counsel, or solicitor; a person licensed to practice law" (*Black's Law Dictionary*).

Leadsheet.   Music manuscript containing a song's melody, text, and chord symbols.

Legal consideration.   "One recognized or permitted by the law as valid and lawful; as distinguished from such as are illegal or immoral" (*Black's Law Dictionary*). The term is sometimes used as equivalent for "good" or "sufficient" consideration.

Legit.   Slang for *legitimate.* Style of music or performance in the classical, formal tradition.

Library service.   A collection of a large quantity and variety of recorded passages that are available for use in productions not using original or "custom" music.

Licensing.   The awarding of rights to perform, reproduce, distribute, or transmit a copyrighted work.

Lift.   In broadcast commercials, a short taped segment drawn from a longer one.

Ligature.   (1) A slur indicating a group of notes sung or played as a connected phrase. (2) The group of notes thus indicated. (3) The device on a clarinet mouthpiece holding the reed in place.

Limiter.   Signal-processing device that reduces peaks but affects overall dynamics less than a compressor.

Live-on-tape.   A television production performed live, with TV recording occurring at the same time for later editing prior to broadcast.

Local.   (1) Branch office of a national union or guild. (2) A market or audience contained within one city or area.

Local marketing agreements.   Agreement whereby a broadcast station owner may "lease" programming and sales to another station. Usually, an LMA leads to a future purchase of the second property by the originator of the agreement.

Logo.   A musical or visual symbol used repeatedly in an effort to reinforce public recognition of a product or organization.

LV.   Laser video.

M

Market.   A particular group of buyers (or a type of audience) that can be identified by demographic research and/or analyses of preferences.

Master purchase agreement.   A contract used by a recording company to obtain exclusive rights in a master tape recording that has been produced by another person, such as an independent producer.

Mastering.   The process by which album tracks are equalized and balanced in relation to each other, then transferred to a master storage device (DAT, CD, cassette, or lacquer disc) to be used as a duplicating master for the purpose of manufacturing recordings.

Material.   "Important; more or less necessarily; having influence or effect; going to the merits; having to do with matter, as distinguished from form" (*Black's Law Dictionary*).

MC. (or Emcee).   Master of ceremonies.

MD.   Music director.

Mechanical license.   Legal permission given by the copyright owner to make a commercial recording of the copyrighted music.

Mechanicals.   (1) Royalties paid by a record manufacturer to the owner of a music copyright. (2) Elements of graphic art assembled for the printer's camera.

Mediabase 24/7.   A data collection service that monitors airplay through a combination of technological and human identification.

Media buyer.   Salaried employee who contracts for print ad space or broadcast time buys.

MIDI.   Musical instrument digital interface. (1) Technology that allows a composition to be transcribed into musical notation by playing it on the keyboard. MIDI notation prepared for one instrument can be used to reproduce similar performances with other MIDI instruments. (2) Standard for exchanging musical information for musical devices including instruments.

Mix.   To combine and equalize, into one or two channels, a larger number of separate tracks of recorded sounds.

Mixer.   (1) Recording technician who operates a console. Often referred to (incorrectly) as an engineer. (2) Electronic equipment that enables the mixing of sounds.

MOR.   Middle-of-the-road type of music, now more commonly referred to as "nostalgia/ big band," that favors instrumentals over vocals and is somewhat similar to easy listening music.

MPA.   Music Publishers Association of the United States.

MSO.   Multiple system operator, a type of cable TV company owning more than one system.

Multiplex.   System for the simultaneous transmission of two or more signals over the same wire or radio frequency channel.

Multitrack.   The recording device or tape on which parallel tracks can be recorded. Each track has separate music or information that can be mixed or edited separately.

Music coordinator.   Production assistant keeping track of musical elements.

Music cue.   Short musical fragment used to bridge dramatic scenes or provide musical background.

Music cutter.   Same as film music editor.

Music house (or music supply house).   A company of composers and arrangers offering creative services (and recording) for buyers of "custom" music.

Music preparation.   Music manuscript proofreading, extraction of parts from the score, collation, reproduction, score binding, and delivery.

Music supplier.   *See* Music house.

N

Narrowcasting.   Contrasts with *broadcasting*: program material produced and delivered to audiences of special tastes.

National account.   Customer of an advertising agency or production company that advertises nationwide.

Needle drop.   Brief recorded passage (orchestral or a sound effect) drawn from a transcription library that a producer uses for a dramatic program or broadcast commercial.

Negative cost.   Expense of producing a movie or TV show and delivering it to a customer; excludes costs of promotion.

Negative tour support.   The advance a recording company may make to pay the difference between the touring costs and touring income, if a band's touring does not break even or make a profit.

Negotiated license.   In the recording industry, a right to record worked out between a music publisher and a record producer. Contrasts with a statutory compulsory license.

Neighboring rights (or related rights).   The rights in a work that don't belong to the author. There are three general categories of neighboring rights: those of performers, producers, and broadcasters.

Neo-romantic.   Any of various movements in the arts considered as representing a return to the artistic styles associated with the romantic period of the 19th century.

Network.   Broadcast service usually distributed simultaneously through more than one station or outlet.

New Age music.   Mellow, mostly acoustic instrumental music with an ethereal, soothing quality, popularized in the 1980s.

New country music.   Music genre that combines elements of country and rock and roll.

New use.   Application of recorded music tape or film to a medium different from the one originally intended, e.g., a record album to be used in a film.

Nielsen rating.   Percentage of the broadcast audience watching a particular program or network, according to A. C. Nielsen, a research company.

NPR.   National Public Radio.

NTSC.   Abbreviation for a standard for TV transmission used primarily in North America and Japan.

O

O&O station.   A radio or TV station owned and operated by a commercial broadcasting network.

Off-Broadway.   Low-budget, often experimental, professional theater, produced in New York City venues but outside its Times Square theater district.

One-stop.   Record distributor/wholesaler offering a large number of recording companies' merchandise to retailers and jukebox operators.

Opticals.   Visual effects created for film or videotape.

Orchestrator.   One who takes music written by someone else and writes or scores the music for the various instruments that play it.

Outboard equipment.   Recording hardware external to the recording console that is patched into it to enhance the mixer's options of controlling sounds.

Overcall album.   Recording requested by label but that was not covered by initial contract.

Overdubbing.   Adding music or sounds to a previously recorded tape.

Overtracking.   (1) Adding sounds to a previously recorded tape. (2) The use of one voice several times or recording one voice several times, then playing them simultaneously on a recording to produce the sound of a larger ensemble.

P

Package deal.   Combined goods and/or services delivered under one price tag.

Pan pot.   Recording console control (fader) used to place a signal to the left, right, or center of the stereo image.

Paper business.   Printed-editions sector of a music publishing company.

Paper the house.   Concert promotion: Issue free tickets to ensure a full audience for a performance.

Pass.   Make a negative judgment; to turn down, reject.

Pay-TV.   Cable television delivery system for which an extra fee is paid, contrasting with *basic*.

Payola.   Money or other compensation illicitly given disc jockeys in return for playing particular recordings.

PD.   (1) Program director. (2) Public domain.

Performance.   A performance occurs any time music is played publicly, whether at a live concert or broadcast over radio, TV, Internet, or other means of transmission.

Performance right, performing right.   Exclusive right given to the creator of copyrighted material to authorize the use of the work in public.

Phonorecord.   Any physical medium carrying recorded music, such as a phonograph record, CD, or prerecorded tape.

Piracy.   Illegal duplication and distribution of sound recordings.

Pit.   Area occupied by the orchestra in a theater, often below the floor level of the audience.

Playlist.   Radio station's recorded music schedule for broadcast.

P.O.P.   Point-of-purchase (merchandising aids).

Power of attorney.   "An instrument authorizing another to act as one's agent or attorney; a letter of attorney" (*Black's Law Dictionary*).

Pay-per-view (PPV).   Television delivery system for which customers pay specific one-time fees.

Print.   Music in printed form.

Production manager.   Business affairs head for a production.

Promo kit.   *See* Promo pack.

Promo pack.   Package of promotional materials.

Proscenium.   Wall arch that separates the stage from the auditorium.

Public domain.   Material, such as music or other intellectual property, available for unrestricted use on which the copyright or patent right has expired or that has no copyright.

Publishing.   In the music industry, publishing is the distribution of printed copies or phonorecords for sale, or the control of the exploitation of a work in a print or nonprint medium (such as recordings or broadcasting).

Punch in.   Interrupt taping or filming with insertion of new (or additional) material.

Punch up.   Add emphasis to music or script.

PVC.   Prerecorded videocassette.

R

Rack jobber.   A merchant paying a rental fee or commission to maintain and sell inventory within the retailer's store.

Rack up.   TV film and tape presets that may then be called up by a technician for broadcast.

Rap.   Lyrics spoken in rhyme to rhythmic music.

Rate card.   Summary of advertising rates for a specific medium (radio stations, TV network, etc.) given to ad agencies, clients, and prospective clients.

Record (album, single).   Generic term for compact disc, audiocassette, or vinyl recording.

Release phrase.   *See* Bridge.

Remedy.   Solve a problem or cure a default under a contract.

Reuse.   (1) Use of a recorded performance after an initial time period is over. (2) Use of a recorded performance in a medium that is different from the medium for which the performance was first used.

Rhythm and blues.   Predominantly black music genre featuring a lead vocalist backed with harmonizing singers, piano, bass, and drums, with harmonic structure adapted from popular and blues forms.

Rhythm section.   The "motor element" of a band or orchestra, normally composed of piano, bass, drums, and guitar.

Right-to-work law.   A state law that makes a closed shop, where union membership is a condition of employment, illegal.

S

Sampling.   (1) Music performances: Technique used by music rights organizations to estimate total performances by examining a limited number of performances.
(2) Music recording: The digital taping of a sound or series of sounds from already

recorded material, for insertion to a new recording so as to enhance that recording's sound; the source sound can be inserted unchanged or transformed by synthesizer or other electronic equipment.

Scale. Specified minimum union wage.

Scaling the house. Determining what quantity of available seats in a performance facility are to be priced the least expensive, the next least expensive, and so on.

Score (a film). Compose, perform, and record music to synchronize with a motion picture.

Second engineer. Assistant to the head audio engineer (technician).

Secondary transmission. Cable TV broadcast of an originating program source, such as from a commercial television station.

Sel sync. The ability of a tape recorder to record on one track at a time in synchrony with previously recorded tracks.

Self-contained group. (1) Small ensemble that writes its own material. (2) An organized ensemble that performs together regularly without outside members.

Selling agent. Person or firm offering printed music or merchandise for sale at the retail level, under a royalty contract or for commission.

Serialism. The method or practice of composing with tone rows.

Session musician. Instrumentalist employed in recording studios and usually paid union scale.

Sforzando. "Stinger" note or chord that brings special attention to specific dramatic action, e.g., to identify a villain, emphasize the sounds of a fight, or suggest the sounds of a beating heart.

Shop tapes. Submit audition tapes to potential buyers.

Side. (1) One side of a recording. (2) One song on a recording.

Sideman. An instrumentalist other than the leader or contractor.

Slate. Chalkboard ID of a filmed or videotaped segment.

Small right. Performance right in nondramatic music.

Song score. A film sound track composed primarily of songs that have the potential to be hits.

Soundcarrier. A phonorecord.

SoundScan.   A data collection service that tabulates sales of recorded product. SoundScan's sales tabulations are generated by a computer network linked to retail outlets and rack jobbers nationwide.

Spec, speculation.   Employed without assurance of getting paid.

Special material.   Music, lyrics, dialogue, and patter specially written for a particular artist's performance.

Split copyright.   Copyright proprietor shares his or her ownership with one or more persons.

Split publishing.   One party shares his or her publishing rights with one or more persons.

Spot.   (1) A broadcast commercial announcement. (2) Theatrical spotlight. (3) To place in a particular position, as in "spotting" a film—deciding precisely where a film should be underscored.

Spotting notes.   Notes given to a composer of motion picture music by the music editor to specify where each cue will happen in the movie.

SRO.   Standing room only, meaning "sold out."

Station.   In radio or television, a station is generally a broadcaster that transmits on one frequency and from one locality. A group of stations is frequently referred to as a *broadcast network.*

Station logo.   Broadcast station's musical signature, identification.

Steward.   Hires performers and supervises enforcement of their union contract with the producer.

Stinger.   Accented chord played by an orchestra to underscore a dramatic moment on the screen.

Stock arrangement.   Published edition; not a custom chart.

Storyboard.   A series of sketches showing the sequence of events for a film or video.

Strip show.   A series of broadcasts scheduled several times a week at the same hour each day.

Studio musician.   Same as session musician.

Subpublisher.   Firm affiliated with a prime publisher in providing publishing services, usually abroad.

Subsisting.   Now in existence, as in subsisting copyrights.

Supervising copyist.   Copyist who directs the services of additional copyists working on the same job.

Sweeps.   Period during which research firms collect data concerning broadcast audience size.

Sweeten.   Record additional sounds by overdubbing.

Synchronization license.   The right to synchronize a composition in timed relation with visual images on film or tape.

Synchronization rights.   The right to use music in such a way that it is timed to synchronize with, or relate to, action on film or video.

Synclavier.   Keyboard synthesizer incorporating a computer terminal, digital processor, and storage unit, with which an operator can create, store, retrieve, and re-create musical sounds.

Syncopated.   Rhythmic placement of musical tones so that their accent does not coincide with the metric accent.

Syndication.   Broadcasts of programs that individual stations schedule to use simultaneously or at times convenient to them.

T

Tail.   End of a tape or film reel.

Take.   One version of a recorded performance, as in "The second take was best."

Teaser announcement.   Brief press release providing preliminary information about a forthcoming event.

Technical rider.   Addendum to a performance contract stipulating requirements for staging, sound reinforcement, equipment, etc.

Telecommunications.   Production and delivery of all modes of entertainment and information.

Term.   The time interval embraced by a legal agreement.

Tessitura.   Prevailing pitch and range of a melodic line.

Tight.   Slang for a well-rehearsed, cohesive performance.

Timbre.   Quality, tone color distinguishing one voice or musical instrument from another.

Time buyer.   Advertising agency employee who purchases time on a broadcast station or network for an advertiser.

Time shift.   Capacity of a VCR to record a TV program off the air and move its playback to a time more convenient for the viewer.

Tin Pan Alley.   The business of popular music most prevalent in the 1920s in New York. Also, style of popular song of that era, usually sentimental, with a verse and chorus form in which chorus predominated.

Track.   (1) One recorded portion of combined tracks, as in "24-track" recording; the sound on one track, as in "the bass track." (2) A single selection on an album.

Tracker.   Label employee following the progress of a record release—airplay, chart action, sales, etc.

Tracking.   (1) An AFM and AFTRA payment category in which performers tape the same notes more than once and the producer or engineer uses each recording simultaneously to produce the sound of a larger ensemble. AFM and AFTRA performers are supposed to be paid for each taped use of their work. (2) A promotion practice of record companies in which the company has employees call radio stations and record stores to see how often a song is played or a recording is sold.

Tracking scale.   Union wage scale for tracking sessions.

Tracking session.   Taping session following the recording of basic tracks; overdubbing.

Trading fours.   Jazz musicians taking turns improvising alternate four-bar phrases.

Transcription.   A copy of recorded music made for purposes other than direct sale to consumers (such as Muzak, in-flight entertainment, and radio syndication).

U

Underscore.   To place recorded music behind a movie or TV program.

Union shop.   An establishment that hires only members of a labor union or those who promise to join a union within a specified time.

Union steward.   An agent who supervises the employment of union artists and provides liaison for them with their employer.

Unison.   Music played or sung by two or more people in which instruments or voices perform identical parts simultaneously in the same or different octaves; the interval formed by two tones of the same pitch.

Up-front payment.   Money advanced prior to completion of a job or production.

Up full.   Background music crescendo to foreground.

V

VCR.   Videocassette recorder.

VDP.   Video disc player.

Venue.   Place of performance or trial.

Verse.   A section or stanza of a hymn or song; a section preceding the refrain or chorus of a song.

Videocaster.   One who broadcasts, cablecasts, or telecasts videos.

Videogram.   Any audiovisual physical medium, such as videocassettes and videodiscs, that contains musical compositions.

Videotex.   Information system for viewers to call up data on video screen.

VJ.   Video jockey, analogous to DJ.

Voice-over.   Words spoken by an actor or announcer who is not seen on the screen.

W

Weighting formula.   Evaluations of a performing rights organization used in determining the relative value of various kinds of music performances in order to judge what royalties are due a writer or publisher.

Work made for hire.   (1) A work prepared by an employee within the scope of his or her employment. (2) A work specially ordered or commissioned for use as a contribution to a collective work.

Y

Yuppies.   Young urban professionals—a desirable consumer market.

INDEX

ABOUT THE AUTHOR

David Baskerville received a Ph.D. in music from UCLA. His background included staff composer-conductor for NBC-Hollywood; arranger for Nelson Riddle, Paramount Pictures, and 20th Century Fox; television producer for the BBC-London; conductor at Radio City Music Hall; trombonist with the Seattle Symphony, Los Angeles Philharmonic, and NBC-Hollywood staff orchestra; Executive Vice President of Ad-Staff, Inc., producer of award-winning broadcast commercials; Executive Editor of Tor Music Publishing Company; and President of Sherwood Recording Studios, Los Angeles (subsequently operated by Warner Bros. Records).

He also served as a consultant to companies in the entertainment industry, such as Walt Disney Productions, and to research and marketing firms, such as Vidmar Communications, Inc., Los Angeles.

As an educator, David Baskerville directed the music management program at the University of Colorado at Denver, where he became Professor Emeritus. He was a guest lecturer, consultant, or clinician at USC, UCLA, Chicago Musical College, Hartt School of Music, the Ohio State University, University of Miami, and Trebas Institute, Canada.

He was a featured speaker at national conventions of the Music Educators National Conference, College Music Society, National Association of Jazz Educators, and the National Association of Schools of Music.

The author (right) receiving ASCAP's Deems Taylor Award,
given each year for outstanding books on music. The presentation is
by Academy Award-winning songwriter Hal David, representing ASCAP.